D1123014

8.
5.

Troublemaker

Troublemaker

The Life and History of A.J.P. Taylor

Kathleen Burk

Yale University Press
New Haven and London

31143006430277
B TAYLOR, A.J.P.
Burk, Kathleen.
The troublemaker : the
life and history of
A.J.P. Taylor

Copyright © 2000 by Kathleen Burk

The right of Kathleen Burk to be identified as author of this work has been asserted
by her in accordance with the Copyright, Designs and Patents Act 1988.

All rights reserved. This book may not be reproduced in whole or in part, in any
form (beyond that copying permitted by Sections 107 and 108 of the U.S. Copyright
Law and except by reviewers for the public press) without written permission from
the publishers.

Set in FFScala by Northern Phototypesetting Co. Ltd., Bolton, Lancashire
Printed in Great Britain by The Bath Press, Bath

Library of Congress Card Number: 00–105012

ISBN 0 300 08761 6 (hbk.)

A catalogue record for this book is available from the British Library.

2 4 6 8 10 9 7 5 3 1

Photographic acknowledgements: © BBC Photograph Library 23, 24;
Kathleen Burk 15; Camera Press Ltd, photo by Tom Blau 25; Robin Darwall-Smith 17;
courtesy of Alastair and Nicola Durroch 4; courtesy of Mrs Pamela Gott 5; courtesy of
Éva Haraszti-Taylor 2, 8, 9, 26, 29; Rick Halpern 16; © Hulton Getty 12, 13, 14, 20,
27, 28; Michael Jewess 6, 10, 11; The President and Fellows of Magdalen College,
Oxford 18, 19, 21; Oriel College, Oxford 3; courtesy of Daniel Taylor 1.

For Michael and Miranda

History has always been my consuming passion: reading history, writing history, lecturing about history.

A Personal History

Every historian should, I think, write an autobiography. The experience teaches us to distrust our sources which are often autobiographical.

A Personal History

Every historian, I think, should write one biography, if only to learn how different it is from writing history. Men become more important than events, as I suppose they should be. I prefer writing history all the same.

'Accident Prone, or What Happened Next'

Contents

Preface and Acknowledgements

A.J.P. Taylor was a profoundly interesting man, who led a life which for years was filled with frenetic activity. Many will not consider teaching, or sitting and writing books and articles, evidence of activity, but those who have taught for successive hours with the concentration which effective teaching requires, or who have written any piece of extended prose – which requires even more concentration – will know that the effort leaves one drained at the end of the day, tired from inside the bones, more tired than if a bout of manual labour had been undertaken. Taylor's ability to combine so much teaching with so much writing, with so much of it so good, can only arouse admiration and envy. He was also a public man, but I have resisted the temptation to overemphasise his public activities; rather, I have tried to convey the interest inherent in scholarly activities and thereby to maintain in the book the balance between the two achieved by Taylor himself. To have done otherwise would have been a betrayal of the meaning of Taylor's life and of the reason why he deserves attention after his death.

I have concentrated on the lineaments of his life, adding as much detail and texture as possible without overwhelming the central core. Besides, this book was never intended to be a two-decker Victorian life and letters: I mean it to be read rather than consulted. I have also organised the story in a slightly unusual way, with more emphasis on themes than on a dogged description of his life day by day. An academic, when looking back on her or his life, thinks in terms of strands: this was my research, this was my teaching, these were my administrative duties, this was my broadcasting or journalism. I have therefore done the same, as this approach shows most clearly the patterns of Taylor's life. But his life also included colleagues and friends, wives and children, politics and walking, music and architecture, and the making of money, and these have not been forgotten.

I knew Taylor reasonably well from 1972 to 1986. He supervised my Oxford D.Phil. from 1972 to 1976, making me, he said, his last research student; he was thereafter my major referee; and from 1980 to 1985 we were two of the co-chairs of the twentieth-century British history seminar at the Institute of Historical Research, London University. He took a detached but kindly interest as a supervisor; he wrote convincing letters as a referee; and he was an assiduous chair for the seminars. He was always kind and helpful to me, he said nice things about me behind my back and occasionally to my face, and he was the model of a distinguished man who had no side. I liked and admired him. But I very much hope that I have been clear-eyed about his weaknesses as well as his strengths, and that my early hero-worship – having Taylor as a supervisor was, to a would-be diplomatic historian, akin to being supervised by God – has been replaced by a more balanced appreciation of his complexities as a man. And I still like him.

As is usual for writers of non-fiction, I have incurred many debts over the eight years spent researching and writing this book. I am grateful for the efficiency of the anonymous staff members of the Harry Ransome Humanities Research Center at the University of Texas, Austin; of the Wheaton College Special Collections, Wheaton, Illinois; of the library of the University of California, Berkeley; of Yale University Library and the Beinecke Rare Books Library; of the Public Record Office at Kew, London; of the John Rylands University Library, Manchester University; of the library of the University of Reading; of the library of Christ Church, Oxford; of the Special Collections of the British Library; of the Modern Records Centre, Warwick University; of the Liddell Hart Centre, Kings College, London; of the BBC Written Archives Centre, Caversham; of the House of Lords Record Office; of the library of the University of Sussex; of the library of Bristol University; of the British Library of Political Science, the London School of Economics; of the Macmillan archives, at their offices in Basingstoke; of David Higham Associates in London; and of Room 132 of the Bodleian Library.

I am particularly grateful to individual archivists. Mr Clifford Smith kindly provided me with all the extant Taylor material from the Bootham School archives; Mrs Elizabeth Boardman of the archives at Oriel College, Oxford helped me decipher some of the college's papers and provided a photograph of Taylor; Mr Simon Bailey of the Oxford University archives dropped everything to help me when I rang and faxed material which I needed immediately; Dr Paul Holder, History Subject Librarian at the John

Rylands Library, located Taylor's uncatalogued Ph.D thesis for me; my work at Manchester was facilitated by the Head of the Department of History, Dr Peter Gatrell; Miss Debra Birch of The Institute of Historical Research, London University provided information on Taylor's seminar; Miss Nazneen Razwi produced the file on Taylor's lecturing at University College, London; Mr Peter Forden of the Oxford University Press archives was extremely helpful, allowing me to get through a massive amount of paper in the shortest possible time; Ms Katherine Bligh, at the House of Lords Record Library (and once the archivist of the Beaverbrook Library) heaped up stacks of material for me, catalogued and uncatalogued; Mr Bruce Hunter of David Higham Associates rode his motorbike to north London to help me get at the Taylor files which were dumped somewhere in a heap in a lock-up garage; and – in a class of his own – Dr Robin Darwall-Smith of the Magdalen College archives facilitated my trawling through everything I wished to see, suggested other material, and rapidly answered the questions I sent to him via email.

A number of private individuals sent me copies of letters from or about Taylor, or allowed me to consult material in their private possession. Mr William Thomas of Christ Church, Oxford, who was both taught and supervised by Taylor, allowed me to borrow his scrapbook of Tayloriana. This provided material for a number of the discussions in the book, most notably that concerning the Special Lectureship which Taylor vacated in a cloud of publicity in 1963. Sir Martin Gilbert, who was taught by Taylor and who remained on close terms with him, loaned to me his thick folder of letters from and about Taylor. This was the main source for the story of Taylor's first *Festschrift*. Professor Chris Wrigley of Nottingham University, the compiler of an exemplary bibliography of Taylor's publications, provided me with copies of many of the letters written by Taylor which he has collected for future publication. Mrs Elaine Koss sent me copies of letters from Taylor to her husband, Professor Stephen Koss. Mrs Pamela Gott provided me with letters from Taylor to her husband, Mr Charles Gott. Mr Brian Pearce sent me a copy of a letter from Taylor. Mr Edmund Roskell provided me with two thick exercise books of notes taken by his mother, then Miss Evelyn Liddell, at Taylor's lectures at Manchester. Professor Klaus Schwabe provided me with letters by one of Taylor's German antagonists, Professor Gerhard Ritter. Mr David Brindley, Headmaster of Buxton Community College, lent me a history of the school as well as bound copies of the school magazine. M. André Etchenique, Directeur of the Hôtel du Quai Voltaire, arranged for me to be shown around the hotel xii • *Preface and Acknowledgements*

and provided me with a photograph. Dr Éva Haraszti-Taylor loaned me the ledger book containing Taylor's list of books read. Mr David Machin was the authority on the pleasure Taylor took in doing his own income tax. Mr Jonathan Lloyd confirmed the period of Taylor's relationship with Curtis Brown. Mr James Richards pointed me towards material on the Wroclaw Conference. Professor Gordon Craig sent his recollections of E.L. Woodward. One of my most enjoyable research excursions was to Penrith, where Mr Alastair and Mrs Nicola Durroch put me up whilst I searched through the papers of Theodore (Jack) Yates, Taylor's close friend from his Oxford days. I now see the attractions of the sort of research which requires extended visits to country houses.

A number of people talked to me about Taylor or provided useful information, sometimes formally into a tape recorder and sometimes informally. I am grateful to Professor M.R.D. Foot, who first sounded me out about my writing this book; to Mrs Doris Fell (Little Dolly), who talked to me about Taylor's early years; to Mr Daniel Taylor, Taylor's youngest son; to Mrs Mary (Crozier) McManus, daughter of the Editor of the *Manchester Guardian*, Mr W.H. Crozier; to Mrs Henrietta Kotlan-Werner, Taylor's Austrian nanny, who talked with me for hours about old Vienna and about Taylor in Vienna, Manchester and Oxford; to Miss Betty Kemp of St Hugh's College, Oxford, who was a student at Manchester when Taylor was there, and a friend and colleague at Oxford; to Mr Alan Baxendale, who wrote to me about Taylor's teaching at Manchester; to Annie and Patrick Eccles, who revealed to me the drill of 'eating dinners' as a preparation for the Bar; to Mrs June Barraclough Benn, cousin of Taylor's friend, Professor Geoffrey Barraclough; to Professor David Worswick, Taylor's colleague at Magdalen; to Mr John Stoye, likewise a Magdalen colleague; to Sir Martin Gilbert, undergraduate student and long-time friend of Taylor; to Lord Dacre and Lord Beloff, both long-time Oxford colleagues of Taylor; to Sir John Coles, a former student; to Mr Gerald Howat, who worked with Taylor on a dictionary of world history; to Dr Dusan Radojicic, a Magdalen colleague of Taylor; to Mr John Steane, a former student; to Professor David Bellos, a Magdalen Prize Fellow (via email); to Professor Paul Ginsborg, the source of the Italian use of one of Taylor's books; to Professor Penelope Corfield, who told me about student reaction to Taylor's last lecture to Oxford undergraduates; to Mr Michael Langham, a local historian in Buxton, who was very helpful in my attempt to make sense of Taylor's schooling; to Mr and Mrs Graham Marten, who live in the Taylor family house in Birkdale, and who kindly showed me round; to Mr and Mrs Adrian Lutte, who live in Taylor's old house in Higher Disley, and who both showed me round and allowed me to read the deeds to the house; to Ms Gillian Bell and Ms Karen Bradley, who live in Taylor's old home in Preston (which sports a blue plaque in his honour); to my colleagues Dr Axel Körner and Mr David Morgan; to Mr Keith Kyle, former BBC Home Service producer; to Mrs Rachel Hemming Bray, London neighbour of Taylor; to Mr Christopher Dunn, source of Taylor's clubland reputation; to Professor Chris Wrigley; and to all of my friends, dinner-party partners and people met at receptions and book launches who increased considerably my store of Tayloriana.

Other friends helped me in a number of ways. Four of my students at different times helped with my research: Dr Giora Goodman kept an eye out for material on Taylor whilst researching his Ph.D on anti-American-ism; Mr Oliver Wright spent part of a summer combing archives in an exemplary manner; Mr Mark Pendleton sped off to find and photocopy articles for me at a moment's notice; and Mr Andrew Taylor spent a day helping me go through the hundreds of David Higham files heaped on the floor of the north London garage, trying to find those on Taylor. Ms Nell Aubrey photocopied articles and checked some references for me. Fräulein Ulrike Wunderle, my research assistant in Tübingen, took over the trans-lation of articles when my baby German proved unequal to the task. Mr Peter Morgan, journalist and friend, voluntarily and selflessly made the initial foray into the BBC archives. Dr Michael Jewess joined me in searching for Taylorian venues, and photographed them; he constructed the 1995 index; he designed and printed out the bar chart and table of Taylor's earnings; and he was responsible for two of the translations from the German. Miss Miranda Jewess read and assessed G.A. Henty's *The Young Carthaginian* for me. Ms Jane Card combed C.S. Lewis's *That Hideous Strength* for me, trying to ascertain which character was based on Harry Weldon. Dr Éva Haraszti-Taylor provided me with photographs of Taylor and his family, whilst Dr Rick Halpern provided me with two photographs of The Mill at Yarmouth.

After the research comes the writing, and it then becomes clear who your friends are, because it is they who are willing to read the chapters. A number who had known Taylor, or who have specialist knowledge about some of the topics covered in the book, read individual chapters, and I am grateful to them for taking the time. Professor Reba Soffer read the chapter on the great books; Dr Giora Goodman read the chapter on Taylor's freelance career; Dr Axel Körner read the chapter on Vienna; Professor

David Worswick, Mr John Stoye, Dr Robin Darwall-Smith, Mr William Thomas and Sir John Coles each read the chapter on Oxford; Dr Michael Jewess read four of the chapters; Dr George Bernard read three of the middle chapters; and Sir Martin Gilbert read the Oxford chapter as well as the *Festschrift* section of the London chapter. Others read most or all of the entire manuscript. Miss Betty Kemp, who knew Taylor for the last sixty years of his life and who shared his academic milieu, read the entire manuscript, indicating where I had gone wrong in the same manner as she had done when I was her pupil at St Hugh's. Professor David Eastwood read all but the final chapter, and commented extensively: his footprints can be found all over the notes. Dr Éva Haraszti-Taylor, and my colleagues Professor David French and Professor David d'Avray, hard man and soft man respectively, also read virtually the entire thing. Ms Jane Card, Head of History at Didcot Girls' School in Oxfordshire, read the entire manuscript; so did Mrs Margaret Evans, my Intelligent General Reader. Mr Jeremy Wormell, close friend and ferocious critic, also read the whole manuscript. And finally, my agent, Mr Bill Hamilton of A.M. Heath, and my editor, Dr Robert Baldock, midwifed the book: I recommend them unreservedly. I am very grateful to everyone mentioned here. The usual disclaimers apply.

Chapter 1

The Child Is Father to the Man
1906–1927

It was ... boring to sit by while the other children were taught their letters. Usually I was given a real book that I read by myself in a corner. The other children became, just like the grown-ups, distant noises that did not disturb my reading. Books were for me real life; people were an interruption and hardly even that.

A.J.P. Taylor, *A Personal History*

Certainly I loved history as far back as I can remember. I cannot explain this. It seems to me natural, just like loving music or the Lake District mountains.

A.J.P. Taylor, 'Accident Prone, or What Happened Next'

A.J.P. Taylor was a child of the north of England. The northern counties combine great natural beauty with commercial and industrial centres which can be grimy and depressing. Taylor was born in Lancashire, and all his life he considered himself a Lancastrian. Although he lost most of his northern accent at Oxford, elements remained, supplemented by a bluntness of speech often at odds with the more ironic and understated Oxford style. He grew up in Southport, Buxton (in Derbyshire) and Preston. He went to secondary school in York. He had a very northern attitude to money – he was quite open about his pleasure in making it – and a devotion to the Lake District of Cumbria. Even in his seventies he continued to walk the Lakeland fells.

An only child, Taylor grew up in comfortable circumstances in a household with plenty of money. More unusual was the fact that this affluent household also developed into a bastion of left-wing radicalism. His father, whom he adored, considered himself a reformist Socialist, while his mother, whom he disliked, leaned more towards revolutionary

Communism. Taylor in his youth supported the idea of revolution which enabled him to strike a pose at school and Oxford, but gradually evolved towards reformism.

During his years at school and university, Taylor was clever and contrary, interested in history and politics, devoted to books rather than to people. Unusual in his accomplishments, he was like many other men and women at the age of twenty-one and at the end of his education: he had very little idea of what he wanted to do.

Taylor was born on Sunday, 25 March 1906 in Birkdale, Lancashire. Both elements of his birthplace were to lose their individual identities: in 1912 Birkdale merged with Southport, of which it became a suburb, and in 1974 this part of Lancashire became part of Merseyside. Taylor took this badly, particularly the change which relegated that part of his beloved county to a lumpen entity called Merseyside: he always held to the old geographical style. Birkdale/Southport fulfilled two functions: it was an up-market seaside resort, and it was a dormitory community for Manchester and Liverpool, especially for cotton merchants and mill-owners. Both of these functions developed because of the railways: railways took the working-class day-trippers to Blackpool, 'a much jollier place' than Southport according to Taylor,[1] leaving the latter largely to the middle classes; and the railway carried businessmen, including Taylor's father, to Manchester and back each day.

Taylor spent most of the first seven years of his life in a house called 'Bicknor', at 18 Crosby Road, Birkdale. Approaching it today, the driver might enter Birkdale from the south, noting the long line of sand dunes on the left (until the late eighteenth century Southport was nothing but dunes) drive up a wide road, cross a railway line – on which Taylor's father rode an electric train from Birkdale to Southport in order to catch the steam train to Manchester – and continue to Crosby Street. His home was a large, detached house built in 1887, with a stained-glass window on the left (west) side of the first floor, a lawn running the length of the east side, and a back yard rather than a garden, with most of the space taken up by a conservatory and a wash house. There were two sitting rooms on the ground floor, along with the kitchen and butler's pantry, and several bedrooms on the first floor, one of which was Taylor's; there was also a series of attic rooms, two of which served as bedrooms for the maids, and in another of which his father built a dark room. In 1913, the year the family moved, the Southport Directory gave the household as the only one in Crosby Road with a telephone.[2]

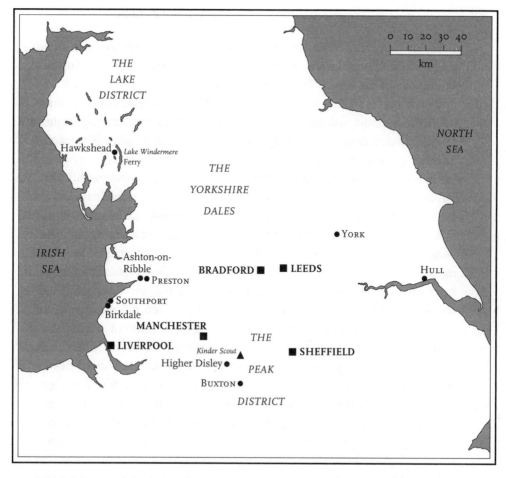

Taylor and the North of England 1906–38
Born and lived Birkdale 1906–13; lived Buxton 1914–19, school 1914–17; lived Ashton-on-Ribble 1919–24; school in York; summer holidays Hawkshead 1919–24; lecturer at Manchester University; lived Higher Disley 1933–8

This was a comfortable, even affluent, household, and it was supported by a complement of servants. There were the two resident maids, a charwoman, who also did the household wash on Mondays, a gardener and occasionally an extra girl who would take Taylor for walks when he was a toddler and small child; there was no governess as such. Taylor remembered one of the general maids in particular, called Annie Clark, who seems to have fulfilled the practical as well as the emotional role of nurse or governess, taking care of him, hugging him and listening to his stories. Hilda, the girl who took him for walks, seems also to have given him his first fumbling initiation into the outwardness of sexual differences: 'the female anatomy had henceforward no mysteries for me.'[3]

Taylor's father, Percy Lees Taylor, was a man of ambiguity, and Taylor was devoted to him; he was less devoted to his mother, Constance Sumner Thompson. They came from different family backgrounds, had wildly different personalities and appear, from Taylor's descriptions, to have made the best of a bad job rather than living together in a marriage of true minds. Taylor certainly differentiated between the family traits of the Thompsons and the Taylors.

Taylor could trace back his Taylor ancestry only to his great-grandfather, Edmund Taylor, a pedlar from Dunblane in Scotland who had drifted down to Lancashire and set up a general store in Heywood, East Lancashire. It was important to Taylor that Edmund was a radical (or at least a Sweden-borgian, a follower of the mystical and nonconforming religious movement, which would indicate that he was an independent thinker); and he always took pride in the fact that an ancestor of his paternal grand-mother had been killed in 1819 at Peterloo near Manchester, during the massacre of men and women gathered to hear a speaker on parliamentary reform (Henry 'Orator' Hunt). His forebears' political activities were important because part of his self-perception as an adult was that he came from a long line of Lancashire radicals. His grandfather, James Taylor, was the one who, in Taylor's words, 'set the family up' both in size and wealth: he had seven sons and four daughters, and he grew rich exporting cotton cloth to India. Taylor surmised that his grandfather's original capital had come to him through his marriage to Amelia Lees, daughter of an old Quaker family. In any case, he prospered quickly: he married at twenty, and six years later he moved his family to Ashton-on-Ribble, which in due course became one of the more prosperous parts of Preston.[4] In 1919 Taylor's father would himself return there to live.

James Taylor was, in the words of his son's obituarist, 'a hard-bitten Lancashire cotton man if ever there was one',[5] and he was also a domestic tyrant. As Taylor described matters, 'Silence had to reign on the news, "Father's back" ... [He] treated his wife abominably. He neglected her, imposed twelve children on her (one died in infancy), and when she was worn out with childbearing and household cares, complained: "Oo's a teaser". He often went off with other women and frequented the brothels in Manchester and Preston.' It was Taylor's belief that his own father was 'soft' towards his wife (Taylor's mother) because he had idolised his own mother and hated the way his father had treated her. Taylor extrapolated from this that he had taken after his own father and treated his wives with too much patience and acquiescence, and that both he and his father would have been better off had they been a bit tougher.[6]

Taylor's father, Percy, was the eldest son of James. He went to Preston Grammar School until he was sixteen, picking up a good grounding in mathematics and acquiring the habit of reading widely in English literature and political history. Upon leaving school he joined his father's firm in Manchester. Eight years later, James Taylor decided that, because he had a weak stomach, he might soon die and should therefore put his affairs in order. He settled enough money on each daughter to provide her with £500 a year for life. His sons were to become partners in James Taylor and Sons when they came of age, on condition they did not speculate on cotton futures. They all did. Three of the brothers fell hopelessly into debt and were dismissed from the firm without a penny after having all of the money they owed paid; four of them, including Percy, kept their speculations within bounds. James retired from business, though he kept the biggest share of the profits and absolute control of the business for twenty-one years.

Percy, as the eldest son, was now in practical terms the senior working partner in the business at the age of twenty-five. He was very well off, never, according to Taylor, making less than £5,000 a year and often more. He was clearly a great catch, if prospective marriage partners did not mind that the money came from trade. At a chapel dance he met a seventeen-year-old girl called Connie Sumner Thompson; he went home and told his brothers that 'I've met the girl I am going to marry.' He was obviously struck by her personality and looks; she was apparently struck by his position and the fact that he could offer her an escape from teaching: Taylor says that she often told him later that she married without love and only to get away from her elementary school (the Thompsons were not as well off as the Taylors, and teaching was frequently the refuge of the female who was educated but relatively poor). She was not impressed by his family; according to her own, the Taylors were 'common'. Taylor's evidence suggests that, for her, it was a marriage of convenience; however, it is entirely possible that it began as something more.[7]

Taylor was clearly of two minds about his Thompson ancestry, approving of the intelligence and drive, disliking the snobbishness, particularly the snobbishness shown towards his father. Coincidentally, the family name of both of his maternal grandparents was Thompson. His maternal grandfather, William Henry Thompson, a gentle man, kept a general warehouse which he neglected in favour of the Methodist Sunday school. According to Taylor, the strength of the family came from his maternal grandmother, Martha Thompson. This branch 'thought themselves rather grand', having 'in their ancestry a rich corn merchant, two of whose sons became solicitors, 'in Preston an almost aristocratic profession', and one of whom created Avenham Park, one of the first municipal parks in England. His grandmother was a stern woman, although kinder to him than to her own children, all of whom had been brought up to believe that they were superior to the riffraff around them: according to Taylor, 'they spoke "proper" and, ignoring their own father, boasted that they had nothing to do with trade. In character they divided three–three between father and mother. William Henry's children were soft and kind, Martha's were sharp-tongued and arrogant. My mother was one of Martha's children. My uncle Harry, cleverest of the lot, was another – in the Lancashire phrase, a clever-clogs.'[8]

Uncle Harry would in due course give him his first job, but as a child Taylor resented the fact that Harry and another of his brothers made fun of Percy Taylor, thinking themselves much cleverer than he was. In fact, they probably were, and Taylor himself sometimes implicitly admits this: he did not read Charles Dickens until he had left Oxford, assuming that because his father read him he could not be particularly good; he also admitted that he had learned quick-thinking and the ability to handle challenging comments from his Thompson relatives. Yet most of his descriptions in his autobiography paint his father in a favourable light, although the occasional bit of shade is allowed.

Taylor's memory of his father in his young days was of a man who always wore a blue serge suit and bowler hat to work and smoked Havana cigars, lighting his first in the morning as he set off. He was often at work, even during the family holidays, although he apparently tried to be home in the evenings to bathe his young son and put him to bed, telling him tales in Lancashire dialect. On Saturdays the two of them would often go into Southport for expeditions to Pleasureland, a seaside fun park with a miniature railway and a deep-sea diver called Professor Powsey, who performed spectacular dives which included one on a blazing bicycle. His father indulged and coddled him, said how fond he was of him and shielded him from his mother's disciplinary episodes. It is not surprising that Taylor was devoted to him.

But he must have sometimes been maddening for his wife to live with. Taylor's explanation was that he was 'a great romancer ... If he turned right on leaving the house in order to buy a newspaper, he would tell my mother on his return that he had turned left in order to buy tobacco. I asked him why he did this, and he said, "It makes things more interesting". ' In short, she could probably never tell for certain when he was being truthful and when not. He grew increasingly deaf, but he often pretended to be deafer than he was, particularly when his wife was likely to be saying something he did not want to hear. Much later Taylor wrote in a private letter that 'my father, though the most angelic man in the world, was devious and a dodger'.9 An inability to trust one's spouse does not make for harmonious marital relations.

In the same letter Taylor also referred to his mother as a bitch. His references to her in his autobiography, while not as venomous as that, are nevertheless by turns dismissive, disapproving and contemptuous. Again, it is not possible to know the truth of the matter, but it is possible, by using Taylor's comments and setting them in context, to modify the portrait with shade and light: rather than cold, snobbish and dull, perhaps she was disappointed, frustrated and intelligent.

It is clear that she was intelligent: in a period when girls' education was not taken very seriously, and coming from a family which was not wealthy, she would not have been kept in school – which would have been paid for after the primary period of education – if she had not been clever. In due course she would become very interested in Marxism, arguably at least partly because of the attraction of the power of ideas. Furthermore, she was a schoolteacher, even if an unwilling one. She read, she went to the theatre, she was very interested in politics, her mind was clearly alive.

She seems to have been something of a romantic. She and Percy married in 1900 and spent six months in India for their honeymoon. Taylor says that they 'made friends with a professional photographer called Tommy Hands who offered my mother the romantic appeal that she did not find in my father. This was the first of her more or less innocent escapades.'10 Taylor's father too must have had something of a romantic streak in him, or he would not have fallen in love at first sight. Nevertheless something was missing: perhaps the lack of sexual experience on one or probably both sides had made the honeymoon a profoundly disappointing period. Taylor certainly highlights his mother's supposed lack of interest in sex; perhaps he drew this conclusion from the fact that while he was still a very young boy his parents went over to twin beds (although there is always the prosaic possibility that one of them snored unbearably).11 In due course she would fall in love – possibly platonically, possibly not – with a younger man, Harry

Sara, an active member of the Communist Party, to whom she would remain devoted for the rest of her life.

She was an active woman. She played a very good game of golf – their house was 'crammed with silver cups that she had won at county championships'. Unfortunately, neither Taylor nor his father liked to play: as Taylor recalled, 'My father was not a keen golfer or a good one. But he was ordered to play. On Saturday mornings I stood at the front gate, looking pathetically after my father, who trailed his bag of golf clubs on the ground and looked pathetically back at me. In the end my mother gave up and found more willing partners' – not surprisingly. Why not just tell her he did not want to play? Why make it clear, week after week, what a bore it was and spoil her play? Taylor's father seems to have combined weakness with petulance. Taylor adds that his parents also played bridge, his father again unwillingly.[12]

His parents often gave large parties, sometimes garden parties for political organisations such as the Liberal Women of Southport, sometimes large dinner parties, sometimes social evenings. During the social evenings, according to Taylor, his father could not follow the general conversation and sat at the back of the room with a book, often Dickens. He does not seem to have objected to the social round, or at least Taylor does not mention it, but his interest must have been semi-detached, if he could not always follow a general conversation. Again, if his mother enjoyed these events, his father's inability to join in fully must have helped to widen the breach.

In short, Taylor's parents frequently did not share the small coin of everyday life. Between the two of them, personal expressions of affection, in spite of his father referring to her as 'Love', as in 'What did you say, Love?', seem not to have been common. They did not spend much of their spare time together, either in weekend activities or during holiday periods. The main beliefs they shared seem to have been political ones, and political activities would in due course take up more of their time, with her growing interest in very left-wing politics and his activities as a local councillor.

They had different approaches to child-rearing, and Taylor's affection for the one and relative lack of it for the other seem to have been based on this. His father frequently expressed his affection to him, spent lots of time with him when he was home, appears not to have disciplined him nor to have set boundaries for behaviour. His mother, he wrote, 'appears to me as a more remote figure. She was the disciplinarian in the household as her own mother had been before her. She was the one who made me sit on my pot or eat up food I did not like . . . In my mother's company I seem to have been always quiet and well-dressed.' Indeed, Taylor remembers that his father prevented his mother from spanking him once by standing between them and threatening that 'If you lay hands on that child I'll never speak to you again.'[13] Taylor never mentions that she played with him, only that she took him with her most mornings on the tram into Southport, where she took coffee and presumably met her friends at Thom's Japanese Tea Rooms in Lord Street. Naturally he preferred going to Pleasureland with his father. However, her influence could not have been entirely negative. After all, someone taught Taylor to read before he was four, and someone read to him for hours at a time, and it was probably not Annie Clark, a working-class girl whose reading skills were arguably not highly developed. Someone had to make certain that, as an only child, his behaviour was not impossible, and that routines were established and limits set. This, however, does not always endear a child to the parent, and particularly when the other parent confines himself to the more enjoyable aspects of child-raising.

Taylor makes a most revealing comparison between the two with regard to the death of his eighteen-month-old sister from tubercular meningitis in 1904, two years before he himself was born. He writes: 'Her death left a permanent mark on my father. He adored Miriam as he often told me and never ceased to grieve for her . . . My mother was less affected. Miriam's death merely increased her dislike for sex and childbearing.'[14] He appears to assume that his mother was less affected simply because she did not repeatedly tell him so. More likely the experience was so devastatingly painful that she could not talk about it – not unlikely when she seems to have been reserved in any case. She might also have thought it a sign of weakness to have referred to it in later years. Taylor, in short, seems to have been much less perceptive when writing about his mother than when writing about historical figures. His relationship with her is important because he used it as a pattern and sometimes as an excuse for his own future relationships with his wives.

Taylor, then, was an only child, his birth bracketed between the death of his sister when she was a toddler and by the stillbirth of a brother. There are disadvantages to growing up an only child: lack of a network of support, lack of experience in sharing, lack of close companions whom you might alternatively love or hate, but against whom you can try your muscles, your wit, your charm, and learn your strengths as well as your weaknesses. Taylor had to wait until he went to infants' school to find such opposition. He mentioned one family, the Blackwells, whose house was full of children – although much older than he was – and books. The Blackwells were, he wrote, the only people he talked to outside his own family. Their warmth and companionship were very important to him: he later equated Mr Blackwell, who ran the Congregational Sunday school that he attended, with Mr Greatheart in *The Pilgrim's Progress*. Yet of equal importance was the fact that 'the Blackwells were the only literate family I knew. Their house was full of books. They alone possessed the works of Beatrix Potter, actually bought as they came out. The books were one reason why I wanted to go to the Blackwells.' The implication is that there were no books in his own home. Yet his father loved Dickens and conveyed this affection to others (though not to his son); in addition, at least in the early 1920s, three of the walls in the Taylor drawing room were covered with books from floor to ceiling. Taylor had clearly forgotten this by the time he came to write his autobiography.[15] Books early on replaced people in his time and affection.

Indeed, it is worth considering what Taylor read and the role reading played in his early life. He could read before he was four and, he says, '*Pilgrim's Progress* was my favourite from the start. I read it again and again in an edition produced by the SPCK [Society for the Propagation of Christian Knowledge] and knew it almost by heart except that I skipped the theological conversations.' Fortunately for the young Taylor, action and talk alternated: for example, Christian flees the City of Destruction, chased by Obstinate and Pliable; Obstinate decides to go back, but 'Christian and Pliable went talking over the plain; and thus they began their discourse.' Taylor could then skip the next two-and-a-half pages, until Christian tumbles into the Slough of Despond and the story resumes.

It is perhaps a mark of his radical heritage that he was introduced to this book at such a young age, since it was the classic radical text. As E.P. Thompson wrote in *The Making of the English Working Class*, 'it is above all in Bunyan that we find the slumbering Radicalism which was preserved through the 18th century and which breaks out again and again in the 19th. *Pilgrim's Progress* is, with [Tom Paine's] *Rights of Man*, one of the two foundation texts of the English working-class movement: Bunyan and Paine, with Cobbett and Owen, contributed most to the stock of ideas and attitudes which make up the raw material of the movement from 1790–1850. Many thousands of youths found in *Pilgrim's Progress* their first adventure story, and would have agreed with Thomas Cooper, the Chartist, that it was their "book of books".'[16]

To our eyes it appears a curious book for a young child to read and reread: the seventeenth-century language is archaic and the theme is so obviously didactically religious. Yet it had a widespread popularity in the nineteenth and early twentieth centuries way beyond the radical English household. In the American Louisa May Alcott's *Little Women*, for example, Meg, Jo, Beth and Amy play at Pilgrim's Progress, leaving the City of Destruction in the cellar, fighting their way up the stairs armed with swords of righteousness and emerging into the Celestial City in the attic. It is also worth remembering that the range and availability of books for children were very much less than now: one of the best-selling children's books of the entire nineteenth century was called *Jessica's Last Prayer*, again very didactic (from which the percipient child could deduce that the good die young). In *The Pilgrim's Progress*, at least, there was fighting and excitement along with the religion. Nevertheless, it appears that Taylor finally outgrew the book: he read it – presumably the whole book now – for the final time when he was twenty-one.

There were other favourites. He confessed to the 'shameful' secret that when young he adored Frances Hodgson Burnett's *The Secret Garden*: 'in recollection it has become utterly detestable, and I had to go out of the room when it was being read to my children'. He liked fairy tales, he liked *Alice's Adventures in Wonderland* and *Through the Looking-Glass*, and he liked Barrie's *Peter and Wendy*, the book of the play *Peter Pan*. He liked reading newspapers, the *Daily News* and the *Manchester Guardian*; but he also liked the *Boys' Own Paper* and the weekly comics.[17] In short, even as a small child he read omnivorously, a habit that would only increase as he grew older and could read more complicated books.

He went off to nursery school at the age of four. This was run by the gentle Misses Annie and Kitty Filmer. It was not stimulating. As Taylor later wrote, 'the school made no impact on me and I can remember little about it. I was already reading grown-up books. It was therefore boring to sit by while the other children were taught their letters. Usually I was given a real book that I read by myself in a corner. The other children became, just like the grown-ups, distant noises that did not disturb my reading. Books were for me real life; people were an interruption and hardly even that.' It is not surprising that he made no friends. Children are not attracted to those who are different and Taylor must have seemed like a being from another world. He did not possess the saving grace of selfless charm nor the ability to hit a ball, either of which might have given him a place in the schoolchild hierarchy. Of course, he may have exaggerated his isolation: the memories in old age of early childhood are bound to be episodic rather than continuous. Nevertheless, it is significant that what he emphasises is his aloneness: 'going home, which was only two streets away, I walked in the gutter so as not to have to talk to the other children who walked on the pavement.'[18]

It all seems terribly pathetic, but is so only if Taylor regretted missing the company of chums. He gave no indication of this. Rather, he spent much of his time, when not alone, in the enlivening company of adults. There was, first of all, his father, and there was Joshua Blackwell; the three of them played cowboys and Indians on the sandhills after Sunday chapel. But most of all there was his extended family, principally his Thompson uncles and aunts. Rather than relegating him to another room as a child, 'they expected me, as the only child in the [Thompson] community, simply to step into it at their level.'[19] They all talked politics, they played card games such as Racing Demon in which Taylor was given no quarter, there was a lot of challenging banter in which he had to learn to hold his own.

The extended family sometimes took holidays together. Taylor remembered going on holiday in 1910 and 1912 to the Isle of Man, principally because sea crossings and seasickness were involved: 'my father had read somewhere that seasickness could be prevented by wrapping blotting paper round the stomach. We all wrapped it round except for my father who was a good sailor. We were all sick. He was not.' These family expeditions, which included both grandmothers, two Thompson aunts, his uncle Harry Thompson, uncle Harold Taylor, Taylor, his mother and Annie Clark, were entirely paid for by Taylor's father. They fished, swam, walked, had picnics, talked and argued and played cards. Taylor admitted of no loneliness.[20]

And then life changed abruptly. Early in 1913 Taylor's mother began spending most of her time in bed; one day he was sent to the Blackwells for a few days, but no one told him why. He was brought back home to find the house full of relatives and doctors and nurses; again, no one told him why. A day or two later he was taken up to his mother who, 'though very weak, greeted me with what was for her unusual affection. She remained in bed for a long time.' He remained in the dark. Eventually piecing together the jigsaw, he realised that his mother had had a stillborn child. There were severe complications which left her very much weakened for the rest of her life: she rested in the afternoons, she no longer played golf and she no longer even shared a bedroom with her husband.[21]

More bewildering for the seven-year-old Taylor, they abandoned their home and Southport entirely. 'Perhaps', Taylor later wrote, 'my parents could no longer stand its associations after a stillborn child on top of the death of Miriam. At any rate I was pulled up by the roots without warning.' A year later they would be living in Buxton in Derbyshire, but in the immediate future the family travelled to Italy. Taylor's mother needed warmth to help her recover, and it was decided that she, her son and Annie Clarke would spend the winter on the Italian Riviera – as Taylor noted, 'in those days, no one except the Italians went there in the summer.'[22]

En route, the family went first to London, where Taylor was taken to the House of Commons, a high treat for him, where he saw the Conservative opposition leader Andrew Bonar Law on the front bench – no memory remained of the Liberals, whom his parents supported. His other memories of his first visit to London are those such as would stick in the mind of any seven-year-old: the hotel on the river Thames, the bright flashing advertisements. Then to Paris and the Gare de Lyon and his first experience of a wagon-lit, which made an abiding and 'romantic' impression on him: for the remainder of his life he would adore sleeping in wagons-lits. When he awoke in the morning he drew the blinds and saw a great lake and the Alps in the distance; when the train reached Modane, the border town situated at the French end of rail and road tunnels leading to Italy, he 'walked self-importantly down the platform with my father in order to unlock our trunks for the customs officials.' From there they travelled to Turin and thence to Alassio. It was not an auspicious arrival: 'we took a carriage from the station to the pension where we were to stay. We were held up at a level crossing. It was raining heavily. I can see the rain beating against the carriage windows. My mother cried and blamed my father for bringing her to such an awful place.'[23]

The Italian, or Ligurian, Riviera is washed by the blue waters of the Ligurian Sea, and – theoretically – the skies are always clear, with a permanently mild climate. The Ligurian Apennines form a mountain barrier against the north winds, while the coast basks in the sunshine. The countryside is covered with pines, cypresses, olive trees, and orange and lemon trees: one of Taylor's few memories of his Italian sojourn was of watching oranges ripening. Alassio itself with its long beach lies along a bay and is sheltered by an amphitheatre of mountains; as a consequence its mean temperature in January is eleven degrees centigrade. Taylor's mother was brought here to rest, to exercise gently, to recover. His father settled them in their pension and, after remaining a few weeks, went back to England and his work.

Taylor remembered very little of his months in Italy. He learned to count in Italian and helped Annie Clarke with the shopping. He remembered his eighth birthday, 25 March 1914, when his mother hired donkeys and they went up a hill to eat lunch, lizards running over the stones at their feet and the blue sea below; his new electric torch made a deeper impression. Beyond that, very little. And because he always had a retentive memory, this argues that very little happened from day to day.

His mother grew bored and, without consulting her husband, decided that they would leave Alassio. According to Taylor, this was the signal for a change in their relationship. She had always depended on her husband to make the arrangements for their travels; in his absence, Taylor worked out the hotel bookings and the train times. As a consequence, 'my mother came to rely on me for planning things, which I did without the arguments and equivocations that my father could not resist. In time she came to depend on me a little for ideas, as soon as I read more serious books than she did.' From this he drew yet another conclusion about his future marital relationships: 'I do not think I ever became fond of her. But unconsciously I slipped into the attitude towards women that my father had before me: that one must look after them and carry out their wishes even if these were unwelcome or foolish. Softheartedness became a substitute for affection, in my case not untinged with irritation.'[24]

They travelled north-east to Milan for two nights, where Taylor saw the first picture that remained in his memory, Leonardo da Vinci's *Last Supper*, and then continued north to Lugano in Switzerland, where they spent some weeks. Lugano is on the lake of the same name, bounded in by the Alps on whose slopes olive trees grow. It made a bit more of an impact on his memory than Alassio had done: he remembered going up a hill and then walking down, and he remembered the reflection of the lights on the lake. Of the journey home he remembered almost nothing. He did remember that there was no home to which they could return, as the house in Birkdale had been given up, and that they had had to stay with his grandmother Thompson, who was living in Lytham. This was a pleasant small town in Lancashire with a windmill and a green next to the promenade, which could be reached by steamship across the Ribble estuary from Southport, undoubtedly a more pleasant journey than the circuitous one necessary by train.

After a short period, the family moved to Buxton, first into a furnished house and then in September 1914 into the house in which Taylor first began to put down some roots. Buxton had been a spa town since the time of the Romans, with its mineral springs celebrated for their healing properties since the sixteenth century. Its development was accelerated during the Victorian period, however, and by 1900 it had reached its heyday as a fashionable spa and resort. Built on the Derbyshire hills, by 1914 it sported dozens of hotels and guest houses, some of great luxury, an opera house, the Pavilion Gardens, a pump room with five massive silvered fountains through which the healing water flowed, thermal baths and a plethora of shops. When the Taylors moved there, at the beginning of the war, the town retained its elegance, but the function of many of the buildings would change and, with the Devonshire Hospital devoted to convalescing Canadian soldiers, a breath of the outside world entered. Twenty-two miles from Manchester, Percy Taylor could travel to work on the '40-minutes' expresses'.[25]

The Taylors lived in a large semi-detached house at 10 Manchester Road, not as large as the Birkdale house and with only one lawn instead of two, but still with such amenities as a butler's pantry and large attics. It was midway down a wide, straight road which was wonderful for bicycle riding – from the top of the road Taylor could freewheel for over a mile – and which during the colder winters was closed off and used as a toboggan run. Taylor remembered the latter practice as being instituted by the Canadian soldiers during the winter of 1916–17, when they waited until the snow had settled and then poured water on the lower slopes, which turned to ice overnight; however, it is clear from old photographs that it was not the first time this had been done. In any case, Taylor found it both terrifying and exhilarating: 'the speed was terrifying, particularly with the knowledge that, if you spilled, you would fall on to hard ice, not soft snow. A good many adults had broken arms and gashed faces. I made myself go down the run again and again, usually alone because I could get no one of my own age to go with me. I thought that if I did this often enough I should stop being frightened. This did not happen, but I discovered that you learn to live with fear just like any other discomfort.'[26]

Taylor liked Buxton very much. He thought it had much more character than Birkdale, both in the amenities and in the buildings. He liked swimming in the warm thermal baths much more than in the cold sea, and he liked going about Buxton, especially once he had learned to ride a bicycle. If, instead of freewheeling down Manchester Road towards the centre, he rode up and away in the opposite direction, he reached the open country in less than half a mile. He could explore the hills and, nearer to home, Corbar Woods.

His social and family life both improved. He made some friends with whom he went around and he 'even had a girl friend' whose hand he daringly held whilst walking back from school. Furthermore, for a period he had siblings of a sort. His uncle Jim Taylor was in Calcutta throughout the war looking after the Taylor firm's interests, and his two daughters came to live with them in Buxton, one a little older, the other a little younger. Taylor notes that 'I almost lost the habits of an only child. I fitted in with other people more and had people of my own age to play games with instead of always waiting for the arrival of some grown up.' All in all, Buxton was a vast improvement on Birkdale: although part of the improvement probably stemmed from Taylor's being older and more independent and therefore able to get around alone, part certainly arose from his having friends his own age and leading a more normal childhood existence.[27]

He was excited about going back to school – it had been eighteen months since he had last attended one. What is unknown is which school it was. Taylor is very clear about it: 'the school was of the sort, then common in England, that took girls to the age of sixteen or eighteen and boys to the age of eleven. It was kept by a Madame de la Motte. Her husband who taught French in the school was Swiss. She, I think, was a native of Buxton.' Unfortunately, there is no trace in the contemporary directories of a school run by Madame de la Motte, although she and her husband certainly lived in Buxton. There was a school for boys not a hundred yards from Taylor's house, called Holm Leigh, and this is close to Corbar Woods, which he remembered as close enough to play in during school hours; however, there were no girls. Another possibility was an institution called the Marlborough College for Girls, which was also situated nearby, but it is unclear whether it took boys.[28]

Wherever he went to school, he seems to have enjoyed it: 'I was pushed up into a class beyond my age and therefore had reasonably interesting things to do. I remember with a vague affection Miss Purvis who taught English and History, not so much because of anything she taught me as because she took her class to Corbar Woods nearby where we played Cavaliers and Roundheads – a variant, supposedly educational, of cowboys and Indians. I do not need to say which side I was on, indeed commanded.'

The fact that he cared which side he was on undoubtedly arose from two sources: his reading, and the strong political beliefs of his parents. As he later wrote, 'Even though I had more social life, I also read more, and more obsessively. Soon after we came to Buxton I discovered the public library. This must have been soon after I was nine, because I remember the difficulty I had in getting a ticket to the adult library at that age.' The library was stocked with the classics, 'the sort of collection you might find in a country house', not with new novels. But he knew what he wanted: he wanted historical novels. He read every novel by Harrison Ainsworth in the library, although he also read the Victorian classics of Charles Kingsley, *Hereward the Wake*, in which a reckless young Saxon retires to the Fens and for a time successfully opposes the Norman conquerors, and *Westward Ho!*, a romance of the Spanish Main which culminates in the destruction of the Armada. None of these could be counted on for historical accuracy, but they were lively and full of action and set in the past, all of which elements attracted him.

His favourite historical novelist, however, wrote another type of book entirely. This was G.A. Henty, and Taylor went so far as to collect these novels himself so that he could reread them at his pleasure. Henty had been a soldier in the Crimea and then a war correspondent in Italy, Abyssinia, Ashanti, Spain and India, and in Paris during the revolutionary uprising of the Commune. An unsuccessful adult novelist, he wrote thirty-six novels for boys, sometimes three or four a year, mainly based on military history, especially that of the Thirty Years War, the Peninsular War and the various wars of the British Empire. (Taylor said that he ignored books on the Empire, having already written off that institution.) Taylor's favourite was *A Roving Commission*, which is about a slave rebellion. One authority refers to Henty's 'didactic influence, conveyed largely through the manly characters of the heroes', which is 'supported by strong narrative and an appearance of historical fidelity.' It is questionable whether Taylor absorbed a sense of manly character in the way Henty presumably intended, but he certainly took note of the driving narrative and the historical detail. As he wrote many years later, 'long, long ago I read the works of Henty with more eagerness, more enjoyment and more application than I did those of any other history writer, perhaps even with more profit.'[29]

Henty's books are certainly full of historical detail. Take *The Young Carthaginian*, the eponymous hero of which is a young nobleman turned soldier called Malchus. The first few chapters focus on the political state of Carthage, after which the reader follows Malchus around the ever-decreasing empire as Hannibal tries to defend it from the Romans. The reader shares with Malchus the last great Carthaginian victories, but the book then takes a personal turn as Malchus is captured, and ends with his marriage to a Gaulish wife and his departure to live in the Alps as a 'barbarian'.[30] Whenever Henty comes to a new people in the march to the eventual battle with the Romans, he stops and spends pages on description:

The Gauls had a passion for ornaments, and adorned their persons with a profusion of necklaces, bracelets, rings, baldricks, and belts of gold. Their national arms were long heavy pikes – these had no metal heads, but the points were hardened by fire; javelins of the same description – these before going into battle they set fire to, and hurled blazing at the enemy – lighter darts called *matras saunions*, pikes with curved heads, resembling the halberts of later times; and straight swords. Hannibal, however, finding the inconvenience of this diversity of weapons, had armed his Gaulish troops only with their long straight swords. These were without point, and made for cutting only, and were in the hands of these powerful tribesmen terrible weapons. These swords were not only those they had been accustomed to carry, which were made of copper only, and often bent at the first blow, but were specially made for them in Carthage of heavy steel, proof against all accidents.[31]

And so on.

Taylor loved these books for their historical descriptions and for the battles. He read 'one book after another about the Thirty Years' war, each one if I remember aright turning on a single obscure battle. The best feature was the battle diagrams with little oblongs for the opposing forces of cavalry and infantry. I reproduced them on the attic floor with my toy soldiers, setting up one dreary battle after another.'[32] Taylor is dismissive of his younger self with his passion for 'dreary' historical detail, but the books fed a mind hungry for facts. There were not the alternatives of today, with shelves of non-fiction history books written specifically for each age group. Once he arrived at Bootham School at the age of thirteen, Taylor would be encouraged to gather together his own historical details. Until then, Henty filled a need.

Taylor, then, was from the beginning history-minded, and his wide reading of historical novels (plus his devotion to *The Pilgrim's Progress*?) gave him a context in which the political theories exemplified by the Cavaliers and Roundheads had real meaning for him. But equally important in giving him a theory with which to approach both history in his early days and politics throughout his life was the influence of his parents. They were Nonconformist in religion and therefore – almost by definition – Liberals; they had discussed politics with Joshua Blackwell, who was a Socialist, and others in Birkdale; but in Buxton both of his parents shot sharply to the left, and took the young Taylor with them. The catalyst was the First World War.

Late in 1914 Percy Taylor came home from Manchester unusually agitated, saying to his wife, 'Asquith and Grey are honourable men. I don't believe they would have lied to us.' He had been reading Bernard Shaw's *Common Sense about the War*, which had come out as a supplement to the weekly political magazine, the *New Statesman*. Shaw argued that 'the Foreign Office, of which Sir Edward [Grey, the Foreign Secretary] is merely the figure head, was as deliberately and consciously bent on a long deferred Militarist war with Germany as the Admiralty was; and that is saying a good deal.' Asquith and Grey 'gave the country assurances which were misunderstood to mean that we were not bound to go to war, and not more likely to do so than usual.'[33] In short, Britain was no better than Germany. According to Taylor, 'it was the beginning of his disillusionment. In no time at all my father had finished with the Liberal party for ever. He did not yet know where to go. At that time it was impossible to become an individual member of the Labour party, and I doubt whether a branch of the ILP [the Independent Labour Party], the only alternative, existed in Buxton. But our house was soon full of ILP pamphlets . . . which I read with unquestioning conviction. My father still held that the war had to be fought now we were in it, but he believed that he and other Radicals had been led into it fraudulently.'[34]

His mother soon went further. In 1916 his uncle Harry decided that he would not obey the (now compulsory) call-up: he was, according to Taylor, among the first conscientious objectors, 'and an "absolutist" at that'. Harry Thompson's stand was not based on party political theory – he was not then a Marxist – nor was he religious: he simply believed in individual liberty and that the state therefore had no right to conscript him. He spent the rest of the war in various prisons. This radicalised his sister. She followed him from court-martial to court-martial and from prison to prison, staying in nearby hotels and supplying him with food and newspapers, and slipping bribes of supplies to guards. It was tantamount to a religious conversion: driven out of chapel by the war-like stance of the preachers, she turned to the conscientious objectors as the real men of God. But she went further than turning against the war: she also turned against established society, and in the name of striking a blow against the war she tried to undermine it by disobeying as many of the petty regulations appertaining to the war as she could find – food rationing in particular. (She struck a blow against war-mongering by hoarding butter.) Taylor certainly absorbed the left-wing and anti-war attitudes of his parents, attitudes which would play a part in future changes in his school career.

By the beginning of 1916, when Taylor was still only nine years old, he had learned everything that his infants' school had to teach him, and it was decided that he should move to the local grammar school, Buxton College. Endowed in the seventeenth century, it had never had the funds to develop into the quality of school that its status implied. Indeed, by the outbreak of the war, it was only the private income of the headmaster, H.S. Lawson, that had enabled electric lighting to be installed; the headmaster himself never received a salary. The college had made some attempt over the previous thirty years to develop into a major public school, but the numbers of boarders, the source of profits for a public school, had never reached the levels required for financial security. It therefore lived under the shadow of having to become a council school.

At the outbreak of the war in August 1914 every member of staff joined up, and an entirely new staff had to be appointed for the autumn term. In November 1915 Lawson too insisted on joining the army, and A.N. Fynes-Clinton, a sixty-five-year-old retired headmaster, became acting head; he died of heart disease within the year, to be succeeded by J.E. Gallaher, who had been a member of staff for less than a year. These rapid changes provided the very sort of uncertainty that parents find alarming, and the decline in the numbers of boarders and the quality of the school accelerated. Certainly when the school was inspected several years later by H.M. Inspectors, they reported that 'the work of the School falls much below what can reasonably be expected in an efficient secondary school'. Taylor must have been sent there because, unless he boarded or went to a state school, which seems not to have been contemplated, there was little alternative.[35]

Two years younger than was usual for admission, Taylor was put in the lowest form, only to be moved up after a term. Catering for the sons of local tradespeople, not of the professional classes, it had always been 'a rough place, and the war had made it rougher', probably because the younger masters, who might have been able to control the pupils, had gone into the forces. Certainly the elderly headmaster, A.N. Fynes-Clinton, was unable to maintain discipline. It might be thought that this was the sort of place where Taylor's precociousness would have provoked bullying, but this was not the case: 'I suppose the bigger boys were not jealous of intellectual achievement and quite ready to seek my help with their home work', while the headmaster was delighted to have a clever pupil. Indeed, Taylor positively enjoyed Buxton College, finding the work interesting and collecting a leather-bound book prize at the end of each term.[36]

Yet after only a year he was abruptly removed from the school. His mother complained that he also was becoming rough in his speech and manners, but it is probable that her real reason for taking him away was her anti-war convictions. Taylor recalled that 'one day in the summer of 1916 I came home with the news that Mr Gallaher had taken us out into the fields and shown us the trenches where the older boys trained in the OTC [Officers' Training Corps]. My mother was horrified. In her mind's eye she already saw me in the trenches or the guardroom. The hateful war was closing in on me. She determined that I must move school at once.' There is no doubt that for a parent with anti-war convictions, Buxton College would have seemed a war-obsessed place. A school cadet corps had been formed, which was recognised by the War Office and attached to the Notts and Derby division; they drilled regularly, went on long marches once a week, formed a drum and bugle band, and during holidays went on extended manoeuvres with other cadet corps. The school was regularly notified of the wounding and deaths of Old Buxtonians, the names of whom were listed in the school magazine.[37]

This, however, would have been the case with most schools during the war. His mother turned first to Manchester Grammar School, which of course also had a cadet corps; the headmaster advised her that she should find a Quaker school (implicitly pacifist) for her son, and suggested Bootham in York. She rushed there, only to discover that they would not admit Taylor until he was thirteen, which was two years away. The Bootham headmaster, Arthur Rowntree, told her that there was a Quaker prep school near Malvern, and the decision was taken to send him there. He would have to board, and his father hated the idea: according to Taylor, he was even unhappier than his son was when he left for school. But Taylor was unhappy enough: 'in January 1917 my parents accompanied me to the Downs School, Colwall near Malvern, and handed me over to Herbert William Jones, the headmaster. In utter misery I watched them disappear through the front gate.'[38]

The contrast between home and school struck Taylor forcibly. At home he had two rooms of his own, a bedroom and the Den, where he read and played; at school he shared everything, sleeping and living space – and furthermore, unlike home, or Buxton College, it was cold. For a loner such as Taylor, this was purgatory. He had great freedom at home: he was free to roam, to read, to be alone or to go out with friends. At the Downs everything was planned, timed and checked. He had had friends, books, warmth and comfort and interesting work at home; at school, some of these elements at least were for a while in short supply.

The Downs was a relatively new foundation, dating only from 1900, and the founding headmaster was also the proprietor; because he happened to be a Quaker, it was considered a Quaker school. Jones and his wife Ethel ran it according to their own lights, often improvising in the early days – at the beginning there were only four boys and they were the only teaching and pastoral staff; by 1918, the end of Taylor's first year, there were forty. Their philosophy implied less attention to the purely academic and more to the whole boy, so activities and hobbies, especially those related to natural history (they were both keen naturalists), predominated. (More unusually for a Quaker school, the Downs was to develop a strong tradition in music.) The concentration on the individual, however, gave scope to Ethel Jones, the dominant character of the two, who imposed her ideas on the daily lives of the pupils.

Taylor characterised them as opposite personalities. He remembered Jones as softhearted and occasionally bad-tempered, but as a reasonably good Classics teacher who gave him lessons in Greek. Others remembered him as happiest teaching complicated mnemonics to help the boys remember the rules of Latin grammar. Nevertheless, the overall picture is vague and soft-edged. Ethel Jones, conversely, left a clear impression on all who came across her. One old boy recalled that 'she hurried everywhere, spoke in high-pitched tones, and used to shout across the lawn to Mr Jones in ungrammatical Quaker English, "Herbert, will thee please come here".'[39] Taylor remembered her as

> a formidable figure. She had a high corsetted bust, swathed in red velvet, and hair piled high ... Character building was her obsession, and for her this meant punctuality and cleanliness. The price of these, she believed, was eternal vigilance, a quality in which she was by no means lacking. Her sharp eyes were never dimmed. Everything and particularly the boys ran to the second, and every activity was meticulously observed. When one of the junior matrons woke us up first thing in the morning, she noted the precise time. We were allowed ten minutes in which to take a cold bath, wash and dress. If we took longer, we missed porridge at breakfast. Instead we had to change back into pyjamas and dressing gown, report to Mrs Jones in the dining room and dress again. The slow dresser missed his breakfast altogether. If we got ready in the prescribed ten minutes, we lined up before Mrs Jones who inspected our hands, teeth and ears, ruthlessly sending us back at the slightest sign of dirt.

She seems to have been obsessed by the number three as well as by cleanliness. The boys' beds were inspected three times while they were being made – bottom sheet on, top blanket tucked in and coverlet on – a mistake and all had to begin again from the beginning. When shoes were cleaned, again there was a three-fold inspection – dirt off, polish on and shoes polished. Each change of activity during the day seems to have engendered its own inspection. When one new master came to the school, he was struck by 'the immaculate tidiness everywhere' – the linoleum was so highly polished that he could see his face in it.[40]

Mrs Jones was also determined that her charges should learn good table manners. Derelictions, such as spilling something or neglecting to notice that your neighbour's plate was empty and thus not passing him food, earned the punishment of 'plain fare', which meant bread and water for a meal. However, the ordinary food was so uninspiring, or even bad – Taylor remembered it as inedible, and it seems to have consisted of cold meat, potatoes and cabbage – that bread and water might not have seemed much of a penalty had the bread not been standard wartime issue. Wheat had to be imported, which meant shipping it from North America or Australia through the German submarine blockade, and so bread tended to be made from other grains such as rye.

Certain elements of the school routine were common amongst Quaker schools, particularly meetings on Sundays, improving literature and nature study. The Quaker meeting house in Malvern, on the other side of the Malvern Hills, was too far to go every Sunday, so meeting was held in the school gymnasium. Mr Jones spoke when the spirit moved him (thought-fully, it also provided him with a manuscript from which to make his impromptu talk), but Mrs Jones never did: instead she kept a close eye on the boys. Taylor, though not religious, enjoyed meeting, because no one was inspecting him or telling him what to do: rather, he could let his mind wander. The forced reading of certain books made him more cross: he particularly disliked the activity (initiated by Mrs Jones) called 'Stiff Reading'. 'For an hour we had to read some solid book, not a work of fiction. I did not mind these solid books, most of which I should have read in any case. But I resented being denied any relief at other times – no Sexton Blake, no comics, nothing but improving works.' Worst of all was nature study, his 'special bugbear', a topic which, over a half-century later, could still arouse his detestation and despair:

I tried one variety after another, always in vain. I tried Aquarium. My tadpoles died. I could not catch newts. My tank smelled. I tried Astronomy and could never identify the stars. I even tried Lichen, the dreariest study known to man. Worst of all was the Flower List. This was a great printed sheet, issued to each boy, with the names of some 200 flowers and space for even rarer ones. We had to collect these flowers on our Sunday walk and then name them to Mr Jones the next morning. Some boys scored well over a hundred in no time. I never got more than half a dozen – daisy, dandelion, buttercup and after that, what? My flowers had all withered by Monday and the water in my jam jar stank. The whole affair was a nightmare to me.[41]

In certain ways Taylor thrived at the school, loath though he might have been to admit it. He did very well in his academic work: his extensive reading, his retentive memory, his developing writing style and his growing analytical powers all combined to ensure that he nearly always came first in his form. Supposedly the other clever boys saw him as the one to beat, their letters home being full of claims such as 'I am first in form order with 72 per cent (5 per cent above Ta 1 [Jones' name for him, short for Taylor 1]).' In due course he won a scholarship to Bootham. He was musical – there are references in his autobiography to practising the piano, and in his final term at the school he played a number of Schumann solos. He had parts in two school plays, Maria in *Twelfth Night* and Puck in *A Midsummer Night's Dream*, and although he later claimed that acting gave him little pleasure, contemporary observers perceived otherwise: his Puck was 'word-perfect and generally reckoned to be outstanding', while his Maria 'was even more impressive, described as cheeky, pert and wicked, never bettered in the experience of one witness'. He gained some ability to handle a ball, bowling underarm and taking three wickets in a cricket match against a rival prep school, also in his final term.[42] But probably the most lasting result was the improvement to his general health.

When Taylor came to the Downs, he was, according to the headmaster, an 'ailing little boy'. Indeed, after a year his Buxton doctor decided that one of his lungs was in danger of collapse and recommended that he should spend all of his time in the open air. This fitted in very well with school tradition, since 'fresh air had always been a Downs panacea' – an earlier pupil, also in rocky health, had sat at a desk outside the open schoolroom window, wrapped up in rugs, overcoat and mittens with his feet in a hay-box with a hot-water bottle, while the master stood at the open window trying to teach him and the rest of the form inside at the same time. The headmaster remembered having on occasion watched this student taking his soup whilst the sleet ran down his nose. They did the same thing with

Taylor: 'the other members of the class must have groaned at having to keep the window open even during the coldest weather, but they were used to a Spartan existence and accepted me as a sort of hero. I also took my meals in the open with the other boys taking turns to provide me with company. This was a highly prized duty – no plain fare, and we could consign the more unattractive items of food to the school boiler.' He must also have slept outside, since a new master upon arrival in 1919 discovered that Taylor slept out on a balcony under an awning.[43]

This regime, unthinkable today, appears to have toughened him. What was probably more useful, however, both for his physical and mental health, was the freedom he gained to wander. His doctor asked whether he liked games, and when Taylor replied that he hated football, the doctor gave him a certificate stating that he had a weak heart. Thereafter, while the other boys played football, Taylor explored the surrounding countryside and walked the Malvern Hills. This may well have consolidated his lifelong love of walking, whether in city or country; it certainly helped him to general good health. He was seldom ill thereafter – except for the 1918 influenza epidemic – until very old age.

The other major development in his interests was in politics, both in theory and practice, and this he owed primarily to his parents and to the Russians. The Bolshevik revolution in October 1917 had led in March 1918 to the making of a separate peace between the Soviets and the Germans. According to Taylor, this caused his parents to swing sharply to the left.

Before this my mother had been vaguely pacifist because of her CO brother and my father had been a Radical disillusioned with his prewar leaders ... The Bolshevik revolution brought a conversion as sudden and complete as Saul's on the road to Damascus. My parents were changed and for ever. While others had talked, Lenin had acted: he had ended the war ... This conversion brought with it a belief in socialism by a side wind. Previously my parents had taken no interest in it. They became Bolsheviks first and socialists afterwards.

His father decided that the revolution had been made by the working class, and thus only they could create a better society. He therefore abandoned middle-class radicalism (and his middle-class friends) and turned himself politically into a working man.

Taylor was hit by the beginnings of this change when he came home for the Christmas break in 1917: Socialist pamphlets lay all around, and his parents talked of their idealistic hopes for a revolution in England. His mother assumed this could happen without bloodshed. Taylor was converted, too, but with the cruelty of youth positively yearned for blood to flow. Through elderly Quaker friends of his parents in Buxton he met their son Walton Newbold, fat, smelly and pompous, a revolutionary on the run who in due course became the first Communist MP. Taylor, characteristically, was rather dismissive: 'it was clear from both his appearance and his smell that he did not wash. If this was the Revolution we certainly were in for a rough time.'[44] As with many middle-class left-wingers, for Taylor the revolution was often more attractive in the theory than in the flesh.

The following year, in the Easter term 1919, he experimented with leading his own rebellion. The context was the attempt by the headmaster to institute a system of guided self-government for the boys as a replacement for the prefectorial system. At the beginning of each term the whole school met and elected, by secret ballot, a half-dozen 'Monitors' who wielded power for the rest of the term. They were formally called the 'Cabinet', but known as the 'Bus'. According to one of the masters, feelings sometimes ran high and unsuitable boys were elected – or as he put it, 'sometimes the most suitable and "weighty" members of the School found themselves thrown out of the government and replaced by others who had nothing like their influence or real authority.' One of these presumably was Taylor.

As the master told the tale:

The climax came in the Easter term of 1919. The School was afflicted, shortly after the beginning of term, with an epidemic of mumps, and it so happened that the majority of the newly-elected 'Bus' were laid low and imprisoned in the sick-room. Being naturally rather jealous of their authority they attempted to govern the School from their beds. As they were completely isolated and messages either way could only be sent through the nurses – apart from ferocious faces made through the window – the result was not very satisfactory and a party soon grew up in the 'free' section of the School rebelling against this domination by the 'occupied zone'. A.J.P. Taylor was the leading spirit among the rebels who proceeded to hold new elections and set up a new 'Bus' to function during the absence of the Mumpers.[45]

Taylor himself gives a slightly different version:

Mr Jones set up a school Cabinet, elected by the boys, ostensibly to advise him on the running of the school. I was one of the five elected. The other four regarded themselves as prefects, reinforcing school discipline. They even claimed and exercised the right to beat the smaller boys. I thought that the function of the Cabinet should be to restrain Mr Jones and relax school discipline. I had a stroke of luck. All the members of the Cabinet except me went down with mumps. I argued that I could not act alone and called a school meeting to elect stand-in members of the Cabinet who I took care were my loyal followers. For the next week or two I had a good time. The Cabinet was out of Mr Jones' control. We abolished beating, whether by boys or by Mr Jones himself. We abolished plain fare. We instituted a right of appeal from staff punishments to the Cabinet.

The schoolmaster takes up the tale:

The School was split into two factions and feeling ran high. Furious letters passed to and fro between the sick-room and the outer world and a vigorous poster war developed. Favours were worn, banners carried, and even armed bands made their appearance and skirmishes took place, Nature having obligingly provided plenty of snow by way of ammunition. Finally the crisis petered out; some of the rebel government went down with mumps and joined their enemies in the sick-room, while the originals recovered one by one and emerged, full of wrath, to avenge their wrongs. The Summer term brought new elections and a 'coalition' government took office; the posters were gradually transformed into paper darts, and the School forgot politics in the joys of cricket.

And in Taylor's version:

At the beginning of the summer term there was a school meeting to re-elect the Cabinet. Mr Jones attended. He named certain boys, principally me, as unsuitable for election. The boys were overawed. None of the rebels was elected. Afterwards Mr Jones summoned each of us in turn and warned us that any further agitation would be severely punished. I did not much mind. If the other boys were too frightened to support me, why should I bother about them? I lost interest in school affairs.[46]

He had obviously had a good time; also obviously he had a standing in the school that is at odds with his later recollection of his time there – 'I do not seem to have had any friends'.[47]

No matter how bad school seems, the student is only there two-thirds of the year. During his first year at the Downs, Taylor had Buxton to look forward to, but unbeknown to him his parents had decided to leave the town, his first real home. Taylor speculated that his mother, with her anti-war beliefs, may no longer have had much of a social life there; it was probably equally the case that with wartime restrictions on cotton imports, his father had much less reason to travel to work in Manchester. In any case, they moved in effect to two places: Taylor's father bought a large house in Ashton-on-Ribble (now part of Preston), the village where both his parents and his ageing grandmother Martha Thompson had lived as children, and where he and his wife now lived during school terms; and they spent long stretches of the year in Hawkshead in the Lake District. Taylor disliked Ashton and loved Hawkshead, and it was this village that he now considered to be his only real home until he left for Oxford in 1924.

Hawkshead is set in the Vale of Esthwaite between Lake Windermere and Coniston Water and is surrounded by wooded fells covered with bracken and heather. Esthwaite Water, where Taylor loved to row and swim and his father to fish, is a mile-and-a-half south of the village, which itself dates from the Norse period. It is a very pretty village, with many seventeenth-and eighteenth-century houses, narrow, twisty streets that lead into little squares and houses which seem almost to grow out of each other. During the period when the Taylors lived there, there were no cars and few visitors. Taylor played with the village boys and roamed the surrounding countryside, which he called 'soft countryside' with its farms, little hills and winding lanes, on his bicycle. There was no public transport, so a cab had to be hired to travel even the five miles to Ambleside. More crucially for Taylor, there was no public library, so he was thrown back on outdoor pursuits.

He remembered the summer of 1919 in Hawkshead as idyllic. His parents took a house for the summer called the Minstrel's Gallery, so called because it had once been an inn and had such a gallery on the first floor. The house is connected on its left, like the bottom part of the letter L, to the Methodist Chapel. Around the back, about twenty feet away, is Ann Tyson's house, where the poet William Wordsworth lodged for part of the time he attended the grammar school in the town. Perhaps Wordsworth never made much impact on Taylor, but Beatrix Potter did, and it is curious that he does not mention in his autobiography the fact that she is also closely associated with the village. What he does remember is endless picnics, swimming across Esthwaite Water, cricket and discussions about Marxism.

These discussions grew out of the other notable element about the summer, which was that their house became, for conscientious objectors, a holiday stop between prison and the open world. The Minstrel's Gallery had plenty of bedrooms, and Taylor's mother filled them with COs selected by uncle Harry; each group stayed a fortnight and then were replaced by another group for another fortnight. One, however, stayed on. This was Henry Sara, an anarcho-syndicalist before the war who had helped to run a weekly paper called the *Spur* (its masthead proclaimed that 'the workers need a spur more than ever'). He was over six feet tall and handsome, with dark curly hair and a powerful physique. He was apparently charming and powerfully attractive to women. One who was so attracted was Taylor's mother, who eventually fell deeply and, according to Taylor, platonically in love with Sara for the remainder of her life. She was probably not aware that he also had a wife in London.

Sara became virtually a member of the family, with Taylor's mother making him an annual allowance and buying his suits. One friend remembered Percy Taylor frequently looking through the appointments book 'and he'd say, "Oh, Sara's coming next week".' The friend would say, ' "What, again? It's not long since he came". And he'd say, "Oh, well he's coming again." ' For some time he was a paid agitator for the Communist Party, going around Britain and travelling to the Soviet Union, China and the US. When he was no longer useful to the party, Taylor's mother and Sara went off on journeys together, sometimes to Paris, and in 1925 (with Taylor as well) to the Soviet Union; she also took him up to London for the theatre. Taylor claimed that his father accepted the situation without complaint, and he also said that Sara's presence was a relief, since he could now fuss over Taylor's mother rather than Taylor himself. But Taylor wrote elsewhere that he resented the situation on behalf of his father, and in later years he repeatedly drew analogies between his mother's falling for Sara and the propensity to similar behaviour in his own first wife.

Taylor's father found his own compensation, however. A fellow member of the Preston branch of the Independent Labour Party was a young man called Sydney Sharples, who had inherited his father's barbershop in the middle of Preston at the age of eighteen. When Percy Taylor discovered that Syd (as he was always called) was a hairdresser, he began to frequent his shop. Syd began to tell Mr Taylor his life story, in particular that he had inherited the care of eight children (two other sisters had died). One, called

Hilda, was ill and fading away; Mr Taylor offered to take her home with him for a few weeks for sunshine and fresh air. While she was there, he suggested that Hilda's younger sister, Doris, who was eleven years old, come out for the afternoon to play too. Doris was round-faced with ginger hair, wholly unintellectual but sweet and good-tempered. Mr Taylor was immediately taken with her – she was, in addition, about the same age as his daughter Miriam would have been – and for the next ten years she filled the part of his life that his wife had vacated and his son did not already occupy. For her part, Dolly always called him Pa Taylor – he was white-haired – and he probably filled the void left by the death of her own father.

The first time he brought Doris – whom he always called Little Dolly – to his home, she met his wife. Mrs Taylor usually retired to bed in the afternoon, but she came downstairs just as Dolly was taking her coat off. She looked at the girl, and said, 'Hello, what have you come for?', striking the child dumb. Dolly did not really know why she had come, and all she could say was 'Well, Mr Taylor asked me to come up.' She was thereafter terrified of the older woman, while Mrs Taylor clearly held her in some dislike and contempt, possibly because her husband made a fuss over her. For the next few years, Mr Taylor had to engage in subterfuge in order to see Dolly. Late at night when his wife was asleep, he would walk over to the Sharples' and sit talking by the fireside until early in the morning – he clearly revelled in family life. The Sharples, especially the children, loved having him there, because he had an endless fund of stories that he was always ready to tell. Taylor was wholly on his father's side, remembering years later that 'I covered up for him. We would set off on a walk together and separate as soon as we were out of sight of the house. We never once exchanged a comment. He assumed that I had no idea where he was going and of course I never asked.' It was years before Taylor's mother discovered what was going on, and then she was indignant and may have been jealous. She probably never equated her own devotion to Sara with her husband's to Dolly: hers was based on intellectual and political attributes, while his was soppy and sentimental.

Dolly remained near the centre of Percy Taylor's life for ten years, after which time she began to feel constrained and restless. In 1930 she turned twenty-one and had the usual party; he did not attend but – just like a father – turned up with his car at 3am to take the girls home. Soon after, Dolly went on a Mediterranean cruise and met a man from over the Pennines; two years later they married, and Percy Taylor, again like a father, gave her away. They saw little of each other for the following seven years. But when the war broke out, and Sheffield, where she and her husband and their two children were living, became a target for German bombs (ammunition was made there), Mr Taylor drove to their house and took Dolly and the children away to stay with her friends. This was to be his last gesture of affection, as he died soon thereafter.[48]

Taylor was permanently affected by the extramarital activities of his parents, although in different ways. About his mother and Sara, he was bitter. In his autobiography he wrote that 'The memory marked me. When I later resented the way the women in my life treated me, it was as much on my father's behalf as my own. I kicked because he had failed to do so and my unfortunate women paid the penalty.' He felt that he was being at least emotionally cuckolded by his first wife and her successive infatuations, while after separating from his second wife he wrote to his cousin that 'It was Henry Sara over again, and in each case I thought – I'm not standing for what my father did.' But he was also aware that his father was a 'dodger' and that he himself had learned from him to be devious and evasive. From his father's relationship with Little Dolly – Taylor later referred to her as the girlfriend 'who consoled him for my mother being so tiresome' – Taylor learned that it was possible and acceptable for a man to find consolation outside of marriage if the marriage itself was unsatisfactory. This was a lesson which he took to heart and would act upon more than once.[49]

It must be said, however, that Sara also made a positive impact on Taylor by introducing him to Marxism and the Marxist classics – Marx's *The Eighteenth Brumaire of Louis Napoleon* and *The Civil War in France* (but not, apparently, *Das Kapital*), Engels's *Origins of the Family* – and later gave him a first edition of John Reed's *Ten Days that Shook the World*, a book, one might say, of applied Marxism. Taylor took it all in and was converted. He read all of the shorter works of Marx and Lenin and 'learnt almost by heart the *Labour Monthly*, a sophisticated Communist periodical ... I believed in Russia. I believed in the coming revolution', and for the next several years would proclaim both to others.[50]

In early September 1919 the family left Hawkshead to travel to their new home in Ashton, and Taylor then went off to Bootham School. This was a formative experience, as he later wrote: 'The five years between 1919 and 1924 when I was at Bootham created me as an individual. I do not mean that Bootham alone did it. In some ways the strange life I led at home stamped me more. But by the summer of 1924 when I left Bootham, I had settled in my ideas and, as far as I have one, in my character. I had become an historian though I did not realize this until long afterwards.'[51]

Bootham School, called officially the York Quarterly Meeting Friends' Boys School, was founded in 1823 as an academic school for Quaker boys, although by the time Taylor arrived fewer than half of the 140 pupils came from Quaker families. The headmaster since 1902 had been Arthur Rowntree, a distant relative of the cocoa-works Rowntrees who had been responsible for admitting non-Quaker boys and for opening up the school more to the outside world. According to the mature Taylor, Rowntree 'had a Gladstonian air and a Gladstonian way of speaking', and he claimed that his memories of Rowntree helped him to understand Gladstone. The school was situated half a block outside the York city walls; York Minster could be clearly seen from its buildings. Bootham traditionally had the same bias as other Quaker schools, which was to emphasise the 'useful' and practical rather than 'barren academic theory'; character and hobbies were the thing rather than scholarship. Nevertheless, it did shine in one area in the nineteenth century, and that was in the natural sciences, producing many Fellows of the Royal Society. By the time Taylor arrived, however, this strength was celebrated more for the manner in which it could occupy the boys than for the science scholarships to Cambridge which the few still won. Certainly a contemporary history of the school celebrates natural history not for the sake of the science but for the healthy outdoor life it encouraged.

As an academic school it was pretty mediocre. There were good reasons for this. First of all, of course, was the fact that scholarship had never been of paramount importance. As significant, however, was the war: this had taken off the younger masters, more likely to be familiar with new scholarship in a subject, leaving the elderly and retired to teach, and none of them were very intellectually challenging. Furthermore, they were wholly unable to keep discipline. Indeed, school policy forbade corporal punishment, emphasising reasoning together and the toleration of differences. As a consequence classes were often a joke and bullying was rife. As Taylor later recalled matters, 'I was a little boy of thirteen thrust into a society of almost grown men, some of whom would have been in the trenches or in prison if the war had not come to an end.' Leslie Gilbert, the young history master who came to the school in 1920 and was the only Bootham master whom Taylor seems to have respected, later told him that the uncontrollable rowdiness in his classes had almost broken his spirit and that he had thought that he would have to leave.[52]

For Taylor the first year or two at Bootham were nearly unbearable. He almost looked back at the Downs with regret: the system had been harsh, but the boys were all right. At Bootham the boys were certainly not regimented – indeed, it might have been better if they had been – but many, given the chance, were bullies. Although Taylor remembered that 'I was more shocked by the bullying of others than bullied myself', others remembered that he had indeed been bullied: 'a group of thirteen-year-olds decided that they would emulate public school prefects by taking it upon themselves to exercise discipline ... They bent [Taylor] over a desk and beat him with a cane.' Because he was very small in comparison to his class-mates, he would have presented no real threat of retaliation. What Taylor had to do, and did, was to find protectors: he did the prep of some of the bigger boys and in exchange they protected him from the others. This allowed him time to establish his own place in the hierarchy, which he did by dint of his cleverness and debating prowess, the latter honed by years of verbal combat with his Thompson relatives.

There were other aspects of Bootham which he hated. First of all, there was the almost total lack of privacy. He had had very little at the Downs, but teenagers feel a growing need for it, and unfortunately he 'had a desk in the big schoolroom and literally nowhere else in the world. I had to keep all my possessions in my desk and sit at it from morning to night except when I was out in the playground.' Secondly, he was always cold: Yorkshire in the wintertime can be unforgiving. There was no heating in the bedrooms and very little hot water; the boys took a cold bath every morning and were allowed a hot bath once a week. (Cold baths at the Downs and at Bootham made an irrevocable impression: for the rest of his life Taylor took a cold bath every morning.) Furthermore, he now had to play football again. Bootham was very keen on sports, and a boy such as Taylor who was relatively hopeless at them had to fight doubly hard to establish his position in the school. Over the years he did so.[53]

He cultivated an arresting combination of cleverness, contrariness and left-wing politics. The first two elements were all his own, but the third was rooted in his home, where politics more and more dominated his parents' lives. Indeed, by the early postwar period it was probably the one interest they shared. His father had taken the opportunity, when the partnership agreement with his own father expired in 1919, of demanding that he be released from James Taylor & Sons with his share of the capital. The settle-ment dragged on until 1920, when he sold out. Fortuitously, he did so at the height of the postwar boom and received £100,000, a very considerable sum in modern terms. Thus he no longer had to travel to Manchester every day but lived off his investments, devoting himself to politics. So did his wife.

At the end of the war both of Taylor's parents had joined the Independent Labour Party (ILP), which Taylor himself joined in 1921, when he was fifteen. According to Taylor, the Preston ILP was very working-class and very left-wing, and took the lead in arguing the case when the ILP considered affiliating to Moscow by joining the Third International; Percy Taylor spoke in favour of the proposal at the ILP's annual conference. The fundamental difference between Taylor and his father is pointed up by their different reactions to this possibility. Taylor's father wanted the revolution, and the Communists wanted the revolution, so he believed that the two should join up. According to Taylor, 'I drew my father's attention to the twenty-one conditions for joining the Third International that Lenin had laid down. My father waved them aside. Just words, he said, like the constitution of the Labour party; the important thing was to unite and fight the bosses.'[54] His father had an ideal, and the means of attaining it were of lesser importance than the goal; Taylor read the document and analysed it, drawing a logical if not entirely palatable conclusion. This was an historian's method.

Percy Taylor turned himself into a working man and then into a politician. As Taylor described it,

My father believed quite simply that the emancipation of the working classes must be the work of the workers themselves. Obviously he must himself become a working man. But how, seeing that he was wealthy and did no work? By joining a trade union of course. The gas works down by the river were the nearest industrial undertaking. So my father became a gas worker, or, to be more precise, he became a member of the General and Municipal Workers' Union, gas workers' branch. He never entered the gas works – indeed I used to tell him that he did not know where they were. But he was accepted unquestioningly by the Brothers.

He became a Labour politician some time thereafter: in 1924 Connie Taylor stood unsuccessfully in the Preston municipal election; a year later, when she was ill, Percy Taylor contested Park Ward as a Socialist in her place and won the seat. He remained a Labour councillor for fifteen years, with a break of a year, dying in harness.[55]

Taylor's mother devoted herself to the political education of the working classes through the medium of the National Council of Labour Colleges. This involved evening classes of a Marxist character, 'education as a partisan effort to improve the position of Labour in the present, and to assist in the abolition of wage-slavery'. This was the goal as Taylor described it; these were also exactly the words printed on his 1922 member-ship card for the Plebs' League, so he was not wholly averse to supporting his mother's activities as well as his father's.[56] Taylor distinguished his father's politics from his mother's by arguing that while his father regarded Communism as a distraction from the Labour movement, his mother 'still hankered to play a great revolutionary role'. Ostensibly she contributed substantial sums to the Communist Party, but in truth she was laundering contributions from a Soviet bank in London. His father's great political friend was George Lansbury, London Labour MP from 1910 to 1912, editor of the *Daily Herald* from 1919 to 1923, and from 1932 to 1935 the pacifist leader of the Labour Party. His mother, however, preferred Henry Pollitt, a Communist agitator who in 1929 became general secretary of the British Communist Party. Pollitt was a warm-hearted man with a twinkling humour, so his personal qualities might well have been nearly as attractive to her as his politics. Taylor and he played whist together.

Taylor enjoyed all the political talk but 'in a detached way',[57] and certainly one gets the impression that his political beliefs were not part of his bones. His father appears to have believed in democratic Socialism gained through the ballot box, not by bloody revolution, and in spite of his twelve-year-old son's belief in the need for blood to run in the streets, there are few clues suggesting that the young Taylor was ever a candidate for the barri-cades. For one thing, he never gave much indication that he was a follower of anyone else; and for another, as soon as it became the orthodoxy he would doubtless have been against it. It is perfectly possible that had Bootham been a left-wing school he would not have been so eager to preach left-wing politics. However, since it was a tolerant, liberal, non-violent school in its aims, preaching the coming revolution exactly fitted in with his dissident and cheeky personality.

In a prize essay entitled 'Communism', which he wrote while at Bootham, he made it clear that he did not believe in Communism for reasons which might make it attractive to Liberals and reformers such as inhabited Bootham – 'the Communist incentive is not an emotional one – they leave it to social reformers to go into hysterics over slum conditions' – but because it was philosopically and historically correct. He based this conclusion, he wrote, on the fact that Marx had used historical methods to elicit the unchallengable explanation, the materialist conception of history, which demonstrated the direction in which history was moving. No one could stand against it, and it behoved the proletariat and those who sympathised with them to facilitate the inevitable revolution. Basically Taylor adopted the methods and arguments of *The Communist Manifesto*, and wrote a careful, and notably unwitty, essay setting them out.[58] If he had maintained this approach in all of the political discussions and debates in which he took part, he would have been ignored and written off as a bore.

Fortunately, in debate he was much more impressive. The Bootham Debating Society met once a fortnight and Taylor often took part. He was known as brilliant and scintillating,[59] and he frequently spoke without notes. He was against authority, for left-wing politics, in favour of female emancipation and against sports and physical exercise. He tried out various rhetorical devices while speaking, experimented with types of argument and in general might have been preparing for his future career on radio and television. He was training himself to think on his feet and to mobilise the contents of his brain for instant use.

Taylor passed Matriculation in 1921, a public examination correspond- ing roughly to General Certificates of Secondary Education (GCSEs) nowadays. He then joined the 'College Class' at Bootham, the school's name for what is now commonly known as the sixth form. This was a relatively recent development at Bootham, and the school was hardly fitted for it. A contemporary history noted that the class was 'hardly a class, indeed, so much as a number of individuals pursuing special and differing courses of work, and involving, therefore, a great strain on the staff, partic- ularly in a school of limited size ... it means a new conception of the purpose and goal of school work'. In short, boys had now to be prepared for university entrance, instead of having their characters and hobbies developed. Unfortunately, there were few masters who were really up to the task.[60]

Taylor had decided that he wanted to sit for a Brackenbury Scholarship at Balliol College, Oxford to read history, and he therefore turned for help to the new history master, Leslie Gilbert. Born in 1892, and therefore twenty-eight when he joined the staff, Gilbert had been a schoolboy at Bootham, where he had captained the cricket XI and won prizes for his essays. He then went to Manchester University, at that time the best in the country at which to study history, where he gained a First. He joined the Friends Ambulance Unit in 1915 and was sent as a nursing orderly to France, working on an ambulance train carrying the wounded from the front lines back to base. After demobilisation Gilbert taught for a short time in Liverpool, and then moved to Bootham as assistant master in history (the only history master). He had a deep personal Christian faith. He eventually developed the ability to influence the boys because of their liking and respect for him, based, one suspects, as much on his continuing athletic prowess and basic fairness as on his teaching ability. Taylor always retained a personal affection for him, the two going on walking holidays together for some years.

Gilbert's suitability as a history master for a boy preparing to sit for an Oxford history scholarship was another matter, although there was no alternative at Bootham. It is true that former pupils have testified to Gilbert's ability 'to impart his own enthusiasm, wide ranging interests and understanding of the significance of events, while at the same time bringing recalcitrant minds to appreciate the necessary rigours of academic discipline: he was sharp with slackness or pretentiousness but always in a way that left the recipient appreciative of the rebuke.'[61] This indeed was good classroom history for the historian and non-historian alike. Gilbert, however, had never taught an Oxbridge scholarship candidate before, and Taylor really required something more than he was able to provide. (In fact, as a man who was on his way to teaching that the hand of God manifested itself in history, Gilbert might well have done Taylor more harm than good in preparing him for Oxbridge.) Taylor could have gone elsewhere – an earlier candidate, G.N. Clark, had transferred to Manchester Grammar School, for example – but by this time he had settled in and did not want to leave Bootham.

According to Taylor, Gilbert doubted Taylor's determination and told him to read some big work of history. 'I silenced his doubts by reading right through Gibbon's *Decline and Fall* in a fortnight and followed this with the eighteen volumes of Samuel Rawson Gardiner on English history in the first half of the seventeenth century, a much drearier undertaking. After this Gilbert set me to read textbooks on European and English history, presumably because he knew nothing better.' This is probably true in essence, but it is difficult, based on the available evidence, to fit it in with the chronology of Taylor's life. Having taken Matriculation in 1921, presumably he began his advanced work on history in the academic year 1921–2, taking the Balliol College scholarship exam (without success) in the late autumn of 1923. According to his list of books read, he did read *Decline and Fall* in mid-1921; however, he did not read Gardiner's *History of the Great Civil War 1642-9* (nine volumes) and *History of the Commonwealth and Protectorate 1649-56* (nine volumes) until late in 1923. (He also read *Decline and Fall* again, in an edition edited by J.B. Bury,[62] but since this was in 1922 it does not help to clarify matters.) It looks as though Gilbert told him to read some big books of professional history during the summer before the entrance exam.

What sort of history books did he read in the two years before his Oxford entrance exam? Textbooks were certainly included, but there were also other history books. He read G.M. Trevelyan, whose books are now largely relegated to the secondhand history shelves, but who in the early 1920s was very highly regarded: he read his *Lord Grey of the Reform Bill* the year after it was published in 1920, his *Life of John Bright*, two volumes of his trilogy on Garibaldi and the unification of Italy, and two books on British history in 1922, and his *Manin and the Venetian Revolution of 1848* in 1923, the year it was published. He read the aforementioned books by Gardiner, as well as his other works: his *History of England 1603–1642* (ten volumes) and his book on Cromwell's place in history, all in 1923. Then there was a volume of Cromwell's letters and speeches, and odd books on various periods, the Roman republic, the Renaissance, the American revolution. Nevertheless, it was hardly a systematic study of any period of history, if one excepts thirty volumes on Jacobean and Cromwellian England, and thus Taylor was probably correct in his assessment of Gilbert's grasp of what was needed.

As a proportion of Taylor's reading, history gave way to literature, though not often novels, except those of H.G. Wells and the political novels of Hilaire Belloc, and some light detective and adventure fiction. What he wanted by this time was ideas rather than facts or delineations of character, and he found these in poetry and plays. He read Homer and Aeschylus, Sophocles and Euripides, buttressed by several volumes of Gilbert Murray on Greek literature and religion. He soaked himself in Shakespeare, reading nine plays one after the other in 1922 and another ten (in two bursts this time) in 1923. He owed to Gilbert his discovery of the plays of George Bernard Shaw (as of the writings of H.G. Wells – he claimed that Gilbert was trying to lure him away from Marxism), and Shaw remained an influence on him for the rest of his life, as much for his writing style as for his ideas.[63] He appears to have read his first play by Shaw, *Heartbreak House*, early in 1922, but before the year was out he had read then all and had moved on to his literary criticism. Shaw introduced him to Ibsen: after Shaw's *Quintessence of Ibsenism* he immediately read seven Ibsen plays. He also tackled volumes of poetry: typically, he would settle upon a poet and read volume after volume of his work, rather than dipping into it. In 1922 he discovered A.C. Swinburne in a serious way, reading four volumes in a matter of days, if not hours; 1923, on the other hand, was a Browning year, and he read ten volumes of Browning (to the Victorians a notoriously difficult poet) in sequence. He also returned to Swinburne and, more seriously, read most of John Milton.

It is perhaps less surprising that he read a great deal of what might be termed politicised non-fiction. At fifteen he read R.W. Postgate's two books on *Revolution 1789–1906* and *The Workers' International*, the following year J.L. and B. Hammond's *The Town Labourer*, John Reed's *Ten Days that Shook the World* (a present from Henry Sara), More's *Utopia*, Machievelli's *The Prince*, *The ABC of Communism* by Buharin and Preobyazhensky, and three volumes on the history of English political thought. By 1923, when he was seventeen, he was reading books produced for his mother's workers' education classes, *Outline of Modern Imperialism* and *Outline of Economics*, *Ethics and the Materialist Conception of History* by the German Karl Kautsky (followed immediately by Browning's *Dramatic Lyrics*), Walter Bagehot's *The English Constitution* and William Cobbett's *Rural Rides*.

But again, none of this gives a real indication of his range and depth. He read the classics of English literature – *Tom Jones*, *Vanity Fair*, *Tristram Shandy*, *The Way of All Flesh*, Boswell's biography of Dr Johnson, his favourite book – but he also read John Buchan, G.K. Chesterton, John Galsworthy's *Forsyte Saga*, J.M. Barrie and a variety of now-forgotten writers. He was an obsessive and omnivorous reader: during his years at Bootham, from 1919 through 1924, he wrote down 861 entries in his list of books read, where an entry might be a single play by Shakespeare or Gardiner's ten volumes. This all contributed to widening, deepening and toughening his brain. He claimed that the greatest influences came from Bunyan, Shaw and Butler,[64] certainly in terms of style, but the fact that religious and political theories and arguments were the motive forces behind the styles must also have contributed to his intellectual development.

His reading also contributed to his eventual success in Oxford entrance, since the ability to cite and manipulate ideas was and is held in high esteem. Nevertheless, while demonstrating this might well have been enough to win a place, it would not have been enough to win an award. To do that, Taylor had to demonstrate his potential as an historian. Indeed, recalling that he himself stated in his autobiography that he became an historian at Bootham, the question is, how? The answer must be church-crawling, and for this Taylor had the flexibility of the school to thank.

Bootham boasted the oldest Natural History Society in the country. Its central importance in the school might well have contributed to his misery as it had at the Downs, but there was a fundamental difference in their approaches to it. For the Downs, natural history meant nature study; for Bootham, natural history included 'archaeology', which appears to have been largely defined as church architecture. In short, Taylor could give up lichen and take up Perpendicular-style windows. He leapt at the chance.

To begin with, Taylor joined parties of boys led by a former Bootham master, Neave Brayshaw, generally known as Puddles – perhaps because he was very short and very fat, and wore loose clothes which must have looked as though they were running off him. He came over to York from Scarborough every half holiday to lead the boys round parish churches; during the winter months they confined themselves to the twenty-seven within York itself, while during the late spring and summer they bicycled out to country churches (Puddles took the train). Taylor rapidly developed a very organised approach to his study of architecture. He had as his constant reference C.E. Power's *English Gothic Architecture*, and he always carried a fifty-foot tape measure and a set square to check the angles of the walls. Taylor wrote that he 'acquired one bad habit from Puddles. He liked us to approach a church with our minds a blank and to discover everything from our own observations. I came to regard it as a point of honour never to consult a guide book.' This meant that he missed much of interest, particularly anything which was unusual. But the relevance to his later work as an historian is obvious. Rather than rely on authorities, he did the research himself and drew his own conclusions. As with his churches, he sometimes went astray, but it also enabled him to write seminal works.

In due course Taylor went out on his own. He spent nearly a year on York Minster, working on the details in weekly visits. During holidays his father took him round the churches of north Lancashire, taking photographs for him, and while they were at Hawkeshead during the summer Taylor spent days at Furness Abbey. The end result of all of this research was a series of archaeology diaries, copiously illustrated with ground plans and photographs. These were exhibited at the school's Christmas show, and Taylor won small money prizes for them; in due course he won the Old Scholars' Exhibition for Archaeology, worth £10, substantial for a school prize. The experience also made him an historian in at least two ways. First of all, he learned research techniques of observation, taking notes, going back to the original sources, drawing conclusions, writing up and publishing (or exhibiting). He also learned a great deal about Gothic architecture, and to this, he always believed, he owed his history exhibition at Oriel College, his springboard to professional history.[65]

During his years at Bootham Taylor increasingly established a position of note in the school. From 1920 to 1924 he was on the committee of the Natural History Society, and indeed was chairman from 1922 to 1924. He was increasingly perceived as extremely clever, and to the approbation of the boys often used this cleverness to argue against the ethos of the school. He could have a great personal impact: to one boy, two years his junior, he was 'a most arresting, stimulating, vital personality, violently anti-bourgeois and anti-Christian'.[66] He was soaked in political theory, largely Marxist, but buttressed by familiarity with a whole range of other writers. Unexpectedly, perhaps, for such an individual, he developed leadership qualities, locally as leader of his room in his boarding house, and school-wide as a reeve or prefect in his final year.

His leadership in 1923–4 of Bedroom 24 of Penn House, one of the boarding houses, grew out of a peculiar Bootham tradition: instead of sharing according to year group, boys of all ages were jumbled together in each bedroom, being allocated to a room on arrival and remaining there until they left. The result, of course, was fierce loyalty to one's bedroom and fierce hostility to the others. Evidence for the warfare to which this could give rise is contained in 'The Chronicles of Bedroom 24', whose provenance is obscure. Ten volumes of these 'chronicles', running from 1921 to 1929, were discovered under the floorboards of the bedroom in 1972; the school archivist wrote to Taylor in 1982 for information, but he had no recollection of them. Nevertheless, much of the first volume is in Taylor's handwriting and thus he was presumably one of the instigators of the tradition, which lasted for at least five years after his departure.[67]

In one section of the 'Chronicles' Taylor wrote a mock-heroic description of the in-house warfare: 'assembling in the Campus Martius under the leadership of the new general A.J.P.T. and his subordinate ... military drill was at once begun ... above all could be heard the voice of the general bellowing out the commands, as he ably directed the movement of the troops.' And later:

the races took place up and down the stairs and in the part set apart for ablutions they partook of a cold bath ...; after leaping into this bath and emerging with more haste than dignity, they covered themselves with all possible dispatch ... and dispensing with all the ceremonial dryings reascended the stairs. The team being wired in series and not in parallel (-bars) it was the object of each member of the team to cover the ground as expeditiously as possible and to hand on the torch to his successor. The barbarous inhabitants of the lower landing for some reason of their own – the psychology of backward races is peculiarly involved and difficult – objected to these feats and made it their practice to waylay, obstruct and otherwise molest the demi-gods of No. 24.

The 'Chronicles' are full of in-jokes, parodies of adult documents and mock-serious, even pompous, prose, all clearly meant to be read aloud for the enjoyment of the bedroom. This example appears in the first volume, which means that Taylor early on established his reputation for being both sharp-witted and witty. He was also clever enough not to get angry when he was teased. Presumably because he was short, his nickname was 'baby', and the 'Chronicle' has a number of references to this. One example is an advertisement: 'Wanted. Nurse for four-month-old baby. If possible, rattle, cot and pram also. Nurse not required to count baby's initials. Apply Taylor, Preston.' Leadership, even in boys' boarding schools, does not always depend on strength: intellectual ascendancy, when combined with humour and challenges to authority, can also win a following. In Taylor's case, he was Odysseus rather than Achilles.

The same year that he became Bedroom 24's leader, he also became a school reeve, or prefect. Bootham, like the Downs, had a measure of guided democracy: the College Class voted on the boys who might be reeves, and the outcome of the vote 'weigh[ed] largely with the headmaster in making the appointment.' Reeves, as in other schools, were part of the control system of Bootham. They took charge of two forms totalling thirty to forty boys whilst they did their prep, and they sat at the head of the table and supervised meals. They had to maintain their authority and exercise control, and Taylor was challenged early on: 'Everyone at Bootham regarded me as very much of a joke, and the younger boys thought that I would be easy game. They soon learnt better. Keeping order is like jumping a horse: it only needs courage and I had plenty of that. After one set-to I had no further troubles.'[68]

Taylor claimed that he had had qualms about accepting such a position of authority, but there is no doubt that he enjoyed, and exploited, his position. He discovered that he was entitled to give a boy exemption from compulsory football, and he promptly gave it to himself; when the headmaster protested that that was not how the rule should be interpreted, Taylor challenged him to point out the restriction, and of course there was none – it had just not been the done thing. He also gave himself permission to wander within York during the afternoon – school rules had stated that it was off-limits after 1.15 pm – and he used the opportunity to good effect. 'For a whole winter, while everyone else played football, I explored the streets of what was still essentially mediaeval York.' More unusually, he learned palaeography, the skill of reading old writing, from a distinguished palaeographer who was then working in York, and this, he claimed, enabled him to read German Schrift (Gothic script) later on without much difficulty.[69]

In his personal relationships he was no longer quite such a loner: not only did he have friends, he even had, in his fourth year, a 'best friend', George Clazy. Clazy was from Edinburgh, a son of the manse, his father having been a minister of the Church of Scotland. They must have presented a startling physical contrast – Clazy was six feet tall and heavily built, Taylor was five feet four – and Taylor emphasised the intellectual differences, especially Clazy's high-mindedness compared to his own schoolboy permissiveness and cynicism. But in this case the opposites sparked off ideas and discussion. Clazy also introduced Taylor to serious walking on the Lake District fells, a pastime he kept up into his seventies. Taylor claimed that Clazy condescended to him, 'a salutary experience'. He was possibly willing to tolerate it because he perceived Clazy as being wholly in control of his life and destiny, in contrast to his own intellectual confusion, 'proletarian Marxism clashing with my intellectual frivolity, theoretical understanding of life combined with an incapacity to understand my own.' The older Taylor is here harsh towards his younger self: playing with ideas is not the same as frivolity, and no schoolboy of seventeen is profound.

The first two terms of his final year at Bootham were dominated by his attempts to win an Oxford history scholarship. In the late autumn of 1923 he tried, in the first instance, for a Brackenbury Scholarship. Balliol then held a predominant position in Oxford – it was supreme in performance in Schools, or final examinations, until 1933[70] – and had a reputation for being attended by the cleverest of their generation, men who would go on to run the country or rule the world, or at the very least gain stature in whatever profession they chose. A Brackenbury Scholar was therefore deemed the highest of the high, and clever boys from all the public schools set out to become one; G.N. Clark, formerly of Bootham and in due course Taylor's tutor at Oriel, had been a Brackenbury Scholar. Taylor later emphasised that he was set apart from all this by his background: 'I had no manners and a rough Lancashire accent.'

His account of the examination ordeal at Oxford rings true, in particular the feeling of going around in a daze:

I remember nothing of the examination except the walk to Keble College where it was held. On the last night I and another candidate were invited to dinner at Balliol high table. Our host was the legendary tutor Kenneth Bell. He asked about my political views. I told him and when he asked what should be done with Oxford in a Communist society, I replied 'Blow it up after I have gone down.' This did not please him. In the common room after dinner – another astonishing experience – Bell asked me and the other boy whether we should come up if we did not get a scholarship. The other boy said No, his father could not afford it. I said, Of course. Bell said to another don ... 'That makes things easy.' The other boy got an exhibition. I got nothing. This was a shocking thing by later standards such as prevailed when I examined for scholarships. Any enquiry into parents' means before awarding a scholarship is strictly forbidden.[71]

Taylor always believed that he had been unfairly deprived of the glory of the Brackenbury, but he (wilfully?) misunderstood the main point of scholarships in those years. Oxford scholarships were originally intended to provide maintenance in college for poor boys – it is worth remembering that in great part the distinction between scholar and commoner was not between clever and ordinary but between poor (and clever) and rich (hence the 'gentleman-commoner' of earlier days). It was true that poor boys of the working classes seldom attended Oxford – during the entire interwar period the sons of semi- and unskilled workers made up just over five per cent of the total – but poor boys of the middle classes, such as the sons of vicars with poor livings, were not uncommon.[72] Scholarships were meant to help the deserving clever, in other words, and therefore it was right and proper in the 1920s for the Brackenbury to go to the less well-off candidate, all else being roughly equal. Taylor's political views may have tipped the balance against him – it is impossible to know – but Balliol was less conservative than many other colleges and may not have particularly minded. Taylor's ideas about scholarships were formed by his examining in the postwar period. Because it had by then become mandatory for all local education authorities to support to a reasonable standard students who had been accepted into university, scholarships were no longer vital to the maintenance of poor students and could be used to recognise quality and promise.[73]

Nowadays there is only one chance a year for Oxford entrance, given the bureaucracy arising from national university entrance which determines the schedule. Things were more relaxed in earlier days, and in March 1924 he tried again, this time at Oriel, chosen because of the presence of G.N. Clark. Taylor, however, sensed that Clark's having been at Bootham was not necessarily an advantage to him. Taylor's explanation was that Clark had become conservative at Oxford and wished to distance himself from liberal and left-wing ideas associated with Bootham. However, given that Clark had left Bootham in order to attend Manchester Grammar's sixth form as preparation for sitting Balliol's scholarship exam, it was equally likely that he had a poor opinion of the history teaching which Taylor would have received at the school.

In any case, it was again an ordeal, possibly because he feared that it would be his last chance, and he hated to face the likely reaction at school and home if he, the clever boy who lorded over all intellectually, should fail. He was ill, both from nervous tension and from the effects of a boil on his left breast, which had been lanced just before he travelled to Oxford.

> I had to dress it unaided, had a high temperature and retired to bed as soon as each day's examination was over. My papers must have been very bad. However I had a stroke of luck. There was a question about Gothic cathedrals, a subject which I knew more about than any other candidate, possibly than any examiner. Even in semi-delirium I could not help writing a good answer. Clark, knowing this was common Bootham stuff, was not impressed. [He had himself won the Old Scholars' Natural History Exhibition in 1905 for his sixteen volumes of archaeological diaries.] Ross, the philosophy tutor, was. Oriel had only two scholarships on offer and both had been filled. Provost Phelps decreed that an exhibition should be created for my benefit.[74]

Provost Lancelot Ridley Phelps could do this because, although the tutors in a college selected those who received existing awards, the head of house traditionally controlled the admission of commoners, and Phelps had the authority and standing in Oriel to decide that a student admitted as a commoner could receive an *ad hominem* exhibition.[75]

Taylor therefore returned to Bootham in triumph. His final term was a thing of joy – summer weather and no work to do. He had certainly made himself a personage in the school over his five years there: head of Bedroom 24 in Penn House, chairman of the Natural History Society, reeve, Oxford exhibitioner and winner of the school's leaving scholarship. He had come to love Bootham. Perhaps he had not been particularly well taught in history, but the school was tolerant and allowed him to grow and develop in his own way. The masters took him seriously as an intellectual equal, and by the end of his time there he even admired Quakers.

The period between Bootham and Oxford was filled with a six-week trip to Germany and France with his mother, Henry Sara and a friend of Taylor's from school, Roger Moore. The contrast between this trip and his two to France as part of Puddles's school journey parties was palpable. With Puddles and the boys he had felt free; now he was constrained by his mother's presence and prejudices – temperance hotels and restaurants, no going out without her, visiting what and when she wished. It was easier to go along with her ideas than to challenge them, and that is what he (and presumably Sara) did.[76] It probably made him even more eager to taste the freedoms of Oxford.

Taylor went up to Oriel in October 1924. Founded in 1326, and therefore one of the older colleges, Oriel's buildings are predominantly seventeenth century. The front giving on to Oriel Square offers little hint of the attractiveness of the quadrangles beyond the porter's lodge. Provost Phelps, aged just over seventy, was the proud possessor of a long white beard and wearer of a morning coat and a black straw hat; he was the son of a clergyman and grandson of a baronet and described himself as the titular head of the Labour Party in Oxford. He had served on the Royal Commission on the Poor Law from 1905 to 1909, and for many years chaired the Board of Guardians of the Oxford Workhouse. He had a lifelong interest in the poor and on his walks up to Headington to the workhouse would greet the tramps, most of whom he knew, with 'Good Day to you, my master', drawing them into 'a free if not very articulate conversation'. His interest in Labour drew Taylor to him; indeed, Taylor's own political inclinations may well have inclined Phelps to offer him the exhibition. Certainly he would have supported Taylor's decision to help the strikers in the 1926 General Strike. The two got along very well, going on long walks and having lunch together in the Provost's lodgings.

Admittedly, this type of social intercourse was much more common then than now. According to his colleague David Ross, Phelps regularly went on long walks with undergraduates, took them on reading parties and talked with them talked late into the night. However, one of these undergraduates remembered that he had techniques which speeded 'the departure of those young men (always a majority, whatever their background) who were unable to get to their feet and take their leave ... He would wait until, from the adjacent Tom Tower, Christ Church began to bang out the hundred-

and-one peals with which ... it assaults the city nightly at five minutes past nine o'clock. The Provost would thereupon stand up and shamelessly declare: "Ah, my dear boys! The witching hour of twelve has struck." ' This combination of and care for their feelings would have greatly appealed to the adolescents in his care, and Taylor would not have been alone in declaring him a warm-hearted human being.[77]

Phelps was also a wit and raconteur, which would have recommended him more highly in the common room than his concern for the feelings of the young. One story was retailed by Dacre Balsdon, a Balliol don: 'When that paragon of austerity, Genner, refused the port after dinner with the remark, "I would as soon commit adultery as drink wine," the Provost of Oriel, Phelps, answered, "There is no accounting for taste, Mr Genner; there is no accounting for taste." ' It was also said of him that every morning before his cold bath he would strike himself on the chest vigorously, muttering 'Be a man, Phelps, be a man.' In short, he was a certified Oxford eccentric, but a kindly man, and his wholehearted care for Oriel, its fabric and estates and its students was a mark of Taylor's time there.[78]

As was the case with most Oxford colleges, Oriel was inhabited predominantly by public school men, who 'had not gone to Oxford to study; that was what grammar-school boys did.' Taylor claimed that 'Oriel had few from the top schools', pointing out that it had only one Old Etonian in his time, who lived apart, attended by his valet. This is a bit unfair to all of the Old Carthusians in the place who had been lured there by the Provost, himself an Old Carthusian and a governor for many years. Charterhouse was, after all, one of the nine 'Clarendon' schools, which included Eton and Winchester. But in essence Taylor was correct, since during the interwar period these nine Clarendon schools accounted for twenty per cent of all male undergraduates at Oxford, with other Headmasters' Conference schools (which included Bootham) accounting for another fifty-four per cent, leaving only a quarter of the places for all of the others. Grammar-school boys were not, of course, evenly spread amongst the colleges, since Christ Church, Magdalen and Trinity were too grand to have had more than a very few, if any. There were many at Oriel, according to Taylor, but they counted for nothing and 'led a sort of underground life'. Other commentators were nastier: Louis MacNeice, up at Oxford at the same time, referred to them as 'monsters – ... those distorted little creatures with black teeth who held their forks by the middle and were set on making a career.' It is difficult to judge to what extent it was due to the efforts of this despised breed that Oriel during the 1920s was one of the top five colleges in terms of examination results.[79]

Taylor was given a set, a bedroom plus sitting room (only Keble and the women's colleges had bed-sitting rooms), on Staircase VIII in the Back Quad at a rent of £14 a year. He was entirely taken care of by his scout. Early in the morning the latter lit the fire after clearing the ashes from the grate, and then brought Taylor a small jug of hot water with which he shaved. The bathrooms, as in virtually all Oxford colleges then, were in a separate building dedicated to the purpose; in his case, they were two quads away, encouraging Taylor frequently to miss out on his formerly habitual cold morning bath. Then at about half-past eight his scout brought in a tray of breakfast. Again, in some of the more old-fashioned colleges such as Oriel, breakfast and lunch were still served in undergraduates' rooms rather than in Hall; this could be jolly, since all the undergraduates looked after by a particular scout on a staircase might eat together. Lunch was invariably bread, cheese and beer, or 'commons', for which undergraduates were charged one shilling; as in the case of cold baths, Taylor absorbed this regime and it became his lifelong regular lunch, taken in his room. The scout then cleared away the debris.[80] Many Oxford memoirs devote a page to the scout, since he could make the undergraduate's life heaven or hell, either covering up for or betraying him, able to produce, wait upon during and clear up after luncheon parties, wiping up the vomit after a night of excess and generally acting as the undergraduate's servant.

At dinner in Hall Taylor sat at the scholars' table, an arrangement whereby all of the scholars and exhibitioners were segregated from the commoners. Close association with those considered the cleverest men in the college should have been stimulating for Taylor, but he found, he said, that with one or two exceptions they had no desire to discuss anything except association football – and certainly not the type of left-wing politics which he then espoused and talked about enthusiastically when he first arrived. He soon learned to keep most of his political opinions to himself and adopted a neutral protective covering – at least until he became something of a rower and therefore worthy of admiration by the non-intellectual.

This is not to imply that he had no companions or was a recluse. His first friend was Norman Cameron, already a published poet; they had sets on the same staircase, and he was the other member of the scholars' table who had no interest in football. Cameron sometimes took him to poets' parties. There were plenty of evenings spent talking and drinking whisky after dinner, and some time into the year he also became close friends with Theodore Yates. Taylor described him as having 'elegance and culture without intellect', while another man also up at Oriel described him as 'your silly friend'. It is indeed true that Yates ended up with a Fourth, but while at Oxford he added to the pleasure Taylor experienced there, especially in his second year: they both loved driving in fast cars, loved good wine and cigars, loved dining at the George – which Yates did every night, although Taylor was more abstemious.

St George's Café and Restaurant – the George – long since disappeared but which was on the corner of the Cornmarket and George Street, had a special place in Oxonian lore. It was the domain of the aesthetes who usually posed as, or were, homosexual. They were led in Taylor's first year by the legendary Harold Acton, who was described by a contemporary as 'slim and slightly oriental in appearance, talking with a lilt and resonance and in a peculiar vocabulary that derived equally from Naples, Chicago and Eton ... who brought with him the air of the connoisseurs of Florence and the innovators of Paris'. He introduced to Oxford the trousers later known as 'Oxford bags' – as broad as twenty-six inches at the knee and twenty-four inches at the ankle, they spread to cover the shoes; they were often in light, bright shades, such as silver, mauve or pink, and sometimes had the effect of a pleated skirt. The George, as described by John Betjeman, who overlapped with Taylor although he was a Magdalen man, was where 'there was a band consisting of three ladies, and where punkahs, suspended from the ceiling, swayed to and fro dispelling the smoke of Egyptian and Balkan cigarettes.' Yates 'had cast himself as a distinguished elderly man', walking with a silver-headed ebony cane, and easily fitted in with that tribe of Oxonians who saw themselves as avatars of culture and decadence. Yates always outshone Taylor in affectation, but he undoubtedly encouraged him to loosen up, and Taylor soon took to wearing Oxford bags – although it is difficult to imagine him in mauve-coloured trousers – and a bow tie. (The more conventional form of dress was grey flannel trousers, tweed jacket, collar and tie.) Taylor also took to dining frequently in the George, although not, perhaps, as one of Betjeman's 'Georgeoisie' ('For life was luncheons, luncheons all the way/And evenings dining with the Georgeoisie'). As Taylor described it, 'waitresses – being safe by their sex from the attentions of the undergraduates – served the food, and painted boys, themselves undergraduates, walked up and down the aisles until they got a free meal in return for their services. I often went to the George but again only as an observer. I never signalled to any of the painted boys'.[81]

Another man who became a close friend in Taylor's first year was Charles Gott, of an army and county family, who was reading Physiology.

He was more serious than Yates, although very agreeable, and it could be said that these two close friends appealed to different sides of Taylor's personality, Yates to the frivolous, Gott to the more practical. Gott was also a Labour supporter. To anticipate, in his second year Taylor also became great friends with a third Oriel man, J.I.M. Stewart, known as Innes, who would eventually become a Student (Fellow) of Christ Church and a writer of novels, a number of which were set in Oxford. A year younger than Taylor, he had come from Edinburgh to read English. According to Taylor, he was the closest friend, apart from George Clazy, that he ever had, although 'our minds were far apart. I was practical, prosaic and, as I thought, politically concerned. Innes was precious.' He laughed at Taylor's politics, especially his Marxism, and his 'excessive' reading of detective stories. (The latter story is piquant in view of the fact that Stewart later became a notable writer of such works under the name Michael Innes.) Stewart also exuded charm and kindness.[82]

It may well have been that the two of them were first drawn together by rowing. It comes as something of a surprise, both because of his height (only about five feet five, but at ten stone nine he was stocky), and because of his hatred of team sports, to learn that Taylor had a moderately success-ful career as a rower. He obviously felt the need for some exercise in the afternoons, after reading in the Radcliffe Camera all morning, and succumbed to the urgent requests of the captain of the Oriel College Boat Club to all freshmen to come out for rowing. He may even have succumbed to the rowing mystique at Oxford. All but two of the new undergraduate intake were wholly inexperienced, but most soon grasped the elements of rowing and the captain decided that the results of the week's practice were very satisfactory. Taylor rowed regularly, and in Torpids, the boat races held during the sixth week of Hilary (winter) Term for the less good boats (the first eights rowed in Eights Week, the sixth week of Trinity (summer) Term), he rowed at the number two position in the second boat.

Boat races in Oxford are of a distinctive sort. The Thames is narrow and sinuous where it runs near and through Oxford, and therefore straight boat races such as are rowed at Henley Regatta or the Boat Race at Putney are not possible. According to James Morris, long ago when oarsmen had pottered down to Sandford for an evening drink, they left to row back to Oxford at different times, and the custom grew of trying to catch each other up. This developed into a very elaborate system of competitive rowing, in which college boats start at equal intervals and try to bump the one in front, thereby taking its place in the next race. There is a week of daily races, and the crew that bumps its way to the top becomes Head of the River.[83] According to the 1924–25 *Oriel Record*, 'the 2nd Torpid was not a bad crew, though the standard of oarsmanship varied greatly within the boat. They raced well, but were too slow at the start, and went down two nights.' The captain in his Book was more direct: for the Second Torpids boat (or Oriel II) they had had problems finding enough rowers to make up a full crew, and as it was one of them had only nine fingers. The boat had finished thirty-fourth on the river.

Taylor persevered, and in his second year was the stroke of Oriel II, while Innes Stewart, a year younger than Taylor and thus in his first year, was the cox. The stroke of a boat is a position of responsibility: while he cannot tell the crew what to do as he could if he were captain, he decides on their tactics and establishes the rhythm and must therefore have the crew's confidence. He must work closely together with the cox, and Taylor and Stewart probably consolidated their friendship in the boat. Taylor's leadership as stroke was appreciated by the boat club captain, who praised the crew's dash and spirit, although 'the standard of oarsmanship left something to be desired in some cases', and some of the crew had not really settled down by Torpids. Nevertheless the performance of Oriel II was much better in 1926 than it had been in 1925. Things began badly – on the first night they were rapidly overhauled and bumped by University II before they had really got going – but on the second night they rowed through, 'a much improved crew ... and indeed gave Univ. II a moment or two's thought.' On the third day they had an exceedingly good row and bumped Exeter II just past the Willows. On the last three days they rowed through, going after Brasenose (B.N.C.) II; on the last night they gained a length on them in about thirty strokes and just missed a bump.[84]

Taylor was felt to have done well and was invited to join the first eight. They began 'tubbing' in preparation for Eights Week and decided to go during the Easter vacation to the Beetle & Wedge Hotel in Moulsford, where there was mile-long stretch of deep water, for a week's practice. They paddled stretches of two-and-a-half miles most afternoons, getting used to rowing together. The other members of the eight were public-school men and Taylor assumed that they found him odd. But he had a car – his father gave him one in his second year – and could drive them into Oxford when they wanted a break from the countryside, which he assumed made him acceptable. Once term began, however, he was less happy with the rowing, possibly because, as he later wrote, the eight was not much good. He was rescued by the advent of the General Strike, which caused eights practice to be suspended indefinitely, and he resigned. When a truncated Eights Week was held later in the term, Taylor's name was not on the crew list.[85]

One thing that struck Taylor forcibly when he first arrived in Oxford was the religious requirement. Chapel was compulsory. It is curious that this came as a shock: after all, attending Quaker meeting had been compulsory during all his years at the Downs and Bootham. He was already an atheist: as he recounts in his autobiography, 'I experienced a conversion during my second year at Bootham. I was sitting in the art room and looking through its big window across to The Minster when I had a revelation just like Saul's on the road to Damascus. A voice said: "There is no God". I had never thought about religion before; I had taken it for granted. From that moment Christian's burden fell from my back for ever.' His reaction at Oxford may be explained by the fact that Quakers did not thrust ritual observances down the throat of the attender at meeting. Taylor had never been to a Church of England service before, and he found it incomprehensible and irrational – even cannibalistic. Nevertheless, he did not at first object to the requirement to attend, on the grounds that it was no more hypocritical than attending meeting had been. What he did, apparently, was to send it up: a friend recalled that Taylor regarded his turn to read the lesson in chapel as an occasion for blasphemous pantomine, a performance which was 'too good to be missed'. Later, Taylor wrote, 'I thought I should strike a blow for freedom and refused to attend. When the Dean summoned me, I explained that I had no religious beliefs and therefore could not consciously attend a Christian service ... He agreed that I could not be expected to attend chapel. He added plaintively, "I hope you will come and talk over your doubts with me". I answered, "I have none". With this my attendance at chapel ended.'[86]

What Taylor did attend, on a weekly basis for three years, was the playhouse. At Bootham he had read plays; at Oxford he both read and saw them. Curiously, perhaps, with his enjoyment of speaking in public, he appeared to have no wish to perform in them, even privately. At Oriel there existed a very active club called the Newlands, or Dramatic Reading Circle, which met together regularly during term to read through a dozen plays both classical and contemporary; the future critic Desmond Shawe-Taylor was a member while Taylor was up. Yet there is no record of his having ever taken a part. He also ignored other college societies that he might have been expected at least to sample: if not the Arnold Debating Society, at least the Prynne Society, which met to listen to papers about and to discuss politics and political economy. However, his name appears in no society minute books as participant.[87]

What he did join, and attended regularly, was the University Labour Club, the secretary of which was A.L. Rowse, an undergraduate at Christ Church. (Taylor claimed that Rowse never attended a meeting, though Rowse's own memoirs are full of the toil associated with being secretary.) The members saw it as a practical rather than theoretical organisation, emphasising co-operation with Oxford City labour bodies and with Ruskin College, home of mature students supported by the trade unions. They were all working for a new social order, with the university men naturally very keen that it 'benefit workers both "by hand and brain" in the very widest sense of the term'. Taylor claimed that he remembered little about what had taken place at the meetings; others, however, recalled his revolutionary speeches.

He also briefly joined the Communist Party, although he also later denied attaching much importance to it; it was of course possible to support the Bolshevik revolution in Russia and something analogous in Britain without actually being a Party member – his father's position, after all. Taylor hung a picture of Lenin in his room, for which temerity his room was wrecked. (One result of this episode was his friendship with Yates, who later wrote that 'I was furious and went out of my way to show him what I thought about this attempted censorship. From that time we became great friends.')[88] Through the party he got to know Tom Driberg, then an Anglo-Catholic homosexual aesthete, since meetings were held in Driberg's rooms in Christ Church. According to Taylor, 'we divided our labours. I looked after the Labour club in the sense of making semi-communist speeches there. Tom did more practical work such as selling the *Workers' Weekly* at the Cowley factory gates, an activity that enabled him to become acquainted with the better-looking factory workers.'[89]

Taylor was to lose what little faith he had in the Communist Party as a result of their lack of activity during the General Strike in 1926. Britain had returned to the gold standard in 1925 at a rate which overvalued the pound, and as a result exports were frequently priced out of their markets. One such was coal, and to bring down the export price the mineowners tried to cut workers' wages. In return the miners threatened to strike, but the government stepped in with a subsidy that enabled wages to be kept at their existing level. However, in April 1926 the government refused to renew the subsidy; and on 2 May the Prime Minister, Stanley Baldwin, broke off negotiations with the TUC; in response the unions declared a general strike, and for nine days (3–12 May) Britain was at a virtual standstill.

University students were encouraged to become strike-breakers, or blacklegs, driving buses, perhaps, or becoming special constables. At Oriel 120 students took part. Somé became special constables in London: their duty was to be shock action troops, who, at the first sign of trouble, would be rushed to the scene of the fight 'where they might be employed to hit everybody and everything very hard.' Others worked the milk run, commandeering lorries, collecting milk from farms, taking it up to the Hyde Park Milk Dump and returning the empties to the farms. Still others went up to Hay's Wharf in London to help unload ships.[90]

Taylor, of course, joined the other side of the barricades. According to his autobiography, his first move was to drive Tom Driberg and himself up to 16 King Street in London, headquarters of the Communist Party of Great Britain, where they expected to receive their orders. The place was locked up, so they resorted to banging on the door. After much rattling of chains, 'an elderly Scotch Communist ... appeared. He eyed us sourly and said: There's no one here. I am only the caretaker. Get along hame with ye.'[91] For Taylor this was symptomatic of the role of the Party during the strike – either useless or a nuisance.

Yates told a more amusing version of the same journey:

'On the first day of the General Strike Alan came to my room and said, 'I am going to London to bring Daily Heralds down here. Would you like to come?' We started off with Alan driving, but as we were crossing Dorchester bridge we met a military convoy. They had with them a number of field kitchens with their chimneys folded down. Taylor thought that this was quite terrible, they were guns being sent by those bastards to shoot down our friends the miners in South Wales. Alan could drive no more and I had my first experience of driving in London. It was splendid because there was hardly any traffic. No trams or buses except one turned over in the road outside Cadby Hall. But the mission failed. For when we got to the Herald offices Tom Driberg appeared on the steps to tell us that though the papers were printed the place was picketed and it would be 'blacklegging' to attempt to distribute them. So we hived off to the Communist offices in King Street to see what could be done. I waited in the car wearing a rather good tweed cap and smoking a pipe with a silver band on, hoping I looked like a young squire.

It was at this point that Taylor and Driberg had their meeting with the caretaker.[92]

Taylor was not attracted by the notion of doing left-wing missionary work in Oxfordshire farming villages, so he decided to take the caretaker's advice and go home to Preston. It was necessary first to get permission from the Dean of Oriel, a muscular Christian who later became Bishop of London. According to Taylor, 'He puzzled over my request and then said: "Other men have gone down to do their duty. I suppose you are entitled to go down to do what you think is yours." '[93]

Taylor and Norman Cameron, who also wanted to help the strikers, drove to Preston, but once there Taylor was at somewhat of a loss as to what he could do. His father pointed out that he and his son were the only members of the Labour movement in Preston who could drive, so each morning Taylor reported to the strike committee rooms in Preston and received his instructions for the day: he might drive union secretaries to meetings, deliver strike pay or take encouragement to committees marooned in Conservative strongholds such as Blackpool. On most days he went to Manchester and collected newsprint for the strike bulletin which Norman Cameron wrote and a jobbing printer set. It was an exciting time, with Preston and most of the surrounding areas solid for the strike. Both he and his father were optimistic about the outcome, but on 12 May Percy Taylor came home with a white, drawn face to tell his son: 'The strike's over. We have been betrayed by our leaders.'

That afternoon Taylor and Cameron went back to Oxford, where they were not beaten up, as Taylor half-expected: rather, all those who had taken part, on whichever side, felt a camaraderie which excluded those who had remained quietly in college. The Editor of the *Oriel Record* wrote that many of those who had acted as special constables returned with 'a diminished respect for the constituted authority of the realm', and the mature Taylor concluded that it might be said that the strike marked the end of unthinking conservative Oxford and the beginning of an Oxford that moved towards the left.[94]

For Taylor, as for many of those up at Oxford, these activities – from rowing to strike-breaking – assumed a greater importance than their academic work. For many undergraduates Oxford was a sort of finishing school in which they gained polish and some knowledge of the world's ways. Those suffering from delayed adolescence, probably the majority, could sow their wild oats and make their mistakes in a contained, supportive atmosphere. Undergraduates went wild with the freedom they enjoyed there compared with school; in response their colleges controlled – or at least made rules about – when they had to be back in the evenings and when they were allowed to leave Oxford itself. Probably a fifth of undergraduates in the 1920s failed to take any kind of degree.[95] Yet academic work was not unimportant, since for a solid section of the undergraduate population a goodish degree was the passport to future prospects. It did not matter terribly how well an undergraduate did if he was destined for the family acres or the family firm; it did matter if entry to the civil service was the hope.

The History school at Oxford was the largest of the arts schools, with roughly thirty per cent of undergraduates reading History.[96] However, the focus was largely mediaeval and early modern: this was deliberate policy on the part of the late nineteenth-century Oxford historians, since they feared that undergraduates studying a subject close to their own time would fall prey to passion and prejudice, rather than devote themselves to the disinterested assessment of the march of history, and especially the march of English history from the swamps of Norman feudalism to the uplands of parliamentary sovereignty and constitutional monarchy. Oxford aimed to provide a liberal and humane education, not to train professional historians – according to one Regius Professor of Modern History, 'the main purpose of the Oxford school is to educate a man to understand modern civilization.'[97] Therefore, the focus in practical terms was English history, and particularly in Taylor's time the history of the mediaeval period and of the seventeenth century, in particular the Civil War and the Glorious Revolution. The knowledge gained was to be deployed first in Schools, the final examinations held at the end of three years, and then in running the country and the Empire. What it did not particularly encourage was specialisation or training in sources and methods for original research. Taylor, therefore, read history books, but he did not learn how to 'do' history.

This is not to say that there was not a desire in Oxford for more modern study. There was, but in 1920 it had been diverted from the History school by the establishment of the new school of Philosophy, Politics and Economics, or PPE. Those who wished to learn about political institutions, or the new theories of economics, or political economy, or what passed for contemporary history, read PPE. Indeed, the two history scholars in Taylor's year at Oriel both changed to PPE.

History at Oxford was very prescriptive. Certain exams had to be passed before a student could embark upon sustained work in history, and in this student choice was restricted. For the historian coming up in 1924, there was the requirement to pass an examination in Divinity ('divvers') and a preliminary examination in History ('prelims') in the first two terms, followed by six terms of tutorials on various periods and topics, followed by revision and Schools (Finals) in the ninth term. This meant that the first two terms could cause some anxiety until the preliminaries were safely out of the way; it meant that a second-year man was one of nature's happiest beings, since there was not yet the threat of Schools looming on the horizon; and it meant that a Schools man was a creature of increasingly haggard mien, whose Oxford career was capped by a week of unforgettable apprehension and pressure.

When Taylor went up to Oxford, he expected to get down to studying history straight away, but was disappointed to learn that he had the two standard exams (Divinity and prelims) to pass first. Theoretically, Divinity required candidates to show their acquaintance either with two gospels in Greek or with the original text of a Greek philosopher (for the non-Christians); by Taylor's time, however, it had degenerated into knowledge of all four gospels in English and an exercise in 'Anglo-Greek', so called, which consisted of passages from Thucydides in English. It was held in such contempt by students that, according to Innes Stewart, 'there was held to be a definite impropriety at passing it at a first attempt. Almost, here was a solecism as grave as wearing a "made-up" bow tie.' The amount of work required, judging by Taylor's book list, was minimal: he read the gospels of Mark, Luke and John, the Acts of the Apostles and *The Story of Greece* by E.S. Shuckburgh – there is no evidence that he bothered reading the *Peloponnesian War* itself. Even this preparation – the work of a day or two? – was enough and, whether he wished it or no, Taylor passed divvers in his first term.[98]

The next hurdle was prelims, which those reading history sat in their second term. On the face of it this was perhaps more challenging: undergraduates were to be examined on the outline of European history 800–1789, on original texts in Latin and French, on unseen translations from one ancient and one modern language and on elements of economic theory. However, the examination statutes suggested the books which students should read over two terms in order to prepare for it. For the outline of European history, four books were recommended, of which Taylor read three – Guizot, Lavisse and Acton; and for the requirement that they had to be able to discourse upon the geography of countries and its influence upon their history, Taylor read a nice little crib entitled *Relations of Geography and History*. For the original texts, Taylor read the Latin text, the *Gesta francorum*, which tells the story of the First Crusade 1095–99, but he appears to have ignored the French requirement, which was either

Philippe de Commines's *Mémoires* or Voltaire's *Siècle de Louis XIV*, apparently contenting himself with reading John Morley's biography of Voltaire. He sat unseen translations in Latin and French, his only preparation for which appears to have been the reading of a number of novels by Anatole France in French. The final part of prelims was a paper on elements of economic theory, for which students were advised to read J.S. Nicolson's *Elements of Political Economy*. Taylor did so in the spring of 1925, and possibly attended a class or had tutorials in the subject from Provost Phelps, who was one of the first dons in Oxford to take up economics and who taught political economy in the college. He passed with no difficulty.[99]

Finally, in Trinity Term 1925, he could begin reading history, or at least begin preparing for the final exam two years hence. All candidates had to study the 'continuous' history of England, including British India and the colonies, both constitutional and political, from the end of Roman Britain to 1885; and they had to study a period of general history, interpreted as European, which might extend, for example, from 476 to 919 or from 1789 to 1878. All those who wished to be considered for a First or Second were, in addition, examined on a special subject, normally based on printed documents in the original languages; on what was termed 'political science', based on Aristotle, Hobbes, Rousseau and Maine; and on economic history with economic theory, based on Adam Smith or John Stuart Mill or Charles Gide.[100]

It was usual in Oxford for candidates to be taught as much as possible in their own colleges, and Taylor therefore began work on his continuous English history with E.S. Cohn and G.N. Clark, Cohn for mediaeval history and Clark for modern. Stanley Cohn was a curious, somewhat shadowy figure who published no books and has left no trace in the *Dictionary of National Biography*. He liked men of action and athletes, and he also liked moving in high society. He wanted passionately to escape from Oxford, which he finally did during World War II. But he 'had a brilliant mind and an enthusiasm for mediaeval history, as yet undimmed', and Taylor learned a great deal from him. Most fundamentally, he learned that the past is a foreign country which the historian must approach on its own terms, neither viewing it as the present in different clothes nor as a quarry for rocks with which to build a present-day house. The former approach is much more common now than it was in the early part of the twentieth century, when history was normally seen as a school for statesmen and citizens. From Taylor's list of books read, it is also clear that Cohn had him study what were some of the most important recent monographs written on the period – it was not only textbooks which were recommended: he read Maitland's *Domesday Book and Beyond*, Vinogradoff's *The Growth of the Manor*, Round's *Feudal England* and Pollock and Maitland's *History of English Law to Edward I* (all of which were still on Oxford reading lists fifty years later). Taylor claimed that he was 'despised by clever Stanley', but this does not accord with the care Cohn took to have him read difficult, important books nor with the time they spent together outside the tutorial hour. Taylor probably did all of his English history up to the sixteenth century with Cohn and possibly some of his other work as well.[101]

For modern English history Taylor went to Clark at first (he was on sabbatical during Taylor's third year, during which most Oriel historians were sent to David Ayerst of Christ Church). Taylor had looked forward to being taught by Clark who, though a youngish man, already had a high reputation: a former Fellow of All Souls, he had published *The Dutch Alliance and the War against French Trade* and was at that time Editor of the *English Historical Review*. According to A.L. Rowse, in personal conversation he was 'alert and vivacious, bubbling with fun and jokes, full of ideas … a busy, fussy little man, compact with energy.' Other students found him equally engaging: one of Taylor's year who was also reading History recalled that 'he was so bright and cheerful, he bore his learning with so unostentatious an air, he was uniformly so considerate that merely to come into his presence was an exhilaration.' What Clark taught this particular student was that, when faced with a statement or an alleged fact, one should always ask, who says so? One should 'regard everything with scepticism; take nothing on trust.' Clark was also considered a safe pair of hands, and the combination of these traits in due course propelled him towards joining the great and the good: founding General Editor of the Oxford History of England, Regius Professor of Modern History at Cambridge, Provost of Oriel and President of the British Academy, the latter three institutional positions taking him away from undergraduate teaching.[102]

Indeed, according to Taylor, he was bored with tutorial teaching – certainly it can become inexpressibly tedious when faced with an unending stream of mediocre undergraduates who have done little work. But Taylor's description of their tutorial meetings – 'he listened to my essays in a detached way and then complained how dreary the business was' – comes as something of a surprise. For one thing it does not accord with other reports, and for another Taylor *was* working, if unobtrusively: he read most of the day in the Radcliffe Camera or in the library of the Oxford Union, where no one would recognise him, rather than in the college library. He knew as well as anyone that it would be fatal to be seen to be working. Oxford celebrated cleverness and Firsts, but it had to be done without apparent effort, since to be considered a swot would ensure condemnation to social oblivion. Taylor was not a swot, but he liked to read and he found history interesting. Furthermore, Oxford required very little of its junior members, but it did require that they show up each week at tutorial with an essay. Again, there is no evidence that Taylor ever failed in this duty. Therefore, Clark had a clever student who read, and thought, and was good at repartee, and the suspicion must be that if Clark had been that bored with Taylor he would not have told him how boring tutorials could be. On the other hand, Clark did tell him that he was not cut out for the academic life, so he obviously thought that something was missing in Taylor's make-up.

According to Taylor, he took him up to 1688, the Glorious Revolution, then told him that 'you know all the rest from the books you read at school' and taught him no more. It may indeed be that Taylor had no teaching at all on the further period up to 1885, on which he would be tested in Schools, but it is unlikely. Clark, after all, was nothing if not responsible. More likely, this was when he went on sabbatical, and Taylor was farmed out to another college for the necessary teaching, something which happened and still happens all the time in Oxford. It is probable that he was taught by David Ayerst at Christ Church, who was not much older than Taylor himself; furthermore Ayerst had been chairman of the Labour Club during the General Strike and was attracted to the Communist Party. For these reasons alone Taylor would have found him agreeable. For his part Ayerst wrote to his mother that Taylor was the only 'first-class man' among his pupils, 'a Communist who suffers from a slightly too rigid North Country fanaticism'.[103]

Taylor had one other tutor with whom he remained for his entire time at Oriel and that was his moral tutor, the philosopher David Ross. The moral tutor provided general advice and kept a benign eye on his charges, in some colleges reading to the student his termly reports from his subject tutors. Ross was an intellectual man, though without much small talk. He had been instrumental in Taylor's receiving an exhibition, having been impressed with his essay on Gothic architecture, and presumably looked upon him with a kindly eye, while keeping a silent tongue. At Oriel moral tutors had one further, and usually onerous, duty, which was to listen to the speculative essays which Oriel required its first-years to produce. Taylor claimed that he would read his out while Ross would smoke his pipe in silence; when the hour was up, he would then say 'Very good' and give him another subject. At the end of the academic year Taylor received the college essay prize, the proceeds from which he spent on an edition of Rabelais – a good way to end his first year at Oxford.

During the summer of 1925 Taylor spent some days in the Lake District with George Clazy, whom he still considered his closest friend. This was a relaxing and stimulating way to wind down from Oxford. But the memorable thing about the summer was his visit to Russia, in the company of his mother and Henry Sara. It was a good time to visit: the borders were open to private individuals, food and hotels were available and suspicion of outsiders had not yet come to dominate the country. They saw the beauties of Leningrad – the once and future St Petersburg – including the Winter Palace, which had become a museum of the revolution. After a week they travelled to Moscow, where, because they carried letters of introduction from British Communist leaders and trade unionists, their visit was treated as semi-official and they were provided with an interpreter and sometimes a car. There were few restrictions, and they could wander in and out of the Kremlin at will. They saw a play and films and athletic events, and they saw the body of Lenin in Red Square. They met Soviet leaders, though not Trotsky – and, curiously, no one mentioned the name of Stalin during the whole of their six weeks in Russia.

Out of Moscow they travelled to Gorki, then called Nijni Novgorod, where the traditional great fair was being held, possibly for the last time. There were merchants from Persia and China with their camels, and peasants, rather than urban industrial workers, thronged the streets. There were beggars and thieving children – Taylor's mother felt as though she was back in India, not in a European country. They were given a banquet, presumably by the local party officials, and Taylor replied to the toasts, although it is unclear in what language. Back in Moscow, Taylor arranged the return journey to England, which was complicated owing to the frontier between the Soviet Union and Poland being closed – they had instead to go via Riga and the Baltic states, which took one night to the Latvian frontier and then three further nights to Ostend.

This visit to Soviet Russia – he had not visited any of the other Socialist republics – made a great and lasting impression on Taylor. He was overwhelmingly impressed by the Russians' spirit and revolutionary enthusiasm, and by their determination to put into practice measures of equality that were only discussed by the few in Britain. It was significant that he was there during the period of the New Economic Policy, when collectivisation and central control policies were in abeyance: for these few years there was plenty of food and goods in the shops. Had he gone in 1927 or 1928, when Stalin was tightening control and enforcing collectivisation on the countryside, he would have found a very different Russia. He would recognise this in due course, but for the next decade Taylor was a confirmed believer in the new Russia and chastised friends who were more sceptical. What he always retained, however, was an admiration for the Russian people, whom he believed deserved better than they got.[104]

He returned to Oriel in October for what was to be a most pleasurable second year. His father had given him a fishtailed, air-cooled, two-seater Rover sports car, the running expenses of which were shared with Yates, which meant that Taylor was one of the very few in college who had an independent means of transport with all that that promised for expeditions on the weekends and out of term. He now had what was required to live a decent life in college. He had friends and was about to acquire another one, Innes Stewart. He enjoyed the rowing and was becoming better at it. And he enjoyed his work.

With Clark away, Cohn organised the tutorial schedules for the Oriel historians, and he did Taylor great good by sending him to F.F. Urquhart at Balliol for his general period of history, which was Europe from 1789 to 1878. Urquhart, known as Sligger – the name was said to be a corruption into prewar dialect of 'the sleek one' – was, according to a long-standing friend, 'cultivated but not highbrow'. He plays a part in a number of Oxonian memoirs, especially those inclining towards the aesthete mode, and his influence was said by the same friend to be 'largely due to a tolerance and a gentleness which he extended to a number of highly strung young men much in need of them.'[105] Taylor said that he was not Sligger's type, being neither beautiful nor smart (presumably in the sartorial sense), but Sligger clearly sensed that Taylor would respond to knowledge and ideas. As a tutor he did not provide much conventional historical knowledge, but 'he knew nineteenth-century Europe at first hand. He had been born in Rome when it was still a papal state. His father [who had been British Ambassador to the Ottoman Empire] ... had championed the Turkish cause and Sligger maintained, very wrongheadedly, that the Ottoman empire was more civilized, even more powerful, than imperial Russia. [This was possibly because Sligger's father had believed that the key to the social problems of the nineteenth century was the Turkish bath.] The European history I learnt from Sligger was not a bit like the European history I had found in the books.'[106] Rather, Sligger stimulated his imagination, putting real human flesh on the bones of history, and steering him in the direction he eventually took as a professional historian.

In his third year Taylor had to settle down and work seriously, if he meant to get a First, an ambition he would never have admitted harbouring. He needed to choose a special subject and he chose a mediaeval one, Richard II, so that he could study the Peasants' Revolt of 1381. It was in the special subject that Oxford came nearest to training historians. The work required Taylor to read a substantial number of printed primary sources in Latin and to practise the art of gobbets: this required taking, say, a paragraph of a document, identifying it, placing it in context and drawing any general implications for the subject which it suggested. Mastering the art of writing gobbets trains the student in gutting a document and wringing all possible information out of it, and is invaluable practice for a future historian. Taylor was soon able to fillet a document rapidly, something absolutely essential for an historian of the modern period, given the abundance of available documents.

This is not to imply that he did nothing but work during his third year. By one account at least he now had something of a name in Oxford and occasionally gave grand parties in his lodgings, attended by many of the literary 'lions' of Oxford student society. At the end of Hilary Term, in a final bash before revision and Schools, he celebrated his twenty-first birthday with a dinner party at the George for his closest friends, Theodore Yates, Innes Stewart, Norman Cameron, Charles Gott and Tom Driberg. According to Taylor, 'Tom [a predatory homosexual] kept slipping out during dinner, a weak bladder I supposed. Then the waiter said, "Can I speak to you privately, sir? I am a respectable married man and unless that gentleman stops coming out to me I shall go home." For the sake of our dinner Tom reluctantly abandoned the chase.' Fifty years later Taylor still enjoyed telling the story.[107]

By the end of Hilary Term he would have moved into revision mode. It was a rule in Oxford that no examiner could examine men from his own college and, given the competition between colleges over exam results, college tutors and their students were united in trying to predict what questions might be asked. Taylor would have spent his time going over his notes – his regular work habits at least meant that he did not have a backlog of reading to make up. His description of Schools, which consisted of two three-hour essay exams a day for a week, rings absolutely true: 'I was very tense, so much so that I had to drug myself for the last three days. I moved in a haze and have not the slightest recollection what the examination papers were about.' For the exams he would have had to wear subfusc, which consisted of a black suit, socks and shoes, white shirt and tie, academic gown and mortarboard under the arm; without doubt putting it on every morning provided a saving carapace. Taylor does not say if his friends met him, with or without champagne, after he finished his final paper, just that he went home.

A month later he returned with his parents for his viva, after which he went off for dinner and champagne with Stanley Cohn. Then it was back to Preston, a sad come-down from Oxford in many ways, even had he not already disliked the place. Finally the telegram arrived, one morning whilst he was cleaning his car: he had got a First. He wrote many years later that 'this news astonished and bewildered me. I really was clever after all. Many years later at dinner in Magdalen I sat next to C.T. Atkinson, who had been chairman of my examiners. He said, "I looked up your marks. They weren't very good, you know".'[108]

Whatever they were – they were destroyed – they were good enough to gain Taylor by far the best history result in Oriel. The two history scholars, who had changed to PPE, did very badly, one gaining a Third and one failing. The total for his year in History at Oriel was one First (his), three Seconds, four Thirds, two Fourths, one Aegrotat and one Failure. He had also done much better than his two close friends in his year, since Yates took a Fourth and Gott a Third (in Physiology). Oriel gave him a prize of £10, with which he bought the complete works of Dickens, a writer whom he had never before read.

Taylor's mature assessment of what he had learned at Oxford was characteristically jaundiced and even profoundly wilful – how to choose a meal in a restaurant; that 1921 was a good year for wine and especially for hock, his then wine of choice: how to drink a lot without getting drunk; how to speak with a long 'a' rather than a short one (thereby 'unintentionally' losing his Lancashire accent). His adamantine devotion to Marxism prevented him, he claimed, from paying attention to any ideas which Oxford had to offer, so that while he gained some knowledge of history he did not improve his understanding of it. What he certainly had not sorted out was what he now wanted to do, other than to leave Oxford and get on with real life, whatever that might turn out to be.[109]

In his first twenty-one years, then, Taylor emerged from his background and even transcended it. There is no doubt that he absorbed from his family two of the themes of his life, Lancashire and left-wing politics. But it also seems that Taylor branched off in a different direction from the parent with whom he identified, his father. His childhood was alternately settled and unsettled – his homes changed, his schools changed, the nature of his parents' marriage changed. The constants in his years from early childhood until he left Oxford seem to have been his and his father's mutual devotion, his love of reading, his self-absorption and his dependence upon his brain to get on in the world and to get him out of trouble. Certainly the final three of these four traits remained intact throughout his active life.

Chapter 2

The Making of the Historian
1927–1934

I picked up one principle from Přibram's lectures: never to forget that diplomats, too, were human beings and therefore to hold the balance between documents and personalities. Přibram also said to me: Do not believe anything merely because it is written down.

A.J.P. Taylor, *A Personal History*, early draft.

No one under twenty-five should publish a book.

A.J.P. Taylor, *Oxford Magazine*, 10 February 1944.

When Taylor left Oxford in the summer of 1927 he had no very clear idea of what he wanted to do. Over the next seven years he made two false starts – as a trainee solicitor and inspector of ancient monuments – before finding his true métier as an historian. Being a professional historian and being a history teacher, at whatever level, are two different things requiring different talents and skills. One person may, as Taylor did, do both, and it is worth disentangling the two strands of his academic life to find out how this came about. Those who took an Oxford First normally plunged straight into teaching, believed to be the most important part of being a lecturer or an Oxford don. Frequently it was only later in an academic's career – and for many it was never – that he or she might find the time to engage in research and possibly publication.[1] Taylor did it the more modern way: his research experience led directly to his first academic job at Manchester University and, although he had a heavy teaching load, he nevertheless kept up the research and soon published his first book. His early publications made his reputation as a coming man and led both to his return to Oxford and to the development of an impressive freelance career. The focus of this chapter, then, is on Taylor's learning how to become an historian. It began when he accepted that history, not law, was his real interest; continued during his two-year research period in Vienna and Paris; and culminated in the writing and publication of his first book in 1934.

Yet these years also saw his evolution from late adolescence to young manhood. He lived abroad for the best part of two years, learning a language and surviving – and thriving – in a foreign culture. He experienced sex, and fell in love for the first time. He discovered music and riding. He distanced himself emotionally from his family and developed the self sufficiency necessary to enjoy a sojourn away from his native land. And he enjoyed it all.

The end of his Oxford years, enjoyable and ultimately successful as they had been, naturally left Taylor in something of a deflated mood. He knew what he liked – even loved – and that was history. But passion for a subject does not necessarily mean that one can turn it into a career and, indeed, the idea of becoming a professional historian does not seem to have occurred to him. Besides, he wanted to escape from the ivory towers and plunge into real life: to him this meant helping the working class and making plenty of money in order to live comfortably. This unlikely combination of goals led him – even more improbably – towards a career in the law.

Going into the law had been suggested to him, in steps, by his uncle Harry Thompson, his mother's brother. Encouraged by contacts made during the war, Thompson had moved his solicitor's practice to London, where, as a leading left-wing lawyer, he soon had plenty of work. However, solicitors require barristers to argue their clients' cases in the law courts, and he had suggested to Taylor during his first year at Oriel that he should become a barrister: he, Uncle Harry, could guarantee him plenty of work. The Bar is the flamboyant, public side of the law profession, attractive to those who like debating; it may well have attracted Taylor for its own sake, as well as for its utility in helping him to fulfil his goals.

Accordingly, Taylor had put his name down at the Inner Temple. The Bar was a much smaller profession in the 1920s than it is now, and it worked on the apprenticeship system: barristers then, as now, would take pupils into their chambers, but in the 1920s there was much less formal training in the law. Those who wished to become barristers had to pick up a good deal of knowledge informally; they also had to find chambers willing to take them as pupils. The four Inns of Court, of which the Inner Temple was one, fulfilled the necessary combination of professional marriage mart plus discussion group. They required that aspiring barristers should keep twelve terms and eat three dinners a term: what this meant was that at least nine times a year Taylor travelled up to London from Oxford and dined in the Inner Temple. The drill was that, after drinks, he would join a table of four, which might include judges, barristers or pupils, and join in the talk, which would range over cases, procedures and law gossip. He was expected to pick up knowledge and advice, and ideally to meet a head of chambers who in due course would invite him to join as a pupil. There were worse ways for him to spend his time, and he probably quite enjoyed it, being a reasonably sociable animal by this time. Taylor kept terms for two years whilst he was an undergraduate at Oxford.

In mid-1926, after the General Strike, Harry had another idea. His law practice was thriving, and naturally he wished it to be carried on by members of his own family. However, his own sons were too young to succeed him as senior partner when he was ready to retire: why should Taylor not join the practice and become a partner, thereby acting as a bridge between father and sons? For Taylor 'it seemed a dreary prospect but I was still eager for self-sacrifice. I also reflected that Harry made a great deal of money and presumably I should soon do the same.' He probably realised that his chosen career – or the one that seemed to have chosen him – might not be as romantic as being a barrister; on the other hand he certainly knew that his financial returns were infinitely more assured as a solicitor than as a barrister. His father very much disliked the prospect of Taylor's dependency on Uncle Harry; his mother was delighted.[2]

In October 1927, therefore, Taylor went to London. His mother, however, had been beforehand him: she set him up in an expensive six-room flat on the edge of Hampstead Heath and installed a housekeeper to take care of him. Whatever pleasure Taylor might have taken in having his own flat in London was mitigated by the suspicion that one of the house-keeper's duties was to keep an eye on him, his activities and his friends. It was also rapidly made clear that his mother planned to use the flat as a London base whenever she wished to come up to town. Taylor seems to have acquiesced passively in all of these arrangements.

In the world in which Taylor still thought he wished to move, that of left-wing movers and shakers, Uncle Harry – W.H. Thompson – was a man of some note. One of his earliest cases was as solicitor for George Lansbury, who had been active in London local government in the borough of Poplar from 1903 to 1910 and then had been an MP from 1910 to 1912; from 1919 to 1922 he was Editor of the *Daily Herald*, a newspaper which he had helped to found. As a former mayor of Poplar he led the Poplarist campaign in

1921, which objected to the inequality of the rates burden between rich and poor boroughs: the Poor Law Guardians of a borough were responsible for their own poor, and a poor borough such as Poplar could be required to impose a heavier rates burden on their ratepayers than richer boroughs, which had fewer poor inhabitants to maintain. The Poplar councillors authorised expenditure which was not supported by income from the rates, and the court held them personally accountable for this overspending; thirty councillors went to prison. In the end the cause was won and new legislation made central, not local, government responsible for supporting the poor. Thompson acted for Lansbury and his colleagues in the case, and it made his name and his reputation amongst the left. He became the leading solicitor for those involved in the Labour movement, his clients including Ramsay MacDonald (Labour Party leader from 1922 to 1931 and Prime Minister in 1924 and again from 1929 to 1935), and the writer H.G. Wells. He specialised in cases arising from workmen's compensation claims after industrial accidents, and this naturally brought him into close contact with the other wing of the Labour movement, the trade unions. Indeed, Thompson's law practice eventually moved into Congress House, the headquarters of the Trades Union Congress.[3]

According to one account, Uncle Harry was as ruthless in his work as he was in ragging those weaker and younger than him. He was tall, energetic and in his familial relations habitually attempted dominance. Such traits certainly contributed to his professional success, but they must have made working for him a somewhat fearsome prospect. He was 'said to employ only solicitors who had lost their membership of the Law Society, so that they could not quit and take their business with them',[4] in short, those whom he could control. Taylor was to be another under his control, at least judging by Taylor's story: 'Before I went to London Harry produced a partnership deed. My father, who had been enslaved by a partnership for twenty years, showed it to his own solicitor who reported that it was slavery of the same kind. Harry agreed to change it but I continued to think that he had tried to cheat me and might do so again.'[5]

Taylor hated being an articled clerk from the beginning. The work bored him to tears, and he spent much of the day in the office reading his prize Dickens and books from the Times Book Club. He wrote that Harry had been used to teasing his father and now took the same line with him, but presumably the successful, thrusting solicitor must have found his non-working nephew intensely frustrating. It might seem surprising that Taylor had not done some intellectual reconnoitring beforehand to see if he liked the law, but his not having done so is in keeping with the passivity of his whole approach to life at that time.

People in jobs which they hate sometimes try to make up for it by a vibrant, or at least interesting, after-hours life. Taylor appears to have failed here as well. He wrote that he did not know anyone in London: what about all those whom he had met in the Inner Temple? It is possible, of course, that he had proclaimed his left-wing convictions to such an extent that he had made few friends in what was a conservative profession. Yet he made little use of those avenues which lay open to him. He refused to join the local Labour Party on the grounds that, coming from an industrial district, he did not wish to mix with Hampstead intellectuals. This is perhaps understandable if, as was possible, he equated the latter with his mother. His uncle put him up for the 1917 Club, which had been started by pro-Bolshevik left-wingers and which met above a bakery in Gerrard Street in Soho, but 'they were now all elderly .... had lost interest in politics and cared only for bridge, at which Harry excelled. I did not. Also the food at the club was very bad.' So every evening he dined alone and sat alone in his flat, not even daring, he claimed, to bring in wine or beer, presumably for fear that the housekeeper would reprimand him in his mother's name.[6]

This hermit-like existence was moderated on Sundays, when he went to the Film Society – he listed thirty-three films seen in 1927 alone. Innes Stewart and Theodore Yates sometimes came to spend the weekend with him, when they would dine and go to the theatre. It is not terribly different from the story of any young person newly arrived in a big city, except that Taylor had a flat and money. Granted, it was not very agreeable when his mother arrived and spent a month with him, but this is also a tale which others have told. The key was the hatred he felt for his working existence. He told his father at Christmas that he should have to leave Harry's office, and his father, with some embarrassment, pointed out that his mother would not be pleased.

Deliverance, literally, came because of a young woman. Tom Wintringham, a middle-class Communist, introduced Taylor to some young Communists in the Hampstead area. One of them was a young girl called Dora, and Taylor began taking her out, even kissing her once. Neither was serious, but Taylor's mother got wind of the relationship, presumably from the housekeeper. She feared that Taylor was the 'prey of a harpy' and became desperate to get him away from London, even at the cost of destroying the partnership with her brother and losing access to the flat. It would have been amazing if Harry had fought against losing Taylor, since the latter was apparently little more than a sullen presence in the office; at any rate, at the end of March 1928 Taylor broke his articles and became, once again, a free man with no idea what he should do. He returned to Preston, but soon decided that the only thing to do was to return to Oxford – there he had been happy and successful, and if his fate was to become a schoolmaster, as had happened to many in his shoes, it was probably easier to do so from Oxford than from Preston.[7]

Taylor wrote in an early draft of his autobiography that he had applied to Oriel to resume his exhibition but that he had received no reply. It was a very strange thing to do and suggests that, even after his three years there, Taylor still did not understand how Oxford worked. Scholarships and exhibitions were awarded to incoming first-year undergraduates to hold for the duration of their first degree course; they were not for postgraduates. In the end, Taylor went into lodgings and simply turned up at Oriel.[8] Innes Stewart was still there, and he immediately had more of a social life than he had enjoyed in London.

But what was he to do during the day? 'By accident', he wrote – did someone suggest it, did he see a poster announcing it? – he discovered that a prize essay had been proposed in a field he found sympathetic and he began his first bout of historical research. Oxford University had a number of prizes in different scholarly fields, and there were at least three important history essay prizes, the Lothian, the Arnold and the Gladstone. For each a subject would be announced, candidates (who had to be within seven years of matriculation) would write essays and they would be judged by senior Oxford academics. Taylor decided to try for the Gladstone Memorial Prize for 1929, due on or before 1 March 1929: the subject was 'The Political Ideas of the Parliamentary Radicals 1832–1868'. He read volumes of Hansard (the bound reports of debates of the House of Commons) and some tracts by Jeremy Bentham and his followers; he did not get the prize, but was, unknowingly, laying the foundation of later research. This period and these historical figures remained a special interest of his, and what he always called his favourite book, *The Troublemakers*, would, thirty years later, cover some of the same ground.[9]

At some point he went to see G.N. Clark, who was not pleased to see him: Clark thought that he should get a steady job and stick to it (he later told the historian E.L. Woodward that Taylor was not mature enough at that time to be brought back to Oxford). However, he also told Taylor that if he was going to be an historian – a comment which can only mean that Taylor had told him that that was what he wanted to do – he would have to learn German. Taylor was attracted by the idea of going to Weimar Germany, supposedly a centre of progressive politics and art, but the contacts proposed by Clark did not materialise.[10]

Taylor also went to see H.W.C. Davis, the Regius Professor of History (the holder of the chair was a Fellow of Oriel), who had an alternative venue to propose: he suggested that Taylor go to 'my old friend Přibram in Vienna'. Přibram, said Davis, was an authority on Cromwell as well as on European diplomacy, and Taylor could write a thesis on some obscure English diplomat of the eighteenth century. Interestingly, Davis was suggesting that Taylor do more than learn German: he was suggesting that he go to Vienna as a research student. This indirectly underlines the fact that Oxford in the 1920s was emphatically not a place where much research was conducted: research was considered a bywater compared with the mainstream of undergraduate teaching. Indeed, it was difficult even to receive structured guidance in the sources and methods of research. A.F. Pollard, Professor of History at University College London and founder of the Institute of Historical Research, told of being invited to Oxford in 1911 to lecture on sources and discovering that lectures which had packed out large halls in University College attracted just one tutor from St Edmund Hall and three students. As Pollard explained in a letter, 'Original investigation is not a strong point at Oxford'. Oxford tutors in history 'don't in the least realize that some notion of historical evidence and of the materials and sources of history is indispensable to anyone who wants to apply critical judgment to historical matters; even undergraduates should be taught how to test the truth of what they learn.'[11] Oxford, conversely, preferred an orderly teaching of facts. Taylor would have to go elsewhere to learn how to do research.

Taylor was immediately attracted by the idea of working with Přibram. Soaked at that moment in the speeches and writings of the parliamentary radicals, he thought that research on their relations with the Viennese radicals in the years before the revolutions of 1848 might well produce an interesting piece of work. Furthermore, Vienna, though not Austria as a whole, held a very special place in the eyes of left-wingers all over Europe, since it was controlled by social democrats and attempted to provide both housing and culture for the working classes. Taylor wrote to Přibram, who replied that he would only be in Vienna for the next few weeks; Taylor jumped on the next sleeper. This was in the third week of May 1928, a lovely time to be in Vienna. Even lovelier was to stay in the Hotel Bristol, the only one Taylor had heard of and the most luxurious in Vienna, with its thick carpets, panelling, gilt and sumptuous restaurant.[12]

Alfred Příbram, born of a middle-class Jewish family, took his name from the small Bohemian town where his father had been a stationmaster; curiously, Příbram himself had been born in Brighton and so had a British passport – a life-saving asset once the Nazis came to power. By the time Taylor met him in 1928 he was nearly seventy years old and a 'delightful character', witty as well as learned, generous and charming. A Viennese professor of history in a country which has a very great respect for professors, fluent in several languages, his house on the Billrothstrasse was a meeting place for artistic and academic friends alike, amongst whom had been the historians Joseph Redlich and Heinrich Friedjung – the latter would indirectly play an important role in Taylor's development into an historian – and Sigmund Freud.[13]

Příbram welcomed Taylor to Vienna and agreed that he could work with him, but broke the news that his own interest in Cromwell had ceased: he was now fully occupied intellectually with the origins of the First World War – as Taylor later wrote, 'a top subject everywhere except in England'. There were at least two reasons for this interest. First of all, the war had been so cataclysmic, so bloody, it had so turned the world upside down, that people wanted to know how it had all begun: who or what had caused it? The second stemmed from Article 231 of the Versailles Treaty, the so-called war-guilt clause: this ascribed to Germany the blame for causing the war. Part of Germany's response had been the publication of diplomatic documents in order to demonstrate that it had not been to blame. In defence or emulation other countries did the same – the Soviets had in fact already begun publication of Tsarist documents, and the French, the British and the Americans followed suit. Within a very few years the unprecedented had happened: the archives had been at least partially opened for the delectation of historians, and within a few years after that the publication of books purporting to explain the origins of the First World War began.

Příbram would have liked Taylor to have worked in the field of late nineteenth-century European diplomatic history, as did others of his students, most notably the American William L. Langer. However, he accepted that Taylor was determined to work on the pre-1848 radicals; he gave him a list of books to read on Austrian history and told him to come back in the autumn. Taylor was 'entranced with the prospect', with the idea of the subject, of working with Příbram and of living and working in

Vienna, which had already 'bewitched' him. He was also relieved that he had something positive to do, at least for the immediate future, having spent half a year in a void as far as his future was concerned. He returned happily to England.[14]

Taylor spent the few remaining weeks of Trinity Term in Oxford and then joined his parents for a holiday in the West Country. It was not a success. They went first to Cornwall, stopping in Bude. This is not the prettiest of Cornish villages – rather, it is a touring centre for the surrounding villages on the Atlantic coast – but it has a beach and grass-topped headlands. Taylor, however, was not to be pleased, describing it in a letter to his friend Charles Gott as 'loathsome', with 'rows of lodging houses, inhabited by broken down missionaries on leave, and nothing at all to do.' Things were made worse by bad weather; this did not bother Taylor, who rather liked getting wet while walking, but 'my mother went into tantrums because it rained and my father couldn't think what to do with her.' In desperation they drove to Dartmoor, staying in an hotel near Princetown, where things were more comfortable. They were then to move to Salisbury and thereafter amble homewards.[15]

One point of this letter was to boast about a romantic adventure to Gott, but the use of childish code emphasises their emotional immaturity: 'the Sussex expedition was attended with all success – she is indeed a fascinating young woman and I shall certainly have the good time with her some time. But the more wuzzy I go, the less I am interested in marriage – I regard myself as quite safe from it. But we both went gug-gug and I daresay if she hadn't been still a little unwell we should have gone nunc-nunc too.' Taylor and Gott, as well as their friend Innes Stewart, would retain a strong interest in gaining sexual experience over the next few years – an interest unsurprising in young men of twenty-one. What is more surprising is their innocence and ignorance: as Taylor himself recalled, later in the summer he, Stewart and George Clazy went on holiday together, during which they visited in Dresden a Swiss girl who had been a governess to some of Taylor's cousins. 'On her table was a wooden mushroom, an instrument that continental women use when darning socks. We had no idea what it was and decided that it must be her contraceptive.'[16] The imagination reels.

Innes Stewart had obtained a First in English and had decided to go to Vienna with Taylor for the following year to study German. The holiday was taken in September *en route* there. The two of them, plus Clazy, travelled first to Berlin, where they stayed for some days; Taylor disliked the city and was relieved that he had decided against going there to study. They moved on to Dresden, notable to Taylor as the venue for his first opera; this, unfortunately, was Richard Strauss's *Die Aegyptische Helena*, which he did not like, but he would have another chance at the Vienna Staatsoper and the next time opera would take. After Dresden they went to Prague, which he disliked largely because he expected to: 'I had been brought up to believe that Germany and Austria were enlightened democratic states, victimized by the peace treaties, and that the succession states were militaristic and reactionary. I therefore decided that Prague was dirty, uncivilized and overrun by soldiers in uniform.' (Later, Taylor came to regard Prague as the most beautiful city north of the Alps and the Czechs as a highly civilised people.) The three of them then travelled to Vienna, and after a few days Clazy left Taylor and Innes Stewart to settle in for the year, Taylor registering with the police on 17 October 1928.[17]

The question then arises, just where did they settle? Taylor in his autobiography is very clear about it: they were 'just behind the Concert House and the open-air skating rink was next door.' However, two letters from Taylor and Stewart to Charles Gott dated 13 and 14 November 1928 give their address as Wasagasse 13, Vienna 9. Wasa Gasse (the proper spelling) is in the university district, while the Konzerthaus and the Wiener Eislaufverein are on Am Heumarkt, at least two kilometres away. What probably happened is that Taylor and his friends lived on Wasa Gasse during their first term in Vienna, and then moved to the Heumarkt after Christmas, when they were joined by Gott, Geoffrey Rowntree, a schoolmate at both the Downs and Bootham, and Peter Mann, an artist (memorable for painting the naked upper half of his girlfriend and exhibiting her in their digs), all of whom stayed until the summer (Stewart left in the spring).[18] Alternatively, Taylor moved there in the autumn of 1929 upon his return from England.

In November 1928, however, they were living as lodgers in the house of Frau Goldschmidt: 'our landlady, having fallen on evil days, had sold most of her furniture except in her own room and our accommodation was somewhat sparse'. This may have been why Stewart described the room as 'about the size of a tennis court'. For their rent of twelve pounds a month they also received five meals a day, '(one inadequate)', and all heat and light. They had their meals separate from the family but sometimes joined them for conversation. The only restriction mentioned was 'lady-friends only in the afternoon', hardly – given the difficulties they were finding in meeting any – an onerous one.[19]

The opposite sex, and sex itself, was a major preoccupation of the two Englishmen and their friends. As Stewart wrote to Gott, 'we are much disturbed by the smell of women here: we constantly meet better men flaunting their mistresses. We do what we can in the way of looking round and have indeed begun seducing two, but as we are shy and unpractised I am afraid the Christmas return to England will arrive before anything is achieved.' Taylor was a bit less elegant about it: 'we go roaming about seeking bitches . . . everyone except us seems to find dozens of mistresses about the place.' They both referred to Viennese girls as 'sleeping dictionaries', and Taylor finally found one, but she only let him remove the top part of her clothing. Taylor and Stewart were both virgins and desperate to lose the label. Finally they purchased help by going to a prostitute, but neither found it very enjoyable. It also carried the risk of venereal disease, and both immediately had a medical check-up.[20]

Taylor's most pressing reason for being in Vienna, however, was to learn German. This he did by a combination of self-help, teaching and a German-speaking girlfriend. His recollection was that he taught himself by first reading a grammar and then history books in German, looking up every word in the dictionary, making lists of vocabulary and learning the words. He had discovered early on that there was no substitute for hard slog in learning a language. It is worth noting, however, that his early forays into German were probably made easier by the fact that the books were *not* heavy tomes of history, but plays, and although his first two were by Ernst Toller and Goethe, his third and fourth were by Shakespeare (*Hamlet*) and Bernard Shaw in translation, two of his favourite authors.[21] He made great strides and, by the following March, of the twelve items on his reading list for that month, ten were in German.

Although reading books might suffice to gain a reading knowledge of German, it was no help at all in learning how to pronounce it correctly. For this he found an English teacher from a nearby school and spent hours and hours with her, practising his vowels until they sounded truly German. (It is as well to remember that this was before the age of tape recorders and language laboratories.) He picked up the local Viennese accent from the grooms at a riding school. He now had written German and the key to its pronunciation; what he needed was practice in conversation. For this purpose his teacher introduced Taylor to a former pupil of hers: this was Else Sieberg, the object of his first love affair.

An English-language correspondent in a Viennese exporting firm, eager to improve her English, Else was just nineteen. Taylor thought that she would be sexually sophisticated, being Viennese; she thought that he would be, being twenty-two; both were almost wholly inexperienced and therefore, according to Taylor, 'never got further than innocent, though intense, embraces.' He assumed that 'she was feather-brained, like most Viennese girls [one wonders whom he had been meeting], whereas she was much more cultured musically' than he was. Rather than take her to concerts, he took her to Russian films and Brecht and Weill's *Threepenny Opera*, both of which shocked her, though neither as much as did Sternberg's *The Blue Angel*.

They grew increasingly fond of each other: 'Else began to speculate whether she would like to live in England .... I began to speculate whether I should like her to do so.' They met every day during her lunch hour, and in the evenings he took her to a restaurant. This was the fatal habit. Else neglected to tell him that in Vienna, while going to the cinema or a concert with a man was respectable, going to a restaurant was not. Things proceeded happily while they went to Schoener's, then the best and most expensive one in Vienna (with a strong pound and a weak Austrian schilling Taylor could afford it); but the night Else wanted a change, and they went to a less expensive restaurant, was the night that they ran into Else's relations by the entrance. Else was told that he was wicked and out to seduce her and was forbidden ever to go out with him again. They continued to meet at lunch time, but her family's repeated arguments apparently began to convince her: at any rate it was over.[22] Taylor does not say whether he was badly affected, but it would be astonishing if he had not been: a first love affair, especially when it ends so badly, can take time to get over. He had no other girlfriend for a year.

He did have other passions, however – horse-riding and music. He began to think about riding in the autumn, writing to Gott in November 1928 that 'we live tolerably expensively, but after Christmas we are going to retrench and, as a result, I shall be able to ride.' He took lessons, sitting on a horse with the stirrups crossed in front of him, his arms folded, being led round and round on a rein. It was painful but he acquired a good seat. By the summer he had progressed well enough to ride by himself down the Haupt Allee, a long, tree-lined path for walking and riding in the Prater. The Prater, an immense green space between the two arms of the Danube River, had once been a hunting reserve for the aristocracy, but had been opened to the public by Emperor Joseph II in the late eighteenth century. It was a favourite place of Taylor's. At the end of the Haupt Allee was a wonderfully equipped jumping field – Taylor later claimed that horse-jumping had given him more pleasure in life than any other physical activity except fell-walking. Also at the end of the Allee was the Lusthaus, the mere name of which reduced Taylor and his friends to chortles. A sixteenth-century former imperial hunting lodge, the Lusthaus had been the location of a celebratory feast by the victorious sovereigns during the Congress of Vienna in 1814, since when it had been a favourite restaurant for Viennese society. It was extremely pleasant to ride or walk through the Prater and then dine at the Lusthaus.

The passion for music hit him unexpectedly. Taylor had clearly decided that he was going to experiment with all sorts of new interests in Vienna and when, upon his arrival, he discovered that the Schubert centenary was in full swing, he immediately booked tickets. He was fortunate in hearing members of the Busch Quartet – whose recordings still form part of the collection of any discerning listener to chamber music – play Schubert trios in his first week. Taylor 'saw the light from that moment and hardly missed a chamber concert during the two years [he] was in Vienna.' He also finally discovered opera in a decided manner. The fifth gallery of the Staatsoper was the bailiwick of the poor but devoted. It was cheap and, because the lights were kept on during performances, many read the score or libretto in order to learn and follow the details. Taylor did this, following along during both Mozart and the *Ring*. He also went to symphony concerts, obtaining a season ticket to the Vienna Philharmonic during his second year in Vienna; this, however, proved a less long-lasting passion than his devotion to chamber music, and his interest in attending symphony concerts would eventually fade along with his youthful devotion to Beethoven. The Schubert Piano Trio in B flat major, Op. 99, was played at his funeral.

During his two years in Vienna, he later estimated, he listened to classical music at least two nights a week. Concerts were of supreme importance in the days before cheap and easily available recordings, and Taylor attended so many, he said, that he soon carried the tunes in his head. This was probably rendered relatively easy because Viennese music impresarios tended to concentrate on a somewhat limited range of music, on Mozart, Beethoven, Schubert, Brahms, waltzes, operettas – nothing so modern as Bruckner or Mahler. Taylor later wrote that he never heard any modern music other than Stravinsky's *Oedipus Rex* – not to be played again in Vienna until after World War II. In short, he gained the musical education and interests which he had failed to obtain in England and which were to provide him with immense pleasure until his death.[23]

One thing he could do in Vienna which was forbidden to him in Britain, and which gave him great pleasure of a different sort – that of cocking a snook at stuffy controls – was to read James Joyce's *Ulysses*. Its publication in Paris in 1922 to literary acclaim, and its subsequent publication – and suppression – in London late in the same year and again in 1923, must have impinged on his consciousness, but he only began to read Joyce during his final months as an undergraduate. He read *Dubliners* and *A Portrait of the Artist as a Young Man* in April and May 1927, possibly as relaxation whilst revising for his final exams. The following March he read Joyce's first published work, the poems gathered together as *Chamber Music*. But only upon reaching Vienna could he and Innes Stewart acquire *Ulysses*, which Taylor enjoyed tremendously, even going so far as to compare himself to, if not to identify himself with, Leopold Bloom. As he wrote to Charles Gott, '*Ulysses* is great fun – I wrote a long letter to my family telling them what a highly moral work it is. Perhaps you would like to buy it from Innes at a cheap rate and he shall smuggle it into England for you. It is an education in itself. I must say I find myself remarkably like L. Bloom, its dirty hero: he had a spirit of scientific curiosity quite in my own line.'[24]

Taylor continued to read Joyce over the next few years. His last great novel, referred to as *Work in Progress* until its eventual appearance in 1939 as *Finnegans Wake*, took Joyce seventeen years to complete. During this period several parts of it had been published separately; Taylor read *Anna Livia Plurabelle* in 1930 and *Haveth Childers Everywhere* twice in 1931. But there is no evidence that he read the whole of *Finnegans Wake* itself – and indeed some evidence that he actively disliked the parts he did read: the author Anthony Burgess, who attended Taylor's history lectures at Manchester in 1937, recalls in his autobiography that 'Taylor lectured to a hundred or so of us and earned my enmity by scoffing at James Joyce's *Work in Progress*.'[25] *Ulysses*, however, the greatest of Joyce's novels, remained a favourite: Taylor read it again in 1938, just before taking up his Fellowship at Oxford, and a third time in 1972, at a time of his life when he read relatively few novels.

One curious omission during his period in Vienna was left-wing politics. As he himself later noted, 'I still thought of myself as a devoted Socialist and it is extraordinary to me looking back that I made no attempt to meet any Socialists of Red Vienna.'[26] The city was a red island in the midst of a blue sea. The new state of Austria, cut off from its hinterlands by the break-up of the Austro-Hungarian Empire in 1919, was fragile in its politics and unstable in its economics. Unemployed soldiers fed the paramilitary groups of both right and left, and politics was dangerously polarised. Austria was Catholic and sharply conservative – but with the coming of universal suffrage in 1919, the voting majority in Vienna became Socialist, with the city itself falling under the political control of the Austrian Socialist Party, the SDAP. The SDAP was determined to transform the lives of its working-class supporters by developing a 'comprehensive proletarian counterculture': the intention was to blend politics and culture, to mix municipal Socialism – new housing, better education, health programmes, sports facilities – with encouragement for and opportunities to improve the self, including inducements to try aspects of high culture. All of these elements in the new life the SDAP was providing for the inhabitants of Vienna were based on the Austro-Marxist concept that culture could play a significant role in the class struggle. For those on the left, it was one of the most exciting places in Europe to live.[27]

Taylor must have anticipated, while still in Britain, becoming part of – or at least finding out about – political life in Vienna. His uncle Harry procured for him a letter of introduction to Otto Bauer from his sometime legal client J. Ramsay MacDonald. Bauer was one of the leaders of the Socialist Party, the philosophical head of Austro-Marxism and a profound democrat who, in his writings, argued for a new federal entity based on the former Habsburg Empire which would accommodate the individual nationalisms inhabiting the same territory. He also argued for a corporatist model of politics, a social partnership which would reconcile capital and labour – a position distinctly at odds with that of the Bolsheviks in the new Soviet Union. Taylor went along to see this profoundly interesting man, but apparently nothing came of their meeting. He could have joined the Socialist society at the University of Vienna, but he failed to do so. He later termed this 'a wasted opportunity',[28] which indeed it was, but perhaps it was not altogether surprising. He was still remarkably unadventurous when it came to meeting new people and seeing new places: he hardly travelled whilst in Austria, and during his first year in Vienna he knew few people, English or Austrian, outside his circle of close friends. The mitigating circumstance, of course, was the language. The time had not yet arrived when the widespread use of English was relatively common, and Taylor took some time to achieve a command of German. The idea of joining a political club was inconceivable when he first arrived; when it did become conceivable Taylor had virtually ceased attending the university and was deep in historical research.

Early in the new year, Taylor returned to historical studies. He had worked hard at his German and now felt confident enough to handle the university. The University of Vienna was still one of the great academic institutions in spite of the Empire's defeat in the war and subsequent disintegration. It represented the summit of the Habsburg intellectual empire, celebrated for its learning, cosmopolitan, with professors drawn from the German-speaking elites of the various Habsburg territories. Taylor registered as a student for the spring term. He went to Přibram's lectures, 'wonderfully impromptu performances that became my model', combining, he later wrote, 'scholarship and excitement';[29] he also attended those of Heinrich von Srbik, whose lectures 'did not impress me'. Srbik's field, however, was the Habsburg Monarchy, and it is not fanciful to posit that it was here that Taylor – virtually a neophyte in modern European history – was introduced to the field which later became the theme of his third book, *The Habsburg Monarchy*.[30] Taylor failed to attend Přibram's seminar, since it was on Cromwell 'and therefore of no use to me'. He probably continued to attend lectures for the whole of that term, if only to improve his German, but he later wrote that at the beginning of the next 'the crowd for registration was too great for me and I did not bother to register again.'[31] He would not have gained the habit of lecture-going at Oxford, where the lectures were optional rather than central to the degree course. Besides, there was now a more alluring prospect: actual research in the Austrian Haus- Hof- und Staatsarchivs, held in the Chancellery where the Treaty of Vienna had been negotiated in 1814–15.

Unaware that Taylor had neglected to re-register at the university, Přibram told him to find a topic for his thesis. Taylor had by now decided against working on the Viennese radicals, but had little idea of what to work on instead. Had he remained in England, and at Oxford, he would probably have been guided towards some topic in English constitutional history, still the major field of research. Possibly he would have been encouraged to specialise in mediaeval history, then considered the most prestigious period in which to do research; possibly the period of the Tudors and Stuarts; possibly even the first half of the nineteenth-century. But what he would not have been encouraged to do was the history of British foreign policy, let alone diplomatic history, not least because there was no one at Oxford doing it; and he certainly could not have easily worked in something so modern as late nineteenth- or early twentieth-century history. Oxford still laboured under the legacy of Bishop Stubbs, the Regius Professor from 1866 to 1884 and a distinguished constitutional historian, who had bequeathed to the university his firm conviction that contemporary history, because it was controversial and therefore might excite the political passions of students, had to be avoided.[32]

Příbram had also suggested that Taylor do research on the origins of the First World War, but Taylor thought that this would be an impossible topic for him. It was not because he feared controversy, though it was indeed a controversial field; rather, it was because, he said, he knew no history after the Congress of Berlin in 1885. Next, Příbram suggested that Taylor investigate Anglo-Austrian relations from 1848 to 1866, the period between the revolutions which had broken out in cities across Europe in 1848 and the Austro-Prussian War, by which the Habsburgs were effectively driven out of Germany. The topic sounded a bit dull to Taylor, but many of the documents would be in French or English, a great advantage, he later noted, 'when my German was still shaky.' He settled down to work in the archives.

Taylor later wrote in his autobiography that neither Příbram nor anyone else had given him the most elementary instructions in how to conduct research, that he had never seen a diplomatic document before and that therefore both form and language were unfamiliar: 'I did not know the difference between an official dispatch and a private letter. I had no idea how to weigh the reliability of historical evidence. I did not even know that I must note the number of each document, an ignorance which caused me much unnecessary labour.' It is, however, arguable that this is an example of a Taylorian trait: a reluctance to admit that he was ever helped, or even influenced, by another historian. In earlier years he was more candid: in 1934 he wrote in the Preface to his first book that 'from Professor Příbram I first learnt what diplomatic history could be and he taught me the elements of scientific research'. As late as 1966 he could still make the private admission that Příbram had 'also taught me the rudiments of technique in studying diplomatic documents.'[33]

However undeveloped his technique in the early days of his research, he did possess an eye for a subject: after he had been reading in the archives for a period, he conceived a new topic, one which centred on a problem rather than covering a period and, more importantly, one which sparked his interest. 'The problem was northern Italy in 1848 as seen by the Austrian administration and by the British and French governments, an international crisis that never quite came off. By chance I had hit upon a good subject.' No one had done it before, the material in the Austrian archives was very rich, and Příbram approved of it.[34]

Taylor and Příbram got along well, frequently meeting socially. When

Taylor arrived, Přibram was working on the Ford Lectures in English History, an endowed series of six lectures given in Oxford each year by distinguished historians invited by the History Faculty. Přibram was scheduled to give them in Michaelmas Term 1929 and, according to Taylor, he helped him with the Englishing of the text; the lectures were published in 1931 as *England and the International Policy of the European Great Powers, 1871–1914*.[35] He gave Taylor good advice on gaining depth as an historian: he ought not restrict himself to reading in the archives, but should travel and 'see the Balkan people',[36] advice which, however, Taylor did not follow as assiduously as he might have done. Přibram always remained his supporter and a year later would be responsible for placing him in his first job.

Přibram's first good turn was to suggest that Taylor apply for a Rockefeller research fellowship to finance another year in Vienna. Přibram was the Austrian representative for the Rockefeller and would obviously only put forward a candidate whom he thought stood a good chance of winning a fellowship. Besides, he told Taylor, no English students ever applied, with the obvious implication that the competition from Britain would be slight. Taylor ran into a problem common amongst research students, however: his thesis topic did not match the requirements of the fellowship. But, as is also common amongst research students, he tweaked his topic to fit it. The fellowship was in the social sciences, but his thesis was 'pure diplomatic history', so he composed an application which emphasised his burning desire to make a special study of British public opinion with regard to Italy – 'the mixture of foreign policy and public opinion was then a favourite topic among social scientists.' (However, when the research was later turned into his first book, he kept belated faith by making some pertinent comments about the impact of public opinion on the making of foreign policy.) He was called for interview, so he returned to London in late spring 1929, where he met J.R.M. Butler, the historian of the Great Reform Act of 1832, at the Oxford and Cambridge Club. Butler was the British representative of the Rockefeller and he proceeded to interview Taylor on his work and proposed thesis. The result was the award of the fellowship, which would enable Taylor to live a reasonably comfortable life in Vienna the following year.[37]

Taylor went home to England for the summer of 1929. His first duty was to go on holiday with his parents, which ordinarily would have been taken in the Lake District – the Taylors had rented a house there every summer since 1919. His mother, however, decided that a change was imperative, and instead they went to Malvern to attend the first festival devoted to the works of George Bernard Shaw. Shaw had long been a favourite of both Taylor and his father, Leslie Gilbert having introduced Taylor to the plays at Bootham; and at Malvern Taylor and his mother saw Shaw himself watching a performance of his play *The Apple Cart*. The Malvern holiday was also notable for a row between his mother and Henry Sara, who usually went to the theatre together whilst Taylor remained in the hotel with his father: 'one evening my mother was waiting impatiently for Henry when he passed the hotel door talking to a girl he had picked up ... There was a terrific row with my father and me more or less literally ducking under the table.' Taylor also remembered a near miss when, after a day spent riding (as he spent nearly every day at Malvern), he came in hot and tired and drank two pints of Herefordshire cider straight off, with the result that by dinnertime he was drunk. He recalled that 'I held on to my chair waiting for the storm to blow. Fortunately my mother was eager to be off and noticed nothing. My father made no comment.'[38]

The most shocking event of the summer for Taylor was his first experience of the death of a friend, and in circumstances as pointless as they were tragic. He was on holiday with Geoffrey Rowntree in the New Forest when Innes Stewart rang from Edinburgh to tell him that George Clazy had committed suicide. Clazy had passed high in the civil service exams and was set for a distinguished career when he fell in love: he wanted to marry the girl, who was very attractive; she was in no hurry and demurred; he threatened that if she did not agree to marry him, he would kill himself; she laughed – probably as much out of embarrassment as of incredulity; he went home and put his head in a gas oven. When he heard the news, Taylor was upset, but he apparently did not reveal just how much; his friend Rowntree later recalled that he was 'not heartbroken'. Yet in his autobiography Taylor wrote that Clazy's death was 'a terrible loss to me', not surprising when it is recalled that Clazy had been Taylor's first, if innocent, love when he was only seventeen, when they wrote ten-page letters to each other daily during school holidays. They had certainly been best friends for the remainder of their schooldays, sharpening each other intellectually and taking tremendously long walks together in the Lake District. With Clazy's death Taylor lost both a close friend and a part of his youth.[39]

The summer was also notable in a positive way for bringing the first job offer that he felt able to greet with some enthusiasm. His father's friend George Lansbury was now First Commissioner of Works (a member of the

Labour government, but not of the Cabinet) and one of his responsibilities was Britain's ancient monuments. The government had plans to increase the number of inspectors of monuments; Lansbury had long known of Taylor's interest in, and indeed expertise in, mediaeval architecture, and he suggested that he might like to become one of their inspectors, assuming that as First Commissioner he would be able to have Taylor selected. Taylor liked the idea, since the work would be interesting. In his old age he claimed that it would be 'totally remote from real life which was exactly what I wanted', which was quite a change from wanting to help the working classes, or even to make money. What is more significant is that he seemed to be following his intellectual inclinations; it is certainly the first time that he admits to doing so.

The main drawback was that he lacked the technical training which would be required; in an attempt to remedy this, Taylor took a number of archaeology textbooks back to Vienna with him in the autumn, determined to spend his evenings studying them. However, it was only in January 1930 that he managed to study anything on the subject, when he read R.A. Smith's *Stone Age Antiquities* (twice) and *Bronze Age Antiquities*. Obviously he had no premonition that when he eventually called in on the Chief Inspector of Monuments, Sir Charles Peers, a few months later he would be told that the government was now economising – the Depression was intensifying – and that no expansion would take place. Yet he was probably saved from a career for which he was unsuited. Normally when he was intrigued by a subject he read lots of relevant books, something he did not do in this case.[40]

What he spent his autumn evenings doing in Vienna was reading a number of books in German, although, it must be said, the literary far outnumbered the historical. The significant exception was *Österreich von 1848 bis 1860* (Austria, 1848–60) by Heinrich Friedjung, Přibram's predecessor at the University of Vienna and an historian who was to have a profound impression on Taylor. Indeed, Taylor's second published book would be a joint translation of one of Friedjung's works. However, this was very much in the future: what seems to have struck Taylor in the autumn and winter of 1929–30 was how alone he was. Rowntree had returned to Vienna with Taylor, travelling along the Adriatic coast to Split, a trip they had made together the previous spring; but Rowntree had then gone back to England. None of Taylor's English friends was now with him in Vienna, and he had irrevocably broken up with Else Sieberg. As he remembered it years later, he had been 'condemned to complete solitude. I did not exchange a word with anyone from morning to night except for waiters and the grooms at the riding stables.'⁴¹ For a period during the dark months of 1929 and 1930, then, his life consisted of work in the archives during the day and either concerts or reading in the evenings. Curiously, this was to be the pattern of much of his life, but it is naturally much more comfortable to know that one has the choice.

In due course he made some friends, two through the agency of Přibram. One was Ian F.D. Morrow, a professional translator, who had lived in various parts of the Austro-Hungarian Empire for many years. Taylor called him a 'remarkable character', although it is unclear whether this was because he spoke fluent German with an 'execrable' English accent or because he shared with Taylor the habit of smoking long Virginia cigars which had a straw down the centre. Taylor learned a great deal from him, something, presumably, about the parts of the old Empire, but also much about the craft of translating. Taylor recalled that he 'shared his work of translating, a good discipline',⁴² but he gives no hint of what he learned or what they translated. It is probable, however, that the book was *Die Entstehung der Deutschen Republik* by Arthur Rosenberg, published in 1931 as *The Birth of the German Republic 1871–1918*. Ian F.D. Morrow is listed as the translator; he would probably have been working on it during 1929, and the topic would have appealed to Taylor. The discipline Taylor mentions must have included close attention to detail and a honing of his ability to grasp the essential as well as the literal meaning of the words, sentences and paragraphs being translated. Certainly this apprenticeship paid off in the near future, when Taylor embarked upon his translation of Friedjung. Morrow also pointed him in the direction of a 'staider' style of life than that of a student when a friend of Morrow's put him up for the Beefsteak Club, at which English businessmen met for dinner once a month at the Grand Hotel.⁴³

Přibram also introduced him to an American, Teddy Pratt, who became a friend for life. Edward J. Pratt had been up at Oxford (where he was known as 'Auntie Pratt') at the same time as Taylor, but their paths had not crossed. This was not surprising: they had been at different colleges – Pratt was a Hertford man – but, even more important, Pratt had been a postgraduate. He had gained his first degree in the States and then come to Oxford in 1922 to work for the B.Litt degree. The B.Litt was a research degree, analogous to the D.Phil. but awarded for a shorter thesis on a smaller subject than was required for the doctorate. Pratt took his B.Litt in 1925, so the two of them had only overlapped for a year in any case. He was a man of private means – he came of a wealthy Boston family and had expectations from various wealthy aunts – who was devoted to food, culture and, at some distance, history. He was in Vienna to learn German and to work on Metternich's Spanish policy, a book still uncompleted at the time of his death fifty years later. In short, he was a dilettante, a good-humoured companion with whom Taylor shared many concerts and restaurant meals in Vienna and many holidays over the years.[44]

Indeed, Taylor's social life widened considerably. He spent Christmas 1929, his first away from home, with his long-standing friend Geoffrey Barraclough in Munich, where Barraclough had gone after Oxford to do research on mediaeval Germany. He was obviously thriving, but his wife Margery was desperately unhappy. Taylor claimed that she had never left Oxford before, let alone England, she knew no German, had no acquaintances in Munich, was alone from morning till night while her husband worked in the archives, and was pregnant. Not surprisingly, she wanted to return home to her parents. Taylor tried hard to cheer her up, making much of her and inviting them to Vienna, and temporarily saved the marriage. In due course they named their first son Alan, but separated ten years later.

A newer friend was Basil Rock, who became his flatmate for some months. Rock was attending the Gzichek School where he was learning how to teach art to children; he was also painting pictures himself. They had a common element in their backgrounds – both had been at Quaker prep schools, Taylor of course at the Downs, Rock at the more famous Leighton Park School in Reading (where the Downs' headmaster, Jones, had lasted only a year in charge). Rock encouraged Taylor's already high opinion of his own legs – Taylor had expressed regret at Oxford that knee breeches were no longer in fashion – by coming into the bathroom and sketching them whilst Taylor was having his morning shower. Taylor remembered him as having a character of 'enchanting innocence': Rock told him that 'the greatest sensual pleasure in life was to put one's foot into a newly-dropped cowpat', a predilection not perhaps shared by everyone. Other young men of their age might have cited sex as a bit more pleasurable, but given that the only sexual exploit of Rock's which Taylor records was his attempt to have sexual relations with a hen, it is easy to see why the cowpat won out.[45] In 1931 he was to be one of the two witnesses at Taylor's wedding.

At some point in late 1929 or early 1930 Pratt introduced Taylor to Margaret Adams, an English girl studying the piano and German in

Vienna. Taylor was ready for another relationship – he had not seen Else Sieberg for nearly a year, and she was in any case about to marry a rich businessman who owned factories in Czechoslovakia. Adams came from a rich, upper-middle-class, Roman Catholic family – though born in India where her father worked, she was educated in an English convent – from which she was attempting to emancipate herself, both in politics and religion. Five feet four inches tall, with blue eyes and long brown hair, she was musical and had a yen for literature, although she was not intellectual, or at least not academic, but, as Taylor later – and inaccurately – stated, 'no intellectual woman attracted me sexually'. Someone who knew her well in the 1930s and 1940s described her as 'a sweet, helpless creature' who was always falling in love.[46]

Over the next months the relationship developed. They attended restaurants and concerts together and gradually fell in love. Taylor 'worried about the future, doubtful whether her religious or family background would consort with mine. She had no such doubts.' They wanted to consummate their relationship and decided to go to Melk to do so. Presumably the lure was artistic and historical as well as romantic: Melk Abbey is the summit of Baroque architecture in Austria, which would have attracted both of them; it had also been the headquarters of Napoleon in 1805 and again in 1809 during his campaign against Austria, which would have attracted Taylor. The abbey sits 150 feet above the Danube, dominating the village, a most romantic situation. Yet the main point of the visit was not fulfilled: 'with total inexperience on both sides', Taylor recalled – but what about the prostitute? – 'nothing was achieved'.[47]

Success followed soon afterwards, however. Taylor was in England for a short period during the spring of 1930, and he and Adams borrowed a car from Charles Gott and spent five days touring the Thames valley. Taylor wrote, somewhat cryptically, that 'Margaret had been to a gynaecologist who had relieved her of her virginity and given her some instruction.' This was apparently necessary but not sufficient, since they still had 'some days of fumbling efforts'. However, success came before the end of the holiday at the Shillingford Bridge Hotel, a large, semi-luxurious hotel of Victorian origins on the Thames near Wallingford in Berkshire (now South Oxfordshire). They then parted, she to return to London, he to the continent.[48]

The reason that Taylor was in England in the spring of 1930 was that he had been offered an academic post in the Department of History at the University of Manchester. He owed the opportunity to Přibram, who had gone to Oxford to give his Ford Lectures and had stayed at All Souls. One of the Fellows there was Ernest Jacob, who had that academic year become Professor of Mediaeval History and head of the department at Manchester. Over dinner one night Jacob revealed to Přibram that he had a problem: the Professor of Modern History had just left and the assistant lecturer had gone off to be married. Come the next academic year, only months away, there would be no one at all to teach modern European history if he could not locate a replacement. Did Přibram know of anyone who might do? According to Taylor, 'I was the only English student he had had for years and was consequently proud of me. He sang my praises to Ernest who jumped at the idea.'[49] The following morning Jacob sent a telegram to Taylor offering him the post of Assistant Lecturer in Modern History. Fate had decided to make him a professional historian.

Taylor claimed that he had hardly heard of Manchester University, unlikely for a man from the north. More to the point for Taylor in deciding to accept or not was whether he had a possible career inspecting ancient monuments. He decided to go to Manchester for an interview: he could call on the Chief Inspector of Ancient Monuments, Sir Charles Peers, on his way through London. Furthermore, he had now finished his work in the Viennese archives and wanted to go on to the French archives, and Manchester would pay his fare from Vienna to London and Manchester and back to Paris. In London he discovered that there were no positions for the foreseeable future in ancient monuments, and the way was therefore open for him to accept the Manchester post, which he did 'without any enquiry or discussion'. Jacob told him when to turn up and what courses he would be teaching. They then bade one another farewell until the autumn and Taylor went to meet Margaret Adams.[50]

A week later he was in Paris, where he took a room at the Hôtel du Quai Voltaire, 'solely for the reason that Oscar Wilde used to stay there'. Looking across the Seine to the Louvre and the Tuileries, the hotel is known for having one of the most panoramic views in all of Paris. Its guests have included – besides Wilde – Baudelaire, who wrote *Les Fleurs du Mal* there; Wagner, who completed *Die Meistersinger* there; and Sibelius; Pissarro painted *Vue du Pont Royal* through its ceiling-high windows. Taylor, however, was almost a pantomine Englishman in his reaction: the hotel may have been attractive in Wilde's day, he wrote, but 'it was very noisy in mine and I cannot think how I put up with it'.[51] (Two lanes of fast traffic run past the entrance to the hotel.) The truth is that it was convenient for work – the archives of the Quai d'Orsay (the French Ministry of Foreign Affairs) were a few minutes' stroll along the banks of the Seine.

The morning hours in the archives were reserved for professors: lesser mortals had to make do with the hours between two and six in the afternoon. This, as it happened, suited Taylor very well. Every morning he went to the Bois de Boulogne, once the former royal forest of French monarchs from the Merovingians to the Bonapartes, but by 1930 the main recreation area of Paris. The Bois is crisscrossed by bridle paths and also boasts a very good horse-jumping field, and Taylor spent a couple of hours every morning riding or working on his jumping skills. He would then enjoy a leisurely lunch, followed by four hours reading in the Archives des Affaires Etrangères. Taylor was looking for evidence of French intentions and actions towards Italy and Austria during the period 1847–9 in order to compare it with the material which he had collected in Vienna. He was now rather more experienced in doing research and therefore more efficient – it takes time to develop a nose for the important document – and he got through the archives in a couple of months. Considering that they closed on 14 July for the summer, this was just as well.

Taylor's characteristic passivity when in a foreign land seems to have continued. He claimed that he never went sightseeing, even on a Sunday. Living as he was on the Left Bank, he only occasionally crossed to the Right Bank to go to W.H. Smith's tea room in the rue de Rivoli – and this with the Louvre just across the river. He did make a friend, the historian Noel Fieldhouse. Born in Sheffield, in 1930 Fieldhouse was based in Montreal. He and Taylor often met for dinner in Paris and cemented a lifelong friendship which lasted in spite (or because) of meeting only rarely. Fieldhouse would, over thirty years later, contribute to Taylor's first *Festschrift*.

After finishing his research in Paris, Taylor returned to his parents' house in Preston, where he settled down to prepare his first lectures. The story of this teaching belongs more properly in the next chapter; this one will instead follow the thread of the research, writing and publishing of his first book, the point at which he can properly be considered to have become an historian.

It was a year before Taylor could return to the archives. In the summer of 1931 he moved to London and plunged into research in the Foreign Office papers, held in the Public Record Office in Chancery Lane. The bibliography of his book would nowadays be considered unacceptably unforthcoming – the particular entry relating to the London period just says 'Manuscript Sources in the Public Record Office. London' – but it is clear from the footnotes that he was going through the correspondence of the British Foreign Secretary, Lord Palmerston, with various British ambassadors.[52] By the end of his time in London, he had completed his primary research in the Austrian, French and British archives, having decided to ignore the Italian archives on the rather curious grounds that Italy was currently being run by a Fascist regime. Now he only needed the time to write.

This he found the following June, when he went off to Austria. He settled down at St Gilgen, a village set in exquisite scenery on the Wolfgangsee near Salzburg. Here, he later wrote, he drafted his book in three weeks, an almost unbelievable rate of production, especially considering that he was 'typing with one finger on an antiquated typewriter'. He also swam in the lake, sunbathed and visited Teddy Pratt and his lover, Paul von Saffin, the son of a former Hungarian officer, who were holidaying in nearly Ischl, once a favourite watering-place of the Habsburgs.[53] In short, Taylor worked hard and played hard. Over the next year he revised and polished the manuscript, utilising the help of friends. Pratt let him consult his own unpublished work on Metternich and checked some references in Vienna for him, while Innes Stewart read the manuscript and gave advice both on details and on the structure of the book as a whole. By early 1933 it was complete and the time had come to look for a publisher.[54]

It is always a hurdle to get a first book published, and Taylor had the usual difficulty. He was fortunate to have the help of Lewis Namier, who had come to Manchester University the year after Taylor as Professor of Modern History. Namier thought highly of him, writing several years later that 'I consider Taylor one of the coming men on pre-War diplomatic history, and, as such, I think he is worth the attention of publishers.'[55] He attempted to smooth the way. He was the General Editor of a new series to be published by Macmillan called 'Studies in Modern History' and he proposed that Taylor's book be included in it. Namier invited Harold Macmillan, the future Prime Minister but then a publisher and MP for Stockton-on-Tees, up to Manchester to meet Taylor, and they discussed the book. There is no indication that Macmillan had read the manuscript, and it is therefore probable that he decided to take a chance on the new author because of his own relationship with Namier: he was Namier's lifelong publisher, and one of Namier's first and very well-informed biographers refers to Macmillan as his patron.[56]

However, having a manuscript accepted and having it published were two different matters: having sent Macmillan his manuscript in March 1933 in order that the firm might estimate the cost of production, Taylor had, with some embarrassment, to turn down the offer of publication. This was made on a commission basis, on which Macmillan, as well as other publishers,[57] often worked in those days: the author would put up part of the costs and would take, say, half of the profits, if any, instead of a royalty. In Taylor's case, the proposal was that he put up £50 towards the cost – one-sixth of his academic salary for the year. Taylor accepted the offer at first, but 'I am afraid I have put myself in rather an embarrassing position', he wrote to Harold Macmillan in mid-May. 'When I saw you, I thought I could raise enough money to offer you a limited guarantee. Since then, I have, unfortunately, bought a house and spent on it – as the way is – considerably more than I expected to do. As a result, much as I would like to accept your offer, I cannot do so because the money is simply not there.'[58] It might well have been there in capital, had he wished to use it, but Taylor probably thought it a sin to touch one's capital. This supposition is based on the reaction of his own children in their adult years to dipping into their investments: by report the very thought was anathema, held with the certainty that comes from early influence.[59] Taylor held shares in 1933, although whether they would have covered what Macmillan required is not known; in any case they were not to be sold.

Manchester University Press came to his rescue. They told Taylor that they would publish the book if he submitted it as a thesis first, and so he duly enrolled as a Ph.D student. According to the regulations, he was required to pursue a course of research for at least two years, to present an acceptable thesis and to satisfy examiners in an oral examination. Namier was registered as his supervisor, and that same year Taylor produced a thesis entitled 'The Question of Lombardy in the Relations of the European Powers during the Italian Revolution of 1848'; the university accepted his years in Vienna as the two years in question (residency in Manchester was not then required). In due course Namier and R.W. Seton Watson, the historian of the Habsburg lands, conducted an oral examination of the thesis. It was a success and the History Department, in its report to the Court of Governors for the 1933–4 academic year, stated that 'the following recommendation for the award of the Ph.D has been made: A.J.P. Taylor'.[60] Yet, 'anxious to avoid being called Dr Taylor, I never took it, much to the indignation of the university administrators'; the Manchester History Department's card on Taylor records only that he 'did not present himself for degree'.[61]

This desire to evade the title is unusual nowadays, but it is possible that at the time he was merely reflecting an Oxford prejudice. The D.Phil. degree had been established at Oxford University only in 1917, partly to attract students from the United States who wished to work for a doctorate away from Germany, where by tradition they had gone.[62] The Oxonian approach was to assume that the man with an Oxford First needed no further training – and, indeed, that the D.Phil. somehow derogated from the pure quality of the First. Certainly relatively few of Taylor's future colleagues in history at Oxford had felt the need to obtain a doctorate. Another possibility was that he was reflecting Namier's prejudice; it is the case that Namier later wrote of himself that he had 'deliberately and carefully avoided that infliction', i.e. the 'foolish title "Dr" '.[63] On the other hand, Taylor's head of department, Jacob, had been one of the earliest mediaeval historians to take the D.Phil., in 1923. (The fact that Jacob was sometimes referred to as 'the (learned or golden) doctor' appears to demonstrate that his was viewed as a somewhat eccentric course to have followed.)[64] The full answer will almost certainly never be known, but most probably the combined prejudices of Oxford and Namier had their effect.

The recommendation that Taylor be awarded the Ph.D was the signal for the Press to commence publication. In 1926 a Tout Memorial Publication Fund had been established in honour of the recently retired head of the History department, Professor T.F. Tout, the distinguished researcher in mediaeval administrative history. A subsidy from the fund enabled Manchester University Press (established by Tout) to publish Taylor's book late in 1934 without any financial contribution from the author and without waiting for him actually to take the doctorate.

It has always been assumed that no copy of the thesis survives: Taylor seldom spoke about it, he spent little time on the experience in his autobiography and it was not entered in the catalogue of the Manchester University Library. However, a copy has been tracked down; it is a typescript, unbound, covered with thick orange paper and entitled 'Europe and Italy 1847–1849'.[65] According to Taylor, Namier 'never in fact looked at a single page' of the thesis. However, he wrote elsewhere that Namier offered to read the book and that he 'savagely corrected chapters one and two and made no comments on the rest.'[66] Certainly in the foreword to the book he thanked Namier for giving him 'advice and criticism with unfailing patience and wisdom'. This implies that changes between thesis and book in the earlier part were made at Namier's suggestion. In fact, the *only* changes made for the published book were the replacement of the first page-and-a-half of the thesis by a single sentence, one or two words changed in the next couple of pages and the provision of an enlarged preface. Otherwise they are virtually identical: in the table of contents, in the contents of the bibliography (although that is slightly differently organised in the book), in the footnotes and in the text. Yet the rewriting of the opening of the book made a real difference for the immediate perception of its quality.

Here is the original text:

The workings of popular taste have restored to favour the nineteenth century. It is no longer disgraceful, it is at worst wistfully humorous, to be Victorian; literary amateurism has even gone so far as to find refuge from the ugly realities of post-war England in the innocent faeryland of the Second Empire. The nineteenth century has become romantic, charming, colourful, tasteful – but it can hardly be called heroic. Its victories were the victories of peace or of warlike preparation; its triumphs were triumphs of organisation and invention rather than of individual daring: the Steam-engine and the Bessemer process, the telegraph and the electric light, limited companies and trade unions. Even Moltke, the one great general of the century, was, characteristically, an organiser rather than a hero. To this general rule there is one exception. In the Unification of Italy the nineteenth century recognised its latter-day epic, and Garibaldi was welcomed in England with demonstrations of popular enthusiasm, such as could then but rarely be aroused by a foreign visitor. In Mr. G.M. Trevelyan Garibaldi found his Homer, and if Italian Unification is now thought to owe more to the methods of contemporary Fascism and of Tammany Hall than Mr. Trevelyan would suggest, depreciation of heroes is yet in itself a form of hero worship.

He continues:

This preoccupation with affairs within Italy has led to a comparative neglect of what is – epical considerations apart – a more important question: the attitude of the great powers to Italy and the effect of their agreements and disagreements on the fortunes of Italian unification. The settlement of Italy was after all the work of the statesmen of Europe, who met in Vienna in 1815, and the interesting question is why they altered, or acquiesced in the alteration of, their work some forty years later. Such a change is obviously the result of many factors: changes in alliances, changes in the public character of the various states, changes in public opinion within those states, to name but a few. In a discussion of such forces it is easiest to isolate and examine them at a time of transition or revolution, and such an opportunity is offered by the events of the year 1848.

Namier would almost certainly have scorned such an opening paragraph, which bore more than traces of the novels Taylor had been reading. Taylor substituted the following sentence for all of the above: 'The Italian problem may, in some sense, be described as the creation of the Congress of Vienna; for it was at Vienna that the powers of Europe as a whole, for the first time, concerned themselves with Italy, and the settlement of Italy after the Napoleonic Wars had a definite European basis.' This is a much stronger opening, and it leads straight into the thesis of the book, without dithering about the nature of the nineteenth century.[67] The few other changes were minor, of the order of changing 'the cry of Legitimacy' to 'the doctrine of Legitimacy', the usual sorts of revision made when polishing for publication.

The Italian Problem in European Diplomacy 1847–1849 is a book of pure diplomatic history, one which concentrates not on domestic matters, nor on events in one country, but on the relations amongst several states as they attempted to deal with a crisis which would have European-wide repercussions. Taylor's overarching theme was the balance of power, which he saw as the dominating factor in international relations of the period: driven by attempts to disturb the balance and counter-attempts to maintain it. The three protagonists were Great Britain, France and the Austrian Empire; those who pulled the strings, or wrote the despatches, were Palmerston, Guizot and Metternich. To the reader today the book can seem old-fashioned: state talks to state, and legislatures and interest groups, let alone public opinion, have relatively little part to play. But it is an interesting book, partly for its groundbreaking nature at the time, partly for its own quality and partly for what it reveals about Taylor's approach to diplomatic history, for most of his academic life a major field of research and publication.

First of all, the type of multi-archival research in which Taylor had engaged is never as widespread as it ought to be. There is much less excuse nowadays, when most countries' archives, or at least those of major powers, become available to historians sooner or later. This was not then the case. As Taylor wrote in his Foreword, 'Only in the last few years has it been possible to study at all adequately the foreign policy of the European states, for only since the War have the archives of the various Foreign

Offices been thrown open to the unrestricted use of scholars.' Even once they were open, relatively few modern historians would have had sufficient command of three languages to be able to take advantage of the opportunity; and, no one had actually done so. As Taylor points out in his Bibliography, 'There are no modern works devoted to a study of the relations of the European Powers during this period, and few devoted to a study of the foreign policy even of a single country. The domestic events of 1848 were, in every continental country, so complicated and so important that historians have tended to forget that foreign affairs were still proceeding, or at any rate have put them very much in the background.' But even those works that had been written were wholly inadequate: 'the opening of the archives in Austria, England and France has rendered incomplete not only pre-war work, written before the archives were open, but also later work, which draws on the manuscript material of one country alone.'

This is actually rather a good approach by Taylor, in terms of emphasising the pioneering nature of his work. No one had done it before. Previous works were incomplete either because their authors had not used archive material, or because they had used the archives of one country only. Using these criteria, he dismisses several of the mere seven secondary sources he thinks even worth mentioning: *The Cambridge History of Foreign Policy* is 'now completely out of date', while two biographies of Palmerston 'are completely worthless as historical studies but both contain extracts of private papers not otherwise available.' He reserves his praise for Heinrich von Srbik's biography *Metternich: der Staatsmann und der Mensch*, published in 1925, as 'the one important work of post-war scholarship on this period'. It was difficult for reviewers to criticise his scholarship, since few were able to match it.

It is, in fact, a most impressive first book.[68] The subject matter will interest few today beyond the more recondite specialists or those interested in the history of history. Yet it is enjoyable to read, and not only for those interested to grasp the origins of A.J.P. Taylor. Those familiar only with the later Taylor, with his short sentences and paradoxes and snappy epigrams, will probably not recognise the style. Consider again the first sentence of Chapter 1: 'The Italian problem may, in some sense, be described as the creation of the Congress of Vienna; for it was at Vienna that the powers of Europe as a whole, for the first time, concerned themselves with Italy, and the settlement of Italy after the Napoleonic Wars had a definite European basis.' First of all, it is long – it is really two sentences. Furthermore, Taylor would soon eschew the regular use of the semi-colon. Indeed, the style is akin to that of the diplomatic despatches he had been reading, at least in the cadences of the sentences. That said, the book is also beautifully epigrammatic, but epigrams are used rather more sparingly than in later books. Taylor's ability to produce the written soundbite was already apparent – except that then it might rather have been called wit: 'Schwarzenberg believed in Austria's strength, or believed at any rate that Austria to exist at all must boast of her strength, whether she had it or not.'[69] His own later characterisation of his style in this book was that it was 'technically old-fashioned, straight political narrative', objective, detached, detailed and without 'behavioural sauce'.[70] Above all, it is lucid.[71]

He included a great many quotations from the archives, sometimes at substantial length. Some were incorporated into the text, but many more found their way into the extensive and voluminous footnotes. He may have adopted this practice because, like many research students, he felt the need to demonstrate his findings. Alternatively, he may have been following the example of Přibram in his book based on the Ford Lectures, *England and the International Policy of the European Great Powers 1871–1914*: in trying to reproduce the policies and principles of the statesmen of the Great Powers, Přibram had noted, 'I should like to point out that I have endeavoured . . . to allow the leading statesmen to come forward and speak for themselves.'[72]

Taylor never had as many footnotes again as he did in his first book, possibly because of the comments of at least one reviewer: while J.P.T. Bury noted in the *Cambridge Review* that Taylor 'quotes liberally from these sources in footnotes which are copious without being unduly obtrusive', and K.R. Greenfield in the *American Historical Review* praised him for the fact that the documents from the archives 'are generously quoted in the footnotes, so that the reader can follow the author in his interpretations with the context in full view', Charles Webster in The *English Historical Review* complained that 'long quotations are placed in the footnotes instead of being digested in the text, so that the reader's attention is constantly distracted, and he has, as it were, to write his own history.'[73] It can only be assumed that this last comment made its intended impact, because Taylor never included such extensive quotations again, either in the text or in the footnotes. He put the gist in the text.[74]

Most interestingly, Taylor set out in his introduction his approach to diplomacy and to diplomatic history. 'At first sight', he wrote, 'the European diplomatic system appears to proceed in the most haphazard way. Personal likes and dislikes ... the accidental delaying of a dispatch, the evil intentions of one diplomat or the levity of another – by these the tranquillity, even the peace, of Europe seem to be determined. And no doubt these personal, these accidental issues have their influence and their importance. But, on a closer view, there emerge more and more clearly certain broad principles, until the petty struggles of day-to-day diplomacy take on the appearance of a battle of Platonic Ideas.' This is not to say that both diplomats and popular opinion do not sometimes fall back upon 'ready-made explanation' – the malignant influence of one diplomat or another, for example. 'But', he goes on, 'it is really not necessary to discover, or to invent, such secret forces: it is rather that the course of national policy is based upon a series of assumptions, with which statesmen have lived since their earliest years and which they regard as so axiomatic as hardly to be worth stating. It is the duty of the historian to clarify these assumptions and to trace their influence upon the course of every-day policy.'[75]

This is another matter in which he may well have been influenced by his Viennese supervisor, Přibram. In his own book, Přibram had characterised the statesmen of the Great Powers as men who saw the interests of their respective countries as ancient and abiding. His focus was on Great Britain, and he emphasised that 'the men in control of British foreign policy held firmly to the basic principles which had ... inspired their predecessors for centuries in their policy towards the Continental Great Powers.' And not only British statesmen: no statesman 'lives in and solely for the day and never raises his eyes from his daily toil to gaze upon the problems that await him on the morrow. Certain fundamental and enduring factors and influences that serve to formulate and condition his policy must be ever present to his mind: otherwise he would never earn for himself the honourable renown of having been a great statesman.'[76] Therefore, beneath the likes and dislikes of diplomats and the changing issues, diplomatic relations exemplify the long-term interests of the countries involved. For example, countries prefer to have weak rather than strong states on their borders. At this particular juncture, Austria was afraid of a strong France in Italy, France was afraid of a strong Italian kingdom on its frontier, and England backed the European balance of power and peace.

Taylor also implicitly emphasised his non-ideological approach. He argued that it is the peculiar fascination of European diplomatic history that the assumptions vary from one country to another, that what is obvious to an English statesman is mere wrongheadedness to an Austrian and *vice versa*. Few European struggles arise from a simple conflict between Right and Wrong – how simple European history would be if they did. The history of Europe is far more often concerned with struggles between two Rights – each side with an unanswerable case … and with no appeal to any course, except to one the standards of which are not those of right and wrong – the arbitrament of war. Here again it is the historian's duty to make the contradictions plain, rather than to provide the appeal court, which had been lacking in real life.[77]

Finally, Taylor fulfilled his Rockefeller pledge to consider the impact of public opinion on the conduct of foreign policy, and here he disagreed with Přibram, who tended to emphasise the importance of public opinion. According to Taylor,

the relation between public opinion and diplomacy is becoming an increasingly popular theme, often with little justification. Statesmen tend to shelter behind public opinion only when they are seeking an excuse for not doing something, which they would not do in any case; public opinion would not allow it, is easier and politer than a simple No. … The opinions of the man in the street on foreign affairs (so far as he has any) are by their nature unascertainable; what usually passes for public opinion is the opinion of a small, politically conscious class – leader-writers … members of parliament and the less instructed members of the Cabinet.

Public opinion is prone to ignorance and sentimentality: it tends 'to want the glory without the suffering and the prize without the pain. It is not prepared to translate the threats of diplomacy into action and yet it is angry when the diplomats do not threaten.' Therefore, to the statesman public opinion is a factor to be allowed for, but hardly a guiding force.[78]

It can of course be argued that in these comments Taylor is now frankly out of date: in 1934 radio was hardly a great motive force in public-opinion formation and television did not yet exist; and although Gallup polls were on the horizon, it would be a generation before statesmen or even politicians took them very seriously. It can also be argued, as David Eastwood has pointed out, that Taylor 'had not yet read the right sources to enable him to comment on the nature, role, and status of public opinion.' Yet it is difficult to disagree with Taylor's resounding conclusion: 'the statesman, unless he is a very poor statesman indeed, adheres to the broad principles of national policy and it is the interaction of the differing national principles which in the long run determines the history of Europe.'[79] The long term, not the contingent and accidental, rules.

The publication of the book established Taylor's reputation as a coming diplomatic historian. One of the earliest reviews to appear was that of the *Manchester Guardian* which, after noting that it was based on 'extensive research ... and only those ... who have gone through this tiring yet enjoyable experience will appreciate what an enormous amount of work has gone into the making of Mr. Taylor's book', made the percipient comment that 'a feeling we have about this book is that it might easily have become a work of general interest.' The review by W.A. Phillips in the *Times Literary Supplement* might almost have been written as a pre-emptive strike against those later critics who accused Taylor of ignoring long-term causes and fundamental forces in his history: the book 'goes behind the petty struggles of day-to-day diplomacy, and reveals the broad principles which in the end always determine national policies in spite of the haphazard way in which diplomacy seems to function'. Indeed, the reviewer points out that in his introduction Taylor 'enlarges on this latter theme with much good sense'.[80]

D.W. Brogan, in his review in the *Oxford Magazine*, picked up on a trait which would increasingly worry certain historians – Taylor's tendency to sweeping generalisations. 'Mr. Taylor', he writes, 'has written an excellent book which starts ominously. References to the Napoleonic empire as "the worst (because the most extensive) tyranny since the time of Attila" and the assertion that France, except for the time she was ruled by the fancies of Napoleon III, has been ruled only by "realpolitikers" while "the statesmen of all other nations appear sometimes to be influenced by sentimental, idealistic, unselfish motives – the French never," are not encouraging, but once Mr. Taylor has unburdened his soul in this fashion, he sets to work to tell his story with great skill and original learning.'[81]

The review in *International Affairs* of September 1935 is a bit problematic. This is not because of criticisms, but rather because there are none: Taylor writes 'lucidly and well', the reviewer states; his judgements are 'always born of careful consideration of all the known factors and are supported by a convincing display of evidence ... The work is a model of scholarship.' In short, this is just the type of review that any author would be pleased to receive; it is only that it would have been more satisfying had the reviewer not been Taylor's friend from Vienna, Ian Morrow.

The first of the heavyweight academic reviews, that in the *American Historical Review*, was one of the best: the book contains 'a fresh and sometimes brilliantly illuminating study of the policies followed by the British, French, and Austrian governments'. There were problems, amongst which were the omission of the parts played in the crisis by Russia and Prussia (an omission noted by other reviewers). But the strength of the book 'lies in the plane to which the author lifts the discussion of diplomatic action … Unsatisfied with the usual account of "day-to-day diplomacy", Mr. Taylor constantly refers the actions of the diplomats to the deep persistencies of interest which to the thoughtful give to international relations "the appearance of a battle of Platonic ideas". '[82]

Over the year other reviews appeared, in English, American, French, Italian and Dutch journals. One or two were hostile, while most naturally had some criticisms, sometimes on the basis of sins of omission: the leaving out of the Prussians and Russians again, the failure to use British Blue Books (relevant documents on a crisis printed by Parliament), the failure to utilise the printed Reports of the Diplomatic Committee of the French Assembly, or the citing of only twenth-three printed and secondary sources in his Bibliography. Others cited sins of commission, in particular the aforementioned printing of extensive quotations in footnotes rather than incorporating them into the text. But on the whole, any young historian would be pleased with such reviews gathered by a first book; furthermore, the writer of one of the very good reviews, E.L. Woodward, would soon prove to be a powerful and important patron.

In the period between 1927 and 1934, then, Taylor had gone from being a trainee solicitor, depressed, resentful and angry but unable to conceive what else he could do besides schoolteaching – which did not attract him – to being a professional historian. It is interesting to consider briefly the type of historian he had become. His university study had concentrated on English history, with something less than a year spent on a period of European history. Furthermore, the nineteenth-century had received relatively little attention. During the months he had spent in Oxford after leaving his uncle's solicitor's practice he had investigated the political ideas of mid-nineteenth-century English parliamentary radicals; he then went to Vienna with the intention of doing research on their relations with Viennese radicals in the years before the revolutions of 1848. Yet at the end of his period in Vienna he emerged an European historian, and by the spring of 1930 engaged as an assistant lecturer to teach modern European history. And by late 1934 he was a published historian, his first book a finely finished piece of diplomatic history. He would continue to concentrate on European history, and particularly diplomatic history, for the subsequent thirty years – with the single important exception of his published Ford Lectures – until he began to write the book which many believe to be his best, *English History 1914–1945*.

Chapter 3

The Manchester Years
1930–1938

The only danger to history today is that historians are sometimes too modest and try to find excuses for their task. It is safer as well as sounder to be confident. Men write history for the same reason that they write poetry, study the properties of numbers, or play football – for the joy of creation; men read history for the same reason that they listen to music or watch cricket – for the joy of appreciation. Once abandon that firm ground, once plead that history has a 'social responsibility' (to produce good Marxists or good Imperialists or good citizens) and there is no logical escape from the censor and the Index, the O.G.P.U. and the Gestapo.

A.J.P. Taylor, 'The Historian', *Manchester Guardian*, 5 August 1938.

With his appointment in the spring of 1930 as Assistant Lecturer in Modern History at Manchester University, Taylor embarked upon his career as an academic. During his first year at Manchester his emphasis had of necessity to be upon his teaching; in the summer between his first and second years he got married; during his second, third and fourth he completed and published his first book; during his fourth he also took the first tentative steps towards his future freelance career while embarking upon his intermittently active public political life. In addition he became a keen vegetable gardener and an even keener father. In short, his years at Manchester saw most of the dominating themes of his life emerge. Taylor himself later said that these were the happiest years of his adult life; they came to an end with his appointment to a Tutorial Fellowship at Magdalen College, Oxford in 1938.

The University of Manchester, as such, was a relatively young institution in 1930, but it already had a national reputation. Founded in 1851 as Owens

College, Manchester, by 1887 it formed one part of the Victoria University (with other constituent colleges in Leeds and Liverpool); only in 1903 did it become the independent Victoria University of Manchester (the 'Victoria' part of the name has since disappeared). The head of the Department of History from 1890 to 1925 was Professor T.F. Tout, who over his years at the university established the fundamental ethos of the Manchester school of history. His legacy was to leave it the leading research-based history department in the country. Taylor was indeed fortunate to find his first position in such an institution.[1]

Tout was a giant amongst historians, one of those who laid the foundations of the research into and teaching of English mediaeval history, especially administrative and constitutional. University teaching of history on the lines followed by Oxford and Cambridge had traditionally concentrated on imparting a body of knowledge, of greater or lesser interest and complexity, to students who would then obediently regurgitate it for their examinations. Tout was one of those, along with certain of the professoriate at Oxford, Cambridge and London, who thought this wholly inadequate. As Head of Department (a position of some power in those days), and as a man who possessed a vision, energy, a strong belief in his own authority and the support of his colleagues, Tout was able to establish a new kind of degree at Manchester, one which included (for Honours students) the study of primary authorities and the writing of a thesis. As he wrote in the essay 'An Historical Laboratory':

> Our [i.e. professional historians'] primary business is to find out as much as we can about the past. Our methods, then, must necessarily be the methods of the observational sciences, and we require as much training in the technique of our craft as any other skilled worker. Nay, more, the educational value of our study lies not so much in the accumulation of a mass of unrelated facts as in training in method, and evidence, and in seeing how history is made. It follows, then, that the study of history should be largely a study of processes and method, even for those to whom history is not mainly the preparation for a career, but chiefly a means of academic education. No historical education can, therefore, be regarded as complete unless it involves training in method. The best training in method is an attempt at research.[2]

Tout was arguing, against the weight of opinion at, for example, Oxford, that even those students who would not go on to become professional historians would benefit by the training required to be able to read and assess primary sources and to weigh evidence.[3] He drew the analogy with the training imparted by reading the classics, for generations celebrated as the best general education for the young Englishman and one uniquely suited to preparing him for citizenship and for ruling the Empire:

> the champions of a liberal education are always expatiating on the merits of the 'classics'; but the advantage which the 'study of the classics' has over most of our history courses is not that it is less, but that it is more, technical. Writing Greek verses may be a waste of time, but it demands a careful technical equipment, and is, therefore, better training to the mind than the woolly half-knowledge by which a smart undergraduate who cannot read original texts is enabled to write plausible answers to questions in examinations. History would be a better, not a worse, exercise to the ordinary man if it were more technical.[4]

This belief in the advantage to students of training in the basic techniques of gathering and weighing evidence, and of the need for their lecturers and professors to be qualified to teach in this manner, had two practical effects on the culture and practices of the department. Firstly, it imbued it with a research culture: as Tout said in a speech to the Newnham College History Society in Cambridge in January 1906, 'The spirit of research is in the air. It has become a commonplace that it is the function of the historical professor, not only to teach, but also to write books.'[5] And not only the professors, but all members of staff, since the best demonstration of an ability to teach these techniques was to publish books and articles arising from such research. As a result, Manchester had, by the 1920s, the most distinguished history department in the country. It is quite probable that Taylor was hired because he was actively researching; certainly he was encouraged to continue and not to put it wholly aside for the sake of teaching. Indeed, he would receive positive approbation for making the effort to write and publish, not something that would necessarily happen at Oxford. But secondly, Tout's, and others', belief in the value of research and the study of its methods also determined the way history was taught at Manchester.

It is worth emphasising that Tout wanted breadth as well as depth. As he wrote in 1906, 'the first business before the student ... [is] that he should acquire as sound a view as he can of the general sweep of all history ... In our academic curriculum ... we ought to throw our main stress on foreign history, mediaeval and modern, though I strongly think that the ancient history should not be excluded ... I would still retain side by side with the foreign history a pretty complete course in the whole of English history.' What he would exclude until a later stage was overemphasis on constitutional or economic history, on the grounds, among others, that 'no one can take up with profit a special aspect of our history until he has some grasp of the general drift of the whole.'[6] The outcome in practical terms was a degree combining lecture courses that covered great sweeps of British or European history, small seminar groups of a half-dozen students looking more closely at shorter periods and, for Honours students, the requirement to study a special subject based on primary sources and to write a thesis.

The department had three kinds of students to teach: those studying for a general degree in another department, such as English or Commerce, but who would attend some History lecture courses; those reading for a Pass degree in History; and those working for Honours in History. The first type of student could come from anywhere in the university, but most of the students came from the Faculty of Arts. In the academic year 1930–1, Taylor's first year, the faculty had 660 students, of which 215 were first years. All first-year students had to take either the Ancient History or the Modern History outline paper (termed, confusingly, an Intermediate course); Taylor taught the latter, and on his first teaching day faced 114 students.[7]

The great majority of students read for a Pass degree, a now nearly extinct creature. Anyone at an English university gaining a Pass degree nowadays will recognise that he or she has had a very near brush with complete failure; conversely, the earlier Pass degree was perfectly respectable and was often called an Ordinary or General degree, and that was what it was: it provided non-specialists with a liberal education.

During the first two years all Pass and Honours students in History followed the same course. This began with what the syllabus grandly called 'The General History of Western Civilisation, Ancient, Mediaeval and Modern'. Examined at the end of two years, it was made up of papers covering outlines of ancient history, which included western Asian, Egyptian, Greek and Roman; of mediaeval history to the French invasion of Italy in 1494; of modern history from 1494 to 1914; of late classical and mediaeval English history from the Roman invasion in 55BC to the death of Richard III in 1485 at the Battle of Bosworth Field; of modern British history from the advent of the Tudors in 1485 to whenever the teacher wished to stop, and including constitutional history; and of original documents and a translation paper. All of the courses except the last would probably have been taught by lectures.

The attentive student would have acquired at least a passing acquaintance with the grand sweep of parts of Western (and a bit of Eastern) history; the less committed might have emerged somewhat muddled. In addition, students had to attend courses of lectures in archaeology, geography, literature, political economy or political science – History students would migrate to lectures in other departments in the same way that English students such as Anthony Burgess came to History lectures. At the end of the two years they then sat a Part I examination; only those who passed were allowed to proceed to Honours. The rest would take another clutch of courses; in the third and final year of the degree, they would take a so-called 'special' course, which would follow a shorter period in more depth and which included the use of some original sources. In other words, although the degree took three years rather than the four allowed for Honours, and although the coverage was broad and therefore superficial, Manchester nevertheless required that every history student 'do' History by using (printed) primary sources.

For the Honours students, Tout had prescribed that all teaching should be based in a library on the seminar method, that the student should study a special subject and that each 'should be encouraged to write some sort of modest thesis'.[8] Their Part II examination, to be taken at the end of their third or fourth year, was focused more on questions to be considered than on periods to be covered. One paper would examine 'General Questions on Historical Problems, Ancient, Mediaeval, and Modern', which gave flexibility to staff to follow their own research interests and teach from strength. Students had to study either the nineteenth century or a course in another subject, such as geography or economics. There were certain set books which could vary from year to year. There was the documents-based special subject. And finally, there was 'An Essay', the thesis required by Manchester but not by Oxford or Cambridge.[9]

The number of Honours students was always limited compared to those taking the Pass degree: between 1882 and 1904, Owens College had produced only fifty-four graduates in History, while from 1890 the department had an average of four Honours students a year. Even a department consisting in 1904 only of Tout and two colleagues (one of whom was the distinguished historian James Tait) would not be stretched by the teaching required by seminars and special subjects for those numbers.[10] By the time Tout retired in 1925, the number of students was greater, but so was the number of staff, and the teaching and research culture fostered by both him and Tait was firmly established.

Tout was succeeded as professor and head of department by another mediaevalist, F.M. Powicke; when Powicke went to Oxford as Regius Professor of History in 1929 he was replaced by yet another mediaevalist, E.F. Jacob, who would in 1930 impulsively hire Taylor by telegram. Jacob, the author, *inter alia*, of *Henry V and the Invasion of France* (1947) and (nearly thirty years after signing the publisher's contract) of *The Fifteenth Century, 1399–1485* in the Oxford History of England series, in 1930 led a department of ten, twelve if Tait, who was an Honorary Professor, and Dr Moses Tyson, the lecturer in Palaeography, are included. The requirement to cover the broad sweep of history ensured that the specialities of the staff were equally wide-ranging.

There were two ancient historians, a story about one of whom, Professor Donald Atkinson, entered Manchester lore: his marriage to an assistant lecturer had coincided with the publication of a piece of research on Etruscan pottery which he had published in a limited-circulation learned journal. The wedding had been announced in the local press, so that when he next walked into the lecture theatre he was greeted with congratulations and the stamping of feet. After the noise had died down, he peered over his glasses and thanked the students: 'I should like to make it clear that I could not possibly have achieved what was done without the help of others.'[11] Atkinson wrote on Roman Britain, his publications including *Three Caistor Pottery Kilns* (1932) – possibly what was in *his* mind, if not in his students'. Atkinson's bride in 1932 was the other ancient historian, Kathleen M.T. Chrimes, an assistant lecturer, who would in 1949 publish a book on ancient Sparta. After her marriage she returned to the department as Kathleen Atkinson, Special Lecturer in Ancient History.

Given that the department was famous for its work on mediaeval history, there was, naturally, a clutch of mediaevalists. One who covered the same general period as Jacob was Bertie Wilkinson, who 'sustained the pure Tout doctrine' according to Taylor (he was the author of *Constitutional History of England, 1216–1399*); he left to become Professor of Mediaeval History at the University of Toronto in 1938. Another was W.A. Pantin, the Bishop Fraser Lecturer in Ecclesiastical History, who would in 1955 publish his book *The English Church in the Fourteenth Century*; he left Manchester for Oriel College, Oxford in 1933, to be succeeded by C.R. Cheney, who in turn also left Manchester for Oxford, in his case for the Readership in Diplomatic, in 1937, the year before Taylor himself left. Manchester was undoubtedly a seedbed for distinguished professional historians. Cheney was a prolific author, whose books included one which soon found its place on most historians' desks, *Handbook of Dates for Students of English History* (1945). Very much less prolific was the ecclesiastical historian A.J. Grieve, who was Lecturer in Early Church History, covering the ancient and early mediaeval Church.

The department also had a group of modernists. Two of them were economic historians, both of whom had studied at Manchester under George Unwin, who had been the first professor of economic history in Britain. One was Arthur Redford, whom Taylor always referred to as Jimmy; he had been appointed to a Readership in Economic History upon the death of Professor Unwin. This was in 1925, at the age of twenty-nine, before his first book appeared (*Labour Migration in England, 1800–1850* was published in 1926), but he then published two further books while Taylor was in Manchester, and another in 1939.[12] Nevertheless, he had to wait twenty years for his readership to be made into a professorship, the university pleading financial stringency. According to Taylor, 'when I first knew him he was gay and highspirited and I watched his growing embitterment with sadness'.[13] The other economic historian, and Taylor's favourite amongst his colleagues, was Edward Hughes, whom he called Ted: 'the son of a Shropshire farmer and himself a skilful gardener, he was a wonderful scholar, though boring as both teacher and writer'. (Hughes's *Studies in Administration and Finance, 1558–1825: With Special Reference to the History of Salt Taxation in England*, which was published in 1934, is probably best thought of as worthy.) Taylor continues, 'he and I shared a room – more like a prison cell than a scholar's study – with unbroken enjoyment'.[14] Hughes moved to a chair at the University of Durham in 1939.

Taylor was very complimentary about Jacob, his head of department, who was only thirty-six in 1930: he was 'not a tyrant as Tout had been and as some of the professors still were. He ran the department as a democracy, a startling innovation for Manchester. We met and allocated the work according to fair rules.'[15] Pantin, too, later wrote of him that he 'managed everything and everybody with tact and consideration, and with a constant consultation of the staff.' Taylor would doubtless have also enjoyed the fact that, as Pantin wrote, 'Jacob was what a mediaeval biographer might have called *dapsilis*; he enjoyed the good things of life, and enjoyed sharing them with others.' But more importantly, again according to Pantin, what struck his colleagues and others most about Jacob's personality was 'his unfailing kindness and charitableness. I [Pantin] do not think anyone ever heard

Jacob speak cruelly or maliciously about anyone, and this was no mean achievement in the academic world.'[16] Jacob, then, was a head of department whom one could like and respect.

According to Taylor, the department had only ten students a year taking Honours in history; 'the rest of the time we were ramming a mob of students through the General or Pass course.' This was not strictly correct, although the general tenor of the remark was. According to the History Department's report to Council, in 1930–1 there were twenty-six first-year, twenty-two second-year and twenty-seven third-year students, for a total of seventy-five Honours students in History. It may have been that Taylor was referring only to those Honours students specialising in modern, as opposed to ancient or mediaeval, history, in which case ten was a perfectly reasonable number. Nevertheless, when compared with the number of Ordinary degree students in both History and other subjects whom they had to teach, Honours students were a distinct minority. According to Taylor, Jacob had made it clear to him in the spring of 1930 that he was being hired to fill the gap left by the departure both of the professor of modern history and the assistant lecturer. (The professor was J.H. Neale, later Sir John Neale, who had moved to University College London.) In any case, this meant that Taylor had immediately to prepare two sets of lectures, rather than the usual one: the early modern European history course, consisting of forty-eight lectures covering the period from 1494 to 1815, and the nineteenth-century European history course, another forty-eight lectures covering the period from 1815 to 1914.[17] ('When he enquired who had covered this considerable time span before, he was given the answer: "Oh Tout. He said that modern history was not a serious subject and anyone could lecture on it."')[18] The majority audience for both of these lecture courses, being 'Intermediate' (i.e. pretty basic), would be students reading for an Ordinary or a non-History degree. This was a somewhat daunting assignment, and upon his return from research in Paris in July 1930, even before taking up residence in Manchester, Taylor settled down at his parents' house in Preston and began to prepare the lectures, to which he devoted the remainder of the summer.

Taylor later recalled:

My own knowledge was slender, really only from the French revolution to the Congress of Berlin [1878]. I had done earlier modern history at school; of the period after the Congress of Berlin, where the Oxford history school stopped, I knew nothing at all. I bought the conventional textbooks (Rivington blue), most of them a generation out of date, and compiled my lectures from them. The prewar history was more difficult. Here there were no textbooks. Of the standard authorities, Gooch and Fay were fairly professional, others were gifted amateurs – Lowes Dickinson, Brailsford and Bertrand Russell. All of them agreed that the Germans had been badly treated. This fitted in with my own youthful recollections, and thus I prepared for future students a ... version of events in which the Great War was all the fault of the Entente Powers.[19]

Rivingtons were a London publisher in the nineteenth and early twentieth centuries. Amongst their publications was a series of eight volumes entitled Periods of European History, covering the years from the fall of the Roman Empire in 476 to 1899, the year of the peace conference at the Hague, with which the last book in the series ended. They were mostly written by historians of some distinction: Tout had produced the second volume, *The Empire and the Papacy, 918–1273*. All were bound in blue cloth, hence Rivington blue. They were clearly intended to be used by university students, and indeed, Taylor had read one of the volumes, A.H. Johnson's *Europe in the Sixteenth Century, 1494–1598*, during his first year at Oxford.[20] In order to cover the period of his two lecture series, Taylor presumably would, in addition, have bought H.O. Wakeman's *Europe 1598–1715*, A. Hassall's *The Balance of Power, 1715–1789* (Hassall was the General Editor of the series), H. Morse Stephens' *Revolutionary Europe, 1789–1815*, and W. Alison Phillips's *Modern Europe 1815–1899* (which had only been published in 1901).[21]

They were a superior sort of textbook, the writer clearly assuming some previous knowledge.[22] They were also of their time. In the first place their approach was strictly political and diplomatic. Wakeman, for example, sets out his conception of the period:

The formation of the modern European states system is therefore the main element of continuous interest and importance in the history of the seventeenth century, that is to say, the acquisition by the chief European states of the boundaries, which they have since substantially retained, the adoption by them of the form of government to which they have since adhered, and the assumption by them, relatively to the other states, of a position and influence in the affairs of Europe which they have since enjoyed. The sixteenth century saw the final dismemberment of medieval Europe, the seventeenth saw its reconstruction in the modern form in which we know it now.

There are no entries in the index for education or printing or population or trade or women, all of which one would expect to find in an analogous textbook a century later – although a certain type of Wakemans' entry could make a welcome comeback: 'Throwing from the window, the, 52' (which refers to the defenestration of Prague which sparked off the Thirty Years War in 1618). The textbooks were also of their time in their prose style: Alison Phillips argued, with regard to Napoleon, that 'the mind of the age itself, dulled with the din of battles and wearied out with efforts that had seemed almost superhuman, felt instinctively that the fall of the man with whose fortunes the affairs of the world had for fifteen years been bound up marked the end and the beginning of an era.'[23] It has been a long time since any modern historian has referred to the 'mind of the age' as an object of serious attention.[24]

Just before term began, Taylor took up residence in Manchester. Once the country's leading centre of political economy – 'Manchester free trade' – as well as an important industrial and commercial centre, Manchester was a town in decline. Taylor's description of it is affectionate if not very flattering: 'it was very dirty, the buildings begrimed, with large smuts coming into the room if you opened a window. Clanking trams from all over Lancashire converged on the centre of the city ... The bales of cotton went along in drays drawn by cart horses. There was a tripe shop on nearly every corner ... The market place was unchanged from 1745 when Bonny Prince Charlie was acclaimed there. In its shops were great Lancashire cheeses, from which you could scoop a taste with a sixpenny bit, and a public house marked "No Ladies Admitted".'[25] Taylor lodged with two French ladies, who provided him with excellent meals; he stayed there from Monday to Thursday and spent the weekends with his parents in Preston. They now had little in common, and he spent his time riding horses on the sands or reading.[26]

The centre of his life, as far as there was one during his first year in Manchester, was the university. The History Department was on the ground floor, just off the large entrance hall, of the new (1926) Arts Building, which Taylor referred to as office-block functional, although it is more attractive than the jibe suggests. The office Taylor shared with Ted Hughes, although attractive – it had a high ceiling and parquet floor, a chimney breast with an egg-and-dart surround within which burned a coal fire, and a half-moon fanlight over the hardwood door – was not very large.[27] It is just as well that he and Hughes liked each other.

Taylor emphasised his isolation during his first year. It is a commonplace for civic universities to more or less empty after five or six o'clock, and Manchester was no exception. According to Taylor, his colleagues all departed for the 'remote suburbs' at five and there was nothing for him to do except return to his lodgings; the one exception was Thursday night, when he went to a concert. Furthermore, he ate his lunch of bread and cheese in his office, rather than going to the refectory. Therefore, he says, he saw his close colleagues only when working, and others not at all.[28]

Yet reports by Honours students in History give a different view of the department, which was more that of a close-knit group of like-minded souls. One account says that 'the students knew each other well, the staff well, the staff knew each other well, and knew the students well. For these particular students the History department was something of a family affair.' Another student recalls going out from time to time for tea with Taylor and his family. It seems clear that as Taylor got a grip on his teaching and his confidence, as he became more established both within and without the department, he assumed his own place in the firmament.[29]

Taylor describes his own first efforts at lecturing:

These vast classes were more like a mass meeting than a university lecture. There were never fewer than a hundred students and often nearer two. The ordeal was at first overwhelming. I simply read out information I had gathered from antiquated textbooks. Soon I decided this would never do. I threw away my notes, chose a topic as I went into the hall and rattled off whatever came into my head. I fear I made little attempt to revise my views on earlier modern history ... The nineteenth century course was much better. I worked hard on this, especially on the period between the Congress of Berlin and the first world war. I do not know whether my students benefited. I certainly did. I taught myself history literally on my feet. I also learnt how to address a mass audience without a tremor.'[30]

Much, though not all, of this rings absolutely true. Few beginning lecturers have the courage to venture beyond their written notes, and this can make for an uninteresting experience for both teacher and student. Certainly the numbers attending the early modern outline course dropped from 114 in Taylor's first year to a hundred in the following year (though they shot back up to 124 in his third year, testimony to his growing command of the lecture hall). It is also true that a lecturer rapidly becomes bored with teaching from the same notes, an important factor in encouraging academics to revise their lectures. Taylor's decision to lecture without notes is more interesting. There were precedents. Přibram in Vienna had done so; closer to home, so had Tout. What is less believable is his comment about deciding on a topic as he entered the hall: this does not entirely accord with a report that his students recognised that he was largely dependent for his approach on the Rivington blue textbook by A.H. Johnson. However, given that he would have followed a rough chronology, it was probably obvious to him, as he walked into the hall, what ought to be the topic of his lecture on any given day. Without firm evidence on his early lectures, however, it is impossible to know for certain how he lectured, what he lectured on and how they were received.[31]

It is, fortunately, possible to say something more straightforward about his later lectures, since there has survived a detailed set of lecture notes on Europe 1494–1815 taken by a student attending his course during 1935–6. First of all, if he had, as he later wrote, merely compiled his first lectures from Johnson, he had indeed thrown his notes away, at any rate by 1935. However, he was probably least at ease with the early years of the course, and thus more likely to hang on to Johnson's ideas for these lectures than when writing about the later centuries: it is therefore interesting to compare the substance of what each had to say, Johnson with Taylor. In the first three pages of his *Europe in the Sixteenth Century*, Johnson sets out his ideas of what distinguishes the modern age from the mediaeval period: the break-up of the mediaeval world Church, the rise of individualism, the growth of nationalities as the new principle of unity, and the rise of the theory of the balance of power, and of diplomacy generally. In Taylor's first lecture on the period, he does the same (he also distinguishes what he calls modern times, i.e. Columbus to Captain Cook, from 'more modern times', i.e. the French Revolution on; it clearly had not occurred to him to call the latter postmodern times). Taylor highlights the change from status to contract, the growing dominance of towns, the growth of the middle or capitalist class and the failure to produce a universal state. The difference in his approach was also highlighted by comments the student noted down, such as 'surplus upsets any economic society – it broke up mediaeval society'. Again, looking at their individual assessments of a particular historical personage, such as Erasmus, there is nothing in the lecture notes which appears to be taken from Johnson. Certainly the following epigram occurs only in Taylor's: 'Erasmus laid the egg that Luther addled.'[32]

In any case, his style developed. One source gives the following account, although there is no indication whether this was very early or later Taylor: 'At the beginning he marched in and started speaking straight away, creating a sense of urgency and purpose. Instead of standing behind the lectern he would pace up and down, very near the front row, projecting his voice to an imaginary listener at the back ... He learned to time his lectures to the dot, so that the bell for the next lesson would ring as he was delivering his last sentence.' Another account states that 'Alan's lectures were said to be well prepared, clearly delivered, and, usually, entertainingly delivered. He was fond ... of witticisms, and explicitly memorable were his epigrams ... [For some students,] their abiding memories of an historical event and of its significance as provided by Alan lay in their memory of some epigram or other with which he would summarise it.' And finally, Jacob, his head of department, wrote that 'I have heard him lecture, and had I been a student in the schools I should never have missed any lectures in his course.'[33]

There were also weekly tutorial or essay classes for the Honours students, and Taylor ran those on nineteenth-century European history. These had no direct connection with the lectures; rather, students would be allocated to a tutor (although presumably they could at least choose the period if not necessarily the teacher), who would then assign essay topics on his or her speciality. Those who had Taylor as their tutor no doubt wrote at least a certain number of essays on European diplomatic history, as well as on the French Revolution and the Napoleonic Wars, another Taylor speciality. He devoted much of his reading time to developing his expertise in the diplomatic history of the later nineteenth century, and in 1936 would break the mould by establishing and teaching a special subject, ordinarily the privilege of the professoriate.

Teaching, then, dominated his life during the first months of his first year as an academic, but there was another abiding interest as well – Margaret. He had encouraged her to return to Vienna the previous autumn to continue her piano studies: 'being full of cranky ideas of marriage, concocted from the writings of Wells and Shaw,' he later wrote, 'I believed that every woman should have a career', and something to do with the piano was apparently Margaret's destiny. It was also his way of putting off any decision. He was apprehensive about her family's class – upper-middle – and their religion – strongly Roman Catholic – and he also believed that any wife of his should be an intellectual, which Margaret was not. But, as he put it ruefully, 'unfortunately no intellectual woman attracted me sexually.' He was also honest enough to admit that the whole enterprise of marriage and setting up a home seemed like too much trouble: 'if someone had provided me with an agreeable house, fully furnished, I should have hesitated less.'[34]

Margaret came back to England for Christmas 1930 and they spent some time in Manchester together. The following Easter Taylor went to Vienna where, *inter alia*, they got to know Bill and Patience McElwee. (A former pupil of Jacob's, Bill McElwee was then working with Příbram. After a period of intense unhappiness as a lecturer at Liverpool University, he found his niche as senior history master at Stowe, the boys' public school.) The four of them became very good friends, and Taylor and Bill McElwee would in due course collaborate on a book.

Some months later, during the summer of 1931, Taylor moved to London to work in the Public Record Office for his first book. Margaret was also in London and, according to Taylor, 'it seemed to me that we must either marry or break. I was reluctant to do either', but he decided to broach the question to Margaret. The episode had elements of farce, as Taylor wrote years later to a friend: 'The only time that I met [X] was one afternoon when I went to make certain proposals to a lady who became my wife. You can imagine that I did not welcome Mr [X's] presence and that I said the most wild and provocative things in order to drive him from the room. I well remember the feeling of desperation as I uttered one absurd and outrageous statement after another and found him still obtusely there, until at last I was reduced to personal offensiveness.'[35] Margaret agreed, and Taylor put their names down at the registry office at Marylebone Town Hall.

On the appointed day, Taylor turned up, with his Bootham friend and Vienna flatmate Geoffrey Rowntree as his best man. Taylor, Rowntree and Margaret walked through to the registry office. According to one account: 'The ceremony began; at the last moment, when Alan was asked to solemnly declare his commitment to Margaret, he answered "No", turned on his heel, and strode out.' Taylor and Rowntree walked to the 1917 Club; apparently all that Taylor would say was that 'he had decided a few moments before not to go through with it.'[36] According to Taylor, Margaret was 'naturally upset', which seems somewhat an understatement – more likely she was distraught. None of the sources give the name of her attendant or even state whether she had one; there is no mention of any of her family being present. It is therefore possible that she was left on her own once Taylor and Rowntree had departed. It was a horribly cruel thing for Taylor to have done, to have waited until the dramatic moment in the ceremony and then to reject her publicly. Margaret immediately fled the country, joining an Intourist visit to the Soviet Union.

Upon her return, the couple met, talked and decided to try again. Taylor's witnesses this time were Basil Rock, his artist friend from Vienna, and Frank Howes, a temporary master at Bootham with whom Taylor had struck up a friendship while still at school and who would in due course become a music critic on *The Times*. According to Taylor, 'neither of them sympathized with my hesitation' and on the first Saturday in October 'we were married without any further fuss.' The wedding feast was a drink in a pub opposite Baker Street station, although they had champagne that evening at the home of Margaret's 'rich aunt Judy', who also gave them a refrigerator, 'then a rare possession'.[37]

The newlyweds spent two days in Preston with Taylor's parents. This was not a success. First of all, his parents had had no advance notice of his marriage, an omission which hurt them – he was, after all, their only child. But even worse, his mother detested his choice: Margaret was Roman Catholic, she was not noticeably left-wing and she was certainly no intellectual. According to Taylor, his mother 'claimed that I had inflicted on her a severe psychological shock and thereafter walked with a heavy limp. Even my father displayed an unexpectedly conventionality. He seemed to think that as we had been married without ceremony in a register office, we had not been properly married at all.' For Taylor, this was underlined by the fact that, until he was prompted by Taylor himself, his father neglected to give them a wedding present. When it came it was hardly in the refrigerator league, but was a set of silver fish knives and forks.[38]

Taylor and his wife set up house in Manchester, first in a furnished flat while they looked around and then in an unfurnished one. This was the top floor of an eighteenth-century house called The Limes, at 148 Wilmslow Road but set comfortably back from the street, located towards the south end of Didsbury, then (according to Taylor) Manchester's smartest suburb.[39] It had four rooms, a kitchen and bathroom. Margaret's mother allowed her to take the furniture she had left in store upon her return to India; an older friend gave them two single beds (very hard ones, of which Taylor approved); and Taylor bought himself an old Victorian partner's desk which he used for the rest of his active life.[40]

Taylor proceeded to organise their married life: he 'duly applied [his] principle of the equality of the sexes.' Margaret had taken cookery lessons in Vienna, so dinner was her responsibility; Taylor prepared the substantial breakfast – coffee made from freshly ground beans, grilled bacon and eggs which were part fried and part grilled. When at home he also prepared tea, with homemade cakes and crumpets with homemade jam. There was, fortunately, no need to quarrel over who would make the beds and do the washing-up: neither did either, since they had the money to employ a daily. They also ran a car, one with a huge V8 engine.

They were able to do so because they were well off. Margaret had some income from money settled on her by her mother. Taylor had his salary of £300 as an assistant lecturer. In addition he had an increasing income from his Stock Exchange operations: he had begun investing that year, using £2,000 from an insurance policy given to him by his father.[41] This, plus Margaret's money, gave them 'altogether over £900 a year, almost as much as a professor'.[42] (When Lewis Namier took up the chair in Modern History at Manchester in 1931, his salary was £1,000 a year.) Within a few years this would be augmented by his income from freelance work. He began reviewing books regularly for the *Manchester Guardian* in 1934: from this in 1935 he earned £57 pounds, nearly £90 in 1936 – which increased his salary by nearly a third – and over £140 in both 1937 and 1938. With his promotion to a lectureship for the academic year 1936–7, his salary was increased to £400. Therefore, with the combination of his salary, Margaret's money, his income from reviewing and his successful Stock Exchange operations, the family income must have exceeded £1,200 per year by the autumn of 1936, continuing to grow thereafter.

Taylor was always very precise about money: he liked making it – he apparently often quoted Samuel Johnson's remark that 'There are few ways in which a man can be more innocently employed than in getting money' – and he was always very precise about how he spent it. He had his home ledger in which he recorded each bit of income and divided it into two, notionally his and hers. He also split the expenses, which meant that each evening Margaret had to recall and relate what she had spent that day. He was also very precise about who owed him money, requiring that it be repaid and that this take place sooner rather than later.[43] He was not altogether a mean man and would spend money on his family and himself – he liked fast cars and good wine – but he liked to know whence his money came and whither it went.

According to Taylor, their first acquisition was an EMG Handmade Gramophone, 'rightly esteemed the finest instrument of its day. It had an enormous papier-mâché horn and used a thorn needle, the point of which had to be clipped after each record. I bought a great stock of records during the nineteen thirties: Schnabel playing all the Beethoven sonatas, some quartet – the Pro Arte I think – playing nearly all the Haydn quartets, the Glyndebourne Opera in the Mozart operas and so on. It was a wonderful musical education though a bit laborious to have to jump up and change the record every four-and-a-half minutes.'[44]

The passion for music awakened in Vienna had continued, and this formed a strong link between him and Margaret. He already had a subscription to the Thursday evening concerts of the Hallé: now they both went. On successive visits to Salzburg in the next years they attended concerts and operas (without having to book – innocent days). Margaret continued her piano studies; within a few years she was in addition playing early music on the clavichord (by the late 1930s she had two). She was also instrumental in bringing regular chamber music back to Manchester. The Taylors after a time moved in moneyed society in Manchester and one of their acquaintances was Philip Godlee, chairman of the Hallé Orchestra. Margaret persuaded Godlee to start the Manchester Chamber Concerts Society with herself as secretary. She wanted the great quartets to perform; they demanded substantial fees; and she therefore charged as much as she could for tickets (£2 each, as much as the best seats at the Hallé) 'instead of as little, the usual principle in Manchester music'. As a result of her determination and drive, Manchester had the opportunity to hear all of the greatest quartets of the day – the Pro Arte, the Busch, the Budapest, the Kolisch. Taylor drove her to the committee meetings, revised her minutes, checked her accounts and 'enjoyed the feast of chamber music'. Their move to Oxford deprived them of the music; and it also deprived Margaret of an absorbing avocation, with devastating results for them both.[45]

But that was in the future: the first year of their married life was most enjoyable. Taylor's confidence in his choice of profession was deepening, with his growing command of the lecture hall and his satisfaction with his research and writing. They had no children to tie them down and could go away at weekends at the prompting of an impulse, sometimes dutifully to his parents', sometimes to Hawkeshead to walk and climb, sometimes to stay with Charles Gott and his wife in Devon. They had enough money to do what they wished, which included summer holidays in Europe. But what makes a place enjoyable is good friends, and they had many, beginning at home: 'our flats provided rich company'.

Immediately below them were Dolly and George Eltenton. Eltenton was an engineer at the Shirley Institute, a large, co-operative textile research centre located in Didsbury. More importantly for Taylor, he was a 'stern

Communist', one who was totally devoted to the Soviet Union, rather than to the British or the international working class. Sometime in the 1930s he went to Leningrad to work at the Institute of Chemical Physics and, 'when thrown out of there on the grounds that the Russians wanted no foreigners however firm their Communist faith', to California, where he entered history. In 1942, while working for the Shell Development Corporation in Berkeley, he was asked by Peter Ivanov, an official at the Soviet Consulate in San Francisco, if he could get information about the work of the Radiation Laboratory at the University of California at Berkeley. Eltenton in turn asked Haakon Chevalier to approach his close friend J. Robert Oppenheimer, a physicist who had just been appointed to head the Los Alamos laboratory (where the atomic bomb would be developed). Chevalier did so in early 1943, telling Oppenheimer that Eltenton had means of getting technical information to the Soviet Union. Although Oppenheimer made it quite clear that he would have nothing to do with this, he delayed or at least neglected to report the approach for some months. This would, after the war, be used as evidence that he was at the very least a 'fellow traveller' (Communist sympathiser) and could not be trusted with such secrets; as a consequence he was stripped of his security clearance and thus forbidden to work on the development of the H-bomb. Taylor drew the moral from this that one should not hide one's beliefs: Eltenton, he said, never did and never got into trouble.[46]

The ground-floor flat was occupied by Malcolm and Kitty Muggeridge, whom Taylor found great fun: they would be firm friends, in spite of later political and religious differences, until death. The Muggeridges were both left-wing: Malcolm had been brought up in a Fabian household, while Kitty was the niece of Beatrice Webb, queen of the Fabians (who once referred to Malcolm's father, with infinite condescension, as 'a Fabian and a very worthy person, though of modest means').[47] Malcolm was lively and stimulating, a man who had the gift of conversation; Kitty, according to her aunt Beatrice, 'has a stiff will and is gifted in appearance, voice and intelligence', while her mother referred to her as 'an atheist and a rebel'.[48] Malcolm was a determined womaniser; in fact both the Muggeridges professed to believe in free love, with Kitty too having the occasional affair. Taylor later wrote that Kitty was 'staggeringly beautiful', a comment in his autobiography that has encouraged some speculation, particularly by Richard Ingrams (one of Muggeridge's biographers), that they might have had an affair. According to Ingrams, Muggeridge was unable to invent characters or place; rather, his novels are thinly disguised autobiographies. The main evidence he proposes for this speculation is a novel published in 1934 called *Picture Palace*, in which all of the characters are taken from his life in Manchester. Rattray, the character based on Taylor, 'was a lecturer in English literature at Accringthorpe University, and lived in a cottage in the country, and took a great interest in his garden, and accumulated a large number of books'. One day he confesses to the main character, Pettygrew (based upon Muggeridge himself), that he is in love with Pettygrew's wife, Gertrude. Pettygrew immediately responds that Rattray must sleep with her: 'you must, you must, it'll strengthen the bond between us.' Rattray makes a pass, Gertrude is repelled but succumbs, Pettygrew is insanely jealous; but in the end he and his wife are reconciled. Rattray, who has been in horrified thrall to his repulsive housekeeper, is due to marry another woman at the end of the novel. Ingrams concludes nonetheless that an affair between Taylor and Kitty Muggeridge was unlikely,[49] and certainly Taylor's previous experience with seducing women was notably patchy. Besides, he was in his early, very happy, years of marriage. What unfortunately remains unrecorded is Taylor's reaction to the novel. The 1934 edition, the subject of a libel suit by the *Manchester Guardian* (which objected to some of Muggeridge's descriptions), was rapidly withdrawn from sale and pulped, but nevertheless Taylor read it in January 1937; however, any comments by him to Muggeridge, or to anyone else, appear lost. By the time it was republished in 1987, Taylor was unable to read anything.

Muggeridge was a leader writer on the *Manchester Guardian*; Taylor in his autobiography referred to him as the 'spoilt child' of the newspaper – he was a favourite of Ted Scott, the editor, until the latter's death in April 1932.[50] Scott was succeeded as editor by W.P. Crozier, who had little time for Muggeridge. This precipitated a break between Muggeridge and the *Guardian*, and he and Kitty decided to abandon England and move to the Soviet Union, where they intended to remain and raise any future children as Soviet citizens. To keep body and soul together, Muggeridge was to work as the *Guardian*'s temporary resident correspondent (although this arrangement fell through soon after their arrival and he was forced to become a freelance). And so, after burning their bourgeois clothes and trinkets and most of their books, and borrowing money from Taylor, they departed, arriving in Moscow in mid-September 1932.

Once there, infatuation with Soviet Communism rapidly evolved into distaste, then into dislike and then into hatred. This was reflected in the articles Muggeridge sent to the *Guardian*, the tone of which was radically at variance with that normally taken by leftist and liberal newspapers and journals, and their publication elicited from Taylor in mid-February 1933 a scathing letter of the utmost self-righteousness. Taylor had, of course, visited the Soviet Union with his mother while still a schoolboy, during the period of the New Economic Policy, when there was food in the shops and the police state was not so pervasive. Things had changed by late 1931 and early 1932, when famine stalked the countryside and Stalin was in unchallenged control. Taylor only reluctantly admitted that famine might be a fact, but in any case it was irrelevant: what was vital was that the Workers' State survive, and Muggeridge's articles might weaken support for it. As far as Taylor was concerned, Muggeridge was missing the point: 'The essential argument between us was already clear enough before you left England – do you remember how indignant you got when I opposed your advocacy of Communism on moral grounds, because it was "better". Well, that is still what is wrong with your attitude – you can't see clearly enough the ruthlessness and the necessity of the class war.' Taylor's attitude was common amongst intellectuals during the 1930s – consider W.H. Auden's poem 'Spain 1937', with its line 'The conscious acceptance of guilt in the necessary murder'[51] – when they celebrated their own 'realism' in the face of someone else's suffering for the higher good.

The benefits for the Soviet worker, Taylor argued, were many:

The Russian worker has a control over his work – through the factory committees – which no worker ever had before: he can criticise, he can control the management: what he says, goes. Then, even from your own moral point of view, look at the fight against illiteracy ... look at the (very wasteful, badly built – but still there) new houses ... the marriage laws which have destroyed the horrible Christian family & made people, for the first time, free in their personal relations ... You'll say that this is all idealistic claptrap, which bears no relationship to the sufferings & privations of the present, which brings me to the peasantry. For the present position is due to the failure of agriculture ... The peasant failure is due to the isolated position of Russia. If the whole world had gone communist in 1919 the workers everywhere would have been in an invincible position: they would have been able to win over the peasantry with the products of industrial Europe & also kill them (economically) with the cheaper foodstuffs from large scale capitalist farms (owned by the workers' state) in America and Australia. But as only Russia went communist, a weak, young working class was left face to face with a backward, individualistic peasantry. It had to buy food from this peasantry & couldn't get the money back again from the peasantry by offering cheap machine made goods, because Russian industry was too backward. As a result the more culpable peasants hoarded money & became, in a small way, capitalists. By 1928, there was a danger that the urban socialism would be swamped by a new capitalism, coming from the Kulaks and that had to be fought, even at the cost of famines. The collective farms weren't started because they would be immediately more efficient, but because – for the Workers' State to survive – the Kulaks & indeed the individualistic peasantry had to be destroyed. There's the problem & that's what you ought to have understood before you began to write about the peasantry, because the famine issue is, in a sense, irrelevant.[52]

This, of course, was the epitome of radical chic, a term unfortunately not then in use. In Taylor's defence, he was only twenty-six; he had been reading and defending Marxist and Communist literature for ten years; he had visited the Soviet Union himself, which gave his opinions a certain weight; and his arguments were wholly in line with the thinking of the progressive establishment. When he wrote to Muggeridge that 'you'll never know Russia until you go to ordinary workers' clubs, rest-homes & so on', he was probably remembering his tour with his mother, during which the letters of introduction they carried gave them an entrée to such clubs. Nevertheless, he had never lived there, trying to exist in squashed conditions, nor been ill but too fearful to go to the hospitals that were little better than deathtraps (Kitty had typhus early on), and certainly he had never walked and walked and looked and looked, as Muggeridge had. The latter's reaction to Taylor's letter must have been complex: almost certainly rage and contempt, but also reluctant recognition of once-shared beliefs. Furthermore, Taylor extended an olive branch: 'Russia won't make us quarrel, although you won't change my mind about it & I suppose I shan't change yours.' This was certainly the case. Taylor remained pro-Soviet for most of his life, although he eventually admitted that the Russian people had deserved better of their leaders. Muggeridge continued in the opposite direction. But they also maintained their close friendship – and the fact that Muggeridge kept the letter is significant.

The loss of the Muggeridges as their neighbours probably encouraged the Taylors to move. According to Taylor, from the moment he went to Manchester he had wanted to live in the country, not surprising given the grubby state of the city, nor given his pleasure in country walking. They first investigated the Lake District, particularly the area around Hawkshead, where he had spent some happy boyhood holidays, but found nothing suitable. This was just as well: it was eighty-five miles from Manchester, and he would have felt obliged to go there every summer rather than to Europe, 'which as a European historian I wanted to do.' A music-loving friend of his then living in Oxford, Alex Moodie, suggested one evening that they try the Peak District, which is on Manchester's doorstep. Moodie's father, a retired bank manager, had once had a cottage there which he had sold on and which was again for sale. Taylor's favourite boyhood home, Buxton, was also in the Peak District and the following day the Taylors went out to look at the cottage. In his letter to Muggeridge of mid-February 1933 Taylor mentions that 'Margaret & I are thinking of going to live in a cottage at Disley! You'd love it – very high and open: miles away from anywhere.' They took the plunge and, for £525, bought it.[53]

Three Gates, the Taylors' name for the house – although it only had one – was situated in the hamlet of Higher Disley. It was two seventeenth-century cottages knocked into one plus a large room at one end added by the Moodies, who had also put in central heating (with the boiler in an outhouse to which Taylor had to struggle through deep snow when he wanted to stoke it in the winter). The Taylors installed electricity, the wiring done courtesy of the local electricity board and condemned as unsafe two years later by the board's inspector. (Taylor neglects to say whether the necessary rewiring was also done by the board.) Eight hundred feet up, north-facing, Three Gates looked across to Kinder Scout from its front windows and, again according to Taylor, had the moor at its back door.[54] There was a farm lane in front of the house, and on the other side was the Taylors' garden, 1,377 ^{2}/$_3$ square yards of it; the left side was devoted to Taylor's vegetable garden, whilst on the right side Margaret grew a lawn and flowers.[55]

Disley itself was, and remains, an outer suburb of Stockport, located about twelve miles from the University of Manchester; having a train station, it served as a commuter community for businessmen and a few academics. It lies in a valley; a mile or so up the hill is Higher Disley, then a rural hamlet. Its closest pub, a necessary amenity for Taylor, was the Plough Boy, some two hundred yards down the hill on Dane Bank. There was a small general store, the owner of which, according to Taylor, 'had been born in the upstairs room and had never spent a night away from it'.[56] Apart from him, their only neighbours were two farmers, who supplied butter, the daily help and advice about growing vegetables, but not much intellectual stimulation. According to a contemporary in Higher Disley, Taylor was called 'Professor' Taylor to distinguish him from a lecturer in industrial chemistry at Bolton Technical College by the name of Jimmy Taylor, who lived nearby in Windy Ridge. 'This sobriquet not only reflected the respect in which the young historian was held, but also the distinction people made between the academic world of Manchester University's History Department and the less respected, vocationally-based one of Bolton's concern with dyestuffs for the moribund cotton industry.' Taylor, he went on, 'was one of the "neet and mornin' buggers" who commuted to and from Manchester and, although the villagers held him in awe, some Disleyites regarded him as a dangerous man who had acquired Continental tastes.'[57]

Taylor loved his house and Higher Disley, and increasingly he loved growing vegetables. In his autobiography he enumerates his exotic produce – mangetout, globe artichokes and other vegetables a million miles away from huge leeks and marrows, the stuff of village produce show competitions. He claimed that his interest in history correspondingly declined except on winter evenings, and that eventually he reorganised his work so that he had only to go into the university for two-and-a-half days a week, with the implication that he spent the remainder of the working week in his garden. The growing season at that latitude and height was short, just May to September, and he lengthened it by the use of protective cloches, while encouraging growth by the use of the ample manure available from the neighbouring farms. He reckoned to grow enough vegetables to feed his family and all of their visitors throughout the year – in which case winter root vegetables must have figured somewhere in the plan.

And certainly they had lots of visitors, with friends staying over nearly every weekend. Usually this was needs must: few had cars, and late-evening trains back into town were not a priority for the railway companies. The Taylors had help: there was the daily, Freda Robinson, daughter of one of their farmer neighbours; and for a while there was a cook. However, according to her nephew, the cook, Eileen Hitchlock, objected to the Taylors' continental tastes, especially his 'habit of drinking beer with his meals and, even more reprehensibly, eating cabbage cooked in beer – a German taste which caused some [Disleyites] to doubt his patriotism and others to doubt his sanity. [She] resigned her post of cook to the Taylors rather than "spoil good food" in that way.' After her departure Margaret

Taylor, who had studied Cordon Bleu cooking, took over the kitchen for all meals except breakfast.[58]

Academic friends from the university visited, as, in due course, did friends from the *Manchester Guardian*; Taylor's students also came for tea, finding themselves greeted by a man in shorts and gardening gloves. The Taylors and their friends ate and drank, particularly the beer he bought by the barrel; but they also walked, Taylor reckoning to take a day-long walk most weekends. A frequent visitor to Three Gates whom Taylor mentions by name in his autobiography was his academic colleague Lewis Namier. He retails a number of stories about Namier, including his risible attempt at nude bathing: 'one summer afternoon we [Taylor and Margaret] and Lewis and the Muggeridges went to a remote field by the River Dane. We and the Muggeridges bathed in the river and ran naked along its bank .... Lewis did not like to be left out. Exclaiming, "There are still young people in the world and I am one of them", he removed his trousers. He soon discovered that, while it is delightful to run naked, the grass tickles when you sit down. Surreptitiously he put his trousers on again.'[59] Namier had played and would continue to play an important part in Taylor's life as both mentor and companion.

'I well remember one summer afternoon,' Taylor later wrote,

> when Ernest Jacob asked me to come over to the common room. Sitting with him was a large man who grasped a tightly rolled umbrella and spoke with a thick accent – Jewish? German?, at any rate a central European. I thought no more of the encounter except to reflect that Ernest had some strange friends. In fact the formidable figure was the great Lewis Bernstein Namier, destined to become professor of modern history at Manchester and for many years a central figure in my life. Ernest had read one day a review by G.M. Trevelyan of the first, and as it proved the only volume of Namier's *England in the Age of the American Revolution* – not as good or as original a book as *The Structure of Politics at the Accession of George III* but a very good book all the same. Ernest went straight across the road to the post office and sent Namier a telegram offering him the chair of modern history – a characteristically impulsive act just like the way Ernest had enlisted me the year before and on a grander scale. Namier accepted, and that afternoon in the common room marked his initiation. Little did I foresee the troubles, the excitements and the enormous pleasure that lay before me with Namier's arrival.[60]

This is interesting. First of all, Jacob clearly had the power to hire whomsoever he wished – no need to worry about advertising the post or ensuring a balanced appointing board. And secondly, in hiring Namier, he was hiring a man who was not a professional academic but a freelance historian: for years Namier had been researching and writing history in his spare time. (As he wrote in the Preface to *The Structure of Politics at the Accession of George III*, 'In 1912 I started work on "The Imperial Problem during the American Revolution"; a year later I had to enter business, but as this carried me across to America, where public libraries are open at night and on Sundays, I was not debarred from continuing my studies.') The Manchester chair was, in fact, his first permanent (and final) academic appointment.

Although Taylor always denied vehemently that he had sat at the feet of Namier, nevertheless it is true that he was greatly influenced. Indeed, certain sentences from his autobiography explicitly admit this. For example: he referred to Namier as one of his two masters (Beaverbrook being the other). 'At Manchester', he wrote,

> I loved Lewis without reserve . . . Lewis was unquestionably a great historian, the only one I have known intimately. Talking to him was an inspiration, always bringing out the best in me and giving me confidence . . . I often stood up to him and sometimes fought with him but there was never a cloud between us [at Manchester and for many years thereafter]. Lewis encouraged me in my work. He rated me more highly as an historian than I rated myself. Indeed I doubt whether I should have persisted in history if it had not been for him . . . Once I was strong enough to stand on my own feet I did not need support from Lewis and simply enjoyed our mutual affection.[61]

Taylor pointed out that he had already been lecturing for a year when Namier arrived and that he always understood much better than Namier how the university worked. He also emphasised that his first book was nearly complete in draft by the time of arrival although, as argued in Chapter 2, Namier influenced its final form, as well as trying to secure its publication. There were possible intellectual influences: 'to enjoy Lewis's company', Taylor wrote, 'you had to believe that the eighteenth-century Duke of Newcastle, Zionism, the European revolutions of 1848, the national tangles of the Habsburg Monarchy and later the loathsome character of the Nazis were the most important topics of the world. I was ready enough to believe this.' However, he continued, 'I did not share the passion for the politics of George III's reign which then consumed him. Both of us derived our views on the Habsburg Monarchy from a book by Otto Bauer on *The Social Democrats and the Nationality Question*. The only difference between us was that I acknowledged the debt and Lewis did not. On the wider themes of international relations I had already arrived there on my own and knew a great deal more about them than Lewis did.' Furthermore, he added, their writing styles were different, as were their methods of research, with Taylor relying more on intuition than Namier.[62]

Namier's biographer, Linda Colley, has argued that 'Namier's work on the nineteenth century remains vivid and suggestive, and his approach to the Second World War has been profoundly – though indirectly – influential. The medium through which this has been exercised is A.J.P. Taylor.' She notes that they were colleagues at Manchester, remaining close allies in the 1940s; both were anti-appeasement and pro-Churchill; both wrote for the *Manchester Guardian*; they shared an interest in wide-ranging European topics, including the German problem, the Habsburg Monarchy and its successor states, wars, revolutions and diplomacy; and each knew the other's work. 'To a quite remarkable degree,' she adds, 'Taylor has written the books that Namier planned to write.' She points out a number of similar positions and arguments, particularly regarding Germany, a question which will be discussed more fully in Chapter 5. And although she never goes so far as to state that Taylor was Namier's acolyte, that is certainly one interpretation of what she does say: 'To point out these similarities of approach and analysis is not of course remotely to imply that Taylor merely borrowed from Namier. But it is the case that Taylor's work has allowed Namier's ideas and insights in the field of modern European history to remain current and widely influential even though the scattered writings in which they were embedded are now largely forgotten.'[63] It is, of course, possible that some of these insights actually were Taylor's rather than Namier's.

She makes a further point about Namier's approach to history without linking it to Taylor, but it seems entirely apposite; this is her comment that 'for Namier iconoclasm was the mark of a great historian'. Once an historian had decided upon and written on a period or problem, Namier insisted, 'others should not be able to practise within its sphere in the terms of the preceding era.'[64] This belief must have come up in discussion between them. Perhaps it encouraged Taylor in his growing habit of attempting to shock the bourgeoisie in his writings and in due course in his broadcasts; in any case Taylor would live up to Namier's injunction with the publication in 1961 of *The Origins of the Second World War*: whether or not one agreed with it, it is incontrovertible that it changed entirely the public's view of and the historian's approach to the war.[65]

Namier must have seemed an elemental force to Taylor when he arrived at Manchester. Namier's longtime friend, Isaiah Berlin, wrote an essay on him after his death which included the following description of his character and personality: he was an

> intellectually formidable, at times aggressive, politically minded intellectual – and his hatred of doctrine was held with a doctrinaire tenacity ... [He] was vain, proud, contemptuous, intolerant, quick to give and take offence, master of his craft, confident of his own powers, not without a strain of pathos and self-pity ... [He] hated all forms of weakness, sentimentality, idealistic liberalism; most of all he hated servility ... [He] fascinated his interlocutors and oppressed them too. If you happened to be interested in the topic which he was discussing ... you were fortunate, for it was not likely that you would again hear the subject expounded with such learning, brilliance and originality. If, however, you were not interested, you could not escape. Hence those who met him were divided into some who looked on him as a man of genius and a dazzling talker and others who fled from him as an appalling bore. He was, in fact, both.[66]

Berlin added that 'I never experienced boredom in his company, not even when he was at his most ponderous', and Taylor implied the same. Partly this was Namier's personality – although Taylor found him aggressive, he also found him fun – but, more to the point, Taylor finally had someone in his own field with whom to talk. Undoubtedly he listened to and learned from Namier: Berlin in the same essay refers to Taylor as Namier's 'friend and disciple'. Undoubtedly Namier encouraged him to question his long-held belief on the victimhood of the Germans, to look at the long sweep of history, to look at past history and current politics as a continuum. But it is also very likely that Taylor too tried out ideas, challenged some of Namier's and eventually held his own with the master.

What is eminently clear is that the two shared a number of intellectual and political interests, and that both derived a great deal of stimulation and enjoyment from their time together at Manchester and later. Taylor's affectionate description of Namier emphasised his clumsiness, his insensitivity to others and his tendency to bore for England. However, a man seems much less of a bore if you share the same ideas. Taylor wrote that 'Lewis and I saw eye to eye over foreign affairs. We were both aggressively anti-Nazi, quite ready to insult any colleague who breathed a word of sympathy with Germany. I remember Lewis coming to Disley one summer Sunday. As the train drew in, he thrust his head out of the carriage window, waved his Sunday newspaper triumphantly and cried, "The swine are killing each other. The swine are killing each other". It was 30 June 1934, the day of Hitler's blood bath.'[67]

It would not be many years before Taylor would be engaged in anti-German or, more specifically, anti-appeasement activities, but his career as a political activist began with a topic closer to home: trade-union politics. For his first two years in Manchester he was 'pretty well detached from politics', presumably having quite enough to do settling into his new job and marriage. He decided against joining the Manchester Labour Party, Didsbury branch, for the same reason that he had refused to join in Hampstead: it was full of middle-class intellectuals. Instead, he followed his father's path and entered politics through the trade-union route. He joined the General and Municipal Workers' Union, which then sent him as one of its delegates to the Manchester Trades Council (his father had been a GMWU delegate to the Preston Trade and Labour Council); he attended every monthly meeting for four years, meetings, he recalled, 'of the utmost tedium'. However, whenever there was a demonstration organised, more often than not Taylor was sent as the Trades Council representative for the university sector.

This led to a formative experience. In June 1934 there was a meeting in the Free Trade Hall in Manchester to protest against events in Austria: as Taylor described it, 'the Austrian Fascist government had overthrown the democratic republic and conducted a civil war against the Austrian Social Democrats. With my Austrian memories still fresh I spoke from the heart.' As reported in the *Manchester Guardian*, Taylor attacked both the Austrian government for firing on the workers and the British government for having agreed to the arming of the Austrian troops and for standing idly by during the attacks. It was the duty of British workers, he said, to learn from the Austrian example, because 'capitalism knew no mercy to women and children when it had to defend its hold over the workers.' It was Taylor's first big public meeting and 'I had only ten minutes. But my voice carried as well as that of any accomplished orator. That Sunday afternoon at the Free Trade Hall convinced me that I too could be a public speaker when I had a cause to believe in.'[68]

During his remaining years at Manchester, he embarked on a gradually accelerating career of public speaking on behalf of political causes. With the odd exception, such as when he was the only member of staff who spoke up for students arrested and threatened with expulsion from the university after a mass trespass in support of opening up the countryside (which had resulted in a battle with gamekeepers), he came to concentrate on issues of defence and foreign policy. The next demonstration which he recalled took place in October 1934. As he described it, it was 'an open-air demonstration against the Incitement to Disaffection Bill, which was supposed rightly or wrongly to have re-introduced general warrants. We spoke in Platt Fields from horse-drawn drays ... My voice was almost inaudible in the open air and this taught me never to speak in the open air again.'

The *Manchester Guardian*'s extensive report makes it clear that it was a not unimpressive event: there was a procession of two to three thousand people who marched to Platt Fields, a crowd accompanying them along the pavements and 'many others' waiting for the meeting in the park, where three platforms were occupied by nearly thirty speakers. They included one of Taylor's most revered colleagues, the Manchester University philosophy professor Samuel Alexander, Arthur Greenwood, MP, Aneurin Bevan, MP, William Gallacher of the Communist Party, a Canon Shimwell and 'Mr A.J.P. Taylor (of Manchester University)'. Canon Shimwell said that the bill was contrary to all he and his brethren in the Church stood for, while Greenwood said that it seemed that those in authority over the fighting forces wanted to deny them their civic rights. 'Mr A.J.P. Taylor said that the Bill was a war measure; a deliberate preparation for the next European war. "Are we going to allow ourselves to be slaughtered," he asked, "or are we going to refuse to fight for capitalism and raise instead the standard of Socialistic England?"' Clearly the *Guardian* reporter heard him if no one else did.[69]

Taylor used the same line of argument – that the only security against war was a socialist government – when speaking in Manchester at an exhibition on the horrors of war which was touring the country during the Geneva Disarmament Conference (1932–4). An anti-war organisation, later called the Manchester Peace Council, was set up and Taylor was 'put on to represent the university, though of course I represented no one except myself and worked out my line as I went along.' He went out once or twice every week to speak to trade-union branches, meetings in church halls, specially organised meetings – but to say what? He opposed rearmament under the government on the grounds that they were more likely to support the Nazis than their opponents; furthermore, the government were anti-Soviet and this made it at least conceivable that such arms would be used against the Soviet Union – and Taylor was 'unshakeably pro-Russian' (as his letter to Muggeridge had demonstrated). So Britain should not rearm – but he also argued that Nazi Germany was basically weak and would collapse if firmly resisted; furthermore, if the Nazis were not resisted, there would come another great war. To cap it all, he said, the League of Nations was useless, a stance which outraged many of those to whom he spoke. All in all, Taylor's audiences could be forgiven if they emerged from the meetings a bit confused.[70]

After moving out of Manchester to Higher Disley, he joined the Disley Labour Party, a ward in the Macclesfield constituency, according to Taylor a great sprawling country area with few Labour speakers. During the run-up to the general election of 14 November 1935, Taylor was second only to the Labour candidate in the number of speeches he gave. He predicted that, if re-elected, the government would betray the League of Nations (which they did with the Hoare–Laval plan the following month); he also argued that a Labour government would have a better foreign policy. Both of these points he believed. But he was trapped by the official Labour policy of support for the League, which he therefore also had to argue for (perhaps with fingers crossed behind his back).

In mid-December 1935 the terms of the Hoare–Laval plan, by which France and Britain were to abandon Abyssinia to the depredations of Italy, became known, and protests blew up around the country. On 17 December five Manchester University societies – the League of Nations Society, the Liberal Association, the Socialist Society, the Anti-War Group and the University branch of the Student Christian Movement – came together in the University Union for a protest meeting. Presiding over the meeting was Professor J.L. Stocks, who had been the Labour candidate for Oxford University, whilst Taylor was the sole speaker. The *Manchester Guardian* printed a good part of his speech, and it is interesting to see how he tailored his arguments to his audience: he combined exhortation, biting wit and an analysis which assumed some knowledge of foreign policy and geography on the part of the listeners. It was, he argued, a matter of great moment that Britain should maintain its reputation as a country prepared to act in defence of small nations. The election had showed the country's desire that the government should continue to support the principles of the League of Nations, but no sooner was the election over than it had turned and made a bargain with Italy. 'If that is what democracy means,' he said, 'then this country is no more democratic than Nazi Germany, for even there they have an election now and then, and the people may vote for Ministers whose policy they do not like.' 'Let us not believe,' he went on,

> that these peace terms were, in the words of a 'Manchester Guardian' leader, an 'aberration'; that Sir Samuel Hoare was outwitted by M. Laval; that he was perhaps tired; that he is not very clever in any case; that he wanted to go on his holiday in Switzerland and did not read what M. Laval put before him. Sir Samuel Hoare may have been tired, but behind his tiredness was his adroit mind; and behind him again was the adroitness of Mr. Baldwin. The peace terms put forward by this Government are the peace terms which this Government has all along intended to put forward. It is no accident that the one bit of Italian territory to be surrendered to Abyssinia is Assab; because Assab, a fortified port, would be a great menace to Aden. This is a convenient way of getting rid of that menace. It is no use trying to believe that this Government has merely blundered. This Government has pursued a policy of buying Italy off in order to pursue its own imperialist aims.

A resolution against the peace terms, to be sent to the Prime Minister, was carried by 234 votes to two.[71]

A growing suspicion by February 1936 that Germany was going to violate the Versailles Treaty by sending its soldiers back into the Rhineland – meant to be a demilitarised buffer zone between Germany and France – caused Taylor to change his mind about the need for Britain to rearm. The Manchester Peace Council held a public meeting to discuss future policy. According to Taylor, one speaker

> gave us all the old stuff about the League of Nations and the oil sanction. I announced a conversion. I said 'This is all dead. Germany is going to occupy the Rhineland [as they did the following month]. What are we going to do? In my opinion rearmament is now all that matters even under the National government.' That ended my connexion with the Manchester peace council .... I cannot claim that I drew any clear moral from my conversion. I should have liked the Labour party to campaign for rearmament which I thought would eventually prove a winning ticket, but of course it did not. I had no faith that the National government would rearm effectively. So I merely lapsed into political inactivity.[72]

This four-year involvement in politics was an important episode in Taylor's development. First of all, he had to learn to speak to, and hold, a non-captive audience. His students had to attend his lectures if they wished to pass their exams; those who go to political meetings need remain only as long as the proceedings are interesting. To make them interesting Taylor had to convey sometimes complex arguments lucidly and arrestingly, and within a short compass of time. This would be useful in his future broadcasting career and in his later role as the most popular lecturer in the country for the Historical Association. Secondly, on the more directly political front, he learned to distrust home-grown Communists; while still convinced that the Soviet Communist Party had the welfare of its country at heart, he came to believe that British Communists cared only for their party, not for the country or the people. This made him immune to the lure of the party, as well as making him much less of a sentimental leftist than many. Furthermore, he learned that demonstrations on their own do not accomplish very much, a proposition which he had to relearn during his involvement in the late 1950s with the Campaign for Nuclear Disarmament. And although he would be involved to a certain extent in anti-appeasement activities once he had moved to Oxford, a move nearly coterminous with Munich, nevertheless February 1936 signalled the end of his first sustained period of political activity.

Other duties soon occupied the time once taken up by politics, the most important of which was fatherhood. On 12 April 1937 his first child, Giles Lewis, was born, named after St Gilgen, where Taylor had spent the summer of 1932, and Namier (who reacted with some embarrassment). Taylor waxed lyrical about his son: 'The first child is a wonderful arrival and remains an only child even when it has brothers and sisters. A first son is also from the beginning the potential head of the family and Giles has been no exception.' (In this context it is notable that Giles is the only Taylor offspring whose photograph appears in his autobiography.) Taylor continues: 'I had been brought up by my parents to regard childbearing as an intolerable hardship inflicted on women by men, which men should spend the rest of their lives atoning for. I did my best to apply this doctrine. It never occurred to me that a woman should look after her baby herself ... We had a Norland nurse complete with uniform. I took over on her day off. I bathed Giles nearly every night and pushed him in his pram round the Black Hill sometimes through deep snow.'[73] This all sounds remarkably like Percy Taylor and the young Alan.

In 1938 the Norland nurse and the Taylors parted company, and she was replaced by Henrietta Werner, a twenty-eight-year-old political refugee from Vienna. Taylor had met her briefly in 1929 when he was a student in Vienna. An acquaintance of Taylor's from Preston, Sydney Sharples (whose sister was something of a surrogate daughter to Taylor's father), had visited Vienna as a delegate to the International Meeting of Socialist Youth being held there in the summer of 1929, and Werner had helped to find him a place to stay. He probably told Taylor about her; in any case, one day Taylor had contacted her, asking to meet. She was not keen and 'resolved to be very stand-offish, meeting a very rich Englishman.' In the event they met only once, since she could not imagine how he would fit in with her Social Democratic friends and colleagues. Then in 1938, having fled Austria for Prague, she came to England and contacted Sydney Sharples. After staying with him and his family for a bit, she was passed on to a secondary school teacher. But she wanted to work and in due course the Taylors, having learned that she had been a political prisoner in Vienna, and of the suicide of her fiancé (also a political activist), asked her to come to Higher Disley to help look after Giles.

Werner was to move to Oxford with the Taylors, staying with them for about two-and-a-half years altogether. She was devoted to Giles, although sometimes oppressed by the responsibility of caring for him, and grateful to the Taylors, not only for giving her work but also for indirectly educating her in how a democracy worked. Her memories give an otherwise unobtainable glimpse into the Taylor household. Taylor, for example, tried according to his lights to practise his Socialism: he did some housework, laid the table, cleaned the shoes of members of the family (and tried to clean Werner's which she would not accept: she wanted her status as a servant to be clear, whilst he tried to blur it). Yet she was only paid fifteen shillings a week rather than the pound others received for the same work – undeniably Taylor was close with his money.

Margaret Taylor was more generous, and probably thought she should have been paid more; she gave her clothes sent by a rich aunt and forbore to scold her when she made a mistake: 'I shall never forget, she was pregnant, she asked me ... would I put a hot-water bottle into her bed. I did it, and the next morning she told me, but in a very kind way, I had not properly closed it, and she had to get up and change mattresses and every-thing, and she was pregnant.' Margaret did the cooking and 'she did it quite well, only, at the end of it she stood in a heap of saucepans on the floor. She also made very good cakes. But she forgot about them when she had put them in the oven, she went back and played: she had a clavichord, she played Bach very beautifully. She forgot it, and I was well experienced in scraping the cake, and put a lot of caster sugar on it, but it was very dry inside.' Margaret believed that she should cook herself and have children, and still find time for art and politics. She was not overwhelmingly interested in the latter, sharing only some of Taylor's ideas, but she was gifted in art and music.

The Taylor progeny were encouraged to call their parents by their first names and discouraged from any interest in religion. 'We [Werner and Giles] went to breakfast, Mr Taylor said "Ah, a new clean overall." "Yes", I said, "it's Sunday." "Ah, Sunday is a day like any other day." And I said, "Don't you believe it, Giles" (Giles was too little to understand). "It's Sunday. Many people needn't work today, they put on their best clothes. And the miners love Sundays because it really is a sun day." And this is how I told Taylor my mind.' He took it from her at least partly because she had more of a claim to be proletarian than he did.

Werner met and listened to an impressive range of people at Taylor's table, often sitting silent during the evening and listening to the talk. There were Taylor's colleagues, including Bruce McFarlane once they had moved to Oxford; and there was Count Michael Karolyi, a democratic Hungarian aristocrat – 'This again was very, very interesting. How would I ever have met a count and his wife?' – who would remain close to Taylor for the remainder of his life. What these two men had in common was a devotion to liberty and democracy. Werner appreciated this, and in particular liked the Taylors for trying to become 'new men', Socialists. But she never quite trusted them, could never forget that they had never been poor, was convinced that Taylor 'would have found it very difficult to be without the security, financial security.'

She doubtless brought a new dimension to the Higher Disley household. She was someone from the political coalface, someone who had suffered badly, as Taylor himself had not, in support of aims which Taylor supported. She had personal principles as well, which she upheld in the face of Taylor's occasional good-humoured scorn. And she was Austrian, a citizen of the foreign country in which he was always to feel most comfortable, a refugee from the country whose history he was currently writing (*The Habsburg Monarchy*). She was to remain a friend of Taylor's until his death, and to maintain her affection for Giles.[74]

From Taylor's own description of his life during his time at Manchester, the reader could be forgiven for thinking that he had given up writing history altogether for gardening, walking, music, friends and childcare. But this was clearly not the case. If he spent only two-and-a-half days a week at the university, this was probably not so much to enable constant gardening as to ensure that he could work. He shared a very small office in the History Department and would be at the beck and call of students: sustained research and writing require space and quiet. In 1934 he had published his *Italian Problem in European Diplomacy*; in 1935 he and Bill McElwee published their translation of *The Struggle for Supremacy in Germany 1859–1866*, for which Taylor wrote an introduction; in 1936 he published an article in the *English Historical Review*; and in 1938 he published his second monograph, *Germany's First Bid for Colonies 1884–1885*. In short, as an historian he was very productive.

There is some mystery as to how he and McElwee came to translate the two volumes of *Der Kampf um die Vorherrschaft in Deutschland, 1859 bis 1866* by the Austrian historian and journalist Heinrich Friedjung, which they published as the single-volume *The Struggle for Supremacy in Germany 1859–1866*. One link was Přibram: he had been close friends with Friedjung, and after the latter's death had completed the writing and publication of Friedjung's last work, *Das Zeitalter des Imperialismus, 1884–1914* in three volumes. *The Struggle for Supremacy* was by common historical opinion a brilliant work, indeed the major work on its subject, and as Friedjung's literary executor Přibram was probably keen on its being made available to a wider audience. As noted above, McElwee was working with him in Vienna when Taylor (and Margaret) returned there at Easter 1931, and it was Přibram who brought the two men together. Perhaps they discussed the book (which Taylor had read in March 1930); at some point McElwee or Taylor suggested that it should be translated.

Taylor admired both the work and the historian. He had read several of Friedjung's books whilst researching in Vienna and was thus qualified to pronounce that this was his best; furthermore, he was not alone in considering him possibly the greatest of all Austrian historians. But greatness alone would probably not have driven Taylor to devote so much time to publishing someone else's book, rather than to writing his own history, on the face of it a strange thing to do. Rather, it is arguable that he was drawn to him because Friedjung combined academic history and journalism in a way that was analogous to Taylor's own yearning. Taylor never wanted to be a straight academic, and for several years he continued to toy with the idea of being a foreign correspondent or a journalist instead. He compromised – or transcended the problem – by choosing to combine the two occupations, as Friedjung had done for a time. He had been a German-speaking, Austrian Jew who had had a chair at the School of Commerce in Vienna, which he combined with active participation in politics. A pamphlet he wrote caused his dismissal from his chair; he went into active politics and became the editor of the *Deutsche Zeitung*, the newspaper of the German Nationalist party; however, because he was Jewish he was driven from his post and had to become a freelance journalist.

The loss of his post had allowed more time for historical work, one result of which was his account of the struggles between Prussia and Austria for dominance of the German states. Taylor notes in his introduction that it was 'primarily a great piece of historical research, but it was also a continuation of Friedjung's political work in another form.' For Taylor, the political drive need not and did not detract from the quality of the book. It is impossible to know for certain, but it is likely that for Taylor the example of Friedjung widened the possibilities for his own work, and certainly more than one of his future books, in particular those on Germany, combined a political with an historical agenda.[75]

What little evidence there is suggests that McElwee translated the work and Taylor wrote the introduction, although it is unknown just how McElwee and Taylor organised the work or when they did it.[76] Taylor's first priority in 1931 presumably was to complete the research for and then to write his book on *The Italian Problem*, which he drafted during the summer of 1932, completing it in early 1933. After going through the motions of writing it as a thesis and having it examined, he at last saw it through the press, writing the Preface in July 1934. He could then concentrate on Friedjung, having already reread the German edition in May 1934. Besides the translation and its polishing, the two decided to add supplementary notes based on material from the Austrian archives to elucidate points which Friedjung had found mysterious or to correct his errors; there are a handful per chapter.

Namier was very helpful. He had agreed to establish and to act as General Editor for a series for Macmillan called Studies in Modern History, and he wanted the Friedjung as the first volume in the series.[77] In November Taylor read the first proofs and then passed them on to Namier, who also read them. Namier also read the text of Taylor's Introduction, which Taylor sent to the publisher in early January 1935. He and Namier both read and corrected the page proofs in January. There had, in the meantime, been a little flurry of correspondence between Taylor and Macmillan over who was to pay for making the index (the publishers paid). Finally, in April 1935, the Friedjung translation, Taylor's second book, was published.[78]

There was a large clutch of reviews in a wide range of newspapers as well as academic journals. Gratifyingly for the translators, all mentions of the translation were favourable; gratifyingly for the ghost of the historian, all reviewers accounted it a work that eminently deserved such translation. The Introduction frequently received particular mention: *Time and Tide* called it 'a little masterpiece of brevity and critical insight', while the *Cambridge Review* stated that 'it is no depreciation of Friedjung's narrative to say that to some readers this introduction, luminous, critical and just, will prove the most interesting part of the whole volume.'[79] No writer could ask for more.

Now it was time to concentrate on a research-based book again. Interestingly, this grew out of work begun back in 1933, probably, in the first instance, for his teaching. As Taylor recalled matters:

> thanks to Lewis [Namier] I trespassed on the field of a special subject, hitherto a professorial reserve. Lewis, himself occupied with his special subject on eighteenth-century British politics, thought that we should have one on European diplomacy as well. This suited me. With *The Italian Problem* out of the way, I was moving on to international relations before the first world war, which had previously been a closed book to me. I bought a set of *die grosse Politik* from a German Jewish refugee, thus accidently profiting from the Nazi regime, and read all its fifty-four volumes during 1933 and 1934. I went on to the published British and French documents until I was one of the best read authorities in the country. I devised a special subject which I began to operate in 1935, much to the disapproval of professors in other departments. This did not distress me.'[80]

Die grosse Politik der europäischen Kabinette 1871–1914 consisted of fifty-four volumes of diplomatic documents from the German Foreign Ministry files, issued by the German government from 1922 on in an attempt to demonstrate that Germany had not been responsible for the First World War. They were soon followed by the *British Documents on the Origin of the War 1898–1914* and by the *Documents diplomatiques français (1871–1914)*. Because a special subject had to be based on primary sources, it was only their publication that enabled Taylor to teach what was considered very contemporary history at the university. He tackled the first two volumes of the German documents in February 1933, reading, according to his list, a total of twenty-two during 1933 and 1934, and a total of thirty-one by the beginning of the war in 1939; in addition he read during the same period twelve volumes of the French documents and nine volumes of the British. (He also read a substantial number of secondary works in all three languages, particularly on relevant German and French history.)[81]

Taylor's special subject, 'International Relations, 1890–1909', was first put on during the academic year 1936–7. Nothing remains of any prospectus or book list; there would not have been lectures, since it would have been taught to a very small group as a seminar, but it is possible to ascertain his approach from his exam papers. Students had to sit three three-hour exams, one of which consisted of gobbets. Traditionally, gobbets terrify students: the whole of the set texts are fair game, and the rules – almost as strict as those governing the sonnet form – preclude waffle. In the case of Manchester, students had to read from the volumes of British and French diplomatic documents, but not the German (one-third of the extracts were in French). Taylor taught his students to assess the documents as reliable evidence; in addition, they had to consider process and not just details of events. Questions included 'How far, with reference to any *one* topic, do you find the *British Documents*, Vol. I–III, adequate?' and 'Compare the influence on foreign policy in France and England of *either* the permanent officials *or* the Cabinet.' These are challenging questions which require broad knowledge to answer satisfactorily.[82]

The need to read the German documents, particularly in tandem with the French and British, led directly to his next book, *Germany's First Bid for Colonies 1884–1885: A Move in Bismarck's European Policy*. As he later recalled, 'going through the French and German documents I was struck by the way in which Bismarck used German colonial ambitions as an instrument in his European policy. Of course there was also a genuine push for colonies in Germany even if Bismarck himself was not affected by it. But my point was worth making, the more so that I could take a jab at the fashionable theories of economic imperialism.' He seems to have begun with the intention of writing an article, but from a long article it turned into a short book. Namier wanted it for the Macmillan series in which the Friedjung had appeared. The final draft was sent to the publisher in mid-November 1937 and published on 1 March 1938.[83]

This was a work of history which, if Taylor is to be believed, achieved a contemporary political relevance which was both unexpected and unintended. His main argument was that Bismarck had not been pushed into trying to acquire overseas territory by the force of German public opinion braying for colonies: rather, his intention was to encourage France into friendship with Germany and, by manufacturing a quarrel with Britain, thereby to soften the French revanchist cry for the return of Alsace-Lorraine. This was plausible because Britain and France were strong imperial rivals (and would indeed nearly come to blows in 1898). Therefore, Taylor's argument goes, Bismarck made claims to 'ownerless territories' which happened to lie near or even alongside British territories, assuming that Britain would threaten war over the claims. Instead, British statesmen, an indifferent lot, fell over themselves to give Bismarck what he seemed to want, and Bismarck found himself with German South-West Africa, the Cameroons, New Guinea and German East Africa on his hands.

Strong themes emerge from the book which many reviewers pounced on for their pertinence to their own times. First of all there was the aggressive nature of German policy and its implementation, threatening and Machiavellian and disruptive to European stability; but secondly was the feeble and incompetent nature of the British response. Germany was a 'made' state, with no tradition but that of Prussian militarism and *raison d'état*, and this was faithfully mirrored by Bismarck's arrogance. Germany wanted colonies and Germany would have colonies, no matter what violence was required to obtain them. And who was to counter Bismarck? A British government headed by Gladstone, whose entire focus was domestic politics, and with a Foreign Secretary in the person of Lord Granville, elderly, ill and with serious financial worries, and with bonhomie as his stock-in-trade: 'That a foreign secretary should have a policy hardly occurred to him; he merely transferred to foreign affairs the principle on which Whig cabinets were held together – personal friendship. His sole endeavour was to be polite and considerate, in the hope that no foreign government would be so cruel as to oppose the wishes of a benevolent old gentleman.' The reaction of a number of reviewers in 1938 to the following can be imagined:

> The British Government had accepted without demur Herbert Bismarck's statement that New Guinea was now the only question separating the two countries; the question of New Guinea had been settled, but Bismarck's policy remained as unfriendly as before; obviously, therefore, there must be some other colonial question in which England had offended, and this too must be removed in order to recover Bismarck's friendship .... But Granville held firmly (or as firmly as he could) to the view that Bismarck was anxious to be friendly to England, if only the English would let him.

Nevertheless, as Taylor later emphasised, he had written these words months before the current Nazi agitation for colonies had been raised, but not before the policy of appeasement had become an object of acute worry to many.[84]

The first review appeared in the *Times Literary Supplement* a mere two weeks after publication, on 19 March 1938. It was the sort of review of which most historians can only dream, and its value was increased by the fact that it appeared in the one journal which everyone for whose opinion he cared would read:

> In his speech to the Reichstag on February 20 Herr Hitler declared categorically that the German demand for colonies would be pressed with ever-increasing vigour in the future. It is, therefore, important that public opinion throughout the world should be informed of the history of German colonization. And it is especially important that the facts in regard to Germany's initial endeavours to obtain colonies should be laid bare. For it is only through the study of the causes underlying the colonial movement in Germany that it is possible to form even an approximately accurate estimate of the part played by it in German national life. For this reason alone Mr. Taylor deserves the gratitude of all students of the present-day colonial problem for his brilliant study of Bismarck's colonial policy during the years 1884–1885 ... His book is timely in its appearance and fulfils the highest standards of scholarship ... His narrative powers and pleasantly ironic style at once arouse the reader's interest and retain it to the close.

There was, however, somewhat of a mixed reaction to the book, as to most books. Its contemporary relevance was commented on by a number of reviewers, and on the whole it was these who tended to write the most favourable reviews. The *National Review* of May 1938 was straightforward about it: 'one striking lesson to be learned from Mr. Taylor's illuminating study is this, namely, to quote his words, the appalling contrast between "Bismarck's far-sighted realism and the helpless benevolence of British statesmen." Let us devoutly hope that when Herr Hitler begins to talk about colonies again he will not find himself in conversation with either a Gladstone or a Granville.' On the other hand, the reviewer in the May issue of the *Oxford Magazine* remained unconvinced by Taylor's argument, based on his own assessment of the extent to which Bismarck was in fact interested in colonies – Taylor's case 'is not quite so good as he thinks'. This particular reviewer was also irritated by the Taylorian 'undergraduate levity': 'What, for example, is the use of writing that "the aggressive Imperialism of the late nineteenth century was merely part of the Diabolism of the Naughty Nineties, with Chamberlain as the Oscar Wilde of politics"?' It is admittedly surprising that that particular sentence got past Namier, but Taylor was now more self-confident about his prose. The paradoxical and epigrammatic quality of Taylor's prose style would increasingly invite comment, which was not always favourable.

One review, but more particularly the reviewer, had an important impact on Taylor's future. This was E.L. Woodward, a Fellow of All Souls and, according to Taylor, 'almost alone at Oxford' in promoting the study of prewar diplomacy (Taylor had written a favourable review of Woodward's book, *Great Britain and the German Navy*, for the *Manchester Guardian* in November 1935). Woodward wrote in the *Spectator* of 26 March that the book was 'a model of the way in which diplomatic history should be written. His introduction is a brilliant little summary of the German attitude towards colonies in general, and British colonies in particular. He writes clearly, and is always master of his subject.' Woodward already knew Taylor's work at Manchester, where he had been an external examiner for a number of years; according to Taylor, Woodward thought that his work was 'much more professional than anything being done at Oxford'. When the occasion arose, then, Woodward was instrumental in bringing Taylor back to Oxford, in this case to Magdalen College.[85]

Taylor always claimed that he had not really wanted to return to Oxford: 'Lewis and Ernest [Jacob] were for ever on at me that I must think of my professional career. For them this meant moving to Oxford. I did not share their taste. Most Oxford graduates at a provincial university were exiles, longing to return. I was not. I liked Manchester and its university. I was happy in my work. I loved Three Gates, Higher Disley. I wanted everything to go just the same for ever.' However, he goes on to admit that 'if I had stayed in Manchester I should never have achieved anything except a few academic books. Without the contacts I made in London, which was easily reached from Oxford, I should never have become either a journalist or a television star. As I had never wanted to be a full-time academic, I suppose my move to Oxford was the best thing for me. All the same it was a painful wrench.'[86]

In fact, he began applying for Oxford jobs within a year of taking up his post at Manchester, beginning in 1931 when the Tutorial Fellowship at Oriel College fell available with the departure of G.N. Clark for the new Chichele chair in economic history (which was tied to All Souls). According to Taylor, he did not even receive an acknowledgement. He tended to blame Stanley Cohn for his lack of success (Cohn was heard to remark of Taylor in 1935 that 'I'll see him dead before he gets into Oxford'), although, according to Woodward, Clark had not then thought Taylor mature enough to be brought back. He next applied for a Fellowship at Corpus Christi, where he was called for interview. According to Taylor, the President of Corpus, Sir Richard Livingstone, said to him sternly, ' "I hear you have strong political views." I said, "Oh, no, President. Extreme views weakly held." ' This application failed as well, although it is unlikely that he fell over that one comment.[87]

Then in the spring of 1938, when Taylor was thirty-two, Magdalen moved to appoint a new Tutorial Fellow in Modern History. Taylor applied, giving as his referees Professors Jacob and Namier from Manchester University and Mr B.H. Sumner of Balliol; in addition Woodward wrote to his friend Stephen Lee, then senior history tutor at Magdalen. Namier's reference ended with personal comments which might surprise those who knew Taylor only in his combative prime:

> He is certainly a man of first-class ability. He has a mind which is both lively and accurate, quick and tenacious; he gets immediately to the essential point and does not lose himself in detail, although he has the proper appreciation for its importance. His knowledge of pre-war diplomatic history is remarkable ... He is in fact one of the coming men for diplomatic history in this country ... While pre-war history is his special subject, he is also very good on the French Revolution, the Napoleonic period, and on 19th Century European history. He has done less at Manchester on British domestic history in the 19th and 20th Centuries, but I do not doubt that he is qualified to teach it and will easily be able to enlarge his knowledge of it. He is a first-class teacher, interesting and stimulating. In talk he will sometimes vent strong views, but when it comes to history work, he attains a very high degree of objectivity and impartiality. He is personally most pleasant to work with; and is a good warm-hearted friend. I do not know of anyone in Manchester with whom he has quarrelled in these seven years.'[88]

Humphrey Sumner of Balliol knew Taylor himself only slightly, through having acted as external examiner at Manchester,

> but I have heard a good deal about him and know his two books, and an article of his in last year's English Historical Review. He strikes me as a

person of very considerable force, with clear and strongly held opinions, incisiveness, and quick grasp. He has a lively, acute mind, and he is a worker. He would take ample trouble with his pupils, and I think his judgement on them would be good. He would be an effective lecturer (and incidently from a University point of view he would be extremely useful as such, in view of the present lack of people lecturing on European history in the nineteenth century) ... He is thoroughly alert and independent, and he writes pointedly and with sting. He will certainly continue to produce historical work, and it should be not only very individual, but of marked distinction.[89]

The final official reference is from Taylor's head of department, who had apparently not been forewarned: 'I am much interested to know that Taylor has made application for the Tutorship in Modern History. There is no doubt that he is entirely first-rate, both as a diplomatic historian and as a tutor of young people. He has developed the study of the 19th century here from a depressed subject into one of the leading periods in the History course. He is now in charge of the Modern Diplomatic Special Subject in our History School and his teaching attracts a good many students.' Because he was a mediaevalist, Jacob disclaimed any special knowledge of the subjects of Taylor's books; nevertheless, he had read them and thought them considerable performances – 'the German one is both witty and learned'. Jacob concentrated on Taylor's teaching and general collegiality: 'he is fully qualified to take over the responsibility for teaching periods of history after 1700. He has a very independent outlook; his judgement, brilliant as it often is, is both sane and central; he is often a little outspoken, but I think that this comes from the force and energy of his nature, for he never says anything for effect, and on the whole he is not lacking in tact. He is an admirable colleague and is greatly liked in the History School here. I do not think I know of any young historian who is better qualified to be a Fellow of a college ... He looks after his pupils most carefully, and knows all about them.' As already noted above, Jacob had heard him lecture and if he were a student, he wrote, would never have missed any lectures in his course; furthermore, Taylor also had considerable experience in tutorials and in supervising research degrees, the latter with great success. Finally, 'I know that this story of his merits is rather tedious, but really, of all younger modern historians I have met, he is definitely one of the best.'[90]

Woodward wrote a private letter to Stephen Lee, in which he discussed various candidates for the post: 'there is a man at Manchester – A.J.P.

Taylor, of whom I think well. He was a pupil of G.N. Clark at Oriel.' Woodward's opinion was that 'Taylor has developed extremely well under Namier's direction. He has just written a v gd little bk on the German colonial hunt.'[91] Woodward would certainly have been privately consulted by the History Fellows at Magdalen, since he was the only one locally in Taylor's field; he may even have been a faculty representative on the appointment committee, which would account for Taylor's belief that Woodward had been instrumental in his appointment. In any case, the other references had hit all of the right notes: coming man in the field; devoted and successful teacher – very important to Oxford with its reliance on the tutorial system; stimulating to talk to – a bore would be very tedious indeed over thirty years of lunch and dinner; and not contumacious in personal relations and therefore easy to get along with – again, very important in the college system, where it is difficult always to avoid colleagues whom one dislikes.

Taylor was called to dinner at Magdalen,

> where Stephen Lee sat on one side of me and Bruce McFarlane, the tutor in mediaeval history, on the other. Afterwards President Gordon came in for a few minutes and looked me over, I thought disapprovingly. Nothing was said about duties or conditions. I, used to the detailed interviews of Manchester appointment committees, assumed that my visit was an empty formality before the appointment of some recognized Oxford figure such as Hugh Trevor-Roper, one of the candidates. I went home to Three Gates and forgot all about Magdalen. One morning, opening my letters in bed, I found one from Gordon to say that I had been elected a Fellow of Magdalen and was expected to present myself at the beginning of the autumn term. Again nothing about conditions or duties, simply an assumption that I should regard my election as a message from Heaven.[92]

He had got what he wanted, but naturally there was sadness at leaving Manchester and particularly at leaving Three Gates. He liked living in the country and assumed that he could do so while at Oxford, but Bruce McFarlane told him that every Fellow had to live near college. The problem appeared to be solved when McFarlane showed him Holywell Ford, a college house a hundred yards north of the main Magdalen buildings, down a lane and on the Cherwell river, secluded and quiet. Taylor, in fact, had caused more difficulties than he was later to admit. McFarlane wrote to the historian A.L Rowse, now a Fellow of All Souls who had supported Taylor's election out of admiration for his gifts, that 'He has climbed down about hours and residence. I was rather sorry, as this trouble has made me feel that we should be well rid of him. However he is going to live in Holywell Ford for three years as soon as the present Groupists have been turned out. He was quite remarkably accommodating and asked if he might call me by my Christian name. I *don't* like him.'[93] Taylor told the Bursar that he wanted the house – no Fellow was then living in it – but the Bursar's response was that 'no Fellow of the College can afford to live in such a house.' However, Taylor insisted, and found a 'cramped' furnished house (in Headington) for the academic year 1938–9 while Holywell Ford was made fit for occupation.

And so the last few weeks of the summer of 1938 were taken up with leave-taking. He stared at Kinder Scout from his garden, not bothering to plant autumn vegetables. He had a last spurt of political activity, when he spoke at a half-dozen political meetings: with the Czech crisis blowing up in the last half of September, the Manchester Peace Council organised protest meetings against Chamberlain and Taylor spoke on the theme of 'Stand Up to Hitler' (with no success: the audience wanted peace, not war). He also made a bit of money: on the day before the Munich Conference the stock markets went mad and Taylor bought some ICI shares which he sold at a good profit a few days later (when the markets had decided that war was unlikely). A few days after Munich the four of them, the Taylors plus Henrietta Werner, packed up and moved to Oxford.[94]

For Taylor, the Manchester years had been formative. Personally, he had married and begun a family, and found that his son was of overwhelming importance to him (as would be all of his children). He enjoyed a happy family life and a group of good friends. Professionally, he had established himself as an historian of present distinction and of even more future promise; he had also developed the lecturing style that would help to make him a household name and learned how to teach small groups of under-graduates and to supervise postgraduates successfully. He had begun the freelance career which would in a few years develop into such a lucrative sideline that its proceeds would dwarf his academic salary. And finally, he had blooded himself in political protest, learning what he could and could not do successfully. Oxford would be very different, not only for him, but even more so for his wife. As a result, his personal life would deteriorate even as his professional life became ever more successful.

Chapter 4

The Oxford Years 1938–1963:
The Good College Man

In England there are no schools of history; there are only individual historians. ... The English historian calls no man master. He works alone, following his own bent, thinking occasionally of the reader (though not often enough), but rarely of his colleagues and never of his critics.

A.J.P. Taylor, 'History in England', *Rumours of Wars*

... foreign affairs – the domain of history in which the 'fact' is at once most attainable and most allusive.

A.J.P. Taylor, 'Ranke: The Dedicated Historian',
Times Literary Supplement, 12 May 1950.

By moving to Oxford, Taylor transformed his future, as he was the first to recognise. Notwithstanding the *post facto* sentimentalising about Manchester in his autobiography, he was a young man on the make: he knew that to get on he had to create a national reputation and that the nearer one was to London the easier this would be. This is not to deny that he had many regrets about leaving Manchester – it is merely to deny that he seriously thought twice about the decision.

His life in Oxford was made up of a number of strands. First of all there was his academic involvement, primarily his teaching and college life. This was important to Taylor. Although he disliked teaching, he never skimped on it, and during term time it came first – indeed he sometimes turned down invitations to speak or to broadcast because of his teaching commitments. Furthermore, he was a good college man: he sat on his full share of committees, he missed only three college (governing body) meetings during his whole period as a Tutorial Fellow,[1] and he happily served as Vice-President during Magdalen's quincentennial year, with all of the extra duties which that entailed. Secondly, there was his war work, which involved the Home Guard, lecturing for the Ministry of Information, writing handbooks for the future British occupying forces and broadcasting for the BBC. Thirdly, there was his personal life, which was dominated by pain and anxiety: his parents died; his first wife fell in love first with a student and then with a poet, and the couple divorced in 1951; his second marriage was sometimes tempestuous. For Taylor, however, his son Giles and the five further children born during the Oxford period made up for most things. A fourth strand was his research and writing, in which respect this period proved his prime; it will be treated separately in the next chapter. And finally, the Oxford years saw him develop his broadcasting and journalism, to the extent that they rapidly became an equal source of satisfaction to, and a more important source of income than, his academic work. These, too, will be treated separately, in Chapter 7.

To go from the University of Manchester to the University of Oxford was to enter another world: from great city to market town, from research university to teaching university, from exuberance to understatement, from metropolitan confidence to parochial smugness.[2] Furthermore, Taylor went from a university to a college. For an Oxonian, whether student or tutor, the centre of life was the college; Taylor would have seen himself as a Fellow of Magdalen College, Oxford, rather than as a lecturer at Oxford University.[3] It was a smaller world, a more self-regarding world, a masculine world, one of some intellectual distinction, but one in which such distinction was not necessarily as highly regarded as might have been expected. Birth and piety held equal if not superior sway in much of Oxford; certainly, this had been the case in Magdalen within the memory of many of the Fellows.

Magdalen College was founded in 1458 by William of Waynflete, sometime headmaster of Winchester School, Provost of Eton, Bishop of Winchester and Lord Chancellor of England. Granted the site and buildings of St John's Hospital immediately outside the east gate of the city by King Henry VI, Magdalen was the wealthiest foundation in the university; in the words of Macaulay, one of Taylor's favourite historians, 'at the time of the general visitation in the reign of Henry the Eighth the revenues were far greater than those of any other similar institution in the realm, greater by one half than those of the magnificent foundation of Henry the Sixth at Cambridge, and considerably more than double those which William of Wykeham had settled on his college at Oxford [New College].' It is still one of the richest colleges in Oxford.[4]

The college grounds extended for more than one hundred acres, considerably more than those of any of the other Oxford colleges, and have from the beginning been celebrated for their beauty. Turning again to Macaulay, he describes Magdalen in the late seventeenth century as follows:

> A graceful tower, on the summit of which a Latin hymn was [and is] annually chanted by choristers at the dawn of May Day, caught far off the eye of the traveller who came from London. As he approached he found that this tower rose from an embattled pile, low and irregular, yet singularly venerable, which, embowered in verdure, overhung the sluggish waters of the Cherwell. He passed through a gateway overhung by a noble oriel [this gateway is now closed], and found himself in a spacious cloister adorned with emblems of virtues and vices, rudely carved in grey stone by the masons of the fifteenth century. The table of the society was plentifully spread in a stately refectory hung with paintings and rich with fantastic carving.[5]

Much building had taken place subsequently, including the New Building of 1733, with its long Georgian windows, parapet and central pediment, in which Taylor was to have his teaching rooms. The college grounds are spectacular, including, as they do, water meadows surrounded by branches of the Cherwell river, and Addison's Walk, which runs along the Cherwell between the college and Holywell Ford and which is named after the statesman and writer of Queen Anne's day. Taylor often took this route, which is a riot of flowers in the early spring, in the early mornings. New Building stands on the edge of the Grove with its herd of deer; once it was full of stately elms, but in the 1970s they were, sadly, depleted by disease.

The college itself had a moment of glory in the seventeenth century, when it defied the King, James II, who attempted to turn it into a Roman Catholic foundation by installing a President and twelve Fellows of that persuasion; James relented and on 25 October 1688 allowed the restoration of the previous incumbent President and Fellows, in an attempt to soften some of the growing opposition to his rule, before fleeing to the continent two months later during the Glorious Revolution.[6] Thereafter the college fell into a torpor, indulging its wealth in great idleness and leading to its denunciation by Edward Gibbon, who was an undergraduate there in 1752 and 1753. As he wrote in his *Autobiography*:

I spent fourteen months at Magdalen College; they proved the fourteen months the most idle and unprofitable of my whole life .... The fellows or monks of my time were decent easy men, who supinely enjoyed the gifts of the founder; their days were filled by a series of uniform employments; the chapel and the hall, the coffee-house and the common room, till they retired, weary and well satisfied, to a long slumber. From the toil of reading, or thinking, or writing, they had absolved their conscience; and the first shoots of learning and ingenuity withered on the ground, without yielding any fruits to the owners or the public.[7]

What one might call the early modern history of the college began in 1885, with the election of Herbert Warren, later Sir Herbert Warren, as President. He set out to change the character of the college, recalling in 1929 for the benefit of *Isis*, the student newspaper, that 'Magdalen had been too much identified with aestheticism, peacocks' feathers and blue china. I had been taught at Clifton and by Plato that the cult of the Muses and the Arts to which I was devoted, should be tempered by politics and athletics. I encouraged the devotees of these.'[8] Certainly by the 1920s Magdalen was a college of hearties. Warren had also set out to transform it in another way. A legendary snob, he encouraged the scions of the aristocracy and the gentry, particularly their wealthier examples, to come up to Magdalen, frequently regardless of their academic potential – a Student (Fellow) of Christ Church later referred to 'Warren's policy of peopling the college exclusively with illiterate lords, who were always sent down long before competing for degrees'.[9] One student was Prince Chichibu, the son of the Japanese Emperor. According to legend, 'On his first day in the college Chichibu, following custom . . . called on President Warren – well-known as an incorrigible lover of blue blood. What, asked Warren, did the name Chichibu actually mean? "The Son of God" came the reply. "Oh well," said Warren, "you'll find we have the sons of many famous men here."'[10] A later Fellow of Magdalen admitted that the college 'did not spurn academic distinction amongst its undergraduates but had hitherto not gone out of its way to demand it.'[11] Magdalen, in short, was something of a finishing school for the rich, well-born and dim.

Yet when Warren retired in 1929 a revolution was already under way, attributed by Taylor solely to one man, the philosopher T.D. Weldon, always known as Harry. According to Taylor:

Harry had come back from the first war an iconoclast, to find Magdalen sleepy, oldfashioned and still much as it had been in Gibbon's day. He had ruthlessly turned it upsidedown, insisting on merit instead of high connexions as the main reason for admission and on efficient teaching rather than piety as the main qualification for a Fellow. By the time I came to Magdalen he had largely succeeded. The college now prided itelf, somewhat excessively I thought, on its intellectual distinction. Underneath there was a great deal of the old Magdalen, complacent and aloof.[12]

Certainly by the time Taylor became a Fellow there was a corpus of distinguished Fellows. One was C.S. Lewis, who had joined the college as Fellow and Tutor in English in 1925, a distinguished literary scholar who eventually became much better known for his spiritual writings, including those for children, the Narnia series. According to Taylor, 'intellectually he was as destructive as Harry and yet professed an urgent Low Church piety which he preached everywhere except in the college common room.' To annoy Lewis, Taylor occasionally proposed that the chapel be turned into a swimming pool.[13] Lewis attracted his share of anecdotes. One relates that he insisted on starting his lectures punctually on the hour; however, he seldom managed to get to the lecture room on time and so would begin whilst strolling up the High Street, entering the hall already well into his third paragraph.[14] Lewis's colleague in English was C.T. Onions, University Reader in English Philology and Leverhulme Research Fellow. According to Taylor, he was probably 'the most distinguished scholar at Magdalen when I went there. Starting as a teacher in a primary school he had become editor of the Oxford English Dictionary and when I knew him, was collecting material for a supplement.[15] This made him more at home with contemporary idioms than any of us were. It also led to an accumulation of "filthy words", which had been excluded from the original dictionary – a curious interest for a pious Anglo Catholic with eleven children.'[16]

There were the philosophers. One was Weldon himself, whom Taylor considered the most stimulating of the Fellows: primarily interested in political philosophy, he began his philosophical life as an orthodox follower of Kant, while ending up approving of the linguistic analysis being done by his colleagues J.L. Austin and Geoffrey Warnock and others.[17] He was to prove a strong supporter of Taylor at moments of minor crisis in 1952 and 1957. Weldon, however, had his detractors amongst the undergraduates. They believed that, on meritocratic grounds, he turned down every single Etonian who applied for admission, and in protest all of the Etonians already up at the college demonstrated in the quad against Weldon, 'the

Red Dean'.[18] There was the considerably more distinguished philosopher J.L. Austin, memorably described by Ved Mehta: 'To look at, he was a tall and thin man, a sort of parody on the desiccated don. His face suggested an osprey. His voice was flat and metallic, and seemed to be stuck on a note of disillusion. It sounded like a telephone speaking by itself.' Taylor, however, had a warmer view of him, recalling that he was 'an abler man than either Harry or Lewis and also a more attractive character. I came to love him though his mind was beyond mine. When I came to Oxford a by-election was on, with Munich as the principal topic of controversy and Quintin Hogg as the pro-Munich candidate. Austin coined the slogan: "A vote for Hogg is a vote for Hitler." I told him that this was the only proposition of his I ever understood.'[19]

Taylor succeeded the distinguished historian of the French Revolution J.M. Thompson, a man with an interesting history of his own. In 1905 he had become Dean of Divinity at Magdalen but had developed Doubts, and in 1911 he published a book, *Miracles in the New Testament*, in which he expressed them. Other churchmen were scandalised and various church dignitaries, including the Bishop of Oxford, tried to get Magdalen to dismiss him; indeed, the Bishop of Winchester, Visitor of Magdalen, withdrew Thompson's licence to exercise a cure of souls in the college, but Thompson was so popular with the other Fellows that he was immediately re-elected to his Tutorial Fellowship. He resigned as Dean in 1915, however, and attempted to engage in war work, but found that he was unacceptable as an army chaplain and went off to teach at Eton instead. He then returned to Magdalen, now purely as Fellow and Tutor in Modern History.[20] Taylor had attended his lectures on the French Revolution as an undergraduate; this was one of his favourite periods of history and it was therefore fortunate that he was at Oxford, since between the wars Thompson was the sole British authority on the revolution.

Thompson was the modern historian; the two other History Fellows were S.G. Lee, a specialist in the Tudor and Stuart periods, and K.B. McFarlane, a mediaevalist. Stephen Lee, Fellow and Tutor since 1919 and Vice-President in 1933–4, has left only a modest legacy as an historian: one book, written with Sir James Berry and entitled *A Cromwellian Major-General: The Career of Colonel James Berry*, published in 1938, and some anecdotes. They include the following description: 'This delightful man, universally known as "Luggins", had a distinguished rowing career and was a rowing coach. As tutor he was not ideal. At the end of an essay he would say "That is very interesting. I have learned a lot".' The writer added that 'Personally I felt that it should have been the other way around. For what was I paying ten pounds per term for tuition?'[21] Bruce McFarlane, a mediaevalist, was an altogether more significant historian. Taylor described him thus:

> McFarlane ... [had] professed Communist views. We were close colleagues for twenty five years and never had a cross word. But we really did not see eye to eye. I thought that a scholar who was any good should write books as his principal task. Bruce, though I am told a scholar of the first rank, put teaching first and published little during his lifetime – whether because he was a perfectionist or because he shrank from criticism I could not decide. As a matter of fact I do not think he was quite of the first rank. He had great learning and took great pains, but it seemed to me that in the last resort he lacked judgement. Also, like most homosexuals, he was neurotic, easily involved with his pupils, whether for or against, and often emotional over college business. While he was alive I hardly confessed these criticisms even to myself. Now I am inclined to think that his admiring pupils have built him up more than he deserved.[22]

McFarlane, who was elected a Fellow by Examination in 1927 and a Tutorial Fellow in 1928, was one of the group of young dons who had supported Weldon's drive to improve the intellectual quality of the Magdalen undergraduates. He spent his entire career at Magdalen, turning down the offer of Jacob's chair at Manchester. Devoted to research, particularly in the administrative and then the social and cultural history of the fifteenth century, he spent thousands of happy hours in archives and record offices, public and private, up and down the land. He was immensely learned. What he could not seem to do was publish. As A.L. Rowse, for decades a close friend, was later to write, 'We all considered that he suffered from a writing-block – as sometimes he did. But that was not it. He was writing away, then rewriting, actually writing out lectures at full length, and giving papers to various societies. Above all he was pursuing research: that was his passion. And he was a perfectionist.'[23]

Gerald Harriss has called McFarlane 'one of the most original and influential medieval historians of the post war years. He reshaped the thinking and research of two generations of scholars about English society in the late middle ages ... In his lifetime he published only one small book, on John Wycliffe, and several seminal articles but his influence and reputation were considerable.'[24] The foundation of this influence was his teaching, through which he trained a number of the most important late mediaevalists of the second half of the twentieth century. Not only did this absorb a good deal of time and energy, but he also cultivated personal relationships with those with whom he shared a love of mediaeval history; Harriss, one of his former students, wrote of him, 'a shy and deeply sensitive man, of somewhat fragile health and temperament, he set a high value on personal relationships and was rewarded by the devoted friendship of many in and outside his academic circle.'[25] It is a curious fact that the fostering came full circle. McFarlane did not publish much during his lifetime but threw himself into training his pupils, and it was only by the efforts of a few of these pupils that his *Nachlass* was turned into books of essays and published after his death, thereby increasing his reputation and ensuring its continuation.[26]

It is difficult to recapture the relationship between Taylor and McFarlane. It was obviously civilised in public. In the early years of Taylor's sojourn at Magdalen it was probably friendly: as already noted, McFarlane was sometimes to be found at Taylor's kitchen table in Holywell Ford for coffee after dinner. It is possible that McFarlane's letter to Rowse, quoted in the last chapter, had been written hastily in a mood of annoyance and that Taylor's friendliness had won him over. It probably helped that they shared to some extent a political ideology (Rowse claimed that the primary reason that he had supported Taylor and had encouraged McFarlane to do so too was to strengthen the left in the History Faculty), although McFarlane seems to have been much more of a Marxist than Taylor ever was – as Karl Leyser later wrote, 'he shared the move to the Left of many English intellectuals of his generation, even to the far Left.'[27] For many years he ran a trade-union summer school in Magdalen. They were both members of the Pink Lunch Club before the war, 'which brought together all of Oxford's donnish left-wingers', including A.J. Ayer, Frank and Elizabeth Pakenham, Isaiah Berlin, Stuart Hampshire, Richard Crossman, J.L. Austin, G.D.H. Cole, James Meade, Roy Harrod, Robert Hall and Redvers Opie,[28] and there is a strong possibility that it was McFarlane who first invited Taylor along.

Judging from his comments, Taylor thought that he and McFarlane were friends. But McFarlane was a critical man, as even his friends admitted. Gerald Harriss has written that 'as a person he was shy, fastidious and aloof, and was feared for his acerbic and deflating comments', while Rees Davies has emphasised an 'intellectual honesty and integrity of almost terrifying proportions . . . Such uncompromising mental honesty cannot have made life easy for him; nor did it always make life comfortable for his friends.'[29] Rowse was to write many years later that Taylor 'gave his senior colleague constant trouble'; and referring to McFarlane's depicting the reformer John Wycliffe as 'rather specifically an academic trouble-maker', Rowse concluded that 'I realised whom he had in mind for this part – his troublesome colleague A.J.P. Taylor.'[30]

The only available primary evidence for McFarlane's feelings about Taylor are his published letters, which begin in 1940. By 1950 he is making almost uniformly disparaging remarks about Taylor. In May 1950, with regard to a review by Taylor in the *Times Literary Supplement* on the nineteenth-century German historian Leopold von Ranke – which had caused quite a controversy and elicited letters from several other historians – McFarlane wrote to Norman Scarfe, 'And did you read Alan Taylor on Ranke in the *T.L.S.*? If he goes on like this, working himself up and dancing like mad, he'll burst; and oh dear where's his judgement?'[31] In June 1954, upon Taylor's declining to be considered for a chair at Edinburgh, McFarlane wrote to Gerald Harriss that this 'doesn't please the President (nor me) so much'.[32] And finally, he commented on Taylor's Ford Lectures at Oxford:

> One thing I've missed today apart from the college meeting is Alan Taylor's fourth Ford Lecture. So far he has provided high class entertainment without either new light or new knowledge. Why he likes 'dissent' becomes clear; it never had to do anything practical; opposition foreign policy, not of the front bench but of the wildest back benchers, is the only kind he feels any sympathy with; it was always against, never for anything; Alan is revealing himself as fundamentally a nihilist; and yet he thinks the liberals of 1848 absurd because they achieved nothing![33]

It seems possible that McFarlane, who must have voted for Taylor when he was offered the Fellowship in 1938, gradually lost his respect for him because of, as he perceived it, Taylor's lack of critical judgement, his pandering to an audience ('high class entertainment') and his lack of new research. The last-named criticism is hardly sustainable – there are other kinds of research than McFarlane's, besides which twentieth-century papers were not yet open to historians – but the first two, being matters of opinion, could certainly be honestly held, and were so by others besides McFarlane. Having said that, it should also be pointed out that, in the same year, Taylor was elected a Fellow of the British Academy, an honour not usually given to the lightweight. It is probably significant, however, that the two clashed in 1942 over the election of a successor to Gordon as President of Magdalen, and from this may have stemmed much of McFarlane's distrust, given that he was an unsuccessful candidate (see below).

But this was in the future. Having been elected in June 1938, Taylor was officially admitted as Probationer Fellow on 12 October 1938. At Magdalen this was hardly a matter of calling in and collecting a key; there was an actual ceremony, as C.S. Lewis had related to his father thirteen years before:

> It was a formidable ceremony, and not entirely to my taste. Without any warning of what was in store for me, the Vice-President ushered me into a room where I found the whole household – it is large at Magdalen [thirty-one Fellows were to attend the day of Taylor's admission]. Warren (the President) was standing, and when the V.P. laid a red cushion at his feet I realised with some displeasure that this was going to be a kneeling affair. Warren then addressed me for some five minutes in Latin. I was able to follow some three quarters of what he said; but no one told me what response I was to make, and it was with some hesitation that I hazarded *do fidem* [I give allegiance] as a reply .... This appeared to fill the bill. I was then told in English to kneel. When I had done so, Warren took me by the hand and raised me with the words, 'I wish you joy'. It sounds well enough on paper, but it was hardly impressive in fact; and I tripped over my gown in rising. I now thought my ordeal at an end; but I was never more mistaken in my life. I was sent all round the table and every single member in turn shook my hand and repeated the words: 'I wish you joy'. You can hardly imagine how odd it sounded by the twenty-fifth repetition. English people have not the talent for graceful ceremonial. They go through it lumpishly and with a certain mixture of defiance and embarrassment, as if everyone felt he was being rather silly, and was at the same time ready to shoot down anyone who said so.[34]

Taylor never related a similar story, so it is possible that it had been toned down with the change of President from Warren to George Gordon in 1929, although Gordon's wife later wrote that 'as a lover of tradition, dignified ceremonial and established forms he did not permit these to be sacrificed to emergency or haste'; certainly a Prize Fellow elected in 1969 recalled that he went through a version of the same ceremony.[35] What

Taylor does relate was that he found the college 'in bad shape', although, he said, he did not immediately realise it.

> The college was … at loggerheads with its bursar. Ten years before the then bursar, an elderly clergyman, had made off with some of the college funds. He was of course dismissed and the college decided this time to appoint an efficient administrator. They imported a civil servant from the Sudan, and he, in true civil servant fashion, thought it his main duty to thwart the Fellows in every way. By the time I arrived every college meeting was a brawl. There was a committee to supervise the bursar, and the bursar protesting against such treatment. Under such circumstances college business fell into chaos.[36]

Another charge Taylor made was that Gordon was a 'lax administrator', curious since Gordon's letters show that he spent a good deal of his life administering; indeed, he served as Vice-Chancellor during the early years of the war. The evidence Taylor adduces was that 'he did not enforce a statute that I must sleep in college for my first three years … a fortunate lapse for I should have resigned at once if he had attempted to do so.' It is likely that Gordon, a happily married man himself, thought it would be ridiculous to enforce the rule on Taylor and quietly let it lapse. Certainly another colleague remembered that 'in the years before the war many changes were effected with very little friction, and this was largely due to the President.' It is likely that this was one of them.[37]

What did continue, however, was the traditional collective social life as exemplified by dining in college. Free dinners were part of a Fellow's remuneration, and married Fellows might well stay to dine after teaching; besides, many of the Fellows were bachelors and Magdalen was their home. In most of the Oxford colleges dress was formal, but this was not the case in Magdalen; black tie was required only on Sundays and then only if the President dined, in which case a note would be sent round to all Fellows warning them. The Fellows gathered in the Senior Common Room for a glass of sherry while the undergraduates took their places in what was (and is) the beautiful Hall. At one end a gallery for choristers and musicians rises above the entrance doors; at the other, a wall of richly carved sixteenth-century panelling can be seen behind the dais, on which stands High Table. At 7.15 pm, the traditional time for dinner in Oxford colleges, the Fellows, all wearing their gowns (as were the students), entered in procession, led by the President or Vice-President, with the rest following in order of seniority. They also took their places at table in order of seniority, which made for a certain sameness in dinner partners. The President, Vice-President or senior Fellow would say a grace in Latin, after which everyone would be seated and dinner could begin.

There is a description of such a dinner by a Magdalen undergraduate of the 1930s:

> College servants carried large trays of food to the high table. Five courses were usually served: soup; an entrée or fish course; meat, game, or poultry; a pudding; and a savoury. Luxuries, such as oysters, smoked salmon, or caviar, would sometimes be served. The food was carried around on large silver dishes from which fellows would help themselves. French or German wine was the most usual drink, but a fellow could order what he liked for himself and his guest, if he had one. The meal was leisurely and the diners talkative .... Dinner at hall, especially in winter, was a lovely sight. The great room was lit entirely by table lamps screened with silk shades. There was sufficient light to dimly illuminate the low-pitched oak roof.[38]

(According to Taylor, the only thing that changed during the war was that four courses rather than five were served; however, his Economics colleague, David Worswick, remembered that the number of courses was reduced to three during the war, raised to four immediately afterwards, but reduced to three again in the late 1940s or early 1950s.)

After the savoury had been eaten, the dons who were going to take wine (called dessert at most other Oxford colleges)

> would hang their gowns up in the vestibule of the Smoking Room, and then move to the candle-lit Senior Common Room next door, where dishes of fruit and nuts were laid, and the decanters looked full. Here the president, if he was present, no longer presided; in the Common Room his status was that of a guest. His place was taken by the vice-president or, in his absence, by the senior Fellow present. At small circular tables, ranged in a semi-circle facing the fire, a guest would be paired with a Fellow other than his host. The vice-president would help himself to a glass of wine, vintage port, Madeira, claret or brown sherry and then the decanters were passed from hand to hand, everyone pouring out a glass. When the table nearest the fire was reached, the decanters were placed in turn on the moving carriage of an ingenious funicular 'railway' which

transmitted them across the fireplace to the table opposite, to continue on their journey from table to table in the other half of the circle, finally reaching the vice-president again. The wines were very good. If someone chanced to empty the decanter without filling his glass he was – and is – entitled to a buzz, an extra glass filled from a fresh decanter.[39]

Meanwhile, 'nuts would be cracked and fruit eaten with silver fruit knives and forks. For many of the older dons, wine in the Common Room was the happiest time of the day. Conversation was far-reaching, and it was not thought correct to talk about one's own professional subject of study. After the wine had been drunk, there came a pinch of snuff and coffee. Then the dons would return to their rooms or houses.'[40]

Taylor enjoyed dinner (although 'the grand dinner on Sunday night I never attended at all')[41] and was known as a witty dining companion. He was not, however, one of those who dined several evenings a week: on the whole he preferred being at home with Giles, and then with his other children (Sebastian, born 1940, Amelia, born 1944, and Sophia, born 1945. Crispin, born 1955, and Daniel, born 1957, his sons by his second wife, never lived in Oxford with their father, but in London). In other ways as well he gradually cut himself off, at least partially, from the social aspects of the communal life. Naturally he breakfasted at home. Furthermore, he never had lunch with the other Fellows, who had a hot meal in the dining room, preferring – as he had done as a student – to eat bread and cheese in his rooms. Throughout his life he insisted that lunch destroyed the working day.

In addition, during his first year the Taylors lived some way from the college, renting a small furnished house on the Marston Road in Heading-ton, a suburb of Oxford east of Magdalen. This was because Holywell Ford, the college house a hundred yards behind Magdalen where he would live until 1953, did not become available until October 1939. The Taylors found their first year in Oxford a bit dispiriting. The music they heard was definitely inferior – amateurish compared with the Hallé; the countryside around Oxford could not compare with Kinder Scout; they knew hardly anyone outside Magdalen, except for the future Labour politician Richard Crossman, then a Fellow of New College, whom they met building a Guy Fawkes's Day bonfire; and they were living in the depressing house in Headington. Early in 1939 Taylor sold Three Gates in Higher Disley, for £825. He and Margaret cheered themselves up by spending a month in Morocco at Easter, leaving Giles at home with Henrietta; Taylor made few trips outside Europe and this was one of them, one he found extremely interesting and enjoyed tremendously – he even wrote about it in the *Manchester Guardian*.[42] However, he never revisited North Africa.

That year the Taylors spent Christmas in Preston, almost the last time Taylor was to see his father: his next sight of him was to watch him die. Percy Taylor wrote to his son in the New Year that he had his usual bronchitis but was shaking it off. The following weekend he went out to pay the household bills, and immediately thereafter developed pneumonia. As Taylor later wrote, 'I was summoned and arrived to see him literally draw his last breath.' He died in February 1940, and Taylor travelled to Preston for the funeral. His father was buried in the local cemetery, and around his coffin was wrapped the Red Flag, 'emblazoned with hammer and sickle ... "Percy Taylor believed man to be naturally good", read his obituary in the *Preston Herald*: "if men behaved anti-socially it was because circumstances, particularly the environment of a capitalist civilisation, had perverted them. He believed an earthly paradise a distinct possibility, but had no belief at all in paradises after this life." Out of the capital of £100,000 which he had acquired by selling his share of the business in the early 1920s, only about £9,000 remained: the rest had been loaned or given away.[43]

The death of his father left Taylor with a practical problem: what to do about his mother. When he had been home for Christmas, his father had told him that she had not long to live; indeed, Taylor believed that his father was wearing himself out looking after her. In any event, she was by now a helpless invalid. Taylor had her brought down to Oxford in an ambulance and installed her in a nursing home. This did not serve: according to one source, she was badly neglected, and when Taylor's uncle, Harry Thompson, and a niece came to visit her, they found that a hot-water bottle had burned through her flesh to the bone. After an unpleasant scene between Taylor and his uncle, she was moved to a house in North Oxford, where she had two nurses to look after her. Harry Sara came to visit her once a month, although she barely recognised him. Taylor himself went to visit her two or three times a week, dutifully rather than affectionately, although this was only to be expected. By one account, he resented the expense of caring for her until she died, in 1946. Even when he later described her death, Taylor added no word of affection for her. This was true of his entire autobiography.[44]

Taylor's main occupation during his first year – and of all his years at Magdalen during term – was his teaching. This was made up of three components, lecturing, tutoring and supervising postgraduate students.

The lecturing system at Oxford (and Cambridge) was (and is) peculiar in that students need never attend lectures and, because they are not examined on the material contained in the lectures as such, many seldom do, preferring to sleep, spend the hours in the library or have coffee with friends. Taylor, however, was rapidly to achieve a reputation as a lecturer for whom it was worth getting out of bed – which he made them do: he was possibly the only lecturer, certainly the only one in the History Faculty, who lectured at 9 am rather than the usual starting hour of 10 am.[45] According to one description:

> he would be informally dressed in a corduroy suit with a bow-tie. He liked to encourage the idea that he had come unprepared; 'Now, what am I going to say this morning?' he asked one undergraduate who walked with him from a tutorial as [he] was on his way to give a lecture. He told Isaiah Berlin that he decided the first half of the lecture while walking around Addison's Walk beforehand; the second half was pure ham. The Hall at Magdalen would be full; indeed later in the War the crush was such that he had to relocate to the Examination Schools, where the largest lecture-hall in the university was to be found. As the bells sounded in Magdalen Tower, [Taylor] walked down the central aisle, pointedly removed the lectern placed on the dais, and leaned back on the top table. He cast a rapid glance over the assembled throng and then began speaking. The voice was strong, clear, measured, flat – no obvious rhetorical tricks, no notes, hardly a gesture, and rarely a pause. When he came to the climax there would be a great surge of sound. The lectures were studded with anecdotes, and the occasional familiar prejudice – 'The Germans have all the ghastly virtues. Clean streets!' – or brilliant aside – 'The chief requirement for anyone accepting ministerial office is the constitution of an ox.' He ended just as the bells rang out once more. At this signal, he announced the topic for the next lecture and strode out.[46]

Taylor lectured on various aspects of European history – for example, the arguments of his book *The Origins of the Second World War* made their first public appearance in 1961 as a set of undergraduate lectures.[47] After the war, he would join Alan Bullock, Fellow and Tutor at New College, and William Deakin, Fellow of St Antony's, to encourage the teaching of modern European history in Oxford. In his first years, however, he was busy getting up his college teaching, which was largely on nineteenth- and twentieth-century English history.

Taylor always made it clear that he did not like the tutorial system, writing in his autobiography that 'there is something to be said for an occasional long session with a really able pupil. The others are far better handled in threes or fours.'[48] Tutorials were usually one-to-one. The student would be given an essay topic, couched in the form of a question – 'To what extent was Disraeli responsible for the destruction of the mid-Victorian party system?' – and a list of books and articles to read; the student would go off to the library, read and think, write an essay of about eight handwritten sides in length and return the following week at the same hour to his tutor. Here he would read out his work and the two of them would discuss it. For the student this could be challenging. For the tutor, talking about Disraeli for, say, the seventh time that week, could be interesting and even stimulating with an able pupil, but deadening with the dull.

Taylor had other criticisms of the tutorial system: 'At Manchester we had been concerned to train historians. Magdalen, like all the other colleges, was interested only in getting high examination marks for the pupils. The Final Honours School was scrutinized like a table in the Football League. How many Firsts did we get? The teaching was geared to this aim. The individual [tutorials] ... were essentially cram sessions. The good tutor was the one who taught his pupils the best tricks for passing examinations. The system, apart from being the reverse of scholarly, was time-consuming. I always resented it.'[49] Nevertheless, he did his duty. Indeed, one of his colleagues confirmed that Taylor never cut corners in his teaching.[50]

Anecdotes abound about being taught by Taylor. A thoughtful and coherent description is that by William Thomas, who was first taught by him in the academic year 1957–8, Thomas's second year: 'He received us in rooms that were sparsely furnished and smelled strongly of stale pipe smoke. There was an L.S. Lowry on the wall to show allegiance to Manchester, and a stuffed owl in a glass dome on a neighbouring bookcase, and no hint of taste in the furniture or hangings. All was austerely utilitarian, College Bursar's issue.' There was material on his stockmarket investments on his desk and a china model of Napoleon III on horseback. 'He usually wore an elephant grey corduroy suit, neither too formal for daily work nor too informal for High Table – the sort of suit a man chooses who is too busy to worry about his appearance.' Sometimes, however, he wore a red velvet waistcoat whilst teaching, and frequently a smart bow tie, not the habit of someone unconcerned about his appearance. 'He was not intimidating, and his quick talkative manner set one at one's ease, but he gave the impression of a man getting as quickly as possible through a duty rather than one enjoying the company and meeting the needs of the young.' Taylor in 1953 was giving tutorials fourteen hours a week, a life of drudgery for one who did not often enjoy it – rather like having to cook meals every day if one does not enjoy cooking. The comparison here must be with McFarlane, who enjoyed teaching.[51]

Thomas recalled Taylor's response as students read out their essays to him. He

> looked at one attentively with those hooded eyes like an intelligent owl, occasionally interrupting if one made a mistake or expressed a matter obscurely, but usually reserving his comments till the end, when he would talk, insistently and rather dogmatically. Then at last one had the feeling of a sharp intelligence playing over a huge store of knowledge, and he would make this knowledge memorable by striking a deliberately provocative attitude. He had plenty to say. One might have misstated an issue at a crucial point in a Cabinet crisis: he would restate it. One might have said [Charles James] Fox was a gambler and a playboy: he would say on the contrary that he was the ablest and most idealistic of the Whigs. He would back up his version with illustrations and quotations. Many of the anecdotes had improved with the telling. Not all of the paradoxes were fresh. But as talk, it was riveting because both vivid and authoritative. Taylor was a born story-teller, and the warm Lancashire vowels, and habit of dropping his voice and retailing some perception of a politician's motivation in a near murmur as if it were a secret to be used discreetly, gave a racy and popular intimacy to the story of High Policy, as if he had been there with Boswell and Horace Walpole, Creevey and Sydney Smith, Charles Greville and Thackeray, and shared their sense of the fascination and absurdity of the world of eighteenth- and nineteenth-century England.[52] He had a way of delivering a criticism with his small tight smile, as if to say, if only you knew. Then abruptly, towards the end of the hour, he would tell us the next essay topic and on the hour we were dismissed. We had had our measure for the week.[53]

Others fill in details:

> Alan sat with his eyes half-closed, stroking a Siamese cat [called Colette] on his lap and often smoking a pipe. Sometimes he would use the stem of his pipe to worry a prominent wart on his forehead. He seemed not to be

listening, though if something in the essay particularly irritated him he might utter a shriek of pain ... He liked being argued with, but not being contradicted – 'Don't you bandy dates with me.' When Karl Leyser, himself later a Magdalen don and professor of medieval history, politely corrected a mistake Alan had made, Alan leapt to his feet and grabbed a volume of *Die Grosse Politik* [sic] from the shelf, brandishing it like a weapon to defend his argument. He was very emotional, almost weeping.[54]

His approach to postgraduate (i.e. graduate) supervision was rather different. He took background knowledge for granted and talked to the student rather more as an equal. On subjects he knew well, such as the Second World War, he took a close interest; on those where his knowledge of the events, and the archives, was less comprehensive, such as Anglo-American relations during the First World War, his interest was more detached, but kindly. What he never did was to push a line, or attempt to create a Taylor school, either for subject or for methodology. As one of his postgraduate students was later to write, 'Of all the historians I have ever met, Taylor possessed the quickest and sharpest intellect. When attacked, he could certainly give as good as he got, and better. But he was never an intellectual bully.'[55] He also let students make their own mistakes – or achieve their own triumphs. He never had vast numbers of research students, though he had enough, but it is worth remembering that for many Oxford (and Cambridge) dons of a certain age, a doctorate was believed to be unnecessary – an Oxbridge First was enough; Taylor certainly told one of his students not to bother with a D.Phil. but just to write a book. Possibly as a consequence it was only some years after the war that he began to have postgraduate students in any numbers at all – by 1967 by he was supervising an average of five a year.[56]

In October 1939 the Taylors finally moved to Holywell Ford. War had begun the previous month, and moving in to Holywell Ford during the blackout had its challenges. Furthermore, in many respects the house was unsatisfactory. As Taylor later wrote, 'the College bursar, who had disapproved of my getting the house [on the grounds that a young Fellow could not possibly afford it – he clearly did not know about Taylor's freelance income], took the excuse of the war to say that the College could not afford any decorating or improvements. So we settled into a house that was shabby, cold, and so badly wired for electricity as to be a constant fire risk.' But, he adds, 'we thought nothing of it.'[57] He also took over the garden and found it harder work than at Higher Disley: it was larger, the soil was heavier and manure was unobtainable. It needed a full-time gardener, but during the war there were no spare men. Undergraduates helped out at first; later he did it all himself and 'the labour nearly killed me, but I raised vegetables for a large household during the war, to say nothing of apples and other fruits. I also kept hens and, when I realised their greater productivity, Khaki Campbell ducks.' The ducks laid their eggs early and were then turned loose on the river, to be fed by people walking along the banks. The livestock were a mixed blessing – profitable, but as bad a tie as children, since they too had to be fed and put to bed, and there were foxes just waiting to pounce.[58]

Although Taylor was given teaching rooms in New Building, once war was declared the college was subject to governmental commandeering. Magdalen had been allotted to the Judicial Committee of the Privy Council in an elaborate plan for evacuating London that was never put into action. By mid-September, as C.S. Lewis wrote to his brother, 'the Fellows have just been informed that New Building will not be used by Govt and that Fellows' rooms in particular will be inviolable.' Taylor recalled that the Bursar had told him that because of the government plans there would be no teaching room for him, and he had agreed to teach at home at Holywell Ford instead; presumably this suited him because, in spite of the availability of New Building, he taught at home for the period of the war. This enabled him to indulge in his favourite form of entertainment for undergraduates: music parties. As he later wrote, 'we had one really large room, perfect for my gramophone with its big horn, and we were soon having music parties for undergraduates once or twice a week.' These were still going on in the late 1950s, but now in his rooms in New Building, as Sir John Coles recalled: 'the musical evening . . . was a weekly affair . . . It consisted mostly of silent listening to Taylor's music and drinking rather ordinary claret.' He also remembered 'Taylor having some of us to dinner in his rooms, when he introduced us to his North country favourites such as black pudding and cheese *with* apple pie.'[59]

Taylor's daily routine was established early on. He was up early and always took a cold bath, as noted earlier, a habit from his prep-school days (although one observer said that 'cold bath meant: jump in and out of the cold water within a second').[60] He went for a brisk walk before breakfast, along Addison's Walk; in summer he and Lewis used sometimes to meet at 7.30 am to bathe at what was called the College Bathing Place in the Cherwell at the other end of Addison's Walk. Then back for breakfast, with lumpy porridge, *sans* milk and sugar for the children. Then to his desk, where he would first deal with his post and his investments. Thereafter came the principal business of the day, at least during term, which was teaching. Lunch was at home, probably in his study, with bread and cheese the main fare; this was followed by a walk; then it was back to work, teaching or writing. In the evening he spent time with family or friends, gardening or listening to music; in addition he sometimes worked, or so he told Magdalen colleagues while drinking Malvern water rather than port after dinner. At 10.15 pm he went to bed.[61]

The other constant element in his routine, as in that of every other Oxford don, was governing the college and administrative duties. During his first year at Magdalen Taylor had nothing to do with most of this owing to Magdalen's custom, shared with a number of other colleges, of considering a Fellow as on probation for his first year; only then was he 'admitted to Actuality'. Taylor began as a Probationer Fellow on 12 October 1938; he was then admitted to Actuality, along with the scientist Peter Medawar (a future Nobel Prizewinner), on 18 October 1939. This coincided with the first month of the war, and by the following March ten Magdalen Fellows had been granted leave of absence for war work, with many others following later. However, the teaching still had to be done: as Lewis wrote to his brother, 'we *are* going to have a term and quite a lot of undergraduates up.' This meant that the administrative work also had to be done and, as one of the Fellows still in Oxford, Taylor took on his fair share.[62]

Oxford colleges are run by their Fellows, who in Taylor's time met three times a term to set policy, elect Fellows and generally deal with all subjects great and small. Their decisions were then implemented by the Bursar and the college staff, who would deal with such matters as estates, finance, student matters, the needs of the Fellows and the college servants, including kitchen staff, scouts, gardeners and cleaners. In other words, a small-to-medium-sized organisation was (and in Oxford still is) run on a part-time basis by Fellows, the bulk of whose energy is absorbed elsewhere. The paid staff often have a sceptical view of the talents of Fellows in this context, and relations, though often warm and mutually regarding, can be cool and tense. It is clear from Taylor's autobiography that the latter was the case in his early years at Magdalen, with warfare sometimes breaking out between the Fellows and the Bursar.

It is piquant to note that Taylor's first post of responsibility was on the Bursarial Committee, set up to oversee the Bursar, to which he was appointed in October 1941. Things had not improved with the appointment of a new Estates Bursar in 1940. As Taylor wrote:

We had at last got rid of our unsatisfactory bursar, only to get one more unsatisfactory still. Mark van Oss was a friend of Harry Weldon's, pushed on us as someone who would make a welcome fourth at bridge. ... Van Oss was an easy-going barrister who had decided that wartime life would be more comfortable in Oxford than in London. He had no qualifications for managing College affairs and little interest in doing so. Much to my regret I was drawn into College administration, a sphere where I soon became efficient, at any rate more so than Van Oss. I sat on most of the College committees and compensated for the waste of time by knitting scarves for the forces, an accomplishment I had acquired during the first world war.[63]

Taylor did not exaggerate his administrative duties. The Bursarial Committee was followed in December 1942 by additional appointments to the Grants and the Fabric Committees, and in May 1943 to a new Fabric and Grounds Committee. In 1943 he became Secretary to the Tutorial Committee, and at the College Meeting held on 13 October 1943, which was attended by only fourteen Fellows – in 1938 there had been forty-two – he was put on a committee of four whose purpose was to decide on the disposition of a legacy of £500 left to the college (they decided to use the income from it to provide the wine at an annual dinner arranged for and by the undergraduates). In December 1943 he was appointed Secretary to the Governing Body, and on March 1944 Secretary of the Fellowship Committee. Presumably arising out of the former position, he took on the task of revising the college byelaws, his draft proposals for which were accepted and immediately implemented and for which the College Meeting minuted their thanks. In November 1944 he was elected Clerk to the College. By February 1945, three-sevenths of his salary from Magdalen arose from his administrative duties.[64]

These were, on the whole, routine duties, but there was one episode that was fraught with politics and emotion. This was the appointment of a new President, following on the death of President Gordon from cancer in March 1942. Taylor took part in the election process and so did McFarlane, and it is from this episode that McFarlane's animosity may date. In the early, informal discussions amongst the Fellows, one name put forward was that of Sir Henry Tizard, former Demy (Scholar) of Magdalen, Scientific Adviser to the Minister of Aircraft Production and Rector of Imperial College, London. Tizard's principal backer was the Chemistry Fellow, Leslie Sutton, but he was backed by non-scientists as well, some of whom welcomed the idea that Magdalen should be the first Oxford college since the seventeenth century to have a scientist as head. However, it is also fair to say that a number of Fellows were hostile, not to Tizard himself but to the idea of a scientist as head of a college. Taylor's view was that 'Tizard was a dynamic force who would awaken the College from its mediaeval slumbers', and he became one of his strongest backers.[65]

There were other candidates. A strong external one was Sir Alexander Carr-Saunders, who fell out of the race when it was discovered that he was bound to remain as head of the London School of Economics and Political Science until the end of the war. According to the Londoner's Diary of the *Evening Standard* newspaper, there were originally several internal candidates – Lewis, Thompson and McFarlane; the last-named, being Vice-President of Magdalen and currently Acting President, was conducting the election. According to McFarlane, however, Lewis was never seriously considered and Thompson had been eliminated early on. There were fierce disputes within the college and, according to Taylor, matters were made worse by the fact that P.V.M. Benecke, Fellow since 1891 and Senior Fellow, presided over the discussions and was congenitally obscure. (Tizard reported to one of the Fellows that 'I have just had a talk with Benecke and I don't know whether I am to be elected President or have no chance.')[66]

Tizard came to dine at Magdalen in April. He was lively and amusing, but nervous, and some of the Fellows thought that he seemed self-important and inclined to show off; furthermore, the rumour was that he tended to be tyrannical at Imperial College, not something that would fit in well with the democracy of a governing body. Others worried that he was too narrowly scientific and by definition less interested in the college as a great and historical institution: they failed to understand his deep devotion to Magdalen and to Oxford, dating from his own days as an undergraduate there. Furthermore, Tizard emphasised that he wished Oxford to gain more influence in public affairs and to bring the scientist more into the mainstream of academic and political life. Others worried that he would continue to spend too much time on his work advising the government, but his allies stressed that he wished to cut down on his governmental work and give more time either to Imperial College or to Magdalen, should he move there. This appears to have swayed a sufficient number of the Fellows and, on 25 July 1942, after much intrigue and manoeuvring, he was elected President.[67]

The decision devastated McFarlane, who wrote to Karl Leyser (then serving in the army as a member of the Pioneer Corps) that

There is not much to tell you about the election. You were here for the real crisis. You saw how little I am hardened, how disgustingly sensitive I am. I am sorry if I was not a very cheerful companion. I did my best. But I was silly enough to be broken by the betrayal of someone I had trusted; silly because I knew that for me to be elected would mean lifelong unhappiness ... Tiz is on holiday. He comes in October and even then will be absent three days a week at least. We have met. I rather liked him. He's crude and uneducated, even simple minded. But he thinks he knows what's what and he is full of push and bounce at getting things done. I think he may do much harm.[68]

McFarlane made his feelings obvious. Tizard had not been to the college for forty years and, according to Taylor, 'ran into difficulties at once. McFarlane, who as Vice-President ought to have guided him, had hoped to become President himself and treated Tizard with a mixture of hostility and contempt. Van Oss took the same line, presumably foreseeing that his days of indolence were drawing to a close. [Van Oss and the college parted company in 1944; he was succeeded by Colin Cooke.] I was the only College officer who served Tizard with loyalty and patience.' He was a difficult man to serve: rather than strong and decisive, he was, according to Taylor, timid and irresolute. He could draft a report but he could not chair a meeting – he could not cope with opposition. Taylor recalled that 'College meetings with their chaotic debates ... terrified him ... Often he was too nervous to introduce the business and I did it for him. Occasionally he even proposed to withdraw some item which might be opposed and I had to threaten to introduce it myself. I could always whip up support with the circular letter I sent to absent Fellows and I also had the advantage of being the only one who understood the business that came up.' This somewhat self-satisfied memory is actually supported by McFarlane, who wrote to Leyser in May 1944 that 'Tiz is as Tiz was and Taylor is his Grand Tizier.' This comment also conveys his contempt for Taylor.[69]

It might seem that teaching and administration would fill his days, but Taylor also had his war work. It is true to say that he had a useful but unheroic war. Unlike many of his contemporaries, he did not decode Enigma intercepts or parachute into Yugoslavia or run a Whitehall ministry. Instead, he wrote and he talked. For almost the whole of the period he remained in Oxford. With the coming of the war European history suddenly assumed some relevance. It was vital that the subject be taught to under-graduates, and later to officer cadets, and as virtually the only European history specialist left in Oxford, Taylor was apparently deemed irreplaceable. Teaching was a reserved occupation, but in any case the university authorities certified his work as of national importance, and he received exemption from military service. Therefore, his main work was to teach anywhere between fourteen and twenty hours a week. Nevertheless, he made a number of attempts to go beyond this, and over the six years of the war he lectured on behalf of the Ministry of Information until he was sacked, he attempted to write guidebooks for the future British Occupation Forces for the Political Warfare Executive until he was sacked, and he broadcast to the forces and to foreigners, as well as to the home audience, over the BBC, from which he was not sacked, but whose management eventually reined him in.

At the outset of the war Taylor was thirty-three. Why did he not join up? He always said that he was not cut out to be a soldier; years later, when his youngest son, left-wing in his political beliefs, asked Taylor why he had not gone off to fight in the Spanish Civil War, he answered that 'I believe in leaving the fighting to other people.' Nevertheless, he and C.S. Lewis joined the Local Defence Volunteers the day it was formed, thereby becoming founding members of the Home Guard. From his brief description of his time as a member, it is not difficult to see how the television series *Dad's Army* emerged:

We had rifles, but of course no ammunition. Whenever there was an air-raid alert, we turned out to guard the gas works, on the assumption that the entire German paratroop force would descend on Oxford. Failing any Germans, our only function was to demand identity cards from passers-by, and many a time we turned back innocent citizens going home across the fields in the gathering dusk. One night I failed to hear the alert and so missed what would otherwise have been the most dramatic event in my military career. By this time our company had acquired one clip of ammunition which was passed with awe from hand to hand and usually entrusted to a veteran of the first war. When the company stood down in the early morning, Frank Pakenham (later Lord Longford), its commandant, asked whether the rifles had been unloaded. The veteran pointed his rifle at the ground and demonstratively pulled the trigger. The effect was literally shattering. It nearly blew Frank's foot off and peppered John Austin [Taylor's Magdalen colleague] in the backside.[70]

There was less amusement as the Battle of Britain reached its climax in late August 1940 and the outcome hung in the balance: 'Just after eight o'clock on the evening of 7 September, the Home Guard stood to arms, having received the signal that invasion was imminent.'[71] After a short period, however, believing that it was now certain that the Germans would not invade, Taylor (and Lewis) quit the Home Guard, Taylor retaining his army boots for use in the garden.[72]

Taylor's more appropriate war work began through the medium of Oxford University's Delegacy for External Studies. Taylor had never been involved in adult education at Manchester, regarding it, as he wrote in his autobiography, 'as a capitalist device for misleading the workers'. But in the autumn of 1939 the tutor of a class at Princes Risborough went off to war, leaving the students in the lurch, and Taylor took it on. This was the beginning of a much larger task: teaching soldiers. The Delegacy was in charge of education for the forces, a grandiose scheme, as Taylor wrote, 'deriving from Cromwell's remark that men fight best when they know what they are fighting for.' For the duration of the war he went out three or four times a week, speaking to audiences ranging from 'three men manning a huge naval gun in the Nore estuary to five hundred at an air camp'.[73] He was also enlisted to lecture to the civil officers who were being trained to administer the future conquered territories, Germany and Italy; his job was to travel to the Civil Affairs Staff Centre in Parkside, Wimbledon [the ANGOT school] where they were housed and lecture on contemporary German and Italian history, with the emphasis on the two types of Fascism. He later recalled that 'there was a dramatic moment when J.R.M. Butler, the commandant, broke into my lecture and announced, "Mussolini has fallen. You won't be here much longer." Everyone cheered.' Taylor, for reasons which he failed to explain, thought his students 'a rum lot'.[74]

Taylor's energy must have been phenomenal, because besides his Oxford teaching and administration and his talks to the forces, he also became a cog in the Ministry of Information machine. As he described the beginning of his involvement, 'among my many romantic notions was the idea that in this great national crisis we should be sending missionaries round the country as the Bolsheviks had done during the Russian revolution, and I aspired to be one. I offered my services to the Ministry of Information, another misguided creation of wartime.'[75] It must be said that it is unclear just what Taylor did and when he did it. His autobiography is a bit opaque on the subject, while he was too unimportant to figure greatly in the surviving papers of the Ministry. Fortunately, however, he got into trouble often enough and in a sufficiently public manner to have left an intermittent trail of evidence.

The Ministry of Information divided the country into regions, each under a Regional Information Officer, who was responsible for implementing the directives of the ministry and for organising most of the talks and events in his domain. Oxfordshire fell into the Southern Region, along with Berkshire, Buckinghamshire, Hampshire, Dorset, the Isle of Wight and the Channel Islands (a curious inclusion, since it was under German occupation). The Southern Regional Office was at Reading, and the man in charge was Sir Arthur Willert, a somewhat elderly ex-journalist on *The Times* who had spent the First World War in Washington, D.C. and was friends with Franklin Roosevelt. Before the war, ninety per cent of the Southern Region had been agricultural, with only five towns – Reading, Oxford, Portsmouth, Southampton and Bournemouth – having populations greater than 100,000. A region of small market towns and a largely rural population, it saw its character transformed with the establishment of war factories, military camps and aerodromes, and the necessary influx of a new population to operate them (not to mention American and Canadian servicemen in due course).[76]

One of the earliest acts of the regional offices was to call for the establishment of Local Information Committees, 'voluntary and advisory bodies' which were intended to include 'representatives of every shade of opinion'[77] and particularly of the three political parties. The members of these committees would provide leadership in keeping up morale, partly by transmitting propaganda but also by supplying information on the war and its associated affairs (as far as the service departments, the politicians and the ministry itself thought it wise to provide it). The Oxford Borough Information Committee was inaugurated on 2 October 1939, although it is unknown whether Taylor was a founding member; he was certainly a member a year later. What he was in any case was a speaker for the committee from its earliest days.

The Ministry had three categories of speaker: Category A (or Class A, as it was sometimes termed) which included party leaders and others with a national reputation; Category B, which included peers, MPs, candidates 'and others of national repute, although not so outstanding as those in category A';[78] and Category C, speakers for smaller meetings which were to be chosen locally. Category A speakers were to be utilised at great national and regional rallies, and their appearances would be organised from the ministry's headquarters at Senate House (the once and future administrative centre of London University). Category B speakers were to speak at town meetings and local demonstrations, while Category C speakers would be sent to open-air and factory-gate meetings and the smaller indoor meetings and lectures. Taylor appears on no Category A or B list and, judging from his own description of what he did, he was probably a Category C speaker.[79]

Taylor later recalled his experience. The nominal head of the Reading Regional Office, Willert, was 'an easy-going elderly man, rather resentful at being consigned to Reading', while its working head was

a former Congregational minister who had become a travel agent. Willert's explanation for employing him was that as a travel agent he must know about Europe. In fact the former clergyman had never been abroad in his life and merely wanted some job when his travel agency collapsed with the war. At least he knew how to arrange my travel schedules. There he was, eager to raise morale and with no one qualified to do it. I was manna from Heaven to him. I was given a free hand. I went to the principal towns in the southern region, contacted the local information committees, which were run by the agents of the three political parties, and offered my services. The party agents, though not very keen, usually acquiesced. I went to the main shops and offices, secured a ten minutes' break and addressed the staff on the war and what it meant ... I never received any instruction as to what to say ... The important thing was to turn in as many reports as possible. I always exaggerated the numbers of those attending and sometimes invented a meeting where I had drawn a blank. In the section marked 'public opinion' I put in whatever appealed to me at the moment: 'Resolute determination to go on until victory' or later: 'Strongly-voiced demand in Aylesbury for the immediate opening of a Second Front.'[80]

At some point Willert suggested that, instead of preaching, Taylor should explain. The letter found this very much more congenial and spent the remainder of his time with the ministry giving war commentaries. Although it is not possible to know for certain, since very few of the Southern Region papers appear to have been kept, Taylor may have become one of the ministry's staff speakers. First of all, staff speakers received a salary of about five guineas per week plus minimal expenses, whilst voluntary speakers usually received nothing except, occasionally, expenses. Taylor also received a salary or fee for his forces' education work, although how much is not known. What Taylor does say is that C.S. Lewis was also engaged in a form of forces' education, religious education, and that they agreed they should not profit from their work, giving their fees to Magdalen for a charitable fund which by the end of the war, according to Taylor, contained nearly £10,000 and which for some years was used for grants. (In 1995 prices this was equivalent to just over £200,000.) If Taylor earned half of that, then it is likely that it came from more than one source. Secondly, a Ministry of Information Minute of April 1943 refers to 'the trio of speakers, Taylor, Wehl and O'Neill, who between them have been responsible for a large proportion of the meetings, many of which tend to be arranged at regular monthly intervals at the same place and time.'[81] Finally, according to the final report on the activities of the Southern Region during the war, 'The War Commentaries of one of the Ministry's staff speakers proved very popular in Oxford, and there was much regret when his name had to be removed from the panel on account of an indiscreet statement which he was alleged to have made during a talk.'[82] Certainly this describes what happened to Taylor.

This indiscretion was not his first. In October 1940, as he described it in his autobiography, 'at Oxford I remarked one day, that, with the Mediterranean closed, the loss of Egypt and the Suez canal would be of little importance. There was a tremendous outcry that the Ministry of Information was defeatist or preparing the country for a compromise peace.'[83] Quintin Hogg, the MP for the City of Oxford, was outraged and asked a question in the House of Commons:

Mr Hogg asked the Minister of Information whether his attention had been drawn to a public speech in Oxford by Mr. A.J.P. Taylor, a member of the local Information Committee appointed by the Ministry of Information, to the effect that a withdrawal from Egypt would not be a major disaster; and whether he is prepared to take steps to prevent members of committees from committing themselves to irresponsible public statements of this nature without consultation with the Ministry?

The Parliamentary Secretary to the Minister of Information (Mr Harold Nicolson): Yes, Sir, the gentleman to whom the hon. Member refers is a member of the local Information Committee of the Ministry of Information but as he was careful to make clear at the time, he was speaking entirely in his personal capacity and not as a member of the local Information Committee. Mr Taylor is neither a civil servant nor in receipt of remuneration from the Government, and he therefore enjoys the same right as any other British subject to express his private opinion on public affairs. [If Taylor did become a staff speaker, and therefore in receipt of remuneration from the government, it was clearly after this date.]

Mr Hogg: … is not the Minister aware of the very grave public disquiet which was caused in Oxford by the irresponsible and ridiculous statement made by a person in a public position? Is he not aware that it led to a very grave misapprehension as to the intentions of the Government?

Mr Nicolson: I am aware that Mr Taylor's statements led to a considerable controversy at the time, but Mr Taylor was speaking as an independent person.

Hon. Members: No.

Mr Hogg: Does not the Minister recognise some responsibility for the people whom he appoints to these committees?

Mr Nicolson: I think my hon. Friend is under some misapprehension as to the functions of these Information Committees. They are not administrative sections of the Ministry of Information. They are voluntary and advisory bodies, and we have taken very great care that they should have on them representatives of every shade of opinion, even if those opinions are not such as to commend themselves to every member of the community.[84]

Hogg was not satisfied and insisted on raising the question of government responsibility for local Information Committees during the Debate for Adjournment, in the course of which Taylor got lost in the larger question. The exchange was reported verbatim in *The Times*.[85]

Taylor was unlucky that this particular indiscretion gained so much unfavourable publicity. Indeed, in his autobiography he recalled a worse one, in Southampton, although no one seemed to have noticed: 'I remarked that it would take years of bombing by the entire German air force to kill all of the inhabitants of Southampton. This, though true, did not look so good when the Germans obliterated the centre of the city only a few nights later. I did not go to Southampton again for some time.'[86]

What Taylor did do was to concentrate on war commentaries, surveying what had happened during the previous month and sometimes speculating on what would happen during the next. He made quite an impression with his first talk at Oxford in May 1941, which he finished by saying 'before we meet again Hitler will have attacked Russia'. Willert had come to listen and he told Taylor, as they walked out, that the Regional Office would have trouble over that particular comment, since someone was bound to accuse

Taylor of revealing secret information. No one did, but Taylor achieved a local reputation for prophecy. He developed a regular round, covering Oxford, Banbury, Aylesbury, Wolverton, Reading, Bournemouth, Swanage and a few other towns. He enjoyed the work – he liked talking about the war and later wrote that it taught him to look at it as history in the making.[87] But in June 1943 it all came to an end when his rhetoric ran away with him.

In February 1943 the Tunisian campaign revived after the winter rains had ceased and the ground was once again dry enough to allow planes to land and troops to move. On 14 February the German general Rommel attacked the US 2nd Corps at Faid and quickly advanced through them, although the corps fought back strongly and by 3 March Rommel's troops were back where they had begun. In one of his war commentaries in April, Taylor remarked that the Americans were still inexperienced and bound to make mistakes. Coming on top of comments he had made some months before about the other major British ally, the Soviet Union, this seems to have decided the Ministry of Information that he was too dangerous to remain on its speakers' list. (Willert had warned him the previous year that 'up in London they don't like anything that draws attention to the Ministry of Information. Never take a line on anything. Otherwise you will be in trouble.') In June Taylor announced in Banbury that he was giving his last war commentary.[88]

The result, according to the *Oxford Times*, was a 'storm of criticism' in several places where he had given his talks. Taylor had told one of his students that 'I won't go quietly', and he tried his hand at stirring up the press, agreeing to speak to an *Oxford Mail* feature writer who had been trying to interview him for some time with no success. The result was his appearance in the regular feature, 'Drawn and Quoted', in which the usually long and sometimes humorous interview was capped with a drawing of the interviewee. Taylor was interviewed as he gardened, surrounded by wife, children, visitors – including A.L. Rowse – and the odd undergraduate. He did indeed emphasise that what was required was not a propaganda ministry, which by implication was what the Ministry of Infor-mation was, but a ministry that stimulated the public to think, as Taylor had been trying to do. At the end of the interview Taylor asked to see the drawing of him that had been sketched whilst they had been talking. ' "Hmmm, yes," he decided. "Now only one thing remains to be done." He took a sheet of paper and neatly pasted it over the features. "Banned by the Ministry of Information," he scrawled in his characteristic hand.' And that is how the picture appeared.[89]

The local Information Committees protested at the sacking of Taylor, and the Mayor of Aylesbury went up to London in person to argue for his reinstatement. The contretemps raised real issues for the ministry, which had to walk a thin line between provocation and boredom. Certainly it was felt by a number in the ministry itself that 'the Ministry's policy of "playing safe" would result in its losing its following in Oxford'. But the fear of raising the ire of the House of Commons was always greater than that of losing its influence in a single locality, and the original order was not countermanded. Taylor's career as a government spokesman was at an end.[90]

Taylor also tried to write for England. During the First World War the Foreign Office had set up within itself a Political Intelligence Department, heavily staffed by historians, who included Arnold Toynbee, Lewis Namier, Charles Webster and E.H. Carr. In 1922 a number of those who had worked in the PID established the Institute of International Affairs, later the Royal Institute of International Affairs, more popularly known as Chatham House. At the outbreak of the Second World War, Chatham House moved to Balliol College, Oxford, and reconstituted itself as a Political Intelligence Department, whose duty was to write reports for use by the government. Taylor offered his services, but was turned down for a regular position; however, he later wrote, he was 'grudgingly given unpaid work and set to write a report on British war aims. This was an instructive exercise. I read all the ministerial statements both before the war and after its outbreak, reaching the conclusion … that the British government had no war aims nor indeed any idea of what they were doing. I was in the process of writing a report on these lines when I was abruptly told to cease work: orders had come from on high that war aims were not to be discussed.'[91]

A second opportunity along these lines came in 1943, ironically enough in the month before he was dismissed by the Ministry of Information. In May, Taylor was summoned to London, where a retired colonel read him the Official Secrets Act and inducted him into the Political Warfare Executive (PWE), 'yet another body pronouncing on foreign countries. The accumulation of information was now enormous. The Foreign Office was doing it; Chatham House was doing it. The Ministries of Information and of Economic Warfare had their research staffs and so had the European and overseas services of the BBC. The PWE now entered the pursuit.'[92]

The PWE was

nominally under the supervision of the Political Intelligence Department of the Foreign Office. Its policy-making was performed by a minis-

terial commission comprising the heads of the Foreign Office and the Ministries of Information and Economic Warfare. The tasks increased with the development of the war but efficient work was hindered by constant collation of the spheres of authority. Thus the Minister of Foreign Affairs [*sic*] was made responsible for policy, for the strategic decisions of the commission, while the Minister of Information was in charge of execution. The units dealing with the individual countries developed the action plans, taking into account the local characteristics. It was in August 1943 that the affair of the so-called 'zone-handbooks' was transferred here from the War Office. The original idea was to provide British soldiers, entering the various European countries during the war, with works offering a comprehensive picture of the countries in question, calling their attention to local customs and traditions, and thus encouraging the population there to look upon the British soldiers replacing Germans not as new invaders but as liberators. The collections of various expressions to be used in everyday situations were also intended to facilitate friendship between the population and the British soldiers.[93]

According to Taylor, the 'PWE presented itself as more practical than the other departments, actually doing things as well as accumulating information ... It was perhaps more relevant that PWE prided itself on being Left wing whereas all the other bodies veered to the Right.'[94]

In 1941 Taylor had published his fourth book, *The Habsburg Monarchy 1815–1918: A History of the Austrian Empire and Austria-Hungary*, which had been very well reviewed. This is probably what led the PWE to call him in, because they wanted a left-wing authority on Hungary. It was deemed necessary to produce a handbook on the country by the autumn, when, it was assumed, British troops would be in occupation and would require guidance. It was also necessary that it be left-wing, because otherwise 'the reactionaries of the Foreign Office would write it and Horthy the Regent would be given a clean bill.' Taylor took four months' leave from Magdalen, receiving the enormous salary of around £1,500 (the equivalent of £31,000 in 1995) – perhaps the main source of his share of the Magdalen grant fund[95] and in any case tax-free because the work was too secret to be revealed to the authorities – and moved to London. He worked in Bush House, which the PWE shared with the European services of the BBC. 'Suitable Hungarian refugees provided me with detailed information on Hungarian administration and economics which I merely turned into good

English.' He drew on his burgeoning friendship with the Hungarian democrat Prince Michael Karolyi to help him compose a chapter on Hungarian politics, although Taylor relied only on himself for the chapter on Hungarian history.[96]

He completed work on the first volume of the proposed multi-volume work by the autumn of 1943, copy being sent off to the printer each day as he completed it; nearly two hundred pages long, it had fourteen chapters, covering Hungary's geography, history, the ethnic and social composition of its population, its system of government, political parties, problems of religion and education, and detailed data on, for example, social insurance, health care and the press.[97] On 15 October the Foreign Office forwarded the manuscript for comment to Professor C.A. Macartney at All Souls, Oxford, an expert on Hungarian history. His response was 'utterly devastating': he considered that the sections on history and politics reflected personal opinions biased against the Regent, Miklos Horthy de Nagybanyathe, and the rest of the very conservative political leadership, while the data published in the book was not as up-to-date as it should have been. Macartney then submitted a text of his own to the Foreign Office. In his memorandum of 11 December on the manual, F.K. (later Sir Frank) Roberts agreed that Taylor's text was extremely biased, while that produced by Macartney 'offered facts without ideological colouring'. He also feared that if the PWE published Taylor's text, it could be seen as the official stand-point of the British government, which might cause difficulties within Britain as well as without. The text accidentally fell into the hands of John O'Malley, the last British ambassador to Hungary before the war, who also felt that the historical sections in particular were propagandist in tone. He was so concerned that he asked the PWE what guidelines were given to authors of the manuals. Elizabeth Barker, the PWE official responsible for the book on Hungary, responded that the guidelines provided by the Foreign Office and the War Office had been very general, adding that 'In a general way we try to tell the truth but having regard to our friendship with Czechoslovakia and Russia and the rather leftish outlook of the British government, we have given the book a bit of a twist to the left.'[98]

In January 1944 the Central Department of the Foreign Office made its final assessment of the revised text, setting out a list of the misconceptions introduced by Taylor. The PWE responded on 4 February. In general terms they accepted the revised text, but argued that the Macartney modifications presented much too rosy a view of interwar politics and history. Compromises were made on both sides and, with Taylorian arguments and descriptions almost entirely expunged, the final version was printed in March 1944. Taylor rightly assumed that the PWE had protested.[99] He also assumed that the handbook was never issued; this was the case, as no British troops ever entered Hungary.[100]

The PWE authorities were dismayed at what had transpired. They tried again, asking Taylor to write a chapter on the Weimar Republic (1919–33) for the handbook on Germany which they were in the process of preparing. According to Taylor, 'I duly wrote my chapter only to learn that I had hit the wrong note again. This time the objection came from PWE itself. I had taken the line, perhaps somewhat exaggerated by wartime feelings, that Germany had not been firmly democratic even in Weimar times and that Hitlerism, far from being an aberration, grew out of what had gone before. This did not suit PWE which with its Left-wing outlook believed fervently in a strongly democratic Germany groaning under Hitler's tyranny. My chapter, I was told, was too depressing to be given to British officers.'[101]

What happened was this. The German historian F.L. Carsten had been an active member of an underground socialist group in Germany from 1933 until 1939, when he fled to Oxford. In 1942 he completed a D.Phil. thesis on early modern Prussian history, looking at the development of the manorial system. He then had to find a job. Duncan Wilson offered him a job in the PWE. His task, as he later recalled, was to help draft the handbook on Germany. 'I was still an "enemy alien", but for the next two to three years I wrote chapters on German administration, local government, the Nazi organisations and ranks, and German politics in general.' But, he adds, 'the contribution of A.J.P. Taylor on earlier German history, which he wrote as an outsider, was so one-sided and partisan that it was rejected on my initiative.'[102] The PWE agreed that Taylor could take his rejected chapter with him, and this later formed part of *The Course of German History*, published in 1945 and which, as a book that met the needs of the time, became Taylor's first best-seller.[103]

By the end of 1943, Taylor had failed in his attempts to speak and to write for England. He remained in only one official outlet: this was the BBC, where his attempts to broadcast for England were still continuing. In February 1942 he had offered himself to the Corporation, and in response Trevor Blewitt, a producer in the Radio Talks Department, invited him to London to audition as a speaker in the series 'The World at War – Your Questions Answered', which was to go out on Forces' Radio.[104] He was successful and he made his first appearance on 17 March 1942. According to Taylor, although 'in theory the questions came from bomber pilots, soldiers in North Africa and naval ratings in the Atlantic', in fact 'they were made up by Guy Chapman, later a professor of history at Leeds.' He clearly enjoyed himself, although he later claimed that he did not think the work very important but that it taught him radio technique.[105]

Taylor made seven appearances, on the programme between March and June 1942. He then ceased to appear until 1944. In August 1944, however, Blewitt wrote to him that he had now taken over the talks on foreign affairs in the Home Talks Department and that he and his colleague would very much like to meet Taylor to 'talk about things'. 'How admirable is your willingness still to contemplate the trouble I should cause you!' Taylor responded eagerly. 'Of course I should like to see you & even to smell the dust of the microphone.' It was agreed that he would join three other speakers for a talk on 'The Future of Germany',[106] broadcast on 26 October 1944, and this indeed might be said to mark the real beginning of his broadcasting career: he made three appearances that year, but twenty in 1945.

Taylor broadcast on the Home Service now and again, but much more often it was for the Overseas Service. One series in which he appeared was 'Freedom Forum' which, as Taylor described it, 'demonstrated to non-existent American listeners our democratic virtues. People like Harold Laski and me wrangled over supposedly controversial subjects. I soon became an expert at the game.'[107] Another series was 'London Calling Europe', for which, in a series of twelve seven-minute talks, he set out 'The Pattern of the News', putting events of the war in context. There were programmes on, for example, 'Poland and France' and 'Europe under Hitler'.

The BBC had continuing difficulties with Taylor. He gently ridiculed their bureaucratic procedures, but more serious for the Corporation was the increasing concern that he would upset people by what he said – the listeners, the Foreign Office, later the political parties.[108] This anxiety would in due course become acute, and in mid-1946 he would be taken off one of the Home Service's current affairs series, 'World Affairs: A Weekly Series'. But this belongs to Taylor's postwar history: suffice it to say that, on balance, from 1942 through to 1945 Taylor pleased more than he displeased the powers in the BBC, an interesting contrast with his relations with government departments.

During the Second World War, then, Taylor served his country according to his own lights, attempting to use his strengths – a knowledge of foreign countries and foreign affairs and a way with words both written and spoken – to help people understand events and to encourage them to think about what they meant. In the process he ran up against individuals and institutions who disliked and distrusted his approach, and more often than not he was silenced. Yet he also honed the skills which would enable him to develop a career in public speaking and writing which would, for some years, be unique for an academic.

The immediate postwar period was inevitably an anti-climax, with great events giving way to more mundane concerns. One was the regrettable tradition in Oxford of shunning the teaching of later nineteenth- and early twentieth-century history. In an attempt to engineer some changes, Taylor ran for election to the Faculty Board for Modern History, but was defeated. He then tried another tack. Taylor, Alan Bullock, later the first Master of St Catherine's College but then a Fellow of New College, and a number of recently demobbed younger colleagues sought to increase the awareness of modern history in the university, at least on an informal basis. Taylor and Bullock organised the Recent History Group, devoted to the study of 'contemporary history', which they appear to have defined as the history of the twentieth century after the First World War. The group, comprising Fellows and research students, met several times a term in the evenings and invited speakers from both inside and outside Oxford to deliver papers which were then discussed. Presumably there was also wine. As a way of giving a scholarly basis to the proposed extension of teaching, Taylor and Bullock compiled *A Select List of Books on European History 1815–1914*, published in 1949, for use by tutors and their students. It was limited to secondary works (not including articles) and was conceived 'as a practical book-list, not as an exercise in academic or bibliographical scholarship'. The Oxford History School gradually crept more and more into the twentieth century, but even by 1970 the latest period of European history studied by undergraduates at Oxford ended in 1939.[109]

For Taylor a more compelling concern even than the teaching of contemporary history was his relationship with his wife, Margaret, to the extent that he called the 1945–50 chapter in his autobiography 'The End of a Marriage'. During his Manchester years his marriage had been strong and happy, but within two years of moving to Oxford things began to go badly wrong. One can only speculate why: the lack of an independent life for Margaret, since the life of the wife of an Oxford don in those years was circumscribed; Taylor's concentration on his work; the availability first of a particularly attractive undergraduate and then of a poet; or sheer chance. Whatever the reason, from mid–1940 Taylor's private life was intermit-

184 • *Troublemaker: The Life and History of A.J.P. Taylor*

tently and then increasingly one of pain and misery. The focus for this was Margaret's infatuations first with Robert Kee and then with Dylan Thomas; the eventual outcome was divorce.

Taylor thought that the origin of Margaret's passion for Robert Kee was a holiday during the summer of 1939. Taylor was then thirty-three, Margaret younger, their son Giles aged two. Robert Kee, then nineteen, was handsome, desired by both sexes, by rumour experienced sexually, clever and interesting. He was one of Taylor's favourite undergraduates, and Taylor never blamed him for what happened. Taylor took his family and their Austrian nanny, Henrietta Kotlan, to Savoy for the months of July–September 1939; they spent July in a house at Yvoire on Lake Geneva and then took a chalet in the mountains at Montriond for August and September. Kee was amongst the visitors who came to stay.

Taylor spent every morning working on his book *The Habsburg Monarchy*; he later claimed that he wrote so well there because he loathed mountains: 'Can't bear them. Particularly the Alps. That's why I invariably choose them! ... Huge menacing reminders of man's insignificance – I couldn't look at them. I closed my windows, drew the curtains, and stayed indoors the whole day, never stirring until it was dark, when I would hurry down to the village for another bottle of brandy at four and six a bottle. The book was finished in no time.'[110] The tale perhaps improved with the telling. In any case, once he had finished work he walked and played with his son Giles (although according to his autobiography he did this in the afternoons). Margaret grew increasingly impatient with Giles and with Taylor's company, spending more and more time with Kee: when they all took walks together, she and Kee strode ahead and were quickly out of sight. According to Henrietta Kotlan, Margaret 'was already in love' with Kee even before the holiday: 'She was a very sweet, rather helpless creature with this falling in love all the time. But she couldn't help it. ... She was very nice, but even I noticed that she lost interest in Giles. For instance she didn't know where his toothbrush was in the bathroom, and little things like that a mother usually does know.' At the time Taylor thought nothing of it, since Kee was good company.[111]

The end of the holiday came abruptly, but for political rather than personal reasons. On one of the few occasions Taylor drew a lesson from history, he was proved wrong in a spectacular fashion. In May he had written to Malcolm Muggeridge that 'One of the few things one learns from history is that chaps can only behave in a given way – despite their resolutions. ... For that reason I don't think we'll have a war. Hitler wins bloodless victories & doesn't know any other way – so he would never start a war.' While they were in Montriond the Nazi–Soviet pact was announced on 21 August, which confirmed Taylor in his belief because 'it ruled out a German attack on Russia and therefore in my opinion the likelihood of any war.' Less than a fortnight later, on 1 September, the Germans invaded Poland and Taylor decided that his party had better run for home. The family plus Kee piled into the car and they drove for the coast, reaching Dieppe on 3 September, the day Britain declared war on Germany. With visions of the rapid arrival of the German army at Dieppe, Taylor saw with alarm the huge queue of waiting cars, abandoned his own (which came over by itself a few days later) and they bolted across the Channel as foot passengers. They spent the night in a hotel at Seahaven, 'full of elderly ladies fleeing from London', and the following month with Margaret's parents on their farm near Bidford-on-Avon. In October they moved back to Oxford, taking up residence in Holywell Ford.[112]

Once they had returned to Oxford, things developed: 'Margaret was falling passionately, unrestrainedly in love' with Kee. She apparently harassed him in his lodgings, once thrusting herself physically on him: by one account they undressed and went to bed together, but failed to go through with it. Taylor eventually found out about her obsession. 'It puzzled me that Robert became increasingly reluctant to come to the house, whether for tutorials or for our evening parties. One day, picking up the extension telephone in my room, I heard Robert say to Margaret: "You know it is impossible for me to come to the theatre with you. I am sending the tickets back." All became clear to me. I understood why Margaret hung about in the hall when she thought Robert might be coming to see me and why she grew listless at our evening parties when he failed to appear.'[113]

Kee left Oxford in 1940 to join the Royal Air Force and Margaret, distraught, followed him to his camp and was sometimes away from home for days. She tried to make contact with him in the evenings and he had to warn the guard against her, cowering in the camp until he was certain that she had left. He then became a bomber pilot and was finally out of reach. Things settled down a bit for the Taylors, but one evening they went to see the film *Brief Encounter*, about a woman who toys with the idea of leaving her family for a stranger (but returns to her husband in the end). Taylor later wrote of how he 'was speechless with agony and walked home feeling as though I were dead. Margaret merely complained that I was rather silent. It was, I think, the bitterest moment of my troubled life.'[114] It was an appalling situation, with the wife of an Oxford don trying to seduce one of his undergraduates. Taylor believed others knew about it and he felt humiliated.

Kee was shot down and became a prisoner of war in Stalag Luft III. At Margaret's urging, Taylor wrote to him regularly, which he did 'more for his sake than for hers. His [Kee's] letters were strange, full of messages to non-existent aunts. After some time a mysterious stranger called, showed me some sort of secret-service card and told me not to be surprised at anything in Robert's letters. The allusions were in fact coded reports by bomber pilots who had been brought down.' This whole episode was turned into a malicious story by Patience McElwee, wife of Taylor's friend Bill McElwee. 'She would describe with relish the layers of black clothing assumed by Margaret when the news arrived that Robert's plane had been shot down. They next heard that the carrier pigeon, a bird which was apparently regularly carried in bombers, had made its way home, whereupon a few layers were removed. Colour was resumed once the news was received that Robert was alive and a prisoner of war.' Margaret threw herself into war work, for two years working at the Morris Car Factory from eight to twelve every morning making shells. She also tried her hand at producing weekly concerts at the town hall, much as she had done at Manchester, although this time she tried to make them as cheap as possible. However, this was not a success: asked in June 1943 why the series of concerts, apparently so successful, was ceasing, 'Not enough people will come to them,' she lamented, 'and the most comical thing of all is that people write me offensive letters saying it's a scandal that I'm stopping them.'[115]

With Kee away, the Taylor marriage appeared to settle down. Taylor rented a room in London to facilitate his war work and Margaret sometimes came with him. They had an active social life and behaved as a normal married couple, even conceiving their last child, Sophia. But things were still wrong, as Taylor discovered when they went to a village in west Wales in August for their first real holiday since the beginning of the war. One day the iron posts which had been set up on the beach in 1940 to deter the landing of German aircraft were removed, the first sign that the war would soon be over. 'Margaret listened to every news bulletin on the wireless with passionate concentration. I realized she was thinking all the time of Robert. ... My hopes and illusions fell from me.'[116]

One day in July 1945 Margaret asked to travel to London with him, only later revealing that Kee was back in the country and would be coming for a drink at eight o'clock. 'We waited miserable and restless until after ten when I went to bed. Robert appeared when I was already asleep. Margaret ... told Robert that our room was available for him if he wanted it. .... Nothing had changed. When I thought Margaret had been setting up the London room for me, she had been preparing it for Robert and planning all along for him to move in. Thus I lost both my London room and my peace of mind.'[117]

Kee began to visit their house in Oxford and Margaret had a period in which she could enjoy his attentions. However, she was soon to be thrown over. Kee invited the two of them to dinner at the Etoile in London. He seemed restless and kept watching the door. 'Suddenly he said, "Here she is" and introduced us to Janetta, already twice married and soon to marry Robert ... who soon wearied of [Margaret's] attentions. Time and again [she] tried to take Robert unawares. .... Robert complained to me. He complained to others and Margaret's infatuation became the common talk of Oxford – or so I thought. I felt humiliated and resentful. My last spark of affection for Margaret was extinguished.'[118]

Taylor later tried to analyse just why Margaret had acted as she had. Her life in Oxford was dreary, certainly compared to Manchester, where they had had an active social life. At the end of the war things became even worse, as their friends who had been exiles in England returned to their own countries – Taylor had had many friends amongst the Eastern Europeans. His real love, however, was for his children, and as Margaret neglected them he and they became a closed circle in which she played little part. His empathy for her was undoubtedly vitiated, then and later, by the way the situation replicated that between his own parents as a result of his mother's years-long infatuation for Henry Sara. Kee's part in all of this is also difficult to understand: was he flattered by the attentions of an older woman? (By one account she was beautiful and elegant, so perhaps there was some reason for his response.) Did he not care that he was effectively cuckolding his tutor and friend? He was later to claim that he had had no idea at the time how much the relationship had hurt Taylor, but this is difficult to believe. Presumably vanity played a part.[119]

Taylor had a respite from Margaret's infatuations for a year, until the autumn of 1946 when Dylan and Caitlin Thomas turned up on their doorstep. Dylan had been an unwelcome visitor before, at Higher Disley. Taylor's Oxford friend Norman Cameron, now an advertising copywriter in London, was often the Taylors' host in London, as they were his in Higher Disley. He moved in poetic circles, and one day early in 1935 he wrote to Taylor 'that a marvellous poet had appeared, young and very poor; it was everyone's duty to support him; would I [i.e. Taylor] have him for a week or two?' Taylor agreed and Thomas duly arrived, 'curly haired and not yet bloated, indeed looking like a Greek god on a small scale.'[120] Margaret appears not to have been attracted immediately; perhaps her marriage satisfied her at that moment.

Taylor disliked Thomas intensely. For one thing, he stayed for a month, not for just a week or two. Secondly, Thomas drank on a monumental scale, fifteen or twenty pints of beer a day, according to Taylor, which created a problem: Taylor kept a barrel of beer in the house and did not intend to provide a constant supply for Thomas, so he tried to ration him. Thirdly, they had little in common: they did not share any literary interests, and Thomas did not like walking. Fourthly, Thomas was cruel, intentionally so. Finally, he was a sponger, and if Taylor disliked any type, it was a man who did not pay his debts – he once wrote that the only thing he believed in was the sanctity of contract. When Thomas left, he told Taylor that he had lost the return half of his railway ticket, which Taylor thought was a lie, and asked Taylor to lend him a couple of pounds. According to his autobiography, Taylor said, ' "I lend once and, unless repaid, once only." Thomas did not repay the money. But this did not matter. I never expected to see Dylan again.'[121]

But here he was again, this time with a wife, Caitlin, who was perhaps even more rambunctious than he was. Their story was that they had been locked out of their flat in London and that Thomas had broken his arm (which was in a sling) trying to climb in to recover their belongings. Margaret took pity on their homelessness and Taylor acquiesced in their taking up residence in the Taylor 'summerhouse' in the garden, which was equipped with gas and electricity although not with water, which had to be carried from Holywell Ford. The Thomases 'lived there in conditions of some hardship, scrounging most of their meals from us. Their daughter Aeronwen shared a room with our two little girls and their son Llewellyn went as a boarder to Magdalen College School. ... Dylan tried to borrow money from me, in which he did not succeed. He would go off to London to give a radio talk and spend the fee on drink before he returned. Then there would be a row with Caitlin. Dylan would cajole her in a wheedling Welsh voice, and Caitlin would succumb.'[122]

Taylor in one sense welcomed the Thomases, thinking they would take Margaret's mind off Kee. Indeed, they did. She had always found literary and musical folk more congenial than university folk, and she now took the Thomases under her wing, giving parties for them, inserting Thomas into various literary circles around Oxford and even inducing Taylor to take him to dine at Magdalen High Table, where Thomas and Tizard, still President, 'sought to impress one another, a very curious conversation'. Margaret was falling for Thomas. Taylor records that one night in the spring of 1947, the night before he and Margaret were due to leave for a visit to Yugoslavia, he remarked to Caitlin that Margaret often appeared unbalanced because she imagined that she was in love with Robert Kee. Caitlin's reply was 'Oh, no. She makes out that now she is in love with Dylan.' Taylor, not surprisingly, was depressed beyond measure at the prospect that there would be no end to Margaret's infatuations. They went off on holiday and Margaret enjoyed the country by day but complained bitterly at night, wanting to be with the Thomases in Italy rather than with Taylor in Yugoslavia.[123]

The following years saw Margaret growing more and more obsessed with Thomas, turning herself into his patroness. For one thing, they paid for all of the Thomases' houses until his death. In spring 1947 Thomas wrote to her from Italy, reminding her about the house in Oxfordshire she was supposed to be finding for him and Caitlin. In the autumn of 1947 she found them the Manor House in South Leigh, ten miles west of Oxford. According to Taylor, he paid for it (a little over £2,000), on condition that she stop giving them money (a condition she utterly failed to fulfil) and that the Thomases paid rent (which they hardly ever did). The house was on the small side, with no electricity, no indoor lavatory (Caitlin remembered that 'we had an outside lavatory with one of those awful tin buckets that had to be emptied regularly') and no means of heating water except over a coal fire. The Thomases moved in in September 1947. Margaret was very pleased because its relative closeness meant that she could keep an eye on Thomas. In fact she bicycled out frequently, as did Taylor; according to Thomas, writing to Caitlin in the spring of 1948, it was hell, with Margaret lecturing them about art and Taylor arriving on his bicycle and making scenes on the road.[124]

Taylor was getting desperate. Reports reached him that Thomas 'was boasting around the Oxford pubs that he had got the wife of a rich don hooked on him. ... Margaret had inherited some money when her mother died in 1941. She spent some of the money on pictures – a Sickert, a Boudin, a Degas, a Renoir, a Utrillo. They now began to disappear along with crystal decanters and the piano. I might not have minded so much if it had not been for Dylan's boasting.' According to one account, the composer Elizabeth Lutyens heard Thomas say, 'I'll have to see if I can squeeze Maggie's left breast and get some money.'[125]

By May 1948 the Thomases were tired of South Leigh: Thomas had convinced himself that he could only write good poetry if he once again lived in South Wales. Margaret had to agree. Indeed, according to one of Caitlin's friends, Margaret had 'visions of returning with them, and setting up a threesome'. Caitlin claimed that Margaret once wrote to Thomas that 'going to bed with you would be like going to bed with a god'. If so, she was truly besotted; Caitlin's biographer in fact judged that 'Margaret's own mental stability [was] sometimes in doubt'. She seems to have wanted to be used, so long as it was in furtherance of Art and Thomas; in return, the poet first sang for his supper but later verbally mauled her. In the early days he encouraged her own writing of verse, sending her long critiques and seeming to take it seriously. But later he was cruel. Once, according to Caitlin, 'she and Dylan were standing in a bar, laughing about poor old Maggs behind her back, when they realised she was there, listening to them, "the tears streaming down her mortified face".' And again, after the Thomases had moved to South Wales, Caitlin wrote to her friend Helen McAlpine about a visit by Margaret: 'it ended as usual, with floods of tears and recriminations, and heliotrope changes of colour, on the main street, on a Sunday, after a few harsh words of truth from Dylan. And she had been so sweet and diplomatic until then. Ebie [Williams, the taxi driver] was simply terrified taking her to the station, clutching a basket of spilling underclothes, and soiled intimacies, her blue hair straggling wildly over her face, her lipstick streaking dangerously down her neck; and the wail of a lost banshee pursuing him to the ends of the earth. He seriously thought the police would arrest him for rape and assault.' Even allowing for Caitlin's habitual exaggeration, this would not have been an edifying sight.[126]

The house in South Wales was the Boat House at Laugharne, which Thomas had coveted in his youth. When it came on to the market, Margaret sold the Manor House at South Leigh, Taylor sold some of her capital for her and with the proceeds she bought the Boat House for £3,000, which was two-thirds of her remaining capital, plus a further £136 for repairs to the roof and verandah. In April 1949 the Thomases moved in. They were supposed to pay rent, although it was difficult for Margaret to extract it; the scene described by Caitlin took place after Margeret had travelled to Laugharne to insist that they continue paying her £2 a week for seven years.[127]

Taylor was becoming increasingly fed up. He wrote to Thomas that he was destroying their marriage and that he should lay off, if only for the sake of the children; Thomas never replied. With Kee she had sometimes been away for days; now it was happening again, if not perhaps for such long periods, with the Thomases, particularly when they were living in South Wales. Taylor recalled that 'often, coming back from London, I found Holywell Ford deserted except for the children and our resident domestic.' He also disliked intensely the fact that she had broken her word over giving the Thomases more money. By 1950 he had decided that they should separate. He had asked for, and received, the promise of a sabbatical during the 1950–1 academic year, which he proposed to spend in London, researching for and writing *The Struggle for Mastery in Europe*. Margaret had suggested that Taylor should lease a house near Regent's Park and let Holywell Ford; Giles could go to Westminster School as a day boy, Sebastian would board at Magdalen College School in Oxford, where he was a chorister, and the two girls would go to a state primary school in London – an interesting contrast. The Taylors spent the whole summer in Oxford, perhaps his first adult year when he had not spent some time in Europe, 'enjoying a family life at Holywell Ford for perhaps the last time. In September we packed up and moved to Park Village East [in London; the house, number twenty-six, was a semi-detached Nash building called Sussex Cottage]. I settled Margaret in her house there and moved to a flat elsewhere. This was the end of my full family life for many years to come.'[128]

In the midst of all of this emotional turmoil, Taylor resumed something of a political life. He was a card-carrying member of the Oxford University Constituency Labour Party, which as a constituency party never met and of which there were not all that many members, though they included the future Foreign Secretary Patrick Gordon Walker, Frank Pakenham (later Long Longford), Bruce McFarlane, Harry Weldon and the Secretary of the constituency party, the economist David Worswick, who in October 1945 became a Fellow of Magdalen – in fact, Magdalen at that time was full of Labour Party sympathisers. Taylor took a full part in the general election of July 1945, speaking on the platform for Pakenham in Oxford and for Aidan Crawley in North Buckinghamshire; Crawley won but Pakenham lost. Taylor knew many of the new Labour MPs, such as Richard Crossman, as well as some of the younger members of the 1945–51 Attlee government, including Harold Wilson, Hugh Gaitskell and Douglas Jay. He saw many of them while he was in London – he spent time there every week writing for the newspapers or broadcasting – and then regaled his colleagues with political and social gossip upon his return to Magdalen.[129]

In 1948 he made a brief foray into international affairs of a sort. Some

Polish intellectuals wanted to renew their ties with the West and proposed a Franco-Polish cultural conference. The Russians were suspicious of the initiative, however, and insisted on taking part, whereupon the Poles sent invitations to most other European countries, excepting Spain (because of Franco) and western Germany, as well as to some Americans. It now turned into a 'World Congress of Intellectuals', to be held in August 1948. In Britain the members of the delegation, most of whom were Communists or nearly so (such as Hewlett Johnson, the so-called 'Red' Dean of Canterbury, and Professor J.B. Haldane), were chosen by the Polish cultural attaché. However, a few non-Communists were included, one of whom was Taylor, on the basis, he assumed, of his pro-Soviet broadcasts, but probably also because of his public reputation as an expert on countries east of the Rhine; others included Edward Crankshaw, a commentator on political affairs, the novelist Richard Hughes (author of *High Wind in Jamaica*), Harold Ould, secretary of the writers' group PEN (Ould was briefed by the Foreign Office on Communist tactics, although he disappointed the FO by failing to do anything with the information) and Sir James Richards.[130] The scientist Julian Huxley, then head of UNESCO, was to act as president of the gathering.

The congress took place in Poland at Wrocław (formerly the German city of Breslau before the postwar change of borders). There were decent hotels and plenty to eat and drink, especially vodka. At the congress itself there were simultaneous translations into four languages, Polish, French, Russian and English, as well as loudspeakers which transmitted the proceedings into the street. It opened with a speech by the Russian novelist Aleksandr Fadeyev, who described how the Soviet Union had single-handedly saved Europe from the Nazi tyranny; he then proceeded to attack Western culture, concluding with the remark, according to Taylor, 'that if monkeys could type they would produce poems like T.S. Eliot's ... The British delegates, even including the Communists, were indignant', although several, including Johnson and Haldane, opposed making any protest. Kingsley Martin and other members, however, insisted they must reply; Taylor determined that they should do so and persisted until he was listed as the first speaker. As he later wrote, 'I had experience of standing up to Communists in pre-war days and now used much the same technique.'

'I was told I must submit my speech beforehand. I answered that I did not work like that but made up my speeches as I went along.' The organisers agreed, and so Taylor's 'extempore' speech boomed out at the congress and onto the streets via the loudspeakers.[131] 'It is a long journey from London', he said, 'and I – for one – did not make that long journey in order to listen to commonplaces or to read slogans which seem to have been left over from the World Meeting of Democratic Youth. We intellectuals are not children; and most of us came here for a serious purpose, the purpose of securing cooperation between intellectuals of all countries. I would like to see the Congress concern itself with the practical problems which intellectuals run up against at the present time. We can't work unless we have free movement'.

He continued:

As intellectuals, we must have some common standards; and I fear that these standards are still lacking. In my opinion, it is our duty as intellectuals to preach tolerance, not to preach hate. In America, and now in England too, more and more people say that there is nothing to choose between the Soviet Union and Nazi Germany, that both want to conquer the world. Many intellectuals, in America as well as in England, have fought against this view. And now, when we come here, what do we find? The same views in reverse. The same bogeys; here it is called American Fascism, over there it is called Russian Bolshevism. We intellectuals, instead of inflating these bogeys, should be trying to bring peoples on both sides to their senses.

If we intellectuals are to work together, it must be on the basis too of truth. As an historian, I cannot sit silent when I listen to history being remade. On this Polish soil an Englishman has the right and duty to say this; we and the French were the only peoples who went to war against Nazi Germany without waiting to be attacked, we and the French alone entered the war in order to liberate Poland. A more flagrant ... example of this historical distortion was when Mr Fadiejew recited the countries which had resisted Hitler – France, Poland, Czechoslovakia, Bulgaria, Albania. One country was missing: yet Yugoslavia had a record of resistance second to none. Now, in order to suit the convenience of a political party, Yugoslav resistence is blotted out. Under this banner of dishonesty I, for one, will not march.

Against? Against Fascism, against Wall Street, against Downing Street, against Kremlin, against all people in authority.

Ah, yes, but what are we for? I know what *I'm* for – for a single humanity, not for British culture, not American culture, not Soviet culture, but for a single human culture. We intellectuals belong to the country of Voltaire and Goethe, of Tolstoi and Shakespeare. But if it must be something less, then Europe – the Europe that is neither Communist nor American.

And his peroration:

I – if alone – am for the freedom of the mind – freedom for the artist to create as he wishes, freedom for the scientist to research, freedom for the writer to express his own ideas. Unless we meet on this basis, we can meet on none. This is not something for intellectuals alone! All peoples ask for freedom from oppression – freedom from arbitrary arrest, freedom from a secret police, freedom to speak their opinion of their own government as well as of others. If we defend this, we defend also the peace of the world and we offer the people of the world what they want. But even if I spoke only for myself, I would still say: without intellectual freedom, without love, without tolerance, the intellectual cannot serve humanity. And in short, here I am, here are my opinions. I could have no others.[132]

Taylor caused an uproar. The Communists were furious, the Poles were delighted and he was lionised at all of the receptions. As one participant later remembered it 'it was astonishing that Taylor should be there at all – it was a very Party-line conference. Then, that he should be speaking! But the miracle was in the speech he gave, to a dumb, stony house – it was dyed-in-the-wool conservative. And then he had the gall to come over to me and whisper in my ear, "I've been dreaming of giving a speech like that since God knows when!"' The Communists tried to arrange a final communiqué criticising American imperialism and only American imperialism. Taylor, Crankshaw and Hughes resisted, Taylor recalling that he himself had said that 'whatever statement is manufactured I shall vote against it.' The upshot was that no agreed statement was issued. At the end of the congress Taylor and Crankshaw flew to Paris, where Taylor found that he was a hero: a reporter from the *New York Times* had attended, and as soon as she had left Poland had sent the story to New York. Taylor became 'the man who had spoken for freedom beyond the Iron Curtain.'[133] The whole episode increased his fame considerably, not only in Britain but abroad. It also, ironically, delighted the Foreign Office. His reputation for independence made him an effective critic, but, they decided, it also made him an unreliable vessel for FO propaganda. Instead they decided to search for other, more pliable figures to 'play the part of an A.J.P Taylor' and infiltrate other gatherings.[134]

Fully fledged academic life also resumed. Two episodes were notable: one was the intrigue and disarray inseparable from the appointment of a new President of the College; the other was the not very serious contretemps arising from the activities of Taylor himself when the time came for the renewal of his Fellowship. The decision of Tizard to resign in November 1946 brought to an end a term of office that had been, on the whole, a disappointment both to him and to the Fellows. The immediate cause of his resignation was the offer late in August of another position, in fact of two positions: Chairman of the Research Committee for the military services and Chairman of the Scientific Advisory Council of the Cabinet, for a salary of £3,000 a year. Tizard's immediate reaction was set out in a letter – significantly not sent – but it indicates the perquisites of his post at Magdalen: 'I am afraid that the whole thing is impossible so far as I am concerned. I am asked to give up my house in Oxford, which I occupy rent and rates free, to move to London at a time when, if one can get a house or suitable flat at all, the prices are prohibitive, to give up, in addition, my special pension rights as President of Magdalen, and the comparative freedom of that office, and to accept by way of compensation a net salary, when income tax has been deducted, rather less than I have at present. ... I lost all pension rights when I left the Civil Service at the age of 44; I cannot afford to lose them again at the age of 61.'[135]

Tizard, in fact, thought hard about the offer, which would return him to the world of Whitehall. He was genuinely attracted, but he was also influenced by the disappointing nature of his reign at Magdalen. According to Taylor he was 'increasingly impatient with the unreasoning opposition he encountered at Magdalen', which could perhaps be characterised by McFarlane's reference in one letter to 'this disagreeable, quarrelsome college and ... the awful Tiz'. Tizard's penultimate position in mid-October was that he was willing to accept the Research Committee chairmanship and combine it with the Presidency: 'To accept both posts', he wrote, 'would certainly involve my resignation as President. On the whole I think it would be best to accept the offer, and resign; but the College Officers, whom I have consulted, have asked me to explore the possibility of combining one Chairmanship with the Presidency. This I have done, and will gladly try it if there is a strongly held opinion among my colleagues that this would be best for the College. I should not like to go away feeling that I had done the College any harm by coming or going.'[136]

The crux of the matter was whether the Fellows wished him to stay; the answer which emerged from a college meeting was that a substantial majority of the Fellows did. But a strong minority wished him to leave; he was vigorously opposed by C.S. Lewis, for example, as well as by many others on the arts side. This was made clear at an Extraordinary General Meeting on 6 November when McFarlane took his revenge. At the meeting Tizard raised the matter but, before he could go on to explain his plan for accepting only one post and continuing as President, McFarlane inter-rupted to say that this was very grave news because now they had only forty days to look for a new President. There was only one response which Tizard could make: he gave formal notice 'of my intention to request you to permit me to retire from my office at the end of this calendar year'. That same evening he wrote to accept the combined posts at the increased salary of £4,500 a year.[137]

Even before this meeting Tizard believed that he had lost Taylor's confidence and support, on the basis of Taylor's opposition to a proposal which he had made a few days earlier. But Taylor was sorry to see him go, later writing that 'there was a creative spark in him which most of my colleagues did not encourage.' Tizard perhaps looked even better in retro-spect because Taylor very much disliked his successor, the elegantly dressed T.S.R. Boase – an art historian, said Taylor, 'of no great distinction' who, as President for the next twenty years, 'initiated nothing and presided happily over a gradual deterioration of both Magdalen's buildings and its academic standing.'[138]

Taylor is being a bit unfair here. The buildings and the academic standing of a college are the responsibility of the Fellows as well as of the head of a college, and in any case the academic standing of Magdalen was high during this period: immediately after the war, Magdalen jumped to the top of the then-prevalent league table of Finals results and remained one of the top three colleges throughout Taylor's period as Tutorial Fellow. Taylor was on firmer ground when speaking of the college's financial position – in 1945 Magdalen had been amongst the three wealthiest colleges, while by the 1970s it had slipped to about tenth – and particularly about the deterioration of college buildings. One example was the state of the Tower, which in the 1970s was discovered to be almost falling down, costing a huge sum to repair it. Another was the state of the chimneys in St Swithun's Quad: they had been restored in the 1950s, but this had left them in an appalling condition, requiring substantial repair work in the 1990s. And then there was the Waynflete Building, by common consent a strong candidate for Oxford's most hated postwar construction – but the Fellow-ship, including Taylor, who was Vice-President at the time, must carry some of the responsibility for the Waynflete. Yet, whilst a head admittedly can do little against the combined wishes of the Fellows, there is no real evidence that Boase attempted to exercise much leadership in these areas. It is also worth remembering the context for Taylor's remarks, which is that he assumed a reciprocal animosity on the part of Boase, writing that 'I must have been the sort of Fellow Boase most disliked and he did what he could to get me out of the College. However as his efforts did not succeed, our relations remained amicable enough on the surface.'[139] In fact, Boase was to outlast Taylor as a resident member of the college.

The semi-serious contretemps over the renewal of Taylor's Fellowship took place on 15 October 1952. In order to understand it fully, it is necessary to return to Taylor's marital history. According to Taylor, he had separated from Margaret at the beginning of his sabbatical year in September 1950, and by his own account had spent that year doing almost nothing but work; supporting evidence for this is that during the year – and on a manual typewriter – he completed the final ninety thousand words of *The Struggle for Mastery in Europe 1848–1918*. Yet he was not always entirely alone: he kept up the friendship, and by now relationship, with the woman who would become his second wife, Eve Crosland.

Eve Crosland does not appear in Taylor's autobiography because of her threat of writs, and thus their two sons appear from nowhere, conceived apparently by parthenogenesis. She herself spoke publicly about their courtship and marriage only twice: once in 1967, when Taylor left her to return to Margaret, and secondly in 1991, on the occasion of the publica-tion of Taylor's letters to his third wife (*Letters to Eva 1969–83*). In other words, the inwardness of the rise and fall of their relationship and marriage is impossible to know. Taylor appears to have first noticed Eve in 1947, the same period when he discovered that Margaret had fallen in love with Dylan Thomas. Was he attracted by a striking young woman who clearly admired him and would prove to be attracted by him as well? He had suffered over the previous eight years, when his wife had had successive love affairs. It is unknown to what extent Margaret's passions were consummated. On the one hand, Taylor referred many years later to her 'wild love affairs'; on the other, he always said that Kee had acted honourably, while Caitlin's temper and ferocious possessiveness with regard to her husband would surely have led her to attack Margaret had she suspected that Margaret and Thomas were sleeping together. Taylor's pride as well as his heart were deeply wounded, and his response – to find another who would admire and love him – is hardly unprecedented.

Eve first caught his attention at a lecture he was giving in 1947, when in her honour he began with 'Lady and gentlemen'; she later consulted him about working for a D.Phil. In the event she became a journalist in the London office of the *Manchester Guardian*, having a 'passionate interest in current affairs (especially international and colonial)' which may well have been what drew them together. However, according to her own account, Eve was at that period 'living with a Canadian who looked just like Cary Grant'. Aged twenty-six, she had a reputation for promiscuity.[140]

She remembered Taylor as being very charismatic, and that 'he had been more or less on his own for two or three years and he needed a woman quite badly. ... Sexually. Very badly.' He took her to the Ivy and the Caprice, restaurants notable as much for their expense as for the quality of the food and wine on offer; he hoped to get her into bed by giving her dinner often enough. He also gave her presents; by April 1948 he was having a special copy of his *The Habsburg Monarchy* prepared for her. He took her to Paris and the south of France. By early 1949 he was trying to wangle an invitation for her to accompany him, John Betjeman and the artist John Piper on a trip to Yugoslavia they were taking for the *Manchester Guardian*; according to Eve – although the chronology does not fit with Taylor's – at this point she asked her older brother, Tony Crosland, the future Labour Foreign Secretary but then a politics don at New College, whether it was true that Taylor and Margaret were separated. When he replied that they were, and that Margaret had departed for London with the four children, Eve decided to go. However, A.P. Wadsworth, still the paper's Editor, did not approve – he liked Margaret – and might have prevented Eve going; but in the event the trip was cancelled. According to one account, 'though she gave out that she was sexually experienced, Eve kept Alan at arm's length until he began to give up hope.'[141] Then she telephoned him in Oxford one day to say that she could not stand her new lover and longed to hear his voice. Taylor rushed down to London and they spent a weekend together in Brighton, the classic venue for such events. It may also have been just before then that the Canadian, who was a journalist, was recalled to Winnipeg. Later that year she moved in with Taylor; according to Eve, 'I thought nothing of it, he wasn't my first lover; but it was considered pretty daring for those days.'[142]

Their relationship developed. Until she moved out of her mother's house into her own flat in October 1949, Eve met Taylor in the upstairs of Robert

Kee's house in Sussex Place, the irony of which would not have escaped Taylor. Taylor began to introduce her to his friends: in December he took 'his girl' to tea with Malcolm Muggeridge, who thought her 'pretty dumb, but better looking than before'.[143] In October 1950, a month after his separation from Margaret, accepting an invitation from the Editor of the *New Statesman*, Kingsley Martin, to speak to the Union for Democratic Control, Taylor asked him to 'be sure to send an invitation to the M.G. [*Manchester Guardian*] and that talented young journalist Eve Crosland can come and write me up.'[144]

Eve then astounded Taylor by demanding marriage. He had thought that she was an emancipated bohemian, and by implication that she would be happy to remain his mistress. Instead, she wanted marriage and a respectable married life. But there was an impediment: Taylor was still married. Furthermore, he insisted that he would never divorce Margaret. According to Eve, she 'blackmailed' him: 'after five years it had come to the point when I said, "It's either/or. I'm not going to be somebody's mistress all my life. If you don't get a divorce I leave."' Margaret was remarkably cooperative, perhaps out of remorse for her own responsibility for the breakdown of the marriage. She offered to give Taylor grounds for divorce, although at this point, by living with Eve, he was giving Margaret grounds herself, had she wished to use them. Once Margaret had agreed to the divorce, he rang up Eve in Manchester where she was working and told her the news. They agreed to marry.

The divorce went through, and three weeks later, in May 1951, Taylor married Eve in the Kensington Registry Office, with the wedding witnessed by Robert Boothby, a fellow performer on the BBC's television programme 'In the News', and Phil Zec, Editor of the *Sunday Pictorial*, a popular newspaper for which Taylor wrote. Taylor and his new wife, who was fifteen years younger than he was, attempted an Italian honeymoon. They stayed first in Alassio, where Taylor had lived for some months as a small boy while his mother was recuperating from the stillbirth, but they found it too hot and crowded and went instead to France. After calling on Michael Karolyi in Vence on the Cote d'Azur, where he was again in exile and attempting (unsuccessfully) to write his memoirs, they went to Etretat, a fishing village a few kilometres south of Fécamp in Normandy. This was an amazing choice: Taylor and his family had spent their holiday there four years before, so it was bound to stimulate memories of times with his children, if not of happier times with Margaret. Presumably Eve did not know about this, since she would almost certainly have been wounded by the idea of their going there as newlyweds.

The return to Oxford and Holywell Ford was equally inauspicious. Eve hated the house – it was cold and damp and almost devoid of furniture, since Margaret had taken most of it with her to London – and she hated Taylor's cat. Although her later memory was that they had been happy together,[145] the marriage seems to have run into difficulties within months, probably because of Eve's unhappiness, not helped by the fact that Taylor did not like having his work disarranged by emotional disturbances. She no longer had a job: she had resigned from the *Manchester Guardian* and found no substitute position with the local Oxford press. She had little social life: a don's wife was still a thing apart from college life, and she was in a particularly difficult position, given her irregular relationship with Taylor before their marriage. Furthermore, it was difficult being Taylor's much younger second wife amongst colleagues who felt sympathy for Margaret; besides this, divorce was still socially unacceptable to many – Taylor later recalled that Rowse, whom he referred to as his oldest friend, had refused thereafter to speak to him. Eve was taciturn, although this may have arisen from shyness, which appears to have prevented her from taking any initiatives to form friendships, even if it did not then stop her complaining that no one came to see her. In short, the life of the wife of an Oxford don appears to have crushed Eve even more rapidly than it had Margaret.

Another bone of contention between them was Taylor's children: he missed them and expected them to spend time in Holywell Ford, particularly during their school holidays; furthermore, his second son, Sebastian, who was a weekly boarder at Magdalen School in Oxford, was often there at weekends. Having no children of her own, Eve found this difficult. What made things worse was Taylor's continuing relationship with Margaret. When he and Eve decided to marry, he had stipulated that he would spend two days a week with Margaret in order to remain part of his children's lives – Sunday evening was sacrosanct for playing with them. (He also stipulated that he would dine once a week at the Beefsteak Club in London.) Margaret telephoned frequently about the children, to which Taylor responded. When Eve complained, Taylor apparently felt that she was being unreasonable (although he was to tell his third wife that Margaret had crushed Eve with her incessant telephone calls and demands). But Eve was right to feel threatened; Margaret was telling her friends that she was trying to win Taylor back – indeed, she wrote to a friend in 1956 that 'Alan and I just jog along and the weeks fly by.'[146]

In some sense Margaret won. In September 1952 Taylor decided that if his children were not to be welcome at Holywell Ford during the holidays, he would have to find another holiday house, one which was to exclude Eve. He explored the Isle of Wight and settled upon Yarmouth on the West Wight: it would provide the opportunity both for seabathing and long walks. Margaret and Sebastian then went down and located a 'snug little house' in South Street, Yarmouth, called Plevna House. It is not clear exactly what was happening between Taylor and Eve, but their relationship was in decline and the following July the break was made: they moved out of Holywell Ford, Taylor into rooms in New Building in Magdalen and Eve to a basement flat north of Regent's Park in London, as it happened a few hundred yards from Margaret's house.

Eve made a number of attempts to find a job, writing for example to Alan Pryce-Jones at the *Times Literary Supplement*: 'I am very anxious to find a job, either whole or part time … I find I have too much time on my hands, and I feel that I might be using whatever brains and intelligence I possess more profitably. The kind of job which, as far as I can see, I am most suited for would be something in the line of editorial assistant to a publisher.' She then outlined the range of her experience in the general area of books and journalism, adding at the end that 'for the past few months I have been answering all likely advertisements in the Times and New Statesman, but it seems rather a forlorn hope. I suspect most of them are filled almost before the advertisement appears.'[147] This application also led to nothing. Eve rapidly declined: she became painfully thin and, after her unsuccessful attempts to find gainful employment, friends worried that she was spending all day reading novels in her flat. Feeling that he could not completely abandon her in her present state, Taylor took to spending one night a week with her, taking her out to concerts and on his trips away from Oxford.

In May 1955, to Taylor's astonishment, they discovered that Eve was pregnant: he had thought that she was unable to have children. With the help of Eve's mother, he bought a house in East Finchley for Eve and their son Crispin, who was born in December. Taylor agreed with Eve that Crispin should have a sibling, and their son Daniel was born in 1957. (For some years the children of the first family did not even know that the second existed; Amelia, for example, only discovered their existence when Taylor brought her to the house and she saw them playing in the back garden.) Margaret, meanwhile, bought a house in St Mark's Crescent, close to Primrose Hill. Here Taylor had his own bedroom and a study behind the sitting room which looked out over the Regent's Canal. Margaret and Taylor also sold Plevna House and bought the Mill, a large – twenty-five bedrooms – seventeenth-century brick house outside Yarmouth overlooking the sea. This was to be his first family's holiday home for years: indeed, his daughters spent so much of their time there that they began to speak with the local accent.

Over the years an unusually complicated private life developed. From Monday to Thursday during the eight-week terms Taylor lived in his rooms in Magdalen, rising early and working late. Then on Thursdays he came to London, staying with Eve and their children and going out in the evening, sometimes with her and sometimes with one or another of his friends. On Friday he spent the day as journalist and broadcaster, writing his regular newspaper column in the morning and broadcasting on 'In the News' in the evening until his appearances were discontinued. On Friday nights he would go to stay with Margaret and their children until Sunday night or Monday morning, when he would roar back to Oxford in his Zephyr convertible.[148]

This, then, was the background to the attack made on Taylor in the October 1952 college meeting. Tutorial Fellowships came up for renewal every five years, a process which was ordinarily a formality. The Senior Fellow would stand up and say, 'Mr President, I nominate X', referring to the Fellow who sought renewal, the other Fellows would raise their hands in agreement and it would essentially go through on the nod. On 15 October all four History Fellows were up for renewal: McFarlane, John Stoye, Karl Leyser and Taylor. The first three went through in the routine manner. When it came time for Taylor, however, the Senior Tutor, Godfrey Driver, Professor of Hebrew, Low Churchman and editor of *The New English Bible*, made an impassioned speech: it was wrong, he said, that a Fellow of the college should be an adulterer; furthermore, he added, Taylor was a writer for a trashy Sunday newspaper. He then sat down.[149]

With regard to the first charge, it is unclear whether Driver objected to the divorce or to Taylor's relationship with Eve Crosland before they were married; Taylor thought that it was the divorce. (The only assumption here must be that Driver was a believer in the indissolubility of marriage.) Taylor also believed, in this case mistakenly, that he was the first Fellow of the college to have been divorced and not resigned his Fellowship; either he did not know or had forgotten about the classicist C.E. Stephens. The 'trashy Sunday newspaper' was the *Sunday Pictorial*. The objection to writing for the press was not confined to Driver: another example was T.S. Eliot who, writing in the *Criterion* in 1938, maintained that the effect of daily or Sunday newspapers on their readers was 'to affirm them as a complacent, prejudiced and unthinking mass'.[150]

The immediate reaction of the Fellows to Driver's interjection was surprise, and silence. Then Harry Weldon sprang up and said that he had never expected to hear such a disgraceful attack by one Fellow on another: if Professor Driver was unable to nominate him, well and good, he would nominate him himself: 'I nominate Mr Taylor,' he said, and sat down. They then voted. One source states that two Fellows voted against Taylor, Driver and Onions, but it is not possible to know for certain. Taylor in his autobiography and private papers made clear his disappointment and long-lasting hurt that none of the Fellows came up to congratulate him on surviving such an attack. According to two of the Fellows present, however, they viewed the whole episode as just one of Driver's idiosyncratic and inexplicable but unimportant actions. John Stoye said that 'every once in a while Driver would stand up and make a strange statement'. One source claims that Taylor was isolated and that many of the Fellows hoped that he would leave the college; if so, they missed their opportunity to press their case.[151]

Taylor had no desire to leave. Indeed, he valued his association with the college, maintained it for as long as he could and was deeply unhappy when he had finally to leave in 1976; by then he had considered his set of rooms in New Building as his home for twenty-three years. On the academic front, in fact, the 1950s were a productive and happy period. He published a number of books: three collections of essays; a very good biography of Bismarck; one of his best books, *The Struggle for Mastery in Europe 1848–1918*; and his personal favourite, *The Troublemakers: Dissent over British Foreign Policy 1792–1939*. These will be discussed in the following chapter. Academic recognition was not all that he might have hoped, however: election to the Ford Lectureship and to the Fellowship of the British Academy on the one hand, but denial of three chairs on the other.

One evening in late November 1954 Taylor returned to his set in New Building after dinner and found a letter inviting him to give the 1956 Ford Lectures, in his own words 'the most prestigious historical lectures in the English-speaking world'. Přibram had given them; Namier had given them; the eighteenth-century historian much admired by Taylor, Richard Pares, had given them; his colleague Bruce McFarlane had recently given them. He was absolutely delighted, writing to his *Manchester Guardian* friend Wadsworth that 'I have been made Ford's Lecturer for next year! ...

It really is the most exciting thing that ever happened in my life.'[152] His surprise was increased by the fact that they were the Ford Lectures on English history and Taylor considered himself, with reason, a European historian. Presumably the basis of his election was his mastery of nineteenth-century English, or British, diplomatic history.

In the circumstances, what could he speak about? According to Taylor, 'I wandered out into the night, encountered Alan Bullock and told him of my plight. He said: "You have always opposed official British foreign policy. Now tell us about the men who opposed it in the past – Charles James Fox, Bright, the Union of Democratic Control, right down to the Left before the second world war." I was intoxicated with delight.' He worked on them throughout 1955. When the time came to deliver them, he claimed, all he did as preparation was to type his quotations onto cards so that he could pull them out as he needed them, which also reminded him where he should be in his argument. This accords with his self-propagated myth of never preparing a lecture. However, there is some oral evidence that, before the time came to give each lecture, he practised before a mirror so that he would have a pretty good idea of what he was going to say. Before the first, he had his son Sebastian over from school to have tea with him and to attend the lecture.

There was a mixed reaction to the lectures. McFarlane, as noted above, was dismissive, and certainly general historical opinion considered them one of the weaker sets of Ford Lectures. According to Taylor himself, however, their worth was underlined by the fact that, unlike previous lecturers, he did not have to move to a smaller lecture room as his audience declined: his audience was as large at the end as at the beginning. They were also to lead to a ground-breaking opportunity, both for history and for Taylor himself: as described in Chapter 7, an ITV producer came to the final lecture and asked Taylor if he thought he could do the same thing on television. Taylor's response, of course, was an eager yes, and the following year he delivered the first ever set of television lectures.[153]

His other honour in 1956 was his election as a Fellow of the British Academy (FBA). Founded in 1901, the British Academy is the learned society which honours those of stature in the humanities. 'Stature' is based on publications and consequently reflects a position of intellectual authority in a given field. According to a Fellow and former President, in Taylor's time the Academy appeared to have as its business its replication by the election of new Fellows; the administration of some public lectures established by private endowment; and the publication of those lectures in its annual *Proceedings*. (Later it would take on the responsiblity for distributing research grants and postgraduate studentships on behalf of the British government.) Election arose from the votes of members of a section; Section II covered all of mediaeval and modern history, the mediaevalists constituting the majority. As the same Fellow explained:

> The hardest problem lies within a section. When it comes to assessing the value of someone's contribution to a subject, the existing members of an academy are likely to be the least unfitted to do it ... The candidate's methodology may be unfamiliar and uncongenial to them, but if its results are fruitful, that will do him good. Yet behind the assessment of an individual lie assumptions about the relative importance of different topics, periods, texts and problems *within* the subject. If an X-ologist is being considered for election and there are only Z-ologists in the section concerned with that subject, there is a danger that they may give priority to one more Z-ologist ... This danger has not always been eluded.[154]

According to Taylor, his election was the outcome of just such a conflict within Section II. The modern historians complained that, being in the minority, they did not get a fair share of their candidates selected as compared to the mediaevalists, and G.N. Clark and Sir Charles Webster, both former Presidents of the Academy (Sir Charles from 1950 to 1954), threatened to resign. Both had in some sense been patrons of Taylor, which probably increased his chances; another Fellow later claimed that Namier had been responsible. Nevertheless, the section was dominated by mediaevalists, and it was therefore probably crucial that the Regius Professor, the mediaevalist V.H. Galbraith, backed Taylor for election: he said that this was because he admired the bibliography of Taylor's *The Struggle for Mastery in Europe 1848–1918*, which lists sources in five European languages. Taylor claimed that Galbraith had another motive, which was to secure Taylor as his successor as Regius Professor in order to deny it to Hugh Trevor-Roper. This fight was, in fact, to take place the following year. Meanwhile, both Taylor and E.H. Carr, whom Taylor referred to later as 'the greatest modern historian living', were elected in 1956. Taylor's response was elation: this, he felt, validated him as a serious historian,[155] and it probably came as an unpleasant surprise to his detractors, both at Magdalen and in the wider academic arena.

But he also suffered academic setbacks during the 1950s, principal amongst which was his failure to be appointed to any of the three chairs (professorships) which he would have liked and for which he was considered, most particularly and publicly the Regius Professorship at Oxford. He had already turned down the offer of three other important chairs, those at Manchester (vacated by Namier), Leeds and Edinburgh. He would have been financially worse off as a professor at a provincial university than he was as a Fellow of Magdalen; he would have had to devote a great deal of time to administration; and he would have been so far away from London that he could not have easily continued his second career in journalism and television. The one chair outside of Oxford which he would have taken was the Stevenson Chair in International History at the London School of Economics,[156] the only endowed chair in diplomatic/international history in the United Kingdom.

The first holder of the Stevenson Chair was Sir Charles Webster, author of the two-volume *The Foreign Policy of Castlereagh*, the British Foreign Secretary during the Napoleonic Wars and the Congress of Vienna. Appointed in 1932, Webster retired in 1952, and the appointments committee set about finding a new professor. Three candidates were interviewed: Taylor, E.H. Carr and Professor W.N. Medlicott. At London University at that time, of which the LSE was a constituent school, half of the members of the committee were appointed by the Board of Studies concerned, in this case History, and half by the institution at which the chair was tenable. According to Taylor, the historians on the committee wanted him, but the LSE, led by its Director, Sir Alexander Carr-Saunders (who ten years earlier had been briefly considered for the presidency of Magdalen), baulked at the possibility. The reasons sometimes given were based on outside activities and personality rather than on a perceived lack of quality in his work. What the committee, and especially Carr-Saunders, objected to was Taylor's lucrative second career writing for the London newspapers, whether tabloids or broadsheets: Carr-Saunders had proscribed all non-academic publication by anyone identifying himself as a member of the LSE, and Taylor refused to give up his role as a journalist, which was contributing to his fortune as well as to his fame. A later commentator who would himself be the Stevenson Professor, Donald Cameron Watt, possibly passing on earlier comments, 'boggled' at what Taylor would have made of the internal politics of the institution. He also added, curiously, that 'Taylor would in addition have lacked the solid weight of his friends and colleagues at Oxford who did so much to shield him from his notorious outbursts of eccentricity and *animus academicus*.' In the end the committee chose Medlicott, who 'never shook the reputation for dull, second-rate worthiness',[157] particularly in comparison with the brightly plumed birds who had also been on offer.

The second missed chair which rankled was that of Professor of Modern History, tenable at Worcester College. 'No offer ever reached me,' he later wrote, 'but gossip, probably ill informed, alleged that I was in the running.' He ascribed his failure to enemies determined to keep him out, in particular J.C. Masterman, the Provost of Worcester. Masterman was an historian of the old school for whom teaching was the highest good – he never published any book of history – and who was famous for his manipulation of patronage. Taylor thought that Masterman disapproved of his political views and of his television appearances, believing that the latter undermined the dignity of the academic role. He was indefatigable in pushing the claims of his protégés – a former History don at Christ Church, he was considered the *capo di capi* of the Christ Church mafia, one beneficiary in due course being Hugh Trevor-Roper. Masterman told Taylor years later that 'I thought Hugh would provide good conversation at dinner', adding apologetically that 'of course you would have done too but I didn't know that at the time'.[158] The remark conveys Masterman's essential dislike of Taylor, expressed in an urbane though trivial manner. This animus would soon again influence the course of Taylor's career.

Masterman's reference to Trevor-Roper was made after the episode of Taylor's third academic setback, his failure in 1957 to be appointed Regius Professor of History – it went instead to Trevor-Roper. Taylor has provided his version, which he pieced together from other people's comments; Masterman has given his own opaque account; and there is material from other sources to add further light and shade. It all began with the imminent retirement of the then Regius Professor, the mediaevalist V.H. Galbraith. According to Taylor, he had hardly noticed, a typically Taylorian aside which is wholly unbelievable; and so far as he did, he assumed that it would go to yet another mediaevalist, as it always did, a comment which *is* believable. The Regius chairs are in the gift of the monarch – hence the name – which in effect means that they are appointed by the Prime Minister. One of Anthony Eden's last acts in office was to ask the Vice-Chancellor at Oxford for a nomination.

Ordinarily, according to Taylor, the Vice-Chancellor commissions some senior historian to sound out opinion, as Masterman had done on the previous occasion. But the current Vice-Chancellor, Alic Smith, the Warden of New College, thought himself fully capable of choosing a candidate, despite being a philosopher, not an historian. He made his selection and confirmed it with Alan Bullock, then a Fellow of New College; he then passed it on to the new Prime Minister, Harold Macmillan. His choice was Taylor.

Unfortunately for Taylor, Smith fell seriously ill the following day and soon after resigned as Vice-Chancellor. His successor was Masterman, who told Macmillan that Smith had been ill for some time and that his judgement was therefore not to be trusted. Masterman offered to find the new Regius Professor for him, but Macmillan wanted to make his own choice. This was Namier – but Namier was beyond the age of retirement. At this point Macmillan resigned the task to Masterman. Masterman duly recommended Trevor-Roper – by one account, only Masterman recommended Trevor-Roper – but other historians – G.N. Clark, Sir Charles Webster, Austin Lane Poole, Galbraith himself and others – had got wind of the matter and intervened to propose Taylor. Indeed, Galbraith was later reported as saying that 'no one beyond Taylor among Oxford's prominent lecturers was worth a "tu'penny fuck" ... he wanted Taylor and only Taylor for the post, because he was a man to whom people would listen.' Macmillan was by now thoroughly confused and decided that Namier should have the choosing, although a senior Oxford don, Herbert Nicholas, wrote that 'No. 10 is said to be prolonging the election because it is finding it so enjoyable.'[159]

At this point Taylor met Namier. Taylor recalled that Namier told him that he was on his way to see Macmillan, although he did not know why. Taylor answered that he was going to choose the Regius Professor, at which Namier seemed embarrassed: this was, Taylor later wrote, because he knew Taylor's record, having backed his election to the British Academy; but against him in Namier's eyes were Taylor's political activities, his television appearances and his popular journalism. At any rate Namier went to Downing Street and recommended that Macmillan choose Lucy Sutherland, the Principal of Lady Margaret Hall (one of the five women's colleges), who had been a pupil of his. Macmillan offered her the chair and Sutherland accepted.

The story, however, continued. Sutherland wished to become Regius Professor whilst remaining Principal of her college – an unprecedented proposal which the university authorities agreed to only reluctantly. A decree was proposed which would allow this. Trevor-Roper then came to Taylor in a state of high indignation at the alleged degradation of the chair; Taylor, while not too bothered, agreed to support his objectives. There was duly an outcry in Oxford, Sutherland withdrew her acceptance and

Macmillan was back to square one. Namier than rang up Taylor and offered to recommend him for the Regius, but if, and only if, Taylor agreed to give up appearing on television and writing for the popular press. If not, he, Namier, would recommend Trevor-Roper. According to Taylor, he replied, 'Lewis, we have been friends for more than twenty years. No shadow has ever come between us. Now your standards and mine are no longer the same.' He then put down the phone and never spoke to Namier again. Trevor-Roper became Regius Professor and the night his appointment was announced Namier dined with him at Christ Church.[160]

The account given by Masterman adds important nuances, not least that of self-satisfied complacency: 'During my term of office [as Vice-Chancellor] two Regius Professorships fell vacant, Modern History and Divinity, and in neither case did the appointment coincide with the majority expectations of Oxford opinion. In the case of Modern History I was in an unusually delicate position since the candidate chosen, Hugh Trevor-Roper, had been my pupil at Christ Church, but on re-reading the papers, my conscience is clear. To one question from the Prime Minister to the Chancellor [then Lord Halifax], and from him to me, I returned a clear answer. In this I said that I thought the office so important that it ought not to be held in plurality with the headship of a college – a choice by the person concerned must be made.' This was clearly a reference to Lucy Sutherland. He continued: 'From Hugh I had a long and impassioned letter urging me to use what influence I had to bring about the appointment of another person (who in the event would not let his name be considered) ... In both these cases [Modern History and Divinity] I was impressed ... by the care and trouble which were taken over them. Every person *whose views were of value* was consulted and every *reasonable* opinion weighed and considered ... No doubt appointment by the Crown is an anachronism, but it works. I must go on record in saying that, by and large, Regius appointments in my time were always as good as and sometimes better than those made by a more democratic method.'[161]

Masterman's reference to a letter from Trevor-Roper is particularly interesting. Trevor-Roper maintained a wide correspondence, and one who was a regular recipient of his letters was Professor Wallace Notestein, an historian of seventeenth-century England who had a chair at Yale University. Trevor-Roper first opened the subject with him in January 1957: 'Here the great speculation is on the Regius stakes: who shall succeed Galbraith? My only concern is that it should be someone very different from Galbraith: someone less parochial, less narrow, and who is not afraid to write.

Galbraith, of course, has his candidate – someone who will continue his sterile tradition ... Galbraith's animosity against me continues unabated.'[162] (Trevor-Roper was quite right in his assessment of Galbraith's feelings. Galbraith wrote to a friend, after the contest was all over, 'In this spirit of *dolce fas niente*, let us waste no words or energy on my successor ... Indeed the only ... comment of real force I've heard is that of Billy Pantin – "Poor old Hitler's got a lot to answer for"!')[163]

Another correspondent of Notestein's took up the story in mid-March: 'The Taylor–Roper–Rowse triangle being virtually exhausted as a topic for speculation, the circle widens to include Lucy Sutherland, Stephen Runciman, [J.H.] Plumb – but opinions differ as to whether any of these should be taken seriously.'[164]

Trevor-Roper continued the saga in May:

As for the Regius Chair – Rowse is now out of the running and is pretending, first, that it was offered to him and refused, and then (when this was proved untrue) that if it wasn't offered, that was because he had made it known that he would refuse; Taylor is out, as too radical in politics; I don't think that the medievalists, try they never so hard, will succeed in getting their candidate in; and all now suggests that it will go to Lucy Sutherland, whom Namier has recommended to the P.M. This prospect depresses me. Lucy is just as narrow as Galbraith and although she is better than Galbraith in her narrow field, I feel that the Regius Chair should not go simply to specialists in ten years of history but to someone who can interest people in historical problems regardless of such cramping frontiers ... I would like to see Stephen Runciman, or even (though I admit he can be irresponsible) A.J.P. Taylor. Unfortunately Taylor lost Namier's support by reviewing the last boring volume by one of the Great Man's little disciples and saying some needed truths. But as a matter of fact I don't think that Harold Macmillan would ever choose Taylor, even if Namier supported him: to him Taylor must seem a vulgar, irresponsible radical, a Little-Englander and a *gamin*. Unfortunately there is some truth in all these charges; but I still think that Taylor's merits rise above his defects.'[165]

Two months later he completed the story:

I must admit that I really think A.J.P. Taylor's qualifications were the highest, and I would have been glad if he had been nominated (Rowse, of course, would have been a humiliating disaster); but I suppose it was impossible, especially since the P.M.'s *eminence grise* in such matters, Namier, seems to have turned against him. The circumstances are, in my opinion, entirely creditable to Taylor. He dared to criticise, in a review in the *Manchester Guardian*, the ridiculous lengths to which Namier's army of industrious hacks are now carrying his methods, 'namierising', at tedious length, the insignificant members of obscure assemblies and their trivial tactics. After that, it seems, all past links were broken: of no avail was Taylor's devoted energy in preparing and writing for that *Festschrift*: the Master requires absolute obedience; and this gesture of independence was fatal. The sad fact is that Taylor is really too independent to have *any* support from *any* Establishment. The Labour Establishment is even more hostile than the Tory: when there was a Labour Government, Herbert Morrison prevailed on the BBC to cut Taylor off the air, and now Lord Attlee has written a mean and factually incorrect review of Taylor's last work (his Ford lectures) dismissing him as 'a well-known television star'. However, if Taylor is, as it seems, simply not *papabile*, and if my other candidate, Steven Runciman, is disqualified as a Cambridge man and a medievalist (but how different from Oxford medievalists!), then who am I to spurn this unexpected crown?'[166]

From this it seems clear that the letter from Trevor-Roper to which Masterman referred set out the former's support of Runciman. It also demonstrates the width and even depth of support which Taylor enjoyed. Indeed, Magdalen 'rallied around its own in quite spectacular fashion'.[167] But what all the evidence shows most baldly is that a small group of men – or even one, with an acquiescent group of supporters – could go against the intellectual consensus and impose a candidate of their own choice, a choice primarily based, it seems, on qualities other than those relevant to the teaching and writing of history. (Galbraith's reaction was that 'Macmillan and Masterman deserve both to be sacked for what they've done!')[168]

Trevor-Roper's comment about Taylor's being too independent to have support from any establishment was perceptive and true. He had appeared to be anti-Communist and therefore right-wing in Poland; he was attacked in Parliament for being anti-American during the Attlee administration (see Chapter 7). But it was his involvement from 1958 in the Campaign for Nuclear Disarmament (CND), a movement which attacked the policies of both the Conservative and the opposition Labour Party front benches, that demonstrated his distance from the political mainstream – and probably underlined for Macmillan his wisdom in not appointing Taylor to the Regius chair.

The Campaign for Nuclear Disarmament was a largely middle-class protest movement, drawing on roots of romantic protest that went deep into English culture, including a suspicion of technology and technocracy, a faith in the idea of community and a belief that the individual mattered and could reform his or her part of the universe. More specifically where CND was concerned, since the war there had been a growing fear of atomic weapons, although it proved to be the advent of the hydrogen, rather than the atomic, bomb which was the catalyst. The US tested its first H-bomb in November 1952, the USSR following ten months later, though in terms of public awareness of the dangers it was the American testing of a bomb in 1954, the fallout from which rained down on a Japanese fishing vessel and subsequently killed one of the crew, which was important. Thus when the government announced in February 1955 that Britain would produce and maintain its own H-bomb arsenal, active concern was stimulated. This was increased by the publication of the 1957 Defence White Paper, which made clear Britain's reliance on nuclear weapons (partly on the basis of cost: it was cheaper than training and maintaining a conscript army). More alarmingly, it stated that 'There is at present no means of providing adequate protection for the people of this country against the consequences of an attack with nuclear weapons.'[169] This was a Tory administration, but it became clear that the Labour Party was not going to oppose the policy when Aneurin Bevan, the leader of the left wing of the Labour Party, announced at the 1957 party conference that he supported the party's pro-nuclear policy. Clearly, any protest was going to have to be extra-parliamentary.[170]

There were two key events that stimulated the founders of CND to act. One of these was the series of six Reith Lectures, which were given on BBC Radio in November and December 1957 by George Kennan. As First Secretary in the American Embassy in Moscow in 1946, Kennan had written the so-called 'Long Telegram', subsequently published anonymously as 'The Sources of Soviet Conduct', the intellectual source of the Anglo-American policy of 'containment' of the Soviet Union. He had already protested that he had not meant containment to be a military strategy, but now in his radio talks he argued that nuclear weapons could never provide the basis of a constructive, as opposed to a destructive, foreign policy, proposing the withdrawal of nuclear forces from continental Europe. Just three days after Kennan's final lecture, NATO authorised the stockpiling of tactical nuclear weapons in Western Europe. Kennan did not advocate disarmament, probably because he realised that it was a hopeless position for which to argue at the height of the Cold War, but his lectures caught the imagination of anti-nuclear groups in Britain.[171]

The other key event was the publication in the *New Statesman* on 2 November 1957 of an article by J.B. Priestley entitled 'Britain and the Nuclear Bombs', written as a riposte to Aneurin Bevan's speech at the Labour Party Conference. This provided many of the major themes of CND: nuclear policy was beyond the democratic control of ordinary men and women, being in the hands rather of 'men now so conditioned by [the] atmosphere of power politics, intrigue, secrecy, insane invention, that they are more than half-barmy'. Only 'an immensely decisive gesture, a clear act of will' could hope to reverse such policy: unilateral nuclear disarmament. This would also return Britain to the role of moral leadership that it had played in 1940, when it had stood alone against Hitler and the Blitz, would help bring peace 'in our time' and would revitalise British society. As Taylor himself was later to write, 'We thought that a British example might influence the world. We failed but it was worth trying.'[172]

At the end of 1957, then, a group of well-known members of the left met in the London flat of Kingsley Martin, the Editor of the *New Statesman*, to discuss mounting a campaign against Britain's nuclear policy. They included both Priestley and, surprisingly, Kennan (who was, after all, a visiting American), along with the philosopher Bertrand Russell, the archaeologist Jacquetta Hawkes, the distinguished physicist and future President of the Royal Society Professor P.M.S. Blackett, and Commander Sir Stephen King-Hall, advocate of a national defence policy based on non-violent resistance. The group agreed on the need for an organisation to fight the production and use of nuclear weapons, and on 21 January 1958 CND officially come into existence. The first, self-appointed, executive consisted of Russell as President, Canon John Collins as Chairman, Ritchie Calder as Vice-Chairman, Peggy Duff as secretary, and James Cameron, Howard Davies, Michael Foot, Arthur Goss, Sheila Jones, Joseph Rotblat, Martin and Priestley. One whom it did *not* include was Taylor, in spite of his claim to the contrary, a claim which probably arose from his later telescoping of the period. He was only invited on to the CND executive on 14 April 1958.[173]

Taylor had in fact already written in April 1954 to the *Daily Herald* opposing nuclear weapons, calling it a question of morals and arguing that

Britain should unilaterally renounce the hydrogen bomb.[174] However, he was probably invited on to the executive in recognition of his resounding success as a speaker. Even before the founding of CND, he had been invited to speak in Coventry on unilateral nuclear disarmament; he had 'given no thought to the subject for many years', but when he did he 'realized at once that this was a subject on which there could be no compromise. The idea of having little atomic bombs or of possessing without using them would not do. These weapons were too dangerous and too evil to be around at all.' The very next day, he later recalled, he read in the *New Statesman* that 'a random meeting at Kingsley Martin's flat had decided to launch a campaign for nuclear disarmament. I rang up Kingsley and offered myself as a recruit.' It is probable that he offered himself as a speaker, which was certainly his strength: at the initial mass meeting on 17 February 1958 at Central Hall, Westminster, he helped to launch the campaign on its dramatic course – a course very different from the one initially envisaged by the founders of CND and by Taylor himself, which was that of a single-issue lobbying group run by its elite core.[175]

The executive arranged advertisements for the meeting, which was to have Canon Collins as chairman and Michael Foot, Sir Stephen King-Hall, J.B. Priestley, Bertrand Russell, Alex Comfort and Taylor as speakers. The response was so huge and so unexpected – five thousand people showed up and a further thousand had to be turned away – that five overflow halls were rented and extra speakers lined up. The speakers rotated from one packed hall to another. According to Peggy Duff, 'The size of the response had its effect on the speakers ... One and all came out with a militant denunciation of nuclear weapons, and Britain's in particular.' Taylor recalled, and Duff confirmed, that he received the most enthusiastic applause when he advised that pro-nuclear MPs be called 'murderers' whenever they appeared in public. His speech was vintage platform oratory: 'He outlined the effects of an H-bomb explosion – so many miles of total destruction, so many miles of partial destruction, so many miles of uncontrollable fires, so many miles of lethal fall-out – paced about in silence and then inquired squeakily: "Is there anyone here who would want to do this to another human being?" A hush descended as though for a count-down, "Then why are we making the damned thing?" Pandemonium.' According to Taylor,

Having worked the audience up to the point of explosion I went home. The audience however did not. It surged out into Parliament Square and swept on to Downing Street. The police, not expecting such a respectable audience to get out of hand, had made no preparations. There were over a thousand people crying 'murderer' on the steps of No. 10 Downing Street before the police appeared. The few police who arrived took fright and called in police dogs, a routine operation against working-class crowds. This crowd was composed of rich, well-dressed people, one of them, Lord Kennet, a member of the House of Lords. Lord Kennet was actually mauled by a police dog. After the resultant outcry police dogs were never used again against a political crowd. That was an achievement of a sort.[176]

Taylor became one of the main CND speakers, addressing audiences, he recalled, in the Albert Hall in London, Leeds City Hall, the Free Trade Hall in Manchester (twice), Sheffield City Hall, the Usher Hall in Edinburgh, Newcastle Town Hall, Birmingham City Hall and others, most of which meetings were reported in the local newspapers. He later wrote that speaking in Manchester, on his home ground, gave him the greatest pleasure, but Birmingham was the most exciting: exactly one hundred years before, his great hero, the nineteenth-century radical politician John Bright, had delivered his speech there denouncing British foreign policy. Birmingham was also memorable because his Bootham history master, Lesley Gilbert, was in the audience. Gilbert gave his impression of the speech a year later in an address to former pupils of Bootham and Mount School: 'Let's think of A.J.P. Taylor, who as a boy was so critical of many of the things the School stands for, of "John Bright and all that". In a crowded meeting last year (Nuclear Disarmament) in Birmingham Town Hall, he made the finest speech of the evening, full of close argument and moral vigour. He reminded the audience of the great speech Bright made in that Hall and how he was proud to have been at Bright's school, and he finished with a peroration which echoed the very accent and words of Bright.' Gilbert took him out to dinner after the speech and, according to Taylor, told him: 'A.J., I know you don't believe in god, but god spoke through you tonight.' For Taylor it was the proudest moment of his life and tears ran down his cheeks. By the end of 1958 Taylor was playing a particularly forceful role in the movement.[177]

A notable feature of CND was the Aldermaston March, which took place for the first time at Easter 1958. This forty-mile march from Trafalgar Square, London to the nuclear weapons research facility at Aldermaston ended on Easter Monday in a wet field outside the plant. Taylor did not go in that year, joining the march, now from Aldermaston to London, only in 1960: 'Forty miles in four days was not a hard assignment. Previously I had kept clear of the march out of intellectual disapproval [he wanted the case to be won by argument, not emotion]. In the end I succumbed and found the march interesting. It was quite pointless and yet psychologically uplifting. As we marched along we really thought that we were bringing the good news from Ghent to Aix. And when we led this great procession into Trafalgar Square, we could not help feeling we were bound to win.' Certainly in 1960 he was still publicly hopeful about the campaign's eventual success, although worried about the lack of support amongst the twenty-five- to fifty-year-olds and the lack of response of students to the moral arguments against the bomb.[178]

This lack of faith in youth contrasts notably with the assessment of Peggy Duff in her memoirs ten years later. Writing that 'From the very beginning there was widespread support among university students and university CND groups rapidly sprouted in every university', she remembered in particular the Oxford University organisation, not least because of the marches they organised to and from the American air base at Brize Norton north of Oxford. They also ran a yearly conference, and usually produced a freshers' leaflet for each new year. Taylor was aware of all of this because he was the Senior Member of the undergraduate CND, which was the largest of the political societies. He would have been acutely aware of their activities when they daubed CND symbols on the walls of Magdalen itself, leading Olive Gibbs, local Councillor and later Chairman of CND, to go down to Magdalen with buckets and scrubbing brushes and clean them off. According to one source Taylor's involvement led some of the more conservative dons to refer to him as '"off the rails": wits compared him to Dr Henry Sacheverell, the Tory Fellow of Magdalen in the early 1700s who had made a reputation as "The Modern Fanatick" for his incendiary pamphlets and sermons attacking in violent terms dissenters, low churchmen, latitudinarians and Whigs'.[179]

And then things began to die away. One reason, thought Taylor, was the drive by local enthusiasts to make the campaign more democratic: they wanted local committees, a formal membership and an elected central committee. As a report of the 1958 CND conference emphasised, in the words of one delegate, 'A number of rank and filers are not prepared to be general hewers of wood and drawers of water without some representation on the executive committee.'[180] Many in fact saw CND as an exercise in participatory democracy as well as a campaign against the bomb, and within a year the rank and file were pushing for this. One historian explained the reaction of Taylor and others as follows:

> For CND's elite leadership, the concept of creative democracy was often difficult to handle. Many members of the Executive found the thing they had created rather frightening. Mervyn Jones [novelist and journalist] recalled standing with Kingsley Martin and watching the columns form for the last day of the 1960 Aldermaston March. As he stared out at the thousands of people, Martin turned to Jones and asked, 'What on earth are we going to do with all these people?' When the political and intellectual luminaries gathered in Canon Collins's study in January of 1958 and declared *themselves* CND, they saw the Campaign as a pressure group working through orthodox political channels and dependent on prestige as much as public support. The Executive decided the Campaign would have no individual members, no local committees, and no affiliated groups. It would avoid the structure, and the reality, of a democratic campaign. At the first public rally at Central Hall in February, however, the Campaign took on a life of its own. It became a mass movement as local groups sprouted all over the country.

When participants achieved their desired formal membership and elected central committee in 1962, Taylor, Collins and Priestley all resigned, 'taking', Taylor said, 'most of the inspiration with them.'[181] As he later recalled, 'I left when it became *democratic*.'[182]

Taylor added other reasons for the waning support for CND, which by the end of 1962 was but a shadow of its former self, although it carried on in some form for many years. One was the fact that the direct action called for by many of the active members, such as marches and sit-ins at Whitehall, achieved no result. Certainly both Taylor and Canon Collins were suspicious of the Direct Action Campaign, organised in fact before CND, and which emphasised extra-parliamentary protest; DAC was the progenitor of the 1958 Aldermaston March, arrangements for which were already in train before CND took it over. Some members spoke of running single-issue parliamentary candidates in competition with Labour, so depriving the campaign of many of its supporters, who tended to be Labour. The final blow, according to Taylor, was the 1962 Cuban missile crisis between the US and the USSR, which showed how irrelevant Britain and its nuclear weapons were. Yet, though CND as such was a failure,

Taylor always claimed that it was his finest and most selfless hour, believing as he did in the cause wholeheartedly.[183]

His efforts on the movement's behalf, combined with his teaching, broadcasting and journalism, might have felled someone with a less organised existence. The explanation, perhaps, was the one repeated by R.W. Johnson: 'Marvelling at this heroic – and sustained – energy, I once asked one of Alan's closest colleagues what, then, had Alan stinted on? "Nothing, really," he said. "He simply had a wonderful economy of effort. He never wasted a minute." ' This was demonstrated to full effect during the academic year 1958–9 at the height of Taylor's efforts for CND. The office of Vice-President at Magdalen was one to which Fellows were elected for two years in order of seniority, the duties usually being of the order of allotting guest rooms and presiding in the common room after dinner. 1958, however, was not an ordinary year: it was the five-hundredth anniversary of the accepted date for the founding of the college. Although it was his turn, Taylor paid little attention until the day it came to his attention that 'elaborate plans' were being laid to keep him out of the post, presumably because he was divorced, appeared on television and wrote for the popular press. From that moment 'I wanted the post badly. I appealed to my good friend Harry Weldon and he threatened the President [Boase] with a contested election if I were not nominated. When the time for nominations came there was a ludicrous scene. Usually the senior Fellow was asked for his thoughts which had been agreed beforehand and everyone acquiesced. This time Driver said he had been unable to think of anyone. Harry nominated me and I was in. Driver had failed to think on principle and was perfectly friendly to me thereafter.'[184]

This was the beginning of what turned out to be two years of quite unexpected interest and even pleasure. He undoubtedly appreciated the moment when President Boase guided the visiting American Vice-President, Richard Nixon, towards Taylor and said, 'Mr. Vice-President, I'd like to introduce you to the Vice-President', possibly leaving Nixon to wonder whether there was a gap in his knowledge of the British political system. Taylor had the clever idea of turning over all of the arrangements for dinners and parties to the chef, leaving for himself the tasks of choosing the fireworks and enjoying the events. There was one sad occasion. Harry Weldon suggested a dinner for all past Junior Common Room presidents, which Taylor thought would be the epitome of dullness but which – thanks to the social graces of the past presidents – turned out to be very successful. Weldon enjoyed it tremendously, but then 'he retired to bed and died peacefully during the night. This was in its way a characteristic act: promoting these complicated festivities and then leaving me [Taylor] to cope with them single-handed, when he had had the best of them. Only a totally selfish man would have died at such a moment. Harry was my best friend in Magdalen. I missed him very much.'[185]

Taylor discovered that he enjoyed administration – as long as he was in charge of it: because President Boase was Vice-Chancellor of the university that year, much more responsibility than usual fell on the Vice-President. Taylor was very good in the role. 'His watchwords were relevance and dispatch. Timewasters at college meetings were cut short by his curt interruption, "We are not here to discuss *that*"; one lasted fewer than ten minutes, a record. Joyce Payne, the college secretary, found him full of fun and very efficient. He came into the college office as it opened at 9.30 in the morning, having dealt with his own letters and perhaps a review or two in his rooms beforehand; when she arrived there was a pile he could point to proudly.'[186] He was so good that he was renominated for a further year by Driver himself, who said that the college had never had a better Vice-President.[187]

But it was not all fireworks. Taylor refurbished the Senior Common Room, taking great pleasure in the fabric chosen for the chairs by his colleague Austin Gill (the Tutor in Modern Languages, who succeeded him as Vice-President) and proudly showing off the result to a History colleague from another college. According to one report, he fostered the abandonment of the age-old custom of the Fellows processing into Hall for dinner in order of seniority (a custom which still obtains in some of the other Oxford colleges); but a colleague of Taylor's recalled that it was the Waynflete Professor of Philosophy, Gilbert Ryle, who was the force behind the change, although Taylor undoubted supported him. And he probably counterbalanced, by this outstandingly successful period as Vice-President, the disapproval which some of the Fellows clearly felt as a result of his CND work. Indeed, John Stoye later referred to his 'memorable reign which included the Quincentenary celebration of 1958, organised by him with such precision and brilliance.'[188]

Throughout all of this external turmoil, the fundamental drive and pleasure of his life – the reading and writing of history – continued unabated. Although he wrote a book of European history during this period, *The Origins of the Second World War*, these years in fact marked the beginning of his switch from European to British history and of the serious work which was to lead to the publication in 1965 of one of his best books,

English History 1914–1945. (Both of these titles will be discussed in some detail in the next chapter.) Taylor was able to read for and to write his *English History* during term time largely because he had held, since 1953, a special university lectureship. This differed from the usual university lectureship, called a CUF (Common University Fund) lectureship, which was (perfunctorily) renewed every five years until the holder's resignation or retirement at the age of sixty-seven. In March 1953 the History Board had invited Taylor to become a special lecturer, which meant that his teaching could total no more than ten hours per week (he was currently doing fourteen). The appointment was for five years from October 1953, with a possible renewal for a further five; this was emphasised in the letter to Taylor offering him the post. The reason for the stated limit was that, at this meeting, the board had also made a change in the regulations, deciding that henceforth ten years was the maximum length of time any recipient could hold such a lectureship. (The reason for the change, according to John Prestwich, then Chairman of the Modern History Faculty, was 'to guard against the natural tendency for such posts to be awarded on the grounds of seniority rather than of faculty needs and individual merit.') McFarlane, who also had a special lectureship, had already held it for four years; he was reappointed at the same time and thus had a windfall of the extra years.[189]

There was an attempt by some members of the History Board to extend Taylor's special lectureship, but this was defeated, and the Board wrote to him to inform him that it would be terminated at the end of the 1962–3 academic year. On 16 October 1962 Taylor wrote to President Boase asking whether Magdalen would agree to his continuing as Fellow and Tutor with the same teaching load, i.e. ten rather than fifteen to eighteen hours a week, so that he might continue with his research. Boase's response was to use the opportunity to rid himself of a troublesome clerk, and he wrote 'Resignation of A.J.P. Taylor' on the agenda for the next college meeting, due to be held on 17 October; Taylor's well-wishers in Magdalen, however, managed to get this item changed.

Meanwhile Taylor tried his hand at orchestrating a press campaign. On 12 October he wrote to the Editor of the *Manchester Guardian*, Alastair Hetherington, that 'I enclose a news item which may be of interest to you. No enquiries or comment until Wednesday please.' This was the announcement that the History Board would not renew his special lectureship. He alerted other newspapers as well, with the result that journalists and photographers from a number of publications, some of them dressed in gowns (as were all of the four hundred or so undergraduates – gowns were mandatory for lectures as well as for tutorials), were in place in the Examination Schools on the morning of Wednesday 17 October. At 9am Taylor began the first lecture of his series 'The Study of History': 'We go on all our lives studying history and very rarely think what we are about. I haven't often spoken about this. If I don't do it now I never will. This will be my last opportunity. The History Board have informed me that they do not intend to renew my lectureship when it runs out next summer. These are therefore the last lectures which I shall give in this university.' This all went over the heads of the students, but they were not his intended audience that morning – the whole performance was for the benefit of the journalists. At the close of the lecture Taylor returned to Magdalen, where he gave interviews to a number of newspapers.[190]

That afternoon Magdalen held its usual Wednesday College Meeting, where Taylor's request to remain a Tutorial Fellow but with reduced teaching was discussed. After some debate the request was refused: other Fellows might seek the same dispensation. However, a number of his colleagues sympathised with Taylor's wish to keep some link with the college while devoting himself to research. Under the statutes there existed the category of Fellow by Special Election where the Fellow was engaged on a research programme that had to be approved by the college. Taylor was half-way through his volume for the Oxford History of England, and researching and writing it would certainly fall into that category. Therefore the meeting accepted Taylor's resignation of his Tutorial Fellowship but decided to look into offering him a Fellowship by Special Election, a proposal that was referred to the Fellowship Committee.[191]

Taylor's fight was with the Faculty Board and through it with the university, not with Magdalen. However, a number of the Fellows felt that Taylor should have done more to make this clear: in fact, the Bursar forced Taylor to write a letter for publication to the *Evening Standard* explaining that it was the university, not Magdalen, which he had accused of acting badly. Furthermore, his Magdalen colleagues were not alone in finding the press campaign distasteful, as well as Taylor's claim that he was asking for special terms because 'I'm a rather special historian.'[192] All of these factors influenced the Fellows as they decided whether to award Taylor his special Fellowship.

In fact, it produced a split within the college. At the meeting of the Fellowship Committee on 31 October, it was decided by a vote of seven to one to recommend that Taylor, 'being a person whose attainments and distinction in the study of Modern History are such as to warrant his election to a Fellowship and who has undertaken to carry on research in Twentieth Century British History, be elected to a Fellowship by Special Election for five years from 1 October 1963, at an annual stipend of £275.' Taylor was apprised of the recommendation, and his immediate response was to refuse it. The stipend was insufficient. He clearly conveyed his reaction to John Morris, one of his colleagues, because even before Taylor's letter of refusal was received Morris had written a counterproposal for the next College Meeting. Taylor had undertaken as a condition of the Fellowship to perform some 'special educational work' within the college, namely the delivery in Oxford of at least sixteen lectures each academic year. He therefore proposed that the stipend be £950 per year: 'The offer of £275 per annum to a man of Mr Taylor's distinction and seniority can hardly be described as generous. And since it is conditioned on an undertaking by Mr Taylor to carry on study or research, it provides him with no inducement whatsoever to continue with his lectures. I regard it as of the first importance that we should offer him some inducement to do so. The figure of £950 is suggested because that is the maximum stipend of a CUF lecturer. … There is no doubt that [Taylor] would welcome some such offer from the College.' In the event the decision of the College Meeting on 7 November was that the proposal be referred back to the Fellowship Committee.[193]

The Fellowship Committee met and decided to recommend to the College Meeting that Taylor be awarded the Fellowship at a stipend of £950 'because they believe that the College will benefit from his continuing to be a Fellow'. But it was supported by only five members of the Committee; the other three wrote a 'Contra Memorandum'. They reminded the meeting that on 13 June the Fellowship Committee had decided that they could not consider the question of offering Senior Research Fellowships at that time: the Fellowship Committee required an increased grant, which would make inroads on the money available, and the governing body was already increasing in numbers. Given that decision, they argued, 'we cannot, without some new policy decision by the College and a survey of possible candidates, support a recommendation now to a Fellowship by Special Election at a stipend of £950.' However, the decision of the College Meeting was in Taylor's favour and he was elected to the Fellowship for five years at the larger stipend, retaining his rooms in New Building and his dining rights.[194]

This, then, was the end of Taylor's Tutorial Fellowship at Magdalen College, a position he had held for twenty-five years. He had made his mark in the two areas of work by which a Fellow is judged a 'good college man' whether or not he is: his teaching and his administrative prowess. No one ever complained that he shirked the former; indeed, his (and McFarlane's) teaching was seen as largely responsible for Magdalen's position amongst the top three colleges for History in the tables drawn up by David Worswick and published in the *Times Education Supplement* and the *Oxford Magazine*.[195] He also did his fair share of the administrative tasks that fall to Fellows in the Oxford college system and he did them well. Likewise with his research, in that era rather less influential than now for assessing the worth of an academic, but nevertheless respected, and even sometimes encouraged: most of his books were very well received, and *The Struggle for Mastery in Europe* spectacularly so, leading directly to the accolade of election to a Fellowship of the British Academy. For all of these attainments he was seen by most of his colleagues as a stimulating and valuable member of the college, full of good talk, kind to junior colleagues and a good man in a fight.

But he was also a complicated man, quick to give and take offence, and with a barely concealed contempt for some of his apparently less productive colleagues: he could never understand, for example, why McFarlane did not write more books. A number of the Fellows found his media activities extremely distasteful: they could stomach the book reviews for the *Observer* and the *Manchester Guardian*, and perhaps for the *New Statesman*, but his columns in the popular press were almost uniformly condemned. Appearing on television also carried limited cachet: television sets for most of the 1950s were seen by many as something owned predominantly by the working and lower-middle classes rather than by the middle classes, and even less by the professional and academic middle class. And finally, his complicated marital and extramarital history provoked mixed reactions.

Taylor was attached to the college, in spite of his occasional mocking comments, and was glad to remain a member. Indeed, he now had the best of all possible worlds: he would still lecture and take on postgraduates, but he would never have to teach Oxford undergraduates again. He was being paid to research and write history. He had his college rooms and, when he wanted it, the camaraderie of the Fellowship. At the same time he was now freer to pursue the freelance career which gave him so much pleasure – and money. Rather than an academic, he was now a professional.

Chapter 5

The Oxford Years 1938–1965:
The Books and their Publishers

Mr. G.M. Young once dismissed diplomatic history as 'what one clerk said to another clerk,' and the details of diplomatic history do indeed seem of irremediable triviality; but, in fact, diplomatic history deals with the greatest of themes – with the relations of States, with peace and war, with the existence and destruction of communities and civilisations.

A.J.P. Taylor, 'Diplomatic History', *Manchester Guardian*, 23 May 1939.

I may be a determinist – I believe in large trends, like the continuous growth of German power before the First World War – but I always write very detailed studies, in which it is the accidents that seem to stick out and make up history. My books, therefore, really turn out to be illustrations of free will.

A.J.P. Taylor, quoted in Mehta, *Fly and the Fly-Bottle*

Taylor loved to write. It was almost a primal urge, and the writer's equivalent of withdrawal symptoms set in if he did not write his thousand words a day. As it happened, what he loved – and therefore loved to write about – was history. The danger of constant productivity is declining quality. Taylor was no different, and it was fortunate for his reputation as an historian that this urge to write had a second channel, that of ephemeral journalism. No one has ever charged him with writing bad serious history books: possibly some were wrong-headed; possibly some material was misinterpreted; indeed, reviewers and readers profoundly disliked some of the books. But no one could claim that they were not carefully thought-out and carefully written. It is on these serious works, written during his Oxford years, that his reputation rests.

A consideration of the vast range of books that Taylor published over his lifetime precludes a tidy reduction of his 'themes'. At some point in his career, Taylor wrote on virtually every European country – a book review, an essay, a book. In his reviewing he seems to have been entirely indiscriminate and to have taken on any and every book which was offered to him. Nevertheless, it is possible to discern three broad areas on which he concentrated during successive periods of his life: the Habsburg Empire and the Successor States during the late 1930s and the 1940s; Germany during the late 1940s and the 1950s; and England from the late 1950s on.[1] These interests overlapped, but each was coherent enough to warrant its separate consideration. Taylor's overarching interest, however, was European diplomatic history, which to a varying degree dominated his work on the Habsburg Empire and on Germany, although not to the same extent his work on English history. A notable aspect of his historical interests was their interrelationship with his current political interests, seen most clearly with regard to his books on the Hapsburg Empire and on Germany.

In spite of the vast range of Taylor's writings, it is still possible to set out recurring preoccupations. These included the use and abuse of power; the relationship between governments and the people they govern; the relationship between states in the international system; and the exercise of power by strong men. Statesmen, he believed, did not plan policies but reacted to external events – a theory which combined the roles of accident and agent into a major explanatory factor in history. He also introduced the concept of the 'invention of tradition'. These ideas will be highlighted when discussing his more significant books. This chapter, then, is organised around Taylor's successive intellectual interests, the products of which made him an historian of distinction. These aspects of his life, including his relationships with his publishers and in particular with the Oxford University Press, should be seen within the context of his life at Oxford.

Taylor's two years at Vienna had been a formative period: he learned German, he learned how to conduct research, he decided that he wanted to be a historian, he discovered diplomatic history and he found an initial geographical area of interest. Becoming a diplomatic historian was an unexpected development. As noted earlier, Taylor's education had concentrated on English history, and he had gone to work with Přibram under the misapprehension that the Viennese professor was still interested in Oliver Cromwell and the English Civil War, the broad area in which Taylor planned to work. Upon reaching Vienna, however, he discovered that Přibram's research interests now lay almost wholly in a different field, that of European diplomatic history in general, and of the origins of the First World War in particular. Once Taylor's German was good enough, Příbram set him to work in the Chancellery archives in Vienna on Anglo-Austrian relations between the revolutions of 1848 and the Austro-Prussian War of 1866. According to Taylor, 'this sounded dull enough and, if I had stuck to it, would no doubt have proved as dull as Příbram's own book on Anglo-Austrian relations between 1898 and 1914'. Nevertheless, he enjoyed the types of documents which he had to read and his supervisor introduced him to the pleasures of diplomatic history; in sum, Taylor found his home.[2]

The guidance of Příbram was therefore crucial, but other factors lured Taylor into working specifically on the Habsburg Empire. First of all, one of the few series of lectures which he attended at the University of Vienna was that given on the Habsburg Monarchy by Heinrich von Srbik, a specialist on Metternich (about whom Srbik wrote a biography) and on the diplomatic history of the Austrian Empire. Another aspect which ought not to be underrated was Taylor's liking for Vienna itself; Vienna 'bewitched' him on his first visit in 1928.[3] A third factor of importance was the simple fact that his first experience of research was working in the Austrian archives, and on a topic dealing partly with the diplomatic history of the Habsburg Monarchy.

An undeniable influence was Heinrich Friedjung – both his books and his life. As described in Chapter 3, Taylor's second publication, in 1935, was the introduction to and joint translation of Friedjung's *Der Kampf um die Vorherrschaft in Deutschland, 1859 bis 1866*, which was published in 1935 as *The Struggle for Supremacy in Germany 1859–1866*. Taylor had read three of Friedjung's books while he was in Vienna, and his profound appreciation of their quality was encouraged by Příbram, who not only discussed them with Taylor, but spoke of his close friendship with Friedjung (he was Friedjung's literary executor). But at least as attractive to Taylor was the story of Friedjung's life, combining as it did outstanding historical research and writing with a second life as a journalist. The work on the translation of, and introduction to, Friedjung's book required further thinking about the Austrian Empire.

There were two further influences which encouraged Taylor's continuing interest in the empire. One was his Manchester colleague Lewis Namier. Taylor had first come across Namier's European work in July 1931, when he read his *Germany and Eastern Europe*, probably after first meeting him in Jacob's office. They enjoyed each other's company and often had long and involved discussions, during which Namier sometimes talked about 'the national tangle of the Habsburg Monarchy'.[4] Of Polish birth himself, Namier was intensely interested in, and knowledgeable about, the history and the current state of the many nationalities that had co-existed in the former Austro-Hungarian Empire. Given his continuing interest in the area, Taylor absorbed Namier's learning and some, at least, of his views. A final influence was the arrival of the Taylors' Austrian nanny, Henrietta Werner, in 1938. Soaked in the politics of Austria, a refugee from the Anschluss (the union of Austria with Nazi Germany), Werner provided for Taylor an example of a victim of these politics, as well as a continuing personal link with Vienna.[5]

But the final influence in writing the book *The Habsburg Monarchy* appeared in the form of a commission from the publisher Macmillan. This came about in a somewhat convoluted manner. The first series of lectures Taylor ever gave in Oxford was on the Habsburg Monarchy. Writing, or even organising, a series of lectures forces one at the outset to think clearly about themes, chronology, causation and consequence. Thereafter lectures can evolve according to the taste of the lecturer: anecdotes, character sketches, detailed analysis and exegesis can be used to convey the themes. When the call came, therefore, Taylor had already worked out his organising principles and developed his views on the main actors in the story of the last hundred years of the Habsburg Monarchy. According to Taylor, it came because Namier could not be bothered to write the short history of Austria he had promised to Macmillan. Namier of course knew about the Friedjung translation, and he probably knew about Taylor's lectures on the Habsburg Monarchy. Therefore, Taylor later wrote, 'Lewis, who never wrote a long connected narrative in his life, passed the idea on to me, and I accepted.'[6] Interestingly, this example forms part of the myth propagated by Taylor that he was as putty in the hands of others when it came to the subjects of his books. As he wrote in his autobiography, 'All my books after *The Italian Problem* were suggested to me by others with one exception ... *The Origins of the Second World ... War* the only book the subject of which I chose myself.'[7]

The documents, however, tell a different tale, revealing that Taylor showed rather more initiative than he later admitted, or possibly remembered. They also reduce Namier's role. In April 1939, a year after the publication of his first book on Germany, Taylor wrote to Macmillans that 'I have been thinking for some time of writing a history of Austria in the nineteenth century, either from 1815 or 1848; it would draw on the latest

German & Austrian works & fill a gap in English history books. It would be one volume and not too learned. I have now been approached by another publisher, not on my initiative, with a request for such a work. After my experience of publishing with you, I should prefer to continue with you; & I should be glad to know whether, and on what terms, a book of this kind would interest you.' Harold Macmillan sent the letter on to Namier for his response. Three weeks later Macmillan wrote to Taylor, offering to publish the book. Taylor, however, was not impressed with the proposed terms, and replied that 'the book I had in mind was of a more popular character' and therefore 'I am afraid I must decline & wait to renew our connection when I have something more serious to offer.' Macmillan replied the following day, but Taylor stood his ground, replying that 'I don't really think there is any misunderstanding. The book I have in mind is not a work of scholarship, but one from which I should make some money; and the other publisher whom I mentioned to you in my original letter, had that sort of book in mind. So I am afraid that I must definitely withdraw the suggestion I made to you.'[8]

This refusal seems to have increased Macmillan's interest – possibly because of the implication that a rival publisher thought it would make a significant amount of money – since the following week he wrote to Taylor, suggesting that he come to Oxford to see him. Macmillan dined with Taylor at Magdalen and must have been more persuasive in person than he had been by letter – perhaps he offered him better terms? – because within a week Taylor wrote to him that 'the terms are perfectly satisfactory to me'.[9] (Taylor later wrote that this was 'the only time I met the future prime minister. It did not occur to me that there was much to him. He told me in his aristocatic way that he and his brother published new books simply for pleasure: "financially we should do better to stick to Kipling and our other classics".'[10] Taylor then set to work, spending the summer writing in Switzerland, and producing eighty thousand words by the following January. A single month of the following summer sufficed to complete the revision of the book, and he sent the manuscript to the publisher in late July 1940. It was published in February 1941.

Here is Taylor's own description of the book, written for Macmillan's spring 1941 catalogue:

This is the first connected history in any language of the last hundred years of the Habsburg monarchy, from the stabilisation achieved at the Congress of Vienna in 1815 to the collapse at the end of the Four Years'

War. The aim is primarily narrative: to recount the fortunes of the monarchy; and the leading topics are carefully discussed – the policy of Metternich; the revolutions of 1848; the personality of Francis Joseph; the Austro-Hungarian compromise of 1867; the struggle of Czechs and Germans in Bohemia; and the forces which drove the monarchy to embark on the War of 1914. But the narrative is not mere chronicle; it seeks also to explain. The key to this century of history is found in the relations of dominant and subject peoples: the dominant peoples (Germans, Magyars, and Poles) free in the exercise of their culture, owners of the land and of industry, and successfully asserting against the dynasty their right to a share of political power; the subject peoples, economically inferior and culturally backward, gradually developing a claim to equality, and seeking freedom from their masters at first in alliance with the dynasty but at last against it. The collapse of the dynasty followed on its failure to give the subject peoples political and economic freedom – a lesson still valuable for any new attempt to give stability to central Europe. Thus this book, as well as satisfying students of history, will appeal to all who believe that only through understanding the past can we make a better future.[11]

This was the first and last time that Taylor tried to justify the writing and publication of a book on the basis that history had some utility: thereafter he stuck to its intrinsic interest. The book illuminates certain of his recurring themes, the use and abuse of power, in this case by the emperors, and the relationship between governments and the people they govern. Indeed, the latter theme is the dominant one of the book, which details just what happens to a government in a time of peril if it does not enjoy the confidence of its subjects: it disintegrates.

The title seems curious at first glance: why not simply the history of the Austrian Empire, or of the Austro-Hungarian Empire? Why the history of a monarchy? There are at least two answers, one historical and one practical, to a question which also exercised Taylor and his publisher. As Taylor wrote:

The difficulty is that the Austrian Empire, which was officially established in 1804, changed its name to Austria-Hungary in 1867; and it is clumsy to run the two together except in a sub-title. The simple title, Austria, 1815–1918, is also misleading, because it might be taken to cover only the later Austria of the republic and certainly excludes

Hungary. I think, therefore, that there is no alternative to the Habsburg Monarchy or some variant on it. Instead of the last Hundred Years we could have The Last Century; or The Decline of the Habsburg Monarchy (but it was declining from the beginning!). I prefer Habsburg Monarchy to Habsburg Empire. But of course I am anxious for your advice.[12]

The advice appears to have been to use as many of the suggestions as was feasible, since the final title was *The Habsburg Monarchy 1815–1918: A History of the Austrian Empire and Austria-Hungary*.

The second answer lies in what Taylor was trying to do with the book. As he wrote in the Preface, 'it is concerned solely with the imperial organisation, with its weaknesses, its difficulties, its successes, and its final failure. It is the history of the Habsburg Monarchy (in the two forms which it took between 1815 and 1918), rather than of the peoples who lived under Habsburg rule.' It is primarily the view from Vienna, the actions – or, rather, reactions – of a monarch and his small, frequently changing coterie as they attempted to preserve the freedom of the emperor to rule, or not to rule, as he chose. The emperors as drawn by Taylor (four in total but only two of any significance) had two concerns only: the preservation of the dynasty and the retention of sole control over the military forces of the empire, and on these two points they were unmovable. Public opinion was, on the whole, a matter of indifference to them; when forced to respond to it, concessions were made only as far as necessary and frequently rescinded when the need had passed. Rather than the view from below looking up, it is the view from the top looking down. In spite of his often proclaimed, and sincerely felt, sympathy for 'the people', Taylor almost invariably concentrated his historical attention on their rulers. With this conception of Habsburg history and consequently of the book in mind, the title seems inescapable.

This is a melancholy book, shot through with historical resignation. It charts the rhythm of Habsburg history in the nineteenth and early twentieth centuries. It concentrates in particular on the relationship between the emperor and his officials and bureaucrats, and the nationalities and political units making up the empire: the process of crisis and compromise, new crisis and new compromise, failure and success, neither complete nor final. The focus is on the emperor. First there was Francis I, who died in 1835. He was succeeded by Ferdinand, 'an imbecile, epileptic and rickety', who abdicated in 1848. Taylor provided the general reading public with Ferdinand's two recorded sayings: 'I'm the Emperor and I want noodles!' and, in 1866 on the occasion of the Prussian occupation of Prague (capital of Bohemia, one of the provinces of the Austrian Empire) during the Austro-Prussian War, 'Even I could have done as well as this.'[13] Ferdinand was succeeded by Francis Joseph, a dim but obstinate man, who is accorded the primary role in the book. He was succeeded by Charles, the last Habsburg emperor, who abdicated in 1918.

The emperor dealt only with his officials, particularly the Imperial Chancellor, the Imperial Prime Minister, the Imperial Commander-in-Chief and the Imperial Foreign Minister. They were eminently expendable and were often expended, but there were always others to take their places. The emperors, in particular Francis Joseph, who came to power during the 1848 revolution and remained Emperor until the middle of the First World War, wanted control and quiet more than they wanted expansion, and they wanted the survival of the dynasty more than they wanted anything else. Taylor followed this thread, bringing in the various subject peoples only as they influenced the success or failure of the emperors' desires. The book has thrust, it has characters and it has ideas.

One interesting historical conception, now widespread but which possibly first makes its appearance in this book, is that of the invention of tradition. Taylor uses it more than once. One example occurs in his discussion of the development of national consciousness amongst the Czechs: 'the professors and journalists who composed the Czech movement grew enthusiastic over the Diet of Bohemia, because – having re-created their nationalism – they were ready to "invent" a political tradition to go along with it.'[14] One result of this Czech enthusiasm was the forgery in the early nineteenth century of putative mediaeval manuscripts, celebrated by Czech nationalists as relics of their true early culture. Taylor cites the exposure by Thomas Masaryk of one of the most famous of these, Vaclav Harka's *Kralodvorsky Rukopis*, as an example both of the existence of such forgeries and of Masaryk's probity. This same example was, in fact, used twenty years later by Prys Morgan in the influential volume of essays *The Invention of Tradition*.[15]

But what really comes through in the book are two of Taylor's major and continuing preoccupations. One was the use and abuse of power. Francis Joseph's concept of ruling was to sign mounds of paper whilst authorising as few changes as necessary – the refusal to take a decision is also a decision. Taylor argues that as soon as a minister showed either (1) signs of even average ability or (2) the desire to change anything which the Emperor deemed fundamental, he was dismissed; indeed, even the implementation of a successful policy frequently invited dismissal. At the same time the empire took on the accoutrements of a police state – but with less than total success: Taylor quotes the observation of the radical Viktor Adler that the Austrian Empire demonstrated 'absolutism tempered by inefficiency'.[16] In other words, the emperor and the officials of the empire frequently tried to abuse their power, but were lamentably inconsistent about it, which probably helped to account for the relative lack of retaliatory rebellion. Power, therefore, was utilised to keep everything the same, in particular the role of the dynasty as the supreme ruler of the empire, its subjects and armed forces.

Secondly, there was the relationship between the dynasty and its subject peoples. Taylor makes the distinction between those nations in the Habsburg Empire with a history – in particular the Magyars, but also the Germans, Italians and Poles – and those without a history – the Slovaks, the Ruthenes, the Croatians, the Czechs, the Romanians. The former were the 'historic nationalities', the latter, all peasant nationalities, were the 'submerged nationalities'. The historic nationalities were conscious of their nationality, through language, through culture, through their co-nationalists having their own state. The submerged nationalities lacked all of these. Taylor emphasises the attempts of the monarchy to suppress, to encourage, to co-opt and to play off against each other the various nationalities, and particularly, as they grew in consciousness and in strength, to play off the submerged nationalities against the historic nationalities. This, one might argue, was a Good Thing, in that the submerged nationalities were thereby encouraged to emerge into the light; but the ultimate outcome was not. As Taylor wrote: 'The legacy of history is such that there is no conceivable settlement of Central Europe which will not involve injustice to some of those living there [because] the privileged historic nationalities and the submerged nationalities who have won their own way to freedom, can never work together.'[17] A prime reason for this, of course, was that none of the nationalities, then in the nineteenth century or in 1941 (when the book was published), was the sole nationality populating any piece of the Habsburg lands. The results of this intermingling, particularly when differing religions were added to the mix, bedevilled – and, indeed, continue to bedevil – a sizable chunk of the empire. The book ends with the break-up of the empire as the subject nationalities formed themselves into more or less national states, an outcome which was given official validation by the Treaty of Versailles.

A final preoccupation was the role of the Great Powers within the international system. For Taylor this primarily meant the role of the six European Great Powers, Great Britain, France, Russia, Prussia (and then the German Empire), the Austrian (then Austro-Hungarian) Empire and Italy (or five: Taylor was always doubtful about, indeed scathing towards, Italy's attempts to play in the Premier League). However, the Empire's foreign policy role received notably short shrift in the 1941 version of the book. Only in times of military crisis – the Austro-Prussian War, for example – do the other Powers make more than a relatively brief appearance. Rather, what dominates is what might be called the internal foreign policy between the monarchy and the various geographically based units of the empire and their resident peoples, and in particular between the monarchy and the Hungary of the Magyars. In fact, Taylor deemed the relative lack of discussion of foreign policy in his 1941 treatment of Habsburg history a fault in the book and moved to rectify it, with somewhat indifferent results, when he revised it in 1948.

The book was published in February 1941 and reprinted the following year. The reviews were on the whole good. The Regius Professor of History at Oxford, F.M. Powicke, wrote one of the first. It is interesting, not only for his very favourable assessment of the book, but also – given the later criticisms of Taylor's prose as sometimes glib – of the writing: 'Mr Taylor has written a very able book. He is not only a master of his subject; he knows how to present it. ... [I]t is worth while to emphasise the truth that a lucid, witty, and epigrammatic writer is the better for the self-discipline which scholarship and industry can give. Mr Taylor's book is an apt reminder of this truth.'[18] Another reviewer began by writing that 'there was a saying in old Austria, one must be Austrian born to understand Austrian policy. Mr. A.J.P. Taylor proves ... that this is not necessarily the case',[19] while a third, Oscar Jaszi (Minister of Culture in the 1918 government of the new Hungarian Republic), wrote in the American *Journal of Modern History* that 'he belongs to that rare class of historians who are able to supplement the factual evidence with a high grade of psychological insight and artistic imagination. ... What we read in his book is not dead history but an often thrilling analysis of personalities and mass psychological insights.'[20]

There were, of course, criticisms. Two reviews followed a similar line. The first began 'A kind critic would call this book scholarly – and it is certainly the work of a scholar. But a juster description would be "academic", a history distilled from other histories, recommending itself by its concise presentation of a very difficult subject', while the second reviewer argued in the *Times Literary Supplement* that 'It is a work of "book learning". He has read widely and understood much ... [and] he has written a book by no means unreadable and fairly accurate.' Taylor replied in the *TLS* 'to the criticism that his book was not based on "first-hand observation" by observing that Gibbon and Macaulay had been similarly handicapped'.[21]

Two other reviewers had more substantial criticisms. The first was the distinguished economic historian Charles H. Wilson. He began by observing that 'This is constitutional history, the study of the distribution of power in the imperial system. ... No objection can properly be raised to this method on the ground of its specialisation ... [But] it does not take sufficient account, it may be suggested, of the economic and diplomatic forces of the period (excluded by Mr. Taylor from his direct inquiry) and their effects upon the Habsburg Monarchy.' The criticism that Taylor had not taken sufficient account of the diplomatic forces was endorsed by Taylor's Viennese mentor, Přibram, then living in exile in Kew Gardens, London. He wrote that 'Little attention is devoted to foreign policy, and this seems to me a defect of the book. The connection between external and domestic policy is close in all states, but nowhere closer than in the Danubian Monarchy.' These were very important points, and Taylor remembered them when the time came to revise the book for a new edition. Nevertheless, Přibram concluded, English readers 'will gain a good insight into the complicated conditions of a now disintegrated Danubian Monarchy from this clear and precise work.'[22]

The Habsburg Monarchy established Taylor as an expert in the modern history both of Austria and of the Successor States. He very much enjoyed the status and, during (and for a few years after) the war in particular, it led to a new circle of interesting and sometimes important friends, to his abortive work for the Political Warfare Executive (PWE) and to unofficial positions as consultant to several of the governments-in-exile, particular those of Czechoslovakia and Yugoslavia. These new relationships had the result of making him considerably more aware of the importance of the subject peoples in both the workings of and the decline of the imperial system, insights which he incorporated into the revised edition of the book. The book's first publication also facilitated his increasingly public career in print journalism and broadcasting, partly based on this area of expertise. The concluding episode was the publication in 1948 of the revised edition of *The Habsburg Monarchy* which, somewhat curiously, signalled his departure from the history of that particular part of Europe.

Taylor's life was in a sense changed, and certainly enhanced, by a meeting late in 1940. As he decribed it, 'I was finishing my book on *The Habsburg Monarchy* and was actually writing about Karolyi's ending of Hungary's connection with the Habsburgs when there was a ring at the door. There stood a tall man with a limp and a cleft palate: none other than Michael Karolyi himself.' Michael [Mihaly] Karolyi, who was thirty-one years older than Taylor, had become President of the Hungarian Republic on 16 November 1918. This was, according to the Foreign Office, 'the will of the people, as a result of his uncompomising anti German attitude and Entente friendship as well as his progressive ideas on social and national problems.'[23] It is immediately obvious from this description that the two men would have shared a fundamental political outlook, that is, their sympathy and support for ordinary people as opposed to their rulers, but what was almost as important was that they shared a sense of humour: 'they were always on the same wave length, they could always tease each other, they could make lighthearted remarks about the most serious things and they found life extremely funny when others would have been hurt or sulky.'[24] The two of them were friends for the rest of Karolyi's life, and Taylor attended his state funeral in Budapest in 1962, giving an oration.[25]

Karolyi widened Taylor's social circle by introducing him to other Hungarian political refugees 'who were crowding into Oxford'. (The Karolyis were living in a flat on Crick Road in Oxford, but soon moved to more opulent quarters in London.) The ones who became closest to Taylor were the Hatvanis. According to Taylor, Baron Hatvani had been a wealthy and powerful newspaper proprietor in Hungary who had managed to bring his fortune with him into exile. The Hatvanis 'provided a lively intellectual centre thoughout the war. Hatvani had been a considerable literary figure and also by repute a great lover, providing many entertaining anecdotes about both. He had been among Michael's [i.e. Karolyi's] close supporters in 1918.' Taylor made a direct connection between this circle and his work on the Hungarian handbook for the PWE: 'Suitable Hungarian refugees provided me with detailed information on Hungarian administration and economics which I merely turned into good English. I wrote a long chapter on Hungarian history and concocted another with Michael's assistance on the political situation.'[26]

Taylor used the knowledge gained from his PWE work to strengthen his links with the *Manchester Guardian* – Wadsworth, the Editor, was happy to take advantage of the information Taylor had gained at the PWE and from his contacts with the exile government leaders. For example, Taylor wrote to Wadsworth in September 1943, with regard to his experience with the

PWE, that 'I have recently had occasion to study contemporary Hungarian politics, and I think that I now know as much of the situation in Hungary as anyone in England. ... I could let you have an intelligence summary for private use, if ever you felt the need for it.' Wadsworth reacted favourably: 'About Hungary it is good to find someone of independent mind who does know something about the place. I wonder whether ... you would do us an early 1,000 words' straightforward account of the present set-up. ... You could do an objective account like that without drawing on any confidential information and it might be very useful in setting people on the right track and forestalling the wirepullers. Crozier would also, I know, welcome very much an intelligence summary such as you suggest.' Taylor sent him the suggested article within a week, adding that 'If ever there is anything really exciting from Hungary and I can be of use give me a ring.' He wrote regularly on Hungary for the remainder of the war,[27] longer pieces on current affairs in the region as well as reviews.

Taylor also became friendly with Hubert Ripka, a member of the Czechoslovak government-in-exile in London, whose family lived in Oxford. From Ripka he learned a great deal about the history and current problems of nationality affairs in central Europe. This friendship led to strong links with Eduard Beneš, President of the Czech government-in-exile, who adopted Taylor as one of his intellectual confidants. According to Taylor, because Beneš was President, even if only in exile, he 'was not allowed to brave the front line in London and had to live in sovereign state at Aston Abbotts – a Rothschild house of, for them, a modest standard. Bored and isolated, Beneš summoned an audience whenever he could and I was often swept over to Aston Abbotts in the presidential car'. Taylor became an unofficial advisor to the group of Czech political exiles on British public opinion and how to influence it, and 'was drawn into pro-Czech propaganda in which I had little faith'.[28]

The upshot was Taylor's first political pamphlet, *Czechoslovakia's Place in a Free Europe*. This began life on 29 April 1943 as a lecture given at the Czechoslovak Institute in London, with Jan Masaryk, the exiled Czech Minister for Foreign Affairs and Deputy Prime Minister, in the chair. The intention of the lecture-cum-pamphlet was to explain to the Czechs themselves, and then to the rest of the public, the glorious and necessary duty they had to the rest of Europe. This duty was defined by geography and confirmed by political system and culture. By their geography the Czechs acted as a barrier to the expansion of Germany, but they also acted as a hyphen between East and West. By the fact that for twenty years they had been the only true and working democracy in the British mould east of the Rhine, whilst having the Slav sense of community, they constituted the marriage of two worlds: they must explain British democracy to the Russians whilst explaining Russia to the West. This meant that everyone would hate them, but this was also part of their historic task. (Taylor's actual words here were 'You must appear to the English people as communists and to the Russians as democrats and therefore receive nothing but abuse from both sides.') And his final paean: 'History lays no heavier tasks on any European people; but no people is more fitted to accomplish them. The very magnitude of their tasks rejoices their hearts; and the Czechoslovak people are not only confident, but cheerful, about the future.'[29] In a sense it was a locker-room pep talk, but it was also meant to lay Czechoslovakia's claim to consideration from the Great Powers in the future.

One outcome of the address was to solidify Taylor's special relationship with Czechs – and with Slovaks. The latter considered themselves a nation apart from the Czechs and had to a certain extent collaborated with the Germans, which had brought them economic benefits. Early in November 1944 Taylor met with the delegates of the Slovak National Council who had just arrived in England from Slovakia – a mixture of Communist, right-wing agrarian and military heads. As he wrote to Wadsworth, they were

> in a tangle. ... Now they want to be a separate Nation, but at the same time they want Czechoslovakia stronger than before, as they realise that without Bohemia they must be dependent on Germany – or on Hungary. I asked them what they meant by being a separate nation. They said they meant culturally independent: their own press, literature, schools. Separate tariffs or economic planning? No. Certainly not. They want a Czechoslovak plan, by which the resources of Bohemia will be used to raise their standards. But suppose the Czechs insist on being a separate nation? That they would not like at all. A separate army? No. But then what is to be the language of command? They were troubled about this and said there would have to be an agreed Czechoslovak tongue for army purposes. Then there is a Czechoslovak nationality? No. And so on.

One can sense Taylor's thought processes here, the questions arising from his work on the Habsburg Monarchy and the nationalities. The issues of the language of state and of the control of the army were germane. So were the questions of social and cultural control. There is here a direct link between his discussion of these issues in a book of history and his discussion of them as current politics. But his comments are also redolent of the experiences of the interwar period, when the group of small Successor States proved no barrier to a resurgent Germany. In the end Taylor told the Slovaks that 'if they wanted security they must go with Russia', but that 'we democratic elements would like them to try to go with us too, though we have not much to offer', said, presumably, with the betrayal of Czechoslovakia at Munich in mind.[30]

Taylor's interest in Yugoslavia had begun as early as 1941: he became associated with the Yugoslav claim to Trieste 'when the Royal Yugoslav government began to run it.'[31] The following year, as he recalled in his autobiography, 'Lewis Namier wrote to me with an odd request. Rebecca West had just published a book on Yugoslavia, *Black Lamb and Grey Falcon*. It had been badly reviewed in *Time and Tide*, a semi-feminist weekly owned by Lady Rhondda of which Rebecca herself was a director. Would I write a long letter giving a more favourable verdict? I greatly admired the book, now I think too much so, and gladly obliged.' Taylor's letter was printed on 7 March 1942. 'It is true', he wrote, 'that Miss West is often inaccurate in her details', but he underlined 'the art with which Miss West accompanies ... her profound purpose, which is to depict the soul of a people as a novelist draws the character of an individual.' He also mentioned that the book lacked a clear chronology and was essentially chaotic, but this was acceptable because she illuminated the past 'by vision'. It is probable that one of his main reasons for liking the book was that West shared his belief that the 'existence and compelling reality of national communities is the fundamental, inescapable fact of European politics both past and present',[32] the theme of his own *Habsburg Monarchy*.

Taylor recalled that 'My letter about *Black Lamb and Grey Falcon* opened *Time and Tide* to me [as a book reviewer]. Lady Rhondda was very keen on the lesser nationalities of Europe and I was the very man for her. I was safe on the Serbs, the Czechs, the Macedonians and such like. I was even safe on Poland's gallant history. But a time came when I received books on what the Poles call the eastern, and the Russians the western borderlands. Here I was on the side of the Ukrainians and the Byelo-Russians and had no doubt that these lands belonged rightfully to the Soviet Union. I said so in my review.' Taylor wrote seven reviews for *Time and Tide* between March and October 1942, assessing books covering both the history and current affairs of the region. It was his seventh, published on 31 October, which caused a furore. This was a review of Bernard Newman's *The New Europe* entitled 'A Europe of Beautiful Wishes'. Referring to the book, which proposed various frontier changes, as 'a blueprint of a new cloud-cuckooland', Taylor reiterated his long-held belief that 'the peoples of Europe can enjoy freedom only under the joint protection of England and Russia; and just as we postulate a group of friendly states in western Europe with similar social and political systems to our own, so does Russia in eastern Europe.' This may have seemed an entirely realistic sentiment to Taylor, but it could hardly have been accepted with equanimity by the Estonians, Latvians, Lithuanians or Poles, or by those who supported their desires for independent nationhood. The response to his review was a spate of attacks; Taylor replied ('It is almost impossible for a mere Englishman to talk sense about eastern Europe without being subjected to a Polish "terror by correspondence"'); the Editor of *Time and Tide* responded to his letter of self-defence with one attacking his arguments; and – excepting one further review that may have already been on the pin and awaiting publication – Taylor was sacked.[33]

Taylor had come to know a number of Slovene refugees 'who had been running their claim underground throughout the period of Italian rule. With their briefing I wrote an article called TRST [sic] for the *New Statesman* some time in the autumn of 1944.'[34] The same year, he was approached by General Vladko Velebit, Marshall Tito's first representative in England, who asked him to write a pamphlet justifying Yugoslavia's claims to Trieste. According to Taylor, 'I was fully in sympathy with these claims though I doubted whether a pamphlet would help them. I said to Vladko, "Get to Trieste before the Allies. That is the only argument that will count." Vladko, with his captivating innocence in worldly affairs, insisted that British public opinion would respond to a fair case. I duly wrote the pamphlet which of course, when published, carried no weight at all.'[35]

The pamphlet was published in 1945 by the Yugoslav Information Office. The core of the argument was that Trieste should be part of Yugoslavia, not of Italy. Taylor supported it with numerical comparisons between Slovenes and Italians, with comparisons between the cases of Danzig and Trieste, with comparisons between the cases of Trieste and Fiume, with historical arguments and with arguments based on rights and justice. His final argument – that to recognise the Slovene, and thus the Yugoslav, claim to Trieste would strengthen relations between East and West – was removed at the request of the Yugoslavs, who knew that the support of the USSR would only strengthen the opposition of the West. During the negotiations over the peace treaty with Italy, Taylor again advised the Yugoslavs, but not surprisingly all the advice in the world availed naught against Western suspicions of a growing communist menace. After a brief life as a Free City, Trieste was awarded to Italy, not to Yugoslavia, and Vladko, who had negotiated the settlement, 'suffered the fate of a fall-guy'.[36]

The pamphlet did not pass unnoticed. It was published shortly before Taylor was due to speak on Trieste in the series 'World Affairs: A Weekly Survey' for the BBC Radio Home Service on 24 September 1945. Even before he spoke, a Dr Massey, Reader in German at Bedford College, University of London, rang up, 'at the request of an MP' whom she refused to name, to protest at Taylor's being allowed to broadcast on Trieste, since it was clear from his pamphlet that he was 'a biassed person on the subject'. Later that day Kenneth Grubb, Controller of the Overseas Division of the Ministry of Information, also rang the BBC and, whilst indicating that 'he did not wish to interfere in the BBC's domestic affairs ... asked whether such scripts were shown to the Foreign Office'. The BBC's answer was no. Some time after the broadcast, Victor Cunard of the Foreign Office's Political Intelligence Department complained that the script was pro-Yugoslavian. The result was a BBC decision to extract from Taylor an assurance 'that he was not going in for pamphleteering and that he would not use or propose to use his talks for the advocacy of special causes'. At the end of October, therefore, R.A. Rendall, the Controller of Talks, and George Barnes, the Assistant Controller, had a long conversation with Taylor. Rendall emphasised that they were not against talks with meat in them, but only against those that 'made a case'; the Yugoslav talk had received much criticism. Taylor, who had probably thought himself very clever in his two-pronged attack, realised that he had overstepped the line and was very accommodating: he appreciated the difficulty, he said, and had been very careful in drafting that part of his script; he also realised that his Trieste pamphlet did in some sense qualify his value to the BBC. They all agreed that the Trieste difficulty must not recur. In the end both Rendall and Barnes 'were impressed by his candour and good sense and his appreciation of our problems in this field'.[37]

During the war and for two years thereafter, then, Taylor continued to learn about and comment on the Habsburg Successor States. Unable to visit the region during the war, he made up for this as and when he could: he went to Czechoslovakia for three weeks in 1946 on behalf of the *Manchester Guardian*; he visited Yugoslavia with Margaret in the spring of 1947, a reward from the Yugoslav government for the help he had given them; and he returned to Czechoslovakia the same year, where, he later claimed, he had a forewarning of the 1948 Czech *coup d'état*. The trip to Yugoslavia made a particular impact: he visited a number of the Orthodox monasteries, which he found a revelation and which reignited his interest in mediaeval church architecture.[38] But the most substantial outcome of this period of learning, thinking and visiting was the revision and republication of his book on the Habsburg Monarchy.

The desire to place his revised thoughts before the world was not, however, what initially motivated Taylor. Rather, it was his outrage at how few copies of *The Habsburg Monarchy* Macmillan had sold. In November 1944 he wrote to Daniel Macmillan, now the effective head of the firm:

> I was surprised to learn from the statement which I received this morning that only 14 copies of the Habsburg Monarchy had been sold during the last year. I could have sold more copies than that by myself; but it is my business to write books, not to sell them. The book is in constant demand ... but no copy is to be found in any Oxford bookshop, nor was there one in two leading London bookshops at which I recently enquired. .... I should be glad therefore to know if this book is still in print. If so, I should like some explanation why it is not stocked by any bookseller; if not, whether you intend to reprint it within the six months specified in your contract. I might also inform you that I have just completed a history of Germany in the ninetenth century; but in view of the disappointments I have had with the Habsburg Monarchy I have offered it to a publisher who is interested in selling books.'[39]

This letter led to a 'frightful' row with Macmillan, and as a consequence they were on 'very bad terms'.[40]

When Taylor wrote again over a year later his letter was considerably milder in tone: 'I imagine that the present edition of The Habsburg Monarchy must be nearly exhausted ... if you are not anxious to bring out a further edition, I am willing to resume my rights and to relieve you of any further responsibility. I quite appreciate that this is not the type of book to the sales of which you attach much importance; but you will also appreciate that I am anxious for a more extensive sale, and it may be to our mutual advantage to bring our present connection to an end.' A month earlier he had proposed to Hamish Hamilton, eponymous head of the publishing firm that had published his *The Course of German History* (see below), that they offer the Habsburg book to an American firm; Macmillans had sold about three hundred copies in the US but had declined to bring out an

American edition. Hamilton demurred, since no publisher would want to take over an unsuccessful book (as it had been in the US).[41] But clearly the idea had taken root in Taylor's mind that he should withdraw from the Macmillan stable entirely and confirm his membership of another that appeared to appreciate him more.

The following year Taylor made his move. Writing to Hamilton in December 1945, he asked

> whether you would like to take over my Habsburg Monarchy. ...
> [Macmillan's] edition of 2000 is now practically exhausted, and they are
> unwilling to bring out a new one, being furious at my desertion. ... It
> sold its first thousand in about nine months. ... It is the only work on the
> subject in English and it will go on being essential to University students
> for a long time – a market not touched yet, as they have all been away at
> the wars. It therefore seems to me a safe steady seller. ... At the same
> time there are a lot of points on which I am not really satisfied with it;
> and if you considered taking it over I'd rewrite it pretty extensively. ... It
> is really the apple of my eye and I'd like to keep it in print and especially
> to get a wider circulation for it. ... It is only now that I understand how
> Macmillans can offer such generous terms after the first 2000: they
> never print or publish more than 2000!

Hamilton's response was cautious: 'Your proposal that we take over your HABSBURG MONARCHY is one which I should like to consider seriously. ... It is hard to say without having read the book how well we could do with a re-issue, but the fact that Macmillan sold so few of the first edition is apt to militate against our chances. Anyway, please try and let me have a copy, and you may be sure that we shall give the proposal our most careful and sympathetic consideration, as we want you on our list for good.'[42]

Some weeks later, Hamilton wrote to let Taylor down as gently as possible: 'I read THE HABSBURG MONARCHY during the week-end with great admiration. It is a great piece of work. ... Quite frankly I am doubtful of our ability to do much more than Macmillan have done, with a reissue of a book of which they still hold over a thousand copies, first published five years ago. ... Furthermore, in Macmillan's present state of mind as described by you, I can imagine that they would be pretty difficult over any question of transfer.'[43]

Taylor, however, was not about to give up without a fight: 'I am afraid that I must have misled you about the figures of the Habsburg Monarchy

1. *Taylor in his Eton collar, Christmas 1916. His personality is already stamped on his face.*

2. *The Taylor 'family' post-1919: Percy Taylor, Alan Taylor, Henry Sara and Constance Taylor.*

2nd Torpid, 1926.

BOW	G. W. PROSSER.	9	11½	4	D. F. CROZIER	12	8½	7	K. M. MONIE	10	13½
2	A. L. EDWARDS	10	12	5	H. R. HERRING.	11	9	STR	A. J. P. TAYLOR	11	1.
3	C. N. EDWARDS	10	10.	6	J. M. CASSELS.	10.	7.	COX.	J. J. M. STEWART	9	10¼

3. The crew of Oriel II – Taylor (seated in the centre of the second row) was the stroke and JIM (Innes) Stewart (seated on the ground in front of Taylor) was the cox.

4. *Taylor's Oxford friend, Jack Yates, about 1930. Although in theatrical costume here, Yates acted the elderly man whilst up at Oxford, even to the silver cane.*

5. *Taylor in 1928, aged 22, before his departure for Vienna.*

6 and 7. The Lusthaus in the Prater (above) and the Chancellery, two landmarks of Taylor's Viennese life. The first stood for pleasure, for horseback riding, good food and fellowship, the second for the research in which he took an ever increasing interest.

8. *Percy Taylor, sometime in the 1930s.*

9. *Taylor, Margaret and (probably) Teddy Pratt (left) in Switzerland in the early 1930s.*

10. *Three Gates, Upper Disley, where the Taylors lived from 1933 to 1938. Taylor never ceased to regret the loss of happiness he had enjoyed there.*

11. *Holywell Ford, the Magdalen College house where Taylor lived from 1939 until 1952, when he moved into a set of rooms in New Building.*

12. *Malcolm Muggeridge in 1953, when he became the Editor of* Punch. *He and Taylor were friends from 1933 until Taylor's death. They even drafted each other's obituary.*

13. *Robert Kee in 1951. An Oxford Lothario, he always claimed that he was unaware of the pain Margaret's infatuation with him caused Taylor.*

14. *The poet Dylan Thomas in 1946. If not quite the Greek god Margaret called him, then he was not always a drunken sot.*

15. *Henrietta Kotlan-Werner in 1991. She came to the Taylors' in Manchester from Vienna as a refugee from the Anschluss. She said that Taylor taught her about democracy.*

16. *The Mill, Great Yarmouth, Isle of Wight, a seventeenth-century brick house overlooking the sea. Taylor bought it in 1955 as the holiday home for his first family.*

17. New Building, Magdalen College, built in the 1730s. From 1952 until his retirement in 1976, Taylor lived and taught here during the week.

18. Harry Weldon, a philosopher and reformer, stimulating and acerbic, was Taylor's closest friend at Magdalen.

19. (above left) *A tutorial at Magdalen: Bruce MacFarlane in 1940 assumes his customary posture whilst listening to Karl Leyser read out his essay.*

20. (above right) *A tutorial at Christ Church: Hugh Trevor-Roper in 1950, apparently about to pounce on the undergraduate reading out his essay.*

21. *The farewell dinner for President Boase in the Hall at Magdalen upon the occasion of his retirement in 1968. The figure at the right end of High Table has been identified as Taylor.*

exactly the most comfortable thing in the world to have a journalist perpetually prowling round your house) was too great. When at last I asked if I could draw him he said, "No." "But why?" I asked. "I can't be of the slightest possible interest to anybody," he said. "But that's absurd," I put forward. "Everyone listens to your commentaries. They would like to see what you look like. What you've got to say for yourself." "You can tell them I look like nothing on earth" (he was gardening at the time, in an old shirt and shorts, and leaning on a hoe), "and all I've got to say is 'No.' Sorry." He didn't look at all sorry.

I wouldn't have minded so much if I could have kept my defeat to myself, but I couldn't. I was in Miss Hermione Baddeley's dressing room one night trying to persuade Mr. Raymond Green, the explorer, to overcome his habitual modesty and be drawn. "If you do refuse," I said, as a final appeal, "you will be the only one who ever has" He wavered, and then, "Oh, no, he won't," piped up a voice; "I did." It was A. J. P. Taylor, of course.

FOILED AGAIN

When I was endeavouring to make Mr. Henry Chennels forget his habitual coyness, I tried the same method. "No one else has ever refused me," I coaxed. "What about A. J. P. Taylor?" came a chorus of voices. Foiled again. The man was everywhere about me, pointing, taunting, grinning, the symbol of defeat. When I died, I decided, A. J. P. Taylor would be found engraved upon my heart.

In my bitterness I became a little malicious. "A. J. P. Taylor," I was heard to say more than once, "thinks he can get more publicity by not being 'Drawn and Quoted'." It was unworthy of me. And it didn't bluff a flea. And then one night the clouds lifted. A. J. P. Taylor, it was borne to me by a rising young spy I know, had been banned by the Ministry of Information. A. J. P. Taylor, with that streak of perversity which constitutes, one had to admit, the major part of his wayward charm, now felt that it was time that his public should be allowed a tantalising glimpse of the man whom the M.O.I. had banished from the public eye; A. J. P. Taylor had something to say.

be / "he might be an official of the Ministry of Information!" We went out into the garden. A. L. Rowse was there, his conversation, for sheer hard glittering brilliance, putting to shame the sequins on the sunlit water. Mrs. Graham Green, with her two children, W. R. Rogers, the Irish poet whose "Awake" has been like a spiritual call to arms. While in the distance Chang Lee, "The Silent Traveller" whose discovery of the English counties has been as exciting for us as for himself, poked about among the flowers and

preserved his customary silence. "Giles," called A.J.P. to an intellectual-looking shrimp who was obviously... "Interviewing"

you collect pictures?" I looked at the Toulouse Lautrec lithograph of Oscar Wilde, the "Sick Duck" of Graham Sutherland, and remembered the Utrillo in the dining room (done at the time when the artist was becoming obsessed with circular posteriors), the Boudin seascape, and the unfinished Sickert in the drawing-room. "My wife's," he explained. "But you must admit that you collect people," I insisted, thinking of the coterie outside. "Why! You can't move a foot in this dovecote without fluttering a poet—Stephen Spender, or Dylan Thomas. It's a positive nest of singing birds!" "My wife's friends," he assured me.

A. J. P. TAYLOR

22. The banning of Taylor by the Ministry of Information as characterised by the Oxford Mail. 'Banned by the Ministry of Information' is in Taylor's own handwriting.

23. The television confrontation over The Origins of the Second World War in July 1961: Taylor, Robert Kee, Hugh Trevor-Roper and the ghost of the protagonist.

AJP TAYLOR
"An unusual kind of star"

24. Where Taylor felt happiest and most confident: in front of the camera.

25. Taken in 1962, this was Taylor's favourite publicity photograph.

26. Éva Haraszti with her two sons in 1958.

27. Taylor with his two daughters, Amelia and Sophia, who married on the same day, 14 May 1966, at St Pancras Town Hall. Amelia, then 22, was an actress and Sophia, 20, was a history student at University College London.

28. Taylor at the opening of the Beaverbrook Library in 1967.

29. Taylor in 1981, in front of his collection of his own titles in their various editions and languages.

30. Taylor depicted by the cartoonist Marc.

... the book will be entirely out of print by the summer of this year and yet it is still selling at the rate of 400 a year, entirely without advertisement or mention of any kind. Macmillans do not claim that the book won't sell. They write: "As you have now left us to go to another publisher, we do not think that we should want to bring out a new edition when the stock of the present edition is exhausted."' Hamilton then capitulated, writing that 'in view of what you tell me of the Macmillan sales of THE HABSBURG MONARCHY and the fact that it will not be necessary for us to negotiate with them for the purchase of over-stock, I shall be glad to republish the book when paper permits.'[44] The principle of publishing having been settled, two major points remained to be decided: what sort of book was it to be, a reissue of the existing version or a rewritten version; and what were the terms to be. There was less argument over the former than the latter.

Taylor presented the alternatives: 'The first would be for you to bring out a small edition, say 2000, of the book in its present form, apart from the correction of a few mistakes; I would be satisfied with a smaller percentage than usual. The other and more ambitious way would be to treat it as a new book: I would rewrite it in large part, make it longer, put in more foreign policy, and polish every sentence for style. Of course then I should expect the usual size of edition and the usual terms.' Hamilton thought that they should choose the first alternative. He then gave Taylor a small lecture on the facts of life in the world of publishing: 'You refer ... to a "small edition of 2000". But this is a very substantial number in the case of a reprint, and even if you were to revise the book completely, we should not have been able to print more to begin with. In the eyes of the booksellers, a "revised edition" differs little from a "new edition"; reviewers seldom devote their space to the book for a second time; and the new version has to make its way slowly with little help from anyone except the publisher.' Taylor acquiesced.[45] Nine months later he had changed his mind: 'looking at the Habsburg Monarchy again, I do not think I should like it to appear in its present form. . . . In fact I should like to rewrite it from start to finish.' Hamilton was agreeable: 'it's up to you to decide whether to re-write, a course which would undoubtedly improve the book's chances of a new life, though involving you in a lot of work. Whatever you decide is O.K. by us.'[46]

The decision was taken: there would be an entirely rewritten version. The other outstanding matter to be settled was the terms of the contract. Taylor opened the batting in November 1946: 'Re terms: I don't think I ought to ask for an advance, unless you are anxious to give me one. I mean to ask for 20% for the next original book I write and I should have got 20%

if Macmillan had brought out a new edition. Do you think 15% on the first 1500 and then 20% would be unreasonable?' Hamilton responded: 'You naturally want to be rewarded for the labour you are putting into a new edition. We for our part have the not inconsiderable expense of setting up a book of over 100,000 words, with the knowledge that, however much it may be revised, the cream of the market has already been largely skimmed by Macmillan, so that much more advertising, circularising, etc. will be needed in promotion. In such circumstances, I would normally have suggested that the 20% should not start before the 5,000 mark, but in view of what you write, I suggest a compromise of 15% to 2500 and 20% there-after.' Taylor was agreeable, adding, 'Don't bother to prepare a contract. I'll write and ask you for one when I get down to the work of rewriting.'[47]

Taylor worked on the revision during the summer of 1947. By November it was complete, and he arranged to hand over it over to Hamilton, adding that 'I should like to settle detail of the contract. ... I don't expect that we shall quarrel on this.' In fact they did, and it took over six weeks to come to an agreement. Hamilton sent the contract to Taylor in February 1948, and Taylor was shocked:

> I am rather in a difficulty in answering your letter. I had assumed that we had settled the terms of the contract and that its signing was a formality. Otherwise I should have pressed for its signature before I had gone to work on my manuscript and certainly before I handed it over to you. As I neglected to do this I must accept your opinion that you can't make ends meet at 15% and agree to a reduction to 12^{1}/$_{2}$%. I do so as a fit penalty for my own carelessness, and shall take good care not to get into this position again. My agreement is, of course, conditional on the other clauses of the contract remaining unchanged, i.e. 20% after the first 3000 and an advance of £100 on day of publication.'

He decided to put off agreeing to the contract until he could speak to Hamilton personally about it. He then wrote to Hamilton himself, who was currently in Paris:

> I think that you are the most wonderful publisher that any author could have. ... I tried to write a good book for you and my main concern is not royalties, but that the book shall come out in a good appearance and in adequate numbers – things that I know you can give. ... At the same time, when it comes to settling a contract, I expect you to look after your

interests and I do my best to look after mine. If you don't like this attitude, you must keep clear of writers who are born in the North of England. ... I suggest that the contract be postponed until I can see you and we can review together the correspondence which has passed between us.

It was to take another five weeks before a contract was signed.[48]

Until the 1970s Taylor tended to negotiate over foreign rights for his books himself. Finding an American publisher for *The Habsburg Monarchy* (1948) proved to be difficult. Coward McCann had published *The Course of German History* in the States, but they did not really want to take *The Habsburg Monarchy* on, since *German History* had not sold very well.[49] Taylor, in fact, was eager for them to release him, because Blanche Knopf, the wife of the publisher Alfred Knopf, was interested in taking it on. By April 1948 the two were in negotiation. She took a copy of the manuscript with her back to the States, but by June had decided against publishing it, giving a somewhat unusual reason: 'Your writing is of such a high quality that I fear we would have difficulty finding a market for THE HABSBURG MONARCHY here.' In the end, Macmillan themselves took printed sheets, but only for a hundred copies. Intended to be published in 1948, and stated as such on the reverse of the title-page, *The Habsburg Monarchy* was held over until January 1949. It then sold two thousand copies in the first six months, a volume felt by both author and publisher to be most satisfactory, particularly for a revised version of a book.[50]

According to the Preface, 'this book is an entirely rewritten version of an earlier work with the same title.' In certain ways it is substantially different. First of all, it is half as long again. This is partly because the dates are different: the 1941 version covers 1815–1918, while the 1948–9 version covers 1809–1918. There is considerably greater detail, with much more context given and more explanation. Many of the sections are thereby extended, and there are new, renamed or shifted chapters. Furthermore, the revised version is illustrated and has an epilogue, absent from the first, which discusses what happened to the peoples of central Europe after the disappearance of the empire.

Secondly, Taylor promised in the preface to the second version to make up some of the deficiencies of the first. In the preface to the first version he had stated that 'the changes in popular life, the awakening of the subject peoples, the growth of new cultures' were referred to only as they impinged upon the imperial system; furthermore, that 'economic changes and development have been taken for granted and emerge in the narrative only when they produced political imperial effects'; and finally, 'though foreign policy is unmistakably imperial, the discussion of it ... has been reduced to a minimum, introduced principally to illuminate the course of internal history.' In the second version economic developments, in spite of Wilson's strictures in his review, still went untreated; indeed, economic developments and political economy remained Taylorian weaknesses. On the other hand, in the Preface to the second version Taylor claimed to have treated 'Austrian foreign policy with greater detail and relevance. The Habsburg Monarchy, more than most Great Powers, was an organisation for conducting foreign policy; and its fate was determined quite as much by foreign affairs as by the behaviour of its peoples. The creation of the Austrian Empire was dictated by Napoleon; the establishment of Austria-Hungary by Bismarck; and the Monarchy fell at the end of a great war, which it had itself helped to bring about.' Certainly there is more detail about foreign policy, but this does not overwhelm the frankly domestic focus.

Where there is a distinct change is in the treatment of the peoples of the empire. In his autobiography Taylor ascribed his growing realisation of their importance to the influence of Karolyi. In any case, he makes his change of mind and approach clear in the revised Preface:

Despite efforts to face reality, the earlier book was still dominated by the 'liberal illusion'; many passages talked of 'lost opportunities' and suggested that the Habsburg Monarchy might have survived if only this or that statesman or people had been more sensible. ... These regrets are no part of the duty of an historian, especially when the story which he tells makes it clear, time after time, that there were no opportunities to be lost. The conflict between a super-national dynastic state and the national principle had to be fought to the finish; and so, too, had the conflict between the master and subject nations. ... The national principle, once launched, had to work itself out to its conclusion.'

Demonstrating this required much more detail, because the complexity of the problem – of languages, religions, ethnicity, geography and history – could hardly be dealt with by use of a broad brush. Indicative of this was the fact that, when referring to places, Taylor now used the name preferred by the dominant nationality, rather than the more familiar German or Italian name as used in the 1941 version: Cilli becomes Celji, Königgrätz becomes

Sadova, Fiume becomes Rijeka and there is a guide to the pronunciation of the unfamiliar name at the bottom of the page.

One of Taylor's new themes grew naturally out of his new preoccupation with the nationalities of the empire: in order for the state of the Habsburg Monarchy to survive as a factor in the European balance of power, there had to be a balance of power within Austria-Hungary. This approach implicitly treated the various parts of the Empire as more or less discrete units; but it also required recognition of increasingly smaller-scale balances of power within these units, in that the dominant personality of a geographical area often depended on the balance between or amongst the nationalities within this area, as, for example, between the Czechs and Germans in Bohemia, as well as within sub-areas, such as cities or towns. Indeed, during the last decades of its existence, the monarchy spent the bulk of its time and effort attempting to create or to maintain just such balancing acts.

Taylor had argued that one reason for entirely rewriting the book was to make it livelier and more readable. In fact, the earlier version is sometimes more arresting: 'History had determined that this great Austrian structure should be built up round the House of Habsburg and yet could now only survive if it ceased to be the monopoly of the House of Habsburg; this is the explanation of the end of Austria' becomes 'The great Austrian structure had been built up round the House of Habsburg; it could survive only if it ceased to be the monopoly of the dynasty.'[51] More often, however, the palm must go to the second version. Compare, for instance, the opening sentences of the respective versions of Chapter 2, 'The Peoples': 'There has never been an Austrian people, only the peoples over whom the House of Austria ruled. Austrian meant an inhabitant of the Empire, or, more positively, one who was loyal to the dynasty'. This became: 'Francis I, told of an Austrian patriot, answered impatiently: "But is he a patriot for me?" The Emperor was needlessly meticulous. Austria was an Imperial organisation, not a country; and to be Austrian was to be free of national feeling – not to possess a nationality.'[52] It was such memorable sentences which helped ensure that for the following fifty years the book would remain in print and that the prose would frequently dominate student essays on the subject.

This second version of *The Habsburg Monarchy* received a number of reviews, rather than being ignored as Hamilton had feared. On the whole these were less favourable than those of the earlier version, reviewers mentioning Taylor's indulgence of 'a dogmatic temper at the expense of a well-considered appraisal of men and things', his 'acid realism and ... professed belief in the fatal inevitably of the events which pass under review', and his 'cock-sureness and ... complete intolerance of those of whom he disapproves, whether living or dead'. At the same time, one reviewer conceded that there was a more adequate treatment of foreign policy, whilst another listed Taylor's merits as a historian: 'acute perception, ability to find a way through tangles, and great skill in making short précis of long sources'.[53]

This was Taylor's last substantial work on the Habsburg Monarchy and its empire, or on the Successor States. Even in his major work on European diplomatic history, *The Struggle For Mastery in Europe 1848–1918*, published in 1954, the Austrian Empire received little attention by comparison with Germany, France and Russia. It is true that he always maintained an interest in the area, enjoyed visiting Yugoslavia and Hungary in particular, and always had a number of friends in or from the various states. But his work was now following a new path, the history of Germany, which would remain his primary interest until the early 1960s.

For Taylor a theme both political and historical that dominated much of his life was the German question – or the German problem, as he was more apt to term it: how to control or at least to contain a country which persisted in being richer and stronger than its neighbours and persisted in exploiting the fact. Certainly for the first fifty-five years of Taylor's life this was an international preoccupation, and unsurprisingly Taylor's interest in German history was further encouraged by the rise of Nazism. His fascination with Bismarck existed independently of current events, as demonstrated by his second monograph, *Germany's First Bid For Colonies 1884–1885: A Move in Bismarck's European Policy*, and by his biography of Bismarck, but his interest was held at least partly because Bismarck knew the power of restraint in his policies, while other German policy-makers seemingly knew only attack. *The Course of German History: A Survey of the Development of Germany since 1815*, published in 1945, grew directly out of the war; *The Struggle for Mastery in Europe 1848–1918* looked at the long-term rise of German ambitions for dominance; *Bismarck*, published in 1955, highlighted the more subtle approach of Bismarck's contribution to Germany's power; and *The Origins of the Second World War*, published in 1961, completed the story of Germany's culpability for what Taylor (and others, such as E.L. Woodward) tended for some years to call the first and second German wars.

Taylor has an enduring reputation as anti-German, but he did not begin that way. This is shown in earlier chapters of the present work. Taylor himself pinned down the point at which he became anti-German in a letter in 1964 to Kingsley Martin, the former Editor of the *New Statesman*: 'I was always against collective security and for a long time against rearmament also. When Germany occupied the Rhineland [7 March 1936], I became anti-German and from that moment held that large rearmament was the only thing that mattered.'[54] Certainly while an undergraduate at Oxford he continued to share the widespread belief that Germany had been hard done by in the Versailles Treaty, and this perception of Germany's recent past remained with him in his earliest teaching years at Manchester. Furthermore, it is worth noting that German was the foreign language in which he felt most comfortable. Neither in his surviving schoolboy essays nor in his earlier book reviews are there comments on Germany that might contradict his memory. His one work on the country before 1936 is the introduction to the translation of Friedjung, but this is largely descriptive, with few *obiter dicta*. Yet he was certainly anti-Nazi and anti-Hitler from their accession to power in 1933. Perhaps 1936 was the year when he began to support rearmament, not when he began to view Germany with suspicion and distaste.

Taylor's first book on Germany, *Germany's First Bid for Colonies 1884–1885*, was discussed in Chapter 3. However, it is worth recalling that it was published in March 1938, and one of its themes was the aggressive nature of German policies and their implementation: threatening, Machiavellian and disruptive to European stability. What also comes through is Taylor's admiration for Bismarck: he liked powerful men – a theme throughout his working life – and he liked Bismarck because he could control Germany. However, he was not under any sort of Bismarckian spell. Near the end of the book he writes: 'It is no discredit to Bismarck that in pursuit of his aims he used means that were as unscrupulous as they were elaborate. ... But he left an unfortunate example to his successors, who imitated his unscrupulousness without possessing his genius.'[55] Within the context of the book, Taylor was referring to Kaiser Wilhelm II and his government after Bismarck had been dismissed in 1890; if the book was intended to have a wider resonance, he could have been thinking of Weimar and the rise of Hitler to power by democratic means.

It must have been the events of the last two years of peace and the years of war which consolidated his darkening views. This would not, of course, have made him much different from many other Englishmen of his time, except that he poured these views into a book of history. The origins of this work – *The Course of German History: A Survey of the Development of Germany since 1815* – in his abortive work for the Political Warfare Executive have been described. The PWE agreed that Taylor could take his rejected chapter and use it in any way he wished. 'The same day', Taylor later wrote, 'I ran into Denis Brogan [later a professor of history at Glasgow University] who was working in the French section of the BBC. He said, "Why not turn your chapter into a book?". I welcomed his suggestion and used my chapter as the ending of *The Course of German History*, my first bestseller.'[56]

Brogan had a meeting with his publisher, Hamish Hamilton, after which Hamilton wrote to Taylor on 9 March 1944 that 'I have just been lunching with Denis Brogan and we discussed the history of Germany which I hope you are going to write for us.'[57] Taylor's response set out the type of book he was planning: 'I had in mind to write a general summary of German history for the layman, such as ought to appear in the works of the various intelligence departments who are producing handbooks on Germany. ... In fact a 1066 and all that in German terms.' He proposed a text of about fifty thousand words.[58] Hamilton responded that he had rather hoped for something more substantial. Taylor in his reply ignored the question of length, but he amplified briefly on the nature of the proposed book: 'I had a talk with Brogan the other day ... I don't think I have either the qualifications or the time to write an extended history of Germany in the nineteenth century, though I agree someone ought to do one. What Denis suggested to me and what I could do is to pick out the salient facts of German history, as a contribution to present political discussion.'[59]

These two comments may appear to confirm what some historians thought Taylor was doing when he wrote the book: that it was intended as either a joke or a political tract. However, there is evidence that he had previously given serious thought to the need for such a book. The German problem predated 1933: it could be said to have begun in earnest for Britain in 1898, with the passage of the German Navy Law. In a review in October 1942 of a book by G.P. Gooch, *Studies in Diplomacy and Statecraft*, Taylor went some way towards repudiating his own intellectual history. The views of Gooch on the diplomacy of the Powers immediately before the First World War, he wrote, had had more influence on informed opinion than those of any other writer. The people who had influenced the young Taylor, whether family or teachers, had imbibed Gooch's opinions and passed them on to him; as noted above, he had in turn passed them on to his own students in his early years at Manchester. He wrote in his review: 'Dr Gooch was a pupil of Acton and a Liberal member of the 1906 Parliament;

in both capacities he was convinced of the civilised character of Germany and this influenced all his scholarship. Germany appeared to him a power like any other, with some faults, but more grievances.' As far as Taylor was concerned, however, by 1942 it should have been clear to all that this view was wrong. He concluded with a clear statement of what was now required: 'The new generation of historians has now the obligation to make a new analysis of the underlying forces in Europe which will be closer to reality and so prepare a British policy which will suffer from fewer illusions and make fewer mistakes.'[60] This is what he proceeded to do in *The Course of German History*.

Taylor set to work immediately and by May 1944 the words were 'pouring out' of him; it was half-completed by July and finished by mid-September 1944, totalling 105,000 words.[61] It was published in July 1945, two months after the cessation of the war against Germany. Taylor introduced it to the reader as a *pièce d'occasion*, stating that although the book was serious history, it would not have been written but for the war; it had been produced to fill the need for some historical background to the political problems of the present. The style is very different from that of Taylor's previous books, the two monographs and the first version of *The Habsburg Monarchy*: he himself said that it was full of paradoxes and epigrams, a feature he ascribed to his being under the spell of Albert Sorel, a nineteenth-century French politician and historian of eighteenth-century France. (He had read Sorel's *L'Europe et la revolution française* in August 1944 and his *Nouveaux Essais* in October.)[62] It is not a book for the beginner: the more one knows the better – or worse – it is, since it is necessary to unpack many of the comments. It is short and vigorous.

Taylor begins: 'The history of the Germans is a history of extremes. It contains everything except moderation, and in the course of a thousand years the Germans have experienced everything except normality.' He emphasises two aspects of German history: the interplay of Kleindeutsch and Grossdeutsch programmes, and the conflict between Germans and Slavs. For him, the 'German problem' has two distinct sides: how can the peoples of Europe be secured against repeated bouts of German aggression? and how can the German people discover a settled, peaceful form of political existence? The solution to the first problem is unity amongst Germany's neighbours and disunity amongst Germans. As for the second problem, non-Germans cannot help: the Germans themselves have to discover the solution.[63]

One of Taylor's a themes is the repeated failure of the German left and liberals to insist on a democratic Germany when the choice was between democracy and unity. Probably the one passage from the book with which most modern historians will be familiar arises from Taylor's discussion of the revolutions of 1848, which Namier had called 'the revolution of the intellectuals':

> 1848 was the decisive year of German, and so of European, history: it recapitulated Germany's past and inspired Germany's future. ... Never has there been a revolution so inspired by a limitless faith in the power of ideas: never has a revolution so discredited the power of ideas in its result. The success of the revolution discredited conservative ideas; the failure of the revolution discredited liberal ideas. After it, nothing remained but the idea of Force, and this idea stood at the helm of German history from then on. For the first time since 1521, the German people stepped on to the centre of the German stage only to miss their cue once more. German history reached its turning-point and failed to turn. This was the fateful essence of 1848.[64]

He carries his investigation of this theme through to the Weimar Republic and the 1930s. About the Treaty of Versailles: it 'gave the final blow to the cause of democracy in Germany ... through the blunders and national passions of the Social Democrats. ... Carried to power through no effort of their own, they wished to prove their patriotism .... Instead of placing the blame for defeat on the old order ... they helped the old order back into power and bore the burden of its disaster.' Or again: 'the republic might have been saved by a united and sincerely democratic Socialist working class. ... All that the Communists achieved was to increase the unscrupulousness of German political life, and to prepare the way for the truly ruthless and unprincipled. When, in 1933, the moment came for the Communists to undertake the battle in the streets to which they had so often appealed, it turned out that they were old-style parliamentary talkers like all the rest.' As for the Centre Party: 'Wherever the dominant current of German political forces led, the Centre would go too – on the clear understanding that these forces would, in return, respect the position of the Roman Catholic Church. ... Long years of exacting concessions by co-operating with the government had sapped its power to oppose.' And finally, he even attacked the only secular political saint the period possessed: Stresemann. 'Even at the moment of signing the Treaty of Locarno, which recognised the Franco-German frontier, he declared ... that his main purpose in signing was to secure revision of Germany's frontiers to the east. Stresemann agreed with the most extreme Pan-German in striving for German supremacy in Europe and beyond; where he differed from the Pan-Germans was in believing that this supremacy could not be won by military power, but must be achieved by the weight of German industry and the preponderance of German organizing power.'[65] In short, the methods of the liberals might be different, but their goals were the same as those in power and for the sake of those goals they had sacrificed their principles. As far as Taylor was concerned, there were no good Germans.

He maintained these arguments, with few modifications, for the remainder of his working life. As is clear from the quotations, however, the book is more of a slashing attack on Germany than a balanced piece of history. Furthermore, it may be that the charge repeatedly made – that Taylor tended to go for the arresting rather than for the strictly accurate sentence – had its foundation here. Certainly he put to use in the book – which was intended for the general public rather than an academic audience – the lessons he had learned while writing book reviews: begin with an attention-grabbing first sentence, write in short sentences and have a strong theme.

The book was a popular success, selling over six thousand copies in the first few months.[66] The reviews, however, were mixed. Namier reviewed it in the *Times Literary Supplement*: not surprisingly, he approved of Taylor's ideas, although not of what he considered to be the half-developed state in which they had been presented: 'his combination of ruggedness and impressionable vivacity renders him also impatient of the careful labour of perfecting and polishing – he discovers precious stones by the handful, and puts them half-cut into circulation. ... The basic ideas of Mr Taylor's book are sound, but would have profited by further careful examination and unfolding.' But Namier added that 'the book should prove of high value in the study of the German problem.'[67] In *International Affairs* the reviewer, after praising the book in its coverage up to 1919, objected to the treatment of the interwar period, writing that 'It is too facile an attempt to discover some continuity in German history which can compare Charlemagne with Hitler' – that is, the attempts of both to unite Europe. In a sentence foreshadowing many of the objections to Taylor's later book, *The Origins of the Second World War*, the reviewer wrote that 'In the effort to make the Nazis, not in large measure the result of this anarchy [i.e. the economic crisis], but a normal development, quite to be expected, of German history,

Mr Taylor nearly succeeds in making them respectable.'[68] In the *American Historical Review*, the reviewer pointed out that 'The profound is mixed with the wisecrack. It has the shortcomings of its virtues. It will shock the scholarly reader but it must challenge him too.'[69]

Indeed, it did shock many. Taylor himself ascribed much of the dislike of the book to the 'shocked disapproval from the older generation of British historians who had learnt their version from the German Establishment, who also voiced disapproval after the war.'[70] Whilst it is worth noting that in the *American Historical Review* the reviewer added that 'A returning American scholar [returning from Germany, presumably] reports that it challenges equally German historians, some of whom admit that it will make them rethink their modern national history',[71] others were indeed outraged. One was the distinguished historian Gerhard Ritter – part of the German establishment – who wrote in some despair to G.P. Gooch that during the time of Hitler, 'German scholars had been ashamed and boiled inwardly at the nonsense written about England, and that no academic historian – as far as I know – had participated. I am correspondingly dismayed and alarmed that even in Oxford, informed history should be displaced in such a high measure by politically motivated history.' Gooch tried to reassure him, writing back that Taylor was the *only* vehemently anti-German British historian and need not be taken too seriously.[72]

It is probable that many of those who objected to the book objected to the point – which would later make its most notorious appearance in *Origins of the Second World War* – that under the liberals Germany would have had the same goals. Taylor expanded on this in a letter to Kingsley Martin:

We are so agreed on the evil and danger of the German right that we do not need to mention it. I should also agree that the German Left, both Socialist and Liberal, had genuinely democratic ideals and that they made some show against Nazi barbarism ... Lack of [a heritage of freedom] may not be the fault of the Germans, but it is a fact, and one which has more and more evil results in every generation. Therefore German liberals, to achieve anything, would have to fight much harder than we [the English] need. The basic issue is whether the German Left were good Europeans – ready to live and let live in Europe. I say that the historical record is against them. ... You, with your Puritan conscience, confuse the issue by thinking in terms of right and wrong. To me the virtues of the German Left are irrelevant. The only question is one of German predominance in Europe, which they favour as much as anyone of the Right.[73]

The book, as Taylor himself noted, made him an Authority on Germany (at least amongst the general public), and his own interest in the country remained deep and abiding. He was by this time a prolific reviewer, especially on German history: between February and late May 1945, for example, seven successive reviews treated of Germany. Certain messages emerged clearly: Hitler was not an aberration, German liberalism had failed, Germany must be kept disunited. He also repeatedly proclaimed his solution for containing Germany, which was an Anglo-Soviet alliance. As the Cold War deepened, this last proposal increasingly irritated the British government, as well as members of the so-called Establishment, in Whitehall and in Westminster and without, who supported the Anglo-American relationship and saw Taylor as damaging and even dangerous. Many historians, too, now considered him unsound, not because of his views on the Cold War but because of his treatment of German history. This was to have minor repercussions.

Taylor had published the first version of *The Habsburg Monarchy* in 1941 and had written *The Course of German History* in 1944. He had not, however, been idle in the intervening years. Along with his teaching, his broadcasting and his war work, he had begun writing a book on European diplomatic history. Two book reviews he wrote in 1942 make clear that he believed strongly that such a book was needed. The first, his review of Gooch's *Diplomacy and Statecraft*, which he saw as absurdly pro-German, has already been mentioned in relation to *The Course of German History*; the reader will recall that Taylor's final sentence was 'The new generation of historians has now the obligation to make a new analysis of the underlying forces in Europe which will be closer to reality and so to prepare a British policy which will suffer from fewer illusions and make fewer mistakes.' This conclusion can also be linked to the approach adopted in his major work on diplomatic history, *The Struggle for Mastery in Europe*. The second review, published a month later, considered *Documents on International Affairs, 1938* and *The Agadir Crisis*. The first book caused him to muse on the lack of perspective and sense of the 'broader picture' exhibited by statesmen as demonstrated by the documents. The nature of the second book stimulated reflections as to why this might be the case. Historians, he charged, had been at fault: 'though innumerable books have been written on isolated episodes, the story of the Struggle for the Mastery of Europe has never been attempted.' As a consequence, statesmen in the 1930s had only thought about the short term, having no context in which to place German policies. Clearly such a book should be written, but by whom? 'German historians cannot do it, because to them the struggle (that is the resistance to German domination) seems merely wrong-headed; American historians cannot do it, because they do not realize what was at stake.' The possibility that such a book might be written by French, Austrian, Russian or Italian historians was not mooted. Whom, then, did that leave? 'It would be a superb opportunity for an English historian, if one could be found with real standards of scholarship and understanding.'[74]

His plan as conceived in 1941 was to begin his narrative in 1878, with a long historical introduction, and to cover the period to 1914; he had written about 100,000 words when he laid the project aside to write *The Course of German History*. At some point he must have mentioned to Hamish Hamilton at least the fact that he was writing a big book, if not its precise topic. In early November 1949 Hamilton wrote to Taylor with regard to his contract for a book of essays, *From Napoleon to Stalin*, which was published in 1950; Taylor had deleted the clause, standard in most book contracts until recently, in which the author promises to let the publisher have first refusal of the next book. This worried Hamilton, who wrote that 'naturally I hope that this deletion doesn't mean that you are contemplating a change of publisher. We have done well with "The Course of German History" and "The Habsburg Monarchy", and we are publishing "From Napoleon to Stalin" largely to please you, so we all hope that you regard us as your permanent publishers, and that there will be a new full length book in the fairly near future.'[75]

A fortnight later, Taylor had still not answered Hamilton's question, and the publisher decided to ask him in a straightforward manner: 'I am much concerned over your silence on the subject of your future work. 'I asked you about this when returning the contract for "Napoleon to Stalin", and again in my handwritten reply to your congratulations on sales of "The Habsburg Monarchy". Please let me have some word soon. I need hardly say that it will be a bitter disappointment to us if, after our success with your two most recent books, you are contemplating a change of publisher.' Taylor was finally driven to answer:

I am sorry if I have alarmed you. I am unwilling to bind myself to you for two reasons. First, I often get asked by a publisher to contribute a single essay or an introduction to a book. ... This is not likely to interfere with my serious work. Second, I am being badgered to take part in the Oxford History of Modern Europe. This will not be a profitable venture for me; but I feel that, if a number of leading Oxford historians take part, I ought not to stay out. After all, I benefit from endowments to do scholarly work and I suppose, once in a life-time, I must try to co-operate with the University. However, the University Press offer such extraordinary terms, in small matters as in great (for instance refusal on principle to deliver galleys), that I have great doubt whether I shall come to an agreement with them. I hope you won't feel that, if I do agree to contribute to this series, it is any reflection on you or any sign of dissatisfaction with you. You know my opinion of your genius as a publisher too well for that. But a scholar is in a rather different position from an ordinary writer: he has obligations to his University which cut across his literary activities.[76]

Taylor's characterisation of his negotiations with the Oxford University Press (OUP) as his being 'badgered' by them was somewhat wide of the mark. In fact, reluctance rather than eagerness was their dominant mood. The Press had begun mooting a series of volumes on European history before the First World War; the idea was again discussed in 1925; but only in 1947 did discussions begin which eventually turned into a firm commitment. The driving force was Alan Bullock, lately arrived at New College as Tutorial Fellow in History. In April 1947 Bullock met at OUP with two of the three members of the editorial staff, Arthur Norrington, then Assistant Secretary but soon to become the Secretary to the Delegates (effectively chief executive), and Dan Davin, then Junior Assistant Secretary but by 1949 Assistant Secretary with responsiblity for history (amongst a number of other fields). Bullock's main point was that nothing did for European history what the Oxford History of England did for English history; 'the reason, no doubt, was the absence of qualified writers'. Bullock argued that this state of affairs was changing: Oxford already had a number of historians interested in European and East European history, and he cited as examples B.H. Sumner, Hugh and Christopher Seton-Watson, Isaiah Berlin, Maurice Bowra and Taylor, adding that 'they may not all be good writers but their influence is important.' Norrington and Davin agreed that there was a need for such a series and were very favourable to the idea if the writers could be found.

In May 1947 Bullock drew up for OUP a 'Memorandum of an Oxford History of Modern Europe', setting out possible intellectual and managerial elements. He included a list of possible authors for each century, in which Taylor was down for the nineteenth century.[77] This memorandum was the beginning of a long haul for Bullock, during which he threatened resignation from the editorial chair at least once. During the subsequent seven years Taylor, perceived initially as a somewhat unreliable trouble-maker, somehow evolved in the eyes of the Press into the star of the series.

Bullock had collaborated with Taylor the previous year on *A Select List of Books on European History 1815–1945* and in the continuing Recent History Group seminars. It was therefore natural that he should ask Taylor for his views; he also asked William Deakin, and the two men independently agreed with Bullock's proposal for a series covering the period 1789–1939. As the OUP summary put it, 'Bullock thinks that by beginning at 1789 we should evade the difficulty that few English historians know much about medieval or late medieval Europe. And by ending at 1939 we have the natural terminus: for the Europe of the 19th century ended there. He thinks that authors can be found as Oxford is fairly strong and getting stronger in modern European history.' Discussions within OUP then focused on possible editors of the series. Bullock should be one with, preferably, one colleague; no definite suggestions were made as to who this should be '(Except negatively: we agreed that A.J.P. Taylor would not do).' In due course William Deakin would join Bullock as Co-editor of the Oxford History of Modern Europe series.[78]

Then followed a long saga. This was partly because OUP kept university terms and therefore virtually nothing was done during the Long Vacation. In addition, however, time was needed to gain the approval of the Delegates,[79] the academics from the university who constituted OUP's board and assessed proposals for new books, and of the History Faculty, some members of which tried to wrest control of the series away from the Press. Whilst working to obtain enough support to establish the series, Davin, Norrington, Bullock and Deakin also laboured to find the necessary authors. Taylor, in spite of his assertion to Hamilton that he was being 'badgered' by the Press, was only intermittently, and then only reluctantly, added to the proposed list.

Taylor was first proposed by Bullock in November 1947 as a possible author of the volume on Germany, but the reaction of the Press and of A.L.Poole, the mediaeval historian and President of St John's College who was the History Delegate, was discouraging: 'A.J.P. Taylor was difficult. Bullock agreed he was difficult but thought him a better historian than his books so far show him.' By the following week he was pencilled in on Bullock's list, but not for Germany: now his proposed task would be the volume on international relations 1848–1914. By January 1948 Taylor was more firmly established on the list as a possible author of the volume on

1848–1914: 'A.J.P. Taylor: he is essentially a diplomatic historian and better on general than regional history. But he would need firm handling.' However, by June 1948 things had changed, and the Editors and Davin decided to approach E.L. Woodward instead, as the minutes of the meeting reveal. 'From our point of view this [approaching Woodward] has the advantage of removing A.J.P. Taylor from the immediate foreground – he was a previous candidate.' But the following week Norrington decided that Woodward would probably not perform.[80]

By 10 November 1948, with the proposal due to go before the Delegates of the Press the following day, Taylor was back on the list. At a preparatory meeting between Bullock, Deakin, Davin, Norrington and Poole, Bullock and Deakin reported that it seemed clear to them that Woodward would not undertake the volume and that, failing him, 'they thought that A.J.P. Taylor [was] the right man. He would not be as dangerous on this subject as he would be on Germany and they [thought] they could control him. [The distinguished historian] Wheeler Bennett consider[s] him "the obvious man".' The following day, in a letter to Poole outlining the proposals to be made to the other Delegates at the meeting, Davin reminded him that 'you were going to introduce tentatively the subject of A.J.P. Taylor if the moment seemed suitable. It may be worth remarking that he would not be asked to write on Germany but on International Relations 1848–1914 where he is a specialist.'[81]

Presumably the Delegates did not bridle at the suggestion, and by May 1949 Taylor had agreed tentatively to write the volume – although he wrote that he would 'be grateful if there was no publicity about my writing this book until I definitely commit myself', presumably because he worried about how Hamish Hamilton would react to the news. However, by early June, 'A.J.P. Taylor seems to be hooked. Deakin let it be known that if he did not want to play, we would look for someone else. He talked to Taylor on the telephone yesterday morning and Taylor said that ... he will perform. In fact, he means to take a year off in order to accelerate matters. I think you can now make him sign on the dotted line.' It was probably this period to which Taylor was alluding when he spoke of being 'badgered'.[82]

There then began negotiations over the contract which continued, with occasional truculence on both sides, for seventeen months. Taylor made it clear in a letter to Davin in mid-October that a major sticking point was the control of translation rights: 'I have always hitherto kept translation rights in my own hands. In any case for you to take 33% for doing nothing seems excessive.' He also wanted galley proofs: 'I know the Press prides itself on driving a harder bargain than any other publisher; and I have agreed to your general terms. All the more reason to meet me over details.' Davin hardly knew how to respond. He turned first to Bullock and Deakin for advice: 'I sent [Taylor] a draft contract ... [but] we cannot give way [over translation rights]. ... This is a special Oxford series and the volumes must be handled as a whole.' But what really angered him was the tone of the prose: 'words fail me for this gratuitous offensiveness. ... We are not engaged in gypsy horsetrading, after all, and if negotiations are going to be carried on in the atmosphere of suspicion which on the whole Taylor's letter breathes, I for my part would sooner he returned to the kind of publishers with whom he appears to have been accustomed to deal.'[83]

After three weeks Davin replied to Taylor's letter: 'I have not answered [your letter] earlier partly because it raised questions of principle which I wanted to discuss with the editors and partly because I found the tone and implications ... so exasperating that I preferred to wait till I was sure of not replying in a manner that would be less than good-tempered.' He then dealt with the points Taylor had raised, refusing firmly to agree to his desire to keep the translation rights. He then ended with a paragraph designed to match Taylor's: 'I hope you will see from this letter that we are being as reasonable as we can. I suggest that it might help us in continuing to be so if you on your part would cease to write as if we were parties to a dubious venture in horse-trading instead of a project which has importance for the future of European history studies and advantages for you as well as for the Press.' Taylor was clearly startled by Davin's response, and his reply of 20 November was softer in tone. Davin put his own gun back in its holster: 'I cheerfully accept your views on the analogy between the sale of a book and that of a horse, though it was not so much the nature of the bargain arrived at as the methods of arriving at it that were the object of my comment. However, the main thing is that we should come to an agreement and get ahead with the series. ... I hope that you can expedite matters with Curtis Brown.'[84]

Taylor (and four of the other authors) had taken on Spencer Curtis Brown as their agent to negotiate and, if necessary, to argue on their behalf with the Press. As it happened, in the fight over translation rights that took place during May and June 1950, Curtis Brown went over to the side of the enemy, a tribute, perhaps, to the prestige which the Press enjoyed. Curtis Brown rang Davin on 11 May to tell him that his authors had now decided that they wanted a clause in their contracts providing that, if translation rights had not been sold after three years, they would revert to the control of the author. Davin had pointed out that the series would take twenty years to publish, and that it would be easier to dispose of the rights after half of the volumes, rather than just one or two, had been published. 'Curtis Brown was very reasonable and readily agreed that this was a valid objection. In fact, he did not seem to see much sense in the clause at all; and I gathered that the originator was our old friend A.J.P. Taylor.' The point had arisen when a colleague of Curtis Brown had discussed the proposed new contract with their authors in Oxford; Taylor had 'claimed all translation rights for himself and persuaded the others that they would like to have them. Curtis Brown thinks that the point is immaterial and that Taylor is being a nuisance but it is difficult for him to do anything.' It was decided that Curtis Brown would propose the new clause to Taylor and see what he had to say; Bullock and Deakin should be warned that there might be a breakdown; and they would arrange through Curtis Brown that the other authors did not make a stand on the same point. Curtis Brown did not think 'that any of them will resist seriously. He says that Isaiah Berlin who has been another troublesome sheep is really quite reasonable, though given to haggling.' Norrington's response to all of this was that 'A.J.P. Taylor is such an infernal nuisance & time-waster that I shd. be glad to see him dropped from the team.'[85]

Curtis Brown called a meeting of the contributors on 20 June at New College, and it was here that battle was joined. The only outstanding issue was the translation rights, over which OUP was unlikely to give way.[86] He put the case for retention of translation rights by the authors and Davin the case for OUP. 'A set-to followed. ... Everyone now turned to me [Davin] and demanded that I should propose a compromise. I could see that the national character was now uppermost and I should have to make some concession to English mores [Davin was a New Zealander].' He proposed that they should reckon in books, not years: after five books were published, if rights in the previous four had not been sold they should revert to the authors.

I think we have gained the substance. Taylor will finish first and we should be able to market his rights successfully. The others when it comes to the point will not trouble. It was a very enjoyable wrangle. Berlin was a valuable reducer of temperatures. Taylor was the chief trouble and I found that if one jumped on him fast and hard he became much less formidable. His main argument that he had accepted our royalty terms at a sacrifice was squashed when I told him roundly that he would still be getting returns on his book in twenty years, that it would sell more because we were publishing and because it would be cheap, and that in any case his terms were very good. Curtis Brown gave him the coup de grace by saying that he would gladly exchange his commission on Taylor's earnings from this book for his commission on any book Taylor liked to publish with another publisher. This had a salutary effect all round. ... I hear from Bullock that the historians are happy & that everyone enjoyed the bandying of home truths by Taylor, Curtis Brown & Davin.

Curtis Brown certainly was happy, writing to Davin – in a way which betrayed his lack of loyalty to his client – that the suggestion 'has solved our troubles and certainly I think we sent Taylor away, if not satisfied, at least without any possible opportunity for making any further troubles whatever.' And by September he could write that 'all the difficult authors, like Taylor, have signed [their contracts] like lambs.' It is probable that Curtis Brown's less than wholehearted support of Taylor against the Press accounted for Taylor's dropping him as his agent.[87]

As noted above, between 1941 and 1944 Taylor had written 100,000 words of a book on European diplomatic history. Once he had completed *The Course of German History*, which was published in July 1945, he turned his mind again to this project. By now, however, his ambition had expanded. He already read German and French very well, and could handle Italian; now he decided that to do it properly he had also to read Russian. In August he completed *Beginning Russian Conversation*, going on to *A First Russian Reader* the following month and completing *A New Russian Grammar* in January 1946. He also settled down to serious reading of monographs and biographies, as well as looking again at printed documents. At the point when he was approached by OUP, he was already well under way.

But the Press did not know this and they could hardly believe how rapidly he wrote. He had been awarded a sabbatical for the academic year 1950–1, which he spent in London, and by September 1952 he had completed 180,000 words. By early the following year he was nearly finished. Bullock had been reading the manuscript, and in March 1953 Davin wrote to Taylor that Bullock had told him 'what a high opinion he had already formed of your book.' By mid-May it was finished. Curtis Brown wrote to Davin in July that 'when we first worked out the contracts for the ... series, I offered to make a small bet with you that A.J.P. Taylor would be first home with his

MS. He has fulfilled my expectations.' Davin's response was that 'yes, Taylor has come in first with his MS, a result which we agreed with you in expecting.' No other author was anywhere near completion.[88]

In October the Editors and the Press had to admit that no progress had been made in commissioning most of the other volumes; 'the only promising line seemed to be a suggestion that A.J.P. Taylor should write International Relations 1789–1848.' Davin wrote to Poole with the proposal: 'I suggested that it might be worth considering Taylor as an author for [it] as well as the volume which is now going through the press. Ever since we got him committed he has shown himself an admirably efficient author and both editors agree that he would do this volume as well as he has done the one we are now printing. ... The only embarrassment might be that he would finish this also before any of the others have come up to the start line. But the prospect of this ironic result might be one of its attractions for him. What do you think?' In December 1953 they decided to ask him, but they only got round to it in May 1955, after *The Struggle for Mastery in Europe 1848–1918* had been published. The answer was vintage Taylor: 'AJP says that he is prepared to write all of the volumes in the series provided that it be called Taylor's History of Modern Europe edited by Bullock and Deakin. So we must let things lie for the time being.' Colin Roberts, by then successor to Norrington as Secretary, wrote in the margin that it was 'nice to see AJP making our points for us'.[89] In fact, it was to be sixteen years before the next volume in the series was published.[90]

The *Struggle for Mastery* was published in October 1954. As traditional diplomatic history, it is a masterful work, its arguments supported by a command of the detail of diplomacy which few have exhibited. Its major theme is the struggle between the Great Powers for the domination of Europe, or more precisely, the struggle by Germany to dominate the continent and the attempts by other Great Powers to prevent it. Taylor begins with his conception of the general context:

> In the state of nature which Hobbes imagined, violence was the only law, and life was 'nasty, brutish and short'. Though individuals never lived in this state of nature, the Great Powers of Europe have always done so. ... However, Europe has known almost as much peace as war; and it has owed these periods of peace to the Balance of Power. No one state has ever been strong enough to eat up all the rest; and the mutual jealousy of the Great Powers has preserved even the small states, which could not have preserved themselves. The relations of the Great Powers have

determined the history of Europe. This book deals with them in the last age when Europe was the centre of the world.[91]

Who were these Great Powers? According to Taylor, the Great Powers who launched the Great War in 1914 were the same Great Powers who had made up the Congress of Vienna in 1815, at the end of the Napoleonic Wars. These were Great Britain, France, Russia, Austria and Prussia, although in the intervening century the Austrian Empire had become the Austro-Hungarian Empire and Prussia had become Germany. Italy was not included in this *obiter dictum*: it was not a state in 1815 and only became a belligerent in 1915. Furthermore, Taylor regarded Italy as a state whose aspirations outstripped its resources, and whose amorality or immorality on the international stage outstripped that of all other Powers: when discussing the general characteristics of diplomacy and diplomats during this period, for example, he noted that 'all diplomatists were honest, according to their moral code', but then added the footnote that 'It becomes wearisome to add "except the Italians" to every generalization. Henceforth it may be assumed.'[92]

Taylor based his list of the Great Powers on a simple test. 'The Great Powers were, as their name implies, organizations for power, that is, in the last resort for war. They might have other objects – the welfare of their inhabitants or the grandeur of their rulers. But the basic test of them as Great Powers was their ability to wage war.'[93] With this criterion in mind, he looked at the relative standing of the Powers with regard to the most important factors in the ability to wage war: population; defence expenditure, including those of the army and navy separately, the armaments expenditure per capita and as a percentage of national income; coal, pig iron and steel production; and manufacturing production. What becomes obvious from this is the rise in the martial capacity of some powers and the decline of that of others. The population of Germany grew the most, whilst that of France grew the least. German army estimates increased the most, those of France and Great Britain the least. Germany led in the percentage growth of defence expenditures, followed by Austria-Hungary and Russia. Russia spent the highest percentage of its national income on armaments, Great Britain the greatest amount per capita.

But Taylor stresses that, whilst these factors might indicate immediate readiness for a short war whose result would be determined by decisive battles, ascertaining the strength of a country requires assessment of its economic resources – a new emphasis for Taylor and one that possibly derived from the earlier strictures of Charles Wilson and others. 'Manpower alone was no sufficient guide: otherwise Russia would never have needed an ally. Europe was reshaped between 1848 and 1914 by the impact of the industrial revolution. This revolution rested on coal; it showed its most revolutionary form in steel. Together these hint at the reality of power which we cannot otherwise measure.' In 1850 Great Britain was the only industrial power of any importance; France was the only continental country where manufacturing industry counted for anything. But between 1871 and 1890 Germany caught up with and, indeed, overtook France in the production of iron and steel; by 1900 it had caught up with Great Britain in steel production, and had surpassed it in manufacturing production by 1910. But Taylor makes the point that these figures also showed that the European era of dominance was drawing to a close: 'Until 1880 the United States counted for little. Then she had the greatest of all industrial revolutions. By 1914 she was not merely an economic Power on the European level; she was a rival continent. Her coal production equalled that of Great Britain and Germany put together; her iron and steel production surpassed that of all Europe. This was the writing on the wall', a statement which foreshadows the story contained in the final pages of the book, when for the first time – but not the last – the New World came to the rescue of part of the Old.[94]

And so – what was the relative standing of the Powers during this period? Germany became the greatest of the land powers, whilst Great Britain remained the greatest of the naval powers. France slipped down the ladder, although less so than Austria–Hungary: indeed, after 1871 neither would have contemplated fighting a war without allies. Russia, because of its history and manpower, was still considered one of the greater of the Great Powers, but showed increasing internal strain; indeed, revolution threatened in Russia after each of its wars, in 1856, 1878 and 1905. Italy never became a Great Power: it only thought – or hoped – it was.

How did these Powers exercise their power? In two ways: war and peace. With the shooting wars Taylor had little to do; rather, he was interested in the attempts to maximise gain or to minimise loss through diplomacy, with the attempts to avert war, with the causes and consequences of war, with settling the outcome of war. These negotiations were carried out by diplomats, a profession dominated by the upper classes, and one which had its own code of honour. As Taylor reminds the reader, 'No ambassador said "No" when the true answer should have been "Yes"; but he might evade the question or, even, if he was clever enough, give a misleading impression. . . .

Nevertheless, although 'many diplomatists were ambitious, some vain or stupid ... they had something like a common aim – to preserve the peace of Europe without endangering the interests or security of their country.' Therefore, because 'diplomacy is an art which, despite its subtlety, depends on the rigid accuracy of all who practise it', it could be easily disrupted by partners who did not abide by the rules. 'To have a great state ruled and run by liars was a unique problem with which the statesmen of Europe were unfitted to deal.' In this case Taylor was referring to the France of Napoleon III and his 'gangster-followers', to whose unreliability he ascribed the 'bewildering diplomacy' of the 1850s and 1860s.[95] Italy was nearly as untrustworthy, partly because it had so few strengths from which to play.

One important diplomatic doctrine, although never codified as such, was that of compensation: if one Power gained, through war or threats of war or negotiation or as a trade-off, the other Powers expected to be compensated. This was entirely predictable, because of the nature of the Balance of Power: 'it seemed to be the political equivalent of the laws of economics, both self-operating. If every man followed his own interest, all would be prosperous; and if every state followed its own interest, all would be peaceful and secure.'[96] The Italians, naturally, went beyond what was deemed acceptable: they 'followed the jackal principle that the more trouble there was in the Mediterranean the more chance for them somewhere.'[97] It was the duty of diplomats to negotiate for and if necessary to demand compensation. Compensation might involve a benevolent neutrality during a war; the promise of support in a crisis along with the promise not to support another Power in the same crisis; support for a territorial claim against another power; or support for the actual acquisition of territory.

Powers were in the habit of transferring land and populations between one another, since for most of recorded history the principle of nationality and its accompanying restrictions had been of little importance either to sovereigns or to their subjects. This was a point underlined by the reaction of Lord John Russell in March 1864 to the proposal that the Elbe duchies of Schleswig-Holstein be divided between Denmark and Prussia according to predominant nationality: 'the idea was "too new in Europe" and ... "the Great Powers had not the habit of consulting populations when questions affecting the Balance of Power had to be settled".'[98] The duchies both went to Prussia, but as the century progressed acceptable compensation became more complicated to arrange as the principle of the right of nationalities to self-determination increasingly took hold. This was encouraged by the spread of literacy and democracy and the decline of press censorship, which forced statesmen increasingly to take public attitudes into account, although 'public opinion', such as it was in most countries, remained comparatively limited.

Other themes arise out of Taylor's narrative. First of all, nothing is determined by fate or history; as he wrote, 'no war is inevitable until it breaks out.'[99] The gulf between that conclusion and the theoretical basis for his approach to Germany could not be more glaring if it were illuminated in neon lights. The culpability of Germany in Taylor's eyes was undoubtedly determined by recent experience: perhaps if the book had been published in 1854 he would have singled out France – the European aggressor at least from the time of Louis XIV through to the Napoleonic period – as the possessor of an ineluctable drive for power.[100] Secondly, what makes the difference is not fate but men, their ideas, their principles (or lack of them), their characters, their energy, their greed and their ability or willingness to react to opportunities as they arose. Bismarck did; Palmerston, British Foreign Secretary and sometime Prime Minister, a man of resolution, and Stratford Canning, 'an outstanding diplomat', both did; Wessenburg, Austrian Foreign Minister, was 'a diplomat of experience and courage'. Others were irresolute and feeble: Malmesbury, British Foreign Secretary, was 'timid'; Buol, Austrian Foreign Minister, 'lacked daring'; Bethmann was 'incapable of consistent policy'; Berchtold, Austro-Hungarian Foreign Minister, was 'feeble'.[101] In his future book *The Origins of the Second World War*, it would become manifestly clear in which category he placed Neville Chamberlain.

Finally, Taylor believed in being clear-eyed and in writing, as the German historian Leopold von Ranke claimed every historian should do, *wie es eigentlich gewesen* (as it actually was). Did Bismarck and Prussia begin the war with France in 1870? Taylor wrote that 'this topic is so overlaid with later controversy and passion that it is impossible to arrive at a detached verdict. I can only say that I have tried to judge according to the contemporary evidence and to resist the later myths, whether created by French resentment or by Bismarck himself. He [Bismarck] later boasted that he had manufactured the war with France; this is evidence of what he thought in 1892, not in 1870.' Or, 'it has been strongly argued that the Germans deliberately timed war for August 1914', as was claimed in Clause 231, the War Guilt clause of the Treaty of Versailles, and by later writers. Was this the case? Taylor thought not: 'the Germans did not fix on war for August 1914, but they welcomed it when the occasion offered. They could win it now; they were more doubtful later. Hence they surrendered easily to the dictates of a military time-table.'[102]

What is most impressive is Taylor's seemingly effortless interweaving of so much information from so many sources. The key to this breadth and depth was his command of the printed primary and secondary material in five languages. This could have led to a long, turgid, indigestible mass, but did not owing to Taylor's system of organising his material. This has been well described by one of his pupils:

His way of enlivening the tedium and formality of diplomatic correspondence was to decide that the central *point* of a despatch, for all the 'flannel' of protocol and diplomatic verbiage, lay in a couple of lines or a single paragraph. He would isolate these nuggets with deft precision, showing that the logic of the situation in which the writer of the despatch found himself proved that that line or paragraph really must be the pith of the matter ... [H]e showed me the method he had used for *The Struggle for Mastery in Europe*. He had, in each period, chosen to hang the narrative on the fullest and most consecutive collection of printed documents. From 1870 this was the *Grosse Politik*. Each important letter was reduced to a line of summary written on one side of the page of a publisher's 'dummy' volume. On the opposite side he would put in notes of other illustrative correspondence, from other printed collections. As he completed his reading, the pages would fill up with little 'shorthand' entries, till they looked like a busy man's appointments diary. But it was a composite diary of the diplomatic activity of the major European Powers, and what prevented it from being a series of random notes was the tight chronology which reflected Taylor's conviction that foreign ministers and their diplomats rarely initiated policy, but more often reacted to international events in a haphazard way. . . . The diplomats responded with varying degrees of acuteness to the logic of the situation. You had to read their minds as you would read the mind of a chess player, from the disposition of the pieces on the board. The state of the board accounted for the mental activity of the players; and the fact that the game of chess involved many players need not be too perplexing, because sudden crises were rare, the normal state of affairs was one of calm, and most foreign ministers were so devoid of foresight that one could easily cope with the few who did show initiative.[103]

Yet Taylor did not neglect the importance of forces which lay beyond the foreign offices of the Powers. As he wrote in the Bibliography, 'Policy springs from deep social and economic sources: it is not crudely manufactured in foreign offices.' Thus he offered in his Introduction, as Paul Kennedy has observed, 'one of the most decisive and penetrating analyses of "what it took to be a Great Power", and what significant alterations occurred between 1848 and 1918 in the population, military and industrial balances which would – in the event of great, modern wars – largely determine the outcome. Here, at least, there is no hesitation at all about the importance of "profound forces".' After quoting the section of the Introduction in which Taylor discussed the fundamental economic and other developments and their impact on the abilities of the various Powers to make war, Kennedy concluded that 'All these were seminal and important points, and it is proper to note just how many later writers have accepted Mr Taylor's basic framework in their own studies of international relations in this period, and in explaining the background to Germany's challenge to the "system" in 1914.'[104] It is possible that historians accused Taylor of neglecting these forces because he did not belabour the point. He himself once remarked, with regard to the Dutch historian Pieter Geyl's view of *The Origins*, that 'Geyl thinks that I ought to keep saying again and again, "Hitler was a wicked man." I tend to think that once I have written a sentence about Hitler's wickedness I have dealt with the subject.'[105]

The basic assumption he made was that there are fundamental causes and causes specific to an event. He later explained this by analogy:

Wars are much like road accidents. They have a general cause and particular causes at the same time. Every road accident is caused, in the last resort, by the invention of the internal combustion engine and by men's desire to get from one place to another. In this sense, the 'cure' for road accidents is to forbid motor-cars. But a motorist, charged with dangerous driving, would be ill-advised if he pleaded the existence of motor-cars as his sole defence. The police and the courts do not weigh profound causes. They seek a specific cause for each accident – error on the part of the driver; excessive speed; drunkenness; faulty brakes; bad road surface. So it is with wars. 'International anarchy' makes war possible; it does not make war certain. After 1918 more than one writer made his name by demonstrating the profound causes of the first World war; and, though the demonstrations were often correct, they thus diverted attention from the question why that particular war happened at that particular time. Both enquiries make sense on different levels. They are complementary; they do not exclude each other.[106]

The whole structure of *The Struggle for Mastery* is informed by the 'profound forces': it is perhaps unfortunate that he often neglected to make their relationship to immediate causes more explicit.

The changes in the configuration of the Powers during the seventy years treated by Taylor form the core of the book. In 1848 the Austrian Empire was a German as well as a Balkan Power, the keystone of the Concert of Europe; there was the German nation, but no Germany; there were Italian states, some of which belonged to the Austrian Empire, and two Italian kingdoms, but no Italy; France was still perceived by all the others as the most powerful, or at least the most threatening, of the continental Powers; and Russia was predominantly a European, not an Asiatic, Power. During most of the period Great Britain saw Russia and France as its great enemies, largely because they challenged its empire, and Prussia and the Austrian Empire as Powers with whom it had no quarrel. And by 1914? The Powers had gone through a diplomatic revolution and changed partners. Germany and Austria–Hungary were linked together in the Dual Alliance, with the half-hearted attachment of Italy to make the Triple Alliance; France and Russia were in alliance against Germany; Great Britain was in alliance with Japan; Great Britain was in tacit though not official alliance with France; and in the wings lurked the United States. The basic force driving the changes was the rise of German aggression and the search by the Powers for security. The end of the book marks the end of this German attempt at *Weltmacht*, but readers knew that the attempt had been made again.

The book was published on 28 October 1954. One of the first reviews, that by Max Beloff in *Time and Tide* in the 13 November issue, led to a somewhat childish contretemps between Taylor and his former supporter E.L. Woodward. In his Preface Taylor had thanked Woodward, along with Nicholas Henderson, Alan Bullock and his wife, for scrutinising the manuscript at different stages. Beloff in his review highlighted this. After remarking that 'the book provides an introduction to the international history of the period as stimulating as it is comprehensive', he went on to add a sneering final paragraph:

> To judge from his Preface, Mr. Taylor is under the illusion that his manuscript was read by Sir Lewellyn Woodward. Had this indeed been the case, so judicious an historian might have persuaded him to avoid pressing an occasional paradox too far and to resist making unworthy gibes at nations which do not figure high on his list of preferences. And so sensitive a writer might have persuaded him not to overwork his

clichés; by the time Mr Taylor's characters have finished putting diplomatic problems 'on ice', he begins to sound like a refrigerator salesman. Mr. Taylor has every quality of a major historian except a sense of the dignity of his subject.

(It is perhaps not surprising that Taylor's brother-in-law, Anthony Crosland, referred to Beloff as 'Alan's great enemy'.[107])

Before writing, Beloff had asked Woodward whether he had in fact read the manuscript, and Woodward had exploded. This may seem strange, given that the latter had been a supporter of Taylor over his appointment to the Fellowship at Magdalen, but an incident in 1947 had since alienated him. Woodward and Rohan Butler were the editors of *Documents on British Foreign Policy 1919–1939, Second Series,* Volume I of which, covering certain topics in 1930–1, was published in early 1947. Taylor reviewed it for the *Times Literary Supplement,* for which he had become a reviewer the previous year (he was 'drawn to *The Times Literary Supplement* when Lewis Namier in his usual fashion became bored with writing for it and handed over to me'). Stanley Morison, the Editor of the *TLS,* had handed the Woodward/Butler tome over to him, saying that the editing was 'shoddy – sycophantic in tone, no minutes reproduced, altogether a cover-up for the foreign office. I [Taylor] wrote a front-page article on this theme. There was a great stir. Woodward was a skilled intriguer. He protested to Astor, the owner of the *Times,* and stirred up the foreign secretary to protest also.' In those days, reviews in the *TLS* were anonymous, and Morison became the scapegoat, losing his position as Editor shortly afterwards.[108]

Taylor's review began in an unexceptionable manner, stating that 'the conflict between secrecy and publicity is the trickiest question in foreign policy. ... Negotiations can only be flexible if they are secret; they will be barren unless they secure popular consent. These are the contradictory propositions which have to be reconciled in modern times by democratic governments.' He then elaborated on the history of the publication of government documents, and posed the question as to whether this was done with the public or historians in mind – that is, were they propaganda or historical record? What is clear is that in this case, for reasons which he elaborated, he thought that their publication verged on propaganda. It was undoubtedly the following paragraph that had enraged Woodward:

Gooch and Temperley, the editors of the previous collection, covering 1898–1914, were scholars of integrity, and they included in every volume from Volume III a statement 'that they would feel compelled to resign if any attempt were made to insist on the omission of any document which is in their view vital or essential ... [T]he editors [of the current volume, Woodward and Butler], do not define their position as precisely as did their predecessors. The accompanying leaflet of explanation states that 'they (the editors) have had complete freedom in the choice of documents for publication'; but in their preface they describe themselves as 'carrying out the instructions of the Secretary of State.' German historians may welcome an official position; it was not hitherto 'the British way' for historians to subordinate their independence to a Government department. Part of the present volume, for instance, seems to have the deliberate purpose of vindicating the British foreign service.[109]

It probably did not take Woodward long to ascertain who had written the review and it is not surprising that he thereafter detested the very idea of an association with Taylor. He immediately fired off a letter to OUP: 'Since I do not remember having ever seen the MS, or indeed, having been asked to look at it, I cannot understand the reference, and I wish strongly to disassociate myself from it.' He then asked the Press what steps they planned to take 'to correct the impression that I am in any way associated with the text of the book.' OUP were bewildered by the letter and asked Taylor what was behind it. Taylor replied that between 1941 and 1944 he had written 100,000 words of a manuscript on European diplomatic history, which Woodward had read and on which he had produced twenty pages of comments. This manuscript was then put aside but in due course formed about half of *The Struggle for Mastery*. For Taylor, 'it seemed elementary courtesy to acknowledge this criticism and help. ... What does he object to? That he scrutinised my manuscript is true; that this was much to its advantage is an opinion which I continue to hold.'[110]

Colin Roberts reported the gist of Taylor's letter to Woodward. There was, of course, no reason for Woodward to connect the half-completed manuscript which he had read, probably in 1944, with the book published ten years later. In any case, Roberts's letter produced only threats from Woodward. 'It is not only that I do not want to be associated with the judgments or statements made in the book – my view of Taylor is that he has certainly not improved in the last ten years. ... For the last seven years I have had what I can only call a long series of malicious attacks ... from Taylor in regard to the editorship of the Documents on British Foreign

Policy 1919–39. These attacks have gone far beyond reasonable criticism – to which of course I do not object; in the earliest and worst of them I had to insist on a public withdrawal of personal allegations ... and if I had not had this withdrawal, I should have taken legal steps to get it.' He feared that people would think that he had gone out of his way 'to give a kind of imprimatur to Taylor's own work. ... I think the Press ought to tell Taylor that he must cut my name out of all the copies of his book, bound or otherwise, and that he ought to write to the Times Lit. Supp. a short notice (of which I should see the text) saying that I had not seen the MS of his book; that I had not been consulted about the book, and that the reference to me in the preface was made without my knowledge or consent.' He also threatened to 'deal with Taylor through a solicitor' ending with 'What a letter – but damn it, what else can I do?'[111]

Then ensued a six-week exchange of letters which, midway through, brought publication of the book to a halt until the problem had been sorted out. Davin proposed to Taylor that the Press arrange to cancel the preliminaries of the unbound copies and put in a new preface which omitted the offending thank you. 'I hope you will not mind our doing this but Woodward is an author of ours and we must preserve as honest a neutrality as we can ... [and] unless you tell me otherwise I shall simply doctor the preface in such a way as to make the passage disappear.' This letter angered Taylor:

You must really bear in mind that I am an author of yours just as much as Woodward; and you have no right at all to doctor my text or even to suggest doing so without my express permission. I have examined my contract and cannot find in it any power for you to alter my text without my consent. I herewith formally withhold this consent. I put in an acknowledgement to Woodward out of ordinary courtesy without any malicious intent, because he had read my manuscript at an early stage and had made valuable suggestions. The only thing I can withdraw is that this was to its advantage. ... I will not tolerate demands. ... I dislike litigation, and of course I want to avoid it. But words such as 'demand' and that you will be 'forced' to this or that do not impress me.[112]

Roberts wrote to Woodward, pointing out that Taylor's statement was so worded that he could defend it as it stood: there was no demonstrable misstatement of fact and no question of libel. (Apparently a thank you was not deemed to be libellous.) He then made various suggestions, but

Woodward refused to budge, saying that he would have to consult with Butler, but that if Taylor refused to do as he wanted he would have 'to take whatever steps may be necessary to protect myself and to ensure that a misleading reference to me is removed.'[113]

Woodward genuinely believed that he had a grievance, but his obstinacy, demonstrated by his unwillingness at that point to compromise, was at one with his 'overbearing, dogmatic style.' Rowse, Woodward's colleague at All Souls (Woodward had been elected a Prize Fellow in 1919, in preference to, among others, Aldous Huxley), wrote of him in the late 1960s, emphasising his meanness, his 'pluralism of College offices that carried an additional salary', including the position of Domestic Bursar, and 'his pleasure at someone's downfall (his prominent yellow teeth grinning over loose wet lips).' Rowse was not a notably generous assessor of character and intelligence, but enough people (such as Taylor's old tutor G.N. Clark and the historian Richard Pares) disliked Woodward to confirm the general likeness of the portrait.[114]

By this time the problem had been put to the Delegates, who made a suggestion as to how the knot might be untied. Furthermore, they had also 'ruled that no further orders for binding or printing can be placed until this question of the preface is resolved.' Roberts then had a long telephone call with Taylor,

as a result of which he has agreed at the Delegates' request to ask us to cut out Woodward's name in all unbound copies and future printings without waiting for Woodward to request it but on the understanding that if this is done both we and Woodward will regard the incident as closed. This is, I think, a considerable concession on Taylor's part and his proviso has been made to ensure that this concession would not be exploited by Woodward. ... It has to be remembered that Taylor is not ready to admit that he has been in any sense in the wrong and won't decline a scrap if it is forced on him, but is anxious to see what he now at any rate regards as a childish quarrel settled. ... I should add that Taylor is very susceptible to anything in the nature of a demand or a threat and I had some difficulty in convincing him that the last paragraph of my letter [in which he had conveyed the Delegates' ruling] was not intended to put pressure on him.

Roberts wrote to Woodward with the proposal and he agreed, thus bringing the 'odd and inconvenient argument' to a close.[115]

Meanwhile, other reviews of the book appeared. One of the earliest, and most favourable, was written by the historian Asa Briggs, who noted that 'one of the most interesting features of this book is its refusal to take German interpretations of recent history on trust or to lean too heavily on the massive supports of *Die Grosse Politik*.' He continued: 'sometimes we need to rest and think three times about his brilliant epigrams; sometimes we pine for a closer study of the economic and social background of diplomacy. ... But whatever we do will be influenced by what he has done, for he has re-opened the nineteenth century rather than closed it down.' Briggs also linked it to the international relations of the twentieth century: 'There are features of the quadrille which not even the square dance has rendered obsolete, and although the music sounds very different now, it still goes on.' Some time later, another reviewer, the American historian of Germany, Gordon Craig, used the same metaphor in his review 'Europe's Perpetual Quadrille': 'What makes this the best study of European diplomacy since W.C. Langer's [Taylor's colleague in Vienna] volumes on the post–1870 period is his ability to keep the major developments of the period clearly before his readers, while at the same time providing them with circumstantial and absorbing accounts of the policies and ambitions of individual powers and statesmen, the changing diplomatic alignments, and the crises and wars which filled the period.' A few months later a third reviewer celebrated Taylor's achievement: 'In working out [his] theme, not in itself novel, Mr. Taylor is original in keeping his eye relentlessly on the ball of power ... and, in dismissing all else as irrelevant to his purpose, and consequently in his caustic judgements upon almost every actor on the stage ... this is the work of a serious, acute and extremely well read writer, who stimulates more than he annoys and redeems his acidity by his zest.'[116]

But one of the most important reviews, that by E.H. Carr in the *Times Literary Supplement*, was more measured. It was hardly a compliment for Carr to state that Taylor 'has not ... written a history of the relations between the European nations: military operations and economic relations are both neglected. His work is diplomatic history in the strictest sense; and such abstraction, while necessary and valuable for the specialist, fits less well into the conception of general history.' Nevertheless, he then goes on to concede that 'what perhaps justifies the detachment of diplomacy during this period is that it in some measure corresponds to the realities of the situation.' He celebrated Taylor's 'detailed and penetrating analysis' and 'the wealth of detail and ... unfailing pertinacity' with which Taylor analysed the subject, and wrote that 'his sharp critical faculty and vigilant readiness to challenge orthodox opinions make it certain that his interpretations and conjectures, whether accepted or not, will have to be taken account of by future historians.' It was 'an outstanding book.' And yet, Carr felt that Taylor's reliance on diplomatic documents prevented him from looking more closely at the societies that had produced them and thus at the more fundamental forces that pushed them towards the First World War – indeed, even Taylor himself had admitted their relevance: '"Policy", he writes, "springs from deep social and economic forces; it is not crudely manufactured in foreign offices".' But he had then failed to incorporate this insight into the body of the book. Carr also believed that Taylor's conception of the European balance of power as limited to the mainland of Europe was itself limiting: 'if we examine the essence of the balance of power in this period, did it not in fact consist in the carefully balanced competitive expansion of Europe into other continents?' Carr, who had his own view of history, regarded Taylor as believing that history was little more than a chapter of accidents, disclaiming 'belief in determining causes or scientifically demonstrable trends' – and in the latter assumption Carr was certainly correct. But this came close to damning Taylor, although Carr's biographer states that only 'those in the top rank were deemed worthy of attack'. And attack, though regretful attack, there was: 'If Mr. Taylor would shed his distaste for ideas, recognise that history would not be worth writing or reading if it had no meaning, and cease to give so many hostages to the assumption that the important explanations in history are to be found in the conscious purposes and foresights of the *dramatis personae*, he would stand in the front rank of living historians'[117] – a conclusion which directly contradicted his earlier comment that Taylor believed history to be a chapter of accidents.

Nevertheless, the reviews were overwhelmingly favourable, with the book even impressing those who professed another field entirely: as noted above, the mediaevalist Galbraith by rumour recommended Taylor for a Fellowship of the British Academy on the basis of the book's bibliography. Taylor himself had changing feelings about *The Struggle for Mastery*. In 1974 he referred to it as 'very scholarly, very learned, with a very good bibliography, but boring to the last degree. I can't think how anyone reads it through'; by 1983 he had softened towards it: the book is

very good as what it claims to be: a work of detailed diplomatic history. Certainly there is little about the 'profound forces' that were then becoming fashionable, though they came in more than might be thought. I agree that public opinion, economic factors and perhaps military calculations counted for more as the nineteenth century wore on. Nevertheless diplomacy ... still had an autonomy which it lost after the First World War.[118] At any rate my book was a success. The reviewers were overawed by my learning especially in the bibliography. I established my academic reputation instead of being merely a public entertainer. However *The Struggle for Mastery* is entertaining as well, or so I thought when I re-read it a few weeks ago.

Furthermore, the book has stood the test of time. Noel Annan, not one of Taylor's admirers, wrote in 1990 that 'his accuracy on matters of fact and scholarship in modern diplomatic history was legendary', and when in 1995 The *Times Literary Supplement* printed a list of the hundred most influential books published since 1945, *The Struggle for Mastery* was on it.[119] Certainly it has retained its stature as one of the most important accounts of modern international history to have been written, a book which repays reading as one's own knowledge of the period increases: it is not a text for beginners.

While the book was being printed, published and reviewed, Taylor was engaged in reading for and writing his next book, *Bismarck: The Man and the Statesman*. In July 1953 he told Hamish Hamilton that the American publisher Alfred Knopf had approached him some time before to write a short life of Bismarck; at that point he had been too busy, but now he was tempted. Would Hamish Hamilton like the English rights? Knopf had offered him $2,500 to buy the manuscript outright, 'but of course I shan't play on that basis – royalties for me.' The answer from Hamilton was of course he would publish it – and he believed it would have a good sale. Also, he suggested, Taylor should remember that Knopf's $2,500 would be for English language rights, and not just American rights: taking a royalty was certainly much better. Knopf, however, held out for buying the rights, offering $1,500 for the USA and Canada, so Taylor asked Hamilton whether he could find him another American publisher who would pay royalties. Hamilton, however, was firm in his refusal: 'I am afraid that the course you propose ... in your letter would effectively terminate our relations with Knopf once and for all! The Bismarck was his idea. ... If I were to endeavour to find a publisher prepared to pay you royalties and word of this reached Knopf, you can imagine his feelings. In the circumstances I think I had better keep out!'[120]

Agreement was finally reached that Taylor would write a book for both

Knopf and Hamish Hamilton that would stand by itself (Knopf had originally intended it as part of a series). There were some problems with the
contract. In October 1953, Taylor wrote to Hamilton that 'Blanche Knopf
certainly likes to keep things moving. The other day she sent me out of the
blue a contract for Bismarck with every detail filled in.' Hamilton was a bit
alarmed: 'I know Blanche Knopf's contracts from long experience. They
usually claim film, and make provision for atomic and Martian, rights. It
would therefore be helpful in preparing our own contract if you would lend
me hers, so that at least we shan't find that you have unwittingly covered
any part of the globe twice. And, if it would interest you, I'll be glad to draw
attention to any provisions in the Knopf contract which seem iniquitous.
(The Society of Authors invariably explodes when presented with one, I
happen to know.)' Taylor, however, had already 'returned the contract to
Knopf for some of the outrageous clauses to be taken out before your letter
reached me.' Adjustments were duly made, and by the end of November
1953 both contracts had been signed.[121]

Meanwhile, Taylor had begun work. He was, of course, intimately
acquainted with Bismarck's political activities – as minister-president of
Prussia and then as Chancellor of the German Empire – as a result of his
work for *Germany's First Bid for Colonies 1884–1885: A Move in Bismarck's
European Policy* and *The Struggle for Mastery*. What he felt less confident
about was Bismarck's private life and psychology. To remedy this, he began
in July 1953 to read a series of biographies of Bismarck, and some
monographs in French, German and English. He also reread Bismarck's
Gedanken und Erinnerungen, which he had first read in 1931 as *Reflections
and Reminiscences*. He then began to write, and by September had written
80,000 words, which left him two more chapters to write. By mid-
November, the month after the publication of *The Struggle for Mastery*, he
had completed another chapter. He worked during the Christmas vacation
and, through a Herculean effort, completed the manuscript (bar the
bibliography), by now 90,000 words, by 3 January 1955. The book was
published in June in both Great Britain and the United States. *The Sunday
Times* had declined serialisation, but negotiations for foreign rights began
(not always successfully – a German edition was only published in 1962)
and within two months Hamish Hamilton were printing a second impression.[122]

Taylor later wrote that *Bismarck* was one of the books which he had most
enjoyed writing: 'I knew all the historical background already. Now I found
Bismarck's personality fascinating as well and he became one of the few I

should like to recall from the dead. It is a very good exercise for an historian to stray into biography – a field seemingly so similar and yet fundamentally different. Perhaps no historian can really handle individual psychology or make an individual the centre of his book. All the same I think my *Bismarck* is the best on him ever written.'[123] His pleasure in the subject comes across in the book, not least his pleasure in delineating Bismarck's character and personality. He had always paid great attention to the characters and personalities of the politicians, officials and monarchs of whom he wrote; now he could do the same thing *in extenso*, it being unnecessary to limit himself to a line of text. In his first chapter, entitled 'The Boy and the Man', he presented a portrait of Bismarck that immediately convinces.

It is a short book, with a lot of ground to cover, and Taylor therefore highlights the broad sweeps of policy in a way that, paradoxically, was not always possible in the longer and more detailed *Struggle for Mastery*. That is, in *The Struggle* the focus was often on the trees, while in *Bismarck* Taylor really had time only for the wood. Again, while the concentration in the earlier book was on foreign policy, in *Bismarck* Taylor had also to look at domestic policy, the aim of which for Bismarck was to ensure his freedom to develop and implement his foreign policy (the German historian Leopold von Ranke's *Primat der Aussenpolitik*). A third difference is that Taylor used the final chapter, entitled 'Into the Grave – and Beyond It', to draw explicit conclusions about Bismarck's sometimes baleful influence on Germany and Germany's baleful influence on Europe.

Taylor had long been interested in Bismarck, one reason why he responded so warmly to the suggestion that he write a biography. He had written in a book review in 1943 that 'to write a life of Bismarck within reasonable compass would be one of the greatest of historical achievements; but perhaps it is impossible. The material is overwhelming; and to make matters worse, Bismarck himself has left, in speeches, conversations or his reminisicences, versions of all the principal events usually deliberately misleading.' Perhaps it was the fact that Bismarck combined a complex personality with the exercise of considerable power over a long span of years, and that it might be possible to peel him like an onion through a rigorous comparison of printed documents, that accounted for the fascination Taylor felt. In 1950 he wrote in another book review that 'the time is coming when a truly historical approach to Bismarck can be attempted, without worrying whether what he did was right or wrong.' But, of course, Taylor made judgements. And for Taylor, Bismarck was not the Junker and Chancellor of iron: rather, he was a complex, urban intellectual, 'the clever, sophisticated son of a clever, sophisticated mother, masquerading all his life as his heavy, earthen father'.[124] Instead of drawing up a careful plan for the reunification of Germany or, more particularly, for his complex system of alliances to keep Germany intact, he took advantage of opportunities, sensing the atmosphere and knowing the limits of the possible. He was an emotional man, prone to sobbing and to throwing crockery in his rages. What gave him stability, purpose in life? Only politics and international relations. And with his sensitive nose and his determination, for many years he was supremely good at them.

The reviews were very good. In Great Britain, the military historian Michael Howard wrote in the *New Statesman and Nation* that 'Mr Taylor carries out his revaluation in the clear, sharp, epigrammatic prose which makes all his work as stimulating as champagne – and which makes one wonder, sometimes, whether it was all really as simple as that. His mind is a convex mirror in which events appear brilliantly coloured, brilliantly distinct, and sometimes a little distorted. He has many of the virtues of Macaulay [Taylor surely liked that comparison], and one or two of his faults. The pattern is too sharply etched; the epigrams are too neat; the judgements are too final; but how refreshing it is to read a historian who is not afraid of patterns, epigrams and judgements!' In the United States Gordon Craig wrote that 'A.J.P. Taylor does two things excellently. He provides a long needed account in English of the main facts of Bismarck's career, an account which is at once readable, up to date ... and balanced. ... In the second place, he paints a fascinating portrait of one of the most complicated personalities in an age which was filled with gifted and original minds ... [The] chapter on the corrosive effects of the Bismarckian tradition in Germany's intellectual development is not the least interesting part of this highly provocative study.' And the German response? Did they agree with Taylor that his book on Bismarck was the best ever written? It was not published in German until 1962, and twenty years later Taylor could write, with regret, that 'no serious German historian ever comments on it.' But one has since: in 1995 Professor Wolfgang Mommsen stated that Taylor's biography was better than any German synthesis.[125]

Taylor's next book was actually the text of his Ford Lectures in English History, published in 1956, which will be considered later. It seems most profitable here to look next at the book that appeared in 1961, Taylor's last important one with Germany as its focus, and the book, moreover, which brought him to the notice of many far beyond the history-reading public. This was *The Origins of the Second World War*, one of his most interesting, most provocative and undoubtedly most controversial books. According to Taylor, he chose the subject himself.

> I wanted to be writing something and decided that I could carry on my diplomatic history from the point where the *Struggle for Mastery* left off. I had, I thought, done most of the research work needed by reviewing the various books of memoirs and the volumes of German and British diplomatic documents as they came out. At that time no original sources were available: no cabinet minutes or papers, no Chiefs of Staff records, only more or less formal documents from the Foreign Office with very occasional minutes. This extraordinary paucity, as it seems now, makes my book a period piece of limited value.[126]

At different times and in different places Taylor gave other reasons for beginning *The Origins* besides the compulsion to write. First of all, he had fundamentally scholarly motives. He had read, since 1947, fifteen volumes of British diplomatic documents, eight of German diplomatic documents and one of Italian diplomatic documents, all covering the 1930s. It would not be surprising if he had decided to write, since no one else had, an analysis of the outbreak of the war based on them – what he himself referred to as 'further thought and new evidence'. Indeed, with hindsight it is possible to trace in outline the development of his main theme. In a review in December 1951 of a volume of German diplomatic documents, he wrote that 'On the one hand the disintegration of Central Europe was so great that Hitler could not resist the temptation to go farther. On the other British and French policy seemed to imply that he could advance eastwards without serious protest from the Western Powers.'[127] In a review in August 1953 of a further volume of German documents, he wrote that 'The reader of these documents will acquit the German diplomatists of deliberately planning a large-scale war of aggression. Why should they? They were getting what they wanted without war; and there seemed no limit to what they could gain by this steady pressure. ... They had the same aims as Hitler's; only more caution.'[128] Finally, in November 1959, in a review of yet another volume of German diplomatic documents, he revealed his theme: 'The war of 1939 seems in longer retrospect to have been the result of miscalculation, not of deliberate policy.' Hitler 'had only to sit up on the Berghof, eating cream buns, and the artificial system of European security fell to pieces before his eyes. Hitler did not plan his victory. It was presented to him by the statesmen of Great Britain, France and Soviet

Russia. Such are the advantages of being in the centre of Europe and having strong nerves.'[129] He was already deep into the book, as he wrote in October 1959 to the former soldier and military historian Basil Liddell Hart: 'I have put my book on English history aside for a year or so in order to write a book on the origins of the Second World War. Mainly to make the point that it was not planned by Hitler but that he stumbled into it by mistake – some his own mistakes, but also the mistakes of others. I'm sure this is right, but it will disturb received notions.' Liddell Hart replied that 'your conclusion that it was accidental coincides with my own ... [F]rom my study of history I [have] come to see that most wars were detonated accidently rather than deliberately.'[130]

There were other reasons, of a more political nature, for his venturing into print on the subject. In his letter Liddell Hart had added that he had emphasised the accidental nature of the outbreak of wars in order 'to correct some arguments that the best way to check any frontier incursions by the Russians or their satellites was to start dropping some atomic bombs.' The Bomb, in fact, was apparently a second impetus driving Taylor to write the book. He produced it in the midst of the initial CND campaign, a strong argument of which was that unintended – that is, accidental – war in an age of nuclear weapons could annihilate the world. By now he believed that the outbreak of the Second World War had been the result of mistakes, or accidents; the book would serve to warn people and perhaps help CND to hammer home its point. As he wrote in the first chapter of *The Origins of the Second World War*, 'I doubt whether much will be gained by waiting another ten or fifteen years; and much might be lost. The few survivors of civilisation may have given up reading books by then, let alone writing them.'[131] This is probably the most blatant example of Taylor's ignoring his own precept that history provided no 'lessons' to be learned.

The other possible political reason was Taylor's fear that mistaken conclusions had been and were being drawn about the causes of the Second World War: that because the failure to stand up to the dictators had led to war in 1939, it was necessary to stand up to the USSR now. Taylor's apprehension was not far-fetched: Prime Minister Anthony Eden had decided in 1956 to confront the Egyptian leader Abdul Nasser partly because of the analogy he drew between Nasser and Mussolini. The result had been the Suez Crisis. For his part, Taylor always believed that the peace of Europe required, as a necessary element in the balance of power on the continent, an Anglo-Russian alliance, rather than confrontation.

Taylor proposed a book entitled 'Outbreak of World War II' or 'The

Causes of World War II' to Hamish Hamilton in late 1958, telling his publisher in December that he would probably write it the following year. He did not mention it again until June 1960, when he wrote that 'I'm in the last stages of The Origins of the Second World War; and a nice, clear typescript should be with you sometime in July.' Hamish Hamilton were delighted: 'No idea you were so near the end of the book and, as you can imagine, we rejoice to hear it.' Taylor had, according to one student, already laid out the arguments of the book in his 9am lectures to Oxford under-graduates during the previous April and May, 'when his voice sometimes had to combat the drone of US bombers passing low overhead.' Once they had the manuscript in their possession Hamish Hamilton were indeed delighted: 'Taylor's approach ... [is] always out to epater. No doubt he'll succeed and it should have a controversial reception and be fallen upon by his rivals.'[132] This was certainly to be the case.

The Origins of the Second World War was published in April 1961, with German and American editions (amongst others) coming out in 1962. The main themes are straightforward. First of all, foreign policies are deter-mined by reasons of state and the need to respond to external threats or blandishments, rather than by internal politics, including those driven by ideology or by economic pressures. Secondly, Hitler had strategic goals but no predetermined master plan as to how and when he would reach those goals. Thirdly, those goals were no different from the goals of other German statesmen such as Stresemann. Fourthly, lacking a precise timetable, Hitler took opportunities as they arose – and the French and British governments gave him those opportunities. And fifthly, Hitler had the support of the German people in overthrowing the Versailles Treaty and invading Poland. In this Taylor challenged and thereby shattered the consensus about the origins of the war which went under the rubric of the Nuremberg Thesis, based on the evidence supplied by the prosecutors in the Nuremberg war trials. This held that Hitler had wanted war, had planned in detail for war and had begun the war; in this he was supported by his fellow Nazis, but not by the German people, who were largely innocent bystanders, if not victims themselves, of the regime and its policies.

The book begins in a measured and careful style, rather as if Taylor wanted to lure the reader into a comfortable relationship with him, a relationship based on the supposition that the book was indeed a continu-ation of *The Struggle for Mastery*, itself a book which had excited admiration for its command of the sources and subject. Like it, *The Origins* was based almost wholly on the published diplomatic documents, memoirs and biographies, supplemented by a number of secondary works. The chapters covering the 1920s attracted almost universal praise for their perceptiveness and judgement. But the further Taylor moved into the later 1930s, the more criticism he attracted, criticism which he virtually invited with his conclusion on the final page of the book: 'Hitler may have projected a great war all along: yet it seems from the record that he became involved in war through launching on 29 August a diplomatic manoeuvre which he ought to have launched on 28 August.'[133]

The first reviews, such as that by Sebastian Haffner in the *Observer* newspaper, verged on the ecstatic: 'This is an almost faultless masterpiece, perfectly proportioned, perfectly controlled. Bitterness has mellowed into quiet sadness and even pity ... fairness rules supreme and of all passions only the passion for clarity remains. ... In spite of all this, it will probably become his most controversial book.' The review ended with the ringing affirmation that 'Mr. Taylor is in the very first rank. He is among English historians to-day what Evelyn Waugh is among English novelists, a rescuer of forgotten truths, a knight of paradox, a prince of story-telling, and a great, perhaps the greatest, master of his craft.' Another was that by David Marquand in the *New Statesman*: 'Mr. A.J.P. Taylor is the only English historian now writing who can bend the bow of Gibbon and Macaulay' – Taylor must have been delighted to have been placed in the same league as his two favourite historians.[134]

A diametrically opposed view was given by Hugh Trevor-Roper (who had been sent a review copy by the publisher) in the July 1961 issue of *Encounter*, a review which attracted a reply by Taylor notable for demonstrating his Renaissance-like skill with the dagger. Trevor-Roper began by outlining the thesis of the book and then set out what he believed was Taylor's general philosophy: 'Mr. Taylor, it seems, does not believe that human agents matter much in history. His story is "a story without heroes, and perhaps even without villains." "In my opinion," he explains, "statesmen are too absorbed by events to follow a preconceived plan. They take one step and the next follows from it." ... The real determinants of history, according to Mr. Taylor, are objective situations and human blunders.' Trevor-Roper proceeded to deconstruct the book, emphasising, for example – as would other critics – that Hitler had stated his programme in 1924 in *Mein Kampf* and on numerous other occasions. 'Mr. Taylor', he wrote, 'hardly ever refers to *Mein Kampf.*' But his main charge was that Taylor had perverted the evidence, which he demonstrated with a number of quotations from the book. His final summation was this:

I have said enough to show why I think Mr. Taylor's book utterly erroneous. In spite of his statements about 'historical discipline,' he selects, suppresses, and arranges evidence on no principle other than the needs of his thesis; and that thesis, that Hitler was a traditional statesman, of limited aims, merely responding to a given situation, rests on no evidence at all, ignores essential evidence, and is, in my opinion, demonstrably false. This casuistical defence of Hitler's foreign policy will not only do harm by supporting neo-Nazi mythology: it will also do harm, perhaps irreparable harm, to Mr. Taylor's reputation as a serious historian.[135]

Trevor-Roper was primarily an historian of the seventeenth century. The reason he had been asked to review the book was because, after spending the war in British intelligence, he had written *The Last Days of Hitler*, whose second edition, published in 1950, was reviewed by Taylor. Taylor gave it an encomium: 'This is an incomparable book, by far the best book written on any aspect of the second German war; a book sound in its scholarship, brilliant in its presentation, a delight for history and laymen alike. No words of praise are too strong for it.' Nevertheless, Trevor-Roper had stumbled in his review of Taylor. Taylor was given advanced warning about it from Robert Kee in mid-June: Taylor and Trevor-Roper were scheduled to debate the book on 9 July in a television broadcast and Kee was to be the moderator.

The assumption was widespread that the confrontation would produce fireworks. As it turned out, although he repeatedly attempted to stick the knife into Taylor, Trevor-Roper apparently came out the worse from the discussion. According to one viewer (an Oxford philosopher), 'Trevor-Roper gave me the impression of spluttering flame under the withering impact of Taylor's mind. Taylor would pinch his nose and take off his glasses as though he had an ulcer or was in pain, and my heart went out to him, while Trevor-Roper appeared nervous, his mouth a little jumpy, his hands writhing. As far as I was concerned, Taylor stole the show.'[136]

In the course of the programme, Taylor defended himself against the charges that he was an apologist for Hitler and for appeasement: 'It's perfectly obvious', he said,

that the wickedness he [Hitler] did, the wickedness he inspired, particularly what went on in Germany – the dictatorship, later on, the extermination of the Jews – these have no parallel in history. I don't dispute this.

But it seems to me that his foreign policy was the least original part of what he contributed, either for good or ill. That in this – and this is all I've been trying to say, not thinking of it in moral terms – that Hitler's policy sprang out of the German history that had gone before. That in one form or another Germany, remaining united at the end of the First World War, was bound to seek to destroy the defeat; was bound to seek to undo the Treaty of Versailles; and that the impetus of success in undoing this Treaty would carry Germany forward, unless it was checked in some way, into being again a great and dominant power in Europe. ... But I don't understand, except that I dislike the Germans, why merely wanting your country to be the most powerful in the world puts you into the head [*sic*] of a wicked statesman. ... The war of 1939 is not the war he planned. It may well be that he planned some different war – a war against Russia, a war in 1943, but the war of 1939 was a war against England and France, it took place against antagonists he'd not planned it to take place against, and it took place at a time when he had not planned it to take place. ... When I judge ... events in the past I try to judge them in terms of the morality which then existed, not of mine. When I say that Munich was a triumph for all that was best in British life, I mean ... by that a triumph for all those who had preached enlightenment, international conciliation, revision of treaties, the liberation of nationalities from foreign rule, and so on.[137]

BBC Radio wanted to get at Taylor. One of the Home Service producers reported a talk with Isaac Deutscher, the biographer of Stalin: Deutscher thought 'it was important to blast the book if only because the two Sunday papers gave it the kind of review one would have given to Macaulay or Ranke. He dismissed the idea of a discussion *with* Taylor – he thought (as I do) that it would become a circus.' There was a rapid reaction: 'Give HELL to AJP?! Let's talk on Monday.' The BBC were keen on the idea of a confrontation – 'what, from a serious historian's point of view, could be thought an unworthy circus might nevertheless make provocative ... broadcasting.' The Head of Talks then suggested a discussion between Taylor and Bullock.

In preparation for 'giving hell' to Taylor, the BBC asked a producer to read the book. The report was unexpected:

[He] has now read [the] book and points out that the press criticism seriously misrepresented it. Taylor does not suggest that Hitler was not expansionist or did not have a list of targets. Instead he claims that Hitler had no master-plan or time-table for reaching these targets, but could not resist exploiting the opportunities presented by the hesitations of the democracies. In other words, Taylor's thesis is less controversial than it has been made out to be and does not lend itself to a discussion on whether he was right to whitewash Hitler, because in fact he does not do so. It seems to me that there is still justification for a programme. Most people will only have read the reviews of the book and it would be reason-able to give Taylor an opportunity to correct the false impression. ... We would advise against Bullock as a speaker, because he has become woolly and lazy over his homework. James Joll is suggested as being more incisive. As it might be difficult to find an outright opponent of Taylor's real thesis, it might be better to have a conversation in which more than one speaker probed Taylor about his attitude with differing emphasis.

Such a discussion programme was never made: instead, Taylor was a 'guest of the week' on 'Woman's Hour', and the Home Service rebroadcast the Taylor/Trevor-Roper confrontation.[138]

Meanwhile, having learned about Trevor-Roper's review in the July *Encounter* from Kee, Taylor sat down and wrote a reply entitled 'How to Quote: Exercises for Beginners', which was published in the September 1961 issue of the journal. It was set out in two columns. The first column consisted of quotations from *The Origins* as cited by Trevor-Roper; the second consisted of the entire sentence from which Trevor-Roper had wrenched each of his citations and, if necessary, the succeeding one. The intention was to demonstate how Trevor-Roper had himself selected, suppressed and arranged his evidence. The final quotation was the sentence that 'It [the book] will do harm, perhaps irreparable harm, to Mr. Taylor's reputation as a serious historian.' Taylor's response was 'The Regius Professor's methods of quotation might also do harm to his reputation as a serious historian, if he had one.' In the same issue of *Encounter* Trevor-Roper replied to Taylor, but the riposte was demonstrably weaker than the initial attack had been.[139] This whole episode, following upon that of the Regius chair, convinced many that Taylor and Trevor-Roper were sworn enemies, when in fact they were not: privately they got along well together.

Trevor-Roper was not the only critic to underline Taylor's lack of emphasis on Hitler's writings, in particular *Mein Kampf*. There were at least three reasons for this lack. First of all, Taylor's method of organising his research precluded it. As already described, he habitually made a diary, as it were, of the activities of his characters based on the books of documents and the material taken from memoirs and biographies. In this there was little room for philosophical musings. Second, the reason there was little room provided was his lack of theoretical emphasis on such musings; given his belief that statesmen did not plan but reacted to external events, writings such as *Mein Kampf* were largely irrelevant: they may have expressed hopes and dreams, but they were not organised blueprints for future actions. But there was a third reason why he referred only four times to *Mein Kampf* and then only in general terms: he had not read it. When recording the books he had read each month, he put everything down: in December 1947, for example, he read Beatrix Potter's *Tale of Benjamin Bunny* and *Tale of Pigling Bland*, followed in October 1948 by *The Tailor of Gloucester*. *Mein Kampf*, which he read in the original German, does not appear on his list until August 1962, evidence which may be taken as conclusive. This was the same month in which he handed the manuscript of his 'Second Thoughts', written for the Penguin paperback edition, to his publisher; the assumption must be that, in reaction to the reviews, he finally read it in order to be able to refer to it.[140]

It is curious that he did not read *Mein Kampf* until after *The Origins of the Second World War* had been written, since he had read Hitler's *Table Talk* twice (once in German and once in English). Certainly some of his reviewers criticised him for not having taken account of it. At least one statement in *The Origins*, that Hitler forbade *Mein Kamp's* publication in English, seems inexplicable. An abridged translation, though with most of the foreign policy section excised, was published in 1933, but a full translation appeared in 1939. Taylor must have known about this, because a full review was published in the *Times Literary Supplment* in March 1939. He *may* have been referring to *Hitlers zweites Buch*, the so-called 'secret book' from 1928, which Hitler had forbidden to be published (and which appeared only in 1961), but this is unlikely. The conclusion must be that Taylor had simply decided that he already knew what Hitler's ideas were without needing to read *Mein Kampf*; after all, as the *TLS* reviewer wrote in 1939, 'It would be easy to comment on the timing of this piece of publishing, to exclaim that at last we have the whole book and to applaud the tearing of the veils of secrecy which are supposed to have hung for so long around certain passages. But the truth, of course, is that it comes late, that the unpleasant essentials have long ago reached the English public, and that many people will be sorry that they can no longer crush all argument with the phrase "as everybody knows who has read *Mein Kampf*". Some English readers may find the original something of an anti-climax.' If Taylor did read the review, at least one comment must have had an impact: 'Herr Hitler's foreign policy has nothing complicated about it. The ends are clear: the methods are obviously to be chosen as occasions present themselves.' Even the appeasing Prime Minister, Neville Chamberlain, had read – and annotated – *Mein Kampf*;[141] Taylor should have done the same.

The Origins of the Second World War attracted a massive amount of attention at the time, whether measured by sales – nearly ten thousand copies were sold in the UK alone before the end of the year – or by reviews, both general and learned. (And in terms of private letters, one example being E.L. Woodward's to G.N. Clark: 'I must, I suppose, read AJP Taylor's book, but it looks to me as though his besetting fault – wh. has got worse with everything he has written – of deliberately standing on his head has now become almost pathological.') Furthermore, between 1971 and 1999 four books analysing Taylor's arguments were published.[142]

A substantial criticism was that he had taken little account of the dynamism of the Nazi state, or of the supposed economic drive towards war. This attack was most famously launched by the young Marxist historian from Oxford, Tim Mason, in the December 1964 issue of the history journal *Past and Present*. Mason emphasised the Nazi state's 'demonic urge'. He objected to – almost denounced – Taylor's dismissing the relevance of German economic patterns, of the concentration on rearmament as the prime objective of the economy, of the drive towards autarky. For Mason, all required war: 'A war for the plunder of manpower and materials lay square in the dreadful logic of German economic development under National Socialist rule.' Taylor had ignored the interdependence of domestic and external factors in the development and conduct of the Reich's foreign policy. Mason made a number of other charges, both important – that Taylor had excluded the profound causes of the war – and trivial – that Taylor used nineteenth-century language, such as calling Hitler 'wicked', which to Mason seemed too pale an epithet to begin to describe the Führer.[143]

Taylor responded. He ignored Mason's animadversions on his use of language. In *The Pilgrim's Progress*, 'wicked' was a strong rather than a weak adjective, but perhaps Mason had not read Bunyan; in any case he could not have known of Bunyan's influence on Taylor. With regard to Mason's argument about rearmament, Taylor rejoined that 'The evidence for economic or political crisis within Germany between 1937 and 1939 is very slight, if not non-existent. Hitler cut German armaments plans by 30 per cent after Munich. He cut them again drastically after the fall of France and was reducing them even after the invasion of Russia. Indeed large-scale rearmament began only in the summer of 1943.' Taylor's serious disagreements with Mason were over the latter's appearing to attribute National Socialism to Hitler alone, with no responsibility attributed to the German people, and his argument that National Socialism itself was responsible for the instability of the European order, rather than considering that the instability already existed, as exemplified by Danzig and the creation of the Polish Corridor. And finally, Taylor responded to Mason's criticism that he had neglected the deeper background factors: 'I fear I may not have emphasised the profound forces. Of course there was a general climate of feeling in the Europe of the nineteen-thirties which made war likely. ... Of course historians must explore the profound forces. But I am sometimes tempted to think that they talk so much about these profound forces in order to avoid doing the detailed work. I prefer detail to generalisations: a grave fault no doubt, but at least it helps to redress the balance.'[144]

Taylor's approach was to receive significant support from the next generation. Thirty years later, D.C. Watt, Stevenson Professor of International History at the London School of Economics, contrasted Taylor's arguments with those of Mason. Taylor, he wrote, argued that Hitler 'simply bluffed, manoeuvred and improvised his way from one crisis to another in a manner dictated by his need to survive as Germany's leader, by the necessities of competition between great powers such as Germany and her enemies, and by the aims of a generation of German nationalists whose views had been formed before or during the First World War ... [He also] believed that Hitler had long term ends, even if they were German in general rather than his own invention.' On the other hand, there were 'functionalist' historians who 'believed that political action was, and is, constrained, if not more, by the economic and social organisation of the society in which the actors live. For this group, Hitler's foreign policy, especially his choice of war in 1939, was not the outcome of a series of deliberate, if not always completely rational or reasoned, choices and decisions, but the product of the internal dynamism of his system of economic rule, an "escape forwards" into international adventure from the social conflicts, economic breakdown and internal muddle of Nazi Germany in the late 1930s.'

Watt's example of a functionalist historian was Mason, whom he believed was wrong. Mason used metaphors as though they were realities.

One example was 'internal dynamism': what did it actually mean in concrete terms? What did he mean by the breakdown in the German economy? Mason had produced evidence to show that the economy was in a bad way in 1938–9, but 'the evidence linking the economic phenomena and conditions perceived by Dr. Mason ... with the chain of decisions which led to the German attack on Poland in August 1939 is simply not there.' The implicit charge by Watt was that Mason's deterministic approach, his belief in the importance of economic factors, allowed him to ignore the evidence, or lack of evidence, required to prove his hypothesis.[145] All in all, Watt preferred Taylor's details to Mason's generalities.

There were a number of translations in the three years following the book's publication in Britain. Although a German translation was only published in 1962, the news magazine *Der Spiegel* reviewed the English edition in November 1961. It pointed out that Taylor had attacked nearly all previous 'argumentations' concerning the outbreak of the war and insisted that the Western powers were also responsible for the events of the late 1930s – an approach that exonerated Hitler. Whilst the greater part of the British press had praised the book, it said, the West German press had unanimously rejected Taylor's views, especially the 'Entdamonisierung' (de-demonising) of Hitler. The reviewer ended by saying that any relation between the roles of historian and entertainer was so alien to the German ideas of a scientist that Taylor's critics in the Federal Republic were extremely suspicious of the idea that he should be taken seriously.[146] Other papers, such as the *Frankfurter Allgemeine Zeitung*, emphasised the fear that the book might become a primer for unrepentant Nazis.

Other reviews were more favourable, but unfortunately they appeared in extreme right-wing papers. In a letter to the *Times Literary Supplement*, the historian Elizabeth Wiskemann revealed that

on April 22 the *Reichsruf*, the organ of the neo-Nazi *Reichspartei* in the Federal Republic, jubilantly welcomed Mr. Taylor's mis-reading of the Hossbach Memorandum and attacked German historians who had read it with greater care. The *Deutsche Soldatenzeitung* of April 28 was happy to note that Mr. Taylor had made nonsense of the Nuremberg trials. The May number of *Nation-Europa* [published in Coburg by Artur Ehrhardt, formerly a Major in the SS, on behalf of the chief neo-Nazi international organisation] was gratified to observe that Mr. Taylor had explained away the responsibility of Nazi Germany for the Second World War. Sir Oswald Mosley has expressed similar appreciation of Mr. Taylor.

Wiskermann's point was clearly that the book was to be known by the sources of the favourable reviews it attracted. Taylor was angered by the implication that he had set out to whitewash Hitler or Nazi Germany, writing that 'to the best of my recollection, those who now display indignation against me were not active on the public platform.'[147] In fact, he remained somewhat baffled by the widespread misinterpretation of his assessment of Hitler's actions, writing a year or two later that 'I ... gave the impression of excusing Hitler. I didn't mean to. All I wanted to say was that he planned much less and improvised much more than people made out at the time. The accumulating evidence of his failure to prepare for war is staggering. He bluffed everyone, including himself.'[148]

Probably the most ferocious German review was that by the distinguished historian Golo Mann in *Der Monat* (Mann was undoubtedly unaware that *Der Monat* had been founded and funded by the CIA). The title of the review, 'Hitler's britischer Advocat', gives a foretaste of it. As far as Mann was concerned, Taylor's whole motivation was to go against the grain: all others agreed on the origins of the war, and therefore Taylor's ambition was to prove Hitler's innocence. According to Mann, the major problem with the book lay in the fact that Taylor did not link foreign and domestic policy, a charge later echoed by Mason. He also implied that Taylor suppressed evidence, leaving out those aspects which did not suit his arbitrarily chosen concept. Furthermore, Taylor had ignored the studies of Bullock and Trevor-Roper, despising them because they had not been written by himself. In sum, Mann charged, Taylor was not interested in discovering the historical truth: rather, he was playing with serious questions only to demonstrate the sophistication of his own mind.[149] Mann's trivialising view of Taylor's motives was shared by Gerhard Ritter, who found the book as bad as he had found *The Course of German History*. Sebastian Haffner, who had reviewed it for the *Observer*, also reviewed the book favourably in Germany, in a periodical called *Christ und Welt*. Ritter wrote to protest: 'Taylor is anything other than a *famous* historian. He counts with all my English colleague-acquaintances as an outsider, not to be taken seriously, and therefore has no prospect of being called to a chair [damning in German academic eyes]. His writing aims to "épater les bourgeois" and under all circumstances to be nonconformist, that is to say, to disconcert and confuse the worthy average opinion of the English public. Under some circumstances he seeks to disconcert by expressing wicked thoughts that other people are ashamed to express openly, as, for example, that Germany's division into two is the greatest luck for England.'[150]

It was not just German historians who were disturbed by the book: so was the German government. Not only was Taylor's book published in the United States in 1962, but also William Shirer's *The Rise and Fall of the Third Reich*, which sold tens of thousands of copies. Furthermore, it was the period of the trial of Adolf Eichmann in Jerusalem for his role in the Holocaust. Bonn officials worried that the combination of the three would discourage the American electorate from supporting Germany by reminding them of the crimes which the Germans had committed only a short time before. The US government shared those worries: the Berlin Wall had been erected in August 1961, and the West needed the Federal Republic to form part of an anti-Soviet phalanx. However, in the event, there was no American reaction of any importance.

The American edition was to be published by Atheneum, but they were apprehensive about the reaction it would draw. As Hamish Hamilton wrote to Taylor, Atheneum 'are particularly anxious that you should write either an introduction or an extra chapter explaining the American role in these important years, for they point out that at present America is almost entirely ignored. I do hope that you may feel like doing this [as it] will clearly make a big difference both to the American critics and the reading public.' Taylor was agreeable: 'As to an introduction on American policy, I can certainly write something. ... But my book already says all there is to say about America, and if I say more it is bound to stir controversy. However, I can try a draft.' He sent them one in June 1961. Hamish Hamilton thought that his American preface 'is very well worth reading and packs an excellent punch in the final paragraph'; Atheneum's reaction was that it was '"Absolutely perfect – stylish, lively, controversial and to the point" ... [and] that it will greatly help the chance of the book in America.'[151]

The Preface was unforgiving. Taylor alluded to the possibility that Americans might complain that there was very little about American policy in the book. This had a simple explanation: 'American policy had very little to do with the British and French declaration of war on Germany.' But this was somewhat curious, since 'The German problem, as it existed between the wars, was largely the creation of American policy.' This was because the United States were a powerful obstacle to any attempt to retard the recovery of Germany; rather, they treated Germany as 'the main pillar of European peace and civilisation.' Things had been made worse by the election of Franklin Roosevelt to the presidency, since this was also a victory for isolationism. American policy was not altogether negative during the last year of peace, but the American government, as well as the French and British governments, dithered. 'It is very hard for a democracy to make up its mind; and when it does so, often makes it up wrong.' Finally, 'I do not believe that a historian should either excuse or condemn. His duty is to explain. I have tried to explain how Hitler succeeded as much as he did and why the British and French governments finally declared war on Germany. If it be objected that Great Britain and France should have counted more firmly on American backing, it is worth bearing in mind that the United States were not drawn into the war either by the fall of France or even by Hitler's attack on Russia, and that we had to wait for the unlikely event of Hitler's declaring war on the United States before they came in.'[152]

According to Roger Louis, the anonymous review by *Time* magazine was typical of the book's reception in the United States. It began with the charge that

A.J.P. Taylor finds excuses for Hitler and reasons to blame nearly everybody else. . . . In Taylor's view it is always somebody else who put poor, passive Hitler in a mood to fight. . . . With scholarly detachment, Taylor states the case for appeasing Hitler and for resisting him, but his sympathies obviously lie with the appeasers. . . . Taylor insists that Hitler was no fanatic. 'Hitler was a rational, though no doubt a wicked statesman,' writes Taylor primly. . . . His nationalism, far from being the common variety, was the most virulent racism the world has ever known. . . . 'A Study of history is of no practical use in the present or future,' Taylor, who likes to be whimsical, once said. As far as Taylor himself is concerned, his book proves his point.

The historian Gordon Craig, reviewing it for the *New York Herald Tribune*, also condemned the book: 'this is a perverse and potentially dangerous book. Mr. Taylor has always shown a tendency to strain the truth in order to achieve striking formulations. But he has never before been so intent upon demonstrating his originality as he is here, or so willing to indulge in exaggeration, oversimplification, quibbling, and sheer willfulness in order to achieve his effects.' Craig concluded with the point made by some of the German reviewers, that Taylor 'also gives aid and comfort to those who would like to rehabilitate the Fuehrer's reputation.'[153]

Was the book lasting? Taylor himself was doubtful, writing in a letter in 1974 that *The Origins* was 'another book I'm not particularly proud of', although in his autobiography he was kinder to his earlier work. Yet without doubt it was seminal in that it broke the log-jam which had blocked any new considerations of the origins of the war. The terms of the debate shifted over time, from the extent to which Hitler was solely responsible for the war to the nature of international relations during the 1930s. In the medium term, according to the historian H.W. Koch in 1968, *The Origins* 'seems to have withstood the mauling of its critics, a test of its quality perhaps'. Robert Young, in an essay published in 1986, wrote that 'it is a mark of this book's impact to be able to say that it remains central to a debate that continues to bubble away over the war's origin'. In the same book of essays, Paul Kennedy noted 'the extent to which many of Taylor's judgments and (for want of a better word) "hunches" have stood the test of time'.[154] It is still in print and still read – something that can be said of few monographs forty years after publication.

Whilst in the midst of working on his last two books on German history, *Bismarck* and *The Origins*, Taylor turned to English history. He had always been a European historian, writing on Great Britain only with regard to its foreign policy (unless he was acting as a book reviewer, in which case his ambit was much wider). The wrench away from the continent began when he was designated the 1956 Ford Lecturer in English History. His appointment and Alan Bullock's suggestion of a topic were discussed above; the focus now is on the book, rather than on the lectures as such. Taylor's Ford Lectures were conceived as lectures, not as chapters in a monograph as most are. Thus, they are considerably lighter than many others, one reason why they disappointed many academics (and produced *Schadenfreude* in many others). Once they were given, Taylor reconstructed them, but he did not write them out first.

Normally the Oxford University Press publishes the Ford Lectures. However: not in this case. In late November 1956, Taylor wrote to Hamish Hamilton:

> I have a book to offer you, under slightly unusual circumstances. You may remember that I gave the Ford Lectures (the premier historical lectures in England) last spring. ... There seemed to be a moral obligation on me, though no strict requirement, to offer these lectures to the University Press; and this had the attraction also of uniform makeup with the earlier lectures. The Press now tell me that they would have to bring out the book at 21/-, and this only by cutting my royalties. I want the book to have a big sale; and I also don't like cutting my royalties, though this is secondary. Could you publish it at 18/- or less, on our usual terms? If so, you can have it. I'd better describe the book to help

you make up your mind. It is 65,000 words or so, which the Press calculate as 192 pages. Subject: The Dissenters of Foreign Policy, i.e. the story of the minority who have opposed official British foreign policy from Charles James Fox to the present day or almost. . . . I think it is much the most exciting and interesting book that I have written, despite its shape as lectures. It held a huge audience. . . . But you may feel that you have had enough of me or that it is too academic. Still, I'd be delighted if you would take it. I offered it to the Press from duty. I would much rather see it in your hands. Let me know what you think.[155]

Hamish Hamilton replied the following day: 'I am delighted to hear of the O.U.P.'s folly and we welcome the Ford Lectures and can easily publish at 18s. . . . The most urgent matter is to have a title – I hope you can find something more attractive than "The Dissenters of Foreign Policy".' Taylor – never brilliant with titles – came up with 'The Other Foreign Policy' and 'The Chosen Few'. In the end, it was Hamish Hamilton who came up with 'The Troublemakers', taken from an expression used by Taylor early in his text.[156] *The Troublemakers: Dissent over British Foreign Policy 1792–1939*, dedicated to Alan Bullock as the 'onlie begetter', was published on 6 June 1957.

Taylor always claimed great affection for this book, 'by far my favourite brainchild and the one I hope to be remembered by'. As the title implies, Taylor surveyed the views and activities of the most prominent of those who had vigorously opposed British foreign policy from the French Revolution to the outbreak of the Second World War. In his first chapter, 'The Radical Tradition', Taylor set out his wares. 'These lectures are a gesture of repentance for having written recently a substantial volume of what I may venture to call "respectable" diplomatic history [The Struggle for Mastery].' This time his intention was to 'discuss aspects of British foreign policy that are left out of official perorations.' He was referring here to those whom he labelled 'the Dissenters', adding that

dissent is a quality peculiar to English-speaking peoples. A man can disagree with a particular line of British foreign policy, while still accepting its general assumptions. The Dissenter repudiates its aims, its methods, its principles. What is more, he claims to know better and to promote higher causes; he asserts a superiority, moral or intellectual. . . . Dissenters have always claimed that the cause of Right (whatever that happened to be at the moment) was also a better way of securing peace, security, and even British predominance in the world. But these practical gains were a sort of bonus, deservedly accruing to the righteous.[157]

Taylor then discussed what he considered to be the Great Tradition, ranging from Charles James Fox, Tom Paine, William Cobbett, David Urquhart (the Turkish-bath believer and father of the Balliol History Tutor Sligger of Taylor's Oriel days) and Richard Cobden, through Gladstonian foreign policy, E.D. Morel and the Union of Democratic Control during the First World War, and ending with the supporters of the League of Nations and those who held a thoroughly confused position during the 1930s; the last-named combined a hatred of imperialist capitalism with a hatred of war, coming out in support for the 'honour of England', whatever that turned out to be. His ramble through the byways of foreign policy was hardly a whitewashing expedition: indeed, it could be argued that Taylor, in the best Dissenting tradition – and he certainly considered himself a Dissenter – dissented from the views of many of those he discussed. His wholehearted affection was reserved for Richard Cobden, whom he called 'the most original and profound of Radical Dissenters; the one who most clearly passed from opposition to the formulation of an alternative foreign policy. The earlier Dissenters – and many later – were distinguished by generous emotion. ... Cobden was sane. Others relied on rhetoric; he reasoned. ... When others grew more passionate, he became cooler. Again and again men had to say of Cobden what Peel said: "You must answer him; I cannot".'[158]

It might be thought that Taylor sought to draw a moral or two from his narrative, particularly with regard to the anti-nuclear movement. But here he remained true to his belief that history was the story of the past, not a school for the present: 'In my opinion we learn nothing from history except the infinite variety of men's behaviour. We study it, as we listen to music or read poetry, for pleasure, not for instruction.' Indeed, the story could be reversed: 'Miss [C.V.] Wedgwood remarked recently that she understood better the Puritan desire to support the Protestant cause in the Thirty Years' war and the bitterness against James I's conciliation of Spain from having herself lived through the Spanish civil war and the controversies over appeasement. The present enables us to understand the past, not the other way around.' The foreign policy of the past, and especially of the nineteenth-century past, revolved round what Taylor called the 'Tribal Gods': John Bull and four females – Britannia, Germania, la France (or Marianne) and Kathleen ni Houlihan. It was clear to him that 'The historian, particularly the historian of foreign policy, finds it hard to escape the Tribal Gods.'[159] The implication, of course, was that he had done so; but what is equally clear is that Taylor himself had his own Tribal Gods, the Dissenters, and in this book he celebrated them.

The reviews were mixed. Indeed, Taylor wrote to Roger Machell at Hamish Hamilton that 'In my innocence I didn't realise how my academic colleagues would hate this book. Never mind. Lord Beaverbrook tells me that he has given away dozens of copies.' Kingsley Martin, Editor of the *New Statesman* (which at the time had Taylor on a retainer as a book reviewer), decided to review it himself: for A.J.P. Taylor, he wrote, 'Every subject has its moral and every moral its refutation. No one, including himself, is allowed to get away with anything. From every opinion there is Dissent; from every Dissent there is another Dissenter. ... Mr Taylor's lectures delivered brilliantly, staccato, without notes, make such points; but they retain their epigrammatic, rather inconsequential, quality in book form.' The anonymous reviewer of the *Times Literary Supplement* wrote that Taylor was 'very nearly an ideal general reader's historian. He tells them exactly what they want to know, briefly, wittily and often wickedly. ... It was at first an amusing trick to invent that *enfant terrible* (which may perhaps be anglicised as an intellectual teddy-boy) to serve as the serious historian's *alter ego*; but the trick can well become an obsession, and the obsession can become involuntary and irreversible.' Furthermore, the construction here was 'slapdash'. The reviewer ended with a particularly cutting comment: 'If he believes, as the dust-cover suggests, that an invitation to deliver the Ford Lectures is the highest honour which an English historian can receive, one could wish that he had been more thoughtful about returning the compliment.' And finally, an American academic review: 'conventions of sobriety and cautious generalization are cast aside as Taylor, in the tradition of dissent, strikes out at the "Establishment" of his profession. The result is a volume which will infuriate or delight the reader, according to his tastes. The reviewer recommends its brilliant half-truths and suggestive paradoxes.'[160]

In spite of Taylor's passion, *The Troublemakers* was one of his least successful books with the public – perhaps the reviews had something to do with it. Nor could a foreign publisher be found for it; several turned it down in America, including the University of Indiana Press. When it went out of print in 1962 and Taylor wanted it reprinted, there was some stalling on Hamish Hamilton's part. Machell wrote to let Taylor know that at that moment Penguin, having originally turned it down, were (in view of the great success of *The Origins*) reconsidering it. 'If Penguin declines we'll certainly bring it back into print ourselves, though for some reason which had always puzzled us, it never sold as well as other of your books.'[161]

A year later Taylor again raised the issue: 'Will there be a second edition of Trouble Makers some time? I know it is not a best seller. But I rate it very high, and should again like to see it in print.' His publishers could not evade the issue, leading to some exasperation inside the firm: 'Here is Taylor *again* raising the question of our reprinting Trouble Makers. As you know, we have been trying to find a paperback publisher for it. ... I wonder whether we ought not anyhow to go ahead and reprint 1000 ourselves?' They then wrote to Taylor: 'We were on the point of reprinting Trouble Makers two months ago when we had an urgent request from Mercury Books to consider it for a paperback, Penguin having most disappointingly declined. I am stirring them up and have been promised a decision tomorrow.' But, 'Mercury Books have declined Trouble Makers so we are at once putting a reprint of our own edition in hand.' It continued in hardback until 1993, when Pimlico brought it out in paperback.[162]

The book was decisive in turning Taylor away from European history and towards his third broad area of concentration, English history. He was by now tired of the nineteenth century and would hereafter write at length only about the twentieth. *The Struggle for Mastery* had drained him. He also decided that 'I've produced so much in recent years that I now need to restore my intellectual capital.' Reading for *The Troublemakers* began this task, but his new course was decided in the spring of 1957. As Taylor later recalled:

G.N. Clark had returned to Oxford after being Regius Professor at Cambridge and was now Provost of Oriel. ... We renewed our old friend-ship, often walking in Wytham Woods together. G.N., James to his intimate friends, had a trick of nervously raising some subject simply to break any silence. One afternoon he burst out abruptly, 'I must do something about a final volume in the *Oxford History of England* [OHE] which I [edit]. [R.C.K.] Ensor (who had written the 1870–1914 volume) started on it but he is dead. Maybe I shall have to write it myself.' I said, 'What about me?'. James heaved a sigh of relief. 'Would you? That would be marvellous'. The idea had never come into my head until that moment or into James's for that matter. But there I was: in, the question settled within thirty seconds and with it my own future as an historian settled also.[163]

When Clark reported to Davin at OUP, a slightly different version of events emerges. As Davin reported in March 1957 to Poole (the History Delegate), Ensor was unable to write the book (he was ill but not, in fact, yet dead), and Clark had decided that he himself had not the mind for it, that it required someone younger. 'In the course of discreet interchanges between himself and A.J.P. Taylor it has emerged that Taylor would be prepared to undertake it and would be ready to give 5 years to the job. As G.N.C. points out, Taylor is not perfectly equipped on topics like philosophy and "thought", but he has as good a range as anyone we are likely to get, and we think we should get a successful book, at least from a publisher's point of view.' There was, however, some difficulty with the Delegates, as Davin wrote to Clark: 'I brought up the question of A.J.P. Taylor for the 1914–?1939 [sic] volume. The Delegates had some qualms about him on home politics, and so rather than rush them into a decision which might have been negative we thought it best to suggest that we bring the proposal up again next term.' Clark replied nearly a fortnight later that 'If on further consideration my suggestion is not accepted, I shall be in a very embarrassing position, because it arose in the course of discussions in which it was impossible for me to conceal the two facts that I thought it was a very good one and that I had not found any other which was satisfactory. ... The writer I had in mind seems to be set on writing some such book.'[164]

The last point, it seems, proved decisive, but only after some wriggling by the Delegates. OUP fought for the book and for Taylor. The Secretary to the Delegates, Colin Roberts, wrote a Minute for the Delegates the following month, pointing out that no other name had emerged from anywhere, that Taylor would write such a book, which would doubtless be both 'distinguished and successful', and that OUP would be sorry to lose it and Taylor to another series. Roberts discussed the matter again with Poole, reporting that he [Roberts] had been 'very emphatic this time and hope that his acceptance of what I said would stay in his mind.' He then told Poole that Taylor would write the book whether or no OUP accepted it, and that it would be a disaster to lose him and the book to Macmillan – particularly if Taylor became Regius Professor. Poole volunteered that Taylor's book would be distinguished and very successful in publishing terms, but he worried that it would be 'partisan' in its treatment of home affairs (Clark, on the other hand, had earlier written to Davin that 'In Taylor's professional historical work I do not think it has ever been suggested that he has intruded his political views'). Roberts replied that they should not expect an historian to write like a White Paper, i.e., in a measured but boring style. Poole had no alternative to suggest but spoke vaguely of 'younger people', who would, Roberts thought, probably turn out to be specialists or journalists. Roberts's assessment was that Poole would finally come round.[165]

By the end of May 1957 Taylor wanted to know what was going on. 'I should like to be sure that the Delegates would not snatch the prize away from me – if prize it is. Would you stir them up to commit themselves?' Clearly he wanted the contract, and was reduced to asking for one, since at OUP little was done with speed. He wrote to Clark in mid-June that 'Yes, I'd like a contract some time. University bodies are notoriously fickle.' He was sent one within days, and returned it by the end of the month: 'I may say that I am staggered by some of the clauses and regard it as outrageous that you, a responsible and presumably honest publisher, should have so imposed upon innocent academic writers. However, as it is a standard contract, I suppose I must sign it.' Davin replied to Taylor in early July that he was sorry that he did not like some of the clauses. 'An aggrieved author can always refer to the Vice-Chancellor as Chairman of the Delegates and have us shaken up that way. Moreover, our policy has always been to provide against the worst by protecting ourselves as far as possible and then relent with remarkable gentleness and liberality from within our stockade.' He added that they were preparing a new general contract more in line with the Publishers' Association Standard Agreement.[166]

Taylor signed, but in December 1957 he warned Clark, as General Editor, that he could only begin serious work on the book in January 1960, once he had finished being Vice-President of Magdalen. According to his intellectual autobiography, 'Accident Prone', his first move was to read the previous fourteen volumes of the OHE, 'though, to be honest, I managed to get right through only five of them' (according to his book list he had finished seven of them before publishing his own volume). He also wrote that he began reviewing more books on English history, and certainly by early 1958 the balance of his reviewing had tipped in that direction. As noted above, he saw himself in this shift in activities as replenishing his intellectual capital as well as preparing to write the book. Two endowed lectures which grew out of this preparation, and which rank amongst his best work, were the Raleigh Lecture in History to the British Academy, entitled 'Politics during the First World War' – which Taylor considered the best lecture he had ever given, 'both in form and in content' – and the Leslie Stephen Lecture in Cambridge, entitled 'Lloyd George: Rise and Fall'. He later wrote that they 'marked my retreat from European and my switch to English history.'[167]

Taylor saw problems with working within the standard Oxford History of England format, in which chronological chapters alternated with topical chapters. Ensor's *England 1870–1914*, for example, begins with three chronological chapters – 'Gladstone's Prime', 'The Rule of Disraeli' and 'The Ascendancy of Parnell' – followed by two cross-chronological ones, 'Economics and Institutions, 1870–86' and 'Mental and Social Aspects, 1870–86'. This pattern is repeated throughout the book, three chronological and two cross-chronological, the latter having the same standard titles with only the dates changed. Taylor asked himself, 'Where was the story line? Each volume presented detached essays about a period, not a continuous narrative. But I was a narrative historian, believing more and more as I matured that the first function of the historian was to answer the child's question, "What happened next?" Of course, when dealing with every aspect of national life – or as many aspects as I understood – I had to stray from narrative now and then. I allowed the reader "occasional pauses for refreshment", but I think the story line is not obscured for long.'

There were other problems. What, for example, should be done about Ireland, Scotland and Wales in a history of England? 'Somehow I sorted it out: the lesser breeds were allowed in when they made a difference in English affairs.' More important, which England ought he to write about? Not the upper classes, 'which is what English history usually amounts to. Maybe the English people had no history until fairly recently. In the twentieth century they had, and this is what my book is about.' Cultural history? 'I accepted the music hall and the cinema as part of English life. ... But what conceivable significance had such writers as James Joyce or Virginia Woolf for the majority of English people? These were coterie interests, irrelevant to history in any serious sense. I ... [was also right] to omit modern philosophy. I fear I was gravely at fault to pass over most scientific advances. Like Johnson, I can only plead "ignorance, madam, sheer ignorance".'

He also regarded it as something of a 'goak' (joke) book. He intentionally parodied the habit of his predecessors of 'delivering the judgement of History in the highest Olympian spirit. I followed their example except that in my judgement the poor were always right and the rich always wrong – a judgement that happens to be correct historically. Some of the details are parody also, as for instance the solemn discussion as to when "Fuck" attained literary though not conversational respectability. I had more fun writing *English History 1914–1945* than in writing any of my other books.'[168]

'Having fun' may have been his retrospective judgement, but he sometimes found it a hard slog whilst he was actually writing. This was reflected in a series of letters he wrote to Clark as the OHE General Editor. By December 1961 he was halfway, seeing his way clear through to the 1931 crisis, though 'I haven't started to think about the Thirties. I haven't even started to read – a terrifying task – about the second World war.' By August 1962, 'I am beginning to think that I shall get this book finished some time.' However, between December and the following August he went through a crisis: he had completed 1918–31 to his satisfaction, but then 'I stuck for a long time in a state of depression.' This was broken by Lord Beaverbrook:

> I had dinner one night with him when I was about half way through my book. Max was in bad shape: hardly able to walk because of gout, falling asleep during dinner and seemingly unaware that I was there. Half awake, he said to me, 'What are you doing now, Alan?' As much to say something as for any other reason, I replied, 'I am writing a book on English History and have got to 1931. Now I am stuck. ... Max saw that I was in trouble. He kicked off his gout shoe, rose from his chair and walked about the room, declaiming about the events of the 'thirties – .... The name of Baldwin occurred again and again, 'What a rascal! He was cunning. He tricked us all.' Much of what he said seemed to me very great nonsense but it inspired me. I thought, 'If this frail old man can get so excited about history, shame on me if I cannot do the same.'[169]

Consequently, by August 1962 he had broken through – he had reached 1933 and saw his way clear to 1936. He decided to stop in 1945 (rather than the proposed 1951), 'if only because the post-war problems are so new and so difficult. At any rate there will be a respectable book, maybe too many ideas and too few facts. I dread the bibliography, though it is always the most interesting task when it comes to the point. At the moment I think of completing in 1965, but probably that is optimistic.' By November he had sent Clark the first ten chapters: he believed that the political part would not need much revision, although thought and art required attention. 'I don't think I shall include science – I don't understand it.' He also had little more to say about religion. 'I hope I've compensated for these omissions by the things I know about and others don't – the press (where I have improved on Ensor) and Leftwing ideologies.' Clark replied promptly with encouragement and constructive criticism, both of which Taylor appreciated.[170]

By March 1963 he had completed the draft down to 1939, with a fully revised draft of 1914–39 (six hundred pages) sent to Clark in early December. Clark thought that in some respects it was a little 'silly', for example on the political influence of the British Legion and Women's Institutes, but he hoped to iron out these imperfections. By February 1964 Taylor saw his way to the end of 1941. 'Then somehow British history comes to an end – eclipsed by the new great powers and one feels what's the point of going on? But then what was the point of World War II? I remember feeling very strongly at the time that it had one and now I can't see what it was. Or nearly so.' Clark tried to help him, suggesting that there were two things readers would want to know about the war: to what extent did what was known at the time really reflect what was going on; and by what stages and to what degree did it prepare the way for the cessation of the colonies? There was also the question of a title. Clark suggested 'English History 1914–1945', since it fitted in well with the contents and with the line Taylor had taken. Taylor liked it, but pointed out that 'we shall have trouble with the Scots. I shall speak for England in the preface.'[171]

Clark on the whole was happy with the way the manuscript was developing, although he told Roberts that 'there were about six *betises* ... which he rather hoped [Taylor] would remove [although Clark's] tone suggested that he is unlikely to take any further action about it. ... One that particularly annoys him is a reference to the British legion [with which Clark had some connection] as a "conservative paramilitary organisation".' Clark sent Taylor some queries, which Taylor answered: 'I don't know a polite phrase about Arthur Greenwood. Drink-sodden will hardly do. There is German evidence for Baedeker retaliation', that is, the bombing of beautiful or historical sites. Taylor was unhappy about the final page: 'I want to say that I like the English people very much and have a poor opinion of those who claim to guide them. I'll get it right in the end.' Clark asked whether there should be a list of office-holders. Taylor replied that he had resolved to cut them out, seeing that they were all in Butler and Freeman [*British Political Facts 1900–1959*, in which Taylor was thanked for his help]. But then 'Roy Jenkins – who represents a typical user – insisted that the lists were necessary, so I think I must include them.' By October 1964 Taylor had sent Clark the draft bibliography, about which the latter had only a few comments ('I suppose you omit Max Beloff's books intentionally, I know Namier thought very poorly of them'). There were further suggestions, to most of which Taylor agreed – 'I have accepted your changes with few exceptions, even sacrificing reluctantly Lloyd George's habit of breaking wind.' By early 1965 the manuscript was in OUP's hands.[172]

There was a final contretemps over the dust jacket. The standard OHE jacket was an austere light blue, giving only the name of the author and the title, and the names of the series and the publisher – no pictures. At the end of July 1965, however, the London office of OUP decided that they wanted an 'arresting' dust jacket for Taylor's volume, at least for the first twelve months. The reason was that it 'would make a substantial difference to the size of the order from W.H. Smith'. Roberts could see that 'there would be a case for cashing in on Taylor's reputation, or notoriety, while not losing sight of the fact that because the volume is in the O.H.E. series there is some guarantee that this is Taylor at his more responsible.' What worried Roberts was the precedent this would set of stressing one volume in the series more than the others. However, by late September Roberts was conceding that 'the London promotion people have convinced me, a little reluctantly, to have a picture jacket, reverting in a year to the standard jacket. W.H. Smith increased their order substantially when they learned of the new jacket.'[173]

But then, amidst the growing excitement, the plan was strangled by Taylor himself. Writing to Roberts at the end of September – three weeks before publication – he told him that he wanted to raise his voice 'most strongly' against the proposed jacket. 'I have acquired, I think most undeservedly, the reputation of being a journalistic, unscholarly writer. This jacket will confirm that reputation. … I have put years of labour into writing this book, partly with the intention of showing that I was a serious scholar. This jacket will ruin all my efforts. … In my opinion, the proposed jacket will be very bad for sales, and for me it will be a catastrophe.' Roberts was rather relieved, writing to Taylor; 'I understand your feelings about the proposed jacket. I agreed to it somewhat reluctantly, at a time when you were not available for consultation, under pressure from our Sales and Publicity people.' Of course the proposed jacket would give an immediate boost to sales, 'but sales aren't everything'. OUP would cancel the jacket and revert to the standard OHE jacket.[174] The book was then published, dustwrapped in the standard austere blue, on 21 October 1965.

The theme of *English History 1914–1945* is straightforward. Within the narrative format, it tells the story of the coming into history of the English people. This is overwhelmingly political history. Taylor had, five years earlier, nailed his colours to the mast: 'Political history provides the acts of drama; and the rest – culture, economics, religion and so on – are refreshing interruptions, like drinks at the bar during the intervals.'[175] In the blurb, Taylor announced what he had done:

During ten of the thirty-one years [covered by the book] the English people were involved in World wars; for nineteen of the years they lived in the shadow of mass unemployment. These themes and the politics which sprang from them shape the main narrative of the book. The author treats also the life of the English people and shows how this took on new forms without conscious direction or often against it. The author believes that even the most recent history can be presented in detachment. His purpose has been to discover what happened and how it happened, not to distribute blame or even praise.

In short, it was politics, in the widest sense, with interruptions.

The inspired beginning of *English History* emphasises the gulf between the state and the citizen:

Until August 1914 a sensible, law-abiding Englishman could pass through life and hardly notice the existence of the state, beyond the post office and the policeman. He could live where he liked and as he liked. He had no official number or identity card. He could travel abroad or leave his country forever without a passport or any sort of official permission. ... For that matter, a foreigner could spend his life in this country without permit and without informing the police. Unlike the countries of the European continent, the state did not require its citizens to perform military service. ... The Englishman paid taxes on a modest scale ... [The] tendency towards more state action was increasing. Expenditure on the social services had roughly doubled since the Liberals took office in 1905. Still, broadly speaking, the state acted only to help those who could not help themselves. It left the adult citizen alone.[176]

The book is in some measure the story of the increasing role of the state in the lives of British citizens.

Indeed, his emphasis again and again is on what 'the people' wanted, what 'the people' did, 'the people' being differentiated from the political and social elites. They supported going to war in defence of Belgium; their patriotism, strength and patience helped England to survive the mistakes of the military and the politicians; and they supported the outsider Lloyd George in his exercise of unprecedented power. In short, the impact of the Great War (the name for it in contemporary parlance, as Taylor notes) was to force the mass of the people to become active citizens. 'Their lives were shaped by orders from above; they were required to serve the state instead of pursuing exclusively their own affairs ... The history of the English state and of the English people merged for the first time.'[177] This was the beginning of the social revolution which culminated in the reforms of the postwar period.

The main thrust of the book is indeed the people's condition, their hopes and fears, their pleasures.[178] But for Taylor this did not preclude a parallel focus on the politicians and their activities in government, or on the military leaders during the two world wars. Yet in the end, the book is notable for the way it interweaves what others might have treated as two separate strands, emphasising the interaction of the people and their leaders, the developments and events which dominated what were, in truth, thirty-one action-packed years. At the end, as in the beginning, the focus is on the people, and Taylor's peroration demonstrates that he had 'got it right':

In the second World war the British people came of age. This was a people's war. Not only were their needs considered. They themselves wanted to win. ... The British were the only people who went through both world wars from beginning to end. Yet they remained a peaceful and civilized people, tolerant, patient, and generous. Traditional values lost much of their force. Other values took their place. Imperial greatness was on the way out; the welfare state was on the way in. The British empire declined; the condition of the people improved. Few now sang 'Land of Hope and Glory'. Few even sang 'England Arise'. England had risen all the same.[179]

The critical response to the book was overwhelmingly favourable. Even those reviewers who took issue with his treatment of certain points or cavilled at what had been left out – and there were many – appeared overwhelmed by the sheer technical mastery and brilliance of the work. The review by Henry Pelling, for example, is famous in the profession for consisting almost entirely of a list of Taylor's mistakes, yet he adds that reading the book was 'a very rewarding experience. The narrative, which is exceedingly skilfully woven, never fails to keep up its pace from the first page to the last.' Peter Stansky castigated Taylor's treatment of literature – 'his accounts are so compressed as to be perfunctory and are sometimes philistine' – yet Taylor's revisionist approach directs the reader 'to much material that has hitherto been allowed to go unexamined.' Noel Annan, who for years repeatedly voiced his dislike of *The Origins of the Second World*

War, nevertheless called English History 'an astonishing tour de force'. He also referred to Taylor as a populist historian, a label which Taylor thereafter wore with pride. Alan Bullock regretted that Taylor had paid so little attention to intellectual history and – an unexpected complaint – he wished there had been more political history (as well as more economic history). Nevertheless, Taylor had 'brought off a double: a masterly account of the most difficult (because the most recent) period of English history, and at the same time a book so well written that it is compulsive as well as compulsory reading.' And finally, there came the review in the Times Literary Supplement, which fulfilled Taylor's expressed hope that this book would re-establish his credentials as a serious historian: it was a book in which 'his undoubted talents as a technical craftsman of wide learning are at last happily yoked, not only with his accustomed brilliance as a stylist, but also with the balance and sensitivity of a mature historical mind.'[180]

The initial print run was 40,000 and the book sold 54,484 copies in the UK in its first ten years, providing Taylor with over £10,000 in royalties in the first year alone. (By way of comparison, The Struggle for Mastery sold 38,600 in its first twenty-one years, from 1954 to 1975.) Indeed, the book became so well known that it was the basis for a New Statesman competition in late 1965. Readers were set the task of providing an extract from the book Taylor had not yet had the opportunity to write, an English History 1946–65. The winner was Henry Pelling, the reviewer who had given the longest list of Taylor's mistakes:

In January 1965 Sir Winston Churchill died. He was given a state funeral – a distinction reserved for royalty since the Duke of Wellington. He had saved his country twice – once by vigour, in 1940; once by sloth, in 1951–4, when England could have joined the Common Market. It was to no avail. With his death, the last vestige of national greatness disappeared. Prime ministers still flew to Washington; opposition leaders lectured at Harvard. No one in the White House or the Pentagon took any notice. Ambassador Lodge attended a 'teach-in' in Oxford, probably to keep the Rhodes scholars in line rather than to instruct the natives. Even the Embassy library in Grosvenor Square was dismantled. British public opinion no longer mattered. British diplomacy faltered. A month's war took place between India and Pakistan. Whitehall ran a firework display at St James's Park. Rhodesia declared independence. The Queen gave the governor a decoration. The Conservatives, if anything, were keener 'Little Englanders' than the government. But there was not much in it. Still, there were the Beatles; if it had not been for them, no foreign schoolchild would ever have heard of England.[181]

Not surprisingly, *English History* also appeared in a number of foreign languages; translated into Italian in 1968, it was still being used in Italian universities as a text for interwar history in the late 1990s.

Taylor responded to the criticisms by making corrections in the second and third impressions, after which he thought that the text should be left as it was for the time being. The British archives covering the period to 1936 had been opened in 1966, and once books and articles based on those archives had been published he intended to produce an entirely revised edition. In February 1973 he wrote that *English History* was due for a new edition and that OUP wanted him to bring the bibliography up to date. This last task had been completed by June, but the rewriting of the book was still to be done, something to which he 'was not looking forward'. It never happened. There were probably two reasons for this. First of all, as Taylor wrote in his autobiography, 'the book is a period piece in both source and outlook. It cannot be revised; it can only be written differently by someone of a different generation.'[182] It is also likely that he was simply tired, both of the work which would be involved in rewriting that particular book and of simply working so very hard. He had decided in 1965 that he would never write another big book; nevertheless, this resolution was followed by his massive biography of Beaverbrook, taken on as an act of piety as much as of scholarship. By the time it was completed he was nearly sixty-five, with a working day taken up with broadcasting, journalism and book reviewing. The prospect of revising *English History* was too daunting, and the intention and expectation that he would ever get round to it gradually drifted away.

Taylor produced, on average, two books of solid worth each decade for forty years. This is a record not to be lightly dismissed and does not take account – as this biography will in the next chapter – of the three valuable books of popular history, the illustrated histories of the First and Second World Wars and of Europe, which he produced in 1963, 1975 and 1966 respectively. He was, he claimed, a 'plain narrative historian', one who tried to answer the child's question, 'What happened next?'. This did not imply a lack of analysis: it meant that analysis came *en train*, providing food for thought for those so inclined but without stopping the story for those who were not. Analysis was also delivered concisely, with comments into which much was packed. Taylor believed that the point of reading history was not to ascertain lessons, whether deep or superficial, but for enjoyment and stimulation.[183] Why should history not be enjoyable to read? Lack of readability does not necessarily imply profoundity – and nor the reverse.

Did Taylor have a philosophy of history? He said not: 'I am not a philosophic historian. I have no system, no moral interpretation. I write to clear my mind, to discover how things happened, how men behaved. If the result is shocking or provocative, this is not from intent, but solely because I try to judge from the evidence without being influenced by the judgements of others. I have little respect for men in positions of power, though no doubt I should not do better in their place.' As for the focus of his interest, 'Englishmen interest me most, and after them Europeans. They may all be of small account now [1956]; but their behaviour in the last century and a half is a subject of some curiosity and even of some importance.'[184]

But of course he did have a 'philosophy', sufficient for a working historian if not for a philosopher of history: 'Certainly the development of history has its own logical laws. But these laws resemble rather those by which flood-water flows into hitherto unseen channels and itself finally to an unpredictable sea.'[185] The focus of these laws is power, the Balance of Power in both international and domestic affairs. As he wrote in *The Struggle for Mastery*, 'Men have tried to supersede [sic] the sovereign state as much by a universal moral law as by an overwhelming force', but it did not work: rather, the Balance of Power worked almost automatically, rather like the laws of economics.[186] This concept suffused *The Struggle for Mastery*, but it also suffused *The Habsburg Monarchy*. In this case, the empire kept together because it formed too important an element in the European balance to be allowed to disintegrate, but the concept could be applied further. Internally, the emperor balanced one unit of the empire against another – Poland against Hungary, Croatia against Serbia – to keep the whole together. Furthermore, the outlook and policies (if there were any) of the individual units were determined by local balances of power within, between cities and countryside, between ethnic groups within the city and within the countryside, between occupations. Indeed, Taylor could have said – though he did not – that in all human relationships, diplomatic, strategic, economic or personal, there is a balance of power. In *The Struggle for Mastery* it was between states; in *English History* it was between the elites and the people. But it was there.

Chapter 6

The London Years
1963–1985

It seems to me that as a scholar I was always solitary, a 'loner', having to work everything out for myself. Also, I discovered that in writing history I was more interested in writing than in the history. In other words I suppose I am more an artist than a scholar, though I happen to be a good scholar as well.

A.J.P. Taylor to Éva Haraszti, 16 June 1975, Letters to Eva

A writer can never give all of himself because his typewriter is really his first love.

A.J.P. Taylor to Éva Haraszti, 16 July 1970, Letters to Eva

Taylor now settled down to a life as a professional writer and broadcaster. He kept tenuous academic links with Magdalen, in particular supervising a few postgraduate students and attending College Meetings, whilst also for some years lecturing for one day a week at University College London and after that at the Polytechnic of North London. Yet teaching was a marginal activity: his time was largely taken up with his biography of Lord Beaverbrook, with writing books of solid but popular history, and with broadcasting and journalism. His earnings increased, but at the same time he believed that his academic stature decreased; more and more Taylor felt forgotten, and this depressed him. Nevertheless, almost alone in all the world he had three *Festschriften* (celebratory volumes) devoted to him, in 1966, 1976 and 1986 (on his sixtieth, seventieth and eightieth birthdays), as well as an entire issue of the *Journal of Modern History* in 1977. But except for the first *Festschrift*, these were all celebrations of past glories rather than of present substance. His life was now made up of lots of little things rather than a few big things.

There *was* one big thing of considerable importance to him, and this was his relationship with Dr Éva Haraszti, an historian of Britain from Hungary. They met in 1960 and were married in 1976, an occasion followed by his happiness and her unhappiness. The latter was caused by Taylor's inability, or unwillingess, to sever himself emotionally from Margaret, his first wife; it was only with Margaret's death that his third marriage settled down to a routine contentment.

The publication of *The Origins of the Second World War*, and its ensuing condemnation, had one unexpected outcome: the production of the first Taylor *Festschrift*. The young man who took the primary responsibility for organising it, and then editing it, was Martin Gilbert, a recent graduate and one of Taylor's favourite pupils. Gilbert later recalled:

> Those of Alan's pupils in 1959 and 1960 who greatly enjoyed his tutorials, and did best in Finals in the subjects he had taught them ... were miffed by the general anti-Alan feeling among their other tutors. His views on the origins of the Second World War were the catalyst. His articles for Beaverbrook [in the *Sunday Express*] fanned the flames. From this anger at the anti-Alan feeling arose the idea of presenting him with a volume of essays. In retrospect, there was clearly something very impertinent about a recent graduate – who did not know most of the historians concerned either personally or professionally – embarking on such a scheme. As for Alan, he was neither consulted nor informed. The whole idea of the volume was to surprise him – hopefully to surprise him pleasantly.[1]

Gilbert drew up a list of historians and sent out his invitations. To his dismay, he received a number of replies casting doubt on the advisability of going ahead with the project: John Roberts, Fellow of Merton, thought that there was no occasion for the volume; James Joll, the Stevenson Professor of International History at the London School of Economics, agreed with Roberts (although by the end of 1963 he was, according to Isaiah Berlin, willing to contribute, and in the end he did). Nevertheless, Gilbert determined to continue: 'it seemed to me that the older generation was being obstructive.' Certain senior historians declined to contribute: it was not surprising that Trevor-Roper declined – how recent had been his and Taylor's *Encounter* encounter? – but it was perhaps more surprising when Bullock said no; Pieter Geyl also declined. Others accepted but failed to carry through: Raymond Carr, who went as far as to agree a title with

Gilbert, Richard Crossman, Michael Foot – who finally appeared in the 1986 *Festschrift* – Henry Kissinger and Arthur Schlesinger, Jr.[2]

Gilbert was indefatigable in pursuing his quarry. One was Isaiah Berlin, who sent Gilbert a series of letters which must have amused even as they exasperated him. Gilbert wrote to Berlin in late February 1962, eliciting this response: 'How can I? Apart from knowing no history and being driven from pillar to post by existing commitments and producing tiny pieces once a year ... the history of ideas is the only thing on which I am a hand at all, and Alan Taylor's distaste for this topic is, if anything, greater than that of Namier who was very unambiguous on that subject.' The following week he wrote again: 'I cannot promise, I really cannot, for unless I have something to say I cannot say it. But I shall think about this and the very next idea that I have – perhaps while I am in America in the autumn – I shall try and present to you in the form of a short essay – but let me warn you, nothing may come of this so do not count on me for goodness sake!' Gilbert kept up the pressure: 'I wish I could participate in the Festschrift, but I cannot, not at all for the reasons allegedly given by Bullock and the others – but simply because I shall not be able to produce it in time, knowing myself as I do. I am terribly unproductive and terribly ashamed of being so: I bear literary children with the irregularity of some particularly ill-conditioned elephant. ... I am as you know extremely fond of AJPT and would like to do him honour, in spite of everything. But no can, no ought. ... I wish I did not know myself so well: the books I have promised to review and have not reviewed stand accusingly on my shelves like so many acts of theft: so do all the broken promises to editors and publishers.' One problem for Berlin was the proposed date of publication, i.e. Taylor's departure from Oxford in 1963, which would require the rapid production of an essay. At his and others' entreaty, this was pushed back to Taylor's sixtieth birthday, in March 1966. The promise of more time finally caught Berlin.[3]

Gilbert was also able to convince Paul Einzig, the writer on political and financial affairs, to contribute an essay, but only after some effort. As Einzig wrote in reply to Gilbert's letter, 'My first reaction was to say no, because Taylor's account of 1931 is hardly worthy of serious criticism. ... But on second thoughts I feel that it would be a huge joke if I did contribute an essay to the presentation volume to Taylor. ... I take it I could be as critical as I liked provided that my criticism is framed in polite scholarly style.' Six months later he let Gilbert know his topic and approach: 'My essay would be called "Mr Taylor and Dilettantism" and would open with a quotation from his broadcast: "I am not an economist, just as I am not a general, but I can describe battles, and I think I can describe this strange economic crisis." I would criticise the BBC for encouraging this attitude by its programmes of pseudo-intellectual parlourgames in which people with an established reputation on a certain subject make fools of themselves over other subjects.' Einzig's essay was so fierce that he feared Taylor's reaction: 'Would it not be wiser to keep my essay as a surprise item and not to give Taylor a chance to mobilise all his connections to bring pressure on you to omit it' – the last thing Taylor would have tried to do. Indeed, when the book appeared Taylor reviewed it in the *Observer* – 'I'm the one man who can be impartial' – and he was particularly complimentary about Einzig's essay, 'the most slashing attack I have ever read on an historian's accuracy, and the maddening thing about it is that most, though not all of it, is justified'. Einzig had eventually decided to begin with the statement that 'English people have always had a soft spot for dilettantism. In no other country are brilliant dabblers in subjects outside their spheres of competence looked upon with so much indulgence as in Britain. . . . Mr A.J.P. Taylor may be regarded as one of the outstanding instances to illustrate the point.' He then went on to outline in devastating detail Taylor's mistakes, some of them egregious. Einzig was, not surprisingly, impressed by the savoire-faire demonstrated by Taylor in his review.[4]

Many who were approached, such as Hugh Thomas, Norman Angell and Noel Fieldhouse, agreed straight away. As already noted, others withdrew. Berlin was certainly tempted to do so: writing to Gilbert in late January 1963, he insisted that 'I am pretty immoveable, yes. Taylor insulted me publicly, so much that even the editor of the paper sent some sort of oblique apologies to me for what even he thought was a little too caddish. Whatever my feelings about Taylor are, therefore, why should I publicly celebrate him? That seems to me too Christian an attitude – humility is a virtue that can be over-done. I therefore do not propose, in my present frame of mind, to do this, and cannot quite understand why you should either: Taylor's latest views about Jews and inter-marriage are worthy of Wells or Joad at their worst. . . . I feel that Taylor was once a friend – but that friend is dead.' Berlin over the years of the preparation of the *Festschrift* gave various reasons for colleagues'. reluctance to contribute. In May 1962 he wrote that 'our beneficiary doesn't make things easier by writing articles in the Beaverbrook papers pleading for a deeper loyalty to the Empire, or praising the enlightened policies of Mr Menzies – at the moment he has really lost the respect of all decent historians, intellectuals, etc. – all save those who are bound to him by an affection that blinds them to what is going on.' A year later he wrote that 'I spoke to Taylor at a meeting of the British Academy; and his exposition of what he was going to say in the last volume of the Oxford History of England *will* set you back, I may tell you; I think probably that he is past mending.' But, he added: 'I am fond of him still, even though insulted by him.'[5]

Upon receiving a significant number of declinations and withdrawals, Gilbert went to see Taylor: he explained what he had tried to do and what the outcome had been, a profoundly embarrassing occasion. Taylor, however, reacted as a gentleman. 'There were no recriminations. Instead, in his usual brisk and business-like way, after saying how flattered he was at the *idea*, he deprecated it, and suggested that he take the Will for the Deed.' When, a little later, Taylor heard that the volume was going ahead, he sent Gilbert some names of those who might replace the drop-outs. These included Fieldhouse and Angell. By the time of publication, rather than too few, there were too many contributors – sixteen – who wrote at too great a length, and as a result Gilbert was forced to leave out his own essay.[6] *A Century of Conflict 1850–1950: Essays for A.J.P. Taylor* was published by Hamish Hamilton in March 1966.

By this time, Taylor had embarked on his final big book, a biography of William Maxwell Aitken, Lord Beaverbrook. The relationship between Taylor and Beaverbrook, press baron and man of ambiguous reputation, was and remains unfathomable. As plain Max Aitken, already by thirty a millionaire, Beaverbrook came to Britain from Canada in 1910 and established a close friendship with the Conservative and Unionist leader Andrew Bonar Law. Within three months he was an MP. He became a peer (against the wishes of King George V) in January 1917 and in 1918 acted as Minister of Information. After the war he devoted himself to the *Daily Express*, which he had bought in 1917, and rapidly built up a newspaper empire. During the Second World War he was successively Minister of Aircraft Production, Minister of Supply and Lord Privy Seal; the basis of his influence was his dynamism and his close friendship with Churchill. After the war he again devoted himself to his newspapers, which now included the *Sunday Express*, for which Taylor was to write a column for twenty-five years. He was a man of great energy and strong prejudices, who used his wealth and his patronage to attract – some said ensnare – politicians, such as Aneurin Bevan and Michael Foot, and others of influence into his ambit. Taylor became one of these.

Michael Foot has described how the two became aware of each other. In October 1956 Taylor read Beaverbrook's two most important books, *Politicians and the War 1915–1916* and *Men and Power 1917–1918*. According to Foot,

Taylor read Beaverbrook's books on politics with fresh eyes. The style, in any case, had a kinship with his own; the taste of the two men for brevity and clarity was similar. But Taylor also set aside the preconceived assumption that Beaverbrook must be a second-rate journalist writing for the hour or the day and for immediate sensation. He wrote a review in the *Observer* [of *Men and Power*] in which, incredibly in the light of all previous academic judgements, he compared Beaverbrook with Tacitus. I was present in the room when Beaverbrook read that review, and his life was transformed. He had indeed always been most modest about his own writings, never expecting to be regarded as anything more than a chronicler, the good teller of a tale which he knew himself to be and had every right to accept as a fair assessment. As for the comparison with Tacitus, utterly flattering as he believed it to be, it meant that a new world and a new friendship had opened before him. Alan Taylor became his intimate confidant on all these questions, his biographer, and perhaps his truest friend.[7]

Why this should be the case remained inexplicable to outsiders. One reason might have been Taylor's liking for powerful men. He wrote about them – Palmerston, Bismarck, Churchill – and Beaverbrook certainly fell into that category, both in government and in his business and private life. Another – and this is related – could well have been that Taylor had such an overwhelming devotion to history that he was drawn to Beaverbrook as an historical figure. At a more venial level, Beaverbrook provided the little luxuries of life, in the nicest possible way, for Taylor and Eve, by then his wife. There were cigars and cases of Château Latour – in the eyes of many, the greatest of the first-growth clarets, certainly the greatest from the Médoc – there were dinners and visits to Cherkley Court, Beaverbrook's country house just outside Leatherhead in Surrey, there was the entrée into a society which had heretofore been closed to Taylor, one which provided new acquaintances to enjoy. But most of all, there was Beaverbrook's personality and sense of fun, his enthusiasm for many of the things that also enthused Taylor. In the end, the heart has its reasons which reason knows not.[8]

Taylor started angling for the opportunity to write a biography of Beaver-brook while his subject was still alive. In October 1962 he hinted to his publisher that he hoped to be asked? allowed? to write such a biography. The project was not mentioned again until May 1963, when he turned down an offer to write a book on diplomacy; his hope was that the biography project would succeed. Shortly before Beaverbrook's death, Taylor said to him, '"Max, would you like me to write your life?" He said grumpily, "I would like it very much" and changed the subject, not welcoming the suggestion that he would die before I did.' (According to one source, Beaverbrook's great-nephew, Jonathan Aitken, was sent by the historian Robert Blake to tell him that Taylor would not be appropriate as a biographer because he would be too favourable, advice to which Beaverbrook did not take kindly.) The death of Beaverbrook on 9 June 1964 brought the matter to a head. In mid-June David Higham, Taylor's literary agent, asked whether they ought to have a discussion on tactics, but Taylor wanted to wait until Lady Beaverbrook and Beaverbrook's heir Max Aitken raised the issue themselves; 'then of course I'll refer them to you for financial terms.' Immediately after Beaverbrook's death both his widow and his daughter asked Taylor to write the life.[9]

Taylor met with Lady Beaverbrook, Max Aitken and the other trustees a few days later. Taylor presented his terms: the book would be entirely his, he would own the copyright and he would have a completely free hand. He would, however, show the manuscript to the trustees and would listen to any recommendations they might make. He would have full access to the papers, which were stored at Cherkley Court. In addition Taylor had a private lunch with Lady Beaverbrook, during which he stated that he did not want a fee – a fee would, of course, tie him to her wishes – but would content himself with royalties. The negotiations were not perfunctory. Aitken probably wanted to retain some control over the book, but he stumbled when he placed an announcement in *The Times* that Taylor was writing the biography. As Taylor assumed, it strengthened his own hand, and in July 1964 the two came to an agreement. Higham then wrote to Hamish Hamilton, who had first refusal to publish the book. In May 1965 Taylor set to work.[10]

There was one other part of Beaverbrook's legacy with which Taylor was involved – the project for a library. Beaverbrook had bought the papers of David Lloyd George and Andrew Bonar Law, both past prime ministers, and had intended that these collections, together with his own papers, would form the core of a centre for historical research at Cherkley. Taylor, too, had argued for this, as he wrote to G.N. Clark: 'I'd like to get all the papers – Lloyd George's for instance – generally available for scholars, but the family are hard to move.' In due course they did agree, and Cherkley became an archive. But difficulties soon arose: there was no room for researchers to work, the nearest food and drink was two miles away, it was a three-hour return journey from London, and Lady Beaverbrook, whom Beaverbrook had hoped would act as custodian of the papers, rapidly grew tired of the archive, the visitors and the responsibility. Soon, as Taylor recalled, 'Sir Max Aitken ... said to me in his abrupt way, "We are moving my father's papers to London, and you're to look after them."' Taylor thought that this was a perfect solution: he would be able to make the Lloyd George and Bonar Law papers available to researchers, and he could more easily get on with his life of Beaverbrook without having to waste three hours of the day in travel.[11]

The Beaverbrook Library was situated in an extension of the *Express* building on Fleet Street, with a separate entrance in St Bride's Street (leading to St Bride's, one of Taylor's favourite City churches). Taylor refused a salary so that he would remain his own master (although he did inquire anxiously of his agent whether he thought that his appointment would endanger the freedom of the biography); he also neglected to inquire into the arrangements for the future endowment of the library, the lack of which would ensure its doom. In the early days, however, what most exercised him was the lack of qualified archival staff. At first, one of Beaverbrook's former secretaries was supposed to be his only assistant; after complaints from Taylor, a secretary from the *Express* pool, Veronica Horne, was added to the staff; and after further complaints an elderly former *Express* employee was provided to fetch the papers for researchers. Only some years later, near the end of its life, did the library obtain the services of a qualified archivist, Katherine Bligh. Inadequately staffed or not, the Beaverbrook Library opened its doors on 25 May 1967.[12]

It was a haven of peace, cool when it was hot outside, warm when it was cool, polished wooden tables (although not many of them), the papers to hand, tea at four o'clock, the whole dominated by the huge Sickert portrait of Beaverbrook and the presence of the Honorary Director of the library, Taylor's official title. Taylor would occasionally emerge from his office to chat briefly with researchers, interested to know what was being discovered, particularly pleased when assured that gold was being mined. During the first eighteen months of the library's life, about 150 researchers worked there, excited and energised by the availability of, in particular, the Lloyd George papers. Taylor set up a seminar as a forum in which the researchers could share their findings. The meetings took place during university vacations from December 1968 until the library closed in 1975. Indeed, the quality of some of the papers was so great that Taylor turned them into a book which he edited, *Lloyd George: Twelve Essays*, published in 1971. The seminar itself moved to the Institute of Historical Research of London

University in 1977 and continued to be chaired by Taylor (in tandem with younger scholars from the university) until 1985.[13]

While the library lasted, Taylor found it a most congenial venue in which to work. He had a secretary for the first time in his life, and she took some of the more mundane administrative tasks off his shoulders, as well as retyping his manuscripts. Furthermore, situated as it was, the library was a good departure point for Taylor's endless walks around the City of London, where he followed historic streets and visited the churches. He was 'drawn into City life even if only on the fringes', dining at the Inns of Court and the Livery Companies. He was also invited to the Lord Mayor's Midsummer Banquet in June 1975, the Lord Mayor adding that 'I am afraid that there is a sting in the tail of this! Do you think you could undertake to respond to the toast "The Arts, the Sciences and Learning"?' Taylor's answer combined pleasure, false modesty and arrogance: 'Your invitation overwhelms me. Though fluent on television I am tongue-tied off it. What is more, I know nothing about art, nothing about the sciences, and am still learning. However, I accept your invitation with becoming modesty. Once I get on my feet I'll be able to ramble away about something.' He went regularly to the lunch-time concerts organised by the City Music Society and in July 1975, to his great delight, was elected its president in succession to the composer Sir Arthur Bliss: 'Your letter contains the most unexpected honour that has ever befallen me. I accept with most humble gratitude as long as you do not expect me to write a symphony for you.' He dined with friends and, functionally a bachelor (he had separated from Eve in 1968), took to eating in his club, the Atheneum. However, 'when I began to dine there I found myself sitting alone at a little table in an almost deserted room and eating badly-cooked food, with good wine as the only redeeming feature. Afterwards I could sit alone in an almost deserted drawing room.' He found this a less than satisfactory solution to the nightly problem of dinner, and switched to the Beefsteak Club, 'where there was always talk even if not highly inspiring.'[14]

But the library was not to last. Taylor had somehow sensed this as early as spring 1973, writing to Éva Haraszti that 'Readers have dwindled to almost nothing. ... I can't help feeling that the Library won't last for ever, even in the sense of for ever for me. Max Aitken is over sixty. When he goes his successors will not be interested in the memory of Lord Beaverbrook and will grudge what the Library cost.' Events did not wait upon Aitken's departure. In the second week of October 1974, Aitken asked to see Taylor to inform him that the library was to close. Taylor took it very badly:

The killing of the Beaverbrook Library on top of my money worries and general political apprehensions has been almost too much for me. I had counted so much on the Library. After the many setbacks I've had in life – not being made a professor, not even being kept on properly at Oxford – I thought: now I really have arrived. Sentimentally, it was good to be doing something for my old friend's memory. Now I feel I have been made a fool of. It is obvious that Max Aitken does not care in the slightest about his father's memory and nor does anyone else. ... Max is cheating me in another way. The story that the [Beaverbrook] Foundation has no money is window-dressing. The truth is that Max wants the floor space to turn into offices [for the *Express* advertising department] and now regards the Library as a waste of space and money. In that case, why did he ever ask me to take it on and devote my life to it? The moral is that you can never trust rich men.

A month later Aitken, while refusing to see Taylor, informed him that the library had to be out by the following April.[15]

The main problem arising out of the closure was what to do with the papers. It took several attempts to find them a home. First of all, Taylor asked the Department of Manuscripts at the British Museum; they were initially keen and agreed, but were prevented from going through with the arrangement by lack of space. He also tried University College London, where he was a Special Lecturer, but nothing came of that either. He then turned to the Public Record Office, which he decided he preferred to the British Museum. Again, there were difficulties, but by mid-December he had found a 'perfect home' for the papers, the House of Lords Record Office. By March 1975 the library was 'being literally torn to pieces. The shelves have gone. The books have gone. Soon the tables and chairs will go, and there will be nothing left except an empty floor.' By early April, the papers had gone to their new home, accompanied by the archivist, Katherine Bligh.[16] Taylor and his secretary, Della Hilton, moved first to an office in the *Express* building and then at the end of the year to a small office in the *Evening Standard* building which required a march through the printing floor to reach it. Here Taylor wrote his reviews and other commissions, here he sometimes saw the postgraduate students whom he was still supervising,[17] here he began to measure out his life in coffee spoons. It is undoubtedly the case that his increasingly depressed view of life in general and of his own life in particular was connected with the loss of the Beaverbrook Library and his position in it.

But all this was in the future when, at the end of December 1964, he began thinking about the biography. This was to be the first book he had written in years for which he would have actually to get his hands dirty by sifting original papers. He was a bit daunted by the size of the collection – 769 boxes of material – and, as he wrote to Clark, 'I am contemplating the Beaverbrook papers with helpless gloom.' By February 1965 he reckoned that he would be able to begin proper work in May, at which point he estimated that it would take from three to five years to complete (although when he wanted to tease Hamish Hamilton he told them it would take five to ten): for the first time since his sabbatical year in 1950–1, he would have no real teaching duties to distract him from spending the major part of his time on a book. In May 1971 he sent Hamish Hamilton the bulk of the manuscript, which he hoped – in vain, of course – might appear in two volumes. Hamish Hamilton were very pleased – 'this is the most exciting event in our publishing history for many years'.[18]

Taylor received a freshly minted copy of *Beaverbrook* on 19 April 1972. Almost up to the day of publication negotiations were still being conducted over serialisation rights: though they were offered first to the *Sunday Express*, the *Sunday Times* emerged as the favourite. There was to be a launch party on 22 June, and there were the usual discussions over the guest list, with possible reviewers – Blake, Bullock, Philip Magnus – taking priority. Taylor did make one unusual stipulation: 'I should not like any public librarians to be present. Indeed, if there are, I shall not attend myself. I regard them as thieves and do not see why we should show them any consideration.' This arose from the feeling, shared by other authors, that a book borrowed was a sale lost, and authors were the ultimate losers. He was therefore glad to help lobby Parliament to change the situation. In June 1973 he himself wrote to ten MPs to ask them to support the following Early Day Motion: 'That this House, mindful of the injustices suffered by authors and other creators through the lending of their works by libraries, without appropriate recompense, urges H.M. Government to amend the Copyright Act 1956 so as to give them the necessary protection under the law.'[19] In due course Parliament was to enact public lending rights which, to a limited extent, did just that.

There were, of course, radio and television appearances: 'I greatly enjoyed listening to your [radio] talk with Michael Foot last night', Machell wrote to Taylor on 14 June, 'and thought you bore up very nobly in the confrontations with those two very odd characters on TV at the weekend.' Sales went very well, as Hamish Hamilton reported to Taylor in mid-August: 'we have sold just over 8,000 copies of Beaverbrook, and are averaging 100 a week, very satisfactory for an expensive book [it was priced at 55/- (£2.75)], which will continue and rise towards Christmas. It was fourth on the Evening News bestseller list last week.' Simon & Schuster published it in the States, where it was a Book of the Month Club Canadian Selection and American Alternative Selection, with a guarantee of $10,000 to the author.[20]

As a publishing event it was clearly a success; it was less so as biography or history. There was, first of all, the question of sources. There existed, of course, the nearly eight hundred boxes of Beaverbrook papers; Taylor also looked through the Lloyd George and Bonar Law papers held in the library. He went through the Beaverbrook files in the Churchill papers, and he looked at the Asquith papers in the Bodleian Library at Oxford. But – and this was a serious omission – he failed to look at any papers in the Public Record Office. Admittedly, he had Beaverbrook's files as put together by his civil servants: but he failed to consult the Prime Minister's files, the Cabinet papers, the Treasury papers – in short, he failed to carry out the research that would be expected of a Ph.D student. It might be argued that he was writing a biography, not a history, and therefore his assessment of Beaverbrook's conflicting tendencies to be sometimes more and sometimes less human was of greater import than a documented assessment of his activities as Minister of Information or Minister of Aircraft Production. But Taylor himself welcomed, and agreed with, the comment that he had written a history of Beaverbrook, not a biography,[21] and within this context it was insufficiently researched.

Secondly, there was the question of style. It was written in a straightforward narrative style, no bad thing in a biography. Anecdote dominated over analysis, which made it very readable, though discussion of motive could be perfunctory. And it was personal: not only was the first-person pronoun sometimes used, but the personal feelings of the writer intruded both implicitly and explicitly. Again, the latter is not without precedent, particularly when the biography is written by someone known to or loved by the subject: Boswell's biography of Johnson leaps to mind. But *Beaverbrook* was an official biography, at least to the extent that Taylor had full access to the material, and it was the biography of someone whose claims to the attention of those outside his own circle of friends arose at least partly from his work as a minister. This required an objectivity, at least about his public activities, that Taylor was seemingly unable to command.[22]

And this was the third flaw: the cloud of hagiography that envelops the book. The book cannot be wholly trusted because, in this case,

Taylor's judgement cannot be wholly trusted. He wrote and said time and time again that he loved Beaverbrook, that Beaverbrook could do no wrong in his eyes, that 'the old man was the dearest friend I had', that his 'friendship enriched me. The joys of his company are beyond description', that 'Beaverbrook was quite a Somebody. Those who loved him have one dream in life: that the telephone will ring again and the familiar voice ask, "What's the news?" '[23] Taylor admitted Beaverbrook's sometimes unforgivable treatment of people, but then smoothed it over by attributing it to his habit of concentrating and then forgetting. He underplayed the irresponsibility of his attempts to use the press to dictate to government. He even dismissed with a tolerant chuckle Beaverbrook's habitual lying – even lying in his writing of history – by ascribing it to his mischievousness, his tendency to become so emotionally involved in his wishful thinking that he took the ought for the is. Perhaps, unconsciously or consciously, Taylor equated it with his father's frequent small lies to his mother – telling her that he was going out for tobacco when he was not, turning left when he said he was turning right: his father had told Taylor that it made life more interesting. Nevertheless, falsification of the historical record surely is the greatest sin of the historian: yet, when caught out, Beaverbrook – and Taylor – treated it as a joke, almost a schoolboy prank. This carelessness about the historian's responsibility to present as far as possible the exact historical truth raises uncomfortable questions about Taylor's own absolute devotion to this truth (the diplomat Nicholas Henderson was to say much the same, as noted below). In short, Taylor ought to have thought twice about writing the book, or at least about writing it in the way he did, if he cared at all for his own historical reputation: he was too close to his subject. As one commentator has nicely put it, '*Beaverbrook* was quite simply the translation of devotion into words.'[24]

It must be said, however, that many of the contemporary reviews were much more favourable. That in the *Times Literary Supplement* was celebratory: Taylor is 'one of the few really original intellects in contemporary historiography – often idiosyncratic, frequently iconoclastic, sometimes wrongheaded, occasionally very wrong indeed, but always interesting, always provocative and always exciting.' In short, the biography was a work of art, and the reviewer in particular cited Taylor's 'refusal to offer simple solutions, and ... the determination to cover all aspects of his subject's life and personality with thoroughness and sympathy.' Tom Driberg, Taylor's friend from his Oxford undergraduate days and himself the author of a biography of Beaverbrook, was more measured in the *New Statesman*. There was some criticism, although put in rather nice terms:

> This biography does not pretend to be objective. As such phrases as 'romantic story' and 'admirable embellishments' suggest, Alan Taylor is prepared to make excuses for his hero's waywardness. ... It is the more to his credit that he has not suppressed some things which might be thought to show Beaverbrook in a less than favourable light ... [It is] a massive achievement. ... It is also wonderfully entertaining. ... His is a much richer, and, obviously more comprehensive book than mine – though, so contradictory was the character that he portrays, he still leaves in some complexity those of us who are neither so adoring as he nor so hostile as, say, the aristocrats of the Establishment whose arrogance Beaverbrook resented.

The final comment should be Taylor's, written in 1976: 'Ten years ago I was looking forward to writing Beaverbrook's life and I enjoyed writing it. Now in retrospect it seems a waste of time: he was not really worth a book on that scale.'[25]

When writing books directed towards the market for popular history after 1963, Taylor produced much more admirable work than his *Beaverbrook*. *English History 1914–1945* (1965) was his last academic book, although even that had been written to be read rather than consulted, the latter being the fate of many in the Oxford History of England series. The popular market is very different from the academic. The popular market requires readability and an awareness of the needs of the public (whether or not the public realises that it needs that particular book). Conversely, the academic market requires the presentation of new research, or the incorporation of others' new research into textbook form. Footnote references are vital for the academic, but are frequently seen as a distraction in the popular, market. The academic must often accept, but resents, the assumption of the publisher that prestige rather than money will be the recompense; the popular writer, rather, is the child of Samuel Johnson: 'No man but a blockhead ever wrote, except for money.'[26] And, if a writer is writing for money, only a blockhead would do so without the help of someone able to extract the maximum from the reluctant publisher. Taylor had always (except in the case of *The Struggle for Mastery*) acted as his own agent, but when approached by George Rainbird, the first of the book packagers (see below), Taylor felt rather out of his depth. At this point he responded to the lure of David Higham that Higham act as his literary agent.

Higham had first approached Taylor out of the blue in October 1957, asking him whether he was 'free to consider a projected book which might prove, in your hands, to be of great importance. ... I should be very glad to have the opportunity of meeting you and discussing possibilities. You may know something of our organisation here and the kind of author for whom we act.' The projected book, on the growth of modern diplomacy (to be called 'Great Strokes of Diplomacy'), had been proposed by an American publisher. It took nearly three weeks for Higham and Taylor to meet, and although Taylor agreed to think about it, in the end he decided that he already had too much planned – at this period, *The Origins*.[27]

It may be that the book was uppermost in Higham's mind, but he also hoped that he might gain such a prolific author as Taylor as a client, an aspiration that soon became more urgent: in early 1958 Higham's associates left the agency, taking other writers with them. Taylor did not bite at the time, but two years later, in September 1959, Higham explicitly suggested that he represent him. Taylor's reaction was not encouraging: 'I don't really see what use an agent would be to me. My journalism is based on personal contacts, and I have to negotiate myself here. I doubt whether there is more to make out of television than I do already. However I'll come around and talk to you about it sometime when I am in London.' There were one or two fruitless attempts to meet, but again Higham failed to land his fish.[28]

Success came in 1961. In late March, Taylor wrote to Higham asking if he would

undertake a negotiation for me? I have been approached by Rainbird, McLean Ltd to produce for an American client (Putnam) a Pictorial History of the First World War. My part in it would be (a) to supervise the choice of illustrations; (b) to write a narrative of about 50,000 words ... Assuming that this is a reputable proposal, I should quite like to do it. The problem is remuneration. They won't pay on a royalty basis; and when they suggested 1000 guineas, I thought it wiser to defer the proposal to you. My difficulty is that I have no scale of values for this sort of thing. ... Obviously my minimum must be more than their offer when your fee has been deducted. ... They know I am consulting you and will therefore expect to hear from you.

Higham 'was delighted to see your letter. .... I shall be in touch with Rainbird as soon as possible and then with you again.' Taylor had made a good decision: Higham got Rainbird to raise his offer by twenty per cent to 1,200 guineas plus one-third of the receipts for subsidiary rights. Higham explained to Taylor that Rainbird McLean 'are people who produce a "package" – that is a complete book which their buyers actually publish. They're therefore not in a position to fix anything finally with you until their proposition is accepted by the buyers. ... So – are these terms acceptable, if they can be confirmed by Rainbird?' Taylor clearly did not know whether they were acceptable or not, since for him – as for most authors then – the concept of a book packager was a new one. Higham had to chase him for an answer, but Taylor finally accepted, promising to try and deliver within the year (whilst at the same time writing *English History 1914–1945*).[29]

The question then arose of a British publisher. Somehow, there was a breakdown in communications between different parts of Hamish Hamilton. In September 1962, Higham proposed the project to them, a suggestion that Hamilton himself received with enthusiasm, although Higham may have been unclear when speaking to Hamish Hamilton as to whether he was suggesting the book with its illustration or just the text. Then, in December, Taylor wrote to Hamish Hamilton that Rainbird was 'still hawking around' the book. This elicited a very proprietorial response from Machell, Hamilton's closest colleague: 'I very much dislike the idea of Rainbird, or anyone else, "hawking around" a text of yours. Why have they never consulted us, I wonder? I should have thought that as your regular publishers we would have been one of the first to whom they should offer it. I don't know on what terms Rainbird functions but we would certainly be keenly interested in publishing an illustrated history of the First World War with a text by yourself and I'd be grateful if you would suggest that they let us have the details if, inexplicably, the rights are still free.' They were, and an agreement was signed. Finding an American publisher was more difficult. Putnam's backed out (Taylor said that they were scandalised by his text) because it was 'thought to be too intellectual for the readers of picture books' and because of the competition from five other books of photographs scheduled to be published the same year; however, they then backed in again. Nevertheless, Taylor found the whole process unnecessarily protracted – 'Publishers are all so casual – so much less prompt and efficient than I am.'[30]

The First World War: An Illustrated History was an easy book for Taylor to write. He knew the material, and he could dash off 50,000 words with his left hand (just as well, since he was writing the Oxford book with his right). The focus was on all of the main belligerents, not just Great Britain, and his approach to it was brutally chronological, with the text divided into six chapters, one for each year of war plus one for peace-making. It included two hundred illustrations, for which Taylor wrote the captions. These were unusually pointed for this type of book. As David Eastwood has noted, they play with the informed reader's perceptions and sensitivities and are, in their way, more subtle than the main text. The text itself is clearly and simply written, with the odd illuminating detail: 'Ludendorf [a German general] was not of high enough rank to hold supreme command. An elderly general, Hindenburg, was dug out of retirement to act as cover for him. The two men met for the first time on Hanover station, Hindenburg buttoning himself into an old uniform that was now too tight.' In the autumn of 1963 it was published in Britain and the following year in the US, attracting good reviews in both countries.[31]

Higham now tried to pin Taylor down, writing to him in early May 1963:

I thought I might just as well put down on paper the points about agency that I made verbally to you [over a good lunch]. Firms such as ours work on the basis of representing an author entirely in whatever fields may be agreed. We are founded basically on the book market and in that market expect to deal with all fields – taking, as it were, the smooth with the rough. So far as other fields are concerned – newspapers, magazines and so forth – that's a matter for arrangement. For some authors we deal completely in that market (often, I'm glad to say, to their substantial profit), for some authors we deal only in the book field ... [S]o far as the future is concerned I hope you will want us to act for you in the book field.

Taylor wrote back immediately:

'I am sorry this misunderstanding has arisen between us. I have acted without an agent for many years, and find that I do not need one in the ordinary way. The First World War was a special case, and I came to you for assistance. I certainly did not mean to commit myself further. As you know, I am at present absorbed in my England book, and cannot think of anything else until that is over. If I then write any popular book, I shall of course come to you rather than any other agent. This is even truer of Beaverbrook, if it comes off. But I can't make a blanket promise. I don't think you need worry. You shall handle any book of mine which is likely to make money.

With this explanation Higham had to be, and probably was, satisfied. Hamish Hamilton were considerably less satisfied at Higham's interposing himself between them and their author: 'What repels me is that *Higham* has somehow got in on the act.'[32]

Taylor wrote to Higham just five months later, this time about a proposal from Thames and Hudson. They wished to publish what they called an illustrated history of Western civilisation, and the Editor of the series, Geoffrey Barraclough, had suggested to Taylor that he write the volume covering 1914–45. Barraclough was an old friend of Taylor's from school, Oxford and Vienna days; whether or not this influenced him, Taylor decided to do it. He made the condition, however, that the date of completion be no earlier than 1966: he wanted to complete his Oxford history before taking on another extended work. Barraclough was willing to wait, and Taylor turned the negotiations over to Higham.

Higham was pleased, of course, and implicitly conveyed to Taylor how much he (Taylor) needed him: 'These people are extremely trying to deal with and I shall fence with great care and commit you to nothing without going into it with you fully.' When he returned to Taylor a fortnight later, he had proven his worth: the delivery date was January 1966, which could slide a bit; and they were now offering an advance of £1,500, rather than £800 as first proposed. Taylor thought that 'their terms are eminently satisfactory' and the deal for *From Sarajevo to Potsdam* was closed.[33]

Taylor then had to decide what 'civilisation' meant, a problem he discussed in the Preface to the book. 'European civilization', he wrote,

is not an easy assignment. Conventionally, Europe extends from the seas and oceans to the Urals, a geographic line of little significance. ... Again, many of our generalizations apply only to western Europe, and more specifically to its wealthier parts. . . . Culturally, the only precise and accurate definition of Europe is 'the area which uses the major and minor diatonic scale'. This is not much use in practice. 'Civilization' is more troublesome still. We usually mean by it moral, peaceful behaviour, or the fancier bits of life – art, literature, and central heating. . . . I interpret civilization to mean the prevailing patterns of communal life, what men do in public ... [T]his book has come out rather political. I can only plead that politics, in the widest sense, had great effects on men's minds. European civilization is whatever most Europeans, as citizens, were doing at the time. In the period covered by this book, they were either making war or encountering economic problems. Therefore war and economics make up their civilization.

Very conveniently, then, civilisation became what Taylor felt most comfortable writing about: even the title was bound by wars.

From Sarajevo to Potsdam is a nice little book, written primarily for that elusive general reader, but destined to find a home as a student textbook. It is a deceptively easy read, deceptive because Taylor wore his learning lightly whilst packing in a lot of interesting ideas – after the First World War, 'civilization was held together by the civilized behaviour of ordinary people. Writers saw only woe in the so-called rise of the masses, but in reality the masses were calmer and more sensible than those who ruled over them.' He divided the book into four starkly titled chapters: 'War', 'Post-War', 'Pre-War', and 'War'. Within these chronological divisions, he interwove political and social events, with more of a bow to culture and the arts than in his *English History*, driven by the need to provide context for the pictures of paintings, architecture and sculpture which leavened the photographs of soldiers and statesmen.

He began with a variation on his opening of *English History*:

In 1914 Europe was a single civilized community, more so even than at the height of the Roman Empire. A man could travel across the length and breadth of the Continent without a passport until he reached the frontiers of Russia and the Ottoman empire. He could settle in a foreign country for work or leisure without legal formalities. Every currency was as good as gold. ... There were common political forms. Though there were only two republics in Europe (France and Portugal – Switzerland was technically a confederation, not a republic), every state except Monaco possessed some form of constitution limiting the power of the monarch to a greater or lesser degree. Nearly everywhere men could be sure of reasonably fair treatment in the courts of law. ... Private property was everywhere secure, and in nearly all countries something was done to temper the extreme rigours of poverty. Civilization was predominantly urban, and the towns had much the same character. The three great symbols of modern architecture were the railway station, the town hall and, on the Continent, the opera house. Trains ran across the Continent with only a short stop at frontiers. ... Citizens of every country and of every class dressed much alike. All Europeans had much the same beliefs. All were Christians except in Turkey. ... All, despite racial differences, looked much alike.

Nevertheless, after this paean to the unity of Europe, he set out the great divisions. 'The first and seemingly most important was class', which he saw as occupational: conflicts between landlords and peasants, between industrial workers and their employers. 'Yet even this class conflict was taking on civilized forms. Trade unions had a legal existence nearly everywhere, and usually some real power. The Socialist parties had become reformist in spirit, if not in phrase. They were part of the political system, often on the point of supporting governments or even forming them. ... The other division was national or, what was not the same thing, the division into sovereign states, but which had few conflicts of a national kind across their frontiers. ... There had been no war between European Great Powers since 1871.' However, 'violence was penetrating life. Rebellion threatened in Ulster. Suffragettes practised direct action throughout Great Britain. Industrial dispute provoked armed conflict in Russia and Italy. The Austrian parliament had been suspended as unmanageable. Most curiously, the traditional standards of art and culture were being broken down, as if artists unconsciously anticipated the destruction of the Great War.'

It is clear from this opening that Taylor was taking 'European' as pan-European, rather than treating countries separately (as he had necessarily done in his *First World War*). The predominant thrust was to make European-wide generalisations; when this was not possible he made comparisons between countries. Thus his characterisation of European external policy: 'Europe dominated the world. Three European powers – France, Great Britain, and Russia – controlled 80 per cent of the world's surface. Three European powers – France, Germany, and Great Britain – had over half the world's industry and half its international trade.' He then threw in his interesting fact: 'Siam was the only country in the world which escaped domination by Europeans at one time or another', an observation that causes the reader to run through all possibilities for escape from this dictum.[34]

As befitted an historian whose preference was for international history, he ended the book with Europe's legacy in the wider world:

Europe was supposed to have lost its hegemony in the world. Yet there was no part of the world which did not become European or at any rate did not aspire to do so. Virtually everyone wore European clothes. Virtually every country had some form of European constitution. Virtually every inhabitant of the globe had European ideas and pursued European ambitions. Everyone wanted social services and his own motor-car. Everyone went to the cinema and watched television. Everyone imagined that universal prosperity had arrived or was just around the corner. Civilization had once been the property of a few: now it was claimed by all. Time alone will tell whether the claim can be satisfied. At any rate, it was Europe's legacy to the world, and only civilization of a European pattern can fulfil it.[35]

Now, much of this is patently ridiculous: even if civilisation *is* defined as exclusively urban, the humble inhabitant of Delhi, for example, was doubtless more concerned to get food than a motor car. Yet in general thrust it was at least arguable, and at the very least, stimulating. As the reviewer in the *Times Literary Supplement* wrote, 'Mr Taylor has had a fine romp. . . . There is the familiar combination of non-fact and debatable statement which irritates the professional historians – but there is also the striking probe, the brilliant summation and the arresting choice of word and phrase which will always excite their envy and admiration.' Published in October 1966, it was an immediate success, selling nearly fifty thousand copies in the US and UK alone over the following twenty years. Even in 1993 it was earning royalties in Lithuania.[36]

While still engaged with *English History*, and after having signed the contract for *From Sarajevo to Postdam*, Taylor agreed to write yet another book, a companion volume to *The First World War*. George Rainbird had been so pleased with the first effort that he wanted Taylor to do the same for the Second World War, that is, to write an essay to accompany a set of illustrations. In April 1964 Taylor agreed to do so, promising delivery by the end of 1967; however, with the death of Beaverbrook in mid-June he wrote that 'obviously I can't do the Second World War.' Higham and Rainbird remained hopeful, however, although Higham had to report in November that Taylor had still not signed the contract. The following July Higham broached the subject again, but Taylor's reaction was firm: 'no arrangement about the SECOND WORLD WAR can be made at present or even, I should have thought, discussed.' Higham reported this to Rainbird, who was 'not too pleased'. In December 1965, however, Taylor held out some hope: 'I'll read a book or two about the Second World War. But no promise that anything will come of it.' Higham, of course, was pleased, and agreed 'no promise understood'. Taylor was a past master in throwing out lures.[37]

Rainbird might have been even more cross had he known that Taylor would agree to write – and would write – another short book whilst working on the Beaverbrook biography. During the spring of 1968 he discussed with Purnell the possibility of his writing 30,000 words to form part of a series entitled 'The History of the Twentieth Century'. In mid-February they came to an agreement, and on 19 October, a fortnight ahead of schedule, he delivered the manuscript for *War by Timetable: How the First World War Began*; it was published in 1969. This book became one of his most influential, largely because of its easily remembered theme. In it he argued that the military plans of the Great Powers in July 1914 depended on their capacity for speedy mobilisation and attack, which were based on transport of troops by rail. The drawback of this increased capacity of movement was its complexity and consequent inflexibility: once the troops were in motion, the interlocking demands of the timetables meant that mobilisation was difficult to halt and the Powers were forced to fight. This was most famously the case with the German plan for marching through neutral Belgium in order to attack France and then Russia, the Schlieffen Plan: when the Kaiser proposed stopping mobilisation, his generals told him that it was impossible. As Taylor concluded, 'When cut down to essentials, the sole cause for the outbreak of war in 1914 was the Schlieffen plan – product of the belief in speed and the offensive.'[38] For some years after the book's publication, what every schoolboy knew was that railway timetables had caused the outbreak of the First World War.

This was not the only non-Beaverbrook work that Taylor wrote during the late 1960s and early 1970s. There were many others – contributions to a series of magazine parts on the history of the twentieth century; a piece on Churchill; contributions to another part series, this one based on Churchill's *History of the English-Speaking Peoples*. One project was a *Dictionary of World History*, the story of which demonstrates Taylor's approach to these multiple-author publications. In October 1966 Gerald Howat, then head of history at Culham College, a teacher-training institution in Berkshire, received a letter from Thomas Nelson and Sons asking him to be general editor of the *Dictionary*, under Taylor as Editor-in-Chief. He was summoned to lunch at the Garrick Club, where he was vetted by Taylor and Nicholas Bentley, Nelson's literary editor. Howat then embarked on the task. After six months Taylor told him that he (Howat) knew what he was doing and that he (Taylor) would not interfere, but was available if Howat needed him. In particular, Howat was to call on him if there were any problems with the in-house editor or publisher.

Taylor was helpful. He put together half of the advisory team, which included Asa Briggs and Max Beloff. He helped sort out unsatisfactory editors, writing to a particularly awkward one not to be so difficult, as he was part of a team. Near the end there was indeed a problem with the publisher. Nelson wanted to pull out, since the volume was becoming expensive. Taylor responded with vigour, telling them that people had given time and substance to the project and Nelson could not play fast and loose with them. More intimidatingly, he sought the advice of the famous lawyer Arnold Goodman, who told Nelson that the authors and editors could not be thrown to the wolves; they backed down.

He also did his duty as editor and writer. He did not demand to see the text in detail, but every so often he wanted to see the copy in order to judge for himself how the project was going. He wrote the entries on the two world wars. In everything he was very efficient. Towards the end, however, there was a difficulty with Taylor's own work. Taylor had agreed to write the Introduction, but the result, according to Howat, was absolutely dreadful: for a publication such as the *Dictionary*, whose intended audience was the general reader, it was not helpful for Taylor to write that history was pointless, that its only use was as entertainment, and in general to convey a very pessimistic tone. Howat went to the mediaeval historian Richard Southern for advice. Southern told Howat that he should take the Introduction back to Taylor and tell him that it was dreadful. Howat did so; Taylor picked it up dramatically and tore it up, telling Howat that he knew that it was rubbish. The Introduction he then wrote was more positive in tone, concentrating, helpfully, on an analysis of the role of facts in history.[39]

Taylor also edited for publication three of the Beaverbrook Library's own holdings. One was *Lloyd George: A Diary*, published in 1971. This was the diary of Frances Stevenson, Lloyd George's secretary and mistress, and eventually his second wife. Taylor followed it in 1975 with *My Darling Pussy: The Letters of Lloyd George and Frances Stevenson 1913–41*. Stevenson had been more than an ordinary secretary to Lloyd George – she was akin to a political secretary, the first female to occupy such a position. She was also intensely feminine. Known as 'the Goat' amongst the political classes, Lloyd George was a danger to the virtue of many women; indeed, Frances Stevenson frequently had problems keeping order and discipline amongst the members of the typing pool during the First World War, a pool in which Lloyd George loved to play. Taylor was certainly intrigued by her, as he wrote to the historian Kenneth Morgan: 'I understood for the first time what was meant by "a mistress by nature". The result for the male was both flattering and sympathetic.' The other Beaverbrook collection which he edited was that of W.P. Crozier, sometime Editor of the *Manchester Guardian*. This was published as *Off the Record: Political Interviews 1933–1943*. For Taylor this was an act of respect and gratitude, though he thought the interviews somewhat pedestrian.[40]

Higham continued to pepper Taylor with proposals. At one point (in March 1970) they had a contretemps, arising from the publication in the US of the Lloyd George essays from the Beaverbrook Library seminar. Taylor habitually only made one copy of a manuscript, and in this case it went to Hamish Hamilton. The American publisher, Atheneum, wanted a copy as well. Taylor was annoyed: 'If they insist, I will get the typescript back from Hamish Hamilton, thus holding up publication in this country, and will produce the required two typed copies, the cost of which will eat up most of my share of the Atheneum royalties.' A fortnight later, he again wrote to Higham, this time in high dudgeon: 'I had the Lloyd George essays copied at the cost of £20.4s.od to myself and dispatched the copy to Atheneum. In return I heard from Michael Bessie [of Atheneum] that he would prefer to have the book composed in London and then sent to him in photo offset. There have been far too many mistakes of this kind in our recent dealings, and this is to give notice that I do not propose to call on your services as agent in any future dealings.' Higham rapidly sent a cheque for the amount to Taylor and then scrambled to find out what had happened. After some correspondence, he discovered that Atheneum had actually requested the copy in order to prepare for advance promotions. Higham sent a copy of the explanatory letter from Atheneum to Taylor, but relations remained tense for some weeks. Consequently, when another chance came to negotiate for Taylor, Higham and his colleague Bruce Hunter pulled out the stops: to their American correspondent agency Hunter wrote, 'As you know, we're having a lot of trouble with him, sparked off by Atheneum's curious behaviour over the Lloyd George book. ... It's obviously important in this case to get the very best we possibly can.'[41] Taylor, had he known this, might have drawn the moral that an occasional show of bad temper towards his agent could reap dividends, but in any event David Higham Associates remained his agent until his death, and the agent for his literary estate thereafter.

Taylor did not finally write the promised book on the Second World War until some time after he had completed *Beaverbrook*. Somewhat amazingly, Rainbird had not given up on Taylor, and negotiations were resumed in early 1972. At that point Rainbird were assuming Taylor would write a rather longer book than had been previously suggested; furthermore, they hoped that Taylor could deliver the manuscript by the autumn. They were rapidly disabused: 'I certainly could not finish a book on this subject by mid-autumn. In fact, I am not prepared to agree to a delivery date at all. If Rainbird like to take the chance on my writing the book and are prepared to wait for it they are free to do so. If they would rather get someone else to do it they are free to do that. Never again will I sign a contract until I have finished the book.' Taylor did not complete the first draft of the manuscript until January 1974, over eight years after he had first more or less agreed to write the book. The outcome demonstrated that Rainbird had been right to wait: published in May 1974, *The Second World War: An Illustrated History* had sold 31,000 copies by the end of the year. It is a very good book, one of the best short histories of the war. The emphasis is on the whole war, beginning with the Sino-Japanese War in 1937; the period from the first shots to the last bomb is bracketed with the run-up to and the aftermath of the war. As C.M. Woodhouse wrote in the *Observer*, 'Three things distinguish his work from any other account of the war: his unfailing grasp of the details on every front, the marvellous succinctness of his narrative, and his acute use of anecdote to concentrate attention on the crucial turning-points. ... The scale and balance of the work make particularly clear the totality of the first total war.' Although Taylor was still to produce two historical picture books, some books of essays and his autobiography, this was his last work of sustained history. It is pleasing that he retired from the field full of honours.[42]

Along with his writing, Taylor did a considerable amount of broadcasting, for both radio and television (see Chapter 7). He also found himself another lecturing position: by leaving Oxford he had deprived himself of his regular fix, but within a year he secured a substitute, University College London. In September 1964, he wrote to Professor Joel Hurstfield, the Astor Professor of British History: 'Would you like to employ me? I don't mean financially. I see you have Veronica Wedgwood as a special lecturer, and I wondered whether there was room for me. I shall not lecture at Oxford again and should welcome some outlet. I am a good lecturer and regular in attendance. If you are interested, I'll come one day and talk to you.' Hurstfield thought it 'extremely generous of you to offer us your help in the way you do', a sentiment shared by the head of the History Department, Professor Alfred Cobban, and the UCL administration. The *Sunday Telegraph* got wind of the appointment, but Cobban and Taylor convinced them that it was 'essentially an academic arrangement', and the newspaper took it no further. His first lecture (of four on twentieth-century dictators) was given in mid-February 1965; the lecture room was packed out.[43]

Taylor was appointed a Special Lecturer, to take effect from the beginning of the 1965–6 academic year, at which point he also agreed to run a weekly discussion class on Europe 1914–45. He settled into a routine of giving four to six lectures plus the class during one of the academic terms, and although in his initial letter to Hurstfield he had suggested that there need be no financial recompense, UCL offered him payment at the rate of £430 per annum. He fulfilled all of the duties required, including writing reports on the students in his class (in January 1971 the highest mark he gave was B++). He sometimes used his lectures, as he had done at Oxford, to work out ideas or to give advance performances of about-to-be published books. He did this, for example, in the autumn of 1968, when his lectures on the origins of the First World War were already in press as *War by Time-Table*.

Taylor continued happily to lecture through the academic year 1978. As he wrote in his autobiography, 'UCL was an agreeable place with agreeable colleagues and the advantage of an excellent bar.' In October 1974 his salary was raised to £795 per annum, and in June 1977 to £1,175. But June 1977 was the beginning of the end of his Special Lectureship. The need to economise in UCL had become painfully clear, and Special Lectureships were seen as a luxury with which it was easy to dispense. The department fought hard to retain him. At one point they appeared to be beaten, and the college wrote to Taylor to inform him that the appointment would not be renewed. When the college then turned around and asked him to give a lunch-time lecture, he refused: 'I am not qualified to give a lecture appropriate for the 150th Anniversary. Further, I shall not be on the staff of the College next year, and my time will be taken up as the Visiting Professor at Bristol. I cannot therefore accept your invitation.' But the department managed 'to smuggle out the money', at least for one further session, that of 1977–8. But that was the last one, as Professor Ian Christie wrote to him in March 1978: 'I have some rather sad news, though I know it is not unexpected, as you anticipated it last year. At that time I managed to snatch back the money for the Special lectureship out of our economy wreck, but I am afraid that I can't do so again.' Taylor accepted the inevitable.[44]

The UCL lectureship was replaced by one at the Polytechnic of North London (now the University of North London), the History Department of which was headed by Professor Robert Skidelsky. As the institution was situated in Kentish Town, Taylor was able to walk to work. His chagrin at the loss of the UCL appointment was also mitigated by the fact that he currently held an appointment as Visiting Professor at the University of Bristol. In March 1976 Taylor had received an approach from John Gross, then the Editor of the *Times Literary Supplement*: would he consider accepting the appointment to the Benjamin Meaker Visiting Professorship for the academic year 1976–7? Taylor was delighted: 'I am attracted by the idea of acquiring a chair after all these years without one.' Each week he travelled by train to Bristol, where he spent two nights. His main duty was to lecture – he filled the largest hall in the university – but he also taught a few students. He was such a success that the appointment was renewed for another year. This was also the year when Taylor began holding a seminar on twentieth-century British history at the Institute of Historical Research.[45]

Although Taylor no longer taught undergraduates at Magdalen, he continued to take an interest in the doings of the college, and as Senior Research Fellow he was entitled to attend and vote in College Meetings. In one notable area of policy, the admission of women to Magdalen, he continued the effort he had begun in 1948. In this early episode, he had convinced the Fellows to allow themselves, on one Sunday a term, to bring into dinner as their guests ladies holding academic positions in Oxford or other universities; Taylor's first guest was the historian Betty Kemp, Fellow of St Hugh's College, Oxford. The admission of women as undergraduates, however, would require repeated attempts over nearly thirty years. Support for the change gradually built up, but attempts were discouraged in the early 1960s by the mutterings – e.g. 'over my dead body' – of some of the more intransigent Fellows.

In January 1970, Taylor made a formal attempt to get Statute I changed: this stated that 'A woman may not become a member of the College.' To put more pressure on the Fellows, he alerted the press. The *Sunday Telegraph* of 28 December 1969, referring to him as 'historian, publicist and Fellow of Magdalen, Oxford', revealed that at the College Meeting scheduled for 21 January Taylor proposed to amend the statutes to allow the admission of women. The change would require a two-thirds majority. At the meeting, Taylor spoke in favour of the proposal from the head of the table, sitting at the right hand of President James Griffith (famous for his unparalleled knowledge of wine from Bordeaux). He pointed out that at first the college had existed only for the clergy; then it had been widened to include members of the Church of England; it had been widened further still to include men regardless of their religion or lack of one; and now – looking around and noting the American Fellow (Keith Griffin) and the Yugoslav Fellow (Dusan Radojicic) – the college was full of foreigners. Women were the next step.[46]

Initial discussion concentrated on whether 'two-thirds' meant two-thirds of persons present and voting, or two-thirds of votes cast, the crux being that the President had two votes; the ruling, and this was to be determining, was that the requirement was two-thirds of votes cast.[47] By one account, the ensuing substantive discussion was only remotely relevant to the main issue: for example, there was an argument over whether the college could afford to install ladies' loos – certainly if Magdalen could not, no college could. In the end Taylor managed to head off the filibustering and get a vote taken. As a Prize Fellow later recalled, 'Joining the old fogey brigade, a brilliant, perverse, and very gay Dutch linguistician ... voted against, and that one vote ... defeated the proposal, since although a majority of fellows were in favour of women, the majority missed obtaining two thirds of votes cast – by one vote. [The vote was thirty-two in favour and seventeen against.] AJPT was incensed. I can't remember quite what he said, but I recall feeling myself in proximity to a diminutive volcano at the end of the table.'[48]

In his last year as a Senior Research Fellow, Taylor made a final attempt. On 21 May 1976 he asked that the following motion be put forward: 'That Statute I be amended by the deletion of the sentence "A woman may not become a member of the College".' In the College Meeting on 16 June the vote was taken: it was twenty-nine for and twelve against. The machinery for change was thereby set in motion, and Taylor could depart from the College with at least one of his radical beliefs accepted and on the way to being implemented. The dissenting Fellows apparently nursed few grudges: when, the following November, the Fellowship Committee proposed that Taylor be elected to an Honorary Fellowship, the vote was forty in favour and only one against.[49]

Another of his academic interests, which continued until 1980, was his activity as a Fellow of the British Academy. Taylor worked hard to get outstanding modern historians elected to the Fellowship, sharing the conviction of other modernists in the Academy that the mediaevalists had more than their fair share of Fellowships. In a note to Clark (a former

President) in 1957, a year after his own election, Taylor passed on the information that he and Richard Pares 'agree Rowse first, Hoskins second. I would like to propose a recent historian off my own bat, but can think of no one at present.' W.G. Hoskins (Reader in Economic History at Oxford and in 1965 Hatton Professor of Local History at Leicester) was not elected, but Taylor tried again, and in 1969 Hoskins became a Fellow. In 1961, Taylor told Clark, 'I put up Trevor Roper for the Academy but got no backers. We settled on Margery Perham, a respectable name.' Perham was elected in 1961, but Trevor-Roper, the Regius Professor, had to wait until 1969. One whose election gave him some trouble was the specialist on the seventeenth century Christopher Hill, whose stoutly maintained left-wing views were, Taylor assumed, a significant cause of the difficulty (Hill had been a member of the Communist Party until the Soviet invasion of Hungary in 1956). As Taylor wrote to Clark in December 1964, 'I continue to have a conscience about Christopher Hill. The Section [of modern historians in the Academy] dodges him every year, and I am sure it is for political reasons. This year I think I'll say so, in my usual provocative way.' It did not work, nor did it work the following year: 'I feel cheated over Christopher Hill, whom we put high and who was passed over, I suppose as younger than some others.'[50] Hill finally became a Fellow in 1966. Taylor was proud of being a Fellow, and entered into the Academy's affairs with gusto.

It was therefore ironic, even tragic, that in 1980 he felt driven to resign as a consequence of its response to the Blunt affair. Sir Anthony Blunt was a specialist on the painter Poussin and former Advisor on the Queen's Pictures. In a book published in 1979, entitled *The Climate of Treason*, Andrew Boyle claimed that alongside the notorious Cambridge spies, Kim Philby, Guy Burgess and Donald Maclean, there had been a 'fourth man'. In November 1979 the Prime Minister, Margaret Thatcher, announced to a stunned House of Commons that Blunt had been a Soviet spy. There was some confusion in the stories that appeared in the press, but it emerged that Blunt had spied for the USSR, then an ally, during the Second World War; he had also alerted Burgess and Maclean in 1951 that they were about to be arrested, thereby enabling them to escape abroad; and he had subsequently protected Philby. It also emerged that he had been arrested himself in 1963 and had confessed, but had been granted immunity in the hope that he could be 'turned'. Blunt was stripped of his knighthood and resigned as a Fellow of Trinity College, Cambridge and of the Society of Antiquaries, both having made it clear that he would otherwise be expelled.

He did not, however, resign as a Fellow of the British Academy: what, if anything, would the Academy do about him?

The man on whose shoulders the greater part of the responsibility lay was Sir Kenneth Dover, the President. When the news broke, Dover later wrote, it did not occur to him that Blunt's Fellowship was in question; however, the historian J.H. Plumb wrote to him to say that he hoped that 'immediate action' would be taken to expel Blunt, because the Academy should not 'harbour traitors'. Nothing could be done straight away: a Fellow could be expelled only by a vote at the Annual General Meeting, which would not take place until the following July; furthermore, this could only be done on the recommendation of the Council (of which Plumb was a member), which itself would not meet until 15 February 1980. The matter was put on its agenda.

When the Council met, all except one of the members spoke at length; a 'straw vote' gave nine to eight in favour of expulsion. Blunt was then invited to the next Council meeting to make a case for retention, but he declined. In the period before the next Council meeting, it became clear that the views of the Council might not correlate with the views of the Fellowship as a whole: many expressed the belief that 'Blunt's folly should not outweigh his services to scholarship'.[51] Taylor told *The Times* that the whole thing amounted to a 'witch hunt' and that he intended to resign from the Academy if Blunt were forced to do so: 'I couldn't be a Fellow of an Academy which uses the late Senator McCarthy as its patron saint. It's not the duty of the Academy to probe into the behaviour of Fellows, except on grounds of scholarship.' Two days later a letter appeared under the name of Max Beloff: 'The expulsion of Professor Anthony Blunt from the British Academy was hitherto a very remote possibility, but Mr A.J.P. Taylor's promise, so portentously reported in your columns today, to resign from the Academy if that event occurred, has now rendered expulsion a virtual certainty.' Beloff assured Taylor that the letter was hoax, and Dover never discovered who had written it. Taylor claimed that it was 'very funny', telling the *Sunday Express* 'I thought the idea of expelling Blunt as a way of getting rid of me was quite brilliant.'[52]

Council met again on 18 March, and by a vote of eight to seven again agreed to recommend expulsion, a decision confirmed without further discussion at the last Council meeting (on 16 May) before the Annual General Meeting. When the agenda for the AGM went out it included, with Council's recommendation, notice of a counter-motion by the economist Lionel Robbins and the English literature specialist Dame Helen Gardner, which 'deplored' Blunt's conduct but proposed that the Academy should not 'proceed further in the matter'. The AGM, held on 3 July 1980, was attended by 187 Fellows, attracting a 'swarm of journalists' who gathered in the courtyard of Burlington House. The discussion went on and on, until L.C.B. Gower proposed that the meeting should 'pass on to the next item of the agenda', a proposal seconded by three Fellows. Robbins withdrew his motion, and the Fellows voted 120 to 42 to pass on. After the meeting, Taylor gave an impromptu press conference on the steps of Burlington House to some of the reporters, calling the decision – or non-decision – 'a splendid outcome ... a victory for good sense. ... It was just like McCarthy all over again. I believe in toleration and I am a freedom man. It is a wonderful thing to realise that we can show patience and tolerance and that we can tolerate the intolerable.' Taylor was not alone in his reaction, agreeing with Ralf Dahrendorf, Director of the London School of Economics, that 'The British Academy is about scholarship, and that was the decision we took – by a handsome majority.'[53]

Matters, however, did not end there: a hostile reaction was growing in the Fellowship, many of whom believed that Blunt's betrayal of scholars in the Soviet Union was indeed a betrayal of scholarship. One Fellow, the historian Norman Gash, resigned, and another wrote to Dover asking if he knew 'of a movement among the Fellows to fight the decision from the inside', adding 'if so, I would gladly support it.' Gash was hoping that Fellows in Scotland would follow his lead in resigning if Blunt were not out by 31 December, while Sidney Allen, a Fellow in Cambridge, wrote to say that he, too, would resign. Dover talked to Gash on 13 December, and his fears of a potential haemorrhage of Fellows were confirmed. The historians J.H. Plumb of Cambridge and Taylor's former colleague at UCL, Ian Christie,[54] were letting other Fellows know of their threats to resign. Gash suggested to Dover that the interests of the Academy would be best served if Blunt himself were to resign, and that Dover ought to ask him to do so.

Dover's 'real feeling about the Allen–Christie–Gash–Plumb combination was the indignant resentment which one feels towards terrorists who threaten to blow up innocent passengers if they do not get everything they want'. Yet there was the reality of at least fifteen resignations, and the possibility of others, if Blunt did not go. Blunt wrote to Dover to express 'his deep distress at the way the *Daily Telegraph* [was] using [him] as a stick with which to beat the Academy' (there had been a spate of letters to the newspaper). Dover wrote to thank him, adding that now that there was no threat that it would expel him he might consider resigning as a means of 'healing the wound' in the Academy. Just before he posted the letter, a journalist from the *Sunday Telegraph* telephoned and read to him a letter from Plumb that was due to be printed the following day and that warned that he would resign if Blunt were not out by the end of the year. Dover feared that this would cause Blunt to refuse. A few days later, Blunt telephoned to say that he was indeed giving serious consideration to resigning but '"The trouble is, there are people who say they'll resign if I do." I [Dover] exclaimed "Good Lord", and he half-laughed and said, "Yes, I know, but that's what they say."'[55] Fortunately for Dover's peace of mind, two days later Blunt telephoned to tell him that he had decided to go.

The news of Blunt's resignation broke on 19 August 1980, and on the same day Taylor wrote a letter to Dover in which he too resigned. Taylor believed that the decision taken at the AGM should have been the end of the matter. 'Instead, by requesting Professor Blunt to resign, you have revived the controversy and enabled a small group of Fellows to thwart the wishes of a substantial majority. I deeply regret this as I have regretted the controversy from the start. But I have no choice. I will not be a party to a witch hunt and therefore tender my resignation as a Fellow.' The historian Richard Cobb also tendered his resignation, but then withdrew it. Dover later wrote that he 'had always admired Taylor for his frequent clarity of perception and exposition – despite his preference for clarity over adequacy of explanation – and the sloppiness of "witch-hunt" was a disappointment.'

In his memoirs Dover also wrote: 'Naturally I did not know at the time, as we now know from his *Letters to Eva*, that Taylor was looking for a pretext for resignation.' This interpretation is debatable. Taylor wrote to his wife on 24 November 1979 that 'Blunt says that his confession was incomplete and that he was still a Soviet agent in 1955. He must enjoy the limelight. He also proposes to resign from his other appointments. I wonder whether he will resign from the British Academy. It would give me an excuse for resigning from it also. There is to be a play on the BBC about Suez, with Eden as its hero. We shall be having one on Blunt next.' This *may* have been a declaration of intent, but since it was written in the month that the news broke, not a year later when the decision was taken, it seems unlikely. It is also the sort of thing which Taylor would put into a letter as an off-the-cuff remark. On the other hand, he did feel strongly about the Establishment, as it were, hounding the nonconformist. In addition, he also believed in horses for courses: academic punishment for academic crimes.[56]

What seems clear is that if he did mean to resign, he was driven by emotion as much as by rationality. Dover stated that the final count for resignations was five, including Blunt and Taylor, and that Taylor later changed his mind. He may have belatedly realised that his charge that Dover had asked Blunt to resign was not strictly true, he may simply have missed the academy. A few years later he wrote to Peter Brown, the Secretary, inquiring whether he might rejoin. 'Brown had to explain that under the by-laws a Fellow could return only by re-election, and Fellows could be elected only under the age of seventy. "Ah well," Alan replied, "I do these things, it is part of my life."'[57]

Taylor by this time was seventy-four years old and perceptibly slowing down; he felt himself crossing the border into old age, saying in March 1980 that 'My mid-old age health has come to an end'.[58] But he had one important reason to bless fate (and he sometimes did): he was not alone. After a love affair, both epistolary and actual, lasting for nearly sixteen years, he had married the Hungarian historian Dr Éva Haraszti. Her reasons for marrying were primarily three: hero worship, sexual desire and love. His reasons were more complex: love and sexual need, yes, but also egotism, and fear of being alone as he grew older. The story is a compli-cated one.

It all began in 1960, when Taylor, the economist Joan Robinson and the ancient historian H.F.D. Kitto were sent by the British Academy on an exchange visit to Budapest. Taylor lectured at the university there and 'visited such historical sights as Hungary could offer', which included the Karolyi Palace. His guide was Éva Haraszti, of whom he took little notice until an official dinner. 'I looked across the table to my guide. I saw what I had not seen before: brown eyes that sparkled with zest and I thought something more.' His interest, once aroused, rapidly increased, particu-larly after a long evening spent talking by the Danube, during which he poured out his unhappy marital story to her. They spent most of his remaining time in Hungary with each other, dining together on the last evening. 'Afterwards Eva suggested we should walk by the Danube before returning to my hotel. I took fright, knowing that I should kiss her and fearing that this might upset me, or perhaps both of us, too much. We went back to the hotel by car and only held hands.' Taylor, of course, was still married to Eve Crosland, and she at least considered that their marriage was still strong. She later said that 'as far as I can gather there was no cor-respondence with the widow [Haraszti] while our marriage lasted', though she was known to refer to Margaret and to 'the other'; Taylor, however, claimed in his autobiography that once back in England he wrote to Éva constantly.[59] This was not something he would have admitted to his wife, and certainly during the following few years anything Taylor might have liked to do was constrained by the fear that he might lose his children. It is, however, eminently possible that this was a useful excuse for his habit, in personal affairs, of drifting along.

Éva Haraszti's own memoir of their first meeting puts a rather different slant on events. She was a historian at the Institute of History (of the Academy of Sciences) in Budapest, happily married and with two young sons. Her husband, though proud of her publications, was not an historian and thus unable to enter into detailed historical discussion with her. Thus meeting and talking with Taylor, a great historian in her own field, was unexpected and exciting: 'I suddenly fell under his spell. I admired his intellect, his kindness and tolerance, his practicality, good humour, the way his mind worked, and his steady nerve. I also liked his face, his profile – everything about him, in fact. He seemed very English to me and I had always liked the way Englishmen behave.' There was a strong sexual attraction between them, and Taylor was not averse to testing the water. There was a dinner, and afterwards Éva, Taylor and one other man were seated together in the back of a taxi: 'I was jammed close to A.J.P. We felt a very great mutual attraction. I could feel through my clothes the way he slowly touched my limbs with his. I trembled, melted and burned. I had rarely ever experienced such feelings.' She agreed with Taylor about the failure to kiss: 'We did not once kiss because we knew that if we did it would have been impossible to stop there.'

Her memory of the talk by the Danube fleshes out Taylor's brief reference to it. Indeed, he must have found the development of the conversation a bit unexpected:

Alan ... told me how unhappy he was at home and how many problems he had with his first and second marriages. As we sat quietly by the Danube, he looked depressed and poured out everything about his life. Everything. It seems to me now [1995] that what he said was slightly exaggerated. I felt vaguely that here was an extremely sensitive and humane man, to whom I was attracted and wanted to help in some way, but I felt no real commitment: I had my two beautiful sons waiting for me to come home as soon as possible. I felt that this man could have told me how to live, how to bring up my children, how to behave with friends and enemies and how to be practical rather than over-analytical. I therefore asked him lots of questions about his children's eating and washing habits, for example, and his relationship with them. It seems to me that, although my questions helped him to shake off his depression and cheered him up a bit, he was not really interested in such maternal matters.

Indeed, as she recognised, they had a different view of the burgeoning relationship: 'We had so many things to say to each other. I was anxious for him to read my articles, which had been printed in Hungary in English. He, on the other hand, was interested in me as a person and as a woman.'[60]
They did not meet again until 1962, when Taylor came to Budapest to give an oration at the funeral of Michael Karolyi. He later wrote: 'I thought this second visit to Hungary would also be a good opportunity to carry further the love affair with Eva Haraszti that I had started, or so I imagined, two years before ... [But] Eva was not, she assured me, the woman I had supposed. She was happily married with two young sons, while I had six children to cope with. The little affair had been a fantasy and was now at an end.' Éva found the attraction still very strong, feeling that 'this was the right man for me.' But it was too dangerous, it might ruin her married life; 'Alan made the same decision.' She told him not to write to her. Nevertheless, each independently attempted to make contact with the other, three years later. This was at the International Historical Congress in Vienna in 1965 and it failed, as neither could find the other.[61]
The crucial period in the development of their relationship was the month Éva spent in London in the summer of 1969, but before that came the break between Taylor and his wife Eve. He had for years divided his time between Margaret, his former wife, and Eve. According to his youngest son, by now Sunday was the day he spent with his second family: during 'Alan's day', he read the papers in the morning, had lunch with them, walked on the heath with the boys in the afternoon, played a family game in the evening – he was extremely competitive and took no prisoners – and then zoomed back to Oxford. (Taylor wanted to be the fastest driver on the road. He loved to overtake a queue of cars, and if a car came from the opposite direction he would merely indicate and cut in. This was a recurring source of tension with Eve. He was aggressive, flashing his lights at any driver who pulled out in front of him. Not surprisingly, he was several times nearly assaulted by other drivers.) When the boys were younger he bathed them as he had bathed those of the first batch, a habit that meant a great deal to Taylor; he only stopped when his youngest son was twelve and had asked his mother to tell his father that he wanted to bathe himself. He read to them regularly as he had read to his children by

Margaret, but the books were perhaps not always well chosen. Taylor judged appropriateness by his own history: he read *The Pilgrim's Progress* to his youngest son when the latter was seven and it terrified the boy. He also had lists of books which he thought his sons should read; Daniel, who was more bookish than his elder brother Crispin, read them but resented the emotional blackmail, whilst Crispin refused.

By one estimate Eve was alone over ninety per cent of the time – effectively a single mother. Furthermore, when Taylor *was* in residence, he spent much of his time working. His son Daniel remembered on one occasion, when aged five, going into his father's study for comfort and Taylor's response was to sit him in a corner and give him a new copy of *The First World War: An Illustrated History* to read, whilst he continued to work. (It is, of course, possible that Taylor believed that no greater comfort existed than to read a new and illustrated book.) Indeed, his son 'remember[ed] him by the pipe smoke rather than by his physical presence.' The walks on Hampstead Heath were didactic occasions: Taylor tended towards giving history lectures, and both boys tended towards shutting them out, as their half-sisters had done earlier. There was little personal talk, little information given about the facts of life, although there was the occasional sly remark: once when he was nine or ten, waiting for his father to collect him from school, Daniel had whiled away the time talking to one of his female schoolfriends; his father commented that he was 'chatting up a tasty bird.' Later he warned him to 'make sure you always use contraception'.

Indeed, as the boys grew older, their father was not averse to sharing – or bragging about – details of his love life with Éva, possibly because he was so relieved to have one at all. Once he had left Eve, she had taken to sharing her flat with tennis coaches, reputedly lovers rather than lodgers, and flaunting them at Taylor as much as to say that she was still desirable and could do what he, Taylor – who was so much older – could no longer do himself. (Tennis played a large part in her life; she sometimes won tournaments, and was an umpire at Wimbledon.) Their marriage had sometimes been tempestuous; Taylor had a temper, and there had been some slight domestic violence (he had apparently slapped her on three occasions; perhaps she had done the same to him).

In September 1968 Taylor and Eve had a final row over his ties to Margaret, and they separated. (In 1976, a few months after they had married, he wrote to Éva that Margaret 'will work persistently to break up our relationship, as she did with Eve.') Taylor wrote to a cousin in December 1968 that 'My second marriage broke up in the autumn mainly because my second wife became increasingly jealous of my first brood of children. Well it was sad. I was fond of her and very fond indeed of my two young sons. But there came a time when I was weary of being nagged at. I'd like to think things would go right again one day, but I doubt it and in a way I don't much care. I'm so busy that I am never at home until late evening, and then it does not much matter where I am.'[62]

Taylor's second marriage was effectively over. As Eve told a reporter on 24 September:

'He has gone back to his first wife, Margaret, in Camden Town. He left this morning. I helped him to pack his books and clothes in the car. I have spent the day walking about the house looking at empty drawers and cupboards and bookshelves. I have known this was going to happen for a long time. But now that it has it is like a limb being cut off. No matter how badly you are getting on with someone, at least if they are there you can row with them. But now I can't.' [She] explained to me [the reporter] that she has always agreed to her husband keeping in touch with his first wife. 'It just didn't work out,' says Mrs Taylor.

However, Taylor then began the same routine with Eve that he had established with Margaret years earlier, when their children were small: he began turning up at Eve's on Saturday or Sunday, spending two nights a week with her and their two young sons.[63] Nevertheless, by the summer of 1969 Taylor was, in a sense, free, although Éva was not.

Éva came to London as the guest of the British Academy to do research at the Public Record Office for a book on British appeasement policy. She had been asked for a list of people whom she would like to consult; at the top of it she put Taylor, and the two finally met in the Conversation Room in the PRO. To Éva, 'Alan looked young and fresh and seemed excited', a perception corroborated by Taylor, who wrote that 'I tracked her down at the Public Record Office and fell in love with her again in one of the waiting rooms.' He was sixty-three, she was forty-seven. They spent as much time as possible together. While in London Éva learned that her husband, who had been ill for some years, had been taken to hospital with a perforated ulcer. Upon her return to Budapest a few days later she discovered the seriousness of it. 'He was', she later wrote, 'still in hospital when I arrived and I immediately went to see him. I did love him and felt guilty at falling so utterly under Alan's spell. I vowed to myself that if only my husband was cured I would never see Alan again.' Some weeks later he had an operation for stomach cancer; it was unsuccessful, and a few days later, aged forty-four, he died.[64]

Taylor wrote Éva a letter of sympathy in December, but did not fly to Budapest, assuming that the last thing she needed at the moment was to worry about him. (Besides, that would have been too decisive.) He had written to her in late November, before the death of her husband, that 'I am not going to keep bothering you by saying I love you. You know it and don't need reminding. My divorce will go through next year [in fact, not for nearly five years]. Thereafter, if you are ever free and want to marry me, I shall be waiting.' Yet, once she was free, and possibly in need of his close support, he made no move to bring them together. His explanation: 'More or less unconsciously I was in a dilemma. Whenever we were together there seemed to be an understanding between us so complete that it guaranteed a perfect life together. After we had parted I saw only the difficulties. Our backgrounds, national and personal, were different. Our ties were in conflict. I had two families to worry over, Eva had two sons. Above all I am lazy about making a change in my life though I have made plenty. So I waited with detached curiosity to see what would happen to me.'[65]

According to Taylor, their relationship the following year was affectionate but remote – although his letters to her came festooned with endearments. However, in the summer of 1970 he was invited to give a lecture at the Ranke Gesellschaft, a prestigious organisation of German historians, which was meeting at Königswinter, a resort on the Rhine near Bonn. He saw it as an opportunity to meet Éva again 'without the embarrassment of a formal assignation' – or the implied commitment? – and suggested to the organisers that she be invited to give a paper as an Hungarian guest. She arrived, they met, 'and from that moment we behaved like innocent young lovers.' According to Éva, she did not allow Taylor to kiss her; she was anxious neither to be a mistress nor to be seen as one. According to Taylor, however, they 'embraced violently on a bench in a dark corner near the river'. In any case, at the end of the conference, Éva remembered, she 'left the small German town feeling happy and enriched. I had somebody behind me, somebody wiser than me, more experienced and tolerant, a good and exciting person.'[66]

The following September, in Salzburg, they became lovers. When discussing the journey, Taylor told Éva to bring her contraceptive device; Éva nearly refused to go, and in retaliation Taylor also threatened not to come. In the end they both went. On their first evening together, Taylor recalled, he said, '"Shall I come to your room?" Éva, slipping in her English a little, replied, "I want." ... She later alleged that she assumed I had wanted to continue our conversation. My assumption was different and things worked out quite differently.' Éva recalled that Taylor had booked two rooms, but that they 'did not in fact need two rooms.' Taylor told her that in her autobiography she had not made it clear that his 'expression of a wish to come to your bedroom was a total surprise to you, and that even when I came you had not expected me to step briskly into your bed. Your surprise makes the story much funnier.' Éva's memory of the episode was more romantic: 'When Alan came to my room I knew that I loved him as a man. Our first time in bed together was unexpectedly beautiful, not just because we suited each other so well, but because he was so unforgettably tender.' They flowed together during the day as well: they went to the Mozart museums, to a Mozart concert and probably to the churches. They had a perfect holiday: they saw the sights during the day, had a good dinner and a cosy talk in the evening, and then retired to bed and made love.[67]

They talked in the intimate manner familiar to lovers. Taylor told her how wonderful it was to have sex again after so many years' abstinence; on the other hand, he was capable of looking on the bright side where that was concerned, since he 'firmly believed that prostate difficulties were caused by too much sex.' But being human, now that he once more had the opportunity, he 'enjoyed love and sex in a healthy and practical way. He knew that he needed it and that it enriched him, but he was realistic enough to know that love can also be an inconvenience. It creates difficulties in that you are involved with someone else instead of being completely independent.' However, Éva added in her memoir of Taylor, 'he managed to be involved and stay independent at the same time', a state of affairs that later came close to causing a final break.[68]

Taylor, whilst sincerely attached to Éva, appears to have considered the Salzburg episode more of a holiday – he later referred to it as 'magical' – than the beginning of a firm commitment to a future together (although he had told Éva that she would 'never be alone again'). Indeed, when they met again the following year in Venice, he considered their time together 'a delight slightly marred by Eva's vague feeling that we ought to be married at once.' According to Éva, her feeling was more than vague: she had already decided that 'as a man, he was the most tender, lovable and satisfactory. And because sex with him was so good, I decided to marry him.' Therefore, she 'went to Venice with the idea that during our stay we would fix when and how we should get married and begin our life together'. It became clear to her that Taylor's priorities were different: 'Alan, I think, came to Venice to have a holiday with me, enjoy my company, make love, make things easier and more interesting for me and show me everything he liked there.'

For Éva, 'Venice nearly became the burial ground of our relationship', once she recognised that he was less eager to marry than she was: 'He had thought of our marrying but I think he was not altogether certain as to how and when he could do it.' He told her that until his younger sons had reached a settled stage in their lives, had grown up enough to have started university or some kind of higher education, he could not even think of marrying. Her belief was that 'he was still escaping from his second wife. He was always taking care of his brood, organized and took part in their summer holidays, spending several weeks every year with his first family on the Isle of Wight and taking his second family either to Ireland or the Lake District.' Éva found it difficult to see where she would fit in in all this, and her unhappiness at not knowing for certain just what, if any, future she had with Taylor cast a pall over the holiday. She felt that he was cheating, that he was trying to get out of the promises he had made in his letters, or was at least putting off their fulfilment. She later became more sympathetic towards his dilemma, deciding that 'for all of his outward frivolity and light-heartedness, he was at heart a worrier, always looking on the dark side of things and a pessimist about how things would turn out'. His own later assessment of his feelings was remarkably close to hers: 'I still had Crispin and Daniel [his two sons by Eve] on my hands; Eva had two adolescent sons to care for in Hungary. I suppose that after so many upheavals in my life I shrank from yet another. . . . I put off the idea of marriage, inclined to believe that something would turn up.'[69]

And so he – and therefore they – drifted on. For the time being, however, they agreed that things could continue as they were, meeting twice a year for a fortnight: Paris in the autumn of 1973, and two visits, to Yugoslavia and Budapest, in both 1974 and 1975. In Budapest he spent a fortnight with Éva in her home, and the relationship deepened: he was accepted by her two sons as a member of the family, and 'clearly for both of us this was no longer a casual or passing affair [with the implication that previously it had been for him?]. When we were together we behaved as though we were married and talked as though we were married. The moment for decision, never a thing I liked, was coming closer. Of course I had problems and as usual saw the problems more clearly than I saw the solution.'

One problem that worried him was the worsening of his personal finances, not so much as a result of declining income, which was not then a problem, but from the decline in his capital arising from the plunge in the stock market – he wrote at the end of August 1974 that 'I have lost a lot of money on the Stock Exchange. Two years ago my shares were worth nearly £100,000. Now they are worth less than £20,000.' Furthermore, Margaret, 'who had been a good friend to me of late years', would naturally be upset if he moved out and remarried. Margaret, in fact, would continue to pose a great, and increasingly divisive, problem for – and in Éva's eyes a profound threat to – their relationship. Taylor seemed unable to make a clean break, often, Éva believed, sacrificing her interests to Margaret's, whilst Margaret still considered Taylor her husband, with some reason: they had, after all, been living together the entire time he was in London ever since his final break with Eve in 1968. Again, he wondered, would Éva really be happy leaving her sons, her work, her home, her country? One problem at least which no longer existed was Eve. After a holiday spent with her and their sons in the summer of 1973, Taylor petitioned for divorce on the basis of a separation of more than five years, and it had been unopposed. It was made absolute in April 1974.[70]

By this time, Éva no longer entirely believed that they would ever build a life together: 'Somehow, although I was absorbed in my love for him, I did not trust him as I had done. [W]hile I still looked forward to his letters and our holidays together, I began to realize that he lived in a world that I did not fully understand. ... The more I got to know about Alan's life in London and Oxford, the more strongly I felt that I did not want to be his mistress. ... I had the feeling that the situation suited him very well as it was, with a mistress in Hungary, a home life in London and a secretary at the office. I felt that things could not go on like this.' Yet it is worth noting, in support of Taylor's honest intentions towards her, that as early as mid–1972 he had made some financial provision for her by making over the royalties of the American edition of *Beaverbrook*, which included its sale to the Book of the Month Club.[71]

Éva began to feel, and she suspected that Taylor did also, that their situation bore – for her – an uncomfortable resemblance to that of David Lloyd George and Frances Stevenson. When Taylor was editing the latter's diary, eventually published as *My Darling Pussy*, he made the first of two comments which must have stimulated Éva's thinking on the subject. The first comment was written in July 1970: 'She was his mistress and secretary for thirty years and put up with every sort of humiliation because she loved him – and also of course because he introduced her to high life and the inside of politics. I suppose the truth is that every woman gives and every man takes. Then he is angry, as no doubt I have been, when the woman tries to reverse the situation. I've always tried to play fair – giving as much as I took. I now think from experience that women don't really like this. They want a master, not an equal partner. But I could never be that.' Four years later, he commented again on the Lloyd George–Stevenson relationship: 'He was certainly cheating her – telling her how wearisome it was to be with his family when he was really enjoying himself.'[72]

Éva drew the obvious conclusion:

Reading *My Darling Pussy* ... I felt that his story was very like ours. I felt that, just as Lloyd George could not give up his wife, Dame Margaret, who lived in Criccieth with their children, so would Alan not be able to give up Margaret and his children – at least not emotionally. Lloyd George could not give up Frances either. ... The similarity between the stories struck me because I was sure that Alan understood and commented so well on the story, not merely because he was so skilful, but because he empathised with Lloyd George's position. I was convinced Lloyd George led his double life because he could not do otherwise; his roots and his love towards his wife were half his life, and the love he felt for Frances was not less, but different. He could not give up Dame Margaret because he was a kind, intelligent and sensitive man. He could not give up Frances because the relationship was as complete as a relationship between two intelligent and loving people could be. Whereas I could understand Lloyd George well enough, I could not see myself in the role of Frances. She flattered him and tolerated the humiliation when she was not accepted or forgiven by the children of the first marriage. I felt I could never play such a role.[73]

And so, for this and for other reasons, she decided to break with Taylor. This was in September 1975, while they were together in Hungary; he looked uncomfortable there, she thought, a misfit, and she certainly resented his lack of interest in her country. One morning she interviewed him formally for an Hungarian publication, during which he was serious and businesslike; for the rest of the day he was so uncommunicative that she hardly knew whether he was fed up with her, with Hungary, or was merely in an unaccountable bad mood. But that night they had, in bed, an overwhelming experience, and she decided that, after all, their fates were bound up together.[74]

Taylor always claimed that he had no such doubts about her, and in

March 1976, when she was again in London with a scholarship, he finally proposed. As before, her account is fuller than his. Taylor wrote: 'I made this proposal to her on the steps of the British Museum. She asked, "What should I be expected to do?" – meaning could she keep on with her work as an historian. I replied "To be a loving wife," which she assured me would not be difficult.' It is clear from what Éva later wrote, however, that there was much more to the proposal than this, for it came after a further crisis. Although she was only in England for a relatively short period, Taylor often left her early to go back to Margaret, which upset her: whom did he love best? Margaret, and Taylor's secretary, seemed to take priority, and she was shaken by this. Éva was convinced that Taylor's secretary had read her love letters to Taylor (which he denied) and that she encouraged Taylor to remain with Margaret. All in all, Éva felt that she was superfluous to requirements, and she told Taylor that she did not want to see him again.

This seems to have driven him to a decision, for the following day he told her that he wanted to marry her:

> I asked him quietly what my duties as a wife would be. I wanted to know whether I should prepare meals for him, whether he needed me as a full-time housewife or whether I would be able to continue with my research and writing; whether I could visit my sons whenever I wanted; whether he would share my life, and so on. 'You have to open your legs,' Alan replied briefly. At first, what he said seemed rude and vulgar. Then I had to laugh. I realised that this was how Englishmen think – at least how this Englishman of mine thought. Alan was practical – why should he take a wife if not for sex? ... There were, of course, the emotional and intellectual aspects as well but the sexual attraction made the whole thing urgent and irresistible.

They both then set out their terms. Taylor wanted to go to the Beefsteak Club once a week, to take Margaret to a concert once a week, to spend one night a week at her house 'as an act of kindness because she was getting old and they were good friends', and to spend a fortnight every summer with Margaret and the children on the Isle of Wight. Éva wanted to spend every Christmas and the summer holidays in Hungary with her sons and to have them to visit once a year. They agreed, and she then returned to Hungary. Taylor arrived in Budapest on 1 September 1976, where the formalities attending their marriage were interminable and were only completed the day before he had to return to England. Much of his time there was made miserable by a virus he picked up swimming: he ran a high temperature, his tongue was infected and he could hardly eat. Pills brought the temperature down, but there was a large yellow spot on his tongue. His weakness was such that his ability to go through with the marriage ceremony remained in doubt – and Éva, at least, assumed that if they did not get married then, they probably never would. In spite of a high temperature, on 15 September Taylor made it to the Council Offices. 'The actual ceremony', he remembered, 'was disappointing. Eva and I were hardly allowed to speak except to say Yes when the registrar ... asked us whether we really wanted to get married.' The following day he flew back to London and rejoined Margaret.[75]

Then came the part he hated: finding a place for the two of them to live. The plan was that Margaret would sell her house in St Mark's Crescent, where Taylor had also been living for part of each week (he had proposed at one point that he and Éva should move into Margaret's house), and buy a smaller one; Taylor would find another one for Éva and himself. (He had been spending part of each week in his rooms at Magdalen, but this would come to an end in mid–1976.) His first thought was that he would get a flat, on the grounds that a house would be too large and they would only need four rooms, but once he saw the actual size of a flat he decided against the idea. In mid-October he found a house he liked in Twisden Road; Margaret had not yet found another house, and he wrote to Éva that he had suggested to Margaret that she might occupy the two rooms at the top of the house. Éva's letters to Taylor have not survived, but her reaction can be imagined. In December 1976 he bought the house, but within a few weeks he began to have doubts on the grounds of expense and its size (it had rooms on three floors). The following week he put it back on the market: 'I mean to live modestly.' If he had not managed to find and furnish something by her arrival, he suggested, Éva could come and stay in Margaret's house. Nevertheless, a letter to Éva in early March 1977 expressed his bewilderment as well as his understanding of the impossibility of their living as a threesome:

I wish I had someone to advise me. I have always let Margaret arrange things and obviously I can't do that this time. She is in a bewildered state. She has looked at various little houses which never quite suit her, and of course she does not want to move until the end of the year. On the other hand, she does not want to be left in her present house without me. It is very sad for her and I understand her reproaches, but I just can't help it.

If I thought she would cooperate fairly I would still urge her to divide a house with us, but she would give us no peace.[76]

Things looked up in mid-March when he received an offer for the house, although to his dismay it would be another four months before the deal was completed. However, he then had other worries: would he find another house for them? If he did, he would hardly know how to furnish it himself; and then there was Margaret, who was not well: 'Of course, if she becomes really ill she will have to live with us.' She had an operation, and Taylor then had to care for her, some details of which he passed on to Éva. He was able to send her good news in June: Margaret had found a house which suited her and had also found a buyer for her current house, so things should be sorted out by the time Éva was due to arrive. Margaret had recovered enough by early August to take it upon herself to look for a flat for Taylor and his wife. Taylor himself, however, found a house himself, also in Twisden Road (whose location he liked) and smaller than the first one, with rooms on two floors rather than three. However, he also told Éva that Margaret wanted to decorate it for them, which must have chilled his new wife a bit. It was Janet Taylor, however, the wife of Taylor's eldest son, Giles, who began to buy things for it. By mid-October 1977 the Twisden Road house was theirs.[77]

Then came an equally worrying period for Taylor: arranging for and keeping an eye on the builders as they modified the house. This became a *leitmotif* in his letters for the next several months, succeeded in due course by his worries over furnishings: what to buy, how many, what style, what colour, how much could they use the leftovers from Margaret's house, what old carpets to use, and where and how they should be laid – there seemed no end to it. By early 1978 Margaret was planning the furnishing of the house, and by mid-March Taylor was complaining that 'Margaret thrusts all sorts of things on me, many of which I don't want, and I cannot refuse for fear of a row.'[78]

When Éva arrived in April, the house was in some sort of order, and Taylor showed her round. He himself liked it very much – as he later wrote, it seemed to him 'a nearly perfect house'. Éva liked it from the outside, but the inside plunged her into a low-key but long-lasting depression. Her assessment was that it had been arranged for Taylor and perhaps a mistress, but not a wife; indeed, Taylor later admitted to her that he had told Margaret that he only loved her, Éva, for her body. (Eve Crosland later claimed that Taylor had wanted to marry Éva so that he would have someone to nurse him when he grew old.) Taylor had a large downstairs room with his Victorian partner's desk for a study; Éva was to have a small desk in a very small upstairs room. But what hurt and angered her at the outset was the impression that the house had been

arranged without care, as if anything would be good enough for me. Margaret had helped to arrange everything in the house and it looked, and still does, like a lower-middle-class, suburban home with no ambition to be up to date. We had a second-hand refrigerator, a second-hand gas cooker, cheap, broken plates mended with glue, and old armchairs that looked as if they had been bought in a jumble sale. ... My little study was dreadful. It was such an insult, I was lost for words. It had the sort of desk that a 12-year-old would use, a terrible thing called a bed, a mattress ['which had a large stain in the middle to remind me of past activities'] and an armchair especially chosen ... by Margaret. The bedroom curtains had been brought from Alan's previous home, where they had been used in the kitchen.

Éva's later assessment was that it had been meant to appeal to Alan rather than to distress her, and he was so pleased that she felt unable to let him know her true feelings. His letters to her had been dotted with remarks to the effect that she could change things when she arrived, a mantra which probably relieved him of any feelings of responsibility for what was being created. But broken plates mended with glue? If he indeed saw them and did not object, it was probably because they appealed to the streak of financial meanness in his nature – certainly he was, from time to time, to chide Éva for spending more than she needed to on some piece of simple kitchen equipment or item of food.[79]

Taylor's behaviour over the following two years was remarkably thoughtless and even unconsciously cruel. He had what he wanted: he loved her and he needed her, and now they were together. But he found it difficult to treat her as an equal, driving her to write in September 1978: 'Alan does not need an equal partner in life, what he needs is a woman who adores him, who surrounds him, who is intellectual and who amuses him at the same time. I did not know this before, because I was happy to entertain him for a fortnight. How can I go on?' And then the realisation came in October that Taylor was 'not really inclined to share his intellectual interests with me. ... Of course he does share his thoughts with me when I ask him to, but he never does it spontaneously. Also he does like people to speak about his works which I cannot do for any great length of time.'⁸⁰ But of greater importance was the fact that he would not give her complete emotional security. She appears never to have doubted his love for her, but she did question whether he was capable of giving her the priority she craved whilst Margaret was still alive. She had lost her country, her sons, and her independent and assured place in society; now she was only a spouse, and a foreign one at that. Taylor's sons and daughters were polite, and his daughters-in-law were welcoming and helpful; but she very much felt that they believed that she had inveigled Taylor away from his rightful place at the side of their mother, who was clearly in a slow decline. Éva brooded, in particular during the days and evenings and nights which Taylor spent with Margaret; she nearly threw in the towel and returned to Hungary; and Taylor appears hardly to have noticed.

Yet it is well to remember that the first year or so of married life can be one of painful adjustments, particularly when the couple is older and each has been used to independence. Moreover, when a couple has met only occasionally and for limited periods, these can be suffused with the aura of a honeymoon, of an unreal moment in time; after that, everyday life, even and perhaps especially between lovers, can come as something of a shock. Éva was trying to cope with a foreign language: whilst she could read English well, her comprehension of the spoken word lagged behind. This made her prone to making mistakes when shopping, and Taylor would sometimes chide her for it; it also limited her enjoyment of social events, because she could not present herself at her best. As for Taylor, he must have felt pulled in separate directions by the two women. Éva perhaps suffered for her strength, since it probably inclined Taylor to consider Margaret the weaker of the two and thus in more need of help and comfort. His amazing lack of sensitivity to the thoughts and emotions of others masked Éva's distress.

The other side of things must not be forgotten. Taylor was extremely happy to have Éva beside him and, although he began as the stronger partner in the relationship, his growing age combined with her growing self-confidence in her ability to survive and perhaps even to flourish in her new home gradually increased his dependence on her. By the time of Margaret's death in July 1980, the relationship was a more balanced one. Shortly thereafter the scales began inexorably to tip in Éva's direction.

The great emotional mystery of Taylor's life was his relationship with Margaret. He clearly never broke the emotional link forged between them during the relatively untroubled early years of their marriage. At least they were untroubled as far as Taylor was concerned; her feelings cannot now be known, but something must have been amiss for her to have fallen for someone else, particular for a callow, nineteen-year-old student. Both of her affairs (platonic or otherwise) happened after their move to Oxford, and her diminished position there, along with his workaholic habits, must carry some of the blame. During the period of her passions for Kee and Thomas, Taylor kept hoping that she would recover and resume a normal married life. What is important is that he had not wanted to divorce her, and it is entirely possible that once Thomas had died they would have slowly come back together. That is, after all, what effectively happened. Perhaps he no longer desired a sexual relationship with her, looking elsewhere for this: such had been the extent of his initial ambition with both Eve and Éva, and both had had to threaten to leave him before he would regularise their unions. Although loving each of them in her turn, he had wanted to keep his primary loyalty to Margaret. By the time Éva and Taylor married, nearly fifty years of Taylor's life had interlocked with Margaret's. He enjoyed her company, she cooked for him, went to concerts with him, shared the news of their children with him and generally treated him as her husband. These ties proved impossible for him to escape and were severed only by her death.

During all of the emotional turmoil, Taylor kept very busy with writing and lecturing, and with some broadcasting. In August 1976 he returned to the television screen to give his first set of lectures for nearly ten years. The series was called 'The War Lords', and it was followed in 1977 by 'How Wars Begin' and in 1978 by 'Revolutions and Revolutionaries'. His final complete series, 'How Wars End', was broadcast in 1984, by which time he ought to have given up: neither his mind nor his body was what it once had been. The late 1970s and early 1980s also saw a continuation of his lecturing to meetings of the Historical Association. The HA is made up partly of professional historians, but predominantly of history teachers and of those members of the public who love history. There are branches all over the country, and Taylor felt a great loyalty to this element of his public; by this period of his life, the only non-academic invitations to lecture which he would accept were those from the HA.

He was busiest with his writing. By the second half of the 1970s, this largely consisted of book reviewing. For Taylor, this was not a second-class occupation. Rather he always considered it to be of the highest importance, very much enjoyed it – frequently putting aside other writing at the arrival of books for review – and continued with it until the very end: his last published work was a book review. He developed his own rules for reviewing, which in 1961 he passed on to Martin Gilbert: 'Serious advice. As a reviewer, weigh your words. But once you've settled them, stick to them. Never apologise or retreat. Above all, remember that as a reviewer you have one duty & one only: to the potential reader. You must tell him the truth about the book without thought whether you are pleasing the author or offending him.'[81] Over his lifetime, Taylor wrote nearly 1,600 book reviews, his final two appearing in 1985.

He did not concentrate on reviews because publishers of books had lost interest in him: rather, he himself gradually lost interest in writing books. In February 1974, Thames and Hudson came to his agent with a proposal that he write a book on the history of Great Britain 1901–1975. This was not to be a shorter, illustrated version of his *English History*: rather, it was to be a manuscript with 'fresh insights'. Taylor was meant to be revising his Oxford history; furthermore, as he wrote in 1973, 'professionally I keep clear of history after 1945'. Nevertheless, he considered this 'a most attractive project' and Thames and Hudson sent him a contract in September 1974. When Higham asked him in July 1975 how it was going, and told him that Thames and Hudson would be pleased if they could have the manuscript by the end of the year, Taylor retorted that there had been no discussions with the publisher, and he would only begin once they made clear to him what they had in mind. He added that he supposed that he would begin writing the book the following year – but that he would not agree to a delivery date.[82]

Taylor began to work on the book in 1976, but it was slow going. By January 1977 he 'had come to dislike' it and laid it aside, having written only one chapter. In June he wrote to Éva that 'I am physically all right but my mind is not working well. I have stopped writing except for reviews and have no interest in ever writing a book again', a comment that may have been stimulated by the lack of time and quiet to write at the Mill on the Isle of Wight, where he was on holiday with his family and taking care of Margaret. In mid-July his confidence was seriously shaken by an incident which happened whilst he was recording a television lecture on the First World War: 'I got so involved that I went on too long and overran my stopping time. Instead of making a quick end I lost my nerve and broke off with an apology, a thing I have never done before. We made a reasonable end afterwards, but it was not the same thing. I have always said there is one thing I can do well and without a mistake, and that is to lecture on television. Now I have slipped, I shall never be so confident again.'[83]

This crack in his armour and his consequent loss of confidence affected his other work. The following month he wrote that 'I no longer have any interesting subject, and I can't organise my life or my mind to go back to revising *English History 1914–1945*. I just do my journalism and let the days go by.' A fortnight later he was still depressed, with the added burden of his domestic imbroglio: 'I have not written a word more about English history and am beginning to think I never shall. I have lost my enthusiasm for it. Indeed, I have lost all interest in writing except for reviews. My mind and my spirit have degenerated, and will not recover until the upheaval in my present life has taken place. I am nervous and worried all day long, though there is nothing I can do about it.' By January 1978 his obsession with the house on Twisden Road was taking over everything: 'I really do no work nowadays except reviewing. I have lost interest in writing history. Also, I am too distracted with the coming move. I lie awake all night counting the number of hooks which will have to be unscrewed and then screwed in again.' In fact, although he reviewed books as they came in and was writing the Diary for the *New Statesman*, he had 'not attempted to write any book or part of one since 1976. Somehow I have lost interest or have nothing to write about.' By August 1978 he had taken the decision: 'I shall abandon *English History in the Twentieth Century*.'[84] He told his agent, Bruce Hunter (who had succeeded David Higham), who told Thames and Hudson that Taylor did not think that he would ever proceed beyond the one chapter which he had written and they had already read. He and they were both happy to let the contract remain on the table: the publisher hoped that inspiration would 'sting you very soon, like an unexpected wasp!'[85] But it did not, and other than turning his television lectures into books, largely by correcting the punctuation, he was never to write another book of history – except for his own.

The first person to suggest to Taylor that he ought to write his autobiography was Hamish Hamilton, who mooted the idea in March 1956. Taylor's response combined gratification with his usual game of playing hard-to-get: 'What extraordinary ideas you do have! I have thought of writing memories some time for my own amusement; & you shall have them when I do. But it won't be until I have accumulated the experiences of a few more years.' In 1967 Isaiah Berlin suggested to an American literary agent that 'one of the most exciting unwritten books of our time would be the memoirs of A.J.P. Taylor himself, an intellectual odyssey that might well receive considerably more attention then, say, the [Harold] Nicolson diaries, as well as outsell them.' Taylor's reaction was straightforward: 'I've learnt enough from history to know that ... few men are gifted enough to write their memoirs – witness Macmillan who was thought to be quite clever until he tried. Nothing interesting has ever happened to me; I have known no one of any interest; and the few episodes I might record would give universal pain. How would the great world like a picture of Dylan [Thomas] treating human beings as a boy pulls the wings off a fly?'[86]

Nevertheless he was moved by Berlin's suggestion, and wrote to him to explain why he had declined to do it. The letter contains a sketched self-portrait and deserves extended quotation:

A proposition came to me the other day that I should write my auto-biography, and I was told it stemmed indirectly from you. I turned it down of course, not regarding myself as a subject of any interest. But I was flattered that you should think I have had an intellectual odyssey and that my memoirs would be more interesting than Harold Nicolson's. To adapt Namier, you must be a very clever man to find anything interesting in me. Harold met many very interesting men and saw all the great events. I have met few and have watched events from afar. My memoirs would be duller than Maurice's [Sir Maurice Bowra, quondam Warden of Wadham College, Oxford and celebrated wit], and one can't say worse than that. I don't think I have travelled much intellectually, indeed far too little. I was at sixteen where I am at 61. I have a blind spot for religion and philosophy. They are as meaningless to me as, I suppose, witchcraft is to you. When I am asked to contribute to volumes entitled What I Believe, I can only reply: I don't *believe* anything. I make certain practical assumptions in life, as that most drivers keep to the lefthand side of the road in this country or that seeds sown in fertile soil will germinate. I have moral habits just as I have appetites and pay my bills with the same routine as I eat my dinner. I like keeping to the rules, but I do not condemn others who break them. Indeed I do not claim any right to judge others and equally deny their right to judge me. Professionally, I am an old-fashioned narrative historian with no gift for analysis or social techniques.

He continued:

I don't like hierarchies and am for the poor against the rich. I can't find much interest in politics except when the call comes unmistakably, as it did for me in the General Strike, Suez, and CND. Then, I think, I am as good a speaker as Bright was, but this is a technical accomplishment I am not particularly proud of. I like making money, not because I want to spend all that much, but simply for the operation of making it. All my life I have driven fast, rather showy cars and am now beginning to fear the days when I shall no longer be able to do so.

And finally:

These are outside characteristics. I doubt whether anyone can write honestly about the inside since Freud. He turned us into psychological hypochrondriacs. I can never have intimate relations with women without noting the symptoms, and it really makes a mess of things. Some strange things have happened in my private affairs, but I don't think it would be a kindness to write about them. My marriage with Margaret was torn apart by two fantasies – the first a war-hero, the second a poet, now, I am glad to say, dead. I ought to have accepted these fantasies, as Lutyens did under similar circumstances. Instead I resented them as irrational and pursued a course which was as destructive for me as for others. Such stories are best left alone. So you won't get your book. I don't think it is there to write despite your flattery. It will be difficult enough for me to make sense of Beaverbrook as a person, particularly as he never made sense of anyone else.[87]

Taylor's attitude was to change, however, and Berlin would be one of the first to know about it.

Roger Machell of Hamish Hamilton inquired again in October 1974: 'have you ever considered writing memoirs? They'd be fascinating to read – and to publish.' By this time Taylor felt that he had accumulated the necessary experience, but recognised that it was of an awkward type: 'I am writing my memoirs in my spare time. I shall call them An Uninteresting Story. Unfortunately I can't leave out my private life and that means the memoirs can't be published while my two former wives are alive. After that I shall be dead and everyone will have forgotten me. So there is something for you to mourn over.'[88]

Taylor had begun work in 1972, as a gift for Éva and to be writing something: 'What shall I do now? I can't face starting a short history of the Second World War straight away. So I must try to write an autobiography for you. I am frightened of this. I don't think I have the gifts. I can't even remember most of the time. What I can remember makes me unhappy and resentful. Either I made other people unhappy or they made me unhappy. I've had an empty frivolous life and not done much that I wanted to do, writing in the void without any real belief in anything. ... I don't like other people much.' Two months later he added that 'I've *promised you to write an autobiography just for you*. Every time I think of it, it depresses me and I put it off. I have enjoyed the isolated incidents of my life very much, but when I consider the general pattern it has been awful: thirty years of living from day to day.' However, by July 1972 he had completed the first chapter, and by the following January had gotten himself to the age of thirteen. As he wrote it, he commented on his former self, usually with a note of surprise: 'Starry-eyed Marxist idealism in a little boy. Belief that the revolution was coming tomorrow and so on.' And: 'As I think back I am amazed how solitary I was – not a single friend while I was growing up, just reading all the time.'

By the end of the year he had completed eight chapters and decided to show them to Berlin for his comments: 'This,' he wrote to Berlin in January 1974,

to be entitled AN UNINTERESTING STORY, is all your fault. You told me to write it, and now you must read it. The task is really beyond me. I can narrate incidents. I can't do characters, least of all my own. I have no idea what went on inside his head. I fear I am often rationalizing or guessing though I have tried not to. The anecdotes, when I can recall any, are genuine. The feelings and beliefs I am not sure about. These eight chapters go up to 1938 when I returned to Oxford. I have no idea whether or when I shall write any more. Later chapters will be embittered by my relations with two wives, each of whom caused me misery and strife. So I do not think they can be published in my lifetime or theirs. Still I'd like your opinion. Treasure this. It is my only copy.'[89]

By the time Machell asked about it, then, he had reached the chapters on Oxford; the need to record his marital troubles accounted for his rather discouraging response.[90] But he kept writing, and by mid-July 1975 the whole draft was finished. By mid-June 1975 he had begun a second autobiography, writing to Éva that 'I have also started my intellectual autobiography though I cannot tell how it will work out.' Called 'Accident Prone, or What Happened Next', this was to appear in a special issue of the distinguished American academic journal, the *Journal of Modern History*, devoted entirely to him. By September he had completed it, although, as he wrote to Éva, 'I badly need a last sentence.'[91]

Word of his memoirs got round to publishers, and in the summer of 1977 Christopher Falkus of Weidenfeld & Nicolson made a bid for it, but Taylor still believed that it could not be published whilst his first two wives were still alive. Once Margaret had died in 1980, however, he got down to re-revising the manuscript: he had first begun to revise it in 1976, though by the end of 1979 he had concluded that the second draft was worse then the first. By June 1981, he decided that it was fit to be seen. In the midst of a publisher's party, he asked Bruce Hunter if he would like to read his autobiography; Hunter's response was, 'You bet I would!' In the event, Taylor held to his 1956 promise to Hamish Hamilton – although he had probably forgotten that he had made it – and offered it to them. Hamish Hamilton's decision was 'of course we must publish it and it will sell a great many copies. It's an extraordinary story.'[92] There followed a healthy recompense. From Hamish Hamilton he received an advance of £15,000, which he wanted to be paid in yearly lumps of £3,000; from the American publisher, Atheneum, he received $10,000; and for serialisation rights from the *Observer* he received nearly £26,000. Given the fact that his age and increasing ill health precluded much freelance work, these sums were a welcome addition to his exchequer.[93]

There then ensued an extraordinary few months, as the book was combed by both the publisher and a libel lawyer. The primary fear was of what Taylor's second wife, Eve Crosland (she had taken back her maiden name by deed poll), would do; she might be indifferent to publication, she might ask for a few changes, or she might sue. They approached her, and she made it manifestly clear that if she was so much as mentioned in the book she would take legal action: 'There is no way I am prepared to give my consent to the publication of anything in Mr Taylor's book concerning me.' In the meantime, and in anticipation of this response, the publisher and the lawyer listed every possible statement which might give rise to a charge of libel – not only those concerning Eve Crosland but also references to other persons who might take offence; these originally totalled seventy-six, but a number proved to be harmless and were allowed to remain. Almost all of the other persons were dead, but Eve was very much alive, and therefore she effectively disappeared from the book.[94]

A Personal History was published in May 1983. In terms of its accuracy, it is riddled with small errors of fact. This is, however, not surprising, given that Taylor wrote it at the kitchen table without any help from diaries or even letters, since his lifelong habit of throwing out letters as soon as he had answered them left him bereft of primary sources. In support of the theory that as one grows older, one remembers the earlier years better than the later, the first hundred pages, out of a total of 275, are devoted to the first twenty-four years of his life. A constant theme of this part of the book is Taylor's dislike of his mother. In the central sections of the book, covering his years as an academic, two dominating themes are his disdain for many of his history colleagues and his celebration of himself for being distinguished. Throughout he emphasises his radicalism. Throughout his bitterness shows through: no Balliol scholarship, no promotion at Manchester, no surcease of the pain caused by Margaret and by Dylan Thomas, no professorial chair and so on.

Some reviewers, such as David Holloway in the *Daily Telegraph* – 'wonderfully lively' – and Byron Rogers in *The Times* – 'not a single dull sentence in it' – enjoyed it, but others, such as John Gross, found it intensely annoying: 'Some of the boasting is merely harmless, perhaps endearing, vanity; some of it takes the form of an unseemly crowing over vanquished rivals and forgotten competitors. And, in retracing his career, Mr Taylor never seems happier than when recalling slights, setbacks and university feuds. The tone is suitably snide: reputations are nibbled away, and compliments wing their way through the air tipped with poison. In many of the disputes he describes Mr Taylor may well have been in the right, but that does not necessarily mean that he was right to dredge them up now.'[95] In general, though many critics and readers enjoyed it, the academic community concluded that Taylor had done his reputation no favours by writing the book.

A dinner given to celebrate the publication showed him at his worst. Robert Kee and Sir Nicholas Henderson, the latter a long-time friend (he had read the manuscript of *The Struggle for Mastery* for Taylor), hosted the occasion, which was attended by a dozen friends, including Michael Foot. After dinner, Foot turned to Henderson and, speaking of Taylor, asked, 'Don't you agree that what he's really renowned for is the pursuit of truth?' Henderson made the mistake of saying what he really thought: allowing that Taylor was certainly influential and stimulating, he said, 'I don't think that truth is what he's been particularly concerned with.' Taylor overheard; and rather than coming back with a riposte of equal bite – as he would have done in his prime – he was deeply offended and snapped venomously that 'There are many things in your life and career I particularly dislike.' He would accept no explanation or apology, insisted on being taken home early, refused to thank Henderson for the party and never spoke to him again.⁹⁶

Taylor's next and penultimate book (the last was the book of the television lectures, *How Wars End*) was a lightweight book of essays entitled *An Old Man's Diary*. Chatto & Windus, an old established publishing house, had first proposed that Taylor's *London Review of Books* Diary pieces be collected together and published. This was in mid-December 1982, and a week later André Deutsch, of the eponymous publishing house, suggested the same thing. Five months later a third publisher, John Spiers of Harvester Press, also suggested such a collection. Taylor was pleased, but suggested that they wait until there was more to show. By May 1983 he thought that there might be enough: twelve Langham Diary pieces published in the *Listener* in 1981; fifteen (eventually seventeen) Diary pieces from the *London Review of Books* for 1982 and 1983; and the Romanes Lecture, which he had given in Oxford in February 1982. Bruce Hunter was free to offer it round. Taylor thought that he would like to have a change from Hamish Hamilton, since *A Personal History* had contained an unacceptable number of printing errors. But Hunter talked him out of this, partly because it would look very strange for him to move publisher after nearly forty years, and *An Old Man's Diary* was published in April 1984 by Hamish Hamilton.⁹⁷

By this time, the deterioration in Taylor's health, increasingly noticeable since 1980, was accelerating. This was especially poignant, because he and Éva had evolved a settled married life, going on day-trips, having friends to dinner, making occasional longer journeys and in general weaving their lives together. But three separate maladies hit him: a prostate operation in July 1982, although there were no unbearable after-effects; a virulent form of Parkinson's disease, which was diagnosed in 1982 and which increasingly manifested itself as the 1980s drew on; and an accident in January 1984, when he was knocked down by a car. Parkinson's disease, which eventually killed Taylor, attacks the part of the brain that controls movement; the most obvious manifestation is a trembling in the limbs, in particular the hands, which can gradually become uncontrollable through shaking. (Taylor's hands never shook.) The disease attacks different people in different ways and, as it transpired, Taylor could type long after his handwriting had become nearly illegible. Another symptom suffered by Taylor was a tendency to shuffle when trying to walk. Drugs can to some extent control its impact, but unfortunately for Taylor these made him nauseous. Worse still, he was one of the approximately one-third of sufferers whose brain is so weakened that they deteriorate mentally as well as physically.

At first the disease seemed to be under control. Indeed, he even felt able to write about it and its consequences in one of his *London Review of Books* Diary pieces. When they went to Budapest in 1982 and consulted a highly recommended specialist on Parkinson's disease, he told Taylor and his wife that 'Professor Taylor, you will be less and less bright, but as you are so clever, nobody will notice it' – and they all laughed. But as Éva described in her diary, 'Alan was hit by a car on January 6 [1984], in Old Compton Street [in Soho, whilst crossing the street after buying some fresh coffee beans]. Since then life is painful and grey, especially for Alan. He fights well; his accident was in a way lucky, because his pelvis was not broken but only hurt and he had to spend three weeks in the Middlesex Hospital. When he came home we made the necessary arrangements in the house and though Alan feels the end is not far away, he tries hard to get back his ability to walk properly.' In April he began to have problems with his bladder, partly as a result of the Parkinson's disease, and after developing a very high temperature he went in an ambulance to University College Hospital. He remained there for three weeks: he developed septicaemia, he became delirious and he lost the ability to recognise people, even thinking that Éva was Margaret. He returned home in May, and after various setbacks recovered, but he could no longer work properly.[98]

Thereafter, he went steadily downhill. The last entry in his list of books read was dated December 1985; that same month he told Éva that his mind was 'disorderly', that he could no longer think in a controlled way. This was particularly tragic. The final sentence of his autobiography had proclaimed his hope: 'Maybe my physical powers will gradually fail, indeed they are failing already. My intellectual powers are undiminished and I intend they should remain that way.' Even more poignant in the circumstances was his statement, as recorded by Éva, that 'in his whole life his principle was that it is not the fairness and niceness of a man that is the most important thing, but his brain.' As the disease took increasing hold, he knew what was happening; he also knew that there was little he could do about it. In March 1986 he could with great effort attend his birthday dinner in the Soho restaurant the Gay Hussar. But the time came when Éva, who had been determined to keep him at home, could control him no longer, and on 12 November 1987 he was admitted to Moss Lodge, a nursing home in Finchley, north London.[99]

Taylor just about knew what was happening, and he hated it. Angry and confused, he tried to run away that night. Two days later he told Martin Gilbert. 'I am compelled to be here.'[100] His decline was uneven, but relentless. Sometimes he would recognise people, sometimes not. For another year he could sometimes write notes, but that ability faded too. He still listened to chamber music, he still loved having Éva around and she usually spent whole days with him. The slow drawing-down of blinds was inexorable, but, mercifully, by that time Taylor was past knowing: his once-magnificent brain had effectively ceased to work.

Chapter 7

The Business History of the History Business: How Taylor Built his Freelance Career 1934–1990

This is a thing all my own. I am a scholar selling my wares.

A.J.P. Taylor, '(Un)quiet Flows the Don:
Alan Taylor Starts a "Revolution" on ITV', *TV Times*, 9 August 1957.

Once I discovered that I could earn money more easily by becoming a journalist I slipped out of teaching history and I can almost say became an historian in my spare time. But I think I remained a good historian: careful about my sources, trying to set down the truth of history as I saw it. I have never belonged to a school of history, whether Marxism or Annales. I am a plain narrative historian and I hope I gave the reader plenty of entertainment as well. For me writing history has been Fun on a high academic level. Add television lectures which combined history and entertainment and my enjoyment was complete. I would not have changed my professional life for any other in the world.

A.J.P. Taylor, *A Personal History*

One of the great and continuing pleasures of Taylor's adult life was his skill and success as a broadcaster on both radio and television. Another was his skill and success as a journalist. The third was the money he made from these activities. He needed this income, for he had some expensive tastes – such as fast cars and fine wines – and he had eventually to support two separate families as well as a third wife. In the writing of books, learned articles and book reviews, he was no different from other academics, except in the level of his productivity. Other historians, such as G.M. Trevelyan, had previously made large amounts of money from books, perhaps serendipitously when a book coincided with popular interest.[1] But Taylor deliberately set out to maximise his income as a 'scholar selling his wares' and exploited outlets for his 'wares' that other scholars were too proud or too unbusinesslike to use. In addition to his academic career, he developed a parallel and equally important career as a freelance historian, possibly the first to run two such careers. By 1950 his freelance income exceeded his academic salary; by 1958 it was probably three times as much. Taylor accomplished this by transferring his lecturing skills from the lecturing hall to the television studio, and by transferring his writing skills from learned book reviews and academic monographs to respectable pieces of *haute vulgarisation*, then to political leaders and finally to columns in the popular press.

Looking over Taylor's freelance career, it is possible to extract certain rules of procedure which the aspiring freelance might usefully ponder. The first step is to build up an area of expertise. In Taylor's case this was, in the first instance, nineteenth-century diplomatic history, with particular knowledge of the Austro-Hungarian Empire and the Successor States, especially Austria, Hungary, Czechoslovakia and Yugoslavia, and then nineteenth-century Germany. The second step is to publish a good book or two. Here one should emphasise the usefulness of a patron, in this case Lewis Namier. During his first three years at Manchester, Namier was instrumental both in getting Taylor's early books published and in setting him on his reviewing career, in the first instance with the *Manchester Guardian*. The third step, arranging a steady sideline in book reviewing, grew out of his *Guardian* contacts; this gave Taylor practice in communicating to non-specialists and indeed to non-historians, and gained him exposure in a national newspaper. The fourth step is to move beyond book reviewing into wider popular and political articles. The fifth step is the crucial leap: becoming a regular radio broadcaster and then television personality. This increased visibility and recognisability made him attractive to the popular press, a most lucrative position to command: he became, for successive newspapers, the house intellectual with the common touch.

The key factor when building a public career such as this is subject: it must be one which is relevant to public interests and concerns. It is of limited use being witty beyond measure about Anglo-Saxon England or Persian carpets. Taylor's field – modern, indeed contemporary, European history – was, in the years surrounding the Second World War, central to public discussion. It is also crucial to be perceived as an expert. Taylor's freelance work began as a result of his expertise in a subject: he did not come to attention only, and certainly not at first, because of the quality and quirky nature of his mind. It was important therefore that he continued to publish, from the 1930s through to the 1960s, at least two books a decade of scholarly worth. His expertise was thereby repeatedly validated, and those who employed him knew that they were hiring someone who was not only skilled at producing the material they required, but was learned enough for his accuracy to be trusted and his opinions generally accepted in the outside world. Taylor's reward? Fame and money.

Taylor first book, *The Italian Problem in European Diplomacy, 1847–1849* (1934), received good reviews. At the time Namier was one of the *Manchester Guardian*'s reviewers, responsible for new history books, but when in November 1934 he could not be bothered to review a biography of Robespierre, he passed it on to Taylor. The Editor of the *Guardian*, W.P. Crozier, looked favourably on Taylor because of Crozier's own close relationship with Namier,[2] but he might also have been influenced by the favourable review that had appeared in his own paper that year of Taylor's own book. (Crozier might also have accepted the substitution because he needed to fill a looming hole in the review section of the paper.) This was not the first book review written by Taylor: in June 1928 he had reviewed *The Life of Dickens* by John Foster for the *Saturday Review*. Taylor himself had made this first contact, calling on the Editor, Gerald Barry, in his office. Barry asked Taylor to show him what he could do. Taylor had over the years read all of Dickens's novels and had just read Foster's *Life*. He wrote a two-thousand-word review which Barry liked so much that he printed it as the principal article of the week. Taylor himself refers to it as 'quite good in its way',[3] and indeed it is. Many such first pieces, because of the inexperience of the reviewer, are grounded in the particulars of the book under review; Taylor, conversely, made large points, not only about the book itself but about the society in which Dickens moved. It was a very confident début.

The review of *Maximilian Robespierre* was not on the same scale as his review of the Dickens biography, but it breathes the same self-confidence. Crozier liked it, and Taylor wrote eleven reviews for the paper the following year. According to Taylor, at first the literary editor gave books to Namier to review and Namier continued to pass them on to Taylor, but soon the editor cut out the middleman and turned directly to him.[4] He became a regular reviewer, and by 1937 a frequent one: that year and the following one, he published twenty-seven reviews, and the resulting payments increased his income during those two years by nearly forty per cent.

Taylor's relationship with the *Manchester Guardian* was crucial to his professional development in a number of ways. First of all, he gained experience in writing book reviews on a number of subjects. It is worth noting, in fact, that he inverted the usual pattern. Ordinarily an academic begins by reviewing for academic journals; only later, and in many cases never, will the academic be invited to review for papers and periodicals which pay for the result. In Taylor's case, he wrote for the *Guardian* for two years before being asked to review for *International Affairs*, a hybrid journal, half academic and half public affairs; only in 1943 did he begin reviewing for the *English Historical Review*, the quintessential academic journal, for which he continued to review (unpaid) for most of his active life.

More important for his career in general was his relationship with A.P. Wadsworth, first labour correspondent and leader writer, then Assistant Editor from 1940 and from 1944 the Editor of the *Manchester Guardian*; Wadsworth early on became Taylor's closest friend in Manchester. More than a journalist, Wadsworth was also a considerable economic historian himself; his own interest in history encouraged him to commission Taylor to write not just reviews but lengthy pieces of history, especially ones drawing out historical parallels, and historical biography. He certainly attuned Taylor to anniversaries: throughout his later career Taylor repeatedly suggested anniversary pieces of one type or another – the death of Napoleon III, the Jameson Raid, the outbreak or the end of wars – to editors and producers.

Beyond giving Taylor the opportunity to write, he was responsible, according to Taylor himself, for teaching him how to write: 'Wadsworth taught me to write taut journalistic prose. He constantly said to me, "An article in the *Guardian* is no good unless people read it on the way to work." I followed his instruction, worrying about my style as much as about my scholarship. In my opinion the writings of an historian are no good unless readers get the same pleasure from them as they do from a novel.'[5] Indeed, any reader tackling Taylor's books in sequence will not fail to notice the development of his prose style, from lucid, elegant and long sentences to lucid, short and snappy ones. He also cultivated an increasing love of paradox in his writing, but this cannot be blamed on Wadsworth. What did emerge from this period was Taylor's trademark approach: begin with a short and arresting first sentence, write clearly, and maintain a strong theme.

In the guidelines for a freelance career set out above, emphasis was placed on developing a field of expertise, and it is worth pausing to consider what Taylor's original field was. He was an historian of modern Europe, of the relations between the European states. He developed an early expertise on the history of Austro-Hungary and its Successor States: anyone working in nineteenth-century diplomatic history had to deal with the Habsburg Empire, since it was one of the Great Powers. The topic on which Taylor did his initial research had the Chancellor of the Habsburg Empire, Prince Klemens Metternich, as a major character; his second book project was translating and providing the Introduction to Friedjung's *The Struggle for Supremacy in Germany 1859– 1866*, which detailed the conflict between Germany and Austria. His two years in Vienna had made a great impact: as noted above, Taylor always felt more at home in Austria than in any other foreign country, as well as most at home in the language. Furthermore, Henriette Werner, his children's nanny, was a Viennese political refugee, and his friendship with the Hungarian aristocrat and political dissident Michael Karolyi cemented his interest in Hungary.

For the needy editor or producer, Taylor's expertise in this field – underlined for them by the publication of his *The Habsburg Monarchy* in 1941 – was of continuing value. During the 1930s crucial political crises centred on these countries: the Austrian Anschluss, the Czechoslovak crisis, the Munich Agreement and the guarantee to Poland in 1939. Taylor could give their historical contexts and explain them to newspaper readers. This remained the case during the war, when he increased and tightened his links with Czechoslovakia and Yugoslavia. After the war, the attention of the world was repeatedly drawn to east central Europe, where the domino theory was played out, as one state after another fell to Soviet-supported Communist governments. Taylor's academic credentials kept him in demand.

But he was not a one-topic man, and it was his other area of expertise, that of German history, which was to emerge as the more important over the long run. The history of Germany was central to the work of any diplomatic historian, and certainly it was a natural progression for Taylor to turn to it after his work on Austria, if for no other reason than it formed the topic of the book by Friedjung he had helped to translate. The immediate outcome was *Germany's First Bid for Colonies, 1884–1885*, published in 1938. Taylor himself noted that the publication date was felicitous: the book, he wrote, 'had a stroke of luck in that, thanks to the usual printing delays, it came out just when the return of the German colonies had become a favourite theme of the appeasers and so provided splendid material for the opponents of appeasement.'[6] It also meant that, for an academic book, it was widely reviewed.

His fame as an historian of Germany was consolidated, however, with his first best-seller, *The Course of German History*, published in 1945. It was written in a 'journalistic' rather than academic style and remains extremely readable; it also ran with the grain of the public's perception of Germany at the end of the war. When this was followed in 1954 by *The Struggle for Mastery in Europe 1848–1918*, in 1955 by *Bismarck: The Man and the Statesman* and finally in 1961 by *The Origins of the Second World War*, Taylor's reputation as an historian of Germany could be matched in editorial and producer circles by few.[7] Therefore, just as the general public's interest in east central Europe began to decline, Taylor's other main area of expertise, Germany, became central. Indeed, Germany, in history and in politics, provided the main intellectual thread running through his career.

With such a wide and increasing range of interests and knowledge at his command, and with his willingness to work, Taylor built up his book-reviewing career during the 1930s. In 1938 he began to write longer and more specifically historical pieces for the *Manchester Guardian*, his first, 'The Case of Mr Eden: An Historical View', drawing historical parallels with previous French and British resignation crises. This was the type of thing very much encouraged by Wadsworth, but they were to bring an unexpected future benefit: many of these pieces would also swell his freelance income in the future when they reappeared as essays in his books. Taylor was to continue to write them for twenty years. The *Guardian* also provided the opportunity to cut his teeth on writing specifically political pieces. In 1944, 'as the staff of the *Manchester Guardian* dwindled,' Taylor later wrote, 'Wadsworth, now its editor, set me on to write leaders, dictating them afterwards over the telephone. This was a glamorous and undreamt of opportunity. Towards the end of the war I was writing most of the leaders on foreign affairs – in May 1945 three in a week.'[8] There were not, in fact, all that many during the war – four in 1944 and eight in 1945 – and as Taylor became more and more publicly anti-American (and pro-Soviet), he lost his usefulness as a leader writer for Wadsworth, who became one of the firmest supporters of the Anglo-American alliance amongst British newspapermen.[9] Nevertheless, the experience was invaluable and would be put to good use during the 1950s, when he began writing political commentaries of a most robust sort for the popular press.

Before he could move into that world, however, Taylor had to become more widely known. He did so largely by means of his early broadcasting career. It was the war which fostered his leap over the print barrier into the world of broadcasting, first radio and later television. This new activity grew out of his war work, lecturing on European history and current affairs to undergraduates, adult education classes, the forces and civilians all around the Thames Valley region. Taylor found that he liked explaining these matters, and decided to try and widen his ambit. As already described, in February 1942 he wrote to the BBC, and in response Trevor Blewitt, a producer in the Radio Talks Department, invited him up to London to audition as a speaker in the series 'The World at War – Your Questions Answered', which was to go out on the Forces' Radio.[10] Forces' Radio, or the Forces' Programme, as it was also called, had been set up in January 1940 specifically to broadcast to British forces at home and abroad, with a remit to be 'lighter' than the Home Service; within two months, however, it had even more civilians than servicemen as listeners.[11] Taylor made his first appearance on 17 March 1942, for a fee of fifteen guineas.

Early on in the war it had become clear that most of the more intelligent listeners were interested in public affairs and not just in dance music; once the Phoney War ended and the fighting war began, listeners in general wanted more information about what was happening. However, what listener surveys, especially of soldiers, showed was that talks as such, even on worthy themes, were not appreciated, and if such things had to be broadcast they should be 'topical and short'. A programme such as 'Your Questions Answered', met these audience requirements.[12] Taylor enjoyed himself, although he later claimed that he did not think this work very important, except that it taught him radio technique.[13] It also gave him access to a new world – and if nothing else, it provided a change from giving tutorials for twenty hours a week at Magdalen. There was then a glamour attached to radio perhaps akin to that now attached to television.

Certainly Taylor worked at his contributions – he drafted and redrafted. Radio technique did not come easily. An internal BBC memorandum dated the day before his first talk indicates what was involved: 'Here is Taylor's script. We are asking him to re-write the introduction: he stresses "guessing" too much. We are also asking him to introduce a breathing space into the script – at present it is tough going for our audience. The script also is too long: cuts will be made.'[14] He would soon learn how many pages of script were required for a programme of ten minutes or fifteen or twenty, a very useful skill for the future. His technique with a microphone also needed work. In the autumn of 1945 Taylor wrote to Blewitt admitting that it took time to become a good broadcaster and that he had some doubts about his own presentation abilities: 'I got off on the wrong foot a little by being nervous.' He added that he should be 'faster and gayer', but that his attempts to pitch his voice lower might 'end by sounding artificial'.[15] The following month Blewitt wrote to Taylor, asking when he would next be in

London 'so that we may have another playback of your discussion and do some hard work on your broadcasting style in the studio.'[16] 'Natural talent' is something of an oxymoron, and Taylor worked hard at mastering broadcasting techniques.

Taylor made seven radio appearances between March and June 1942, all on the same programme, 'Your Questions Answered'. He then ceased to appear until 1944. There were two possible reasons for this. One might have been as a result of Communist pressure: he wrote to Blewitt on 4 September 1942 that 'the Communists are running a campaign against me in Oxford and are saying, amongst other things, that as a result of my answer about the *Daily Worker*, I have been barred from the BBC. I assume this is quite untrue, but I should like to be sure.' No answer remains in the files, but it may well have been that he *was* barred from the programme, although not from the BBC. The other, more probable, reason was that he and the BBC producers could not agree on what he could or should do. Blewitt wrote to him on 7 December 1942 to ask if they could meet in order to 'discuss one or two ideas for programmes'. On 25 September 1943 Taylor was asked to give a talk on Austria, but he turned it down: 'I have always been reluctant to be connected with propaganda to Austria, as I think that anything except propaganda to the Social Democrats will have dangerous consequences. The best thing for Austria would be to become part of Czechoslovakia, but that is not a practical proposition; and the alternative, sooner or later, is that it will again become part of Germany.' In February 1944 there was some discussion as to whether Taylor should broadcast on France – did he know anything about it, did he like France, was he any good at the microphone? – and then a decision against Taylor's proposal that he should talk about the Anglo-French Entente on its fortieth anniversary in favour of someone with 'practical experience'.[17]

He did not broadcast again until 26 October, when he joined three other speakers for a talk on 'The Future of Germany'.[18] This was the real beginning of his radio career: he made three appearances that year, but twenty in 1945. He broadcast on the Home Service now and again, including once on 'The Brains Trust' in January 1945, but he broadcast much more often on the Overseas Service. This had begun broadcasting in December 1932 as the Empire Service, had become the General Overseas Service in 1943 and would in due course turn into the World Service.

The BBC had continuing difficulties with Taylor. The Corporation was very bureaucratic, and this fed into programme-making: for example, for a fifteen-minute programme of commentary on foreign affairs with Vernon

Bartlett (journalist on the *News Chronicle* and experienced broadcaster) and Barbara Ward (author and Assistant Editor of *The Economist*), the producer expected Bartlett to draft questions, Taylor and Ward to write answers and Bartlett then to write his comments on their comments – and then all of them to read the resulting script and pretend it was spontaneous. Taylor's response was that 'the scheme sounds rather complicated. I do not think that there is time in a quarter of an hour for three people to say much worth saying' – and besides, such comments would hardly be related to the points the others were making.[19]

More serious for the Corporation than his modest ridicule of their procedures was their increasing concern that Taylor would upset people by what he said – the listeners, the Foreign Office, later the political parties. One example arose from his speaking on Trieste in the series 'World Affairs: A Weekly Survey' for the Home Service on 24 September 1945, shortly after he had published the pamphlet arguing that Trieste should be part of Yugoslavia, not Italy. Taylor realised that he had overstepped the mark and hastily tried to pacify and reassure the Controller of Talks. He was successful on this occasion, and he continued to broadcast for the 'World Affairs' series into mid–1946, speaking on, for example, Soviet policy, the Middle East and postwar policy. By May 1946, however, Blewitt had decided that they should not use Taylor again in that particular series, a decision presumably triggered by his talk on 8 May entitled 'The First Year of Victory'. This was, Blewitt explained,

> not so much because he is a cause of anxiety every time we put him on, as because I think his admirable qualities (courage, intellectual brilliance, if not profundity, ability to avoid the claptrap of the age, whether from Right or Left, vigour) are vitiated by a certain cynicism which is out of place in an objective and ultimately educational series for the ordinary listener. The cynicism has been kept in check in the past, but possibly because Taylor has not been granted his request for a higher fee, or because in any case he feels broadcasting is not worth while, or even because he has been irritated by the inevitable whittling-down process involved in getting a script on the air, he does seem to me to have let his cynicism 'rip' – and it is apparent in his tone of voice at the microphone as much as in the 'tone' of his script.

George Barnes, the Assistant Controller of Talks, agreed, adding that he objected to Taylor's 'stating his conjectures and opinions as objective facts'.[20]

Therefore, Taylor's broadcast on 12 June, 'The Problem of Germany', was his last for the series. However, no one at the BBC told him so, and he was left to dry on the vine. He was finally driven to write to Blewitt in September, pointing out his absence from 'World Affairs' and asking whether he would be used again. 'I don't expect the BBC to invite me if they don't like what I say; but I think that, since I have worked regularly in the series and aroused interest in some listeners, I deserve the courtesy of some explanation instead of being ignored as though I had committed some crime.'[21] This seems a reasonable request, but there is no record of an answer from Blewitt.

What appears to have been decided was that Taylor should be shunted out of the Home Service into the newly established Third Programme, where, Blewitt wrote, he would be extremely useful.[22] He was not, the BBC decided, the man for a mass audience. The Third Programme, which began broadcasting in September 1946, was directed at a 'highly intelligent minority audience', and had programmes at 'a high cultural level devoted to the arts, serious discussion and experiment'.[23] The target Third Programme listener could be expected to cope with Taylor's stimulating but provocative ideas; the fact that it would be broadcasting only between 6pm and midnight could be expected to eliminate the less-sophisticated daytime listener. In August 1946, therefore, Blewitt wrote to Taylor with the request that he write and broadcast in a series called 'The Roots of British Foreign Policy'; other broadcasters would include E.H. Carr and Arnold Toynbee. Taylor agreed.

Taylor's four programmes, one on the need for controversy in public debate on foreign affairs – i.e. in favour of clear thinking and against a stifling consensus – and three on Britain's relations with the US, with Russia and with Europe respectively, caused an uproar. Of particular concern to the government was Taylor's unfavourable comparison of the US with the USSR: the US economy would soon collapse, he had predicted, whilst the Soviet economy went from strength to strength; at the same time, he said, Russia had neither the power nor the will to follow any aggressive foreign policy. As printed in the *Listener*, Taylor argued that the only way the UK could 'remain prosperous and a Great Power, is the policy of the Anglo-Russian alliance'. He rammed the point home with what was, by then, a typical peroration: 'the advantages of co-operation between Russia and England are so obvious and ... the dangers of association with America are so blatant that I am amazed that even the fog of a century of suspicion, thickened up by the smoke of ill-informed anti-Marxism, is enough to keep England and Russia apart.'[24] In another of the talks he described American foreign policy as one that would become 'increasingly selfish, harsh and self-interested', in that US strategic policy cared not for Britain as an ally but only for its use as 'an aircraft carrier from which to discharge atomic bombs'. Therefore, he advised Britain to dissociate itself from the 'present policy of becoming an economic and military satellite of the United States ... [which] is neither necessary nor workable.'[25]

Politicians reacted with an attack upon Taylor in the House of Commons. Chunks of his talk were read out in the House by Henry Strauss, MP for the Combined English Universities, while Herbert Morrison, the Lord President of the Council, called them 'anti-American, anti-British and not particularly competent'.[26] Taylor had hit a particularly tender nerve of the Labour government, relations with the US. Indeed, the Foreign Office was very much concerned in the early postwar years about the damage that expressions of British anti-Americanism might do to Anglo-American relations, and Taylor's remarks had not helped.[27] The Foreign Office may well have insisted that the BBC take him off the air, as Taylor was later to claim in his autobiography: certainly the Foreign Office Index in the Public Record Office shows that two letters on Taylor were sent by the Information Department of the Foreign Office to the BBC, although the letters themselves were not preserved in the PRO nor can they be located in the BBC Archives.[28] This episode damaged his relations with present and future Labour grandees, and may have helped to ensure that Taylor never received any position, honour or gift in the hands either of the Crown or of the politicians.

Others joined in the condemnation. The next speaker on the programme was R.C.K. Ensor, journalist and historian (he had written *England 1870–1914* in the Oxford History of England series), broadcasting on 'Difficulties of Modern Diplomacy'. During his talk he made a remarkable attack on Taylor: 'What I disapproved in him was not merely the substance of his talks, but the manner. The substance to my thinking consisted too largely of shallow half-truths, more dangerous than plain untruths because more specious, yet not a bit more trustworthy to build on. But I also, if I may say so without needless discourtesy, objected profoundly to his jaunty cocksure manner.'[29] Ensor clearly felt that this was just the sort of discourtesy which Taylor required.

Taylor was driven to respond. He wrote to Harman Grisewood, the Director of Talks, that 'it almost appears that since I have been attacked in the House of Commons the BBC also welcomes the opportunity to have a jab at me. . . . I daresay that it did not occur to you or others that I had feelings to be hurt, but I have.' He wanted to answer Ensor, but Grisewood refused to give him the chance, responding: 'I do not feel that what Ensor said exceeds the limits that are appropriate to a series of this kind in which speakers have been frankly critical of their predecessors, and of other personalities that are connected with the subject in hand.' Taylor had to accept this, but he made it clear to Grisewood that he was not mollified: he still thought personal abuse on the air was a bad thing, 'but respect precedent for me!'[30]

Taylor had found the need to keep up with current affairs 'almost a full-time job', and this, plus his suspicion that the BBC had run out of patience with his provocative comments on these subjects, encouraged him to turn to a safer and less time-specific field: history. On the same day in September that he wrote to Blewitt complaining about being dropped from 'World Affairs', he also wrote to Barnes that 'I am anxious to escape from the controversies of political commentary into the more serious talks of history and I think I have some suggestions that might appeal to you.' He received an encouraging response from Grisewood, who wrote that he was 'positively interested' in a series on prime ministers, for which he would like Taylor to be general editor.[31] Whilst launching Taylor into a new type of broadcasting, this series too, was not to be without its problems.

Taylor proposed six programmes on British prime ministers of the nineteenth century. His first suggestion was that he himself should give all six lectures; in the end, however, it was decided that he would begin and end the series, with lectures on Lord John Russell and Lord Salisbury. Difficulties soon arose as Taylor and Blewitt tried to commission the other lectures. A.L. Rowse and Lord David Cecil, who had both shown some interest, cried off. Taylor explained matters to Blewitt: 'You see, you are dealing with academic persons, not with journalists, and they need months of preparation to write the simplest article. To the academic mind a month is too short notice; besides they fear any kind of public appearance.'[32] Or looked at another way, for anyone who has a full range of academic duties, the request to produce such a piece within a month, for an unfamiliar medium and to a high standard, could seem daunting. Furthermore, for many in academic life, it might seem irrelevant: as Peter Laslett, a BBC producer (and future historian of *The World We Have Lost*), wrote in 1950, few people in university society paid much attention to radio, and even those who did 'would read what had been broadcast rather than listen to it.'[33] Besides, for many, such a public performance would seem vulgar.

Taylor's own script on Lord John Russell seemed to him – or so he wrote to Blewitt – 'a little academic and dry, but I thought that the Third Programme might be interested in ideas'. They claimed to be, but Taylor had the wrong sort. Delivered on 7 March 1947 (and published in the *Listener* on 20 March), the talk aroused quite disproportionate anger and disgust in the BBC. For George Barnes, now Controller of the Third Programme, the script raised two questions: how history could effectively be dealt with in broadcasting, and Taylor's suitability. For the question of history in general, he had no immediate answer, beyond castigating Taylor's script as 'dogmatic': 'in a 20-minute broadcast', he wrote, 'where one cannot rely upon much background knowledge, even in an educated audience, such dogmatic phrases stick in the mind'. Neither Taylor nor his producer, Blewitt, Barnes wrote, had thought about this fundamental problem. As for Taylor himself, 'his business is to shock – an appropriate one for an audience of undergraduates whose business is to read the sources on which Taylor draws, but a dangerous method for a listener without background'. Barnes particularly disliked Taylor's comment that 'theology and classics are the most useless studies known to man.'[34]

The cause of all of this was hardly an iconoclastic, fire-breathing piece: the text of the talk is thoughtful and interesting, and whilst a number of comments are arresting, it is favourable and even a bit affectionate towards Russell. When one remembers that the Third Programme was intended to appeal to 'a highly intelligent minority audience' with programmes at 'a high cultural level devoted to ... serious discussion', the anxious patronising of listeners' capacities by Barnes and his colleagues seems inexplicable. Asa Briggs provided at least part of the answer when he wrote in his history of the BBC during the period 1945–55 that 'It was the function of "Talks", *inter alia*, to stimulate and to reassure, and it took a long time for a place to be left in Talks policy also for provocation or shock.'[35]

Barnes himself gave in an internal BBC paper in 1948 his preferred definition of a broadcast talk as one that 'does not quite speak like a book ... it is thinking aloud'.[36] What he wanted was more dependable thoughts. Laslett had shot over to Cambridge to try and interest Michael Oakeshott and Herbert Butterfield in giving talks – 'we'll do all right with the really good men' – and whilst there he discovered how much out of favour Taylor was: he was 'one of the names which has caused trouble in the Cambridge Historical Faculty'. It is impossible to know to whom Laslett spoke: as far as Taylor was concerned, the criticism 'came from those who would have liked to do the talks themselves, and even from some who declined to take part in them and then objected to others doing so.' Whoever it was, their strictures only reinforced both Barnes and Grisewood in their assessment of Taylor as 'second-rate or [at least] has made himself so'.[37]

After Taylor's second talk, on Lord Salisbury, Grisewood wrote to him: 'I would like to pass on to you a number of complaints that we have received about the Prime Ministers series, which I must say did a good deal disappoint us in the result.' In response Taylor cited Vita Sackville-West's review in the *New Statesman*, adding 'perhaps the BBC dislike talks which arouse too much interest'. This letter 'startle[d] [Grisewood] into indignation for a moment', but he then wrote ponderously that 'I shall return to this when we meet, if you do not think it humourless and ponderous of me. I would like to give you grounds for your belief to be otherwise than it now appears.' Barnes was more straightforward in his reply to the letter Taylor had written to him on the same day: to Taylor's charge that 'I think I am now permanently out of favour with the Talks Department. Praise from the Radio Critic of the *New Statesman* has been my ruin', Barnes told him that any fool could be provocative. He had his doubts not only about Taylor personally but more broadly about how the BBC should approach history: history was not a matter of snap judgements, and 'these talks did not make me alter my opinion that a lecture, however skilfully potted, will never obtain the interest of the critical listener in history'. If radio history was to contribute anything to the critical assessment of historical events, there was a lot of hard thinking to be done about methodology first of all.[38]

The decision had already been taken that they did not like Taylor's approach, and he had little future in radio talks as long as Barnes, who became Director of the Spoken Word in February 1948, controlled them. Indeed, Taylor hardly appeared in this capacity on the Home Service or the Third Programme over the next several years, although he started to broadcast more frequently for the Overseas Service. Yet in 1948 and 1949 he appeared on two programmes that were to lead him eventually to his real métier, television: these were 'The Brains Trust' for the Home Service and 'London Forum: Talking at Large' for the Overseas Service, programmes in which Taylor's ability to think on his feet and produce unexpected comments were rather more welcome.

'The Brains Trust' was the more famous programme: first broadcast in January 1941 and called then 'Any Questions', meant to be 'serious in intention, light in character', it was soon one of the BBC's more popular programmes.[39] Taylor had already appeared once before, in January 1945, and he made his second (and final) appearance in October 1948. His performances testified both to his ability to handle questions and to his name-recognition amongst the audience. It was probably his success here that led Grace Wyndham Goldie, a television producer, to respond favourably to his suggestion – a remarkably far-seeing and indeed forward one for an Oxford don – in December 1949 that he might embark upon a new medium: 'I wondered whether you ever had an opening for a lively talker on current affairs in television. As you know, I can do very nicely in impromptu discussion; and if you are ever thinking of this sort of thing, I'd be grateful if you'd think of me. I realise it is a new trade, but I'm not too old to learn it.' Wyndham Goldie wrote back: 'I am enchanted to hear that you might be induced to take part in some television discussions on current affairs. I am hoping to embark on some illustrated debates rather than discussions. The plan of them is not yet at all definite but when, in December, it was agreed that I should undertake some this spring, I had you very much in mind as a possible speaker if you could be persuaded into television.'[40] Taylor was viewed considerably more favourably at Alexandra Palace than at Broadcasting House, and within eight months he would indeed appear on television. In the event it was not this contact with Wyndham Goldie but 'London Forum: Talking at Large', a discussion programme with three participants, which led directly to his television debut. This was because it was run by Edgar Lustgarten, former news analyst, currently successful broadcaster and future editor of 'In the News', the vehicle for Taylor's rise to television fame.

The origins of 'In the News' lay in the need felt by Norman Collins, the Controller of Television, for a programme that would stimulate discussion rather than merely inform and that would at the same time entertain (his model was based on American programmes primarily involving interesting talking heads). Once the February 1950 general election was over, he 'determined that a regular series of topical discussions should be started on television.' Collins brushed aside any difficulties. 'It would be a very simple operation. All that was required was a more or less permanent team of informed people who would regularly discuss matters in the news. If the talks department could not undertake it he would make other arrangements. He considered that it should be possible to hire people from outside the television service and get them to work on contract. Edgar Lustgarten ... could be responsible for getting the people together and could possibly take the chair himself. John Irwin, an experienced television director, now freelancing, could be employed to direct the programme.'[41]

Lustgarten recruited the debaters he had used on radio. The first programme was broadcast on a Friday evening, 26 May 1950, with a team of four speakers: two Members of Parliament, the Conservative Robert Boothby and the left-wing Labour member Michael Foot; W.J. Brown, who had been an Independent MP; and the economist Donald McLachlan, Assistant Editor of the *Economist*. Taylor first appeared in the third programme, broadcast in August, and when in October 1950 'In the News' settled down to a weekly slot with a regular team, Taylor was one of them, the others being Boothby, Foot and Brown.

Taylor recalled that 'the BBC, usually so cheese-paring, treated us lavishly'. John Irwin's idea was to engender stimulating discussion between the speakers before recording, which would then carry over into the studio: 'the meeting place at the Albany is convenient both to Fleet Street and the House of Commons. Here, in comfortable surroundings and with some refreshment offered by Mr Lustgarten, the speakers have their preliminary discussion. At 6 : 30, a pleasant two-minutes' stroll to the Ecu de France, where they are given an agreeable meal in pleasant surroundings. At 7 : 30, into the motor-cars which take them to Lime Grove.'[42] The cameras were set and the lighting and sound adjusted, and then they were off for another break, this time in The British Prince, a pub at the end of Lime Grove. Then they went on the air at 10pm for a half-hour's spirited discussion. Finally, they all retired to John Irwin's flat in Holland Park to hear a playback of the recording of the programme over a nightcap. Judging from the reaction by the public, the result was most entertaining and very watchable. Judging by the reaction from the politicians, neither the speakers nor the content were necessarily what they wanted to watch. The BBC, and especially George Barnes, tried to rectify matters.

The BBC was meant to be independent, but it was also meant not to give preference to any particular political tendency. The problem with 'In the News' in this regard was that

> while it was not originally intended to be of political significance it rapidly became one of the most important political programmes regularly transmitted by the BBC. It was also immensely popular. The regular team of Boothby, Brown, A.J.P. Taylor and Michael Foot seemed, in combination, to provide a remarkable effervescence of wit, common-sense, intellectual honesty and political passion. Week after week matters in the news were discussed by intelligent men who seemed to be thinking independently, not merely mouthing the clichés of routine

party politics. But, paradoxically, since in creating a team which would discuss topical subjects it was felt necessary to maintain some sort of balance of political alignment, with Boothby and Brown considered to be roughly on the Right and Taylor and Foot roughly on the Left, the discussions quickly took the form of arguments of Right versus Left.'[43]

This was the signal for the political parties to take a close interest in the programme, especially in who spoke on it: surely, they thought, representatives of mainstream party opinion ought to appear, not those who clung to the rims of the parties. George Barnes, who had become Director of Television in mid-October 1950, certainly agreed, and he immediately insisted on this, writing to the Controller of Television on 30 October his

views on In the News at present: 1) It is a good idea and at its best is a good example of frank discussion. It has an excellent public relations side ... in that it brings MPs into contact with the Television Service and with the programmes which they so seldom see. 2) Policy: The personnel must change. The BBC's trust of impartiality in politics requires not only that the main parties should be balanced but that there should not be a single representative of each party over a long period of time ... the members should change one at a time pretty frequently. 3) Choice of speakers: The importance of choosing representatives of the main body of each political party must not be lost sight of in the programme value of the skirmishers on the flanks of the parties.[44]

Barnes's insistence was based not on his strength but on his timidity: as Wyndham Goldie put it, 'his combination of temperament and experience made him wary rather than courageous in his handling of the relationship between television and politics'.[45]

Over the next months, the political parties brought increasing pressure on the BBC. Should MPs appearing on 'In the News' (and other programmes) be regarded as representing the political party to which they belonged? If so, should their appearance be balanced by a representative of another party? And who should choose them? In March 1951 the Chairman of the BBC wrote to Barnes that 'The P.M.G. [Postmaster-General] was very interested in In the News and in the MPs who are used. He would like to go up to the studios and have a talk to you on this, and I assume other matters. I said I felt sure you would be glad to see him.' They may even have discussed Taylor, given that, at least in 1947, he was on Conservative

386 • Troublemaker: The Life and History of A.J.P. Taylor

Central Office's list of left-wing broadcasters, and he had done nothing since to ameliorate this reputation.[46] The pressure applied both directly and indirectly led Barnes to insist on lists of speakers for 'In the News' being drawn up and classified according to their political affiliation, since he was concerned about balance both between and within the parties. In February 1951 he asked a member of the News Division to remind Lustgarten 'of the need to get in an occasional straight Conservative', while in April he was concerned about the Labour balance: 'I see from this morning's newspapers that Mrs Castle, Driberg and Foot are supporting Bevan in the N.E.C. [the National Executive Committee of the Labour Party]. This of course makes it impossible for In the News between now and 25th May: (a) to use any two of these people together; (b) to have one of them in each of the remaining programmes.'[47] By October lists such as the following were appearing:

26 October: Hailsham (Orthodox Con)
    Brown (Indep. supporting Con.)
    Hynd (Orthodox Labour)
    Taylor (Indep. supporting Labour on this occasion)
2 November: Boothby (Con)
    Byers (Liberal)
    Hynd (Labour)
    Taylor (Left-wing Indep)[48]

By December 1951 Barnes was directly consulting the Conservative Chief Whip, Patrick Buchanan-Hepburn, about 'promising Conservative Members who might take part in the weekly political discussion on television entitled "In the News" ', and in February 1952 Buchanan-Hepburn, as a result of 'another talk with the Whips and the Central Office', sent Barnes an amended list of possible speakers.[49]

By September 1952 it had been decided that the regular team would only appear once a month, and that overall the 'appearance of the "regulars" would be limited to an average ratio of one in two for Brown and Boothby and three in four *between them* for M. Foot and Taylor.' Thereafter Taylor appeared seven times in eighteen programmes. (Between May 1950 and May 1952 he had appeared thirty-eight times plus once as chairman.) Taylor became increasingly worried about how the programme was going: 'I can't go on indefinitely being the only non-politician in a programme which is becoming more and more a party debate,' he wrote to Barnes in

October 1952. Barnes wrote back soothingly: 'Do not worry. If In the News becomes as dull as a Party debate we shall have to take it off but I do not myself share your misgivings about this tendency.'⁵⁰ The following month, Taylor took things into his own hands. He objected strongly both to the policy of 'dilution' of the original team and to the attempt by the political parties to 'manipulate' the discussion, and in a dramatic moment during the programme on 15 November 1952 he made his objections clear.

> When one of the Tory MPs referred, somewhat confusingly, to 'you Leftish organisations', Alan interrupted: 'I am no organisation. I represent absolutely nobody, I'm glad to say, but myself, nobody nominates me, though many people try to prevent my appearance.' The discussion turned to the subject of the Rent Restriction Acts. Alan took no part in the debate, besides saying that he differed fundamentally on the issue from the Labour MP, the future Prime Minister James Callaghan. The argument became increasingly heated, with Callaghan interrupting and taunting one of the Tory MPs. Then Alan intervened. Horrified at the purely political statements being made, he denounced the politicians on the panel: 'When I was invited to take part in this programme, I thought that four individuals were to sit round the table and express their individual points of view, but this is too much like total-itarianism – except instead of there being one official party, there are two. No one seems to be allowed an individual belief.' The others were behaving like party 'automata'.

He announced that he would take no further part in the discussion and turned half away from the rest, presenting his back to them and his profile to the camera, looking grim and sulky. Callaghan tapped him on the shoulder, but Taylor kept stubbornly tight-lipped and silent for the three or four minutes of the programme that remained. The others continued their discussion until the end of the programme, at which point the Conserva-tive MP Marlowe got in his dig. Before he came in, he said, several people had asked him whether he could silence Taylor. 'I am glad that I have found a way of doing so.'⁵¹

When the broadcast ended, the BBC telephone switchboards were swamped with calls from viewers, whilst over the next few days what the director John Irwin described as Taylor's 'expression of vehement emotion' provoked 254 letters, some criticising Taylor, some the chairman and some other members of the team. Irwin himself defended Taylor as well as his own decision to keep him in shot: 'it seemed to me that he had not been rude to the viewers, and as the other members of the panel were in a position to comment on his attitude there was no need for me to exclude him from the screen. ... Whatever the ramifications this incident may have, it was TELEVISION.'[52]

The ramifications included what Barnes called 'resting' Taylor and what Taylor himself called being banned: as the minutes of the BBC's Board of Management put it, they 'approved [Barnes's] recommendation that, in view of Mr Alan Taylor's publicly expressed dislike of this programme as now constituted, he should be rested from it during the next quarter, or longer, and that he should be so informed after his next appearance in the programme on December 10th.' Barnes's letter to Taylor informing him of this was somewhat disingenuous: 'we have decided after much cogitation to retain In the News for the present on the lines on which it is run now, and we are now engaged in inviting the speakers for the next quarter's programmes. As you have expressed to me personally as well as in public your dissatisfaction with the programme as it is I have assumed that you will prefer not to take part until some alteration is made.'[53] He was not to appear on it again for nine months, after which he was invited occasionally, e.g. three times in 1954. The effect of Taylor's withdrawal was 'to diminish the appreciation index by five points, although the number of viewers remained fairly constant'.[54] The programme itself eventually died of boredom in 1954.

Taylor's appearances on 'In the News' shot him to fame, although, as Taylor himself put it, fame 'of a limited kind. There were only a few hundred thousand television sets in all. Few middle-class people had them and certainly no intellectuals. Most of the viewers came from the more prosperous, skilled working class – taxi drivers ... artisans, waiters and such like. ... I was hailed as the Plain Man's Historian, a description I did not disdain.'[55] It was to lead to a new life for Taylor as a Fleet Street columnist, but at the same time he widened his scope on television. He owed this opportunity to John Irwin, the director of 'In the News', who was to lead him first to the new independent television and then into giving television lectures.

Barnes had found the whole 'In the News' episode so nerve-wracking that he decided that the BBC had to take complete control of the programme; therefore, when in December 1952 Lustgarden and Irwin's contracts ran out, they were not renewed. In response, the pair immediately began to plan a rival programme to appear on commercial television, featuring the old team and called 'Free Speech' for reasons which the BBC would understand. In the event, many of the same people came together for 'Free Speech' as had been involved in 'In the News'. One was Norman Collins, who as BBC Controller of Television had acted as midwife for the discussion programme based on the American model. Because radio was believed by most BBC policy-makers to be the more important medium, the development of television was controlled by those whose interest and experience lay in radio. Collins had fought for more independence for television from control by radio from within the BBC and had become increasingly disenchanted; when in October 1950 a new Director of Television was appointed, and it was George Barnes rather than him, Collins immediately resigned. (In due course he became Vice-Chairman of the Associated Broadcasting Company, which became ATV.) Within months he was in contact with the Conservative Party broadcasting group, who were calling for competition for the BBC; in May 1952 the White Paper on broadcasting included the sentence 'The present [Conservative] government have come to the conclusion that in the expanding field of television provision should be made to permit some element of competition.'[56] Certainly the historians of both the BBC and of independent television believe that 'in the years between the White Paper of May 1952 and the enactment of the first Television Bill he [Collins] was to play a key role; and he probably did more than any other single man to achieve the creation of ITV'.[57]

Taylor actively campaigned for commercial television, serving as a Vice-President (along with eleven others) of the Popular Television Association. Many of the backers of the move for independent television were business interests, but others shared an animosity towards the BBC. Taylor was certainly one of this number, referring continually to the need for independent television as an alternative to the BBC in order to ensure 'freedom of the mind': as he wrote in an article published in the *Contemporary Review* in December 1953, the BBC was 'highly tolerant in whatever does not matter', the implication being that it was repressive in whatever did.[58] The opposition to independent television, led by the National Television Council, was organised and dominated by 'the great and the good', or what Taylor had in 1953 called 'the Establishment' (some time before Henry Fairlie had used the term in his famous *Spectator* article). The Council was formally set up in the home of Lady Violet Bonham Carter, and Vice-Presidents included Lord Beveridge, Julian Huxley, Bertrand Russell and Sir Harold Nicolson. While the watchword of the Popular Television

Association was freedom, that of the Council was 'the power of television for good', and the importance of moral responsibility in the television output.[59] The Labour Party naturally opposed the bill and threatened to nationalise any commercial television company upon their return to power. In the end the Conservative government opted for freedom over a moral tone, and the (Independent) Television Act was passed in July 1954.

Commercial television began broadcasting on Thursday, 22 September 1955. Three days later, on a Sunday afternoon, the first 'Free Speech' went out. According to Taylor, 'at first we had even more fun. We were experienced, even famous, and had fewer restraints. ... We were better paid and even more lavishly treated. This time it took place on Sunday afternoons, usually on the empty stage of an abandoned music hall. We had a superb lunch and staggered home afterwards to recover.'[60] The key to the popularity of the programme was its reuniting of the old team. Depending on what was in the news that week, the discussions could be ferocious. As the *Observer*'s television critic wrote in December 1955, the 'team seemed to be not only on the verge of, but actually, losing their tempers with each other over the desirability or otherwise of the House of Lords. Boothby boomed, Foot fumed, Taylor trephined, with apparent real malice. ... Anyway it was first-class television.'[61]

'Free Speech' continued to be broadcast for four years, until, as Taylor described it, 'Norman Collins, our patron from the beginning, turned against us. No doubt, like all television directors, he wanted a change. Also he developed political ambitions. The party organisation disliked *Free Speech* as much as it had disliked *In the News*, and it was hinted to Norman Collins that he might find a constituency available if he killed *Free Speech*, which he duly did in 1959.'[62] 'Free Speech' was important to Taylor: it was a most satisfactory revenge on the BBC and particularly on George Barnes; it brought him back into the popular, national media limelight, which paid dividends in both fame and money; and it provided a stepping stone to a more important and longer-lasting media position, that of the first television lecturer. In this, as in earlier Taylor advances, John Irwin was to prove the crucial man.

It all began with the Ford Lectures in English History. W.J. Brown and John Irwin came down to Oxford to hear the final lecture and dine with Taylor afterwards in Magdalen. As Taylor described it, 'I thought John Irwin had come just for a night out. Actually he had come professionally. I had told him I lectured without notes. He did not believe me. Having seen me in action, he was convinced and said to me, "If you can lecture like that, can you do it on television?" I said of course I could.'[63]

There was, of course, more to it than that. Irwin was certainly convinced: he was later quoted as saying that the lecture hall was packed, and that 'I've seen nothing like it. That audience was hypnotised by Taylor's dynamic personality, his passionate sincerity, his wit, his command of words, his brilliant sense of timing, and his complete mastery of the subject – without a single note.'[64] But there were others who also needed to be convinced, particularly Lew Grade, the Deputy Managing Director of ATV. Grade later described how he called Taylor in and asked him to talk to him about history.

> I was talking to Bill Ward, who was my Programme Controller, I said we need something for Sunday afternoon. He said, well, John Irwin saw a professor at Oxford give a lecture. I said, what does he lecture about? He says, history, he's a great historian. I says, I'm not sure whether I fancy that, but I'd like to meet him. Ask him if he'll come up to see me for ten minutes. He said fine, and then he fixed up a meeting, and he [Taylor] walked in, and seemed a nice man, he sat down, I said, what do you think you would like to do? He said, well, I'd like my first lecture to be on Russian history. I said, well, you know that will be very difficult for the public to understand. Why don't you tell me a little about it? And he started, and I was absolutely enthralled. I was actually born in Russia, I came here when I was five-and-a half years of age, and I learnt things I had never known, and it was put so simply, and so easily understandable, which was the secret of his success. You knew that here was a star, an unusual type of star.'[65]

The first lecture, transmitted on Monday (not Sunday), 12 August 1957, from 6 to 6.30pm, was carefully staged. ATV had its own studio, the Wood Green Empire, once a cinema, which it filled with an invited audience. A series of curtains was pulled back, one by one, to reveal an empty stage; at a signal Taylor began walking into the spotlight, eyes on his feet to avoid tripping over the cables, whilst the announcer portentiously intoned the 'Challenge': 'ATV presents an experiment. Can a brilliant historian talking about a fascinating subject hold the attention of a television audience of millions for half an hour? That is the question, and the answer lies with YOU. Our subject is the Russian Revolution, this evening's theme The End of the Tsars, our historian, Alan Taylor, Fellow of Magdalen College, Oxford.' Taylor then reached the middle of the stage, made an abrupt head-only bow, clasped his hands together in front of him, said 'Good evening' and began to tell the story of Lenin and the Swiss students in the last days of December 1916 when Lenin predicted that there would be no revolution in his lifetime. Periodically the camera moved from him to show the audience, made up of old and young, now looking serious, now smiling. He spoke for a half-hour, then walked carefully off the stage, trailing the cable behind him.

Taylor had felt – or at least stated that he felt – that 'It's not only me on trial, but the whole idea of lecturing on TV. . . . It is conceivable that I will be so bad that some of [the audience] will switch over to the BBC, but that is setting my sights very, very low.'[66] As it happened, the reverse was the case. ATV was clearly happy with the critical response and the viewing figures: they announced at the end of Taylor's third and final talk that he would be giving a longer series of lectures in the autumn. This was 'Alan Taylor Lectures: When Europe Was the Centre of the World', which consisted of eleven half-hour and two twenty-minute lectures on topics such as 'The Fall of the Bastille', the 'Revolutions of 1848', 'International Socialism', and 'The End of the Story: 1914'. Transmitted between 23 September 1957 and 10 March 1958, it drew an average audience of 750,000, a very good figure: it is estimated that at the end of 1956, 2,656,000 homes in London, the Midlands and the north were capable of receiving ITV.[67] It was the considered opinion of one experienced broadcaster that the magic lay in Taylor plus history: if Taylor 'chose to talk about a blade of grass he could keep his audience spellbound', but he talked about history – and 'history is interesting'.[68]

According to Taylor, for the next ten years he gave at least one, and sometimes two, series of six lectures each year. There was then a hiatus for ten years – his regular producer, John Irwin, retired, and as Taylor himself wrote, 'such is the rule in life: you must have a patron somewhere in the organization. Otherwise you slip down the ladder.' It is also probable that television decision-makers had decided that they were bored with Taylor and his unchanging approach to television. Some of these lectures are now lost forever – even their titles have been forgotten – but enough remain in archives to allow some consideration of style, both televisual style and Taylor's own.[69] Between July and September 1960, for example, Taylor gave another series for ATV, this time on British prime ministers. Consider the beginning of the lecture on Disraeli. It opens with a photograph of Number 10 Downing Street, in an endearing attempt by the producer to provide some pictorial context and interest, whilst trumpets sound and then fade as Taylor comes on stage – the music was certainly not written to time. By 1961, when he gave a series on the First World War for ATV, the producer's style had developed: each lecture begins with archive film of soldiers going over the top accompanied by period music played on a single harmonica – it is consciously atmospheric.

Taylor did not lecture only for ATV. Two of the series, that on the 1920s in 1962 and that on 'Men of the 1860s' in 1963, were in fact for the BBC, but this was because his producer, John Irwin, had left ATV and Taylor always worked with him whenever he could. He then lay dormant as a television lecturer from late 1967 until 1976. Again, Taylor owed his rejuvenation to a patron, in this case a former Oxford history student, Eddie Mirzoeff, who had attended Taylor's lectures as an undergraduate. Mirzoeff was now a BBC producer, and he approached Taylor, asking him why he was not lecturing on television.[70] The result was six lectures on 'The War Lords', which, compared to the 1960s lectures, demonstrated a great leap forward in television graphics and music: the introductory material was prepared to order, in colour, and with music cut to fit the visuals. Taylor also had a prop for each of these lectures: a gold-coloured cast of the appropriate face, whether Churchill's or Mussolini's. This was followed by a series of six lectures in 1977 on 'How Wars Begin' and then by another six in 1978 on 'Revolutions', both for the BBC. By the time he presented his last complete series, six lectures on 'How Wars End' given in 1984, the introduction had been developed to perfection: it combined colour graphics, newspapers and archive film both still and moving. This was accompanied by a motif played on a single plangent cello. The 1984 lectures also demonstrated an apotheosis of sorts, this time for Taylor himself: whereas each lecture of the war lords series had featured a cast of the appropriate leader, for these lectures the only appropriate face was apparently that of Taylor himself, and a glowing oval-shaped photograph appeared in the upper right-hand corner of the television screen as Taylor began to talk.

Television's presentation of talking heads – or at least the introductory matter – had clearly developed apace over the course of the nearly thirty years during which Taylor performed. But what about Taylor's style? Did it develop as well? The answer is, yes and no. Whilst viewing these lectures, one cannot help but notice little things, the habits and tics. Returning to his lecture on Disraeli for the prime ministers series in 1960: Taylor walked straight forward out of the dark into the light, stopped, coughed, rubbed his hands together in front of him, said 'Ladies and gentlemen' and began by comparing Disraeli to a giraffe. He did not know what to do with his hands:

within fifteen seconds of starting, he had rubbed them together, put them briefly into his pockets and then removed them, stuck them behind him in a manner which suggested that he was supporting a bad back, and then fiddled with his watch band. This continued whenever he talked alone on a naked stage for his lectures. The changed approach of the 1970s and 1980s, when he stood next to a cast or a picture, constrained him, and he neither fiddled with his hands so much, tending to keep them clasped in front of him, nor bounced up and down on the balls of his feet, nor turned so much from side to side. He had been chained.

But these are the small change of lecturing: in essence the style remained the same. As noted above, Taylor transferred his lecturing skills from the lecture hall to the television studio. What were the components of this style? The presentation was done without notes; it ran strictly to time; it was driven by stories and anecdotes: had he been a religious teacher, he would have used parables; it was only rarely historiographical; and it appeared to be produced on the hoof. It was probably the first two elements that most astounded the average viewer (and possibly the average lecturer). Taylor had been lecturing without notes since his second year at Manchester University: he would now probably have found it difficult to follow a written script. He always lectured for television on topics which he knew extremely well and therefore he did not have to *learn* (and take the chance of forgetting on air) new material: he merely had to put existing knowledge in order. He always prepared the first and last sentence of a lecture, so that he knew just how long it would take him to wind up and therefore when he should begin to do so. He wrote out on a card any quotations which he intended to use in the order he intended to use them: this, of course, provided an excellent crib for his argument should one be needed. Even Taylor was very occasionally at a loss for words, as he admitted to Lady Longford one day at a Foyle's literary luncheon. 'Do you never get absolutely dried up?' she asked him. 'What do you do?' His answer: 'Well, occasionally I do, but I find that there's one way of dealing with it: I just say something, even the word however, or nevertheless, just something and that starts the flow up in the brain.'[71] Such techniques can be learned. What was more impressive was his apparent ability to time his lectures to the second. But here as well he had a stratagem: the large clock used by the weatherman was wheeled in and placed next to the camera.[72]

Where Taylor's television lectures differed markedly from his Oxford ones was in the content. For television they were lightened, both in subject matter and in treatment. They were heavily biased towards the biographical – prime ministers, men of the 1860s, war lords – or towards exciting events – wars, revolutions, parliamentary crises – and virtually all lent themselves to narrative and story. This was doubtless a wise decision. What did the average viewer care about historiographical debate, or deep analysis of social movements or discussion of profound versus immediate causes of events? Taylor gave the viewer enough to provide a taste of the subject, interesting without being overwhelming; for those who wanted to know more, there were books to read, by Taylor or by other historians. Judging by the number of people from all walks of life who recall watching his lectures, and in particular by the number of schoolteachers who remember being riveted by Taylor's television lectures and then turning to his books, he amply fulfilled his goal of bringing history to the people. He did not necessarily convince them to question the Establishment, the ruling elite – one of his stated goals – but he certainly conveyed the pleasures of history.

His television lectures also differed from his academic ones in their style. His university lectures were analytical: *The Origins of the Second World War*, which began its public life as a series of Oxford lectures, has never, even by its enemies, been called devoid of analysis, just wrong. His Raleigh Lecture of 1959, 'Politics in the First World War', was a brilliant and influential analysis of its subject, as was his Leslie Stephens Lecture of 1961 on 'Lloyd George: Rise and Fall'. His television lectures were of a different order, heavily narrative and larded with memorable stories. They almost never discussed the views of other historians: the most he might say was that 'many historians think X'. What the viewer got was Taylor on the topic, an interesting, sometimes amusing, sometimes (though not always) riveting, always linear tour, but not a very deep analysis, arguably appropriate for Mondays at 6 or 10.30pm.

Finally, he appeared to be making it up on the spot. Sometimes he was: as he later wrote, lecturing 'provided the excitement of discovering new ideas while I was talking'.[73] Joan Bakewell, writing in the *Radio Times*, commented that 'it was not often that you could see people thinking on television . . . A.J.P. Taylor thinks as he talks. No script, no notes; just himself thinking and talking.'[74] It is the sort of thinking many academics do when trying to explain something to students, particularly when trying to give a full and logical answer to an unexpected question: you think on your feet. Taylor had been reading hundreds of books a year since boyhood; he was blessed with a very good memory; he had been employed as a professional explainer, as it were, for decades; and he enjoyed performing.

Taken together, these circumstances would account for his surface insouciance and the self-confidence.

And of course, he did prepare. In his case, however, this did not involve writing out a text, at least not for television (although he had had to do so in his early days in radio). Consider his record: he published over the years at least ten books of solid worth, plus hundreds of essays; but what must also be remembered is the nearly sixteen hundred book reviews. He had a virtual library full of thoughts about historical topics. Preparation for him meant pulling out these thoughts and deciding which ones to use and in what order. But his style also incorporated coming up with an original view of a familiar topic. This was particularly true in the earlier years of his television career, when he was still an active researcher, thinker and writer. Later on, in the later 1970s and the 1980s, when even his book reviewing was slowly winding down, his intellectual capital was being used up with little to replace it. What remained was his way with words and with thoughts, but the thoughts were less original, and in a sense Taylor was feeding on himself.[75]

Yet the later period saw a development in his freelance career related directly to his television lecturing which he had not exploited when he was in his prime. This was the turning of his lectures into books. In the early commercial television days, pamphlets containing all or part of two of his lecture series had been published by the television companies themselves: the three lectures of his first ATV series in 1957 on the Russian Revolution and four of the ten lectures on World War given in 1966 for Rediffusion Television. But no commercial publisher produced a whole series. Hamish Hamilton suggested doing so in 1962: 'Your talks on "The Twenties" make the mouth water. Are they going to be enough for volume form?' But Taylor's response was that 'My television lectures are too ragged to make a book ... and in any case they are fragments from my projected volume in the Oxford History of England.'[76]

By 1976, however, when he was no longer writing books of original history, Taylor's attitude had changed. His second chance was provided by his 1976 BBC series on the war lords. Roger Machell of Hamish Hamilton wrote to Taylor in August of that year that he had 'been enjoying enormously your "Mussolini" in today's *Listener* and must certainly watch the rest of the series on TV. How about a book on the whole "War Lords" series, with many illustrations? We'd very much like to publish this if it seems feasible.'[77] Taylor naturally agreed, and Hamish Hamilton published the hardback in 1977, Penguin issuing a paperback edition in

1978. Machell also arranged a book club edition and an American edition by Athenaeum. Taylor received around £1,700 for giving the lectures and (over the years 1977–94) around £13,500 from this one book, which he had not even had to write, just speak. The same type of arrangement was made for three further complete series of television lectures, 'How Wars Begin', 'Revolution' (published as *Revolutions and Revolutionaries*) and 'How Wars End'; this was a valuable addition to his income, at a time when he was no longer receiving an academic salary. In the circumstances, it is perhaps understandable that he had forgotten his 1938 dictum that 'Books should be books and not radio scripts.'[78]

Taylor, then, had a long innings as a broadcasting star, first in radio and then on television. He even began a further series of television lectures for Channel 4 in 1984, but by then his Parkinson's disease rendered completion impossible. Nevertheless, it was a tribute to his fame and perceived attractiveness for television audiences that he was asked to give them when he was so clearly in decline. With regard to television's role in his freelance career, it made a substantial contribution to his income, particularly between 1951 and 1967. Furthermore, the fame arising from his appearances made him much more marketable in other areas than would have been the case had he remained known primarily for his academic work. The most lucrative area was the popular press, where opportunities arose because of his television appearances and consequent growing fame amongst the general public.

Taylor had been writing political commentaries for newspapers since the mid-1940s, and by the early 1950s was still writing more or less regularly for the *Manchester Guardian* and occasionally for other publications, such as the *New Statesman*. However, both the *Guardian* and the *New Statesman* appealed to a relatively narrow segment of the reading public, and it is therefore ironic that it was a *New Statesman* lunch which provided the occasion for Taylor's leap into the arena of a mass readership. As Taylor himself described it, 'I used occasionally to attend the *New Statesman* weekly lunch, a function which with my dislike of lunch I did not much enjoy. One day Philip Zec was there. He was a cartoonist who ... was [now] editing the *Sunday Pictorial* (later the *Sunday Mirror*). On a sudden impulse he asked me how I should like to rival W.J. Brown as a rustic philosopher.' This was in January 1951, just four months after 'In the News' had settled down with its regular team, including Taylor and Brown (and four months before Zec would be a witness at Taylor's second wedding). Taylor continued, 'though I did not think I was suited to the part, like others I could not resist the lure of Fleet Street.' The money, he said, seemed 'astronomical' compared with what he was used to getting from the *Manchester Guardian*.[79]

He threw himself into the writing – Friday was his media day. He spent the morning at the *Sunday Pictorial* and the evenings on 'In the News', and the connection between the two was underlined by his newspaper by-line: 'A million people see and hear this man on Friday nights'. In the same way that he would soon modify his lecturing skills for the television studio, he pared down and exaggerated his writing style to adopt it for columns in the popular press. He already habitually began with an arresting first sentence, wrote in short rather than involved sentences and maintained a strong theme; he now began with a short title which, more often than not, ended with a question or an exclamation mark, and wrote a punchy polemic. Indeed, his very first column was entitled 'UNO Has Failed!', arguing that the Korean War was the outcome of American attempts 'to steal the United Nations and use the organisation for its own policy'.[80]

Over the year in which he wrote for the *Sunday Pictorial* he outlined the long-standing British fear of Russia ('Fear of Russia' – 11 February); argued that the decline in religious belief was the 'biggest thing that has happened in the twentieth century' ('So the Churches Are Empty Again Today!' – 1 April); argued against Communist witch hunts and in favour of people of independent judgement ('We Must Not Silence our "Reds"!' – 24 June); maintained that 'Freedom is in more danger from attacks from within than from attacks without' ('Secret Police? Britain Has Them Too' – 16 September); and denounced Adenauer's plans for German rearmament whilst urging a settlement with the Soviet Union ('What Sort of Friend Can This Man Be?' – 9 December). What is notable is that, notwithstanding the fact that the style was popular, the topics he wrote about were on the whole serious ones, with a bias towards foreign policy. He enjoyed the work, the exposure and the money, but it all ended in February 1952: his patron, Phil Zec, was sacked as Editor, and as Taylor counted as Zec's man he was soon sacked as well (although he received a case of champagne to show that there was nothing personal in it).[81]

He only rested for a year. Another popular newspaper, the *Daily Herald*, 'had for once', Taylor wrote, 'an enterprising features editor, Dudley Barker, who was usually a writer of novels and biographies. He hired me to write a weekly column called "As I See It" [later called "I Say What I Please"].' In its 1 January 1953 issue the paper advertised his column on the front page. The link with his television stardom was made directly:

'A.J.P. Taylor, the blunt spoken Oxford don who was sacked from television's "In the News" is to write a weekly commentary. ... Viewers know that Taylor says what he thinks – and it is always forthright, provocative and original.'[82] According to Taylor, writing for the *Daily Herald* 'was a pretty grim task. I gave offence to the regular journalists by bouncing in once a week and writing my column in a couple of hours. Moreover the trade-union directors disapproved of my frivolity even though I conformed to their rules by joining the NUJ, an obeisance to the closed shop that has never brought me much advantage.'[83]

Taylor wrote for the *Daily Herald* for three and a half years, from January 1953 to June 1956, during which period the quality of his columns was more mixed than it had been for the *Sunday Pictorial*. It was not that Taylor thought that his audience was ignorant or stupid. He later wrote that 'I do believe that the British public has an appetite for things which are intellectually interesting and stimulating to the mind',[84] and he never expressed any contempt for his popular readership. Nor was it that he wrote down in terms of style: ever since he had begun writing for the *Manchester Guardian* in the mid–1930s he had placed a premium on clarity and accessibility of expression. But there is no doubt that assertion began to supplant argument in his pieces. One problem was the need to produce a piece every week whether or not he had something to say. Or, to be more precise: he always had something to say, but it was not always of great importance.

Some of his pieces must certainly have caused ironic snorts amongst those who knew him. Take his column of 25 April 1953, 'Don't Tell Us: Show Us!', which castigated a major feature of the modern age, the craving for publicity. This from A.J.P.Taylor! Or his column of 14 March of the same year, 'Save Us from These New Elizabethans', in which he argued that 'there is only one path which will lead us to a great future. That is the path of international Socialism.' In Britain, 'all the resources of the community must be planned to serve the community and for no other purposes.' On the other hand, in his column of 18 July, 'Leave Us Alone!', he claimed that 'I detest the idea that other people know how to run my life. I detest just as much the idea that I know how to run other people's lives.' Did he have a consistent argument here? Did it matter to him, or to his readers?

What did matter to him was that he was read. When Kingsley Martin had written to him in 1951, castigating him for a piece in the *Sunday Pictorial* and warning him that the serious papers would no longer want to use him if he continued in that vein, Taylor had replied:

Of course the problem of writing for the Sunday Pic has exercised my mind. But I ask myself: ought I to be content with teaching ten or fifteen undergraduates in Magdalen or even with writing for the fairly limited readers of the New Statesman and the Manchester Guardian? If Phil gives me the chance of addressing five million people, ought I to take fright at the shade of Joad and turn it down? It is a difficult job that takes me a long time to learn; and I daresay that I shall make lots of mistakes before I get better. But I surely ought to try. For my own part, I'm content if once every two months or so, I can get in a piece advocating a more independent foreign policy and appeasement with Russia, but especially with China.'[85]

And this is what he did: he interspersed pieces with a more serious intent with those of a consciously lighter vein. After all, one of his mottoes was that 'the Editor is always right',[86] and it seemed clear what the popular papers required. He always prided himself on being good at whatever job he was doing, and he certainly believed that he had mastered the popular style and approach. But it ended abruptly, and he was dismissed from the *Daily Herald* with only twenty-four hours' notice.[87] It is unclear why this happened. The then Editor, Sydney Elliott, was hardly one of the great visionary editors of Fleet Street, and he might simply have acted on impulse. Taylor was dismayed at the time, believing that it signalled the end of his career as a popular journalist. This was a blow both to his ego and – equally important – to his pocket, since he was by now supporting two complete families, and his freelance earnings constituted the significantly larger portion of his total income. But Taylor was later to write that 'the *Daily Herald* did right to get rid of me. As I once wrote about Bernard Shaw, I had a great gift of expression and nothing to say. I had lost faith in Socialism after the experience of the Attlee Labour government. The Cold War destroyed my hopes for a better international future.'[88] This is one of the comments in his autobiography that is best taken with a pinch of salt. He implies that he needed a period of lying fallow, or perhaps the appearance of something new in which he could have faith; he would soon find a political movement in which he could again believe with the advent in 1957 of the Campaign for Nuclear Disarmament, but in the meantime he hardly lay fallow. He wrote a few pieces during the remainder of 1956 for *Reynolds' News*, described by Taylor as 'a Leftwing Sunday paper now defunct',[89] and he wrote a number of pieces for the *News Chronicle* and the *Sunday Graphic*, in addition to a number of *New Statesman* London Diaries. He liked the smell of newspaper offices.

Then in October 1957 came the first piece for the popular newspaper with which he maintained his longest and closest connection: the *Sunday Express*. The proprietor of the Express Newspapers was Lord Beaverbrook, but Taylor insisted that 'I settled into the *Sunday Express* before I ever met Beaverbrook though he surely became my patron thereafter.' Rather, 'I was taken up by John Junor who had recently succeeded John Gordon as editor of the *Sunday Express* and, I suppose, wanted some new blood. I had hardly ever looked at the *Sunday Express* before and regarded it as implacably Rightwing. To my surprise I found myself writing radical articles – not of course socialist ones and certainly not any against the Empire. But there was plenty of common ground between Junor and me. By the end of 1956 I was on the *Sunday Express* with an annual contract and remained so until 1982.'[90] This contract barred him from writing anything for other papers except book reviews for the *Guardian* and the *Observer*.

This version of events lacks a certain plausibility. Taylor met Beaverbrook soon after he wrote the adulatory review of the latter's *Men and Power 1917–1918*, which was published in the *Observer* on 28 October 1956. Taylor's first piece for the *Sunday Express* appeared almost exactly a year later, on 27 October 1957. It is, of course, possible that Beaverbrook had in the interim made no attempt to meet for a second time the man who had transformed his life, but this is unlikely. It is also, of course, possible that it never occurred to Beaverbrook that Taylor might make a good columnist on one of his papers: after all, the link between them was history, not politics. At this distance, it is of course impossible to know for certain.

Accepting for the moment Taylor's story that it was all due to Junor, how might Junor have come across Taylor? Newspaper editors read the competition, and so Junor would have been familiar with Taylor's journalism. He probably watched him on 'Free Speech' and was therefore familiar with his rumbustious style. August–September 1957 also saw Taylor's first television history lectures: Taylor was now, in Lew Grade's words, 'a star, but an unusual type of star'. In short, it is easy to see how Junor might have decided to hire Taylor; it was not even an adventurous appointment as it had been for Phil Zec and the *Sunday Pictorial*. However, it might have been thought a politically unusual offer for Taylor to accept. The *Sunday Pictorial* later became the *Sunday Mirror*, a stalwart Labour Party supporter, while the *Daily Herald* was forty-nine per cent-owned by the TUC. The *Express* newspapers inhabited the other half of the political spectrum. However, it was not as strange a decision on Taylor's part as it might have seemed. Although he was always loyal to the party, and in fact was a member for over sixty years,[91] he was disillusioned with mainstream Labour: his own natural home, he felt, was more to the left, particularly in foreign policy, although there were many areas of domestic policy, such as support of the BBC, with which he could not sympathise. Furthermore, he liked writing popular journalism, both the work itself and the fame following from it: as he wrote in his autobiography, 'I enjoy journalism – the challenge of a new subject, the urgency of the deadline (which I have never missed) and the reward of getting immediately into print.'[92] And he wanted and needed the money.

According to *Sunday Express* folklore Taylor's position within the newspaper was more functional and less exalted than he probably imagined. Peter Oborne, sometime columnist for the *Express on Sunday*, related that, 'he was not regarded within the paper as a star writer. As far as I can tell, he was foisted on the *Sunday Express* by Lord Beaverbrook. The editor John Junor was glad to make use of Taylor's services. But he valued him chiefly for his speed and efficiency and treated the famous historian as a hack writer who could churn out copy at a moment's notice. In the words of a colleague, "JJ did not have much time for Alan Taylor except as a useful functionary. He used him as a fallback when there was nothing doing politically." Taylor once told columnist Alan Watkins that he regarded Junor as a "blockhead" and the feeling was possibly mutual.' Junor always insisted that 'Taylor "never put up an idea of his own" ... but he was more than ready to churn out copy on anything he was asked.'[93]

Consequently he wrote a variety of types of pieces for the *Sunday Express*, retaining his interest in foreign policy issues but increasingly taking up more populist themes. During his first complete year as a regular commentator for the paper, three of his ten pieces dealt with Germany, two argued against the United Nations and one praised Khrushchev. The others called for the scrapping of the House of Lords, praised the freedom of the press, argued in favour of commercial television and demonstrated the relative unimportance of Cabinet ministers. In 1963, a year during which he published fourteen pieces in the paper, four still dealt with foreign policy issues and seven with national issues, whilst three looked at lesser issues: in one of the last-named, for example, he blustered that it was absurd that so many people had to take their holidays in August, and demanded that educational institutions begin in January, with examinations to take place in November and December. The probability that this would merely shift the 'holiday madness' from one month to another obviously slipped his notice. But even though the themes of the other eleven articles were relatively serious, they were mostly treated in a deliberately provocative manner. In the context of the Vassall (espionage) affair, he argued that homosexuals were a security risk and should be treated accordingly; he denounced taxpayers' subsidies of minority culture, in particular the Third Programme on the BBC and opera (the title of the column was 'Why Must *You* Pay for the Culture Snobs?'); and he argued against the recommendations of the Robbins Report on the future of universities, writing that 'every increase of students means a lowering of standards', and agreeing with Kingsley Amis that 'more means worse'. He continued in this vein, and it is probable that those readers (and non-readers) who regarded his output as trivial did so because of the way he treated his themes, not because of the themes themselves.

The number of articles he wrote per year varied across his career with the *Sunday Express*, which ran from 1957 to 1982. He was on an annual contract to write twenty articles a year for one hundred pounds each, generous wages by the standards of the day but rather less than occupants of the leader page like Enoch Powell, Reginald Maudling and Quintin Hogg. In practice Taylor wrote considerably less than the twenty articles a year. But he made sure he got paid for all twenty come what may. The great historian, who was careful with his money, would ring up each New Year regular as clockwork demanding payment for those unwritten pieces.[93] Some years Taylor wrote on average more than once a month (1959–63, 1967, 1971), but during most years he contributed less frequently: in 1965 he wrote nine, in 1966 and 1968 seven, in 1972 only two. In November 1972, in fact, he decided that he had been dropped by the paper because 'it has become too right-wing to employ me, a loss of over £2,000 a year', and he wrote the editor a letter of farewell. However, as a consequence the editor 'rang up, said he could not bear to part with me and agreed to take fewer articles but at a higher fee. So I shall get £1,200 or so instead of £2,000.'[94] In 1973 he wrote six pieces, but thereafter he wrote an average of three a year, until the final break came in 1982. Funnily enough, his membership of a trade union now finally paid off. The Assistant Secretary of the National Union of Journalists wrote to their solicitor that 'Mr Taylor, one of the Union's more distinguished members, gave the Sunday Express his exclusive services for more than two decades and then had his contract terminated without due notice or any compensation.'[95] Full circle, from left to right and back again.

This survey of the development of Taylor's freelance career has emphasised a series of events, but the effect was not so much sequential as cumulative. For example, he began by reviewing, he continued to review and he ended by reviewing. Emphasis has been laid on the importance of reviewing for the *Manchester Guardian* in providing the foundation of his extra-academic work, and he continued to review for the *Guardian* for almost as long as he continued to write. But there were other papers which demanded his time and were willing to pay a retainer for it. In March 1948 he published his first review in the *New Statesman and Nation*, followed by four others that same year; by 1953, whilst writing eighteen reviews for the *Manchester Guardian*, he wrote sixteen for the *New Statesman*, and the Editor, Kingsley Martin, decided to tie him as closely as possible to the publication: 'The point is that we want you to do more reviewing for us, and not to review the same kind of books in other papers that you do so well in the N.S. The best solution would be to offer you a retainer, which would mean that you would not review, in the ordinary way, books for rival publications that we would want you to review for us. I looked up our payments to you over the last ten months, and find that ... you now make about £150 a year from us.' He suggested a retainer of £300 per year. Taylor agreed, adding that 'you will have to specify that you get first refusal except for the *Manchester Guardian*. If they fail to get in first, *tant pis* for them.'[96] Taylor continued to review for the *New Statesman* for the next twenty-five years, although his output varied from year to year – twenty-four reviews in 1954, ten in 1958, four in 1960, but sixteen in 1963. From 1967 on, however, the number of reviews each year was in single figures, as low as one in 1972 and two in 1978.

Kingsley Martin wanted Taylor to review for the *New Statesman* because they shared a number of political ideas and because of the quality of his writing; it is doubtful that he was influenced by Taylor's growing television-led prominence. This was not, however, the case with the *Observer*. Taylor began reviewing on an occasional basis for the Sunday broadsheet in 1953, writing five reviews that year. By 1957 he was writing one every three weeks, the rate at which he continued, and that he occasionally surpassed, for the next twenty years. An agreement was reached between Taylor and the paper that he review regularly for them, but the Editor, David Astor, only reluctantly agreed to the arrangement. In fact, Astor actually wrote to Terry Kilmartin, the literary editor, in October 1957 that 'I want formally to record the fact that I regret the closer association with [Taylor] that we are engaged in and look forward to the time when we can only use him infrequently for things that he is specially qualified to do. I know it was me who suggested taking him on fully, but that was in the phase ... epitomised with the phrase "we are all businessmen, aren't we?" I was influenced by the idea that A.J.P. would give us circulation, but I really think that he is rather a terrible little man, although brilliant.'[97] The quality of Taylor's reviews for the *Observer* is consistently high – it was hardly in the same style that he employed for the popular press. Perhaps the date is important: Astor's letter was written two days after Taylor's first piece for the *Sunday Express* appeared. Yet the fact that, even though Astor had figuratively to hold his nose, he still felt compelled to pay is an important indicator of Taylor's drawing power.

The work was cumulative in yet another way. Many of his longer journalistic pieces, particularly those written for the *Manchester Guardian*, made a second appearance in one of his books of essays. But Taylor went further than that: some of his later books of essays are compilations taken from previous collections. *From Napoleon to Stalin* (1950), *Rumours of Wars* (1952) and *Englishmen and Others* (1956) were the quarries out of which were hewn *From Napoleon to Lenin: Historical Essays*, published in the United States in 1966, and *Europe: Grandeur and Decline*, published in Britain by Penguin in 1967, which share some (though not all) of the same essays. He was the Rossini of history writing.

A brief look at Taylor's freelance work in 1957 will demonstrate how the opportunities in the different areas arose because of the cumulative nature of his fame and perceived attractiveness to the reading, listening and viewing publics. He published a book, *The Troublemakers*; he made two radio broadcasts, gave eleven television lectures and appeared regularly on 'Free Speech'; he wrote seven book reviews for the *Manchester Guardian*, fifteen for the *New Statesman* and nineteen for the *Observer*; and he wrote two columns for the *Sunday Express*, one for the *Sunday Graphic*, three for the *News Chronicle* and three London Diaries for the *New Statesman*. Anyone who read a paper or watched television would have had some difficulty in avoiding Taylor.

He worked phenomenally hard because he enjoyed it and because he needed the money. He had two complete families by 1957, his ex-wife Margaret and their four children, and his current wife Eve with their two, and they had to be supported – neither wife worked outside the home, and some of the children were still young. His academic salary had been £1,350 in 1950, the first year in which his freelance income surpassed it. By 1957, when his salary had risen to £1,700, it was dwarfed by a freelance income of over £4,000 – in 1995 terms more than £50,000. This pattern continued for the remainder of his career.

One justification for having paid so much attention to the ways and means by which Taylor made his money is that little information is available about the earning power of freelance media performers in any field during this period, and certainly almost nothing is known about the earnings of the academic performer. But it is also important because an interest in money was a significant part of Taylor's make-up. Reference works for investors were kept on his desk in Magdalen, and he was an active dealer in shares for much of his life. He kept a very close eye on his fees and royalties, writing to his publishers or to his agent when payments were late. He even liked doing his income-tax return: when discussing a publication schedule with an employee of the publishers Jonathan Cape some time in the 1970s, he demurred at an early April date, saying that 'I always reserve the first week of that month for doing my tax return. It's one of the things I enjoy most in the year.'[98]

Taylor's freelance earnings are impressive. From 1950 until 1966, when he turned sixty, at least half, and usually more than half, of his income in every year came from book reviews, broadcasting and journalism taken together. Thereafter, his income from those sources diminished in real terms and was consistently less than that from book royalties (which grew sharply in real terms from 1960 to a broad peak between 1967 and 1975, followed by a very substantial tail until after his death in 1990). A model of lifelong prudent financial planning, Taylor admirably achieved his apparent objective of using book royalties as a 'deferred pension'. From 1934 to 1966 he earned from his freelance work about £71,000 in absolute figures; in 1995 prices this was about £900,000. Eighty per cent derived from the combination of book reviewing, broadcasting and journalism, and only twenty per cent from book royalties. Thereafter, until 1990 when he died, he earned from his freelance work a further £285,000 in absolute figures, or about £1,000,000 in 1995 figures, with the proportions reversed – i.e. eighty per cent now came from book royalties and twenty per cent from book reviews, broadcasting and journalism.

What is even more impressive is the range of activities generating these earnings. Taylor began by responding to an opportunity which fell into his lap – the invitation to review the biography of Robespierre for the *Manchester Guardian* – but thereafter to a large extent he made his own opportunities. He initiated the contacts with the BBC in 1942 and the television producer Wyndham Goldie in 1950. He worked hard on his technique, whether it was in writing lucidly and arrestingly for the *Manchester Guardian* in the 1930s, or in mastering broadcasting techniques in the

Taylor's Freelance Income 1934–90 in 1995 Prices

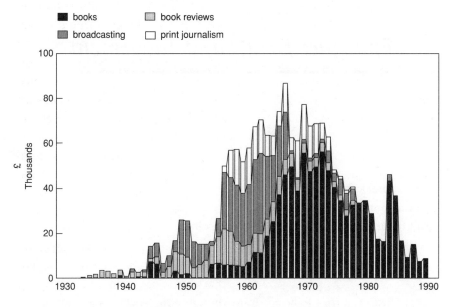

1940s, or in discovering how best to write for the popular press in the 1950s. As for the range of his knowledge, and interests, this stemmed from his habits since boyhood of hard work and wide reading, plus an openness to new fields of inquiry. When to these are added the quality and quickness of his mind and a profound self-confidence, the ingredients for a lucrative freelance career were all there. All he needed were patrons and opportunities, and he had the luck to find plenty of both. Or perhaps personality plus intelligence plus hard work provided the luck?

Epilogue: Death and Judgement

Break, break, break,
At the foot of thy crags, O Sea!
But the tender grace of a day that is dead
Will never come back to me.

From Tennyson, 'Break, Break, Break'

Every historian tries to be accurate, though none succeeds as fully as he
would like to. Style is colouring and something more: it sets its stamp on
the whole work. As [Samuel] Johnson says, application is the main thing.
Writing history is like W.C. Fields juggling. It looks easy until you try to
do it.

A.J.P. Taylor, 'Accident Prone, or What Happened Next'

On 7 September 1990 Taylor died. Ten days later, the funeral service took
place at Golders Green Crematorium. His eldest son, Giles, began the
service with a welcome, after which a number of friends and relatives
talked about him or read aloud from writings that he had particularly
enjoyed: Kee reminisced about the years at Magdalen; Taylor's elder
daughter, Amelia, read E.V. Knox's humorous poem 'The Everlasting
Percy'; and his younger daughter, Sophia, read Shelley's 'The Mask of
Castlereagh', which describes the Peterloo Massacre of 1819. Another
former pupil, Pat Thompson, a Fellow of Wadham College, Oxford, gave
the tribute, after which Blake's 'Jerusalem' was sung. Finally, one of
Taylor's favourite pieces of chamber music, the second movement from
Schubert's Piano Trio in B flat, Op. 99, was played as his body disappeared.
The following April, a memorial service was held at Magdalen. This was an
occasion dominated more by friends than by family: Michael Foot, Alan
Sked (a former postgraduate student), Robert Skidelsky and Arthur Adams

(the former Dean of Divinity) all spoke about him; Cynthia Kee (Kee's second wife) read from Beatrix Potter; Richard Ingrams played an organ solo. The main family contribution was the reading of Tennyson's poem 'Break, Break, Break', by Taylor's granddaughter, Rosa Howard. Once again, Schubert's Piano Trio in B flat was played, this time by the Magdalen String Trio.

Taylor left an estate of just over £307,000. The Trustees were Éva, Giles Taylor (the eldest son by his first wife), and Crispin Taylor (the eldest son by his second wife). The house, the published and unpublished works and their copyrights, and one-third of the residue of his estate (with a minimum of £50,000) went to Éva. The remainder of the estate was divided evenly amongst Taylor's six children and two stepsons, each of whom received just over £10,000.[1]

On the whole the obituaries were kind, particularly the one by Hugh Trevor-Roper in the *Sunday Telegraph*. Many depended on Taylor's own *Personal History*, although one or two, such as Trevor's-Roper's and James Joll's for *The Times* (the latter updated by Martin Gilbert), showed a more intimate familiarity with both his personality and his writings. Some three years later, reviews of two biographies provided the occasion for a regaling of stories about Taylor with, in one or two cases, the settling of old scores. A.L. Rowse wrote in the *Evening Standard* that 'A serious historian must abide religiously by what is true. So no wonder universities would not appoint Taylor to the chairs he was anxious to get. He never seems to have understood why not, nor why his dreadful book about Hitler's war shocked so many people. An Oxford colleague called him "a dishonest historian".' The military journalist and historian John Keegan, writing in the *Daily Telegraph*, was scathing about Taylor's books on English history: 'His gritty, disrespectful, stay-at-home world contains nothing of the elements which made Britain the power whose passing he regretted – the derring-do of its soldiers and sailors, the colonial dynamism, the Kiplingesque ethos of its "imperial" working class. His is indeed a Little England, and one deformed by his insensitivity to anything aesthetic or spiritual in the way life is lived.' Taylor's influence, he charged, conveyed contempt for 'everything that the word "Establishment" stands for'; worse, by means of his influence on schoolteachers, gained through his lectures to branches of the Historical Association, 'a whole generation of schoolchildren was indirectly exposed to his wicked shafts of doubt and deflation.' Furthermore, this influence 'permeated the polytechnic world and that of the teacher training colleges', as well as directly touching 'a coterie of notable journalists who had been his pupils'. His dislike even extended to Taylor's appearance: 'Once seen, never forgotten. Small – very small, in fact – stooped, bright-eyed, bushy about the brows and ears, with disproportionately large and knobbly feet, AJPT looked very much like a Hobbit.' Finally, Richard Overy, certainly a serious historian, catechised his personal faults in the *Observer*: 'As he got older, he got more bitter about the way life had treated him, but he had always had a vindictive streak. For all the insouciance and cheery helpfulness, Taylor was possessed of a quite extraordinary vanity. He was self-centred to the point of parody; insensitive, prickly, miserly and he hated real responsibility.' Yet Overy finished by quoting Taylor on Macaulay, one of Taylor's two favourite historians, and drawing the obvious conclusion: 'Macaulay, Taylor thought, was not a very profound historian; he concentrated on the great rather than the crowd; he could be grossly unfair to his subjects, but he had a prodigious knowledge and was, above all, a great writer, "the most readable of all historians". Warts and all,' Overy concluded, 'Taylor remains the Macaulay of our age.'[2] It remains to be seen whether subsequent generations will wish to read a Macaulay.

A.J.P. Taylor was possibly the greatest, and certainly the most famous, diplomatic historian of the twentieth century. How and why he was great is a difficult question – he initiated no new methodology, opened up no new field of research, left no school of disciples. His range was wide, covering nineteenth- and twentieth-century British and European history, but this is hardly unknown amongst historians. He was certainly extraordinarily productive, and his books are very readable, but these traits do not necessarily add up to greatness. Perhaps one should begin with the fact that he was a wonderfully intuitive historian, an intuition grounded on wide reading and hard thinking. Trusting his intuition, Taylor assumed the mantle of iconoclast. He knew that he was good; he saw himself as basically a dissenter; and the result was a stream of books and essays in which he took delight in questioning accepted historical truths.

How and why he was famous is easier. Abroad, it was the books. In Britain it was certainly the books – all twenty-three of them, some of which were books of essays which included some of the more than six hundred essays and articles he had written as well as some of the nearly sixteen hundred book reviews – but it was also the pure journalism and the broadcasting. Taylor pioneered the role of the telly don: his television lectures must have enabled thousands to relate their lives to their times, as well as providing the historical context for recent events.[3] Finally, there were his hundreds of lectures to branches of the Historical Association. It is not necessary to accept Keegan's characterisation of their influence as baleful: they provided information as well as pleasure.

In his prime, Taylor was charismatic and authoritative in his speech and demeanour, in spite of being barely five feet six inches tall. He was hugely and fiercely intelligent, ferociously articulate and aggressive. He had a retentive mind, an analytical mind, a mind which worked wonderfully quickly and played over his large store of knowledge gained from a lifetime's reading – over 7,100 books listed between 1914 and 1985. He could see connections which others had missed, he anticipated the conclusions which others arrived at only after spending hours and days in the archives. On the other hand, the quickness of his mind sometimes encouraged him to be superficial, not to be as deeply probing as he might have been. This tendency increased as he grew older. However, he retained his command of prose, which in his hands was powerful rather than poetic. From about 1940 his use of paradox grew rapidly, a habit of which he himself became increasingly dismissive and even disapproving as he grew older. What he never stopped being was readable.

He had developed this readability by writing book reviews. The need to make his points in a short piece encouraged arresting statements made in increasingly shorter sentences. This style gradually took over his longer pieces, including his books. As he himself described it, 'Since then [the 1930s] my style has been my own. It has however changed with my writing instruments. With a pen you write words. With a typewriter you write sentences. With an electric typewriter . . . you write paragraphs. In military terms: bow and arrow, musket, machine gun. I try to keep up a continuous fire.' Reviewing itself never lost its pleasures for him – 'Every book that arrives on my desk for review excites me.'[4] He built up a great store of miscellaneous knowledge from these reviews, which his memory retained, as well as pithy judgements about myriads of men, women, movements, crises, revolutions, wars and peace, judgements that he could pull out of his mental filing cabinet and utilise in his on-the-hoof lectures and comments.[5]

His wide-ranging knowledge and pithy judgements also came into play in his teaching. He tried to lead his more mediocre students, and those whose interest in history could best be described as tepid, towards a genuine desire to learn, enlivening his tutorials with the entertaining anecdote, the apposite judgement. He gave the full measure of his time, but, unsurprisingly, not the extra spark. Those of his undergraduate and postgraduate students who shared his love of history and were prepared to work, however, he swept off on a voyage of discovery, sharing with them his discoveries, his techniques, his sheer interest and pleasure in history. He also showed genuine interest in their own work, their discoveries, their techniques, treating his postgraduate students, once they had proved themselves to be true historians, as colleagues rather than acolytes. He was never condescending, and he never appropriated their findings.[6]

Taylor the historian and don, then, is of tremendous interest, but there was also Taylor the man of affairs. He saw himself as a man of the left, though he always insisted on deciding for himself just what that meant. From his youthful aid to the strikers during the General Strike in 1926, through his light-hearted attempts on countless occasions, during the Second World War and thereafter, to subvert the official line, and ending with his prominent role in the Campaign for Nuclear Disarmament, Taylor attempted to live out his family heritage as to the Dissenting manner born. He took a perverse pride in his lack of political success, referred to himself as an 'impotent Socialist' and claimed that his activities made him a marked man. Indeed, he ascribed his lack of academic laurels to the hostility of the elite, not always mistakenly, but he claimed not to mind – though of course, he did; rather, he took pride in his fame as a 'populist historian'. It enabled him to see himself as yet another of 'The Trouble-makers', and thus of the line of his nineteenth-century Dissenting heroes, Cobden and Bright.

Finally, there was Taylor the private man. He was very complicated. On the one hand, he was lively and bright, stimulating and amusing, warm and generous, patient and tolerant, and devoted to his friends, his children and sometimes his wives. He was a wonderful raconteur, someone with whom it was a pleasure to dine. He was kind to the less powerful and to the powerless: schoolchildren and members of the public who wrote to him always received an answer; had he lived in an earlier age he would have been kind to the servants. He was democratic in his private life, at least according to his lights. On the other hand, he seems to have found it difficult to keep many of his friends over the years, alienating them person-ally or politically; he was quick to take offence, capable of cutting off old friends who had offended him, and unforgiving. He was basically indiffer-ent to most people. He was conceited and self-righteous, self-absorbed and self-contained, insensitive and thoughtless. His vanity increasingly led him to talk about himself and his own works rather than encouraging other people to talk. (In this, of course, he was akin to one of his heroes, Churchill.) He could be mean about money, dispersing it with some reluctance (except on cars, travel and wine: at Oxford he learned to drink a great deal without becoming drunk) and charging his friends interest on loans he made to them. Yet there was another side, as the episode of the University of London's 1973 Creighton Lecture showed: he forwent his fee on the understanding that the amount would be reviewed and substantially raised before the next lecturer was appointed.[7] He was a man of settled habits: only reluctantly did he change his lunches, his spending habits, his houses or his wives. He did not like his mother and, indeed, had little respect for her, and this appears to have coloured his attitudes towards women. Where they were concerned he was frequently indecisive, and sometimes weak and resentful. Yet he claims to have preferred the company of women to that of men.

Most of all, he enjoyed the company of his six children. The sometimes strained and prickly relationships of his first two wives with various of his children were in both cases partly responsible for the breakdown of the marriages. Margaret's repeated abandonment of their children when following first Kee and then Thomas angered him greatly; Eve's inability to accept his desire to have them around him was a major factor in his estrangement from her. He referred to his daughters as 'my darlings', but he apparently provided less for them than for his sons. When Margaret and the four children moved to London, Giles was sent to Westminster School, a prestigious and expensive independent school; Sebastian went as a boarder to Magdalen College School in Oxford; but Amelia and Sophia went to the local state schools. When the boys were older, he went on long walks with them, happy that those of the 'first batch' and of the 'second batch' got along well together. The girls were not included – although it is, of course, possible that they did not wish to come. But Taylor never wrote that he had invited them. He repeatedly took the boys abroad; he never mentioned taking the girls. The girls had few early memories of their father, since their parents had separated when they were very little; thereafter he was, naturally, absent most of the time. One memory was that he 'took them for walks in Regent's Park and talked to them about the Kings and Queens of England',[8] appropriate parenting, he probably thought, on the part of an historian. Sophia, his younger daughter, resented the fact that he was not always around, as well as his authoritarian mode of behaviour when he was. Her relationship with him was always somewhat prickly on her side. Her elder sister was more easy-going and remained on better terms with her father. Taylor's relationship with his third son, Crispin, was considerably more difficult than with his other sons: Crispin took his mother's side in her arguments with Taylor, and when a young man he more or less absented himself from his father's life for several years, to his father's distress. Conversely, Crispin's younger brother, Daniel, who did not get along very well with his mother, tended to side with his father.[9] What is not in doubt is that he was proud of his children and loved them dearly. Always his children came first.

Taylor had many private pleasures. His love of music was one, and during the evening he frequently attended concerts or listened to gramophone records of chamber music. Late in life he wrote that buildings and walking had provided his two greatest pleasures. He loved church architecture, in particular the Saxon churches of England, the early Christian churches in Rome and the Yugoslav monasteries. He was a serious walker. From his schooldays he had walked in the Lake District, and before his death he claimed that he had been up every major peak with the exception of Steeple, expeditions whose pleasure was increased by his discovery of the guides by Wainwright.[10] His greatest enjoyment was the companionship of his sons once they were old enough to join him on various long-distance walks – the Pennine Way as far as Hadrian's wall, Offa's Dyke Path as far as Llangollen. He tramped many of London's streets, walking daily from his home in north London to Fleet Street, as well as spending most lunch-times wandering and exploring. He particularly enjoyed introducing his sons to Venice and Rome. Other interests faded after a time. One was riding, which he loved as a young man but which he gave up from lack of time and money once he had to establish himself in his career. Another was gardening, a great pleasure in Higher Disley, less of a pleasure in Oxford and non-existent in London.

One pastime which he enjoyed from his time at Oxford as an undergraduate until his mind and body faded was going to a pub. He was a frequent visitor to the local in Higher Disley, where he also bought beer by the barrel for home consumption. He liked lecturing at UCL partly because it had a good bar where he could find excellent company. After they were married he and Éva often went to a nearby pub, where they would talk for hours. His friends and former students recall his habit of sweeping them off to go for a beer and talk. Pubs were the obvious place to go with friends and students: less formal and certainly less trouble than inviting them home. The author remembers being swept off in that very manner to go to a pub with Taylor and a friend of his whom he introduced as Maurice; only later did the realisation dawn that this had been Sir Maurice Oldfield, a former pupil who was then the head of MI6.

The final question must be that of his lasting significance. Part of his contemporary influence arose from the number of his books combined with the ubiquity of his public appearances, in print, on television and radio and in person. He made history matter to hundreds of thousands of people. The books could last; the rest will not, except as a phenomenon of twentieth-century British social and cultural history. Which books? Not the ephemera based on his television lectures; possibly for a generation the compilations of his better essays and reviews, useful as they are to students and attractive as they are to the history-reading public; also for a generation, *The Habsburg Monarchy* and *Bismarck*, as readable as the essays and even more useful for students; and for more than a generation his three greatest books. Many consider *The Struggle for Mastery in Europe 1848–1918* his masterpiece and one of the greatest of all works of diplomatic history. *The Origins of the Second World War* was one of the most influential books of the postwar period, stimulating, thought-provoking and maddening. At the very worst it was an example of fertile error. And finally, *English History 1914–1945* is a period piece of the best sort: a wide-ranging portrait and analysis of Taylor's beloved England, a history of the recent past written by a man steeped in the past. For this, and for its prose, it will surely last. In the end, these three books will be Taylor's enduring legacy.

Appendix

Taylor's Freelance Career: How Much Money He Made and How He Made It

As seen from the following table (presented as a bar chart in Chapter 7), Taylor made a substantial amount of money from his extra-academic work. The reader should know, however, that the evidence on which these totals are based is necessarily questionable. The ledgers of his agent, David Higham Associates, provide the sums he received for a period of his life (1964–90) arising from book royalties and fees, but the agency never handled his broadcasting or his journalistic arrangements, and therefore do not have records of those payments. They also do not cover the first thirty years of his career. Some evidence is available from the records of his various publishers, since he frequently made arrangements for deferring payment of his royalties. Partly this was to minimise tax, but Taylor also treated his royalties as a kind of deferred pension: if he decided that he had already received all of the money he required in a year, he had the rest kept back by the publisher until he needed it. There is some evidence in the BBC archives, especially the letters in which Taylor complained about mistakes in payments made by the BBC. In addition, there are comments made by Taylor in other letters.

Every scrap of evidence found has been entered into a database and sorted both by source and by year, and the results appear below. A great deal of extrapolation was involved. If Taylor wrote that he received fifteen guineas for a twenty-minute talk on the radio, the sum of fifteen guineas was entered into the database for every such talk until there was evidence that the payment had changed. He wrote in 1972 that he used to make £2,000 per year from his television work, and this figure was therefore entered into the database for 1957 through 1967, although it is likely that the figure is wrong for the earlier years. Therefore, these figures can only be regarded as plausible indicators.

The amounts given for his television and radio work are certainly underestimated. The total for his television work comes to £34,738, while that for radio is £8,507.39, but the BBC records follow a thirty-year rule and thus the period from 1970, one of rising prices and fees, cannot be accurately tracked. However, Keith Kyle, one of Taylor's radio producers from 1951 to 1953, recalled that 'at some relatively early stage (it was certainly later than the period when I was dealing with him) he adopted as a fixed rule that he would not appear for under £100.' Another bit of evidence to support the theory of underestimation is a letter from his publisher in May 1972 referring to 'the high fees which you normally command for television.'[1] It is also worth noting that the fees for his work on independent television could not be ascertained and thus they do not appear in the table.

In general, virtually all of the totals given in the table are smaller than they ought to be: the one exception is that for books, where greater confidence is possible because of the harder nature of the evidence. For the other columns, substantial information is missing, and where there was no information at all the number entered was zero. The other examples of years with zero are the early years, where obviously no fees were earned in a given category, such as the television column before 1950.

In order to interpret the information thus assembled, it was necessary to index it to allow for inflation. Between 1934, the first year in the table, and 1990, prices in the United Kingdom rose about twenty-five-fold. Indexing, for all its well-known imperfections, was necessary if even the gross trends over such a long period were to be discernible. All of the absolute values were therefore converted into 1995 terms so as to give a reasonably current impression of the contribution which Taylor's freelance income made to his financial well-being. An average index for each year in the period was constructed by linking the 'All items' cost of living index 1914–47 to the 'All items' retail prices indices for 1947–52, 1952–56, 1956–62, 1962–74, 1974–87 and 1987–96 in official publications.[2] The index thus constructed is given in the penultimate column of the table.

Taylor's freelance income 1934–90 (italicized values in 1995 prices)

YEAR	books	book reviews	broadcasting radio	broadcasting tv	print journalism	TOTAL INCOME IN YEAR	index (1995= 4128.9)	TOTAL INCOME IN YEAR 1995 PRICES
1934	0.00	5.25	0.00	0.00	0.00	5.25	141.0	153.73
1935	0.00	57.75	0.00	0.00	0.00	57.75	143.0	1667.43
1936	0.00	89.25	0.00	0.00	0.00	89.25	147.0	2506.82
1937	0.00	141.75	0.00	0.00	0.00	141.75	154.00	3800.44
1938	0.00	141.75	0.00	0.00	0.00	141.75	156.00	3751.72
1939	0.00	99.75	0.00	0.00	0.00	99.75	158.0	2606.68
1940	75.00	94.50	0.00	0.00	0.00	169.50	184.0	3803.50
1941	0.00	57.75	0.00	0.00	0.00	57.75	199.00	1198.20
1942	15.00	141.75	73.50	0.00	0.00	230.25	200.0	4753.37
1943	45.00	99.75	0.00	0.00	1.10	145.85	199.0	3026.11
1944	36.90	120.75	40.00	0.00	0.00	197.65	201.0	4060.06
1945	365.62	86.50	273.45	0.00	0.00	725.57	203.0	14757.57
1946	323.75	168.00	304.50	0.00	0.00	796.25	203.5	16155.36
1947	0.00	147.00	204.75	0.00	0.00	351.75	204.8	7090.53
1948	3.15	296.00	261.30	0.00	0.00	560.45	218.6	10584.17
1949	187.50	481.50	262.50	0.00	0.00	931.50	224.7	17114.76
1950	105.00	533.50	709.09	168.00	0.00	1515.59	231.6	27016.61
1951	155.00	452.00	321.75	693.00	0.00	1621.75	252.7	26494.16
1952	0.00	345.50	423.60	380.00	0.00	1149.10	276.0	17192.15
1953	5.25	454.50	567.60	63.00	0.00	1090.35	284.6	15819.76
1954	0.00	623.00	385.50	84.00	0.00	1092.50	289.7	15571.32
1955	500.00	612.50	135.30	0.00	0.00	1247.80	302.9	17010.86
1956	555.25	927.50	635.25	0.00	0.00	2118.00	317.7	27525.61
1957	500.00	1347.50	36.75	2000.00	200.00	4084.25	329.5	51172.63
1958	500.00	1268.75	25.65	2000.00	1000.00	4794.40	339.5	58306.76
1959	500.00	924.00	121.75	2000.00	1300.00	4845.75	341.4	58608.63
1960	500.00	756.75	0.00	2000.00	1200.00	4456.75	344.8	53368.10
1961	650.00	687.75	400.65	2000.00	1400.00	5138.40	356.6	59488.57
1962	1083.50	747.75	21.00	3000.00	1300.00	6152.25	366.0	69407.63
1963	1083.50	795.75	26.75	3350.00	1400.00	6656.00	379.2	72481.44
1964	1833.50	731.25	226.75	2500.00	900.00	6191.50	391.6	65280.78
1965	2583.50	905.25	80.00	2000.00	900.00	6468.75	410.3	65101.05
1966	3932.64	881.25	365.00	2000.00	700.00	7878.89	426.4	76297.86
1967	4998.85	756.75	285.00	2000.00	1400.00	9440.60	437.0	89200.75
1968	5651.29	680.25	100.00	0.00	700.00	7131.54	457.5	64364.52
1969	4652.00	656.25	25.00	0.00	2000.00	7333.25	482.4	62770.32
1970	7101.38	587.25	185.00	0.00	2000.00	9873.63	513.1	79451.50
1971	6630.42	666.00	140.00	0.00	2000.00	9436.42	561.4	69399.31
1972	7423.33	642.00	260.00	0.00	2000.00	10325.33	601.3	70898.92
1973	9164.39	692.25	220.00	0.00	1200.00	11276.64	656.6	70913.76
1974	9031.81	680.25	205.00	800.00	1200.00	11917.06	761.6	64604.69
1975	9496.51	601.50	295.00	600.00	300.00	11293.01	946.2	49277.02

YEAR	books	book reviews	broadcasting radio	tv	print journalism	TOTAL INCOME IN YEAR	index (1995= 4128.9)	TOTAL INCOME IN YEAR 1995 PRICES
1976	9424.53	680.25	295.00	1700.00	300.00	12399.78	1102.8	46426.13
1977	8817.34	873.75	475.00	1800.00	400.00	12366.09	1277.6	39965.54
1978	11189.16	601.50	120.00	1800.00	200.00	13910.66	1383.5	41513.16
1979	13083.18	0.00	0.00	0.00	0.00	13083.18	1568.9	34431.86
1980	15947.79	0.00	0.00	0.00	0.00	15947.79	1851.0	35572.55
1981	14807.48	0.00	0.00	0.00	0.00	14807.48	2070.8	29524.58
1982	9675.35	0.00	0.00	0.00	0.00	9675.35	2249.1	17762.28
1983	9529.90	0.00	0.00	0.00	0.00	9529.90	2352.2	16727.79
1984	26492.57	0.00	0.00	1800.00	0.00	28292.57	2469.5	47304.36
1985	23776.39	0.00	0.00	0.00	0.00	23776.39	2619.7	37473.90
1986	11162.17	0.00	0.00	0.00	0.00	11162.17	2708.8	17013.69
1987	6546.82	0.00	0.00	0.00	0.00	6546.82	2821.8	9579.30
1988	11136.10	0.00	0.00	0.00	0.00	11136.10	2960.3	15532.20
1989	6182.00	0.00	0.00	0.00	0.00	6182.00	3190.1	8001.18
1990	7587.99	0.00	0.00	0.00	0.00	7587.99	3492.0	8972.00
total								
1934–90	265047.81	23341.50	8507.39	34738.00	24001.10	355635.80		1899855.71
%	75	7	2	10	7	100		
total 1934–90 at 1995 prices	994077.25	259529.64	105062.80	325383.44	215802.58	1899855.71		
%	52	14	6	17	11	100		

Notes

1 *The Child is Father to the Man*

1 Taylor *A Personal History* (London: Hamish Hamilton, 1983), p. 1.

2 Adam Sisman, in his *A.J.P. Taylor: A Biography* (London: Sinclair-Stevenson, 1994), p. 10, notes a large bellboard in the kitchen which, he wrote, 'could summon the servants to any room in the house.' However, according to the current owners, Mr and Mrs Graham Marten, these (electric) bells, replacing an earlier mechanical system, were only installed after 1929.

3 Taylor, *A Personal History*, pp. 9–11. Taylor called her Jane in his autobiography in order to spare her blushes.

4 *Ibid.*, pp. 1–3; Taylor, 'A Southport Childhood', *Spectator*, 20 Sept. 1980, pp. 15–16.

5 J.F.B., 'Town Council's Double Loss', *Preston Herald*, 1 March 1940, p. 2.

6 Taylor, *A Personal History*, p. 3.

7 *Ibid.*, pp. 3–6.

8 *Ibid.*, pp. 5–6.

9 *Ibid.*, pp. 8, 12; Taylor to Éva, 8 Nov. 1974, *Letters to Eva 1969–1983*, edited by Éva Haraszti-Taylor (London: Century, 1991), p. 211.

10 Taylor, *A Personal History*, p. 6.

11 *Ibid.*, pp. 7, 8.

12 *Ibid.*, p. 11.

13 *Ibid.*, p. 8.

14 *Ibid.*, p. 7. Percy Taylor always claimed that she got it from a blow to the head: she had just begun to walk, she crawled under a table, stood up quickly and crashed the top of her head under the table. Interview with Mrs Doris Fell, 2 Feb. 1991.

15 Taylor, *A Personal History*, p. 10; interview with Mrs Doris Fell, 2 Feb. 1991.

16 E.P. Thompson, *The Making of the English Working Class* (New York: Random House, 1964), p. 31. Thanks to David Eastwood for pointing this out.

17 Taylor, *A Personal History*, p. 12. From 1921, when he was sixteen, through to 1985, after which his Parkinson's disease took firm hold, Taylor kept a list of every book he read (and from 1927 every film he saw). For the years 1921 through to 1925, he noted down the titles in the back of small yearly engagement diaries; these can be found in File Personal Memorabilia (Diaries) in the A.J.P. Taylor Papers held in the Harry Ransome Humanities Research Center, University of Texas, Austin. The list for 1926 is missing; the lists for 1927 through to 1985 were written in a large, partly leather-bound ledger book, now in the possession of his widow, Dr Éva Haraszti-Taylor.

18 Taylor, *A Personal History*, p. 16.

19 *Ibid.*, p. 14.

20 *Ibid.*, pp. 15–16.

21 *Ibid.*, p. 17.

22 *Ibid.*, pp. 17, 19.

23 *Ibid.*, p. 19.

24 *Ibid.*, p. 20.

25 Mike Langham and Colin Wells, *Buxton Waters: A History of Buxton the Spa* (Derby: J.H. Hall and Sons, 1986), *passim*; *Official Guide to Buxton* 1934, for train information.

26 Taylor, *A Personal History*, p. 23. There is no longer a 10 Manchester Road. After some investigation it was discovered that the road was renumbered in the 1920s and the Taylor house is now number 6.

27 *Ibid.*, pp. 22–4.

28 *Ibid.*, p. 21. The 1912 Buxton Directory lists Vital de la Motte as well as the Marlborough School for Girls; the 1916 Kelly's Directory also lists de la Motte as well as Holm Leigh boarding school. Letter from Mike Langham to the author, 19 Feb. 1997.

29 Taylor, *A Personal History*, pp. 21, 24–5. Margaret Drabble, ed., *The Oxford Companion to English Literature* (Oxford: Oxford University Press, 1985), p. 454. 'Prince of Storytellers', a review by Taylor of Guy Arnold, *Hold Fast for England: G.A. Henty, Imperialist Boys' Writer*, *Observer*, 13 April 1980.

30 I am grateful to my daughter Miranda Jewess, who read the book to give me the plot and more precisely to give me the reaction to it of a clever and history-loving eleven-year-old. She found it rather heavy-going and 'over-descriptive'; 'you have to be interested in details of battles, politics and scenery.' While reading it she commented dismissively that there was 'lots of detail about flowers along the trail'.

31 G.A. Henty, *The Young Carthaginian: A Story of the Times of Hannibal* (London: Blackie and Son, 1887), p. 97. It included five full-page illustrations.

32 Taylor, *A Personal History*, p. 25.

33 George Bernard Shaw, 'Common Sense about the War', *The New Statesman Special War Supplement*, vol. IV, no. 84 (Saturday, 14 Nov. 1914), p. 7.

34 Taylor, *A Personal History*, pp. 27–8.

35 R. Bolton King, *Buxton College 1675–1970* (Privately printed, 1973), pp. 22–43, quotation from p. 43. Buxton College was eventually amalgamated into Buxton Community School and is now part of the state sector. I am very grateful to the current headmaster, Mr David Brindley, for lending me a copy of Bolton King's history, as well as a bound copy of surviving issues of the school magazine, the *Buxtonian*.

36 Taylor, *A Personal History*, pp. 26–7. The school magazine, the *Buxtonian* (Aug. 1916), p. 14, records A. Taylor as receiving the prizes for Form IIIa and IIIb in the Lent and summer terms.

37 Taylor, *A Personal History*, p. 29; *Buxtonian* (Aug. 1916), p. 12.

38 Taylor, *A Personal History*, pp. 29–30.

39 E.J. Brown, *The First Five: The Story of a School* (privately published, 1987), pp. 1–12, p. 5 for the quotation.

40 Taylor, *A Personal History*, p. 32. Geoffrey Hoyland, 'Downs in Times Past: Second Series', *Badger*, no. 15 (spring 1941), p. 22.

41 Taylor, *A Personal History*, pp. 33–4.

42 Sisman, *A.J.P. Taylor*, pp. 23, 24, 30.

43 H.W. Jones, 'The Downs during the War', *Badger*, vol. V, no. 11 (spring 1938), p. 13; Taylor, *A Personal History*, p. 35. Hoyland, 'Downs in Times Past: Second Series', *The Badger*, no. 16 (spring 1942), p. 23.

44 Taylor, *A Personal History*, pp. 36–7.

45 Hoyland, 'Downs in Times Past', no. 16, p. 25.

46 Taylor, *A Personal History*, pp. 39–40; Hoyland, 'Downs in Times Past', no. 16, pp. 24–5.

47 Taylor, *A Personal History*, p. 34.

48 Interview with Mrs Doris Fell (Little Dolly), 2 Feb. 1991; Taylor, *A Personal History*, pp. 56–7; Sisman,

A.J.P. Taylor, pp. 72–3.

49 Taylor, *A Personal History*, p. 57; Taylor to Karin Wood, 16 Dec. 1968, quoted in Sisman, *A.J.P. Taylor*, p. 350; Eva Haraszti-Taylor, *A Life with Alan: The Diary of A.J.P. Taylor's Wife Eva from 1978 to 1985* (London: Hamish Hamilton, 1987), p. 176; Taylor to Eva, 9 Nov. 1975, *Letters to Eva*, p. 267.

50 Taylor, *A Personal History*, pp. 37–8, 41–3, 54 for quotation.

51 *Ibid.*, p. 45.

52 F.E. Pollard, *Bootham School 1823–1923* (London: J.M. Dent & Sons, 1926), pp. 12, 161, 170–1. Taylor, *A Personal History*, pp. 45, 48.

53 Taylor, *A Personal History*, p. 45; Sisman, *A.J.P. Taylor*, p. 35. Mr Clifford Smith, Keeper of the Bootham School Archives, also believes that Taylor was bullied. I am grateful to Mr Smith for supplying the extant material on Taylor from the Bootham Archives.

54 Taylor, *A Personal History*, pp. 53–4.

55 *Ibid.*, p. 55; Sisman, *A.J.P. Taylor*, p. 38; *Preston Herald*, 1 March 1940, p. 2.

56 Plebs' League membership card found tucked inside the front cover of his 1922 engagement diary, File Personal Memorabilia, Taylor Papers, Ransome Center.

57 *A Personal History*, pp. 55–6.

58 A.J.P. Taylor, 'Communism', in *The Observer: The Collected Writings of the School Essay Writing Society*, second series, vol. XXIV, part II, pp. 1737–47.

59 Interview with June Barraclough Benn, 9 Oct. 1992.

60 Pollard, *Bootham School*, pp. 170–1.

61 Michael Rowntree (1932–6) quoted in J. Philip Wragge, ed., *Leslie Howard Gilbert 1892 to 1987: An Appreciation* (York: The Ebor Press, 1988), pp. 3–4. The previous paragraph is based on Wragge, pp. 1–9.

62 Still the definitive, scholarly edition, according to John Kenyon in *The History Men* (London: Weidenfeld

and Nicolson, 1983), p. 174.

63 Taylor, *A Personal History*, pp. 59–60. Books cited taken from Taylor's book lists found in File 5.11, Taylor Papers, Ransome Center. Textbooks which he read in preparation for the Oxford entrance exam included Mary Hollings' *Europe in Renaissance and Reformation* in 1921; Sir John Marriott's *England since Waterloo*, Sidney Herbert's *Modern Europe 1789–1914*, A.D. Innes's *England under the Tudors* and Sir John Seeley's *The Expansion of England* in 1922; and A.F. Pollard's *The History of England*, Marriott's *English Political Institutions* and L.C.A. Knowles's *Industrial and Commercial Revolutions in the Nineteenth Century in Great Britain* in 1923.

64 Taylor, *A Personal History*, p. 59.

65 *Ibid.*, pp. 50–1, 63, p. 50 for the quotation.

66 This was Geoffrey Barraclough, who later held chairs at, *inter alia*, Liverpool and Oxford. Interview with his cousin, June Barraclough Benn, 9 Oct. 1992.

67 Clifford J. Smith to Alan Taylor, 22 July 1982; Taylor to Smith, 7 Aug. 1982; 'The Chronicles of Bedroom 24', 1921, all in Bootham School Archives.

68 Pollard, *Bootham School*, p. 172 for the quotation; Sisman, *A.J.P. Taylor*, pp. 47–8. Taylor, *A Personal History*, p. 62.

69 Taylor, *A Personal History*, p. 62. Professor David d'Avray, an experienced mediaeval palaeographer, insists that no one can read German Schrift easily.

70 Brian Harrison, 'College Life, 1918–1939', in Brian Harrison, ed., *The History of the University of Oxford. Volume VIII: The Twentieth Century* (Oxford: Oxford University Press, 1994), p. 105.

71 Taylor, *A Personal History*, p. 62.

72 Daniel I. Greenstein, 'The Junior Members, 1900–1919: A Profile', in Harrison, *The History of the University of Oxford*, Table 3.3:

'Father's Occupation of Oxford Men and Women in 1900–1913, 1920–1939, 1946–1967', vol. VIII, p. 56.

73 However, from 1902 local education authorities offered grants to all students, although the amounts varied, and by 1937 about twenty-five per cent of those in residence at Oxford held such awards. Greenstein, 'Junior Members', p. 46.

74 Taylor, *A Personal History*, p. 63; Pollard, *Bootham School*, p. 169.

75 The holding of a college award had not quite the scarcity value it later acquired: during 1900–39 between a quarter and a third of all men who matriculated held college scholarships and exhibitions. Greenstein, 'Junior Members', p. 46.

76 Taylor, *A Personal History*, pp. 64–5.

77 *Ibid.*, p. 68; J.I.M. Stewart, *Myself and Michael Innes: A Memoir* (London: Victor Gollancz, 1987), p. 37 for the witching hour.

78 Dacre Balsdon, *Oxford Now and Then* (London: Duckworth, 1970), p. 142; Harold Hobson, *Indirect Journey: An Autobiography* (London: Weidenfeld and Nicolson, 1978), pp. 120–1; entry on Phelps by W.D. Ross, *Dictionary of National Biography*.

79 Taylor, *A Personal History*, pp. 67–8; Greenstein, 'Junior Members', p. 47; according to Table 3.2, p. 53 in Greenstein's chapter, during 1920–9 the secondary school origins of male undergraduates were just under seventy-two per cent from independent schools, just under twelve per cent from maintained schools, just under thirteen per cent from direct grant schools, just over three per cent from other assisted and under one per cent private tuition. Louis MacNeice, *The Strings Are False: An Unfinished Autobiography* (London: Faber, 1965, 1966 pb), p. 104; Harrison, 'College Life, 1918–1939', p. 92.

80 Room Rents 1916–28, Ref. II. L. 24; Quarter Book, Ref. T152, both Administrative Records, Oriel College Archive. Taylor, *A Personal History*, p. 69.

81 The description of Acton is from Evelyn Waugh, *A Little Learning* (London: Chapman and Hall, 1964, Sidgwick and Jackson pb, 1973), p. 189; description of Oxford bags from Martin Green, *Children of the Sun* (New York: Basic Books, 1976), p. 153; description of The George from John Betjeman's chapter in Ann Thwaite, ed., *My Oxford* (London: Robson Books, 1986 pb), p. 65; the Georgeoisie from Betjeman's *Summoned by Bells* (London: John Murray, 1960), p. 93; *A Personal History*, p. 74.

82 *A Personal History*, pp. 74–6.

83 James Morris, *Oxford* (London: Faber, 1965), p. 16.

84 Captain's Book of the Oriel College Boat Club, entries for 1924–5 and 1925–6; *Oriel Record*, vol. IV, no. 9 (June 1925), pp. 284–5 and vol. IV, no. 11 (June 1926).

85 Captain's Book, entry for 1925–6; Taylor, *A Personal History*, p. 79.

86 Taylor, *A Personal History*, pp. 47, 67. The friend was Geoffrey Barraclough. Interview with June Barraclough Benn, 9 Oct. 1992. Barraclough was two years behind Taylor, which means that Taylor was still attending chapel in his third year. His blow for freedom clearly came late in his Oxford career.

87 The surviving Minute Books of the Newlands, Arnold and Prynne Societies reveal no mention of Taylor as having spoken at any meetings. While clearly not being ordinarily attracted to the Plantagenet Society, which heard literary papers, he might have attended an evening devoted to Samuel Butler, one of the writers to whom he was devoted. Those who merely formed the audience were not, of course, listed, so there is no way of knowing.

88 John Theodore (Jack) Yates, fragments of a draft autobiography, held by his great-niece Mrs Nicola Darroch, to whom I am very grateful for giving me full access to his notes and papers. The typewritten draft was lent to an historian and never found its way back to its home; what remains are scattered notes and some pages of a draft.

89 Taylor, *A Personal History*, pp. 72–3; A.L. Rowse, *A Cornishman at Oxford* (London: Jonathan Cape, 1965, 1974), p. 131; M.P. Ashley and C.T. Saunders, *Red Oxford: A History of the Growth of Socialism in the University of Oxford* (Oxford: Oxford University Labour Club, 2nd edn, Jan. 1933), pp. 27–9.

90 Three reports by students of their activities during the strike, 'The Oriel Special Constables', 'The Milk Dump Arranged at Aynho for South Northants and North Oxon' and 'Hay's Wharf', all in the *Oriel Record*, vol. IV, no. 11 (June 1926), pp. 329–34.

91 Taylor, *A Personal History*, p. 80.

92 Yates, draft autobiography.

93 A.J.P. Taylor, 'Class War: 1926', *New Statesman*, 30 April 1976, p. 572.

94 *Ibid.*, pp. 572–3; Taylor, *A Personal History*, pp. 80–1; *Oriel Record*, vol. IV, no. 11 (June 1926), p. 329.

95 Estimate based on Greenstein, 'Junior Members', pp. 58–9.

96 In 1913–14, thirty-six per cent of men and forty-two per cent of women taking Schools read History; this excludes the passmen. In 1932, twenty-nine per cent of men and twenty-seven per cent of women took Schools in History. Robert Currie, 'The Arts and Social Studies, 1914–1939', in Harrison, *History of the University*, Vol. VIII, pp. 110, 116.

97 F.M. Powicke, 'Historical Study in Oxford', inaugural lecture at Oxford, 8 Feb. 1929, reprinted in F.M. Powicke, *Modern Historians and the Study of History: Essays and Papers* (London: Odhams Press, 1955), p. 172; Reba N. Soffer,

Discipline and Power: The Universities, History, and the Making of an English Elite 1870–1930 (Stanford: Stanford University Press, 1994).

98 Stewart, *Myself and Michael Innes*, p. 41. The Divinity exam was finally abolished in 1931.

99 Guizot, *History of Civilization in Europe*; Lavisse, *Vue général de l'histoire politique de l'Europe*; Acton, *Lectures in Modern History*; and Bryce's *History of the Holy Roman Empire*, which Taylor ignored. Book lists, File 5.11, Taylor Papers. Taylor, *A Personal History*, p. 68.

100 *The Examination Statutes ... Revised to July 10, 1926, Together with the Regulations of the Boards of Studies and Boards of Faculties for the Academical Year 1926–1927* (Oxford: Clarendon Press, 1926), pp. 107–19. Smith was obviously *The Wealth of Nations*, Mill was his *Principles of Political Economy* and Gide was likewise *Principles of Political Economy*. With regard to political history up to 1885, the regulations state helpfully that candidates would be expected to show in the examination 'such knowledge of the general outlines of the Political History of England as may be gathered from a modern textbook', p. 109.

101 Taylor, *A Personal History*, pp. 70–1.

102 A.L. Rowse, *Historians I Have Known* (London: Duckworth, 1995), pp. 20–1; Hobson, *Indirect Journey*. pp. 158–9. For Clark as a safe pair of hands, see Chapman to Brierly, 11 June 1929; about Clark's becoming the General Editor of the OHE: File OHE General 1929–31, Oxford University Press Archives, Oxford.

103 Sisman, *A.J.P. Taylor*, p. 66.

104 Taylor, *A Personal History*, pp. 76–8.

105 C.M. Bowra, *Memoirs* (London: Weidenfeld and Nicolson, 1966), pp. 119–20.

106 Taylor, *A Personal History*, p. 71. According to Anthony Kenny,

David Urquhart, Sligger's father, believed that 'in earlier less hygienic centuries ... though the rich had exploited the poor, they had not actually despised the poor because rich and poor had both alike smelt. Now, however, the rich had started to take regular hot baths, and to look down on the poor as the great unwashed. The solution was to build Turkish baths for the poor; that would make them actually cleaner than the rich, who misguidedly soaked themselves in tubfuls of their own dirty water. Accordingly, Urquhart campaigned for the installation of Turkish baths in Irish villages.' Anthony Kenny, *A Life in Oxford* (London: John Murray, 1997), p. 57.

107 Interview with June Barraclough Benn, 9 Oct. 1992; Taylor, *A Personal History*, p. 82.

108 Taylor, *A Personal History*, p. 84.

109 Schools list for June 1927 in Modern History, *Oriel Record*, vol. IV, no. 14 (Dec. 1927); Taylor, *A Personal History*, p. 84.

2 *The Making of the Historian* 1927–1934

1 See e.g. J.C. Masterman, *On the Chariot Wheel: An Autobiography* (Oxford: Oxford University Press, 1975), pp. 149–50.

2 Taylor, *A Personal History*, p. 85.

3 Sisman, *A.J.P. Taylor*, pp. 68–9. Lansbury was again an MP in 1922–40 and leader of the Labour Party 1931–5.

4 *Ibid.*, p. 69.

5 Taylor, *A Personal History*, p. 86.

6 *Ibid.*

7 *Ibid.*, p. 87.

8 Professor David Eastwood finds all of this inherently implausible, and the author sympathises with this reaction, but there is no obvious reason to think that Taylor was lying. Comment by Eastwood on a draft of this chapter.

9 *The Examination Statutes .... for the Academical Year 1928–1929* (Oxford: Oxford University Press, 1928). The examiners for the Gladstone Prize for 1929 were the Vice-Chancellor of the University, Francis William Pember of All Souls; the Regius Professor of Ecclesiastical History, Edward William Watson of Christ Church; and the Chichele Professor of Modern History, Sir Charles Oman of All Souls. Taylor, *A Personal History*, pp. 87–8.

10 *Ibid.*, p. 88: Woodward to S.G.L[ee], n.d., File FD/2, Magdalen College Archives, Magdalen College, Oxford. It would be interesting to know whether there was an Oxford view that the foundations of professional history were German, or whether this was purely the view of an historian who himself worked on European history.

11 Pollard to his father, 22 and 29 Jan. 1911, quoted in Soffer, *Discipline and Power*, p. 159. This same 'conflict' between teaching and research as the primary duty of an academic still occasions discussion. Students themselves increasingly have their own view on the question: one final-year engineering student was quoted (anonymously) in a draft report for the Higher Education Funding Council of England as follows: 'non-research-active staff *teach students to pass exams*, whereas research-active staff *teach students the subject.*' Ronald Bennett, Kelly Coate and Gareth Williams, *Annex A (Draft): Academic Activity*, March 2000, for the HEFCE Fundamental Review.

12 Date of departure based on the Foreign Office stamp dated 21 May 1928 on the photo in his passport. File Personal Memorabilia (Passports), Taylor Papers, Ransome Center. The Hotel Bristol remains luxurious.

13 Haraszti-Taylor, *A Life with Alan*, p. 186; Taylor, *A Personal History*, p. 88 for the quotation; Sisman,

A.J.P. Taylor, p. 76.

14 Taylor, *A Personal History*, p. 88 for all three quotations. Langer later wrote, among other books, *European Alliances and Alignments 1871–1890* (1931) and *The Diplomacy of Imperialism 1890–1902*. Taylor cites both of these books in the annotated bibliography of his *The Struggle for Mastery in Europe 1848–1918*, where he refers in particular to *Alliances and Alignments* as 'outstanding', though he states that in both books Langer sees everything through German eyes. It is worth pointing out that, in his bound list of books read, the only entry on Austria was Grant Hartig, *The Genesis of the Austrian Revolution*, listed under May 1928. Either the list is not comprehensive – difficult to believe – or memory has drawn a veil over a summer of reading primarily devoted to fiction.

15 Taylor to Charles Gott, 9 July 1928, letter in the possession of Mrs Pamela Gott.

16 Taylor, *A Personal History*, p. 89. David Eastwood commented on a draft of this chapter that 'Most of the northern working class had them [wooden mushrooms]. Taylor's assumption that these were continental instruments is v. revealing of his social observation (or lack of it).' Betty Kemp added to the draft that 'so did many of the mid or "upper" class who had learned to darn or sew – or solder.'

17 Taylor, *A Personal History*, pp. 89–90.

18 Sisman, *A.J.P. Taylor*, p. 77 for information about Rowntree and Mann.

19 Taylor, *A Personal History*, p. 90; Innes Stewart to Charles Gott, 13 Nov. 1928, letter in the possession of Mrs Pamela Gott.

20 Stewart to Gott, 13 Nov. 1928 and Taylor to Gott, 14 Nov. 1928, both letters in the possession of Mrs Pamela Gott; Sisman, *A.J.P. Taylor*, p. 76.

21 His first German book, read in September 1928, was a play by Toller, *Die Wandlung* (1919), about the horrors of war and the need for a social revolution; this was followed by plays by Goethe, *Iphigenie auf Tauris*, Shakespeare, and Shaw, *Captain Brassbound's Convention* (*Kapitan Brassbound's Bekehrung*) in October 1928. Only in November does the first history book appear on his reading list, *Das Jahr 1845* by Heinrich Reschauer.

22 Taylor, *A Personal History*, pp. 90, 92–3.

23 *Ibid.*, pp. 90–2.

24 Taylor to Charles Gott, 14 Nov. 1928, letter in the possession of Mrs Pamela Gott.

25 Anthony Burgess, *Little Wilson and Big God: Being the First Part of the Confessions of Anthony Burgess* (Harmondsworth: Penguin Books, 1987, 1988 edn, p. 171.

26 Taylor, *A Personal History*, p. 92.

27 Helmut Gruber, *Red Vienna: Experiment in Working-Class Culture 1919–1934* (Oxford: Oxford University Press, 1991), p. 5 for the quotation, and *passim*.

28 Taylor, *A Personal History*, p. 92. I am grateful to my colleague Dr Axel Körner for his help on Bauer. Bauer had an intellectual if not political influence on Taylor, in that Taylor (and Namier, according to Taylor) derived his views on the Habsburg monarchy from Bauer's book *The Social Democrats and the Nationality Question*. Taylor, *A Personal History*, p. 113.

29 Taylor to Robert Cole, 19 Feb. 1966, cited in Robert Cole, *A.J.P. Taylor: The Traitor within the Gates* (Houndmills: Macmillan Press, 1993), p. 5.

30 Taylor was impressed with Srbik's writing if not his lecturing: in his first book, *The Italian Problem in European Diplomacy, 1847–1849* (Manchester: Manchester University Press, 1934), *Srbik's Metternich: der Staatsmann und der Mensch* (1925) is one of only seven 'secondary authorities' which

Taylor lists in his bibliography, noting that it was 'the one important work of post-war scholarship on this period'.

31 Taylor, *Personal History*, p. 90.

32 Soffer, *Discipline and Power*, p. 89.

33 Taylor, *A Personal History*, pp. 90–1. *The Italian Problem*, pp. vii–viii; Taylor to Robert Cole, 12 Jan. 1966, cited in Cole, *A.J.P. Taylor*, p. 10.

34 Taylor, *A Personal History*, pp. 90–1.

35 Taylor, 'Accident Prone, or What Happened Next', *Journal of Modern History*, vol. 49, no. 1 (March 1977), p. 6. However, it is worth noting that in the acknowledgements which Přibram made in his book of the help which 'Several of my younger friends' had given with the translating, he named Ian F.D. Morrow, Dr Walter Edge and Dr Carleton Sprague Smith, but not Taylor.

36 Cole, *A.J.P. Taylor*, p. 5.

37 Taylor, *A Personal History*, p. 91; Stamp on passport, file Personal Memorabilia (Passports), Taylor Papers, Ransome Center.

38 Taylor, *A Personal History*, p. 94.

39 *Ibid.*, pp. 93, 60–1; Sisman, *A.J.P. Taylor*, p. 80.

40 He wrote in 1977 that 'I took serious steps to become an inspector of ancient monuments, a post for which, apart from my knowledge of Gothic architecture, I was totally unqualified.' 'Accident Prone', p. 5.

41 Taylor, *A Personal History*, p. 94. List of books read, in the possession of Dr Éva Haraszti-Taylor.

42 Taylor, *A Personal History*, p. 94.

43 *Ibid.*, p. 96.

44 *Ibid.*, p. 95.

45 *Ibid.*

46 *Ibid.*, pp. 96–7, 93, 105; Sisman, *A.J.P. Taylor*, pp. 80–1; interview with Frau Henrietta Kotlan-Werner, Vienna, 21 June 1991, for description of the 'sweet, helpless creature'. At least one intellectual woman attracted him: his third wife

was also an academic historian. There may have been others.

47 Taylor, *A Personal History*, p. 97.

48 *Ibid.*, p. 98.

49 *Ibid.*, p. 97. As is often the case with Taylor, the chronology does not entirely match up. It is true that nowadays the Ford Lectures take place in Hilary Term, i.e. January–March, but Přibram's were given in Michaelmas Term 1929 according to the title-page of the printed version, i.e. October–December 1929. However, Taylor should know when he consummated his relationship with his future first wife and got his first post, so perhaps Přibram had stayed on in Oxford for research.

50 *Ibid.*, pp. 97–8.

51 *Ibid.*, p. 98. I am grateful to M. André Etchenique, the Directeur of the hotel, for providing information on its history and an old photograph.

52 The classes were FO 7, 27, 30, 44, 64, 67 and 73.

53 Taylor, *A Personal History*, p. 122.

54 Taylor, *The Italian Problem*, p. viii.

55 Namier to Harold Macmillan, 31 October 1937, quoted in Sisman, *A.J.P. Taylor*, p. 96.

56 Linda Colley, *Lewis Namier* (London: Weidenfeld and Nicolson, 1989), p. 10.

57 In order to get *The Hobbit* published, J.R.R. Tolkien made a deal with Allen and Unwin to pay half the cost of his books and take half of the profits. This was standard procedure at Allen and Unwin at the time (1937) and for years afterwards. Nicolette Jones, 'Will Royalties Remain King?', *Bookseller*, 6 Feb. 1998, p. 23.

58 Taylor to Macmillans publishers, 1 March 1933 and Taylor to H. Macmillan, 17 May 1933, for quotation, both Macmillan Publishers' Archives, Basingstoke.

59 'What puzzled me most, both at the beginning and later, was that every member of Alan's family was so frugal in spite of the fact that they all had investments, which they did not wish to touch – they were

sacrosanct.' Éva Haraszti-Taylor, *Remembering Alan: A Love Story* (Privately printed, 1995), p. 110.

60 Taylor, *A Personal History*, pp. 122; University of Manchester, *Report of the Council to the Court of Governors, November 1933–October 1934* (Manchester University Press, November 1934).

61 Taylor, *A Personal History*, p. 122.

62 Harrison, *History of the University of Oxford*, vol VIII, p. 6.

63 Namier to A.P. Wadsworth, 25 March 1946, quoted in Sisman, *A.J.P. Taylor*, p. 96.

64 Information from Professor David d'Avray, and from David Morgan, who had been a research student of Jacob's at Oxford. 'Golden' came from d'Avray, while Betty Kemp thought it might have been 'learned'. David Eastwood points out that the episode reflected 'a double Oxford prejudice – against the doctorate, and against non-Oxford degrees'.

65 Reference no. TH 11642, John Rylands Library, Manchester University. The author was the first person ever to have consulted it. I am most grateful to Dr Paul Holder, the History Subject Librarian, for having found it. The library was not yet called the John Rylands in 1934. Title given on card on Taylor held in the Department of History, University of Manchester. I am grateful to Professor Peter Gatrell, the Head of Department, for giving me access.

66 Taylor, *A Personal History*, pp. 122, 112.

67 His original first paragraph would have made a brilliant opening for a book review, and indeed smells strongly of one. David Eastwood has pointed out that the statement 'if Italian Unification is now thought to owe more to the methods of contemporary Fascism and of Tammany Hall than Mr. Trevelyan would suggest, depreciation of heroes is yet in itself a form of hero worship' is highly characteristic of Taylor's 'mature' style and shows, more than anything else in the first version, or in the functional substitute sentence, that Taylor was going to be a great historian and a fine writer. He calls the sentence 'echt Taylor'. Comments on a draft of this chapter.

68 With regard to his later pronouncement about the minimum age for publishing a book, Taylor was twenty-eight.

69 Taylor, *The Italian Problem*, p. 3.

70 Taylor to Cole, 12 Jan. 1966, cited in Cole, *A.J.P. Taylor*, p. 9.

71 Taylor wrote in *A Personal History*, p. 113, that he had worked hard from the moment he began to write to make his style simple.

72 A.F. Přibram, *England and the International Policy of the European Great Powers 1871–1914* (Oxford: Clarendon Press, 1931), p. xii.

73 *Cambridge Review*, vol. 56, No. 1380 (3 May 1935), p. 351; *American Historical Review*, vol. 41, no. 3 (April 1936), p. 539; *English Historical Review*, vol. 51, no. 4 (October 1936), p. 747.

74 David Eastwood has made the pointed comment that 'Taylor's mature methodology – though he would always deny it – rested on allowing no-one to speak for themselves'. Comment on draft of this chapter.

75 Taylor, *The Italian Problem*, p. 1. It is worth pointing out that this particular approach, i.e. the attempt to recover the cognitive maps of statesmen, to go behind their words to their unspoken assumptions, is seen as cutting-edge history today.

76 Přibram, *England and the International Policy of the European Great Powers*, pp. 150, 1.

77 Taylor, *The Italian Problem*, pp. 1–2.

78 *Ibid.*, p. 8.

79 *Ibid.* Comment by David Eastwood on draft copy of this chapter.

80 'A Study in Diplomacy', *Times Literary Supplement*, no. 1720 (17 Jan. 1935), p. 27.

81 *Oxford Magazine*, no. 53 (2 May

1935), p. 553.

82 Kent Roberts Greenfield in *American Historical Review*, vol. 41, no. 3 (April 1936), pp. 539–40.

3 The Manchester Years 1930– 1938

1 By the 1870s Owens College had so prospered that, according to Tout, it felt limited in its course development by its external validating body, 'the so-called University of London, for whose examinations its students had perforce to prepare. About 1877 it started an agitation for a Manchester University, but Yorkshire opposed this in the imagined interests of the Yorkshire College, Leeds, while Liverpool also objected, though there was then no college in that city.' A compromise was adopted by which there was established in Manchester a degree-giving institution, called the Victoria University, of which Owens College was the first college and which was joined by the University College, Liverpool in 1884 and the Yorkshire College, Leeds in 1887. By the last years of the century, however, the pressures for the establishment of three independent universities became overwhelming, and in 1903 the decision was taken to dissolve Victoria University. The first head of the Department of History in the new Victoria University of Manchester was T.F. Tout, who as head of the department of Owens College since 1890 had been amongst those who had worked most strongly for its re-establishment as an independent university. T.F. Tout, 'The Future of Victoria University', *The Collected Papers of T.F. Tout; With a Memoir and Bibliography* (Manchester: Manchester University Press, 1932), p. 45.

2 T.F. Tout, 'An Historical Laboratory', *The Collected Papers*, p. 80. For information on the Manchester University history department and Tout's place in it, see Peter R.H. Slee, *Learning and a Liberal Education: The Study of Modern History in the Universities of Oxford, Cambridge and Manchester, 1800–1914* (Manchester: Manchester University Press, 1986), chapter 8.

3 Rather the sort of training now required by the British GCSE examination in history, taken at age sixteen.

4 Tout, 'An Historical Laboratory', *The Collected Papers*, p. 82.

5 Tout, 'Schools of History', *The Collected Papers*, p. 96.

6 *Ibid.*, pp. 98–9.

7 *The Victoria University of Manchester Calendar 1930–1931* (Manchester: Manchester University Press, 1930), pp. 364–83; for numbers of students, University of Manchester, *Report of the Council to the Court of Governors*, Nov. 1931 (Manchester: Manchester University Press, 1931).

8 Slee, *Learning and a Liberal Education*, p. 157. Until 1920 Honours students took two special subjects.

9 All information on the syllabus taken from Manchester University Calendar for 1929–30, 1930–1 and 1931–2. The prescribed set books for all Honours students in 1930–1 were Aristotle's *Politics*, Locke's *Civil Government*, Rousseau's *Contrat social*, and Dante's *De Monarchia* (in English); all but the Dante were the set texts in the Oxford History School's Political Theory paper as followed by the author in 1970–1. The special subjects available in 1930, when Taylor took up his post, were (1) The Transition to the Roman Empire 59BC to 37AD and the Empire under Augustus, 29BC to 37AD; (2) The Period of the Conciliar Movement, 1378–1448; (3) The Age of Constitutional Experiment. English History 1783–1801; and (4) The Age of Economic Reform. British Economic History 1830–1848.

10 Slee, *Learning and a Liberal Education*, p. 5, n. 9, p. 154.

11 Sisman, *Taylor*, p. 84.

12 *Economic History of England 1760–1860* (1931), *Manchester Merchants and Foreign Trade* (1934) and *The History of Local Government in Manchester* (1939–40).

13 Taylor, *A Personal History*, p. 103.

14 *Ibid.*

15 *Ibid.*

16 W.A. Pantin, 'Ernest Fraser Jacob 1894–1971', *Proceedings of the British Academy*, vol. 58 (1972), pp. 455, 463, 462.

17 Taylor, *A Personal History*, p. 103. The Assistant Lecturer was Mabel Phythian, a Manchester University BA, who had gained an Upper Second in 1919. H. Hale Bellot, Reader in Modern History, had also left, to take up the Commonwealth Fund Chair in American History at University College London.

18 Chris Wrigley, 'Alan John Percivale Taylor 1906–1990', *Proceedings of the British Academy*, vol. 82 (1993), p. 499.

19 Taylor, *A Personal History*, pp. 98–9. G.P. Gooch, *Recent Revelations in European Diplomacy* and H.N. Brailsford, *The War of Steel and Gold*, both read in January 1931 and, in the case of Brailsford, reread (first read in 1924); Gooch, *Modern Europe 1878–1919* and S.B. Fay, *The Origins of the World War*, both read in February 1931; there is no mention of either Dickinson or Russell in his book lists covering 1921 on, though 1926 is missing.

20 It appears that they were also used by schoolboys: the main early modern textbook at Stockport Grammar, at least during the 1930s and early 1940s, was A.H. Johnson. Letter from Mr Alan Baxendale to the author, 17 May 1998.

21 The cost of the complete set of eight volumes was £2.8s.0d.

22 Indeed, the author owns copies of two of the volumes in the series, and in both is the bookplate of 'Adolphus William Ward, Kt, Litt.D, F.B.A. Master of Peterhouse', the Editor of the *Cambridge Modern History*, the *Cambridge History of English Literature* and the *Cambridge History of British Foreign Policy*.

23 Henry Offley Wakeman, *Europe 1598–1715* (London: Rivington, Percival and Co., 1894), pp. 2, 393; W. Alison Phillips, *Modern Europe 1815–1899* (London: Rivingtons, 1901), p. 1.

24 But see David d'Avray on the 'weak *Zeitgeist* principle', *Death and the Prince: Memorial Preaching before 1350* (Oxford: Clarendon Press, 1994), pp. 223–4. Administrative historians of the modern period, however, do occasionally refer to the 'official mind'.

25 Taylor, *A Personal History*, p. 104.

26 *Ibid.*, p. 101.

27 These offices have now been taken over by university administrative staff.

28 Taylor, *A Personal History*, pp. 101–2.

29 Quoted from a letter from Mr Alan Baxendale to the author, 17 May 1998. The student who took tea was Miss Betty Kemp, interview with the author.

30 Taylor, *A Personal History*, pp. 103–4.

31 For numbers of students, *Report of the Council*, 1930–1, 1931–2 and 1932–3; it must be admitted that the conclusion drawn from the numbers of students cited necessarily assumes that the number who might have enrolled was constant, a point mentioned by David Eastwood in his comments on a draft of this chapter. Information on Tout's lecturing taken from V.H Galbraith's entry in the *Dictionary of National Biography*, in which he writes that 'He was a fine lecturer. He carried his subject in his head, speaking always without notes or even immediate preparation, but with illuminating digressions suggested by his own special studies or his travels.' On student recognition of Taylor's

source, letter from A. Baxendale to author, 17 May 1998.

32 A.H. Johnson, *Europe in the Sixteenth Century 1494–1598* (London: Rivingtons, 1925 (7th edn, 9th impression)). The notes were taken by Miss Evelyn Liddle, an Honours History student at Manchester 1935–8; she married a fellow student, J. Roskell, later Professor of History at the university. I am grateful to their son, Mr Edmund Roskell, for giving me the lecture notes. As a very old man, Professor Roskell still remembered Taylor's lectures, in particular that he lectured from memory, that he had prodigious powers of factual recollection, that the lectures were very popular and that his style was 'narrative and observations thereon'. Professor Roskell's notes on a letter to him from the author, 10 Feb. 1998. Based on Miss Liddle's notes, Taylor's forty-eight lectures turned out to be forty-five, with the final eight, all given in the third term, entirely devoted to the French Revolution and Napoleon. According to Betty Kemp, the Erasmus quotation was already in circulation.

33 First quotation from Sisman, *A.J.P. Taylor*, p. 86; second quotation from a letter from Mr Alan Baxendale to the author, 19 May 1998; and third quotation from E.F. Jacob to Bruce McFarland, 8 May 1938, File FD/2, Magdalen College Archives.

34 Taylor, *A Personal History*, p. 105.

35 Taylor to Kingsley Martin, 25 Nov. ?1944, Box 15, File 2, Kingsley Martin Papers, Sussex University.

36 Sisman, *A.J.P. Taylor*, p. 89. Sisman does not give his source, but presumably it was Rowntree.

37 Taylor, *A Personal History*, p. 106. The wedding was announced in *The Times* of 5 Oct. 1931.

38 Taylor, *A Personal History*, p. 107.

39 The area is no longer quite as smart. The house now forms part of a nursing home.

40 The author bought the desk at Sotheby's and is writing this biography on it.

41 Chris Wrigley, ed., *A.J.P. Taylor: From the Boer War to the Cold War. Essays on Twentieth-Century Europe* (London: Hamish Hamilton, 1995), p. xvii.

42 Taylor, *A Personal History*, p. 107. One knowledgeable estimate is that he possibly earned, say, £100 per annum from the investments, which would make Margaret's contribution £500 per annum. Comment by Jeremy Wormell, August 1998. Depending on just when his father gave him the policy, it may be that this was his wedding present. By the late 1930s he and Margaret both had shares in Unilever (although she may have inherited hers). Interview with Henrietta Kotlan-Werner in her home in Vienna, 22 June 1991.

43 Sisman, *A.J.P. Taylor*, p. 90; Taylor, *A Personal History*, pp. 107–8; see, for example, Taylor to Malcolm Muggeridge, 16 June 1933: 'When you pay me some interest in September, may I suggest that you pay me £10–£20 of the principal as well, according to taste?' Malcolm Muggeridge Papers, Wheaton College, Wheaton, Illinois.

44 Taylor, *A Personal History*, p. 108.

45 *Ibid.*, pp. 108, 114, 121, 128–9. Interview with Henrietta Kotlan-Werner, 22 June 1991, for the clavichord.

46 Taylor, *A Personal History*, pp. 108–9. The Shirley Institute was the Cotton, Silk and Man-Made Fibres Research Association. David Holloway, *Stalin and the Bomb: The Soviet Union and Atomic Energy 1939–1956* (New Haven and London: Yale University Press, 1994), p. 103, n. 55. Peter Goodchild, *J. Robert Oppenheimer: 'Shatterer of Worlds'* (London: BBC, 1980), pp. 69–70.

47 Malcolm Muggeridge, *Chronicles of Wasted Time. Part I: The Green Stick* (London: Collins, 1972), p. 141.

48 Beatrice Webb's assessment is from her diary entry for 1 August 1932, while Rosalind Dobbs's is in the entry for 21 October 1933, both from Norman and Jeanne MacKenzie, eds, *The Diary of Beatrice Webb. Volume Four. 1924–1943: The Wheel of Life* (Cambridge, Mass: Harvard University Press, 1985), pp. 287, 315.

49 Malcolm Muggeridge, *Picture Palace* (London: Weidenfeld and Nicolson, repr. 1987), pp. 69, 50; Richard Ingrams, *Muggeridge* (London: HarperCollins, 1996 pb), pp. 60–1.

50 Taylor, *A Personal History*, p. 109.

51 This line appeared in the first edition of May 1937. However, after it was criticised by George Orwell in 1940, on the grounds that it could only have been written by someone 'to whom murder is at most a *word*', Auden changed it to 'The conscious acceptance of guilt in the fact of murder' for his 1940 collection *Another Time*. Humphrey Carpenter, *W.H. Auden: A Biography* (London: George Allen and Unwin, 1981), p. 219.

52 Taylor to Muggeridge, 13 Feb. 1933, Muggeridge Papers, Wheaton College.

53 Taylor, *A Personal History*, p. 117. Taylor to Muggeridge, 13 Feb. 1933, Muggeridge Papers, Wheaton. I am grateful to Mr and Mrs Adrian Lutte, in 1997 the owners of Three Gates Cottage, for showing me round the house and allowing me to read the series of deeds of the cottage: Mr Moodie had paid £20 for it, not £25 as Taylor said; it cost Taylor £525, not £500 as he later remembered; and when Taylor sold it in 1939 he received £825.

54 This may have been poetic licence, and it is certainly not true now: to the side and behind is a converted barn, while immediately behind Three Gates is another, newer house. Then comes the main road, with houses on the further side of the road. Only then is there open

country. The Luttes have raised the roof of the house and altered some windows, but Taylor would still recognise it.

55 Taylor was dispirited by the changes when he saw the house in 1982. Taylor, *Personal History*, p. 272. The farm lane, called Corks Lane, is now tarmacked. The left-hand part of the land, which stepped down and was his vegetable garden, is now occupied by a house called Kinder View. Margaret's flower garden is now occupied by a garage and privately tarmacked parking space belonging to the owners of Kinder View, plus some lawn. The garage entirely blocks the view of Kinder Scout from all but the most western window of Three Gates.

56 Taylor, *A Personal History*, p. 118.

57 Mark A. Bloomfield, letter to the *Independent* printed as a supplement to Robert Skidelsky's obituary of 8 Sept. 1990.

58 Taylor, *A Personal History*, pp. 118–20; Mark A. Bloomfield to the *Independent*, supplement to the obituary of Taylor by Robert Skidelsky, 8 Sept. 1990.

59 Taylor, *A Personal History*, p. 112.

60 *Ibid.*, pp. 104–5. *The Structure of Politics at the Accession of George III*, 2 vols (London: Macmillan and Co., Limited, 1929) and *England in the Age of the American Revolution* (London: Macmillan and Co., Limited, 1930). Trevelyan's review had appeared in the *Nation*, 15 Nov. 1930.

61 Taylor, *A Personal History*, pp. 112–14.

62 *Ibid.*, pp. 111–13.

63 Colley, *Lewis Namier*, pp. 99–100.

64 *Ibid.*, p. 46. Namier's comment is taken by Colley from Lucy Sutherland, 'Lewis Namier and Institutional History', *Annali della Fondazione Italiana per la Storia Amministrativa*, no. 4 (1967).

65 David Eastwood, a social historian, argues that 'the point profes-sionally, surely, is that *Origins*

demonstrated the limitations of traditional diplomatic history in interpreting the origins of the second world war.' Comment on draft chapter.

66 Isaiah Berlin, 'L.B. Namier', *Personal Impressions* (London: The Hogarth Press, 1980), p. 70.

67 Taylor, *A Personal History*, p. 126. This became known as the Night of the Long Knives.

68 *Ibid.*, pp. 115–16; *Manchester Guardian*, 25 June 1934, p. 11.

69 Taylor, *A Personal History*, pp. 120, 116; *Manchester Guardian*, 22 Oct. 1934, p. 11.

70 Taylor, *A Personal History*, pp. 124–6.

71 *Ibid.*, p. 127; *Manchester Guardian*, 18 Dec. 1935, p. 5.

72 Taylor, *A Personal History*, pp. 127–8.

73 *Ibid.*, p. 131.

74 Interview with Frau Henrietta Kotlan-Werner, in her home in Vienna, 21 and 22 June 1991.

75 Heinrich Friedjung, *The Struggle for Supremacy in Germany 1859–1866*, translated by A.J.P. Taylor and W.L. McElwee (London: Macmillan and Co., 1935), p. xvi.

76 Professor Chris Wrigley remembers Taylor telling him that he had suggested that the book be translated. Wrigley, 'Alan John Percivale Taylor 1906–1990', p. 499.

77 Professor Chris Wrigley speculates that the whole idea for the translation arose because Namier needed books for the new series and Taylor came up with the idea of the Friedjung. Telephone conversation with author, 11 Jan. 1999.

78 Taylor to Macmillan, 13 Dec. and 20 Dec. 1934, 25 Jan, 15 Feb. and 9 April 1935, Macmillan Publishers' Archive. In 1966 the book was reissued in America. McElwee's daughter wrote that 'After Bill [her father] died, Alan Taylor sent me a cheque for a little over £2 with a note expressing the hope that "it

made me feel rich".' Harriet Hall, *Bill and Patience: An Eccentric Marriage at Stowe and Beyond* (Lewes, Sussex: The Book Guild, 2000), p. 89.

79 *Time and Tide*, 15 Sept. 1935 and *Cambridge Review*, 11 Oct. 1935.

80 Taylor, *A Personal History*, pp. 122–3.

81 Johannes Lapsius *et al.*, eds, *Die grosse Politik der Europäischen Kabinette 1871–1914: Sammlung der diplomatischen Akten des Auswärtigen Amtes* (Berlin: Deutsche Verlagsgesellschaft für Politik und Geschichte, 1922–); G.P. Gooch and Harold Temperley, eds, *British Documents on the Origins of the War 1898–1914* (London: HMSO, 1926–38); Ministère des affaires étrangères, *Documents diplomatiques français (1871–1914)* (Paris: Imprimerie Nationale, 1929).

82 University of Manchester, *Faculty of Arts Examination Papers, 1937*, pp. 306–8 for Taylor's questions.

83 Taylor, *A Personal History*, p. 123. Taylor to Macmillan, 19 Nov. 1937; Summary of *Germany's First Bid*, 1,500 copies printed, sold for 7s.6d., out of print 24 June 1950, both Macmillan and Co. Archive, Basingstoke.

84 Taylor, *Germany's First Bid for Colonies 1884–1885: A Move in Bismarck's European Policy* (London: Macmillan and Co., 1938), pp. 21–2, 84–5. Taylor, *A Personal History*, p. 123.

85 Taylor, 'Accident Prone', p. 8 and *A Personal History*, p. 133.

86 Taylor, *A Personal History*, p. 132.

87 Sisman, *A.J.P. Taylor*, p. 76 for the Cohn comment; Woodward to S.G. Lee, n.d. but probably May 1938, Magdalen College Archives; Taylor, 'Accident Prone', p. 8.

88 Namier to the Secretary to the Tutorial Board, Magdalen College, 9 May 1938, File FD/2, Magdalen College Archives.

89 B.H. Sumner to Bruce McFarlane, 8 May 1938, File FD/2, Magdalen College Archives.

90 E.F. Jacob to Bruce [McFarlane], 9 May 1938, *ibid.*

91 Woodward to Lee, n.d., *ibid.*

92 Taylor, *A Personal History*, p. 133.

93 Richard Ollard, *A Man of Contradictions: A Life of A.L. Rowse* (London: Allen Lane, The Penguin Press, 1999), p. 78. According to Ollard, Rowse continued to acknowledge Taylor's gifts 'in his furious denunciations of their misuse'. *Ibid.*

94 Taylor, *A Personal History*, p. 134.

4 The Oxford Years 1938–1963

1 These took place on 22 May 1946, 5 December 1951 and 28 June 1954. Of course, he missed those that took place during his two periods of sabbatical leave, the academic years 1950–1 and 1960–1, which he spent largely in London. College Orders, CMM/2/7, CMM/2/11, CMM/2/12, CMM/2/15 and CMM/2/20, Magdalen College Archives.

2 Sir John Coles takes issue with this description, arguing that everyone then thought of Oxford as 'national', not 'parochial'. Coles to the author, 19 April 1999.

3 Oxford is a federal university and Magdalen is one of over thirty separate, and significantly autonomous, colleges. Madgalen in the academic year 1938–9, Taylor's first, had 221 undergraduate students, all of whom would have received the bulk of their teaching in Magdalen itself. There were forty-two Fellows and ten Lecturers, as well as ten Honorary Fellows, including Sir Frederick Kenyon, Director of the British Museum; the Right Hon. and Most Rev. Cosmo Gordon Lang, Archbishop of Canterbury; Geoffrey Dawson, Editor of *The Times*; and Reginald Lane Poole, the historian.

4 Thomas Babington Macaulay, *The History of England from the Accession of James II* (London: Longman, Brown, Green and Longmans, 1849), Vol. 2, pp. 288–9. Historical information on Magdalen from A.R. Woolley, *The Clarendon Guide to Oxford*, new edition (Oxford: Oxford University Press, 1979), pp. 42–9, certainly the most learned of the general guides to the university.

5 Macaulay, *The History of England*, vol. 2, p. 287.

6 'When President Clerke died in 1687 James II ordered the Fellows to elect a Roman Catholic, Anthony Farmer, whose vicious life was notorious and who had been expelled from Cambridge. Farmer was disqualified not only by his evil reputation but also by the fact that he had never been a Fellow of either Magdalen or New College, as the statutes required. The College respectfully begged the King to excuse them and waited as long as the statutes allowed in the hope that James might make a more suitable nomination. When none came they elected John Hough whom the Visitor at once admitted to office. This infuriated the King, who called the Fellows before the Court of High Commission, and who now ordered them to elect Samuel Parker, Bishop of Oxford, who was also unqualified. The Fellows pointed out that there was no vacancy, Hough having been properly elected and admitted. James then came to Oxford and sent for them to come to the Deanery at Christ Church, where he furiously rated them as they knelt before him and told them that unless they did as he bade them, he would not only turn them out but would bar them for ever from any preferment in the Church; that is to say he would deprive them of all means of livelihood. Only three Fellows submitted to him ... but the contest had raised such feeling that a public subscription was raised to help the ejected, and the King's own

daughter, Mary, gave £200. ... But the popular enthusiasm aroused by the acquittal of the Seven Bishops in June, the dismay caused by the birth of the Old Pretender, and the movement to put William of Orange on the throne, caused James to begin, too late, to retreat. He permitted the restoration of Hough and the expelled Fellows on 25 October 1688, a day ever after celebrated at Magdalen as Restoration Day. Two months later his exile began and the reign of the Stuart kings had ended.' Woolley, *The Clarendon Guide to Oxford*, pp. 45–6.

7 *Autobiography of Edward Gibbon* (London: Oxford University Press, World's Classics edn, 1907), pp. 36, 40. Angus Macintyre, Fellow and Tutor in Modern History at Magdalen, offered in 1994 a gloss on Gibbon's remarks: 'On 2 April 1752, a boy not yet 15, small and slight, with a large head and prodigiously unathletic body, unevenly educated and brilliantly precocious, was entered as a gentleman commoner of the College. ... Our gentleman commoner, in his "elegant" three-room set in New Buildings, had high, indeed unrealistic, hopes. They were rapidly dashed. ... He got on personally quite well with his tutor, Dr Thomas Waldegrave, whose "mild behaviour had gained my confidence". But Waldegrave unfortunately devised no coherent plan of study for his pupil. He set Gibbon to construing the comedies of Terence rather than helping him to learn Arabic and so enabling him to plunge into the excitements of Oriental scholarship which the University could have provided so abundantly. Since he found his lessons "devoid of profit or pleasure", he simply apologised and absented himself, on which Dr Waldegrave "gently smiled." This lack of guidance and discipline was compound by his bad relations with

his second tutor Dr Thomas Winchester, who gets the most savage treatment in the *Memoirs*: "Dr **** well remembered that he had a salary to receive, and only forgot that he had a duty to perform".' Using other sources, Macintyre makes an effort to demonstrate that Magdalen comes out rather better in other works. 'Edward Gibbon and Magdalen', *Magdalen College Record* (1994), pp. 54–5. My thanks to David Worswick for bringing this article to my notice.

8 Cited in Bevis Hillier, *Young Betjeman* (London: John Murray, 1988), p. 128.

9 Hugh Trevor-Roper to Wallace Notestein, 28 Jan. 1951, Box 8, Folder 747, Notestein Papers, Yale University Library.

10 R.W. Johnson, 'Diary', *London Review of Books*, 8 May 1986, p. 21.

11 Karl Leyser, 'Kenneth Bruce McFarlane: A Memoir', in K.B. McFarlane, *Letters to Friends 1940–1966* (Oxford: Magdalen College, Oxford, 1997), p. xxii. William Thomas has pointed out that the crucial thing about Magdalen's conservatism before 1914 was that it had only three Presidents between 1789 and that date. Thomas to the author, 12 April 1999.

12 Taylor, *A Personal History*, p. 139.

13 *Ibid*. Swimming-pool comment by Professor David Eastwood, who had it from a former Fellow of the college, Angus Macintyre.

14 Johnson, 'Diary', *London Review of Books*, 8 May 1986, p. 21.

15 This was *The Oxford Dictionary of English Etymology* (1966). Onions died as the volume was going through the press. According to the Publishers' Note at the front of the volume, Onions had drafted nearly all of the entries himself.

16 Taylor, *A Personal History*, p. 140.

17 Fellow and Tutor in Philosophy 1923–58, Vice-President 1937, Weldon had been awarded the M.C.

and Bar in 1918 and was to serve as a wing commander in the R.A.F. at Bomber Command Headquarters 1942–44. He was the author of *Kant's 'Critique of Pure Reason'* (1945), *States and Morals* (1946) and *The Vocabulary of Politics* (1953). According to Taylor, 'there is a very good, but malicious, portrait of him' in C.S. Lewis' novel *This Hideous Strength*. This character encourages a young Fellow to sell his soul to the devil, and then, when the bargain goes wrong, says, 'My dear fellow, it was your decision. What else did you expect?' Taylor, *A Personal History*, p. 139. This is all very confusing. First of all, Taylor quotes Weldon elsewhere (*ibid.*, p. 161) as saying 'Well, what did you expect?', which he clearly sees as Weldon's catchphrase. Furthermore, he states that Weldon embraced logical positivism and carried it to extremes, upon which 'all value judgements became for him matters of taste, neither true nor false', a belief to which Lewis may well have taken exception. On the other hand, no character in the novel utters the words Taylor quotes. The closest character might be Curry, the Sub-Warden of Bracton; it might be Lord Feverstone; or the two of them might divide Weldonian traits. The only certain thing is that Taylor never read the book himself; in fact, based on the evidence of his list of books read, he never read any C.S. Lewis at all. His statements can only have been based on Senior Common Room gossip.

The following e-mail of 26 April 2000 was sent by the C.S. Lewis Foundation with regard to Weldon's being a model for Lord Feverstone (Dick Devine):

Devine is 'probably' also a composite, though he is most often associated with T.D. (Harry) Weldon, a philosophy tutor at Lewis's college at Oxford and his nemesis. Weldon was a pro-gressive and a free thinker, and he and Lewis took opposite sides, not only in philosophical matters, but also in the college's political affrays. At some points their relationship became so strained that they were barely on speaking terms. Lewis particularly disliked Weldon's arrogance in debate, his deliberate rudeness such as we see in Feverstone's treatment of Canon Jewel and others. If Weldon really were the model for Devine, then Lewis's satire here is especially pointed; he gives Weldon's nickname, Harry, to the half-witted boy whom Devine tries to kidnap before deciding to take Ransom instead. However, it would be a mistake to associate Devine too closely with Weldon. After all, the latter was an academic and a trained philosopher, one whose intellectual credentials Lewis seemed to assume with a begrudging respect. Devine, on the other hand, is a breezy man of the world, an intellectual dilettante whose only interest lies in getting ahead (though he was elected to a fellowship under mysterious circumstances). One cannot imagine Devine, even for a moment, stopping to consider the historicity of the Gospels or the nature of morality. His natural milieu is not a university town but London. In fact, Devine is the incarnation of the values that Lewis associated with boyhood. Lewis explains that Ransom felt for Devine 'that sort of distaste we feel for someone whom we have admired in boyhood for a very brief time and then outgrown'. Devine had entertained his schoolfellows 'with that kind of humour which consists in a perpetual parody of the sentimental or idealistic clichés of one's elders'. His flippancy and cynicism, his worldly and sophisticated air, the 'varnished vulgarity' of his speech were, arguably seen by Lewis as characteristically Weldonian.

I am very grateful to Jane Card, who attempted to follow the trail Taylor laid and thereby to ascertain the identity of the supposed Weldon character. Letter from David Worswick to the author, 9 April 1999. Warnock was a Prize Fellow at Magdalen from 1949, and Fellow and Tutor in Philosophy, 1953–71.

18 Johnson, 'Diary', *London Review of Books*, 8 May 1986, p. 21.

19 Ved Mehta, *The Fly and the Fly-Bottle: Encounters with British Intellectuals* (New York: Columbia University Press, 1983 pb), pp. 57–8; Taylor, *A Personal History*, pp. 139–40.

20 Thompson wrote his autobiography in verse. His comment on his change of subject: 'Finding the changing fashion of the Schools/ Called for new tutoring, I changed my tools, /Unyoked my mind from theologic mystery,/And hitched it to the sober car of history.' *My Apologia* (Oxford: Alden Press, June 1940). Cited in Hillier, *Young Betjeman*, p. 137. Information on Thompson and his Doubts from Dr Robin Darwall-Smith, Archivist of Magdalen College. According to Taylor, when Thompson reached sixty, 'Weldon and others, who cared nothing for his eminence as a scholar and only knew that he was a bad tutor, turned him out. This was a discreditable transaction at which Thompy was rightly aggrieved. I am glad that I made amends later by having him elected an Honorary Fellow – against considerable opposition.' Taylor, *A Personal History*, p. 141. David Worswick points out that sixty was the retirement age specified in the Statutes at that time. Letter to author, 9 April 1999.

21 Peter Smithers, 'Bruce McFarlane – A Prince among Tutors', *Magdalen College Record* (1994), p. 78. One informant has told the author

that the brightest undergraduates destroyed Lee. Private information.

22 Taylor, *A Personal History*, p. 140.

23 Leyser, 'Kenneth Bruce McFarlane', p. xxii; Rowse, *Historians I Have Known*, p. 67.

24 G.L. Harriss, 'Introduction to the Letters', in McFarlane, *Letters to Friends*, p. xxix. *John Wycliffe and the Beginnings of English Nonconformity* (London: English Universities Press, 1952).

25 G.L. Harriss, entry on McFarlane in John Cannon *et al.*, eds, *The Blackwell Dictionary of Historians* (Oxford: Basil Blackwell, 1988), p. 261.

26 *Hans Memling* (Oxford: Oxford University Press, 1971); *Lancastrian Kings and Lollard Knights* (Oxford: Oxford University Press, 1972); *The Nobility of Later Medieval England* (Oxford: Oxford University Press, 1973); and the collected essays in *England in the Fifteenth Century* (London: Hambledon Press, 1981). This work by his pupils was presumably at the expense of their own research and writing, a mark of the devotion that McFarlane inspired.

27 Leyser, 'Kenneth Bruce McFarlane', p. xiii. Ollard, *A Man of Contradictions*, p. 78.

28 Quotation from Michael Ignatieff, *Isaiah Berlin: A Life* (London: Chatto and Windus, 1998), p. 70. Elizabeth Durbin, *New Jerusalems: The Labour Party and the Economics of Democratic Socialism* (London: Routledge, 1985), p. 98. Interview with Lady Longford (Elizabeth Pakenham), 27 July 1998. Lady Longford said that Cole was not a member, as he was a different generation, and that she never saw McFarlane there. Ignatieff cites Cole as a member.

29 McFarlane, *Letters to Friends*, pp. xxix, 252.

30 Rowse, *Historians I Have Known*, p. 66.

31 'The Dedicated Historian: Leopold von Ranke's Correspondence', *Times Literary Supplement*, 12 May

1950, pp. 285–6; letters from Noel Annan, G.P. Gooch, Pieter Geyl and Howard Brogan, as well as a reply by Taylor to Annan, in *ibid.*, 26 May, 2 June and 23 June 1950. McFarlane to Scarfe, 16 May 1950, McFarlane, *Letters to Friends*, p. 76.

32 McFarlane to Harriss, 7 June 1954, McFarlane, *Letters to Friends*, p. 104.

33 McFarlane to Harriss, 8 Feb. 1956, *ibid.*, p. 126.

34 W.H. Lewis, ed., *Letters of C.S. Lewis* (London: Geoffrey Blas, 1966), p. 103. Sir John Coles states that 'I wish you joy' remained at least until the late 1950s, when President Boase said it to him. Coles to the author, 19 April 1999.

35 M.C. Gordon, *The Life of George S. Gordon 1881–1942* (London: Oxford University Press, 1945), p. 159. 'I sat the "Prize Fellowship" and Examination in January 1969 and in February, as I was going in to Exeter (where I was a PG student) the porter called me over and said there was a message for me from Magdalen: it just said "please attend the President's Lodgings at 6 pm for sherry. Gown and subfusc." So I turned up, and was greeted by the barrel-shaped Griffiths, given a glass of ghastly sherry and then told to follow. I processed behind the sweeping & smelly gown through the cloisters and into a little doorway I had never noticed before and found a collection of ... men in gowns standing in two rows, and at their head a kind of knee-cushion, but as the centre room was candle-lit it was quite hard to see just what was going on. The president went to the head of the little gauntlet and I followed instructions to KNEEL in front of him whilst he intoned some abracadabra. And that was that: I was a fellow of the college. I never ever had anything in writing, such as a job offer, a letter of congratulations – don't even mention a contract!' David Bellos to the author, 24 March 1999. According to John Stoye, Taylor's colleague as

History Tutor, the ceremony remains pretty much as Lewis described it. He queried Bellos's description of the sherry as 'ghastly', however, noting that Griffiths was a noted connoisseur of wines. John Stoye to the author, 23 April 1999.

36 Taylor, *A Personal History*, pp. 138–9. The civil servant from the Sudan was Arnold John Forster (1885–1968), who had worked in the Sudan 1906–30, mainly in the financial departments. He was Estates Bursar 1930–40.

37 *Ibid.*, p. 138; Gordon, *The Life of George S. Gordon*, p. 114, quoting Canon Adam Fox, then Dean of the Divinity School. M.C. Gordon, ed., *The Letters of George S. Gordon, 1902–1942* (London: Oxford University Press, 1943), *passim*. According to Robin Darwall-Smith, the Magdalen Archivist, there are about thirty files of Gordon's presidential correspondence, which betokens at least some official work. Darwall-Smith to the author, 8 April 1999.

38 George Sayer, *Jack. A Life of C.S. Lewis* (London: Hodder and Stoughton, 1977 pb), pp. 192–3.

39 This evocative description is by John Stoye. Letter to the author, 23 April 1999.

40 Sayer, *Jack*, pp. 193–4; for three courses by 1976 see A.J.P. Taylor, *An Old Man's Diary* (London, Hamish Hamilton, 1984), p. 142, diary of 18–31 Aug. 1983 for the *London Review of Books*.

41 He adds that 'The Sunday night dinner is dead now [1983] – killed off by the general spread of marriage and the lack of domestic servants.' Taylor, *A Personal History*, p. 142.

42 Deed of house, seen by kind permission of Mr and Mrs Adrian Luttes of Three Gates Cottage on 9 Feb. 1997. Taylor, *A Personal History*, pp. 142–3. About Morocco he wrote that it was 'one of the greatest works of civilisation', *Manchester Guardian*, 15 May 1939.

43 Taylor, *A Personal History*, p. 149; Sisman, *A.J.P. Taylor*, pp. 129–30 for the obituary.

44 Taylor, *A Personal History*, p. 149; Sisman, *A.J.P. Taylor*, p. 130 for Taylor's resentment.

45 Colleges do encourage students to attend the lectures covering the material on which they will be examined in Prelims; these are arranged by the History Faculty Board. The stipends of CUF Lecturers, who give the majority of the series of lectures, are paid by the university, one reason perhaps why the colleges have never enforced attendance.

46 Sisman, *A.J.P. Taylor*, pp. 139–40.

47 R.B. Bosworth, *Explaining Auschwitz and Hiroshima: History Writing and the Second World War* (London: Routledge, 1993), p. 39.

48 Taylor, *A Personal History*, p. 138. His colleague C.S. Lewis felt the same, alluding in 1931 to the 'long tedious hours of tutorials'. Stephen Schofield, 'Oxford Loses a Genius', in Schofield, ed., *In Search of C.S. Lewis* (South Plainfield, N.J.: Bridge Publishing, 1983), p. 150.

49 Taylor, *A Personal History*, p. 138. John Stoye pointed out that the most famous Oxford league table, the Norrington Table, first appeared only in 1964, after Taylor had ceased to be a Tutorial Fellow. However, David Worswick compiled his own and stated that Magdalen came top or in the first three for some years after the end of the war.

50 Interview with John Stoye, 30 June 1998. Stoye was appointed Fellow and Tutor in Modern History at Magdalen in July 1948.

51 William Thomas, 'Recollections of A.J.P. Taylor', *Contemporary European History*, Vol. 3, no. 1 (1994), p. 62. William Thomas has been a Student (i.e. Fellow and Tutor) in Modern History at Christ Church since 1967. John Steane to author about the waistcoat and the Napoleon III model whilst both were researching in the Magdalen Archives. For hours of teaching, Taylor to the President, 30 March 1953, File FD/2, Magdalen College Archives.

52 The author has a vivid recollection of Taylor revealing to her in the same murmur that Frances Stevenson had been Lloyd George's mistress.

53 Thomas, 'Recollections of A.J.P. Taylor', p. 62.

54 Sisman, *A.J.P. Taylor*, pp. 132–3. No source is given, but presumably at least part of it came from Leyser, who had been appointed in July 1948.

55 Paul Addison, 'Wizard of Ox – Paul Addison Pays Tribute to A.J.P. Taylor', *London Review of Books*, 8 Nov. 1990, p. 4.

56 Taylor never told the author that he did not think she had a workable D. Phil. topic, which would have been crushing; as a result she continued to dig in the archives and discovered that she had a very rich topic. The student who was told not to bother writing a D. Phil. was Martin Gilbert. For numbers of postgraduate students, Taylor to Malcolm, 5 June 1967, File FD/2, Magdalen College Archives.

57 Taylor, *A Personal History*, p. 147.

58 *Ibid.*, pp. 147–8.

59 Lewis to his brother, 10 Sept. 1939, in Lewis, ed., *Letters*, p. 168; Taylor, *A Personal History*, p. 147; letter from Sir John Coles to the author, 17 Oct. 1998. Thomas, curiously, wrote that 'between tutorials, there was no socialising', 'Recollections', p. 62.

60 Éva Haraszti-Taylor to the author, 15 April 1999.

61 A.J.P. Taylor, 'The Fun of the Thing', in Schofield, *In Search of C.S. Lewis*, p. 117 for the swim; Sisman, *A.J.P. Taylor*, p. 135 for the porridge; interview with David Worswick, 19 Aug. 1997, for water over port.

62 College Orders, 1936–40, File CMM/1/11, Acta: Wed. 12 Oct. 1938;

Wed. 18 Oct. 1939; Wed. 6 March 1940. Lewis to his brother, 10 Sept. 1939, Lewis, ed., *Letters*, p. 168. Magdalen was not the only college requiring a year's probation for new Fellows.

63 David Eastwood takes a jaundiced view of Taylor's version, writing that 'I simply don't believe this. It's a typical Taylor affectation. I don't want to do these things, but when I do I turn out to be better than others … in other words this is Taylor's version of effortless superiority.' Comment on draft of chapter, 8 July 1999. Taylor, *A Personal History*, p. 161.

64 File CMM/2/1, Acta: Wed. 15 Oct. 1941; Wed. 2 Dec. 1942; Wed. 26 May 1943; Wed. 23 June 1943; Wed. 13 Oct. 1943; Wed. 8 March 1944; Wed. 1 Dec. 1943; Wed. 18 Oct. 1944; Wed. 8 Nov. 1944. Taylor was receiving £400 per year as a Fellowship Stipend and £300 as an Official Stipend, Acta: Wed. 14 Feb. 1945. Taylor, *A Personal History*, p. 161.

65 Ronald W. Clark, *Tizard* (London: Methuen and Co., 1965), p. 313; Taylor, *A Personal History*, p. 162. The last scientist who had been head of a college was William Harvey, the discoverer of the circulation of blood, who had been imposed on Merton by Charles I in 1645 but withdrew in 1646.

66 McFarlane, *Letters to Friends*, p. 11; Taylor, *A Personal History*, p. 162.

67 Clark, *Tizard*, pp. 313–14.

68 McFarlane, letter of 1 Sept. 1942. *Letters to Friends*, pp. 10–11.

69 Taylor, *A Personal History*, p. 162; McFarlane, letter of 4 May 1944, *Letters to Friends* p. 12. David French has pointed out that, given Tizard's background as a very senior civil servant and Rector of Imperial College, London, Taylor's picture is at worst highly unlikely and at best overdrawn. Van Oss ceased being Estates Bursar in 1944, being succeeded by Colin Cooke, Senior Bursar 1944–70.

70 Interview with Daniel Taylor, 6 April 2000; Taylor, *A Personal History*, p. 154.

71 Sisman, *A.J.P. Taylor*, p. 141.

72 Taylor, *A Personal History*, p. 156.

73 *Ibid.*, p. 152.

74 *Ibid.*, p. 166. Butler had interviewed Taylor in 1928 for the Rockefeller Scholarship.

75 *Ibid.*, p. 159.

76 'Survey of Activities of the Southern Region No. 6, Ministry of Information, 1939–1945', INF 1/297/54303, Ministry of Information papers, Public Record Office, London.

77 Hansard, *H.C. Debs, 1939–40*, vol. 365, 24 Oct. 1940, col. 1144.

78 Ivison Macadam, 'Public Meetings', Ministry of Information Regional Administrative Division Regional Circular No. 37, Feb. 1940, INF 1/294A, p. 2.

79 Ministry of Information Home Publicity Division, 'Public Meetings. Instructions to Local Information Committees (Enclosure with Regional Circular No. 12)', 17 Sept. 1939, INF 1/294A; list of Category A and Category B speakers, Appendix A of George Meare to Mr Rhodes, 5 Dec. 1940, INF 1/294C. The Leader of the Opposition, Clement Attlee, who was one of the three speakers on the category A list, had his name spelled Atlee.

80 Taylor, *A Personal History*, p. 159.

81 S.S. Semneer, 'Public Meetings Expenses', 23 April 1943, INF 1/301.

82 'Survey of Activities', INF 1/297.

83 Taylor, *A Personal History*, p. 159.

84 Hansard, *H.C. Debs, 1939–40*, Vol. 365, 24 Oct. 1940, cols 1143–4.

85 *Ibid.*, 5 Nov. 1940, cols 1293–7; *The Times*, 25 Oct. 1940. David Eastwood has suggested that Hogg's intervention was given a particular edge because of Taylor's stance on Munich and the Oxford by-election of 1938.

86 Taylor, *A Personal History*, p. 160.

87 *Ibid.*

88 *Ibid.*, p. 165 for Willert's comment; Stanley Parker, 'Drawn and

Quoted: A.J.P. Taylor or My Waterloo', *Oxford Mail*, 17 June 1943, p. 2; *Oxford Times*, 11 June 1943, p. 4.

89 *Oxford Times*, 11 June 1943, p. 4; Parker, 'Drawn and Quoted', p. 2.

90 Taylor, *A Personal History*, p. 165; 'Survey of Activities of the Southern Region', INF 1/297/54303, p. 4.

91 Taylor, *A Personal History*, p. 153.

92 *Ibid.*, p. 170.

93 Attila Pók, 'British Manual on Hungary in 1944', in Pók, ed., *The Fabric of Modern Europe: Studies in Social and Diplomatic History* (Nottingham: Astra Press, 1999), p. 202.

94 Taylor, *A Personal History*, pp. 170–1.

95 Taylor later wrote that his salary, those of his secretaries and the printing costs amounted to over £5,000 in four months. *A Personal History*, p. 172. David Eastwood has suggested that if Taylor did indeed donate the money to the college, it ran counter to the McFarlane gibe that Taylor would do anything, even talk to the College History Society, if money was involved. Comment on a draft of this chapter.

96 Taylor, *A Personal History*, p. 171.

97 Pók, 'British Manual on Hungary', p. 203.

98 *Ibid.*, pp. 203–4.

99 *Ibid.*, pp. 204–5, 171–2.

100 Taylor wrote to his wife Éva on 3 November 1977 that 'I am interested to hear that my handbook on Hungary has survived. But your young colleague must be careful. After I had written it and it had been set up in proof, the FO deleted most of the history and politics and substituted versions written by Macartney. I suspect that your colleague found Macartney's version. I alone retained the original proof and now I have destroyed it.' Taylor, *Letters to Eva*, p. 367.

101 3 November 1977, *Ibid.*, p. 172.

102 Francis L. Carsten, 'From Revolutionary Socialism to German History', in Peter Alter, ed., *Out of*

the Third Reich: Refugee Historians in Postwar Britain* (London: I.B. Tauris, 1998), pp. 31–2. Carsten later became Professor of Central European History at the School of Slavonic and East European Studies of the University of London.

103 Taylor, *The Course of German History: A Survey of the Development of Germany since 1815* (London: Hamish Hamilton, 1945).

104 Blewitt to Taylor, 19 Feb. 1942, Radio Contributors, Talks, A.J.P. Taylor, File 1, 1942–6, BBC Written Archives, Caversham.

105 Taylor, *A Personal History*, p. 165.

106 Blewitt to Taylor, 21 Aug. 1944; Taylor to Blewitt, 23 Aug. 1944; Boswell to Taylor, 27 Aug. 1944, all Radio Contributors, Talks, A.J.P. Taylor, File 1, 1942–6, BBC Written Archives.

107 Taylor, *A Personal History*, pp. 165–6.

108 See Blewitt to Taylor, 9 March 1945 and Taylor to Blewitt, 10 March 1945 for the ridicule, both in Radio Contributors, Talks, A.J.P. Taylor, File 1, 1942–6. For a fracas over his views on Trieste, see record of telephone conversations between Massey and Barnes, 24 Sept. 1945; memo by Rendall re telephone call by Grubb, 24 Sept. 1945; memo by Barnes re complaint by Cunard, 1 Oct. 1945; and memo by Rendall re interview with Taylor, 30 Oct. 1945, all Radio Contributors, Talks, A.J.P. Taylor, File 1, 1942–6, BBC written Archives.

109 Sisman, *A.J.P. Taylor*, p. 161. Alan Bullock and A.J.P. Taylor, eds, *A Select List of Books on European History 1915–1945* (Oxford: Clarendon Press, 1948). A thoroughly revised second edition was published in 1957. According to the preface in the first edition, it included 'works in the major languages of western Europe, including English, but not those written in Dutch, or the Scandinavian or east European languages. We have made this distinction on

the grounds that knowledge of these languages is still too limited to make inclusion useful in a practical work. The result is an inevitable lack of proportion, but this (it is only fair to add) reflects the lack of proportion in the attention histories in western Europe have so far given to the history of eastern Europe, Scandinavia, and certain smaller countries like the Netherlands and Portugal.' Because of length the history of ideas 'has scarcely been mentioned ... we have done all we can to make the list representative on the social and economic as well as the political side of history.' The proportions are revealing: nine pages to books on international relations, three pages for economic and social history. The remainder are devoted to the histories of individual countries: Austria and Austria-Hungary, four pages; Balkans and the Eastern Question, seven pages; Belgium, two pages; France, nine pages; Germany, six pages; Italy, eight pages; Netherlands, one page (seven books listed); Poland, one page (seventeen books); Russia, two-and-a-half pages; and Scandinavia, one-and-a-half pages.

110 Interview with Henrietta Kotlan-Werner, 21 June 1991; Parker, 'Drawn and Quoted' p. 4.

111 Taylor, *A Personal History*, p. 145; interview with Henrietta Kotlan-Werner, 21 June 1991.

112 Taylor to Muggeridge, 1 May 1939, Muggeridge Papers. Taylor, *A Personal History*, pp. 146–7.

113 *Ibid.*, pp. 145; 149 for the quotation; Sisman, *A.J.P. Taylor*, pp. 133–4 for going to bed together, Sisman gives no source, but presumably it was Kee.

114 Taylor, *A Personal History*, pp. 164 for quotation, 177.

115 Hall, *Bill and Patience*, p. 110; Parker, 'Drawn and Quoted', p. 4.

116 Taylor, *A Personal History*, pp. 173–4.

117 *Ibid.*, p. 175.

118 *Ibid.*, p. 177.

119 *Ibid.*, pp. 177–8; Sisman, *A.J.P. Taylor*, p. 135 for Kee's ignorance.

120 Taylor, *A Personal History*, pp. 129–30.

121 *Ibid.*, pp. 130–1, 188–9 for the sancity of contract.

122 *Ibid.*, pp. 184–5.

123 *Ibid.*, p. 185. Taylor's visa for Yugoslavia was dated 10 April 1947. Stamp in his passport issued 2 March 1939, renewed 15 May 1947. File Personal Memorabilia (Passports), Taylor Papers, Ransome Center.

124 Paul Ferris, *Caitlin: The Life of Caitlin Thomas* (London: Pimlico pb, 1995), pp. 97, 99, 102; Caitlin quotation cited in Lynne Mills, 'Under the Influence', *Limited Edition: The Magazine of Oxfordshire*, no. 54 (April 1991), pp. 7–8; Taylor, *A Personal History*, p. 188.

125 Taylor, *A Personal History*, p. 188; Ferris, *Caitlin*, p. 97 for the breast-squeezing.

126 Ferris, *Caitlin*, pp. 122 for Margaret's mental stability, 97, 122. Caitlin to Helen McAlpine, 6 March 1952, Thomas letter copied by the author while on view at Sotheby's, London before its auction on 13 Dec. 1994.

127 Taylor, *A Personal History*, pp. 191–2; Ferris, *Caitlin*, p. 104; Caitlin to Helen McAlpine, 6 March 1952, Caitlin Thomas Papers, Sotheby's. Taylor, *A Personal History*, pp. 188–9.

128 Taylor, *A Personal History*, pp. 188–9, 193; Taylor to the President, 25 April 1949 and the President to Taylor, 27 May 1949, both File FD/2, Magdalen College Archives. William Thomas recalled that once when Taylor had him to dine in Magdalen, Emrys Jones, then Tutor in English, mentioned a recent life of Dylan Thomas; Taylor's response was that 'I know more about Dylan Thomas than any other man living – and it will die with me.' William Thomas to the author, 12 April 1999.

129 Interview with David Worswick, 19 August 1997.

130 Minute by J.P. Cloake, 14 Oct. 1948, PR693, FO1110/271, FO Papers. Cited by John Jenks in his unpublished paper, 'Fight Against Peace? Britain and the World Peace Council', given on 10 July 1996 at the Institute for British History Conference, London. I am grateful to Mr Jenks for making a copy of his paper available to me.

131 Taylor, *A Personal History*, p. 192; *The Times*, 27 Aug. 1948.

132 'Speech of Professor Taylor at the Intellectuals' Congress', in possession of Éva Haraszti-Taylor. Taylor did not write it or he would not have referred to himself as Professor; the fact that Fadeyev's name is spelt in the Polish manner argues for a contemporary transcription of the speech.

133 Mehta, *The Fly and the Fly-Bottle*, p. 168 for the quotation; Taylor, *A Personal History*, pp. 192–3.

134 Minute by R.M. Hankey, 18 March 1949, PR749/92/G, FO1110/271, cited in Jenks, 'Fight against Peace?'

135 Clark, *Tizard*, pp. 383–4.

136 Taylor, *A Personal History*, p. 187; McFarlane, *Letters to Friends*, p. 26; Clark, *Tizard*, p. 384. The letter was dated 10 October.

137 Private information for Lewis's opposition; Sisman, *A.J.P. Taylor*, p. 161; Clark, *Tizard*, p. 385.

138 Taylor, *A Personal History*, pp. 187–8.

139 David Worswick to the author, 9 April 1990; Taylor, *A Personal History*, pp. 187–8.

140 Angela Lambert, interview with Eve Crosland, 'My Husband, his Other Wives, and Me', *Independent on Sunday*, 7 July 1991. Interview with Daniel Taylor, 6 April 2000.

141 Sisman, *A.J.P. Taylor*, pp. 191–3.

142 Interview with Crosland, 7 July 1991. For Taylor's separation from his wife taking place as early 1949, see 'History Man'. *Evening Standard*, 25 June 1991; for Taylor's

memory of the date as September 1950, see *A Personal History*, p. 193.

143 Unpublished entry, diary of Malcolm Muggeridge, 21 Dec. 1949, quoted in Sisman, *A.J.P. Taylor*, p. 193. It would be interesting to know whether Muggeridge's 'better looking than before' referred to Eve's becoming prettier, or to a previous woman.

144 Taylor to Martin, 3 Oct. 1950, Box 15, File 2, Kingsley Martin Papers, *New Statesman* Papers, Sussex University.

145 According to Eve Crosland's later recollection, although the marriage could be 'tempestuous', they were happy together until the late sixties: 'we were good companions; we were *fine* sexually.' Interview with Eve Crosland, *Independent on Sunday*, 7 July 1991.

146 Margaret Taylor to Bill and Helen McAlpine, 15 June 1976, Caitlin Thomas Papers, Sotheby's.

147 Eve Taylor to Alan Pryce-Jones, 4 July ?1952, Box 17, Folder T, General, 1927–86, Alan Pryce-Jones Papers, Uncat. MS Vault 571, Beinecke Rare Books Library, Yale University.

148 Sisman, *A.J.P. Taylor*, pp. 199–201, 207–9, 226, 279–80; Taylor, *A Personal History*, pp. 199–200; Taylor to Bursar, 27 April 1953, Bursar to Taylor, 27 April 1953, Taylor to Bursar, 28 April 1953, all File OXF/139/1, Holywell Ford, A.J.P. Taylor, Magdalen College Archives. Taylor retained the so-called 'garden hut', where the Thomases had lived, tramping over to it every morning to make a cooked breakfast; he also sub-let it, one tenant being Professor L.R. Palmer of Oriel in June 1963. For some years the house next to Sussex Cottage in Park Village East, called Winchelsea Cottage, was lived in by the Hemming family. Rachel Hemming Bray recalled playing with an aggressive little boy called Clive, the son of the (Italian or Moroccan) maid of the house. All of

the neighbours assumed that Taylor was the father of the child. Rachel Hemming Bray to the author, 29 March 1999. Other rumours abounded in London as to Taylor's putative womanising. One man who worked behind the counter in the Regent Street branch of the National Westminster Bank, where Taylor banked, recalled the amusement at Taylor's financial affairs: a lot of money came in and a lot went out in different directions; the bank staff assumed it went to support his affairs. Certainly the gossip in clubland was that Taylor had a number of women over the years. Christopher Dunn to the author, 28 March 1999. None of this, of course, is provable. Interview with Daniel Taylor, 6 April 2000.

149 Acta, Wednesday, 15 Oct. 1952, File CMM/2/12, Magdalen College Archives. Interview with David Worswick, 19 Aug. 1997.

150 Interview with David Worswick, 19 Aug. 1997. Taylor wrote later that Driver was objecting to his reviews for the *Observer* – unlikely, since Taylor did not begin writing for the *Observer* until 1955. *A Personal History*, p. 199. Eliot quotation in John Carey, *The Intellectuals and the Masses: Pride and Prejudice among the Literary Intelligentsia, 1880–1939* (London: Faber and Faber, 1992 pb), p. 7.

151 Interviews with David Worswick, 19 Aug. 1997 for the details and John Stoye, 30 June 1998, who supports Worswick's assessment of the fundamental unimportance of the occasion; Sisman, *A.J.P. Taylor*, p. 200 for the private desire of Magdalen colleagues that Taylor would leave of his own accord.

152 Taylor to Wadsworth, 22 Nov. 1954, File B/T/19/263, Wadsworth Papers.

153 Taylor, *A Personal History*, pp. 209–10. The appointment was announced in *The Times*, 22 Nov. 1954. Taylor also delivered them on BBC Radio, and they were pub-lished as a book, *The Troublemakers*, by Oxford University Press.

154 Kenneth Dover, *Marginal Comment* (London: Duckworth, 1994), pp. 135–6.

155 Taylor, *A Personal History*, pp. 210–11. According to Taylor, he at once campaigned for splitting the History section; he would have been happy with two, but 'thanks to the obstinate resistence of the mediaevalists we finally got three – mediaeval, early modern, late modern' in 1968. It was the Elizabethan scholar and professor at UCL, J.E. Neale, who wrote in 1962, 'Though I like the man in a way, he is quite impossible and behaves as no scholar – certainly no F.B.A., for which honour Namier was responsible! – should behave. Television, the sublimation of the scholar and easy riches in cheap journalism have a lot to answer for.' Neale to Notestein, 20 Nov. 1962, Box 6, Folder 536 (Neale), Notestein Papers.

156 Taylor, *A Personal History*, p. 205.

157 Taylor, *Ibid.*, p. 206; comments by D.C. Watt at the Conference on International History, the LSE, June 1993; Kathleen Burk, 'Britische Traditionen internationaler Geschichtsschreibung' in Wilfred Loth and Jürgen Osterhammel, eds, *Internationale Geschichte: Themen–Ergebnisse–Aussichten* (München: Oldenbourg Verlag, 2000).

158 Taylor, *A Personal History*, pp. 206–7. Masterman's books included *An Oxford Tragedy* (1933), a novel; *To Teach the Senators Wisdom: An Oxford Guide-Book* (1952), a strange little book intended to interpret Oxford to three visiting American senators; *The Double-cross System in the War of 1939–45* (1972); and *On the Chariot Wheel: An Autobiography* (1975), which conceals much but reveals more between the lines than he probably intended.

159 Interview of Galbraith by Cole, 18 Dec. 1969, quoted in Cole,

A.J.P. *Taylor*, p. 168; Number 10 quotation from Herbert Nicholas to Wallace Notestein, 13 March 1957, Box 6, Folder 545, Notestein Papers.

160 Taylor, *A Personal History*, pp. 214–17. According to private information, the L.M.H. governing body meeting at which Sutherland asked her Fellows to support her bid to hold the principalship *with* the Regius chair was leaked by one of them to Piers Mackesy, who told Trevor-Roper.

161 Masterman, *On the Chariot Wheel*, p. 296. Emphasis added by the present author.

162 Trevor-Roper to Notestein, 17 January 1957, Box 8, Folder 747, Notestein Papers.

163 Billy Pantin was W.A. Pantin. The reference to Hitler presumably refers to Trevor-Roper's *The Last Days of Hitler*, which enjoyed a large sale and wide fame. V.H. Galbraith to Doris Stenton, 3 July [prob. 1957], File 8/1, Frank Stenton Papers, University of Reading Library. I owe this reference to George Bernard. Doris Stenton was also a mediaeval historian.

164 Nicholas to Notestein, 13 March 1957, Box 6, File 545, Notestein Papers.

165 Trevor-Roper to Notestein, 2 May 1957, Box 8, Folder 747 (T-R), Notestein Papers.

166 Trevor-Roper to Notestein, 25 July 1957, *ibid.*. The review was probably Taylor's review of John Brooke, *The Chatham Administration 1766–1768* (London: Macmillan, 1956) in the *Manchester Guardian* of 16 November 1956. The *Festschrift* was Richard Pares and A.J.P. Taylor, eds, *Essays Presented to Sir Lewis Namier* (London: Macmillan, 1956); it includes a major essay by Taylor entitled 'The War Aims of the Allies in the First World War', pp. 475–505. David Eastwood made the following acute comment on a draft of this chapter: 'It's interesting that Taylor makes no mention of his

academic differences with Namier. Did he not know of N's response? Unlikely if T-R and others did. Is it not true? I suspect it is (& Taylor was right about Brooke, and Brooke was probably Namier's favourite Namierite). We are left again with the *leitmotiv* of Taylor's constructing himself as an outsider, as a dissident. The great fact in Taylor's self-presentation (& perhaps too in his own self-evaluation) is his popular journalism. Thus in Taylor's own version Namier's sole objection must be to his continuing to combine popular journalism & serious scholarship. Taylor offers us a narrow version of scholarship (Namier's and the academic establishment) and the wide vistas of his own audience, academic and popular. Taylor invites us to choose, knowing (or rather believing) we must warm to his moralized populism and despite the narrow-mindedness which denied him the academic recognition which he wanted.'

167 Johnson, 'Diary', *London Review of Books*, 8 March 1986, p. 21.

168 V.H. Galbraith to Doris Stenton, 3 July [?1957], File 8/1, Stenton Papers.

169 *Defence: Outline of Future Policy: 1957*, Cmnd 124 (London: HMSO, 1957), pp. 2–3. This has distinct echoes of the National Government's conclusion in the 1930s that 'the bomber will always get through'.

170 The material for this paragraph comes from Meredith Veldman, *Fantasy, the Bomb, and the Greening of Britain: Romantic Protest, 1945–1980* (Cambridge: Cambridge University Press, 1994), Introduction, Part II.

171 The Reith Lectures were subsequently published as *Russia, the Atom Bomb and the West* (London: Oxford University Press, 1958). Veldman, *Fantasy, the Bomb, and the Greening of Britain*, pp. 131–2. *The Autobiography of Bertrand*

Russell 1944–1969 (London: George Allen and Unwin, Ltd, 1969), pp. 138–41. The 'Long Telegram' from Moscow of 22 February 1946 can most conveniently be found in Kenneth M. Jensen, ed., *Origins of the Cold War: The Novikov, Kennan and Roberts 'Long Telegrams' of 1946* (Washington: United States Institute of Peace, 1991); for 'The Sources of Soviet Conduct', written by 'X', see *Foreign Affairs*, no. 25 (July 1947), pp. 566–82.

172 Taylor to Michael Howard, 27 January 1975, Box 2, Folders 5&6, Taylor Papers, Ransome Center.

173 Taylor, *A Personal History*, p. 226 and Taylor, 'CND: The First Twenty-Five Years', *Observer Magazine*, 20 February 1983, pp. 13–14. For the evidence of his attendance see CND Executive Committee Minutes, 21 January 1958 and 14 April 1958, both MSS 181, CND Collection, Modern Records Centre, University of Warwick, England, cited in Veldman, *Fantasy, the Bomb, and the Greening of Britain*, p. 133.

174 'There's No Dodging the H-bomb', *Daily Herald*, 29 April 1954, p. 4.

175 Taylor, *A Personal History*, pp. 225–6.

176 Veldman, *Fantasy, the Bomb, and the Greening of Britain*, p 134; Peggy Duff, *Left, Left, Left: A Personal Account of Six Protest Campaigns, 1945–1965* (London: Allison and Busby 1971), p. 124; Richard Taylor, *Against the Bomb: The British Peace Movement 1958–1965* (Oxford: Clarendon Press, 1988), pp. 26–7 for the numbers at Central Hall. He also reports that there were several hundred at the sit-down protest at Downing Street and that five were arrested. Taylor, *A Personal History*, p. 228; Richard Gott, 'Great History, Little England' (an obituary of Taylor), *Guardian*, 8 Sept. 1990 for the quotation from his Central Hall speech.

177 'Presidential Address to the Joint Meeting of the Mount Old Scholars'

Association and Old York Scholars' Association 6th June, 1960', in Wragge, *Leslie Howard Gilbert*, pp. 34–5; Taylor, *A Personal History*, p. 229; R. Taylor, *Against the Bomb*, p. 35.

178 Taylor, *A Personal History*, p. 229. 'How They Brought the Good News from Ghent to Aix', by Robert Browning, describes a purely imaginary incident. Taylor, 'Campaign Report', *New Statesman*, no. 55 (21 June 1960), pp. 799–800.

179 Duff, *Left, Left, Left*, pp. 160–1; Sisman, *A.J.P. Taylor*, p. 309. Taylor did not mention the Youth Campaign for Nuclear Disarmament, which was started early on in the campaign by his eldest son, Giles, and Duff's son Euan. While officially the age limits were from 12 to 25, most of the members were under 20, with many still at school. Duff, *Left, Left, Left*, p. 161.

180 R. Taylor, *Against the Bomb*, p. 34.

181 Taylor, *A Personal History*, p. 230; Veldman, *Fantasy, the Bomb, and the Greening of Britain*, p. 148.

182 Interview with A.J.P. Taylor in April 1978, R. Taylor, *Against the Bomb*, p. 60.

183 Taylor, *A Personal History*, p. 230.

184 Johnson, 'Diary', *London Review of Books*, 8 May 1986, p. 21: Taylor, *A Personal History*, pp. 222–3. Taylor was nominated on 6 November 1957; Acta, File CMM/2/18, Magdalen College Archives.

185 Thanks to Martin Gilbert for the Nixon story. Taylor, *A Personal History*, pp. 223–4.

186 Sisman, *A.J.P. Taylor*, p. 268.

187 Driver nominated him to be Vice-President for 1959 on 5 November 1958; Acta, File CMM/2/18, Magdalen College Archives. Taylor, *A Personal History*, pp. 224–5.

188 The colleague was Betty Kemp, Fellow and Tutor in History at St Hugh's College, who had been a student at Manchester while Taylor lectured there; she had briefly attended his outline lectures on modern European history and had

not been very impressed by them. Taylor had been one of those who had welcomed her to Oxford in October 1946. Kemp note to the author. Sisman, *A.J.P. Taylor*, p. 268 for the processing. Taylor's colleague the economist David Worswick wrote that a change to the regulation about proceeding into Hall by order of seniority required a resolution in a College Meeting. The first proposal for such a change was made by Ryle, but it was defeated. A certain period had to elapse before the proposal could be brought up again, when it was successful. Worswick to the author, 9 April 1999. John Stoye, review of Sisman's *A.J.P. Taylor, Magdalen College Record* (1994), p. 84.

189 Taylor to the President of Magdalen, 30 March 1953, and the President to Taylor, 30 April 1953, both File FD/2, Magdalen College Archives. Letter from J.O. Prestwich, Chairman of the Board of the Faculty of Modern History, to the *Oxford Magazine*, 1 Nov. 1962, p. 40.

190 Sisman, *A.J.P. Taylor*, p. 321; Taylor to Hetherington, 12 Oct. 1962, cited in Sisman, *A.J.P. Taylor*, p. 318; *Manchester Guardian*, 18 Oct. 1962; *Oxford Mail*, 17 Oct. 1962; George Gale interview with Taylor, *Daily Express*, 18 Oct. 1962. Professor Penelope Corfield, who was present at the lecture as a student, commented to the author over lunch on 12 July 1999 that Taylor's announcement meant absolutely nothing to the student audience.

191 Acta, Wednesday, 17 October 1962, File CMM/2/22, Magdalen College Archives; interview with David Worswick, 19 August 1997.

192 Private information; *Observer*, p. 14 for the quotation.

193 Acta, 'Report by Fellowship Committee for College Meeting', 1 Nov. 1962; Taylor to the President, 5 Nov. 1962; note by J.H.C.M., 2 Nov. 1962; Acta, Wednesday, 7 Nov. 1962, all File CMM/2/22,

Magdalen College Archives.

194 Acta, CES, ELJ, PLG, DterH, CWMcM, 'Election of Mr A.J.P. Taylor, Memorandum to the Governing Body', 28 Nov. 1962; TSRB, NRK, GR, 'Contra Memorandum to the Governing Body', 28 Nov. 1962; Acta, Wednesday, 5 Dec. 1962, all File CMM/2/22, Magdalen College Archives.

195 Worswick compiled the tables for results in Finals, analysed by college and subject, from the end of the war until 1964, when he ceased doing them. The Norrington Table, which first appeared in 1964, tabulated all subjects together.

5 The Oxford Years 1938–1965

1 In short, the great books on all three subjects were written during his Oxford years, broadly taken; in strict terms, his last great book, *English History 1914–1945*, though mostly written during his years as a Tutorial Fellow at Magdalen, was only completed the following year and published in 1965. David Eastwood has remarked that 'when Taylor ceased to teach history seriously he ceased to write serious history.' Comment on draft of chapter.

2 Taylor, *A Personal History*, p. 90.

3 *Ibid.*, p. 88.

4 *Ibid.*, p. 111. Taylor had read *Der Krimkrieg und dee Österreichische Politik* and *Österreiche von 1848 bis 1860* in October 1929 and *Der Kampf um die Vorherrschaft in Deutschland 1859 bis 1866* in March 1930.

5 David Eastwood has suggested that there is a certain tilting at windmills here, in that there was no obvious reason why Taylor should have abandoned the Habsburg Empire in the 1930s; he had no other research project in mind. He argues that the move to German history

was driven by the Second World War, which 'centred "the German problem" in the most awesome way, and it created the circumstances which led directly to *The Course of German History*.' Comment on draft chapter. This is, of course, true, but the reasons for the attractions for him of Habsburg history are still interesting.

6 Taylor, *A Personal History*, p. 145.

7 *Ibid.*, pp. 99, 233.

8 Taylor to Mr Macmillan, 17 April, 8 May and 10 May 1939, all Macmillan Archive. There is no clue as to who the other publisher might have been.

9 Taylor to Macmillan, 2 June 1939, Macmillan Archive.

10 Taylor, *A Personal History*, p. 145.

11 David Eastwood claims, for reasons that remain obscure, that the use of the name 'Four Years' War' was 'very much a diplomatic historian's discourse'. Comment on draft chapter.

12 Taylor to Macmillan, 26 July 1940, Macmillan Archives.

13 The alternative first saying is 'I'm the Emperor and I *will* have dumplings!' Taylor, *The Habsburg Monarchy 1815–1918: A History of the Austrian Empire and Austria-Hungary* (London: Macmillan and Co., 1941) [hereafter *The Habsburg Monarchy* (1941)], p. 47. For the description of Ferdinand, Taylor, *The Habsburg Monarchy 1809–1918: A History of the Austrian Empire and Austria-Hungary* (London: Hamish Hamilton, new edition 1948) [hereafter *The Habsburg Monarchy* (1948)], p. 47, and for the second quotation pp. 76–7.

14 Taylor, *The Habsburg Monarchy* (1941), p. 53.

15 Prys Morgan, 'From a Death to a View: The Hunt for the Welsh Past in the Romantic Period', in Eric Hobsbawm and Terence Ranger, eds, *The Invention of Tradition* (Cambridge: Cambridge University Press, 1983, 1984 pb), p. 99.

16 Taylor, *The Habsburg Monarchy*

(1941), p. 32.

17 *Ibid.*, pp. viii, 26–7.

18 'Austria of the Day', *Manchester Guardian*, 28 March 1946, p. 6.

19 No name, no date, pasted into Taylor's cuttings book, Box 2, Folder 44, Taylor Papers, Ransome Center.

20 *Journal of Modern History*, vol. 14, no. 4 (Dec. 1942), pp. 538–40.

21 First review, no name, no date, Taylor's cuttings book, Box 2, Folder 44, Taylor Papers, Ransome Center; second review, 'Dynasty in Fetters: Why the Habsburg Monarchy Fell', *Times Literary Supplement*, no. 2038, 22 Feb. 1941, p. 88. Taylor letter cited in Chris Wrigley, *A.J.P. Taylor: A Complete Annotated Bibliography and Guide to his Historical and Other Writings* (Sussex: The Harvester Press, 1980), p. 68.

22 Wilson's and Přibram's reviews in Taylor's cuttings book, Box 2, Folder 44, Taylor Papers, Ransome Center.

23 'President and Members of the Hungarian Council in Great Britain', 1944, FO371/39247, cited in Éva Haraszti, 'Michael Karolyi: a Friend', in Chris Wrigley, ed., *Warfare, Diplomacy and Politics: Essays in Honour of A.J.P. Taylor* (London: Hamish Hamilton, 1986), p. 232.

24 Haraszti, 'Michael Karolyi', p. 232.

25 Karolyi became the Hungarian Minister to France after the war, but was eventually forced into exile. Upon his death he had been buried in the Isle of Wight, but was exhumed and reinterred in Hungary. Taylor, *A Personal History*, p. 239.

26 *Ibid.*, pp. 157, 171.

27 Taylor to Wadsworth, 3 Sept. 1943, B/T19/8; Wadsworth to Taylor, 9 Sept. 1943, B/T19/10; and Taylor to Wadsworth, 13 Sept. 1943, B/T19/11, all Wadsworth Papers.

28 Taylor, *A Personal History*, p. 158.

29 A.J.P. Taylor, *Czechoslovakia's Place in a Free Europe* (London: Czechoslovak Institute in London, 1943).

'This booklet contains the substance of the lecture given by A.J.P. Taylor'; presumably someone was taking notes. This pamphlet was finally run to ground in the Rare Pamphlets collection in the library of the University of California, Berkeley. David Eastwood has commented that this episode 'reveals the intensely *serious* side of T's political engagement. In a sense, he was always posturing when working on modern German history, & this posturing became mere polemic when writing popular pieces on Germany. On the Habsburg lands, & perhaps even on Austria, T. was always more serious & less eager to strike a posture.' Comment on draft chapter.

30 Taylor to Wadsworth, 4 Nov. 1944, B/T19/32, Wadsworth Papers.

31 Taylor to Sir Geoffrey Cox, 6 Feb. 1978, Box 4, Folder 19, Taylor Papers, Ransome Center.

32 Taylor, *A Personal History*, p. 166; quotation from *Time and Tide*, vol. 23, no. 10 (7 March 1942), pp. 195–6.

33 Taylor, *A Personal History*, pp. 166–7. *Time and Tide*, vol. 23, no. 44 (31 Oct. 1942), p. 873; vol. 23, no. 45 (7 Nov. 1942), pp. 887–8 for anti-Taylor letters from F.B. Czarnomski, Adam Pragier, Z. Grabowski and H.C. Stevens; and vol. 23, no. 48 (14 Nov. 1942), p. 907 for Taylor's response and a letter attacking Taylor's arguments from the Editor of *Time and Tide*.

34 Taylor to Sir Geoffrey Cox, 6 Feb. 1978, Box 4, Folder 19, Taylor Papers, Ransome Center. The article was 'Trieste or Trst?', *New Statesman*, vol. 28, no. 720 (9 Dec. 1944), pp. 386–7.

35 Taylor, *A Personal History*, p. 173.

36 Taylor, *Trieste* (London: Yugoslav Information Office, 1945). Reprinted in *From Napoleon to Stalin: Comments on European History* (London: Hamish Hamilton, this edition for The Right Book Club, 1950), pp. 179–208. David Eastwood has commented: 'Isn't

there something of Versailles & 1919 in this kind of argument? T. was fond of speaking up for the rights of relatively powerless peoples politically, whilst rejoicing historically in describing the triumph of *realpolitik*.' Comment on draft chapter.

37 Record of telephone conversations between Massey and Barnes, 24 Sept. 1945; memo by Rendall re telephone call by Grubb, 24 Sept. 1945; memo by Barnes re complaint by Cunard, 1 Oct. 1945; and memo by Rendall re interview with Taylor, 30 Oct. 1945, all Radio Contributors, Talks, A.J.P. Taylor, File 1, 1942–6, BBC Written Archives.

38 Taylor, *A Personal History*, pp. 182–6.

39 Taylor to D. Macmillan, 20 Oct. 1944, Macmillan Archives.

40 Taylor to Hamilton, 3 Nov. 1944, Box DM 1352, Correspondence with A.J.P. Taylor 1944–76, Hamish Hamilton Papers, Bristol University Library.

41 Taylor to D. Macmillan, 4 Dec. 1945, Macmillan Archives; Taylor to Hamilton, 3 Nov. 1944 and Hamilton to Taylor, 6 Nov. 1944, both Box DM 1352, Hamilton Papers.

42 Taylor to Hamilton, 20 Dec. 1945 and Hamilton to Taylor, 21 Dec. 1945, both Box DM 1352, Hamilton Papers.

43 Hamilton to Taylor, 15 Jan. 1946, *ibid.*

44 Taylor to Hamilton, 17 Jan. 1946 and Hamilton to Taylor, 28 Jan. 1946, *ibid.*

45 Taylor to Hamilton, 17 Jan. 1946; Hamilton to Taylor, 28 Jan. 1946; and Taylor to Hamilton, 30 Jan. 1946, all *ibid.*

46 Taylor to Hamilton, 9 Oct. 1946 and Hamilton to Taylor, 26 Oct. 1946, both *ibid.*

47 Taylor to Hamilton, 3 Nov. 1946; Hamilton to Taylor, 6 Nov. 1946; and Taylor to Hamilton, 8 Nov. 1946, all *ibid.*

48 Taylor to Hamilton, 21 Nov. 1947;

Taylor to Hamilton, 19 Feb. 1946; Machell to Taylor, 24 Feb. 1948 (two letters, first not sent); Taylor to Machell, 25 Feb. 1946; and Taylor to Hamilton, 25 Feb. 1946, all *ibid.*

49 According to Hamilton, Coward McCann 'must have lost a good deal of money' on the German book. Hamilton to Taylor, 11 Dec. 1947, *ibid.* Knopf was one of the publishers who had turned it down.

50 Taylor to Machell, 8 April 1948; Knopf to Taylor, 1 June 1948; Hamilton to Taylor, 15 Feb. 1949; Hamilton to Taylor, 8 April 1949; Hamilton to Taylor, 3 Nov. 1949; and Taylor to Hamilton, 3 Nov. 1949, all *ibid.* The book was also turned down by Oxford University Press in New York, Yale University Press and Harper.

51 Taylor, *The Habsburg Monarchy* (1941), p. 231 and *The Habsburg Monarchy* (1948), p. 184.

52 Taylor, *The Habsburg Monarchy* (1941), p. 16 and *The Habsburg Monarchy* (1948), p. 22.

53 'The Austrian Empire, *Times Literary Supplement*, no. 2456 (26 Feb. 1949), p. 132; F.W. Deakin, 'The Habsburgs', *Manchester Guardian*, 4 March 1949, p. 3; C.A. Macartney, *History*, vol. 37 (Oct. 1950), pp. 273–4; *TLS* as above; *History* as above, all citations taken from Wrigley, *A.J.P. Taylor: A Complete Annotated Bibliography*, pp. 71–2.

54 No date but '?1964' written in pencil. Box 15, File 2, Kingsley Martin Papers, *New Statesman* Archive, University of Sussex.

55 Taylor, *Germany's First Bid for Colonies*, p. 99.

56 Taylor, *A Personal History*, p. 172.

57 Box DM 1352, Hamilton Papers.

58 Taylor to Hamilton, 11 March 1944, *ibid.*

59 Hamilton to Taylor, 15 March 1944 and Taylor to Hamilton, 28 March 1944, both *ibid.*

60 *Oxford Magazine*, 15 Oct. 1942, pp. 15–16.

61 Taylor to Hamilton, 3 May, 24 July and 13 Sept. 1944, all Box DM 1352, Hamilton Papers.

62 Taylor, *The Course of German History*, p. 7; *A Personal History*, p. 172; list of books read.

63 Taylor, *The Course of German History*, pp. 13, 8–9.

64 *Ibid.*, p. 68. Namier used the term as the title of his 1944 Raleigh Lecture, subsequently published as Sir Lewis Namier, *1848: The Revolution of the Intellectuals* (London: Oxford University Press, 1946).

65 Taylor, *The Course of German History*, pp. 187, 193–4, 200.

66 Hamilton to Taylor, 28 Jan. 1946, Box DM 1352, Hamilton Papers.

67 *Times Literary Supplement*, 29 Sept. 1945, pp. 457–9.

68 R. Birley in *International Affairs*, 1 Jan. 1946, pp. 136–7.

69 Sigmund Neumann in *American Historical Review*, vol. 52, no. 4 (July 1947), pp. 730–3.

70 Taylor, *A Personal History*, p. 172.

71 Neumann in *American Historical Review*, p. 733.

72 Ritter to Gooch, 17 Feb. 1948 and Gooch to Ritter, 28 Feb. 1948, in Klaus Schwabe and Rolf Reichardt, eds, *Gerhard Ritter: Ein politischer Historiker in seinen Briefen* (Boppard am Rhein: Harald Boldt Verlag, 1984), pp. 445–6. Thanks to Michael Jewess for the translation.

73 Alan to Kingsley Martin, 25 Nov. ?1944, Kingsley Martin Papers.

74 'Pre-War', *Time and Tide*, vol. 23, no. 48 (28 Nov. 1942), pp. 955–6. David Eastwood has commented that it is odd that 'T. thought historians are governed by normative national imperatives – his own self-perception was as a rebel, as an intellect who transcended the follies of the British Establishment, & did so because he understood historical processes.' Comment on draft chapter.

75 Taylor to D.M. Davin, 7 Nov. 1954, File Oxford History of Modern Europe [hereafter OHME]: A.J.P. Taylor, Oxford University Press Archives, Oxford. Hamilton to

Taylor, 1 Nov. 1949, Box DM 1352, Hamilton Papers.

76 Hamilton to Taylor, 16 Nov. 1949 and Taylor to Hamilton, 20 Nov. 1949, both Box DM 1352, Hamilton Papers.

77 Two-page proposal for a series on European history, n.d. but pre-1914; G.N. Clark and A.L. Poole, 'Suggested Scheme for a Series of European Histories', 5 Feb. 1925; note of discussion at OUP between Bullock, Arthur Norrington and Dan Davin, 8 April 1947; Alan Bullock, 'Memorandum of an Oxford History of Modern Europe', 6 May 1947, all File OHME General: 1947–61, OUP Archives.

78 Minutes of meeting of Bullock, Davin and Norrington, 17 Oct. 1947 and minutes of meeting of A.L. Poole, Norrington and Davin, 11 Nov. 1947, both File OHME General: 1947–61, OUP Archives.

79 A Department of Oxford University, 'the Press' was governed, in lieu of a Board of Directors, by fourteen Delegates, all members of Convocation appointed (or delegated) by the university. They included the Vice-Chancellor, the two Proctors and the Assessor, plus ten other Delegates. The Vice-Chancellor served for two years and the Proctors for one, so the continuing responsibility fell on the ten other Delegates. Five were 'ordinary Delegates', appointed by the Vice-Chancellor and the Proctors for seven years, and five were 'perpetual Delegates', selected by the Delegates themselves from amongst the ordinary Delegates. The latter served until death. In 1945 one delegate, the classicist Cyril Bailey, had served since 1920 (until 1946); another, Sir David Ross, moral philosopher and Provost of Worcester, since 1922 (until 1952); a third, Sir Cyril Hinshelwood, scientist and linguist, since 1934 (until 1967); a fourth, the philosopher and Master of Balliol, Sandy Lindsay, since

1937. The Delegacy was dominated by a certain conservatism. A.L. Poole was the history Delegate. See Keith Ovenden, *A Fighting Withdrawal: The Life of Dan Davin. Writer, Soldier, Publisher* (Oxford: Oxford University Press, 1996), pp. 216–17.

80 Bullock to Norrington, 26 Nov. 1947 for the initial list; document listing proposed authors and initialled by Davin, n.d. but after 1 Dec. 1947 and by 16 Jan. 1948; minutes of lunch meeting of Deakin, Bullock and Davin on 2 June 1948, document dated 3 June; and comment by Norrington on minutes dated 3 June 1948, 8 June 1948, all File OHME General: 1947–61, OUP Archives.

81 Meeting 10 Nov. 1948 and Davin to Poole, 11 Nov. 1948, both *ibid.*

82 Taylor to Davin, 24 May 1949, File OHME: A.J.P. Taylor, and Norrington minute on meeting with Deakin of 2 June 1949, 3 June 1949, File OHME General: 1947–61, both OUP Archives.

83 Taylor to Davin, 16 Oct. 1949 and Davin to Deakin, 21 Oct. 1949, both *ibid.*

84 Davin to Taylor, 14 Nov. and 24 Nov. 1949, both File OHME: A.J.P. Taylor, OUP Archives.

85 Davin note to Norrington, 12 May and 24 May 1950, File OHME General: 1947–61, OUP Archives.

86 Davin to Deakin, 14 June 1950, *ibid.*

87 Memoradum by Davin, 21 June 1950, Curtis Brown to Davin, 22 June and 6 Sept. 1950, all *ibid.* Jonathan Lloyd confirmed to the author that 'According to our records Spencer Curtis Brown made only one agreement for AJP Taylor, that for THE STRUGGLE FOR MASTERY IN EUROPE.' Jonathan Lloyd of Curtis Brown to the author, 29 Sept. 1999.

88 Taylor to Davin, 10 Sept. 1952; Davin to Taylor, 25 March 1953; Curtis Brown to Davin, 13 July 1953; and Davin to Curtis Brown, 14 July 1953, all File OHME: A.J.P. Taylor,

OUP Archives.

89 Davin minutes of meeting with Deakin, Bullock and Colin Roberts, 20 Oct. 1953; Davin to Poole, 21 Oct. 1953; Davin minutes of meeting on 7 Dec. 1953 of the Editors, Poole, d'Entreve, Raymond Carr and Roberts, 9 Dec. 1953; Davin minutes of meeting on 24 May 1955 with Deakin, Bullock and Roberts, 25 May 1955; and Davin minutes of meeting with the Editors, 15 Dec. 1955, all File OHME General: 1947–61, OUP Archives. Roberts, a classical scholar and papyrologist, Fellow of St John's College and OUP Delegate since 1946, succeeded Norrington as Secretary to the Delegates in 1954. Ovenden, *A Fighting Withdrawal*, p. 257.

90 The volume covering 1789–1848 was not published until 1994: Paul W. Schroeder, *The Transformation of European Politics, 1787–1848* (Oxford: Clarendon Press, 1994).

91 Taylor, *The Struggle for Mastery in Europe 1848–1918* (Oxford: Oxford University Press, 1954), p. xix.

92 Taylor, *The Struggle for Mastery*, p. xxiii. In his small classic *Diplomacy*, Harold Nicolson, the son of an ambassador and a former diplomat himself, has this to say about the Italians: 'It [Italian diplomacy] is more than opportunist, it is based upon incessant manoeuvre. The aim of Italy's foreign policy is to acquire by negotiation an importance greater than can be supplied by her own physical strength. ... Italian diplomatists make a speciality of the art of negotiation. Their usual method is first to create bad relations with the country with whom they wish to negotiate and then to offer "good relations." She combines, on the one hand, the ambitions and the pretensions of a Great Power with, on the other, the methods of a Small Power. Her policy is thus not volatile only but essentially transitional.' *Diplomacy* (London: Oxford University Press, 1939), pp. 152–3.

93 Taylor, *The Struggle for Mastery*, p. xxiv.

94 *Ibid.*, pp. xxv-xxxi.

95 *Ibid.*, pp. xxiii, 81n.

96 *Ibid.*, p. xx.

97 *Ibid.*, p. 286n.

98 Quoted in *ibid.*, p. 151.

99 David Eastwood points out that 'T. made much of this in *Struggle* & more of it in *Origins*. Nevertheless patterns of contestation are, or become, structural. *Struggle* implicitly acknowledges this, but *Origins* more or less explicitly denies it. To that extent, *Origins* represents Taylor's approach in its most conceptually extreme form: the study of diplomacy with the history left out.'

100 Very Herderian – communities have a moral energy which inclines them to develop further in a direction once begun – although there is no evidence from his book list that he ever read Johann Herder.

101 Taylor, *The Struggle for Mastery*, pp. 10, 518, 20, 47, 520.

102 *Ibid.*, pp. 202, n. 2, 520, 527. One of the later writers was R.C.K. Ensor in his volume in the series, the Oxford History of England, *England 1870–1914* (Oxford University Press, 1936), pp. 469–70, 482.

103 Thomas, 'Recollections of A.J.P. Taylor', pp. 63–4.

104 Paul Kennedy, 'A.J.P. Taylor and "Profound Forces" in History', in Chris Wrigley, ed., *Warfare, Diplomacy and Politics*, pp. 21–2.

105 Mehta, *The Fly and the Fly-Bottle*, pp. 174–5.

106 Taylor, *The Origins of the Second World War*, (London: Hamish Hamilton, 1961), pp. 102–3. The political scientist Jack S. Levy has pointed out the – doubtless unintended – relationship between Taylor's work and that of the distinguished systems theorist Kenneth Waltz. He pointed out that Waltz's theory identified three levels of outcome determinants: the individual, state and system levels: 'Waltz's three levels are reflected in

A.J.P. Taylor's analogy between the causes of wars and automobile accidents (the individual driver, the nature and condition of the vehicle, and road and weather conditions).' Levy, 'The Theoretical Foundations of Paul W. Schroeder's International System', *International History Review*, vol. 16, no. 4 (Nov. 1994), p. 717.

107 Anthony Crosland to his mother, 10 Nov. 1954, File 10/1, Anthony Crosland Papers, London School of Economics.

108 Max Beloff, 'Balance of Power', *Time and Tide*, vol. 13, no. 46 (13 Nov. 1954), p. 1517; Taylor, *A Personal History*, pp. 179–80. The book passed from Namier to Taylor was Harold Nicolson, *The Congress of Vienna*: *Times Literary Supplement*, No. 2317 (29 June 1946), pp. 301–2.

109 'The Secrets of Diplomacy', *Times Literary Supplement*, no. 2358 (12 April 1947), pp. 165–6 (quotations from p. 166).

110 Woodward to Roberts, 30 Oct. 1954; Davin to Taylor, 4 Nov. 1954; and Taylor to Davin, 7 Nov. 1954, all File OHME: A.J.P. Taylor, OUP Archives.

111 Roberts to Woodward, 8 Nov. 1954 and Woodward to Roberts, 9 Nov. 1954, both File OHME: A.J.P. Taylor, OUP Archive. Taylor wrote reviews of fifteen volumes of the British documents between 1947 and 1954, common themes of which were the lack of any documents other than those of the Foreign Office and the selection of formal papers only, excluding all minutes. This line of attack may have had an effect, since in his final review in 1954 Taylor criticised the editors for printing only selected minutes – but at least there were minutes. All three 1948 volumes were reviewed for the *Times Literary Supplement*, so the paper had not been put off by the reaction to Taylor's first review. Thereafter his reviews appeared in the *Manchester*

Guardian and the *New Statesman*.

112 Davin to Taylor, 15 Nov. 1954 and Taylor to Davin, 16 Nov. 1954, both File OHME: A.J.P. Taylor, OUP Archives.

113 Roberts to Woodward, 18 Nov. 1954 and Woodward to Roberts, 23 Nov. 1954, both *ibid.*

114 Ollard, *A Man of Contradictions*, p. 50. 'Was it Pares who composed the verses, pencilled on the outside of an envelope in which Rowse collected some of Woodward's letters? "Plato was a Levantine/in the abbé's eyes/So were Aristotle/Socrates likewise/Sophocles or Sappho/The abbé would despise/That they were not approved of/Among the really wise/And they would hear that they were dagos/with extreme surprise." Woodward's All Souls nickname was "the Abbé".' Ollard, p. 50. On the other hand, Professor Gordon Craig, whose B. Litt thesis Woodward had supervised during the years 1936–8, liked him very much, later recalling 'many a pleasant lunch with him, eating oysters out of a paper sack and drinking American chablis.' However, he also recalled that Isaiah Berlin 'likened him to a Restoration abbé and intimated that he was richer in ambition than in talent.' Craig 'regarded him as a fine historian with a healthy suspicion of cleverness, and a gay companion.' Craig to the author, 19 Oct. 1999.

115 Roberts to Taylor, 2 Dec. 1954; Roberts's circular letter to members of the Finance Committee of the Delegates of the Press, 6 Dec. 1954, which contains the report of his telephone conversation with Taylor; Roberts to Woodward, 11 Dec. 1954; and Roberts to Taylor, 12 Dec. 1954, for the 'odd and inconvenient quarrel' quotation, all File OHME: A.J.P. Taylor, OUP Archives.

116 Asa Briggs, 'Before the Ball Was Over', *New Statesman and Nation*, vol. 48, no. 1235 (6 Nov. 1954), pp. 586–8; Gordon Craig, 'Europe's Perpetual Quadrille', *Saturday Review*, vol. 38

(16 July 1955), p. 28, quoted in Wrigley, *A.J.P. Taylor: A Complete Annotated Bibliography*, p. 83; and C.W. Crawley, *History*, vol. 61 (Oct. 1956), pp. 263–4.

117 'European Diplomatic History', *Times Literary Supplement*, no. 2756 (26 Nov. 1954), pp. 749–50; Jonathan Haslam, *The Vices of Integrity: E.H. Carr, 1892–1982* (London: Verso, 1999), p. 207.

118 David Eastwood has commented that 'This is profoundly correct – and again makes *Struggle* a more compelling work than *Origins*.' Comment on draft chapter.

119 Alan to Éva, 18 Oct. 1974, *Letters to Eva*, pp. 206–7; Taylor, *A Personal History*, p. 198; Noel Annan, *Our Age* (London: Weidenfeld and Nicolson, 1990), p. 273.

120 Taylor to Hamilton, 7 July 1953; Hamilton to Taylor, 9 July 1953; Taylor to Hamilton, 1 Sept. 1953; and Hamilton to Taylor, 2 Sept. 1953, all Box DM 1352, Hamilton Papers.

121 Taylor to Hamilton, 30 Oct. 1953; Hamilton to Taylor, *Private and Confidential*, 2 Nov. 1953; Taylor to Hamilton, 17 Nov. 1953; and Taylor to Hamilton, 29 Nov. 1953, all *ibid*.

122 Taylor to Hamilton, 1 Sept. 1954; Taylor to Hamilton, 11 Nov. 1954; Taylor to Hamilton, 3 Jan. 1955; Hamilton to Taylor, 19 Jan. 1955; Taylor to Machell, 25 Aug. 1955; Machell to Taylor, 26 Aug. 1955; and Taylor to Machell, 22 Aug. 1955, all *ibid*.

123 Taylor, *A Personal History*, p. 207.

124 Review of Eric Eyck, *Bismarck, Volume I* in the *English Historical Review*, vol. 58, no. 229 (Jan. 1943), pp. 113–15 and review of Eric Eyck, *Bismarck and the German Empire* in the *Manchester Guardian*, 25 July 1950, p. 4, both quoted in Wrigley, *A.J.P. Taylor: A Complete Annotated Bibliography*, p. 86; Taylor, *Bismarck: The Man and the Statesman* (London: Hamish Hamilton, 1955), p. 12.

125 Michael Howard, 'The Iron Chancellor', *The New Statesman and Nation*, vol. 50, no. 1270 (9 July 1955), pp. 47–8; Craig quotation from review in Wrigley, *A.J.P. Taylor: A Complete Annotated Bibliography*, pp. 86–7; Taylor, *A Personal History*, p. 207; Mommsen comment heard by the author at a seminar at the German Historical Institute, London, 16 June 1995.

126 Taylor sent up his compulsion to write by entitling the chapter in his autobiography covering these years 'Scribble, Scribble, Scribble, Mr Gibbon, 1960–65', a reference to George III's remark to the earlier historian. Taylor, *A Personal History*, p. 233. Along with the fifteen volumes of British diplomatic documents that he had reviewed between 1947 and 1954, Taylor also reviewed the eight volumes of German diplomatic documents and the one of Italian documents that had appeared during that period.

127 'The Heyday of Appeasement: German Policy From Munich to Prague', *Manchester Guardian*, 20 Dec. 1951, p. 4, reprinted in Taylor, *Rumours of Wars* (London: Hamish Hamilton 1952), p. 200.

128 'The Appeasement Years: Germany and her neighbours', *Manchester Guardian*, 28 July 1953, p. 4, reprinted in Taylor, *Englishmen and Others* (London: Hamish Hamilton, 1956), p. 156.

129 'Hitler's Secret', *New Statesman*, vol. 58, no. 1496 (14 Nov. 1959), pp. 682–3.

130 Taylor to Liddell Hart, 1 Oct. 1959 and Liddell Hart to Taylor, 5 Oct. 1959, both File A.J.P. Taylor 1957–67, 1/676, Basil Liddell Hart Collection, The Library, King's College London.

131 Taylor, *The Origins of the Second World War*, p. 16.

132 Taylor to Hamilton, 9 Dec. 1958; Taylor to Hamilton, 22 June 1960; and Machell to Hamilton, 1 Aug. 1960, all Box DM 1352, Hamilton Papers. Bosworth, *Explaining Auschwitz and Hiroshima*, p. 39 for the bombers.

133 Taylor, *The Origins of the Second World War*, p. 278. David Eastwood has referred to this as 'an epigram too far'. Comment on draft chapter.

134 Haffner, 'Mr. Taylor's Masterpiece', *Observer*, 16 April 1961, p. 30. In February 1949 a reviewer of *The Habsburg Monarchy* had made the same comparison. As Taylor wrote to his publisher, 'I liked being called the Evelyn Waugh of historians, but I wonder whether Evelyn Waugh is equally pleased.' Taylor to Hamish Hamilton, 16 Feb. 1949, Box DM 1352, Hamilton Papers. David Marquand, 'The Taylor Doctrine', *New Statesman*, 21 April 1961, printed in Wm Roger Louis, *The Origins of the Second World War: A.J.P. Taylor and his Critics* (New York: John Wiley and Sons, 1972), p. 65.

135 H.R. Trevor-Roper, 'A.J.P. Taylor, Hitler, and the War,' *Encounter*, July 1961, reprinted in Louis, ed., *A.J.P. Taylor and his Critics*, pp. 44–58. The review, together with Taylor's reply and Trevor-Roper's reply to Taylor, were also reprinted in Esmonde M. Robertson, *The Origins of the Second World War: Historical Interpretations* (London: Macmillan, 1971 pb), pp. 83–104. As soon as Taylor was appointed the author's D.Phil. supervisor, friends sent her straight to the Bodleian Library with instructions to read the *Encounter* exchange.

136 Mehta, *The Fly and the Fly-Bottle*, p. 119.

137 Quoted in *ibid.*, pp. 120–2.

138 Kallin to Comacho, 15 June 1961; note, 16 June 1961; Comacho to Kallin, 19 June 1961; Clark to Head of Talks, 22 June 1961, all Radio Contributors, Talks, A.J.P. Taylor, File 5, 1958–62, BBC Written Archives. Taylor appeared on Women's Hour on 12 July 1961, and the repeat on the Home Service of the television discussion took place on 30 July 1961.

139 For Kee's telling Taylor of the review, see Mehta, *The Fly and the Fly-Bottle*, p. 176. Taylor's review of *The Last Days of Hitler* appeared in the *New Statesman and Nation*, vol. 40, no. 1009 (8 July 1950); quotation taken from Wrigley, *A.J.P. Taylor: A Complete Annotated Bibliography*, p. 33. Taylor's reply to Trevor-Roper and Trevor-Roper's reply to Taylor's reply are also found in Louis, ed., *A.J.P. Taylor and his Critics*, pp. 58–63. For a description of the Taylor/Trevor-Roper BBC clash on 9 July 1961, see the following day's *Daily Telegraph*.

140 Taylor to Machell, 26 Aug. 1962, Box DM 1352, Hamilton Papers. With regard to Taylor's failure to read *Mein Kampf*, David Eastwood has commented that 'If this is right – and your evidence is very strong – it suggests that Taylor's research technique was more obviously selective, even by the late 1950s, than has often been supposed.' Comment on draft chapter.

141 'Complete Translation of "Mein Kampf" ', unexpurgated edition, translated by James Murphy, *Times Literary Supplement*, no. 1938 (25 March 1939), p. 170. For the expurgated edition see Adolf Hitler, *My Struggle* (London: Hurst and Blackett, 1933), 285 pp., with no translator named. In fact, he was Edgar Trevelyan Stratford Dugdale, the husband of Mrs 'Baffy' Dugdale, daughter of Lord Balfour. The 1939 translation had 567 pp. For the story of the various translations, and of the efforts of various German agents to interfere, see D.C. Watt, 'Introduction', Adolf Hitler, *Mein Kampf* (London: Pimlico pb, 1992), pp. xl–xliv. For the story of the Chamberlain annotations see p. xlvii. *Hitlers zweites Buch, ein Dokument aus dem Jahr 1928, eingeleitat und Komm. von* G.L. Weinberg (Stuttgart, 1961). *Hitler's Secret Book*, trans. S. Attanasio (New York, 1962).

142 Woodward to Clark, 17 May 1961, File 39 (OHE General), Clark Papers. The four books were

Robertson and Louis, already cited; Gordon Martel, ed., *The Origins of the Second World War Reconsidered: The A.J.P. Taylor Debate after Twenty-Five Years* (Boston/London: Allen and Unwin, 1986); and Gordon Martel, ed., *The Origins of the Second World War Reconsidered: A.J.P. Taylor and the Historians* (London: Routledge, 1999), essentially a second edition of the above book, but with several new essays.

143 T.W. Mason, 'Some Origins of the Second World War', *Past and Present*, vol. 29 (Dec. 1964), pp. 67–87, reprinted in Robertson, *The Origins of the Second World War*, pp. 105–35, esp. 125, 108–9. David Eastwood has pointed out that 'Tim, in fact, hugely admired T. as a historian. He regarded *Origins* as an aberration.' Comment on draft chapter.

144 Taylor, 'War Origins Again', *Past and Present*, vol. 30 (April 1965), reprinted in Robertson, *The Origins of the Second World War*, pp. 137–8, 140.

145 Watt, 'Introduction', *Mein Kampf*, pp. xlvii–lv.

146 'Adolf Hitler – Weder Held noch Schurke? Neue Thesen über den Ausbruch des Zweiten Weltkriegs', *Der Spiegel*, no. 48 (1961), pp. 45–51. I am grateful to Ulrike Wunderle for the translation of this and of the Golo Mann review below.

147 Wiskermann letter printed in Louis, ed., *The Origins of the Second World War*, pp. 36–7; Taylor, 'Second Thoughts', *Origins of the Second World War* (London: Penguin pb, 1964), p. 26.

148 Taylor to Kingsley Martin, 24 July ??, but between 1961 and 1964, Box 15, File 2, Kingsley Martin Papers. David Eastwood has pointed out that 'it all depends on what we mean by war. That H. didn't plan WW2 is palpable, though the point needs making. WW2 was a *consequence* not an intention. That Germany & Hitler planned a series of military interventions, & a type of war (*Blitzkrieg*) is obvious, & Taylor's treatment of this rather willful.' Comment on draft chapter.

149 Golo Mann, 'Hitler's britischer Advocat: A.J.P. Taylors Revision des Geschichte', *Der Monat*, no 11 (96), pp. 79–86. The intention of the CIA was to 'address, and to stimulate, the German-reading intelligentsia of Germany and elsewhere, with the world-views of American writers and thinkers.' The result was *Der Monat*, 'a monthly journal of philosophical-cultural-political debate which first appeared in October 1948. . . . It was an instant success, capitalising on the lack of intellectual debate in post-fascist Germany, and providing an alternative to the wide-ranging Soviet-sponsored pro-communist press.' Giles Scott-Smith, 'The Organising of Intellectual Consensus: The Congress for Cultural Freedom and Post-War US-European Relations (Part I)', *Lobster*, no. 36 (Winter 1998), p. 12. Thanks to Scott Newton for the reference. For more information specifically on *Der Monat*, see Giles Scott-Smith, ' "A Radical Democratic Political Offensive": Melvyn J. Lasky, *Der Monat*, and the Congress for Cultural Freedom', *Journal of Contemporary History*, vol. 35, no. 2 (April 2000), pp. 263–80.

150 Ritter to Giselher Wirsing, 2 May 1961, in Schwabe and Reichardt, *Gerhard Ritter*, p. 548. Translation by Michael Jewess.

151 Hamilton to Taylor, 13 April 1961; Taylor to Hamilton, 19 April 1961; Taylor to Machell, 2 June 1961; Machell to Hamilton, 5 June 1961; and Hamilton to Taylor, 12 June 1961, all Box DM 1352, Hamilton Papers.

152 Preface to the American edition (New York: Atheneum, 1962), pp. v–x.

153 *Time*, 12 Jan. 1962, reprinted in Louis, *A.J.P. Taylor and his Critics*, pp. 104–5; Gordon Craig, 'Provocative, Perverse View of Pre-1939',

New York Herald Tribune, 7 Jan. 1962, reprinted in *ibid*., pp. 110–14.

154 Taylor, letter of 28 April 1974, *Letters to Eva*, p. 178; Taylor, *A Personal History*, p. 233; H.W. Koch, 'Hitler and the Origins of the Second World War: Second Thoughts on the Status of Some of the Documents', Robertson, *The Origins of the Second World War*, p. 158; Robert J. Young, 'A.J.P. Taylor and the Problem with France', Martel, *The Origins of the Second World War Reconsidered: The A.J.P. Taylor Debate*, p. 97; and Paul Kennedy, 'Appeasement', Martel, *ibid*., p. 140. Indeed, the argument still rages over the role of Hitler, the culpability of the German people, and so on.

155 Taylor to Hamilton, 28 Nov. 1956, Box DM 1352, Hamilton Papers.

156 Hamish Hamilton to Taylor, 29 Nov. 1956; Taylor to Jamie, 30 Nov. 1956; Hamish Hamilton to Taylor, 10 Dec. 1956; and Hamish Hamilton to Taylor, 11 Dec. 1956, all *ibid*.

157 Taylor, *The Troublemakers: Dissent over British Foreign Policy 1792–1939* (London: Hamish Hamilton, 1957), pp. 12–14.

158 *Ibid*., p. 50.

159 *Ibid*., pp. 23–24, 11.

160 Taylor to Machell, 26 July 1957, Box DM 1352, Hamilton Papers. Reviews quoted in Wrigley, *A.J.P. Taylor: A Complete Annotated Bibliography*, pp. 92–3.

161 Taylor to Roger, 2 May 1962 and Roger to Taylor, 7 May 1962, both Box DM 1352, Hamilton Papers.

162 Taylor to Roger, 12 May 1963; Machell to Hamilton, 14 May 1963; Machell to Taylor, 14 May 1963; and Machell to Taylor, 16 May 1963, all Box D 1352, Hamilton Papers. Ledger Records on A.J.P. Taylor, David Higham Agency Papers, Higham Office Records, London.

163 Taylor to Hamilton, 18 Sept. 1957, Box DM 1352, Hamilton Papers; Taylor, *A Personal History*, p. 220.

164 Davin to Poole, 6 March 1957, File

OHE General: 1931–61, OUP Archives. Ensor had written to Clark in September 1956 that the doctor had come to see him that day and 'I must throw in my hand'. Box 30 (A.J.P. Taylor), G.N. Clark Papers, Bodleian Library, Oxford. Davin to Clark, 11 March 1957, File OHE General: 1931–61 and Clark to Davin, 24 March 1957, File OHE: A.J.P. Taylor 1957–65, both OUP Archives.

165 Roberts's draft, 26 March 1957, which became a Minute for Delegates, 'Oxford History of England – 1914–1950', 29 April 1957, File OHE: A.J.P. Taylor 1957–65, OUP Archives; Clark to Davin, 12 March 1957 and Roberts to Clark, 30 March 1957 reporting discussion with Poole, both File 30 (A.J.P. Taylor), Clark Papers.

166 Taylor to Clark, 3 May 1957 and 11 June 1957, both File 30 (A.J.P. Taylor), Clark Papers; Taylor to Davin, 29 June 1957 and Davin to Taylor, 3 July 1957, both File OHE: A.J.P. Taylor 1957–65, OUP Archives.

167 Taylor to Clark, 6 Dec. 1957, File 30 (A.J.P. Taylor), Clark Papers; Taylor, 'Accident Prone', p. 14. The other volumes in the series that he read were May McKisack, *The Fourteenth Century* (1959); Jacob (1961); J.D. Mackie, *The Earlier Tudors* (1952); J.B. Black, *The Reign of Elizabeth* (1936); Godfrey Davies, *The Early Stuarts* (1937); Sir George Clark, *The Later Stuarts* (1934), the first in the series to be published; and Basil Williams, *The Whig Supremacy* (1939).

168 Taylor, *A Personal History*, pp. 236–7. 'Goak' = joke, a spelling Taylor took from the writings of the nineteenth-century American humourist Artemus Ward.

169 Taylor to Clark, 20 Dec. 1961 and Taylor to Clark, 25 Aug. 1962, both File 30 (A.J.P. Taylor), Clark Papers; Taylor, *A Personal History*, pp. 237–8.

170 Taylor to Clark, 25 Aug. 1962; Taylor to Clark, 28 Nov. 1962; and

Taylor to Clark, 6 Dec. 1962, all File 30 (A.J.P. Taylor), Clark Papers.

171 Roberts memorandum for Davin, 28 March 1963, File OHE: A.J.P. Taylor, OUP Archives; Taylor to Clark, 23 Oct. 1963, File 30 (A.J.P. Taylor), Clark Papers; Roberts to Davin, 9 Dec. 1963, File OHE: A.J.P. Taylor, OUP Archives; Taylor to Clark, 9 Feb. 1964; Clark to Taylor, 4 March 1964 and Taylor to Clark, 5 March 1963, all File 30 (A.J.P. Taylor), Clark Papers.

172 Roberts for Davin, 2 April 1964, File OHE: A.J.P. Taylor, OUP Archives; Taylor to Clark, 12 June 1964, Clark to Taylor, 14 July 1964, Taylor to Clark, 18 July 1964, Clark to Taylor, 5 Oct. 1964, Taylor to Clark, 31 Dec. 1964 and Taylor to Clark, 10 Feb. 1965, all File 30 (A.J.P. Taylor), Clark Papers.

173 White to Davin, 30 July 1965; Roberts to White, 2 Aug. 1965; and Roberts to Clark, 21 Sept. 1965, all File OHE: A.J.P. Taylor, OUP Archives.

174 Taylor to Roberts, 26 Sept. 1965 and Roberts to Taylor, 27 Sept. 1965, both File OHE: A.J.P. Taylor, OUP Archives. The author possesses what must be a rare copy of the first issue of the book with its W.H. Smith-friendly dust jacket (copies thus wrapped had been sent out to reviewers and could not be recalled). It is a darker blue than the standard OHE jacket, with five photographs on the front: soldiers carrying a colleague on a stretcher during the First World War; Lloyd George and Churchill walking together during the same war; Hitler saluting in his characteristic manner; Roosevelt, Churchill and Stalin at Yalta; and soldiers disembarking during the Normandy landings. It could hardly be more chaste.

175 Taylor, 'Unlucky Dip', review of *The New Cambridge Moden History*, *Observer*, 22 May 1960, p. 21, quoted in Wrigley, *A.J.P. Taylor: A Complete Annotated Bibliography*, p.

103.

176 Taylor, *English History 1914–1945* (Oxford: Clarendon Press, 1965), p. 1.

177 *Ibid.*, p. 2.

178 Indeed, as George Bernard has pointed out, Taylor's command of the specialised detail is impressive. In the book (p. 234) he wrote that the BBC issued regular news bulletins, which worked in well with the changes apparent in newspapers. 'The evening papers printed the racing results, and therefore still had news value; they remained predominantly local in circulation.' Bernard noted that 'in Reading in the early 1960s, the Evening News and Evening Standard would arrive by train several times a day; they would be taken to nearby sheds where chaps with John Bull style printing sets would print in the Stop Press columns the latest racing results, and every half hour or so a new batch of papers would be taken by van or cycle to the vendors in the main streets – so that at 4.15 you could buy a paper with the 4.00 Newmarket result in it.' Bernard to the author, 21 Oct. 1999.

179 Taylor, *English History*, p. 600.

180 Henry Pelling, 'Taylor's England', *Past and Present*, vol. 33 (April 1966), pp. 149–58; Peter Stansky, *Journal of Modern History*, vol. 39, no. 3 (Sept. 1967), pp. 329–31; Noel Annan, 'Historian of the People', *New York Review of Books*, vol. 5, no. 9 (9 Dec. 1965), pp. 10, 12; Alan Bullock, 'England from Asquith to Attlee', *Observer* (24 Oct. 1965), p. 26; and 'History Taylor-Made', *Times Literary Supplement*, no. 3329 (16 Dec. 1965), pp. 1169–70.

181 Henry Pelling in the *New Statesman*, 17 Dec. 1965.

182 For publication numbers, Jenny McMorris of OUP to the author, 31 May 1996 and Tony Morris of OUP to the author, 1 July 1996; for Italian usage, Paul Ginsborg, Professor at the University of Florence, to the author, April 1999; Taylor to

Clark, 21 Sept. 1966, File 30 (A.J.P. Taylor), Clark Papers; Taylor to Eva, 18 Feb. 1973 and 16 June 1973, both *Letters to Eva*, pp. 116 and 133; and Taylor, *A Personal History*, pp. 244–5.

183 Taylor, *A Personal History*, pp. 273–4.

184 Taylor, *Englishmen and Others*, Preface.

185 Taylor, *Bismarck*, p. 70.

186 Taylor, *The Struggle for Mastery*, p. xx.

6 *The London Years 1963–1985*

1 Martin Gilbert to Adam Sisman, 3 Sept. 1991, Martin Gilbert Papers, in private possession, London.

2 *Ibid.*, William Thomas to Gilbert, 28 April 1962 and Berlin to Gilbert, 30 Nov. 1963; list of writers and titles, 25 March 1966, all Gilbert Papers. Mehta, *The Fly and the Fly-Bottle*, p. 163.

3 Berlin to Gilbert, 2 March, 8 March, 1 May, 14 May and 18 June 1962, all Gilbert Papers.

4 Einzig to Gilbert, 9 May, 15 Nov. and 5 Dec. 1962, all Gilbert Papers; Einzig had not seen the broadcast, but had read the text, 'The Great Depression', in the *Listener*, 22 March 1962, p. 505. Taylor to Machell, 15 Nov. 1966, Box DM 1352, Hamilton Papers; Taylor, 'Received with Thanks', *Observer*, 20 Nov. 1966; Paul Einzig, 'The Financial Crisis of 1931', Martin Gilbert, ed., *A Century of Conflict 1850–1950: Essays for A.J.P. Taylor* (New York: Atheneum, 1967), pp. 234–5; and Sisman, *A.J.P. Taylor*, p. 342, for Einzig's being impressed.

5 Hugh Thomas to Gilbert, 16 March 1962; Norman Angell to Gilbert, 27 Nov. 1964; H.N. Fieldhouse to Gilbert, 1 April 1962; Berlin to Gilbert, 22 Jan. 1963, 21 May 1962 and 28 April 1963, all Gilbert Papers.

6 Gilbert to Sisman, 3 Sept. 1991 and Gilbert to Taylor, 13 May 1966, both Gilbert Papers. The other two *Festschriften* were Alan Sked and Chris Cook, eds, *Crisis and Controversy: Essays in Honour of A.J.P. Taylor* (London: Macmillan, 1976) and Chris Wrigley, ed., *Warfare, Diplomacy and Politics: Essays in Honour of A.J.P. Taylor* (London: Hamish Hamilton, 1986).

7 Michael Foot, 'Alan Taylor', in Wrigley, ed., *Warfare, Diplomacy and Politics*, p. 9; A.J.P. Taylor, 'Lord Beaverbrook as Historian', *Observer*, 28 Oct. 1956, p. 16.

8 Or as Pascal actually wrote in the *Pensées* (iv. 277): 'Le coeur a ses raisons que la raison ne connaît point.'

9 Taylor, *A Personal History*, p. 246. Taylor to Hamish Hamilton, 23 Oct. 1962, Box DM 1352, Hamilton Papers. Memo by Higham, 3 May 1963, File 657, 'T' General/1963; Taylor to Higham, 11 June 1964, File 728, Taylor, A.J.P./1964, both Higham Agency Papers, Ransome Center. For the Blake story see Anne Chisholm and Michael Davie, *Beaverbrook: A Life* (London: Hutchinson, 1992), p. 511.

10 Higham Memos, 17 June and 22 June 1964; Higham to Taylor, 13 July 1964; Taylor to Higham, 18 July 1964; Higham to Taylor, 23 July 1964; and JK to IVA, 24 Aug. 1964, all File 728/Taylor/1964, Higham Agency Papers, Ransome Center. Machell to Taylor, 1 Feb. 1965 and Taylor to Machell, 6 Feb. 1965, both Box DM 1352, Hamilton Papers.

11 Taylor to Clark, 18 July 1964, File 30 (A.J.P. Taylor), Clark Papers; Taylor, *A Personal History*, p. 246.

12 Taylor to Higham, 4 Feb. 1965, File 812/Taylor/1965, Higham Agency Papers, Ransome Center; Taylor, *A Personal History*, pp. 246–7.

13 Taylor, ed., *Lloyd George: Twelve Essays* (London: Hamish Hamilton, 1971). At the IHR the seminar on twentieth-century British history

was co-chaired by Taylor with Martin Ceadel, John Ramsden and John Turner; when Ceadel left London for Oxford in 1980, he was succeeded by the author of this biography, the only one of the Taylor co-chairs who continues as a co-chair of the seminar.

14 The Lord Mayor, Sir Murray Fox, to Taylor, 13 Jan. 1975 and Taylor to Fox, 16 Jan. 1975, Box 3, Folder 13i; and Ivan Sutton, Chairman of the City Music Society, to Taylor, 18 July 1975 and Taylor to Sutton 21 July 1975, Box 3, Folder 16, all Taylor Papers, Ransome Center. Taylor, *A Personal History*, pp. 247–8.

15 Taylor to Éva Haraszti, 3 March 1973, 3 Nov. 1974 and 17 Nov. 1974, *Letters to Éva*, pp. 118, 208–9, 212. By the following April the truth had emerged: 'I have now learnt why the Library was killed, and it has nothing to do with the shortage of money. Apparently they are installing new machinery on the floor below the advertising department and did not allow for the fact that the machinery was too tall to be accommodated on a single floor. In fact, the machinery stuck up into the office above. New space was needed for the advertising offices. None could be found so they simply grabbed the Library.' Taylor to Eva, 8 April 1975, *ibid.*, p. 233.

16 Taylor to Éva Haraszti, 18 Oct., 3 Nov., 8 Nov., 1 Dec. and 13 Dec. 1974, 30 March and 8 April 1975, *Letters to Eva*, pp. 205, 209–10, 214, 232–3.

17 Including the author, who remembers marching through the print works in order to reach his office, accompanied by wolf whistles and suggestions for activities of doubtful repute.

18 Taylor to Clark, 23 Dec. 1964, File 30 (A.J.P. Taylor), Clark Papers; Taylor to Machell, 6 Feb. 1965; Taylor to Hamilton, 7 Jan. 1967 and 24 May 1971; and Hamilton to Taylor, 26 May 1971, all Box DM

1352, Hamilton Papers. David Eastwood comments that *Beaverbrook* was 'his only archively-based work of (quasi) British history.' Comment on draft chapter.

19 Taylor to the Secretary, Society of Authors, 26 June 1973; list of Members of Parliament who signed Early Day Motion 203 before 11 June 1973; and Victor Bonham-Carter to Taylor, 28 June 1973, all Box 5, Folder 31, Taylor Papers, Ransome Center.

20 Taylor to Machell, 9 March 1972; Taylor to Hamilton, 21 April 1972 for librarian quotation; Machell to Taylor, 14 June 1972; and Hamilton to Taylor, 15 August 1972, all Box DM 1352, Hamilton Papers. Ober Associates (Higham's preferred American literary agency) to Higham, 10 April 1972, Garage Box (Higham Papers discovered in a north London lock-up garage – with many thanks to Bruce Hunter, who facilitated my search, and to my former student, Andrew Taylor, who helped in the search), Higham Agency Papers, London.

21 Kenneth Young to Taylor, quoted by Taylor in his Introduction, *Beaverbrook: A Biography* (New York: Simon and Schuster, 1972), p. ix.

22 David Eastwood takes issue with the harshness of this judgement, pointing out that Taylor never claimed that it was an official biography, and therefore, 'implicitly at least, might reasonably expect it to be judged on its own terms.' But see note 25 below. Comment on draft chapter.

23 Taylor, *Beaverbrook* (New York), pp. xvi, xvii and p. 671.

24 Cole, *A.J.P. Taylor*, p. 232.

25 'The Great Fixer', *Times Literary Supplement*, no. 3670 (30 June 1972) and Tom Driberg, 'In the Sight of the Lord', *New Statesman*, vol. 83, no. 2154 (30 June 1972), both quoted in Wrigley, *A.J.P. Taylor: A Complete Annotated Bibliography*, pp. 114–15. Taylor to Éva, 2 Feb. 1976, *Letters to Eva*, p. 288.

With regard to Taylor's comment that the scale of the book had been wrong, David Eastwood considers that 'Had it been a life and times, properly contextualized & research-ed, then its scale might have been justified, or at least less dispro-portionate.' Comment on draft chapter.

26 Uttered on 5 April 1776, aged sixty-seven: James Boswell, *The Life of Samuel Johnson, LL.D* (London: Bliss Sands, 1897), p. 263 in the author's copy.

27 Higham to Taylor, 10 Oct. 1957; Higham to IVA, 29 Oct. 1957; and Higham to Taylor, 28 Oct. 1957, all File 251.21/T General, Higham Agency Papers, Ransome Center.

28 Ovenden, *A Fighting Withdrawal*, p. 279. Higham to Taylor, 17 Sept. 1959; Taylor to Higham, 4 Oct. 1959; Higham to Taylor, 16 Nov. 1959; and Taylor to Higham, 17 Nov. 1959, all File 392.19/T General, Higham Agency Papers, Ransome Center.

29 Taylor to Higham, 23 March 1961; Higham to Taylor, 5 April 1961; Higham to Taylor, 10 April 1961; Higham to Taylor, 18 April 1961; and Taylor to Higham, 19 April 1961, all File 520, Taylor/1961, Higham Agency Papers, Ransome Center.

30 Taylor to Hamilton, 8 Sept. 1962; Hamilton to Taylor, 10 Sept. 1962; Taylor to Hamilton, 10 Dec. 1962; Machell to Taylor, 12 Dec. 1962; Taylor to Machell, 14 Dec. 1962; and Machell to Taylor, 23 Jan. 1963, all Box DM 1352, Hamilton Papers. Taylor to Higham, 8 Aug. 1962, File 603/T General/1962/DH for the first quotation and Taylor to Higham, 23 March 1963, File 657/T General/1963/DH for the second, both Higham Agency Papers, Ransome Center.

31 Taylor, *The First World War: An Illustrated History* (Harmonds-worth: Penguin, 1972), p. 38. See reviews by Alan Clark in the *Spectator* of 8 Nov. 1963, the anonymous review in the *Times Literary Supplement* of 5 Dec. 1963 and the review by Taylor's old friend Geoffrey Barraclough in the *New York Review of Books* of 14 May 1964. Comment by David Eastwood on draft chapter.

32 Machell to Hamilton, 28 June 1963, Box DM 1352, Hamilton Papers.

33 Taylor to Higham, 31 Oct. 1963; Higham to Taylor, 1 Nov. and 18 Nov. 1963; and Taylor to Higham, 20 Nov. 1963, all File 657/T General/1963/DH, Higham Agency Papers, Ransome Center.

34 Such as Korea and Afghanistan.

35 Taylor, *From Sarajevo to Potsdam* (London: Thames and Hudson, 1966), pp. 7–14, 17, 62, 198.

36 'Picture Past', *Times Literary Supplement*, no. 3381 (15 Dec. 1966), p. 1163, quoted in Wrigley, *A.J.P. Taylor: A Complete Annotated, Bib-liography*, p. 109. File cards and cash ledger book, Higham Agency Papers, London.

37 Taylor to Higham, 12 April and 18 April 1964, and note by Higham, 2 November 1964, all File 728/AJPT/1964/DH; Taylor to Higham, 24 July 1965, note by Higham, 1 Oct. 1965, Taylor to Higham, 7 Dec. 1965 and Higham to Taylor, 8 Dec. 1965, all File 812/AJPT/1965/DH, all Higham Agency Papers, Ransome Center.

38 Taylor to Higham, 24 Jan., 19 Feb. and 16 Sept. 1968, all File 1069/AJPT/1968/DH, Higham Agency Papers, Ransome Center. Taylor, 'War by Timetable', reprinted in Chris Wrigley, ed., *A.J.P. Taylor. From the Boer War to the Cold War. Essays on Twentieth-Century Europe* (London: Hamish Hamilton), p. 180.

39 Interview with G.M.D. Howat, 9 April 1995.

40 Frances Stevenson, *Lloyd George: A Diary*, edited by A.J.P. Taylor (London: Hutchinson, 1971); Taylor, ed., *My Darling Pussy: The Letters of Lloyd George and Frances Stevenson 1913–41* (London: Weidenfeld and

Nicolson, 1975); and W.P. Crozier, *Off the Record: Political Interviews 1933–1943*, edited by A.J.P. Taylor (London: Hutchinson, 1973). Taylor to Morgan, 12 Jan. 1981, quoted in Sisman, *A.J.P. Taylor*, p. 352. It is interesting that none of these volumes was published by Hamish Hamilton. Taylor wrote to Higham on 21 Jan. 1974 that 'Christopher Falkus was here the other day. I showed him the LG letters. He is very eager to get them for Weidenfeld & Nicolson. To tell you the truth I think Hutchinsons are rather a stodgy firm whom I should be glad to escape. Nor do I think Hamish Hamilton made much of Beaverbrook and should therefore be glad to escape them also.' Garage Box Higham Agency Papers, London.

41 Taylor to Higham, 13 March and 31 March 1970; Higham to Taylor, 1 April and 13 April 1970; CMS to Higham, 6 April 1970; IVA to Higham, 9 April 1970; and Hunter to IVA, 14 May 1970, all File 1195/AJPT/1970, Higham Agency Papers, Ransome Center.

42 Higham to Taylor, 10 Feb. and Taylor to Higham, 11 Feb. 1972, Box 3, Folder 10, Higham Agency Papers, Ransome Center Taylor to Higham, 23 Jan., 15 Nov. and 4 Dec. 1974, Higham Agency Papers, London. C.M. Woodhouse, 'World War II in Perspective', *Observer*, 13 April 1975. The picture books are *The Last of Old Europe: A Grand Tour with AJP Taylor* (London: Sidgwick and Jackson, 1976) and *The Russian War 1941–1945* (London: Jonathan Cape, 1978), first published in Czech in 1975. David Eastwood suggests that 'The sheer volume of T's writing in semi-retirement is a comment, in part, on the relative impoverishment of his private life – a consequence, in part, of uncultivated friendships & sometimes willful indifference.' Comment on draft chapter. This comment, while perceptive, does not allow for the sheer force of Taylor's need to write (and to earn money).

43 Taylor to Hurstfield, 15 Sept.; Hurstfield to Taylor, 24 Sept.; Cobban to Taylor, 4 Dec.; Taylor to Cobban, 18 Dec. and 22 Dec., all 1964, Department of History Papers, UCL. I am grateful to the Departmental Secretary, Miss Naz-neen Razwi, for finding the papers and making them available to me.

44 Cobban to Provost, 24 Feb. 1965; College Secretary to Taylor, 14 April 1965; Taylor to Hurstfield, 5 June 1968; Hurstfield to Taylor, 13 June 1968; Reports, 7 Jan. 1971; Assistant Secretary (Personnel) to Dear Colleague, 28 Oct. 1974; Assistant Secretary (Personnel) to Taylor, 17 June 1977; Taylor to Hill, 3 June 1977 for 150th Anniversary, Christie to Taylor, 13 June 1977 for smuggling out the money; and Christie to Taylor, 22 March 1978, all Department of History Papers, UCL. Taylor, *A Personal History*, p. 245.

45 Taylor to Gross, 30 March 1976, Box 4, Folder 19, Taylor Archive, Ransome Center. Sisman, *A.J.P. Taylor*, p. 380. Institute of Historical Research, *Annual Report*, 1977–78.

46 Acta, Wednesday, 19 May 1948, File CMM/2/9, Magdalen College Archive; David Worswick to author, 2 Jan. 2000; and Dusan Radojicic to author, at lunch in Magdalen, 1997.

47 Taylor later queried this, writing the following year to Professor W.J. Mackenzie of the Department of Government and Administration, Glasgow University: 'A dispute has arisen in the College over our procedure in changing Statutes. The Act of 1923 says that a Statute can be changed by "the votes of a two-thirds majority of those persons present and voting". We have always interpreted this as a two-thirds majority of the votes cast, and

the President has two votes. Recently a proposal to amend Statute I and thus permit the admission of women received 32 votes to 17. James then declared that the amendment was not carried. It has now been suggested that although 49 votes were cast, 48 persons were present and that 32 is a two-thirds majority of 48. We are in the process of asking the Visitor for his true interpretation.' Was he aware of a 1930s correspondence on the same subject? Taylor to Mackenzie, 2 Dec. 1971, Box 4, Folder 18, Taylor Papers, Ransome Center.

48 David Bellos to author, 24 March 1999.

49 Letter from Taylor proposing the change, 21 May 1976 and Acta, 16 June 1976, both Magdalen College Archives. My thanks to Dr Darwell-Smith for transcribing these for me.

50 Taylor to Clark, 6 Dec. 1957, 8 Jan. 1960, 17 Jan. 1961, 23 Dec. 1964 and 7 Dec. 1965, all File OHE Taylor 1957–65, Clark Papers.

51 Dover, *Marginal Comment*, pp. 212–14.

52 *The Times*, 24 June 1980; *Sunday Express*, 29 June 1980, quoted in Sisman, *A.J.P. Taylor*, p. 390.

53 Dover, *Marginal Comment*, pp. 215–16. The three Fellows were John Crook, Colin Roberts and T.C. Skeat. Reported in the *Daily Telegraph*, 4 July 1980, quoted in Sisman, *A.J.P. Taylor*, p. 391.

54 Another link: as an undergraduate at Oxford, Christie had been taught by Taylor.

55 The bulk of the material in the above two paragraphs, including all quotations, is from Dover, *Marginal Comment*, pp. 216–18. *Daily Telegraph*, 20 Aug. 1980. Dover revealed the gist of the above exchange in an interview with Ann Morrow of the *Daily Telegraph* 21 Aug. 1980.

56 Sisman, *A.J.P. Taylor*, p. 392 for letter to Dover; Dover, *Marginal Comment*, p. 218; Taylor to Éva, 24

Nov. 1979, *Letters to Eva*, p. 405.

57 Dover, *Marginal Comment*, p. 220; Sisman, *A.J.P. Taylor*, p. 393.

58 Entry for 17 March 1980, Haraszti-Taylor, *A Life with Alan*, p. 104.

59 Taylor, *A Personal History*, pp. 230–1; Angela Lambert interview with Eve Crosland, 7 July 1991, *Independent on Sunday*.

60 Éva Haraszti-Taylor, *Remembering Alan: A Love Story* (Privately printed, 1995), pp. 3–5.

61 Taylor, *A Personal History*, pp. 239, 241–2; Haraszti-Taylor, *Remembering Alan*, pp. 8–9.

62 Interview with Daniel Taylor, 6 April 2000; Taylor to Éva, 14 Dec. 1976, *Letters to Eva*, p. 320; Taylor to Karin Wood, 16 Dec. 1968, quoted in Sisman, *A.J.P. Taylor*, p. 350.

63 'AJP Taylor Goes Back to his First Wife', *Daily Mail*, 25 Sept. 1968; 'History Man', *Evening Standard*, 25 June 1991.

64 Haraszti-Taylor, *Remembering Alan*, pp. 16, 21–2; Taylor, *A Personal History*, p. 252.

65 Taylor to Éva, 11 Dec. and 24 Nov. 1969, *Letters to Éva*, pp. 1–3; Taylor, *A Personal History*, p. 253.

66 *Ibid.*, pp. 261–2; Taylor to Éva, 24 July 1981, *Letters to Eva*; and Haraszti-Taylor, *Remembering Alan*, pp. 25–6.

67 Taylor to Éva, 24 July 1981, *Letters to Eva*, p. 433; Taylor, *A Personal History*, p. 262; Haraszti-Taylor, *Remembering Alan*, p. 30; Haraszti-Taylor, *Choices and Decisions: A Life* (Nottingham: Astra Press, 1997), p. 205.

68 Haraszti-Taylor, *Remembering Alan*, p. 30.

69 Haraszti-Taylor, *Choices and Decisions*, p. 207; Taylor, *A Personal History*, pp. 262–3; Haraszti-Taylor, *Remembering Alan*, pp. 29–32, 35.

70 Taylor to Éva, 31 Aug. 1974, *Letters to Eva*, p. 198; Taylor, *A Personal History*, pp. 262–3; *Daily Telegraph* 26 Jan. 1974.

71 Haraszti-Taylor, *Remembering Alan*, p. 49; Taylor to Éva, 16 April 1972,

Letters to Eva. pp 71–2.

72 Taylor to Éva, 16 July 1970 and 17 Feb. 1974, *Letters to Eva*, pp. 13, 168.

73 Haraszti-Taylor, *Remembering Alan*, p. 55.

74 *Ibid.*, p. 58.

75 *Ibid.*, pp. 63, 70; Taylor, *A Personal History*, pp. 66–7.

76 Taylor to Éva, 25 Sept. 1976, 1 Oct. 1976, 11 Oct. 1976, 26 Nov. 1976, 14 Dec. 1976, 21 Jan. 1977, 28 Jan. 1977, 4 Feb. 1977, 3 March 1977, all *Letters to Eva*, pp. 307, 308, 310, 320, 327, 328 for living modestly, 329, 333 for needing someone to advise him.

77 Taylor to Éva, 18 March 1977, 2 April 1977, 10 June 1977, 29 July 1977, 5 Aug. 1977, 16 Aug. 1977, 30 Sept. 1977 and 9 Oct. 1977, all *Ibid.*, pp. 335, 340 for Margaret being ill, 347, 355, 356, 358, 362, 363.

78 Taylor to Éva, 20 March 1978, *Ibid.*, p. 389.

79 Taylor *A Personal History*, p. 267; Haraszti-Taylor, *Remembering Alan*, pp. 92–3.

80 Entries for 25 Sept. and 22 Oct. 1978, Haraszti Taylor, *A Life with Alan*, pp. 33, 39.

81 Taylor to Gilbert, 16 May 1961, Gilbert Papers.

82 Higham to Taylor, 27 Feb. and 10 May; Taylor to Higham, 15 May; and Higham to Taylor, 4 Sept., all 1974; Higham to Taylor, 10 July and Taylor to Higham, 11 July, both 1975, all Higham Agency Papers, London. For keeping clear of post–1945, Taylor to Hamilton, 9 Jan. 1973, Box DM 1352, AJPT 1944–76, Hamilton Papers.

83 Taylor to Éva, 21 Jan., 28 June and 12 July 1977, *Letters to Eva*, pp. 327, 351, 353.

84 Taylor to Éva, 12 July and 29 July 1977, 9 Jan., 2 Feb. and 3 Aug. 1978, *ibid.*, pp. 353, 355, 379, 382, 391.

85 Stanley Baron to Taylor, 11 Sept. 1978, Taylor Papers, House of Lords Record Office.

86 Higham to Taylor, 22 March and Taylor to Higham, 23 March, both 1967, Higham Agency Papers, Ransome Center.

87 Taylor to Berlin, 24 March 1967. Thanks to Chris Wrigley for supplying a copy.

88 Machell to Taylor, 18 Oct. and Taylor to Machell, 21 Oct., both 1974, Box DM 1352/AJPT 1944–76, Hamilton Papers.

89 Taylor to Berlin, 22 Jan. 1974, copy from C.W. Wrigley

90 Taylor to Éva, 10 Jan. and 20 March, both 1972; 6 Jan., 20 Jan., 1 Feb., 2 Dec., all 1973, *Letters to Eva*, pp. 55–6, 67–8, 108, 111, 113, 158.

91 Taylor to Éva, 16 June, 23 July and 1 Sept., all 1975, *Letters to Eva*, pp. 247, 253, 259. *Journal of Modern History*, vol. 49, no. 1 (March 1977), pp. 1–18.

92 Taylor to Éva, 30 Sept. 1977, 21 Oct. 1976 and Christmas 1979 Journal all *Letters to Eva*, pp. 312, 363, 425. Hunter to Taylor, 4 June 1981, Higham Agency Papers, London; Taylor to Machell, 29 June 1982; Box DM 1352/126i, Hamilton Papers.

93 Taylor to Éva, 30 Sept. 1977, 21 Oct. 1976 and Christmas 1979 Journal, all *Letters to Eva*, pp. 363, 312, 425; Hunter to Taylor, 4 June 1981, 13 Aug. and 21 Dec., both 1982, and Cash Ledger, all Higham Agency Papers, London; Taylor to Machell, 29 June 1982, Box DM 1352/126i, Hamilton Papers.

94 Machell to Kelly, 29 Sept. 1982, File DM 1352/126i, Hamilton Papers. Taylor said, in the Preface to *A Personal History*, that 'I had hoped to atone for some of my graver acts of selfishness and lack of consideration. But the opportunity has been denied me.' When he wrote this, had Taylor forgotten the tone and content of some of his original remarks?

95 David Holloway, 'Odd Historian Out', *Daily Telegraph*, 26 May 1983; Byron Rogers, 'Histories Make Men Wise?', *The Times*, 2 June 1983; and John Gross, 'Media Star and Major Historian', *New York Times Book Review*, 25 Sept. 1983, cited in

Sisman, *A.J.P. Taylor*, pp. 399–400. David Eastwood adds that 'There is not only little esteem for most professional historians, there is very little sympathy for history as a discipline. Actually I suspect the *reality* was different, as his reading shows, but his cultivated image was one of professional detachment bordering on indifference.' Comment on draft chapter.

96 Henderson on the BBC2 television programme 'Reputations: A.J.P. Taylor – An Unusual Type of Star', transmitted 22 January 1995.

97 Hunter to Taylor, 10 Dec., Taylor to Hunter, 14 Dec. and Hunter to Taylor, 21 Dec., all 1982; Spiers to Hunter, 20 May 1983; Taylor to Hunter, 28 May and 12 June, Hunter to Taylor, 16 June, Taylor to Hunter, 8 Aug., Hunter to Taylor, 11 Aug., 28 Sept. and 20 Oct., all 1983, all Higham Agency Papers, London.

98 For the *London Review of Books* piece, see Taylor, *An Old Man's Diary*, p. 143; Éva Haraszti-Taylor to the author, 13 Jan. 2000, for the Budapest specialist. Entries for 15 Jan., 15–18 April, 17 May and 22 May, all 1984, Haraszti-Taylor, *A Life With Alan*, pp. 193, 196–7, 198–9.

99 Entries for 22 May 1984, and 30 May and 18 Dec. 1985, Haraszti-Taylor, *A Life with Alan*, pp. 199, 221, 239.

100 Gilbert note of visit to Taylor, 14 Nov. 1987, Gilbert Papers.

7 *The Business History of the History Business*

1 Trevelyan's *British History in the Nineteenth Century*, published in 1922, had sold 68,000 by 1949; his *History of England*, published in 1926, had sold 200,000 copies by the same year; they were both trumped by his *English Social History* which, published in 1944,

had sold more than half a million copies by the early 1950s. See David Can-nadine, *G.M. Trevelyan: A Life in History* (London: HarperCollins, 1992), p. 23. Taylor's sales never approached these.

2 Interview with Mary Crozier (Mrs McManus), daughter of W.P. Crozier, 2 Nov. 1994.

3 Taylor, *A Personal History*, p. 87. A.J.P. Taylor, 'Robespierre', *Manchester Guardian*, 21 November, 1934, p. 5.

4 Taylor, *A Personal History*, p. 112. 'Forster's Dickens', *Saturday Review*, 16 June 1928, p. 774. According to Mary Crozier, there was no such position as 'literary editor': 'a member of the staff … took the books, somebody else took the theatres, and the person who took the books arranged the reviews. … And each night a list, it was just a small flimsy, of who the books had gone to for review was sent to my father late at night, and he scanned it and if a book was designated for anyone he didn't approve of it going to, he struck it out, had a word with the man who took the books and suggested somebody else. So he obviously approved of Alan being chosen as a book reviewer, because if he hadn't approved he would have said so.' Interview, 2 November 1994.

5 Taylor, *A Personal History*, p. 124.

6 *Ibid.*, p. 123.

7 Hugh Trevor-Roper, because of his *The Last Days of Hitler*, and Alan Bullock, because of his biography of Hitler, were also in the running; however, in 1961 the BBC Talks Department declined to invite Bullock to speak on Taylor's *Origins of the Second World War* 'because he has become woolly and lazy over his homework.' T. Clarke to Head of Talks, 22 June 1961, Radio Contributors, Talks, A.J.P. Taylor, File 5, 1958–62, BBC Written Archives.

8 Taylor, *A Personal History*, p. 166.

9 I owe this suggestion to Dr Giora

Goodman.

10 Blewitt to Taylor, 19 Feb. 1942, Radio Contributors, Talks, A.J.P. Taylor, File 1, 1942–6, BBC Written Archives.

11 Asa Briggs, *The History of Broadcasting in the United Kingdom. Volume III: The War of Words* (London: Oxford University Press, 1970), pp. 125–58.

12 *Ibid.*, p. 130.

13 Taylor, *A Personal History*, p. 165.

14 Lloyd Williams, 16 March 1942, Radio Contributors, Talks, A.J.P. Taylor, File 1, 1942–6, BBC Written Archives.

15 Taylor to Blewitt, 29 Sept. 1945, *ibid.*

16 Blewitt to Taylor, 1 Oct. 1945, *ibid.*

17 Taylor to Patrick Smith, 25 Sept. 1942; Director of Talks to Blewitt, 14 Feb. 1944; Blewitt to Taylor, 17 Feb. 1944, all *ibid.*

18 Blewitt to Taylor, 21 Aug. 1944; Taylor to Blewitt, 23 Aug. 1944; and Boswell to Taylor, 27 Sept. 1944, all *ibid.*

19 Blewitt to Taylor, 9 March 1945 and Taylor to Blewitt, 10 March 1945, both *ibid.*

20 Memo by Blewitt, 9 May 1946, and draft letter by Barnes to Taylor, 15 May 1946 (not sent), both *ibid.*

21 Taylor to Blewitt, 27 Sept. 1946, *ibid.*

22 Memo by Blewitt, 9 May 1946, *ibid.* The three divisions of BBC radio came to be known by the names Home, Light and Third.

23 Asa Briggs, *The History of Broadcasting in the United Kingdom. Volume IV: Sound and Vision* (Oxford: Oxford University Press, 1979), pp. 52, 65.

24 'British Policy towards Russia', *Listener*, vol. 36, no. 937 (26 Dec. 1946), p. 919.

25 'Britain's Relations with the United States', *Listener*, vol. 36, no. 936 (19 Dec. 1946), p. 873.

26 Hansard, *HC Deb.*, vol. 431, cols 1237–40, 1285.

27 Giora Goodman, ' "Who is Anti-American?" The British Left and

the United States 1945–1956' (University of London Ph.D thesis, 1996), pp. 107–9.

28 Taylor, *A Personal History*, p. 181. The Index numbers of the two FO jackets referring to letters on Taylor are from the Information Department, P1110/2/907 and P1140/2/907. I am grateful to Dr Giora Goodman for the information on the Taylor entries.

29 'Difficulties of Modern Diplomacy', *Listener*, vol. 37, no. 939 (9 Jan. 1947), p. 63.

30 Taylor to Grisewood, 4 Jan. 1947; Grisewood to Taylor, 9 Jan. 1947; and Taylor to Grisewood, 22 Jan. 1947, all Radio Contributors, Talks, A.J.P. Taylor, File 2, 1947–9, BBC Written Archives.

31 Taylor to Boswell, 15 March 1946 on keeping up with current affairs; Taylor to Barnes, 27 Sept. 1946; Grisewood to Taylor, 14 Oct. 1946 and 7 Nov. 1946, all Radio Contributors, Talks, A.J.P. Taylor, File 1, 1942–6, BBC Written Archives.

32 Taylor to Blewitt, 28 Jan. 1947, Radio Contributors, Talks, A.J.P. Taylor, File 2, 1947–9, BBC Written Archives.

33 Briggs, *The History of Broadcasting*, Vol. IV, p. 555.

34 Minute by Barnes, 12 March 1947, Radio Contributors, Talks, A.J.P. Taylor, File 2, 1947–9, BBC Written Archives. Giora Goodman has pointed out that Taylor's comment echoed his hero Cobden's radical critique of nineteenth-century Oxbridge. Letter to the author, 16 April 1997.

35 Briggs, *The History of Broadcasting*, Vol. IV, p. 578.

36 *Ibid.*, p. 580, n 6.

37 Grisewood to Barnes, ?12 March 1947, for Laslett in Cambridge and for Taylor being second-rate; minute by Peter Laslett on A.J.P. Taylor on Lord John Russell, 17 June 1947; Taylor to Grisewood, 10 May 1947, all Radio Contributors, Talks, A.J.P. Taylor, File 2, 1947–9,

BBC Written Archives.

38 Grisewood to Taylor, 8 May 1947; Taylor to Grisewood, 10 May 1947; Grisewood to Taylor, 13 May 1947; Taylor to Barnes, 10 May 1947; Barnes to Taylor, 16 May 1947, all *ibid*. It is clear from a 1997 Radio 3 programme that Barnes was indeed trying to experiment with e.g., semi-dramatised episodes in history and the utilisation of readings from contemporary diaries and writings in order to engage the listener more deeply than a lecture was likely to do.

39 Briggs, *The History of Broadcasting*, Vol. III, pp. 318–20.

40 Taylor to Mary Adams, Head of Television Talks, 13 Dec. 1949; Goldie wrote 'excellent' on the letter; Wyndham Goldie to Taylor, 6 Jan. 1950, both A.J.P. Taylor, TV Talks, File 1, 1949–62, BBC Written Archives.

41 Briggs, *The History of Broadcasting*, Vol. IV, p. 599 and (for the quotations) Grace Wyndham Goldie, *Facing the Nation: Television and Politics 1936–76* (London: The Bodley Head, 1977), p. 68.

42 Taylor, *A Personal History*, p. 96; Irwin to H.Tel.P., 13 Sept. 1950, File T32/215/1, In the News, File 1, 1950–1, BBC Written Archives.

43 Wyndham Goldie, *Facing the Nation*, pp. 70–1.

44 Barnes to C. Tel.P., 30 Oct. 1950, File T32/215/1, In the News, File 1, 1950–1, BBC Written Archives.

45 Wyndham Goldie, *Facing the Nation*, p. 69.

46 Letter dated 1 March 1951, File T32/215/1, In the News, File 1, 1950–1, BBC Written Archives. For Central Office list, see obituary of Lord Annan by Tam Dalyell, *Independent*, 24 Feb. 2000. Annan was also on the list.

47 Barnes to Balkwill, 7 Feb. 1951 and 27 April 1951, both File T32/215/1, In the News, File 1, 1950–1, BBC Written Archives.

48 Cecil McGivern, Controller, TV Programmes, to D. Tel. (Barnes), 1

Oct. 1951, *ibid*.

49 Wyndham Goldie, *Facing the Nation*, p. 76.

50 Lustgarten to Barnes, 1 Sept. 1951 and list of all those appearing on In the News, probably June 1952, both File T32/215/1, In the News, File 1, 1950–1; Taylor to Barnes, 9 Oct. 1952 and Barnes to Taylor, 17 Oct. 1952, both A.J.P. Taylor/TV Talks, File 1, 1949–62, all BBC Written Archives.

51 Sisman, *A.J.P. Taylor*, pp. 205–6; *Daily Telegraph*, 16 Sept. 1952.

52 Irwin to Barnes, 15 Nov. 1952, A.J.P. Taylor/TV Talks, File 1, 1949–62, BBC Written Archives.

53 Secretary to Director of Administration to HP, 5 Dec. 1952 and Barnes to Taylor, 15 Dec. 1952, both *ibid*.

54 Briggs, *The History of Broadcasting*, Vol. IV, p. 604.

55 Taylor, *A Personal History*, p. 196.

56 *Broadcasting: Memorandum on the Report of the Broadcasting Committee 1949*, Cmd.8550 (London: HMSO, 1949), para. 7; Wyndham Goldie, *Facing the Nation*, p. 69.

57 For quotation see Bernard Sendall, *Independent Television in Britain. Volume I: Origin and Foundation, 1946–62* (London: Macmillan Press, 1982), p. 14; Briggs, *The History of Broadcasting*, Vol. IV, p. 223.

58 *Ibid.*, pp. 905–13 (quotation on p. 913).

59 *Ibid.*, pp. 903–5.

60 Taylor, *A Personal History*, p. 210.

61 Maurice Richardson in the *Observer*, 18 Dec. 1955, p. 9, quoted in Wrigley, *A.J.P. Taylor: A Complete Annotated Bibliography*, p. 25.

62 Taylor, *A Personal History*, p. 219. It is unclear whether this story is true; if it is, Collins never found a constituency.

63 *Ibid.*

64 Fred Cooke, 'It's a Great Experiment – Taylor Vision!', *Reynolds News*, 26 May 1957, p. 8, quoted in Wrigley, *A.J.P. Taylor: A Complete*

Annotated Bibliography, p. 27.

65 Quoted on the BBC2 television programme 'Reputations: A.J.P. Taylor – An Unusual Type of Star'.

66 Quoted in '(Un)quiet Flows the Don', *TV Times*, 9 Aug. 1957.

67 Viewing figures given in the introduction to *The Russian Revolution* (London: ATV Library Series, n.d. [early 1958]. The number of television receivers comes from Sendall, *Independent Television*, p. 135.

68 Norman Swallow, *Factual Television* (London: Focal Press, 1966), pp. 135–6, quoted in Sendall, *Independent Television*, pp. 350–1.

69 Taylor, *A Personal History*, p. 220. It is instructive here to remember the number of times the equivalent controllers of BBC Radio 4 have attempted to change the 'Today' programme on the grounds that a new approach was required. In addition to those mentioned in the text there were through 1967 a series of lectures on the First World War, broadcast by ATV probably in the late 1950s; a series on 'The Twenties' for the BBC, broadcast February–March 1962; a series for the BBC on 'Men of the 1860s', transmitted in May–July 1963; a series of six lectures broadcast on commercial television (at 10.30–11pm on Monday nights) on 'The Big Rows' (about parliamentary reforms plus attendent general elections), November–December 1964; a series of ten lectures on 'World War', transmitted by Rediffusion in the summer of 1966; and five lectures on 'Revolution 1917' broadcast September–October 1967 on commercial television.

70 Sisman, *A.J.P. Taylor*, p. 380.

71 Telephone interview with Lady Longford, 27 July 1998.

72 Whether or not this was done from the beginning or only when age had begun to take its toll is impossible to say.

73 Taylor to Eva, letter of 19 Nov. 1973, *Letters to Eva*, p. 154.

74 Joan Bakewell, 'Preview', *Radio Times*, 22 July 1977, p. 15.

75 Joseph Hone, the *Listener*'s reviewer, wrote on 12 Aug. 1976 that 'A.J.P. Taylor wasn't his normal, perky best on Mussolini in *The War Lords* (BBC1). He retains all his great mental gifts as an instant, straight-to-camera historian. But a lot of the physical bite from his earlier performances was missing here. He is 70 this year – and that is no fault of his.' Taylor's reaction to this review was that 'I think they are exaggerating the liveliness of my lectures all those years ago, but I was depressed all the same. It will make it more difficult for me to get a contract for another series. Oh, no, they will say, he is too old. The lectures looked all right to me, except that I was rather in a hurry, having too much to say in half an hour. But once people get an idea in their heads, they never get it out.' Taylor to Éva, Letter of 17 Aug. 1976, *Letters to Eva*, p. 302.

76 Jamie to Alan, 5 Feb. 1962 and Alan to Jamie, 6 Feb. 1962, both Box DM 1352, Correspondence with A.J.P. Taylor 1944–76, Hamilton Papers.

77 Machell to Taylor, 6 Aug. 1976, *ibid*.

78 'Lively History', a review of Paul Frischauer, *England's Year of Danger*, *Manchester Guardian*, 22 March 1938.

79 Taylor, *A Personal History*, pp 196–7.

80 *Sunday Pictorial*, 28 Jan. 1951, p. 5.

81 Taylor, *A Personal history*, pp. 204–5.

82 Quoted in Wrigley, *A.J.P. Taylor: A Complete Annotated Bibliography*, p. 26. Here is the sort of connection Taylor himself relished: his father, Percy Taylor, had backed the *Daily Herald* financially because of his friendship with George Lansbury. Taylor, *A Personal History*, p. 52.

83 *Ibid.*, p. 205.

84 '(Un)quiet Flows the Don', *TV*

Times, 9 Aug. 1957.

85 22 Aug. 1951, Box 15, File 2, Kingsley Martin Papers.

86 Taylor to Kingsley Martin, 13 Feb. 1953, 'In any case I'd never dispute the right of an editor to judge the best interests of his paper.' New Statesman Editorial Correspondence, File T, *New Statesman* Papers, Sussex University.

87 Taylor to Wadsworth, 13 July 1956, File B/T19/264, Wadsworth Papers.

88 Taylor, *A Personal History,* p. 205.

89 *Ibid.,* p. 214.

90 *Ibid.*

91 Taylor, *An Old Man's Diary,* p. 101.

92 Taylor, *A Personal History,* p. 180.

93 Peter Osborne, Foreword to *Professor A. J. P. Taylor on Europe: The Historian Who Predicted the Future* (London: The Bruges Group, 1997), pp. 1–2.

94 Taylor to Éva, letters of 11 Nov. 1972 and 6 Jan. 1973, *Letters to Eva,* pp. 99 and 109–10. Osborne, Foreword to *Professor A. J. P. Taylor on Europe.*

95 The letter continued, 'The Sunday Express appears to be implying that he repudiated the terms of the contract, but in doing so seems to be reading more into the contract than actually existed.' Robert Norris to Mark Stephens, 3 Nov. 1982, Taylor Papers, House of Lords Record Office, London.

96 Martin to Taylor, 16 Nov. 1953, and Taylor to Janet, 22 Dec. 1953, both Editorial Correspondence – File T, *New Statesman* Papers.

97 Astor to Kilmartin, 29 Oct. 1957, *Observer* Archive, quoted in Richard Cockett, *David Astor and the Observer* (London: André Deutsch, 1991), p. 171.

98 Letter from David Machin to the author, 17 April 1997.

Epilogue

1 Taylor's will and testament, signed by Taylor on 9 January 1987, dated 5 April 1991. Taylor was already in the nursing home, Moss Lodge, when he signed the will, but his signature was still quite recognisable.

2 Hugh Trevor-Roper, *Sunday Telegraph,* 16 Sept. 1990; James Joll and Martin Gilbert, Stock Obit., Gilbert Papers; A.L. Rowse, 'History and Hot Air', *Evening Standard,* 20 Jan. 1994; John Keegan, 'A Great Little Englander', *Daily Telegraph,* 22 Jan. 1994; and Richard Overy, 'Riddle Radical Ridicule', *Observer,* 30 Jan. 1994. David Eastwood has commented about Keegan's piece that 'This mean-spirited assessment sits very uneasily alongside, say, [Taylor's] *Essays in English History.* Of course he affected to despise the Establishment, but he did offer a celebration of certain popular values & civic virtues.' He notes further re Keegan's excoriation of the 'polytechnic world' that this 'world' 'was much more the world of E.P. Thompson & radical social history that it ever was the world of Taylor & diplomatic history.' Comments on chapter by David Eastwood.

3 He also provided a role model of a lecturer for some academics: Alastair Parker and David d'Avray, for example, have said as much.

4 Taylor, 'Accident Prone', pp. 16, 2.

5 David Eastwood has noted that, as I imply elsewhere, this 'did mean that much of his professional reading became increasingly unsystematic.' Comment on this chapter.

6 Comments by Paul Addison and Martin Gilbert, for example, and by the author herself.

7 Taylor to the Vice-Chancellor, 13 Nov. 1973 and the Vice-Chancellor to Taylor, 15 Nov. 1973, both Box 2, Folder 3, Taylor Papers, Ransome Center.

8 Sisman, *A.J.P. Taylor,* p. 280.

9 Interview with Daniel Taylor, 9 April 2000.

10 With regard to Taylor's invocation of Steeple, David Eastwood writes

that 'I don't believe this. Steeple isn't a peak: it's really a striking point on the Pillar ridge. If he'd climbed Pillar (which is a major peak) he must have walked onto Steeple. All this is clear in Wainwright – whose style & outlook are, in many ways, strikingly Taylorian.' Comment on draft chapter.

Appendix

1 Keith Kyle to the author, 2 Oct. 1996. He adds that 'The only other person whom I knew to have such a rule at the time was Enoch Powell.' Roger Machell to Taylor, 16 May 1972, Box DM 1352, Hamilton Papers.

2 Central Statistical Office, *Retail Prices 1914–1990* (London: HMSO, 1991) and Office for National Statistics, *Retail Prices Index – October 1996* (London: HMSO, 1996).

Bibliography

MANUSCRIPT SOURCES

United Kingdom
A.J.P. Taylor Papers (private possession)
Public Record Office, Kew, London
    Foreign Office Papers
    Ministry of Information Papers
House of Lords Record Office, London
    Beaverbrook Papers
    A.J.P. Taylor Papers
British Library, London – Macmillan and Co. Papers
Bodleian Library, Oxford
    G.N. Clark Papers
    Oxford University Archive
Oxford University Press Archives, Oxford
Christ Church College, Oxford Archive – Tom Driberg Papers
Magdalen College, Oxford Archives – College Papers
Oriel College, Oxford Archives – College Papers
John Rylands University Library, Manchester University
    Lewis Namier Papers
    A.P. Wadsworth Papers
Modern Records Centre, Warwick University, England
    CND Collection
    Michael Foot Papers
Bristol University Library
    Hamish Hamilton Papers
    Penguin Books Papers
Sussex University Library
    New Statesman Papers
    Kingsley Martin Papers
    David Levy Papers
Reading University Library – Frank Stenton Papers
King's College London Library – Basil Liddell Hart Papers
University College London – Department of History Papers
London School of Economics, British Library of Political Science Anthony Crosland
    Papers
BBC Written Archives, Caversham
Macmillan and Co. Archives, Basingstoke – Macmillan Publishers'. Archives
David Higham Agency Papers, London

Caitlin Thomas Papers, Sotheby's, London (private possession)
Sir Martin Gilbert Papers, London (private possession)
York – Bootham School Archives

United States
Harry Ransome Humanities Research Center, University of Texas, Austin
  David Higham Agency Papers
  A.J.P. Taylor Papers
Yale University Library
  Wallace Notestein Papers
  Alan Pryce-Jones Papers, Beinecke Rare Books Library
Wheaton College, Illinois – Malcolm Muggeridge Papers

PRINTED SOURCES

Broadcasting: Memorandum on the Report of the Broadcasting Committee 1949, Cmd. 8550
  (London: HMSO, 1949).
Central Statistical Office, *Retail Prices 1914–1990* (London: HMSO, 1991).
Defence: Outline of Future Policy: 1957, Cmnd 124 (London: HMSO, 1957).
Dictionary of National Biography
Hansard, *Parliamentary Debates*, 5th series
Institute of Historical Research, London University, Annual Reports, 1977–8, 1984–5.
Manchester University, *Faculty of Arts Examination Papers, 1937*
  *Report of the Council to the Court of Governors, 1930–1931; Ibid., 1931–1932; Ibid.,
  1932–1933*
  *The Victoria University of Manchester Calendar, 1929–1930; Ibid., 1930–1931; Ibid.,
  1931–1932*
Office for National Statistics, *Retail Prices Index – October 1996* (London: HMSO, 1996).

BROADCAST SOURCE

'Reputations: A.J.P. Taylor – An Unusual Type of Star', BBC2, transmitted 22 January
  1995.

SECONDARY SOURCES

Addison, Paul, 'Wizard of Ox – Paul Addison Pays Tribute to A.J.P. Taylor', *London
  Review of Books*, 8 November 1990.
Alison Phillips, W., *Modern Europe 1815–1899* (London: Rivingtons, 1901).
Annan, Noel, *Our Age* (London: Weidenfeld and Nicolson, 1990).
Ashley, M.P. and C.T. Saunders, *Red Oxford: A History of the Growth of Socialism in the
  University of Oxford* (Oxford: Oxford University Labour Club, 2nd edition, January
  1933).
Balsdon, Dacre, *Oxford Now and Then* (London: Duckworth, 1970).
Berlin, Isaiah, 'L.B. Namier', *Personal Impressions* (London: The Hogarth Press, 1980).
Betjeman, John, *Summoned by Bells* (London: John Murray, 1960).
Bolton King, R., *Buxton College, 1675–1970* (Privately printed, 1973).
Boswell, James, *The Life of Samuel Johnson, LL.D* (London, Bliss Sands, 1897).
Bosworth, R.B., *Explaining Auschwitz and Hiroshima: History Writing and the Second
  World War* (London: Routledge, 1993).
Bowra, C.M., *Memoirs* (London: Weidenfeld and Nicolson, 1966).
Briggs, Asa, *The History of Broadcasting in the United Kingdom. Volume IV: Sound and
  Vision* (London: Oxford University Press, 1979).

————, *The History of Broadcasting in the United Kingdom. Volume III: The War of Words* (London: Oxford University Press, 1970).

Brown, E.J., *The First Five: The Story of a School* (Privately published, 1987).

Bullock, Alan and A.J.P. Taylor, *A Select List of Books on European History 1915–1945* (Oxford: Clarendon Press, 1948).

Burgess, Anthony, *Little Wilson and Big God: Being the First Part of the Confessions of Anthony Burgess* (Harmondsworth: Penguin Books, 1987, 1988).

Burk, Kathleen, 'Britische Traditionen internationaler Geschichtsschreibung' in Wilfrid Loth and Jürgen Osterhammel, eds, *Internationale Geschichte: Themen – Ergebnisse – Aussichten* (Munich: Oldenbourg Verlag, 2000).

Cannadine, David, *G.M. Trevelyan: A Life in History* (London: HarperCollins, 1992).

Cannon, John, et al., *The Blackwell Dictionary of Historians* (Oxford: Basil Blackwell, 1988).

Carey, John, *The Intellectuals and the Masses: Pride and Prejudice among the Literary Intelligentsia, 1880–1939* (London: Faber and Faber, 1992 paperback edition).

Carpenter, Humphrey, *W.H. Auden: A Biography* (London: George Allen and Unwin, 1981).

Carsten, Francis L., 'From Revolutionary Socialism to German History', in Peter Alter, ed., *Out of the Third Reich: Refugee Historians in Postwar Britain* (London: I.B. Taurus, 1998).

Chisholm, Anne, and Michael Davie, *Beaverbrook: A Life* (London: Hutchinson, 1992).

Clark, Ronald W., *Tizard* (London: Methuen and Co., 1965).

The Examination Statutes . . . Revised to July 10, 1926, Together with the Regulations of the Boards of Studies and Board Faculties for the Academic Year 1926–1927 (Oxford: Clarendon Press, 1926).

Cockett, Richard, *David Astor and the Observer* (London: André Deutsch, 1991).

Cole, Robert, *A.J.P. Taylor: The Traitor within the Gates* (Houndsmills: Macmillan Press, 1993).

Colley, Linda, *Lewis Namier* (London: Weidenfeld and Nicolson, 1989).

Currie, Robert, 'The Arts and Social Studies, 1914–1939', in Brian Harrison, ed., *The History of the University of Oxford. Vol. VIII: The Twentieth Century* (Oxford: Oxford University Press, 1994)

D'Avray, David, *Death and the Prince: Memorial Preaching before 1350* (Oxford: Clarendon Press, 1994).

Dover, Kenneth, *Marginal Comment* (London: Duckworth, 1994).

Drabble, Margaret, ed., *The Oxford Companion to English Literature* (Oxford: Oxford University Press, 1985).

Duff, Peggy, *Left, Left, Left: A Personal Account of Six Protest Campaigns, 1945–1965* (London: Allison and Busby, 1971).

Durbin, Elizabeth, *New Jerusalems: The Labour Party and the Economics of Democratic Socialism* (London: Routledge, 1985).

Ensor, R.C.K., *England 1870–1914* (Oxford: Oxford University Press, 1936).

Ferris, Paul, *Caitlin: The Life of Caitlin Thomas* (London: Pimlico paperback edition, 1995).

Friedjung, Heinrich, *The Struggle for Supremacy in Germany 1859–1866*, translated by A.J.P. Taylor and W.L. McElwee (London: Macmillan and Co., 1935).

Galbraith, V.H., 'T.F. Tout', in the *Dictionary of National Biography*.

Gibbon, Edward, *Autobiography of Edward Gibbon* (London: Oxford University Press, World's Classics edition, 1907).

Gilbert, Martin, ed., *A Century of Conflict 1850–1950: Essays for A.J.P. Taylor* (New York: Atheneum, 1967).

Goodchild, Peter, *J. Robert Oppenheimer: 'Shatterer of Worlds'* (London: BBC, 1980).

Goodman, Giora, ' "Who is Anti-American?" The British Left and the United States 1945–1956' (University of London Ph.D thesis, 1996).

Gordon, M.C., ed., *The Letters of George S. Gordon, 1902–1942* (London: Oxford University Press, 1943).

———, *The Life of George S. Gordon 1881–1942* (London: Oxford University Press, 1945).

Green, Martin, *Children of the Sun* (New York: Basic Books, 1976).

Greenstein, Daniel I., 'The Junior Members, 1900–1919: A Profile', in Brian Harrison, ed., *The History of the University of Oxford, Vol. VIII: The Twentieth Century* (Oxford: Oxford University Press, 1994).

Gruber, Helmut, *Red Vienna: Experiment in Working-Class Culture 1919-1934* (Oxford: Oxford University Press, 1991).

Hall, Harriet, *Bill and Patience: An Eccentric Marriage at Stowe and Beyond* (Lewes, Sussex: The Book Guild, 2000).

Haraszti, Éva, 'Michael Karolyi: A Friend', in Chris Wrigley, ed., *Warfare, Diplomacy and Politics: Essays in Honour of A.J.P. Taylor* (London: Hamish Hamilton, 1986).

Haraszti-Taylor, Éva, *Choices and Decisions: A Life* (Nottingham: Astra Press, 1997).

———, *A Life with Alan: The Diary of A.J.P. Taylor's Wife Eva from 1978 to 1985* (London: Hamish Hamilton, 1987).

———, *Remembering Alan: A Love Story* (Privately printed, 1995).

Harrison, Brian, 'College Life, 1918–1939', in Harrison, ed., *The History of the University of Oxford. Volume VIII: The Twentieth Century* (Oxford: Oxford University Press, 1994).

Harriss, G.L., 'Introduction to the Letters', in K.B. McFarlane, *Letters to Friends 1940–1966* (Oxford: Magdalen College Library, 1997).

Haslam, Jonathan, *The Vices of Integrity: E.H. Carr, 1892–1982* (London: Verso, 1999).

Henty, G.A., *The Young Carthaginian: A Story of the Times of Hannibal* (London: Blackie and Son, 1887).

Hillier, Bevis, *Young Betjeman* (London: John Murray, 1988).

Hitler, Adolf, *Mein Kampf* (London: Pimlico paperback edition, 1992).

———, *My Struggle* (London: Hurst and Blackett, 1933).

Hobson, Harold, *Indirect Journey: An Autobiography* (London: Weidenfeld and Nicolson, 1978).

Holloway, David, *Stalin and the Bomb: The Soviet Union and Atomic Energy 1939–1956* (New Haven: Yale University Press, 1994).

Ignatieff, Michael, *Isaiah Berlin: A Life* (London: Chatto and Windus, 1998).

Ingrams, Richard, *Muggeridge* (London: HarperCollins, 1996).

Jenks, John, 'Fight against Peace? Britain and the World Peace Council' (Unpublished paper given at the Institute for Contemporary British History Conference, London, 10 July 1996).

Jensen, Kenneth M., ed., *Origins of the Cold War: The Novitov, Kennan and Roberts 'Long Telegrams' of 1946* (Washington: United States Institute of Peace, 1991).

Johnson, R.H., 'Diary', *London Review of Books*, 8 May 1986.

Johnson, A.H., *Europe in the Sixteenth Century 1494–1598* (London: Rivingtons, 1925).

Jones, Nicolette, 'Will Royalities Remain King?', *The Bookseller*, 6 February, 1998.

Kennan, George, *Russia, the Atom Bomb and the West* (London: Oxford University Press, 1958).

Kennedy, Paul, 'A.J.P. Taylor and "Profound Forces" in History', in Chris Wrigley, ed., *Warfare, Diplomacy and Politics: Essays in Honour of A.J.P. Taylor* (London: Hamish Hamilton, 1986).

———, 'Appeasement', in Gordon Martel, ed., *The Origins of the Second World War Reconsidered: The A.J.P. Taylor Debate After Twenty-Five Years* (Boston/London: Allen and Unwin, 1986).

Kenny, Anthony, *A Life in Oxford* (London: John Murray, 1997).

Kenyon, John, *The History Men* (London: Weidenfeld and Nicolson, 1983).

Koch, H.W., 'Hitler and the Origins of the Second World War: Second Thoughts on the Status of Some of the Documents', in Esmonde S. Robertson, ed., *The Origins of the Second World War* (London: Macmillan, 1971 paperback edition).

Langham, Mike, and Colin Wells, *Buxton Waters: A History of Buxton the Spa* (Derby: J.H. Hall and Sons, 1986).

Levy, Jack S., 'The Theoretical Foundations of Paul W. Schroeder's International System', *International History Review*, vol. 16, no. 4 (November 1994).

Lewis, C.S., *That Hideous Strength: A Modern Fairy Tale for Grown-Ups* (London: John Lane, 1945).

Lewis, W.H., ed., *Letters of C.S. Lewis* (London: Geoffrey Blas, 1966).

Leyser, Karl, 'Kenneth Bruce McFarlane: A Memoir', in K.B. McFarlane, *Letters to Friends 1940–1966* (Oxford: Magdalen College Oxford, 1997).

Louis, Wm Roger, *The Origins of the Second World War: A.J.P. Taylor and his Critics* (New York: John Wiley and Sons, 1972).

Macaulay, Thomas Babington, *The History of England from the Accession of James II*, 6 vols (London: Longman, Brown, Green, and Longmans, 1849–1861).

Macintyre, Angus, 'Edward Gibbon and Magdalen', *Magdalen College Record* (1994).

MacKenzie, Norman, and Jeanne MacKenzie, eds, *The Diary of Beatrice Webb. Volume Four, 1924–1943: The Wheel of Life* (Cambridge, Mass.: Harvard University Press, 1985).

MacNeice, Louis, *The Strings Are False: An Unfinished Autobiography* (London: Faber, 1965, 1966 paperback edition).

Martel, Gordon, ed., *The Origins of the Second World War Reconsidered: A.J.P. Taylor and the Historians* (London: Routledge, 1999).

———, ed., *The Origins of the Second World War Reconsidered: The A.J.P. Taylor Debate After Twenty-Five Years* (Boston/London: Allen and Unwin, 1986).

Mason, T.W., 'Some Origins of the Second World War', *Past and Present*, vol. 29 (December 1964), pp. 67–87.

Masterman, J.C., *On the Chariot Wheel: An Autobiography* (Oxford: Oxford University Press, 1975).

McFarlane, K.B., *Letters to Friends 1940–1966* (Oxford: Magdalen College Oxford, 1997).

Mehta, Ved, *The Fly and the Fly-Bottle: Encounters with British Intellectuals* (New York: Columbia University Press, 1983 paperback edition).

Mills, Lynn, 'Under the Influence', *Limited Edition: The Magazine of Oxfordshire*, no. 54 (April 1991).

Morgan, Prys, 'From a Death to a View: The Hunt for the Welsh Past in the Romantic Period', in Eric Hobsbawm and Terence Ranger, eds, *The Invention of Tradition* (Cambridge: Cambridge University Press, 1983, 1984 paperback edition).

Morris, James, *Oxford* (London: Faber and Faber, 1965).

Muggeridge, Malcolm, *Chronicles of Wasted Time. Part I: The Green Stick* (London: Collins, 1972).

———, *Picture Palace* (London: Weidenfeld and Nicolson, reprinted 1987).

Namier, Lewis, *1848: The Revolution of the Intellectuals* (London: Oxford University Press, 1946).

Nicolson, Harold, *Diplomacy* (London: Oxford University Press, 1939).

Official Guide to Buxton (1939).

Ollard, Richard, *A Man of Contradictions: A Life of A.L. Rowse* (London: Allen Lane, The Penguin Press, 1999).

Onions, C.T., ed., *The Oxford Dictionary of English Etymology* (Oxford: Clarendon Press, 1966).

Ovenden, Keith, *A Fighting Withdrawal: The Life of Dan Davin. Writer, Soldier, Publisher* (Oxford: Oxford University Press, 1996).

Pantin, W.A., 'Ernest Fraser Jacob 1894–1971', *Proceedings of the British Academy*, vol. 58 (1972).

Parker, Stanley, 'Drawn and Quotes: A.J.P. Taylor's, My Waterloo', *Oxford Mail*, 17 June 1943.

Pók, Attila, 'British Manual on Hungary in 1944', in Pók, ed., *The Fabric of Modern Europe: Studies in Social and Diplomatic History Essays in Honour of Eva Haraszti Taylor on the Occasion of her 75th Birthday* (Nottingham: Astra Press, 1999).

Pollard, F.E., *Bootham School 1823–1923* (London: J.M. Dent and Sons, 1926).

Powicke, F.M., *Modern Historians and the Study of History: Essays and Papers* (London: Odhams Press, 1955).

Přibram, A.F., *England and the International Policy of the European Great Powers 1871–1914* (Oxford: Clarendon Press, 1931).

Robertson, Esmonde M., *The Origins of the Second World War: Historical Interpretations* (London: Macmillan, 1971 paperback edition).

Rowse, A.L., *A Cornishman at Oxford* (London: Jonathan Cape, 1965, 1974).

———, *Historians I Have Known* (London: Duckworth, 1995).

Russell, Bertrand, *The Autobiography of Bertrand Russell 1944–1969* (London: George Allen and Unwin, 1969).

Sayer, George, *Jack. A Life of C.S. Lewis* (London: Hodder and Stoughton, 1977 paperback edition).

Schofield, Stephen, 'Oxford Loses a Genius', in Schofield, ed., *In Search of C.S. Lewis* (South Plainfield, N.J.: Bridge Publishing, 1983).

Schroeder, Paul, *The Transformation of European Politics, 1787–1848* (Oxford: Clarendon Press, 1994).

Schwabe, Klaus and Rolf Reichardt, eds, *Gerhard Ritter: Ein politischer Historiker in seinen Briefen* (Boppard am Rhein: Harald Boldt Verlag, 1984).

Scott-Smith, Giles, 'The Organising of Intellectual Consensus: The Congress for Cultural Freedom and Post-War US-European Relations (Part I)', *Lobster*, no. 36 (Winter 1998).

———, ' "A Radical Democratic Offensive": Melvyn J. Lasky, *Der Monat*, and the Congress for Cultural Freedom', *Journal of Contemporary History*, vol. 35, no. 2 (April 2000).

Segal, Edward, 'A.J.P. Taylor and History', *Review of Politics*, 26 Oct. 1964, pp. 531–46.

Sendall, Bernard, *Independent Television in Britain. Volume I: Origin and Foundation, 1946–62* (London: Macmillan Press, 1982).

Sisman, Adam, *A.J.P. Taylor: A Biography* (London: Sinclair-Stevenson, 1994).

Slee, Peter R.H., *Learning and a Liberal Education: The Study of Modern History in the Universities of Oxford, Cambridge and Manchester, 1880–1914* (Manchester: Manchester University Press, 1986).

Smithers, Peter, 'Bruce McFarlane – A Prince Among Tutors', *Magdalen College Record* (1994).

Soffer, Reba N., *Discipline and Power: The Universities, History, and the Making of an English Elite 1870–1930* (Stanford: Stanford University Press, 1994).

Stewart, J.I.M., *Myself and Michael Innes: A Memoir* (London: Victor Gollancz, 1987).

Stonor Saunders, Frances, *Who Paid the Piper? The CIA and the Cultural Cold War* (London: Granta Books, 1999).

Sutcliffe, Peter, *The Oxford University Press: An Informal History* (Oxford: Clarendon Press, 1978).

Taylor, A.J.P., 'Accident Prone, or What Happened Next', *Journal of Modern History*, vol. 49, no. 1 (March 1977).

———, *Beaverbrook: A Biography* (London: Hamish Hamilton, 1972).

———, *Beaverbrook: A Biography* (New York: Simon and Schuster).

———, *Bismarck: The Man and the Statesman* (London: Hamish Hamilton, 1955).

———, 'CND: The First Twenty-Five Years', *Observer Magazine*, 20 February 1983.

———, *The Course of German History: A Survey of the Development of Germany Since 1815* (London: Hamish Hamilton, 1945).

———, *Czechoslovakia's Place in a Free Europe* (London: Czechoslovak Institute in London, 1943).

———, *English History 1914–1945* (Oxford: Clarendon Press, 1965).

———, *Englishmen and Others* (London: Hamish Hamilton, 1956).

———, *The First World War: An Illustrated History* (Harmondsworth: Penguin, 1972).

————, *From Napoleon to Stalin: Comments on European History* (London: Hamish Hamilton, 1950).

————, *From Sarajevo to Potsdam* (London: Thames and Hudson, 1966).

————, *Germany's First Bid for Colonies 1884–1885: A Move in Bismarck's European Policy* (London: Macmillan and Co., 1938).

————, *The Habsburg Monarchy 1815–1918: A History of the Austrian Empire and Austria-Hungary* (London: Macmillan and Co., 1941).

————, *The Habsburg Monarchy 1809–1918: A History of the Austrian Empire and Austria-Hungary* (London: Hamish Hamilton, 1948).

————, *The Italian Problem in European Diplomacy, 1847–1849* (Manchester: Manchester University Press, 1934).

————, *Letters to Eva 1969–83*, edited by Éva Haraszti-Taylor (London: Century, 1991).

————, ed., *Lloyd George: Twelve Essays* (London: Hamish Hamilton, 1971).

————, *An Old Man's Diary* (London: Hamish Hamilton, 1984).

————, *The Origins of the Second World War* (London: Hamish Hamilton, 1961).

————, *The Origins of the Second World War* (New York: Atheneum, 1962).

————, *A Personal History* (London: Hamish Hamilton, 1983).

————, *Professor A. J. P. Taylor on Europe: The Historian Who Predicted the Future* (London: The Bruges Group, 1997).

————, *Rumours of Wars* (London: Hamish Hamilton, 1952).

————, *The Russian Revolution* (London: ATV Library Series, n.d. [early 1958]).

————, *The Second World War: An Illustrated History* (London: Hamish Hamilton, 1975).

————, *The Struggle for Mastery in Europe 1848–1918* (Oxford: Oxford University Press, 1954).

————, *Trieste* (London: Yugoslav Information Office, 1945).

————, *The Troublemakers: Dissent over British Foreign Policy 1792–1939* (London: Hamish Hamilton, 1957).

————, *War by Time-Table: How the First World War Began* (London: Macdonald, 1969).

————, 'War Origins Again', *Past and Present*, vol. 30 (April 1965).

Taylor, Richard, *Against the Bomb: The British Peace Movement 1858–1965* (Oxford: Clarendon Press, 1988).

Thomas, William, 'Recollections of A.J.P. Taylor', *Contemporary European History*, vol. 3, no. 1 (1994).

Thompson, E.P., *The Making of the English Working Class* (New York: Random House, 1964).

Thompson, J.M., *My Apologia* (Oxford: Alden Press, June 1940).

Thwaite, Ann, ed., *My Oxford* (London: Robson Books, 1986 paperback edition).

Tout, T.F., *The Collected Papers of T.F. Tout; With a Memoir and Bibliography* (Manchester: Manchester University Press, 1932).

Veldman, Meredith, *Fantasy, the Bomb, and the Greening of Britain: Romantic Protest, 1945–1980* (Cambridge: Cambridge University Press, 1994).

Wakeman, Henry Offley, *Europe 1598–1715* (London: Rivington, Percival and Co., 1894).

Waugh, Evelyn, *A Little Learning* (London: Chapman and Hall, 1964; Sidgwick and Jackson paperback edition, 1973).

Woolley, A.R, *The Clarendon Guide to Oxford*, new edition (Oxford: Oxford University Press, 1979).

Wragge, J. Philip, ed., *Leslie Howard Gilbert 1892 to 1987: An Appreciation* (York: The Ebor Press, 1988).

Wrigley, Chris, *A.J.P. Taylor: A Complete Annotated Bibliography and Guide to his Historical and Other Writings* (Sussex: The Harvester Press, 1980).

————, *A.J.P. Taylor: From the Boer War to the Cold War. Essays on Twentieth-Century*

Europe (London: Hamish Hamilton, 1995).

——, 'Alan John Percivale Taylor 1906–1990', *Proceedings of the British Academy*, vol. 82 (1993).

——, ed., *Warfare, Diplomacy and Politics: Essays in Honour of A.J.P. Taylor* (London: Hamish Hamilton, 1986).

Wyndham Goldie, Grace, *Facing the Nation: Television and Politics 1936-76* (London: The Bodley Head, 1977).

Young, Robert J., 'A.J.P Taylor and the Problem of France', in Gordon Martel, ed., *The Origins of the Second World War Reconsidered: The A.J.P. Taylor Debate after Twenty-Five Years* (Boston/London: Allen and Unwin, 1986).

NEWSPAPERS AND PERIODICALS

American Historical Review
Badger
Bookseller
Buxtonian
Cambridge Review
Contemporary European History
Daily Express
Daily Herald
Der Monat
Der Spiegel
English Historical Review
Evening Standard
Foreign Affairs
History
Independent
Independent on Sunday
International Affairs
International History Review
Journal of Contemporary History
Journal of Modern History
Limited Edition. The Magazine of Oxfordshire
Listener
Lobster
London Review of Books
Magdalen College Record
Manchester Guardian
Nation
New Statesman
New York Herald Tribune
New York Review of Books
Observer
Observer: The Collected Writings of the [Buxton] School Essay Writing Society
Oriel Record
Oxford Magazine
Oxford Mail
Oxford Times
Past and Present
Preston Herald
Review of Politics
Saturday Review

Spectator
Sunday Express
The Times
Times Literary Supplement
Time and Tide

INTERVIEWS

Mr Alan Baxendale; Mrs June Barraclough Benn; Professor David Bellos; Mrs Rachel Hemming Bray; Sir John Coles; Professor Penelope Corfield; Lord Dacre; Professor David d'Avray; Mr Christopher Dunn; Mrs Doris Fell; Professor M.R.D. Foot; Sir Martin Gilbert; Professor Paul Ginsborg; Dr Éva Haraszti-Taylor; Mr Gerald Howat; Miss Betty Kemp; Dr Axel Körner; Mrs Henrietta Kotlan-Werner; Mr Keith Kyle; Mr Michael Langham; Mr and Mrs Adrian Lutte; Mr and Mrs Graham Marten; Mrs Mary McManus; Mr David Morgan; Dr Dusan Radojicic; Mr John Steane; Mr John Stoye; Mr Daniel Taylor; Professor Chris Wrigley; Professor David Worswick

Index

Steane, John, 439
Stenton, Doris, 210, 454
Stephens, C.E., 202
Stevenson, Frances, 333–4, 351–2
Stewart, J.I.M. (Innes), 50–1, 57,
    62–3, 70, 74–6, 91
Stocks, J.L., 132
Stoye, John, 202–3, 219, 438–9, 444
Strauss, Henry, 379
Sumner, B.H., 144–5, 257
Sutherland, Dame Lucy, 208–10, 445
Sutton, Leslie, 168
Switzerland, 3, 14–15, 184–5, 228

Tait, James, 107–8
Taylor, Alan John Percivale
    and administration, 148, 158,
        167–70, 195–7, 223, 301, 434
    appointment to chairs, 206–7,
        336–7, 365, to Regius, 205–11,
        to Stevenson, 206–7
    and architecture, 40–1, 43
    and book reviewing, 223, 225,
        254, 279–82, 309, 314–16,
        320, 358–60, 370–2, 374,
        403–5, 411, 444, 453–4
    books edited: Dictionary of
        World History, 332–3; Essays
        Presented to Sir Lewis Namier,
        445; Lloyd George: A Diary,
        333–4; Lloyd George: Twelve
        Essays, 318, 334; My Darling
        Pussy: The Letters of Lloyd
        George and Frances Stevenson
        1913–1941, 333–4, 351–2; Off
        the Record: Political Interviews
        1933–1943, 334
    books read: 10–11, 16–18, 31,
        37–9, 57–9, 76, 79, 85,
        111–12, 115, 262, 287–9, 411,
        420–2, 426–7, 430

    books written: A Personal
        History, 360–6, 409;
        'Accident Prone, or What
        Happened Next', 363–4; An
        Old Man's Diary, 366;
        Beaverbrook, 309, 311, 315–17,
        321–4, 335, 351, 460, 462;
        Bismarck: The Man and the
        Statesman, 203, 248, 277–80,
        295, 374, 415; Czechoslovakia's
        Place in a Free Europe, 236–8;
        English History 1914–1945,
        220, 299–310, 314–15, 324,
        326, 328, 359–60, 415, 447,
        458, 469; Englishmen and
        Others, 405; Europe: Grandeur
        and Decline, 405; From
        Napoleon to Lenin, 405; From
        Napoleon to Stalin, 256, 405;
        From Sarajevo to Potsdam,
        309, 328–31; Germany's First
        Bid for Colonies 1884–1885,
        137, 140–3, 248–9, 278, 373;
        How Wars Begin, 397; How
        Wars End, 366, 397; Letters to
        Eva, 342; Revolutions and
        Revolutionaries, 397; Rumours
        of Wars, 405; The Course of
        German History, 181, 245,
        248, 250–6, 262, 373–4, 448;
        The First World War: An
        Illustrated History, 309, 325–7;
        The Habsburg Monarchy
        1809–1918, 198, 241–8, 256,
        310, 415, 455; The Habsburg
        Monarchy 1815–1918, 81, 136,
        179, 184, 227–35, 241–3, 251,
        255, 310, 373; The Italian
        Problem in European
        Diplomacy 1847–1849, 95–101,
        137–9, 227, 371, 428; The
        Origins of the Second World